United States Lawn Tennis Association
OFFICIAL ENCYCLOPEDIA OF TENNIS

United States
Lawn Tennis Association

1817

OFFICIAL
ENCYCLOPEDIA
OF TENNIS

Edited by the Staff of the U.S.L.T.A.

HARPER & ROW, PUBLISHERS

New York, Evanston, San Francisco, London

Acknowledgments

The compilation of this volume required the aid of many people. For example, we at the United States Lawn Tennis Association wish to thank Lawrence A. Baker, James H. Van Alen, Edwin S. Baker, George W. Gowen, Joanna Davenport, Eve F. Kraft, John Conroy, Marjorie Gengler, William Colson, Russ Adams, Ron Bookman, F. E. Sturer, Barry Lorge, Harold O. Zimman, and Clifford Sutter for their great cooperation in making this book possible. In addition we wish to thank Robert Scharff, David John, and Mary Puschak for coordinating the material in the book. Finally, a word of thanks must go to Michael J. Burns, Alice Valentine, Frances Freese, and the other members of U.S.L.T.A.'s staff. We, of course, received assistance from various manufacturers as well as many other people whom we failed to mention above—to all of these, many special thanks.

ROBERT S. MALAGA, Executive Director, U.S.L.T.A.

Excerpts of records in Section V and Section VI, pages 221 to 226 and 333 to 364, taken from *United States Lawn Tennis Association's Yearbook and Guide.* Copyright 1971 by United States Lawn Tennis Association.

Excerpts in Section I, pages 59 to 67, on lawn tennis history taken from *The History and Interpretation of Amateurism in the United States Tennis Association.* Copyright 1966 by Joanna Davenport. Reprinted by permission of the author, Joanna Davenport.

Excerpts in Section IV, pages 216 to 218, on court courtesy taken from *The Quick and Easy Guide to Tennis.* Copyright 1962 by the Crowell-Collier Publishing Company. Reprinted by permission of the publisher, The Macmillan Company.

FIRST EDITION

STANDARD BOOK NUMBER: 06-014479-3

LIBRARY OF CONGRESS CATALOG CARD NUMBER: 71-181644

Contents

Section I.   History of Lawn Tennis, 1

Lawn Tennis Becomes a Major Sport—Lawn Tennis Comes to the United States—
Development of the Game in the United States—Founding of USNLTA—Men's
Championship Play Before World War I—International Team Competitions—The
Ladies Enter the Scene—The Golden Era of Tennis and Beyond—Men's Double Play
After World War I—Women's Play in the Golden Era of Sports—The European
Golden Age of Tennis—The Davis Cup Moves About in the Twenties and Thirties—
The Start of the Wightman Cup—Other Cup Competitions—The Olympic Games and
Tennis—Men's Play in America After World War II—Women's Play After World
War II—Wimbledon After World War II—The Professional and His Part in Lawn
Tennis—Open Tennis Tournaments

Section II.   Lawn Tennis Equipment, 70

The Tennis Ball—*Specifications*—*How Balls Are Made*—*Buying and Caring for Balls*
—The Tennis Racket—*Weight of the Racket*—*Balance of the Racket*—*Size of
Handle*—*Frame Material*—*Flexibility of the Racket*—*Type of Strings*—*Care of the
Racket*—Tennis Clothing—*Shoes and Socks*—*Suggested Women's Outfits*—*Suggested
Men's Outfits*—Practice Devices—*Practice Board*—*Rebound Net*—*Ball-Throwing
Machine*—*Rebound Ball*—The Tennis Court—*How to Lay Out a Tennis Court*—
Court Material—*Selection of Tennis-Court Surfaces*—*Grass Courts*—*Clay Courts*—
Concrete and Asphalt Courts—*Wood Courts*—*Other Surfaces*—Where to Play—
Winter Tennis—Tennis Camps and Their Selection—Tips for Parents

Section III.   Principles of Lawn Tennis, 93

Fundamentals of Tennis—The Grip—*Eastern Grip*—*Continental Grip*—*Western Grip*
—Tennis Form—*The Swing and Hitting the Ball*—*Footwork*—*Timing*—Tennis
Strokes—Forehand Ground Strokes—*The Flat Forehand Drive*—*Topspin on the
Forehand*—*Slice and Chop Strokes*—Backhand Ground Strokes—*Topspin and Under-
spin*—Lobbing—Volleying—*Horizontal Volleying*—*Smashing and Overhead Volley-
ing*—*The Lob Volley*—*The Stop Volley*—*The Drop Shot*—*The Half Volley*—The

Service Stroke—*The Grip—The Stance—The Ball Toss—The Swing—The Slice Service—The Flat Service—The Twist Service—Service Strategy*—The Return of the Serve—Changing and Correcting a Stroke—Court Tactics and Strategy—Player Position and the Placement of the Ball—*The "Center Theory"—Depth and Net Clearance*—Playing on Different Surfaces—Playing the Wind—Tennis Strategy and Psychology—*Match Play—Practice*—Taking a Tennis Lesson—*Kinds of Lessons—The Teacher's Methods—Learning Takes Time—Kinds of Practice—Understanding the Learning Process*—Doubles Play—Service Strategy—Return-of-Service Strategy—Strategy During Rallies—Doubles Tips—Mixed Doubles

Section IV.   Rules and Etiquette of Lawn Tennis, 165

United States Lawn Tennis Association (USLTA)—USLTA Sectional Associations—International Lawn Tennis Federation (ILTF)—Rules of Lawn Tennis—Scoring—Conventional Scoring System—*Scoring the Game—Scoring the Set—Scoring the Match*—Nine-Point Tie-Breaker Game—*Singles—Doubles*—Twelve-Point Tie-Breaker Game—*Singles—Doubles*—VASSS (Van Alen Simplified Scoring System)—*Rules of VASSS "No-Ad"—Rules of VASSS "Single Point"—Nine-Point VASSS Tie-Breaker Rule*—Handicapping in Lawn Tennis—*VASSS Handicap Rules*—Par Tennis—Competition and Tournaments—Types of Tournaments—USLTA Amateur-Player Ruling—*Enrollment in the USLTA*—USLTA Championship Tournament Regulations—How to Make the Draw—Seeding the Draw—*Where the Seeds Go—The Rest of the Draw—"Foreign" Seeds—Rankings*—Other Types of Competitions—*Single Elimination Tournament—Double Elimination Tournament—Consolation Tournament—Round-Robin Tournament—Handicap Tournament—Move-Up Move-Down Tournament—Ladder Tournament—Pyramid Tournament—VASSS Round-Robin Medal Play*—Team Matches—First Aid on the Courts—Duties and Jurisdictions of Officials—Duties of Referee, Umpire, and Linesman—*Net Umpire—Foot-Fault Judge*—The Tennis Umpires' Association—Tennis Etiquette—Twelve Unwritten Rules of Good Courtmanship—Etiquette for the Gallery

Section V.   Results of Major Tournaments and Lawn Tennis Championships, 221

USLTA Champions—*Men's Singles*—USLTA Open Champions—*Men's Singles*—USLTA Amateur Champions—*Men's Singles*—USLTA Champions—*Men's Doubles*—USLTA Open Champions—*Men's Doubles*—USLTA Amateur Champions—*Men's Doubles*—USLTA Champions—*Women's Singles*—USLTA Open Champions—*Women's Singles*—USLTA Amateur Champions—*Women's Singles*—USLTA Champions—*Women's Doubles*—USLTA Open Champions—*Women's Doubles*—USLTA Amateur Champions—*Women's Doubles*—USLTA Champions—*Mixed Doubles*—USLTA Open Champions—*Mixed Doubles*—USLTA Amateur Champions—*Mixed Doubles*—USLTA Champions—*Junior Singles—Junior Doubles—Junior Singles (Grass)—Junior Doubles (Grass)—Boys' 16 Singles—Boys' 16 Doubles—Boys' 14 Singles—Boys' 14 Doubles—Boys' 12 Singles—Boys' 12 Doubles—Girls' 18 Singles—Girls' 18 Doubles—Girls' 16 Singles—Girls' 16 Doubles—Girls' 14 Singles—Girls' 14 Doubles—Girls' 12 Singles—Girls' 12 Doubles—Father and Son—Men Seniors' Singles—Men Seniors' Doubles*—USLTA Open Champions—*Men Seniors' Doubles*—USLTA Amateur Grass Court Champions—*Men's Singles—Men's Doubles—Women's Singles*—

Women's Doubles—Men Seniors' 55 Singles—Men Seniors' 55 Doubles—Men Seniors' 60 Singles—Men Seniors' 60 Doubles—Men Seniors' 65 Singles—Men Seniors' 65 Doubles—Men Seniors' 70 Singles—Men Seniors' 70 Doubles—Women Seniors' Singles—Women Seniors' Doubles—USLTA Champions—*Mother and Daughter*—USLTA Indoor Champions—*Men's Singles—Men's Doubles—Women's Singles—Women's Doubles—Mixed Doubles—Junior Singles—Junior Doubles—Boys' 16 Singles—Boys' 16 Doubles—Girls' 18 Singles—Girls 18 Doubles—Girls' 16 Singles—Girls' 16 Doubles—Seniors' Singles—Seniors' Doubles—Men's 35 Singles—Men's 35 Doubles—Men Seniors' 55 Singles—Men Seniors' 55 Doubles—Men Seniors' 60 Singles—Men Seniors' 60 Doubles—Men Seniors' 65 Singles—Men Seniors' 65 Doubles—Men Seniors' 70 Singles—Men Seniors' 70 Doubles—Women Seniors' Singles—Women Seniors' Doubles—Seniors' Mixed Doubles*—USLTA Hard Court Champions—*Men's Singles—Men's Doubles—Women's Singles—Women's Doubles—Mixed Doubles—Junior Singles—Junior Doubles—Boys' 16 Singles—Boys' 16 Doubles—Boys' 14 Singles—Boys' 14 Doubles—Boys' 12 Singles—Boys' 12 Doubles—Girls' 18 Singles—Girls' 18 Doubles—Girls' 16 Singles—Girls' 16 Doubles—Girls' 14 Singles—Girls' 14 Doubles—Girls' 12 Singles—Girls' 12 Doubles—Father and Son—Men Seniors' Singles—Men Seniors' Doubles—Women Seniors' Singles—Women Seniors' Double—Seniors' Mixed Doubles—Men's 35 Singles—Men's 35 Doubles—Men Seniors' 50 Singles—Men Seniors' 50 Doubles—Men Seniors' 55 Singles—Men Seniors' 55 Doubles—Men Seniors' 60 Singles—Men Seniors' 60 Doubles—Men Seniors' 65 Singles—Men Seniors' 65 Doubles—Men Seniors' 70 Singles—Men Seniors' 70 Doubles—Women's 35 Singles—Women's 35 Doubles—Women Seniors' 50 Singles—Women Seniors' 50 Doubles*—USLTA Clay Court Champions—*Men's Singles—Men's Doubles—Women's Singles—Women's Doubles*—USLTA Amateur Clay Court Champions—*Men's Singles—Men's Doubles—Women's Singles—Women's Doubles*—USLTA Clay Court Champions—*Junior Singles—Junior Doubles—Boys' 16 Singles—Boys' 16 Doubles—Girls' 18 Singles—Girls' 18 Doubles—Father and Son—Men's 35 Singles—Men's 35 Doubles—Men Seniors' Singles—Men Seniors' 50 Singles—Men Seniors' 50 Doubles—Men Seniors' 55 Singles—Men Seniors' 55 Doubles—Men Seniors' 60 Singles—Men Seniors' 60 Doubles—Men Seniors' 65 Singles—Men Seniors' 65 Doubles*—USLTA Interscholastic Champions—*Men's Singles—Men's Doubles*—USLTA Women's Collegiate Champions—*Singles—Doubles*—National Intercollegiate Champions—*Men's Singles—Men's Doubles*—Colleges Winning Intercollegiate Championship—(Men's Singles)—Winners of both Intercollegiate Championship and National Singles (Men's Singles)—National Public Parks Champions—*Men's Singles—Men's Doubles—Women's Singles—Women's Doubles—Mixed Doubles—Junior Singles—Junior Doubles—Boys' 16 Singles—Boys' 16 Doubles—Boys' 14 Singles—Boys' 12 Singles—Girls' 18 Singles—Girls' 18 Doubles—Girls' 16 Singles—Girls' 16 Doubles—Girls' 14 Singles—Girls' 12 Singles—Men's 35 Singles—Men's 35 Doubles—Men Seniors' Singles—Men Seniors' Doubles—Women Seniors' Singles—Women Seniors' Doubles*—Record of Church Cup Matches—Record of Sears Cup Matches—U.S. Title Matches of Leading Events (1965–1971)—American Tennis Association Champions—*Men's Singles—Men's Doubles—Women's Singles—Women's Doubles—Mixed Doubles*—U.S. National Professional Champions—*Men's Singles—Men's Doubles—Women's Singles—Mixed Doubles*—Title Matches of Leading Contract Pro Events (1969–1971)—United States Major Tournament Summary (1966–1971)—United States Professional Tournaments (1967–1971)—Australian Championships—*Men's*

Singles—*Men's Doubles*—*Women's Singles*—*Women's Doubles*—*Mixed Doubles*—
Canadian Championships—*Men's Singles*—*Men's Doubles*—*Women's Singles*—
Women's Doubles—*Mixed Doubles*—French Championships—*Men's Singles*—*Men's
Doubles*—*Women's Singles*—*Women's Doubles*—*Mixed Doubles*—German Champion-
ships—*Men's Singles*—*Men's Doubles*—*Women's Singles*—*Women's Doubles*—*Mixed
Doubles*—All-England Championships—*Men's Singles*—*Men's Doubles*—*Women's
Singles*—*Women's Doubles*—*Mixed Doubles*—British Hard Courts—*Men's Singles*—
Women's Singles—British Covered Court (Indoor) Championships—*Men's Singles*—
Women's Singles—Irish Championships—*Men's Singles*—*Women's Singles*—Italian
Championships—*Men's Singles*—*Men's Doubles*—*Women's Singles*—*Women's Doubles*
—*Mixed Doubles*—New Zealand Championships—*Men's Singles*—*Women's Singles*—
South African Championships—*Men's Singles*—*Women's Singles*—Welsh Champion-
ships—*Men's Singles*—*Women's Singles*—Other Major World Championships (1968–
1971)—Professional World Tournament—Davis Cup—Challenge Rounds—Challenge-
Round Standings—Finals and Interzone Play—United States Rivalries—Kings Cup—
Dubler Cup—Stevens Cup—Mitre Cup—Galea Cup—Annie Soisbault Cup—Sunshine
Cup—Wightman Cup—Federation Cup—United States Federation Cup Rivalries

Section VI.   Lawn Tennis Greats, 367

National Lawn Tennis Hall of Fame—World Tennis Roll of Honor—Leading Tennis
Players of Today—Age of Men National Champions—USLTA Rankings (Men)—
USLTA Rankings (Women)—*Leading Members of the First Ten*—All-American
Top Ten World Rankings (Men)—World Rankings (Men and Women)—*Leading
Members of the World's First Ten*—All-Time Records—*Men's Singles*—*Men's
Doubles*—*Women's Singles*—*Women's Doubles*—*Mixed Doubles*—Longest Sets
(*Men's Singles*)—Longest Sets (*Men's Doubles*)—Longest Sets (*Women's Singles*)—
Longest Sets (*Women's Doubles*)—*Most Games Won in Succession*—Shortest Set in
a Tournament Match—The Grand Slams of Tennis—USLTA Tennis Awards—*The
William M. Johnston Award*—*Junior and Boys' Sportsmanship Award*—*Girls' Sports-
manship Trophy Award*—*The Samuel Hardy Award*—*The Harold A. Lebair Memorial
Trophy*—*The John T. McGovern Umpires' Award*—*The Service Bowl Award*—*New
England Winners*—*National Winners*—*Seniors' Service Award*—*The Colonel James H.
Bishop Award*—*Tennis Educational Merit Award*—*The Ralph W. Westcott Award*—
The Leadership Award for Women—*The Maureen Connolly Brinker Award*—Lead-
ing Achievers in Davis Cup Play—*Davis Cup Stalwarts of All-Times*—*Davis Cup Stal-
warts Among the Leaders*—*Challenge-Round Stalwarts*—*Vital Challenge-Round
Matches*—*Longest Davis Cup Matches*—*United States Davis Cup Who's Who*—
American Davis Cup Highs—Wightman Cup Leaders—*United States Wightman Cup's
Who's Who*—*Leading British Wightman Cup Players*—Federation Cup Leaders—
All-Time Federation Leading Players—*Longest Federation Cup Matches*—Prize
Money List (Men's)—Prize Money List (Women's)—Pepsi Grand Prix.

Section VII.   Glossary of Lawn Tennis Terms, 457

Index, 468

SECTION I

History of Lawn Tennis

Lawn tennis, as we know it today, is a relatively young game, having been in existence for around a hundred years. Nevertheless, varied forms of the sport were known centuries ago, and the actual game of lawn tennis borrowed characteristics from several different games.

One of these was the "royal and ancient" game of court tennis. This game goes back for centuries; most historians agree that the sport started in France in the early part of the fourteenth century. But whether the French invented the game, or whether it is an adaptation of a ball game introduced from the East after the Crusades, perhaps from the Byzantines, is a matter of surmise. The Romans and Greeks are known to have played a game under the name of *sphaeristeria* (a Greco-Latin word meaning a courtyard where a ball game was played), which was similar in many ways to the early form of court tennis played in France.

Earliest records in France indicate that court tennis, considered as a type of handball, was played in open courtyards or monastery cloisters. During the mid-fourteenth century, closed courts were built for the practice of the game, and these closed courts multiplied with amazing rapidity throughout the country, although the outdoor game still continued. The game in France was called *jeu de paume* (game of the palm of the hand), and gradually the indoor game came to be known as *jeu de courte paume* (short tennis) and the outdoor game as *jeu de longue paume* (long tennis).

Some maintain that the word *court* originated from the description of the indoor game. The outdoor game apparently passed into England, as we find there descriptions and illustrations of an outdoor game of "open, or long, tennis." This was undoubtedly copied directly from the game in France.

The original outdoor game, as previously mentioned, consisted of hitting the ball with the bare hand, or the hand covered by a glove; however, when the indoor game became prominent, crude rackets were invented to extend the player's reach. These early court tennis rackets were called *battoirs,* and we find them described by Antonio Scaino, the Italian author of the first known book of tennis, *Trattato del Ginoco della Palla,* published in Venice in 1555, as being of various shapes. The heads of the battoirs were later hollowed out and covered with parchment, and owing to this practice many precious manuscripts fell prey to the battoir makers and tennis players of the time. Later, stringing took the place of parchment, and in this way the racket in tennis was evolved. For many years, however, tennis was played both ways, and there are old accounts of matches where players with rackets played opponents without rackets, and vice versa.

The ball used in court tennis was a leather-covered affair stuffed with wool.

In court tennis, from the earliest times, the number fifteen has been the scoring unit. Scaino informs us in his book that even in his time (the sixteenth century) each stroke won

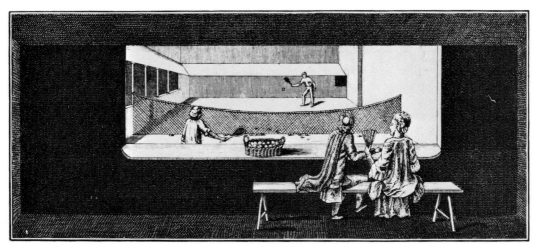

The play of court tennis was very popular in the sixteenth and seventeenth centuries.

scored fifteen for the winner: that is, for the first, fifteen; for the second, thirty; for the third, forty-five; or at one (*a una*), meaning only one stroke necessary to win; and at two (*a due*), when the game is "set" at two strokes to be gained for winning. The term *a una* is now obsolete, but *a due* is still preserved in the French expression *à deux,* and in the English equivalent "deuce." The term "advantage," in Italian *vantaggio,* like *avantage* in French, was also used at that time. The only change that has taken place during the course of centuries has been the contraction from forty-five to forty, a change undoubtedly made merely for the sake of brevity and ease in calling the score.

Regarding the mysterious counting by fifteen, Scaino states at the very outset that after most diligent search he has been unable to find any literature, ancient or modern, on the subject. Tennis historians, even today, cannot decide upon any definite reason for the fifteen counting system. Many, however, agree with Jean Gosselin's treatise written in 1579 which contends that the numbers fifteen, thirty, forty-five, etc., could not have been arbitrarily chosen, but must have been taken from some definite measure, familiarly known to those who first practiced the game. This measure is said to have been borrowed from astronomy: A physical sign (or sextant) being the sixth part of a circle, and itself consisting of 60 degrees, each of which is divided into 60 minutes, and each minute into 60 seconds,

it seemed likely that scoring at tennis imitated this division of the circle. For the physical sign equals four times 15 degrees, as four times 15 makes a game of tennis, and four games made a set according to the practice in France at that date. (The six-game set was instituted in the early 1700's.)

During the late fifteenth and sixteenth centuries tennis became *the* game among the wealthy people of France, especially in Paris, where it is on record that over 1800 courts were to be found in that city alone. In England its popularity also increased, especially under the reign of King Henry VIII (1509–1547).

During the early nineteenth century in England, royal tennis was played in a roofed and walled court of 110 by 38 feet, across which was stretched a net 5 feet high at the posts. Along both back walls and one side wall, and somewhat less than halfway up, narrow roofs sloped inward. The server hit the ball over the net and onto the sloping roof, along which it rolled until it fell off into the striker's (receiver's) court; the striker, hitting the ball either before it bounced or on the first bounce, returned it across the net to any part of the court, provided it did not hit above a play line marked on the rear and side walls. The method of scoring was 15, 30, 45, and game, and both the server and receiver could obtain scoring points.

Today court tennis, or what the English purist would call tennis, or *real* tennis, is not widely known. A grand total of about 38 courts are now in existence throughout the world.

The second game that had an influence on lawn tennis was the game of racquets, or rackets. While court tennis was considered the game of the wealthy, racquets was actually a slum sport, originating in the yards of eighteenth-century English debtors' jails. In the early 1800's it moved out of the jails into private sport clubs and became fairly popular. It was played in a walled court without a net, the ball being alternately hit against the front wall by the opponents, and scoring was based on a 15-point game. (One point was awarded for a fault or missed shot, but only the server could obtain a scoring point.) The modern games of squash rackets and squash tennis are an outgrowth of "lowly" racquets.

The next game to come into vogue that has some bearing on lawn tennis was badminton, named after the Duke of Beaufort's home in Gloucestershire, where apparently it was first played by the fashionables of the 1850's. Originating in India, this game was to have several effects on lawn tennis. Its play was similar to the game of badminton of today.

Another wall game, called "fives," was

Court tennis is still played today on approximately 38 courts throughout the world. The above court tennis match in progress was at the Royal Tennis Courts in Melbourne, Australia.

played at such English schools as Harrow and Eton, and while played somewhat like modern handball, it also had an influence on the modern game of lawn tennis.

But who invented tennis? In the early 1870's several independent groups of players were experimenting with an outdoor game which would take the place of croquet, then losing popularity in country-house circles owing to the necessity of excellent turf for its pursuit. It is on record that in the 1860's Major T. H. Gem and L. B. Perera were playing a form of "real" tennis on a lawn and they called it "lawn tennis or lawn pelota"; and in June, 1873, the house of James Lillywhite announced a new outdoor Indian lawn game "prettier, healthier and merrier than croquet" to be known as "lawn racquets." Maybe this prompted Major W. C. Wingfield to step into the field and issue his now famous pamphlet introducing his game "Sphairistike" to the Christmas party at Nantclwyd in December of that year. At all events, Wingfield can claim to be the chief pioneer when he exploited the game of lawn tennis by filing a specification for the invention of "a new and improved court for the playing of the ancient game of tennis," though it will be noted that he did not profess to have invented a new game, but a new *court*.

However, most historians credit Walter Clopton Wingfield with the invention of the modern game of lawn tennis. Actually, he took the basic principles of court tennis and adapted them to outdoor play where there were no walls. It was played on grass, the net from badminton was employed, the ball was borrowed from fives, and the scoring technique was taken from racquets. In order to make the novelty his own so that it could be of financial benefit, Wingfield called the invention "Sphairistike, or Lawn Tennis," from the ancient Greek game, and designed the shape of the court in the form of an hourglass, with a high net and wings on both sides. In February, 1874, Wingfield received a patent for his game. In the specification for requesting this patent, Wingfield claimed the invention to be ". . . a new and improved portable court for playing the ancient game of tennis." He then hired an agent to manufacture the sets in quantities. These sets consisted of rackets, balls, and a net, and on them were

Major Walter Clopton Wingfield—the man most historians credit with the invention of the modern game of lawn tennis.

printed the words, "Dedicated to the party assembled at Nantclwyd in December, 1873." The game was an immediate success and soon became the most popular lawn game in English society.

Wingfield also published an eight-page pamphlet entitled *Sphairistike or Lawn Tennis*. This booklet contained the first rules formulated for the game, and they were quite different from the ones of today. The hourglass court was 60 feet in length and at the widest part, the base line, it was 30 feet in width. The shape of the court can be visualized by noting that even though the base line was 30 feet in width, the net was only 21 feet wide. The net was low, 4 feet 8 inches at the center, but was 7 feet high at the sides. A small box or crease was marked in the middle of the court on each side of the net. This was the place where the server stood to serve the ball. The object of the server was to send the ball into a space behind this crease in the opposite court. The receiver was allowed to strike the served ball either on the volley or on the first bounce. The scoring was similar to the method used in badminton today whereby only the server can win points, and a game consisted of 15 points.

In August of 1874, Wingfield published another pamphlet concerning some new rules. The service crease was no longer included as court measurements but the shape of the court was still in the form of an hourglass and the game was still called by the difficult name of "Sphairistike." This title was a failure, as the word was not only difficult to pronounce but could not be remembered by most people. It soon earned itself the nickname "Sticky." Eventually, after much criticism of the name, Wingfield published another pamphlet in which "Sphairistike" was omitted and the game was called "lawn tennis."

It is necessary to mention that Major Wingfield received much criticism during his lifetime concerning his invention of lawn tennis. Many felt that he did not deserve the credit for originating a new game because he had incorporated ideas from so many other sports. Furthermore, they resented the fact that he made a considerable profit from his ingenuity by the sale of his patented sets. Even though the game he introduced was not completely original, he deserves the same honor that is associated with James Naismith in relation to basketball.

LAWN TENNIS BECOMES A MAJOR SPORT

In 1875 the Marylebone Cricket Club in England published a revision of Wingfield's tennis rules. There were still the hourglass court, the racquets system of scoring, and a net slightly higher at the edges. These 1875 rules, however, did include some very important changes, and a few of them are regulation in the world today. The length of the court was established at 78 feet. The server was now required to serve from the back line instead of the middle of the court. Also, the serve could no longer be taken on the volley, and a let in service was counted as good.

But the birthplace of the sport of lawn tennis may be said to have been on the grounds of the All England Croquet Club at Wimbledon. As was stated earlier, croquet is a game which demands extremely true turf, and it was while admiring the magnificent velvety square at Worple Road, Wimbledon, that three otherwise sober-minded gentlemen decided it would make an ideal surface for the lusty new game "Sphairistike," which was then sweeping England.

So the lively three began agitating for the right to invade those sacred lawns and to stage the first Lawn Tennis Championships. Sphairistike was too clumsy a name and, as previously stated, it soon gave way to the one by which the game is known today. The agitators were very persuasive, and so the honor of promoting the first "Wimbledon" was entrusted to a committee of four gentlemen, all of whom deserve the gratitude of lawn tennis players the world over. Three of them—Julian Marshall, an eminent authority on royal (or court) tennis, Henry Jones, widely known as the expert "Cavendish," and C. G. Heathcote, a fine player himself and the stipendary magistrate at Brighton— formed the subcommittee which set up a pattern, followed ever since, by studying the rules then prevailing, deciding they were impossible, and so drawing up a completely new set. The fourth member of the committee was J. H. Walsh, editor of *The Field* magazine, in whose offices at 346, The Strand, London, W.C.2, the All England Club had been founded. It was Walsh who introduced lawn tennis into the program and who, with B. C. Evelegh as seconder, carried the motion to hold a championship meeting. *The Field* presented a silver challenge cup of a value of 25 guineas, which was subsequently won outright by William Renshaw.

Until 1877 there were almost as many sets of rules as there were tennis courts, although the primary set in use on most courts had been the rules drawn up by the Marylebone Cricket Club's Tennis Committee in 1875, which were the subject of much controversy. Messrs. Heathcote, Jones, and Marshall decided they would have none of this, and so they framed a virtually new set of conditions and rules. History has fully justified them.

Three of the main principles laid down have stood the test of time and are still basic foundations on which the game is built, a

The early game of tennis as played in England.

splendid testimony to the foresight and wisdom of the revolutionary three men. These include, for example, abandonment of the hourglass court and adoption of the rectangular one. The size of the court was also set at 26 yards (78 feet) long by 9 yards (27 feet) wide, which are the present measurements. The net was suspended from posts 3 feet outside the court. Also, one fault on a serve was adopted, a let on a serve was still considered legal, and the server was allowed to stand astride the base line. The most dramatic rule change was the discarding of the racquets system of scoring and adoption of the court tennis method so that the game would be scored ". . . by fifteens, games, and sets."

The original notice to the outside world that the championship meeting was being staged was given in *The Field* of June 9, 1877. Over the signature of Henry Jones, honorary secretary of the Lawn Tennis Sub-Committee, it read: "The All England Croquet and Lawn Tennis Club, Wimbledon, proposes to hold a lawn tennis meeting, open to all amateurs, on Monday July 9 and following days. Entrance fee, one pound, one shilling. Two prizes will be given—one gold champion prize to the winner, one silver to the second player." Notice that the Club added "Lawn Tennis" to its name in 1877.

Of the 22 players who entered, the majority were more or less familiar with tennis scoring, a circumstance which Heathcote declared fortunate for the legislators. The winner and first champion, S. W. Gore, an old Harrovian and eminent racquets player, was naturally adept at all ball games. He possessed great mobility, a long reach, and a strong, flexible wrist which he used to great effect on the volley. It must be remembered that, with the net much higher at the sides (5 feet) than it is today (3 feet 6 inches), the down-the-line pass was impossible and covering the net, therefore, much easier than today. So C. G. Heathcote, whom Gore beat in the final, later wrote: "Gore was the first to realize, as the first and great principle of lawn tennis, the necessity of forcing his opponent to the back line, when he would approach the net and, by a dexterous turn of the wrist, return the ball at considerable speed, now in the forehand, now in the backhand court, till, to borrow the expression of one of his opponents of the year, his antagonist was ready to drop." So was born the net rusher!

If volleying was decisive from the start, service was not. All entrants to the first championship used the side service used in racquets, and it was not until the following year that A. T. Myers introduced the overarm service to lawn tennis. Nevertheless, there were a fair number of aces, not because of speed but because the court, for all its smooth appearance, was terribly rough compared with the "tennis only," carefully coddled Centre Court of the new (1922) Wimbledon. Of the 601 games contested in the 70 sets played at

that historic first Wimbledon, 376 went with service, 225 against. The players changed ends only at the end of the set, which had a "sudden death" after 5-all, the winner of the next game taking it. About 200 people paid one shilling each to watch the play and the championship was adjourned during the Eton-Harrow cricket match, a great social occasion in those far-off days.

The history of tennis, like the history of war, has shown that methods of attack are, sooner or later, countered by new systems of defense. P. F. Hadow, another old Harrovian, on leave from tea planting in Ceylon, produced the answer to Gore's net attacks the following year in 1878. (These were made from so close to the net that he frequently volleyed the ball before it had reached his side. This caused a long stoppage the first time it happened. His shot was judged fair but the rule was amended in 1880 to the present one forbidding intrusion of the opponent's side.)

Gore's closeness to the net, then 4 feet 9 inches high at the posts, gave Hadow, a

The lawn tennis meeting at Wimbledon in 1882.

patient base-liner, the clue to success—a series of lobs hoisted over Gore as he rushed netward. So Hadow won the Challenge Round, abolished in 1922, 7–5, 6–1, 9–7.

Earlier L. Erskine and C. G. Hamilton played out before 700 spectators the first five-set match at Wimbledon, Erskine winning after saving two match points.

Wimbledon was now firmly launched, although interest ebbed and flowed over the next decade or so. The year 1881 produced one record which has stood ever since—the shortest men's singles final, or Challenge Round, as it was then called. Willie Renshaw took only 37 minutes to beat the Reverend J. T. Hartley. Willie Renshaw won the singles seven times in all, another record among men, although Helen Wills Moody Roark won the women's singles a total of eight times.

The first overseas winner of Wimbledon did not travel far. W. J. Hamilton crossed the Irish Channel in 1890 to beat Willie Renshaw in the last Challenge Round ever played by that illustrious stylist. One year later William Baddeley, 19, became the youngest winner of the men's singles, a record which still stands.

The first "Centre Court full" notices were posted in 1894, and royalty, in the person of Crown Princess Stephanie of Austria, made its first visit in 1895. In 1907 all the titles—men's and women's—went overseas and, in 1909, A. W. Gore became, at 41 years 7 months, the oldest man ever to win the singles.

Thanks to the British efforts and the popularity of Wimbledon, lawn tennis spread round the world. Tennis clubs started in Scotland (1875), Brazil (1875), India (1875), Germany (1876), Ireland (1877), France (1877), Australia (1878), Sweden (1878), Italy (1878), Hungary (1878), Peru (1878), Denmark (1880), Switzerland (1880), Argentina (1881), the Netherlands (1882), Jamaica (1883), Greece (1885), Turkey (1885), Lebanon (1889), Egypt (1890), Finland (1890), and South Africa (1892).

LAWN TENNIS COMES TO THE UNITED STATES

A few months after the game of Sphairistike was patented, the British garrison stationed in Bermuda obtained some sets of equipment. An American visitor, Mary Ewing Outerbridge, of Staten Island, New York, tried the game and became very interested in it. When she returned home in the spring of 1874, she brought with her a net, some balls, and several rackets that had been given to her by some of the British officers. Upon arriving at the port of New York, she had difficulty in getting her tennis set through the customs house, as no one knew what it was, and consequently could not classify it for duty. But her brother, A. Emelius Outerbridge, was prominent in shipping circles, and she called upon him for assistance, and he helped her get the set through the customs. Outerbridge was an active cricketer and a director of the Staten Island Cricket and Baseball Club, which had its grounds at Camp Washington (later St. George), Staten Island. He obtained permission from the Club to allow his sister, shortly after her return from Bermuda, to set up her net and mark out a court in one corner of the grounds. Most tennis historians agree that this court on Staten Island, which was laid out in 1874, was the first lawn tennis court in America.

However, some accounts claim that prior to this court at Staten Island, a court was erected at the summer home of William Appleton in Nahant, Mass. The following evidence conclusively indicates that the court in Nahant was made following the event at Staten Island. The earliest account on record concerning Miss Outerbridge's introduction of the game to the United States appeared in 1887 in a historical sketch of the Staten Island Cricket and Baseball Club. It told of Miss Outerbridge's return from Bermuda and stated: ". . . armed with a net, a set of rules, rackets and balls, (she) returned to America and paid the United States Customs duties on the first lawn tennis set ever brought into this country." She lost no time in interesting her friends in the pastime, and obtained a ready assent from the members of the club to erect a net on their grounds; for it must be remembered that at this time the famous ladies' club had not come into existence.

In 1890, three years after this article and

approximately fifteen years after the event itself, Richard D. Sears, first tennis champion of the United States, proclaimed in a published story that a court had been laid out in Nahant in August of 1874 and thus was the first court for lawn tennis in America. Malcolm D. Whitman, also a national champion, proved by construction contract dates that the Nahant court was erected one year later during August of 1875, and since the court in New York was put up in the spring of 1874, the Staten Island court was therefore the earliest lawn tennis court of any kind, public or private, in the United States.

Even though there is this slight question as to which court was the first one in this country, there is complete agreement that the first two tennis players of any prominence in the country played in Nahant. One was James Dwight, who some years later became the president of the United States National Lawn Tennis Association and has been often called the "father of American lawn tennis." The other person was F. R. Sears, Jr., who was the elder brother of the first United States national tennis champion.

Soon courts were constructed at Newport, R.I.; Plainfield, N.J.; and Tuxedo, N.Y. It is important to keep in mind, however, that the game of tennis was played by relatively small numbers during its first few years in America. Tennis was a sport for wealthy people who either belonged to clubs that had grass areas or who owned estates with suitable lawns so that a court could be laid out on the premises. In addition, what little popularity the game acquired was limited to the eastern area of the United States.

Development of the Game in the United States

The American players were, at first, completely dependent upon England not only for the necessary equipment but also for the regulations of the game. Each rule change that was drafted in England soon became tennis law in the United States. As a result, the early rules in America paralleled those of England. Nevertheless, numerous local variations in the rules and equipment were seen. The rackets were of different sizes, some triangular, some square, and some bent like a shovel. In the book *Fifty Years of Lawn Tennis in the United States,* these early rackets were spoken of as "exaggerated fly-swatters." The balls were of different weights despite the fact that each tennis dealer stamped his particular brand "Regulation." Even court dimensions were not always the same, and the height of the net varied with the locality. The early game itself was a somewhat leisurely one for several reasons. First, the players' dress consisted of regular street clothing and leather shoes. For the women this meant that their apparel was a full, long skirt and many petticoats. As a result, both men and women were hampered in their movement. Another reason for the slow pace of the game was that there were

Dr. James Dwight, an early tennis player, who has often been called the "father of American lawn tennis."

only two basic strokes employed, a sliced drive and a chop. In addition, the serve was moderate in speed since it was done either underhand or at the shoulder level. It was not uncommon to see eight players in a match standing still on the court patting the ball back and forth without its touching the ground.

In September, 1878, an article appeared in *Harper's Weekly* on "This elegant and pleasant pastime, lawn tennis, which has become popular in this country within a short time." But it gave the width of the court as 30 feet at the base line, and said it might be reduced to 24 feet at the net. It put the height of the net at 5 feet at the posts and 4 feet in the middle. It described the rackets as 27 to 30 inches in length, and suggested covered balls for fine weather and uncovered ones for rainy days. It noted that two, four, or eight could play at once, and kept the racquets method of counting. It did not accept the new Wimbledon rules.

An ordinary outfit, including four rackets, a net, poles, and balls, said this article, could be purchased in any city for 15 dollars.

This novel game of tennis, however, was not treated with much respect at first. Most looked upon it as a curiosity, for very few even knew what it was called. Many newspapers sent their reporters to write humorous articles about the gentle pastime and had ". . . artists draw comic sketches of the queer implements and aesthetic postures of the players." People scoffed at the sport, thinking it fit only for women and unathletic men. One author stated, "No other game was treated with so much indifference and to so many slurs." An example of this scorn is shown by the following excerpt taken from a letter that appeared in *The Harvard Crimson* on April 5, 1878.

Allow me a little space to expostulate, not ill-naturedly I hope, on a kind of athletics that seems to be gaining ground very fast at Harvard. I mean to say Lawn Tennis. There are now four clubs, and perhaps five, that have come into existence here this year. These clubs are generally composed of eight members each; that is, we have now at Harvard from thirty to forty men who devote their leisure hours to Lawn Tennis. Many of these men were formerly seen on the river, forming part of the club fours and sixes; now they have deserted these posts, where as much energy is needed as the College can supply, for a sport that will do themselves little physical good, and can never reflect any credit on the College. Is it not a pity that serious athletics should be set aside by able-bodied men for a game that is at best intended for a seaside pastime? The game is well enough for lazy or *weak* men, but men who have rowed or taken part in a nobler sport should blush to be seen playing Lawn Tennis.

Many historians feel that this early attitude was fostered by use of the word "love" in the scoring process. The general public gathered from the word that there was ". . . something languorous or love-sick" to the game. In a short time, however, the growing popularity of tennis in America was shown by an article that appeared in England's *Century* in 1879. The article stated:

The game is also winning favor in America, and it has so much in it that is commendable that it will, no doubt, supersede croquet as a garden recreation there as it has already done in England.

Even so, some of the cricket clubs where tennis played a minor role were beginning to worry that this new game might supplant the old one. The *American Cricketer*, in the late 1870's, stated under the headline "Let Us Face The Music":

If the success of lawn tennis gives warrant to anticipate such a result, the matter is indeed a serious one. Frankly, the *Cricketer* does not deem the thing is even remotely a possibility.

Despite the critics and scornful articles the game took hold and steadily increased in popularity. With an increased growth of tennis, competition was stimulated. The first tournament on record in the United States was played on the private court of William Appleton in Nahant, Mass., in August, 1876. It was a local round-robin affair with 15 entries, although only 13 players took part. Since James Dwight and F. R. Sears, Jr., were decidedly superior to the other contestants, handicaps were given to the players. Despite the handicapping system in use from England, Dwight beat Sears by a score of 12–15, 15–7, 15–13.

Both, as we said, were at scratch. All of the other matches were decided by a single set, and racquets scoring was used.

For the sake of the record we give the scores of the matches played by Dwight with the handicap allowed the other players. Dwight beat H. Curtis, (4) 15–8; Dan Curtis, (4) 15–8; Louis Curtis, (5) 15–8; R. Grant, (7) 15–7; W. Otis, (7) 15–8; H. G. Otis, (9) 15–10; Guild, (11) 15–13; Merriam, (11) 15–11; Ellis, (12) 15–12; Greenough (13) 15–13; Post, (13) 15–13.

Soon local matches sprang up between various neighboring clubs. In 1879 the Belmont Cricket Club in Philadelphia issued a challenge to the neighboring clubs and stated that a tournament would be played "under such regulations as to size of court, etc., as may be hereafter agreed upon." Local tournaments were also held at Newport, Boston, Philadelphia, and Staten Island.

In 1880 Emelius H. Outerbridge was the secretary of the Staten Island Cricket and Baseball Club. Upon his suggestion, it was decided to hold a tournament at the Club. The tournament was to be open to any player in the United States, and the winner was to be called the "Champion of America." Both singles and doubles matches were to be played.

The tournament, which was held on September 1, 1880, presented some difficulties. For instance, the few clubs where tennis was played then had no uniform rules and no uniform balls. Some were playing with uncovered rubber balls; some with balls made by Wright and Ditson; some with balls made by Peck and Snyder of New York, all of different sizes and weights, none of them true. Realizing this condition, the committee gave notice in advance to each entrant that the tournament would be played under Wimbledon rules and with the Ayers (British) ball, which was then the standard.

In spite of the warning, difficulty arose early in the tournament. Players who were not doing as well as they had anticipated were ready to lay their troubles to the difference in the balls from those they were used to. Their opponents were quite willing to give them a break by playing with any balls they might choose. But the Tournament Committee, called upon to decide, ruled that such a change could not be permitted. A tournament could not be carried on with a dozen different kinds of balls on the different courts. The players must conform to the rules of play or withdraw. Some of the complainants withdrew, but the tournament went on to a most successful ending as reported by the following press article:

The Staten Island Lawn Tennis Club inaugurated their first open tournament under the most auspicious circumstances. The recent rains had put the grounds in perfect playing condition, and the entries for the competition included the names of some of the finest players in America.

The tournament which was open to all drew many famous players from far and near and the main object that the Staten Island Club had in view when they organized the meeting was to invite players from distant clubs to play on their grounds under their rules.

In America nearly every club has its own rules. The Staten Island Club have made up a set of rules from the Marylebone and All England Clubs, supplemented by some trifling additions of their own, and their aim is to have the Staten Island tennis game the standard game throughout America.

There are in all 33 entries. Seven sets of tennis were laid out on the terrace and on the cricket ground. The sets were all "15 up" and two sets were played in each match. The aggregate number of points instead of number of sets won, deciding who is winner.

The final match was between O. E. Woodhouse, a ranking English player, and J. F. Hellmuth, of Toronto, Canada. Woodhouse won by the scores of 15–11, 14–15, 15–9, 10–15, with two sets–all, but 54 points against 50.

James Dwight and R. D. Sears had come down from Boston but had found the balls different from those they had been accustomed to and had stayed out of the singles. In the doubles, Dwight lodged a protest against the balls, claiming they were lighter, smaller and softer than the regulations demanded. He and Sears were beaten by W. M. Wood and A. F. H. Manning of Morristown, N.J., 15–9, 15–2. The latter team was defeated in the final in straight sets by James Rankine and W. M. Donald, of Staten Island.

Another newspaper account described Woodhouse, who was runner-up at Wimbledon in 1879, as "asparagus stalk, about six

The first "National" lawn tennis tournament on September 1, 1880, on Staten Island, New York.

feet two or three in height with an enormous reach." Before the end of the first set the Englishman's high overhand service was commented upon by players and gallery alike. The only service in this country at the time was known as the "Lawford service," negotiated from low to the ground up with a direct cut.

Some weeks after this event, a club match was held between the Staten Island Cricket and Baseball Club and the Young America Cricket Club of Philadelphia. Here again, discussion arose because the clubs had been accustomed to nets of different heights, and balls of different size. These difficulties at the matches caused not only confusion but began to point the way to dissension among the clubs, which was not helping to promote the growth of tennis. Knowing from the experience of England that tournaments and interclub matches were a necessary feature of the game, the leaders in New York, Philadelphia, and Boston decided that if the sport was to grow in popularity, the rules must be standardized. Outerbridge took the lead in this matter and received permission from the directors of the Staten Island Club to form an association in order to regulate the game. The decision to establish such an organization marked the end of the first stage of development of tennis in the United States.

FOUNDING OF USNLTA

On May 5, 1881, the *American Cricketer* printed a proposal which stated that all organized tennis clubs and clubs playing tennis were invited to send representatives to a convention.

. . . for the purpose of adopting a code of rules and designating a standard ball, to govern and be used in all lawn tennis matches or tournaments throughout the

United States, with a view of enabling all clubs or individual players to meet under equal advantages.

The leaders behind this idea were representatives of three prominent tennis centers in the country. They were Emelius H. Outerbridge of the Staten Island Cricket and Baseball Club, James Dwight from the Beacon Park Athletic Association in Boston, and Clarence M. Clark from the All Philadelphia Lawn Tennis Commission.

The convention to form the association met in Room F of the Fifth Avenue Hotel, New York City, Saturday evening, May 21, 1881. At this first meeting of what was at the time known as the United States National Lawn Tennis Association, there were represented 34 tennis clubs, either by direct delegates or by proxies. These clubs were grouped mainly about the Middle Atlantic and New England seacoast, running as far afield as midwestern Pennsylvania and upstate New York. They included 12 clubs in Pennsylvania, where the interest centered in and around Philadelphia but extended to Harrisburg, Pittsburgh, and Johnstown; six located in and around Boston;

seven in the growing suburban towns of New Jersey; five in various places on Staten Island, Long Island, and in New York State; the remainder scattered through Connecticut and Rhode Island. Incidentally, the present name of the Association—United States Lawn Tennis Association—was adopted in 1920.

During the first session of USNLTA, it was decided that the person nominated for the president should not be chosen from the Staten Island Club nor from either Boston or Philadelphia. There was to be no feeling aroused that these larger clubs were trying to dominate things. So came about the choice of General R. S. Oliver from the little tennis club at Albany, New York, as the first president. Among other items adopted at the meeting was the selection of an Executive Committee with Outerbridge, Dwight, and Clark as members. The All-England Marylebone Rules for 1881 were selected as the "official" rules and the purpose of the organization was read and accepted, ". . . to develop a national scope, to govern the eligibility of clubs and thus to have control over the qualifications of tournament players." Thus

Tennis as it was played at the Newport Casino in 1881.

was created one of the first amateur sports-governing bodies in the United States and the first lawn tennis association in the world.

The Executive Committee met soon after the first gathering and decided upon the use of a uniform court, the adoption of the 15, 30, 40 method of scoring, and the use of the Ayers ball in all national tournaments. It was also decided to hold the first National Men's Championship at the Newport (R.I.) Casino, August 31 to September 3, 1881.

Men's Championship Play Before World War I

The first USNLTA Men's Singles Championship was held at Newport in August, 1881. Twenty-five hopeful aspirants for the title showed up at the tournament. They were all Americans, not a visiting foreign player in the lot. Most of them were from the three big eastern cities—New York, Philadelphia, and Boston, where tennis had been played in the

old and established cricket clubs for several years. (For example, the Seabright Lawn Tennis and Cricket Club was organized as Shrewsbury, New Jersey, in 1877.) There was no seeding of the draw, opponents being drawn entirely by chance. If a player from the Staten Island Cricket Club drew a man from his own organization, he knew pretty well what he was up against and the same went for the Longwood and Germantown Club members; but if the man across the net happened not to be from his own club, he was all in the dark as to his type of game.

There were no grandstands. The very select gallery of what are now termed "socialites" was accommodated on rows of wooden chairs placed round the edge of the court by the club steward. The ladies were gowned in the elaborate summer frills of the period, and each one protected her delicate complexion from the destructive rays of the sun by a fluffy silk and lace parasol. The male spectators sweltered in formal attire, boiled shirts, and stiff

Richard Dudley Sears (*left*) and Henry W. Slocum, Jr. (*right*), the first two United States Singles Champions.

Oliver Campbell defeating Fred Hovey in 1891.

derbies or boaters. They stood for the most part to watch the matches, as that was the only way they could get a view of the proceedings over the tops of the parasols.

The matches were played on a lovely stretch of emerald turf beside the old Newport Casino. It was beautiful turf, much greener than any you could find on the much-used courts of the big tennis clubs today, where all the resources of electric sprinkling systems and rollers are required to insure a blade of grass being left for the finals of the big tournaments. The net was 4 feet high at the posts and 3 feet in the middle, which encouraged cross-court shots which did not have to be lifted over the high part of the barrier. The net was not reinforced by iron strips and tended to sag. This did not matter much as none of the players had a devastating service, which would have swept the flimsy thing away at the first crack. Players changed courts only at the end of a set.

There was no loudspeaker for the umpire, and he did not need one, since his audience was grouped so closely about him. The club did not provide a press box, the papers being not much interested in tennis championships and could well wait until someone dropped into the office to tell them what happened at Newport. The club did not have to worry over parking space either, for automobiles had not been invented and the guests came in their carriages, which the coachmen took away, or they walked to the matches from the nearby "cottages."

Nobody was much surprised when Richard Dudley Sears won the singles title. He was given a medal. Sears had been leading the tennis in the Longwood Cricket Club in Boston, for which he had persuaded his family to give a clubhouse site. Sears won the title the next year too and was given a silver cup. It was announced that another cup would be put up to be given outright for the first consecutive three-year win. For seven consecutive years Sears met and defeated all challengers of his supremacy. Then in 1888 Sears did not defend his title because of an injury, and Henry W. Slocum, Jr., winner for the second year of the All-Comers, succeeded him as national singles champion. It is important to note that in 1884 the challenge round which permitted the holding champion to stay out of the tournament and meet the winner of the All-Comers in a final challenge round was adopted. The challenge round was abolished by the 1912 annual meeting of the USNLTA.

During this first decade of championship play, lawn tennis itself was changing. The overhand serve was in full use, and the players had found out about lobbing and volleying. In 1890 Slocum had to bow to the net game of Oliver S. Campbell, who had wisely figured out that back-court play would not in the future be sufficient to win a national singles championship. Campbell held the title three years, retiring from match play in 1892 after defeating Fred Hovey and winning permanent possession of the trophy.

Campbell's retirement opened the way for Robert D. Wrenn, winner of the 1893 All-Comers', to succeed to the title, which he won four times—though he was defeated in 1895 by Fred Hovey, Wrenn came back in 1896 and 1897.

The Spanish-American War seems to have had little effect upon the national championships; it did affect some local affairs, however. There may have been tennis players at Manila Bay or San Juan Hill, but this was not total war. Malcolm D. Whitman, winner of the All-Comers', became the national singles champion by the failure of Wrenn to defend his title. This was the first of three national singles wins which were to place Whitman on the first United States Davis Cup team in 1900.

The following year, 1901, brought to the top in the national singles a player who was destined to take his place among the nation's greatest exponents of the game. William A. Larned, who as a student at Cornell had won the intercollegiate title, had been knocking at the door of national championship honors for eight years. A sterling player but one who had hitherto been inclined to sacrifice safety to brilliance, Larned had been runner-up on four different occasions before he won the 1901 All-Comers' and automatically became national singles champion on Whitman's failure to defend. Larned defended his title successfully the following year against the challenge of Reginald "Big Do" Doherty but was defeated in 1903 by Hugh "Little Do" Doherty. Holcombe Ward (developer of the famous American twist service), Beals Wright, and William J. Clothier were the title holders in 1904, 1905, and 1906 respectively, and then in 1907 Larned came back for the first of five successive years of championship, which were to bring his total winning of the title up to seven, a record equaled so far by but two other players—Sears and Tilden.

In 1909 two young players from the Pacific Coast made their appearance at Newport as contestants in the tournament. By courtesy the two visitors—Dr. Melville Long and Maurice McLoughlin—were assigned the center court for their match. There they staged a brand of tennis bred of the fast hard

Stars of the early 1900's: (*left to right*) Holcombe Ward, Beals C. Wright, Paul Dalshields, William A. Larned, and William J. Clothier. Incidentally, this group was the United States 1905 Davis Cup team.

courts of their native San Francisco which for dynamic power and sheer excitement outdid anything ever seen on those hallowed Eastern courts. Before the thrilling five-set encounter was over, the fashionable gallery had ceased to talk and many were standing up on their chairs for a better view of the court. Speed had injected into tennis the punch that was all it needed to make it one of the most fascinating of spectator sports. For Newport as a tennis center, the sands were running out. Another half-decade and the championships would be played at Forest Hills, where they would be more accessible to the thousands of new fans who were eager to see them.

But not before 1912, when McLoughlin proved, after his defeat by Larned the previous year, that the fiery brand of tennis of which he was master could win a national title and hold it for two years. The last championship at Newport was won by Dick Williams in 1914. By that time the clouds of World War I were gathering over Europe. Still we thought it could not happen here, and in 1915 the national championship was staged as usual, only this time under the auspices of the West Side Tennis Club at Forest Hills. For the first time the gallery saw an all-Pacific Coast final, William M. Johnston then starting his famous career, defeating McLoughlin. Dick Williams scored again in 1916 with Johnston as runner-up.

By 1917 America was in the war, and the United States National Lawn Tennis Association was faced with the decision of holding or dropping the national championship. It was finally decided to hold what was called a Patriotic Tournament, the proceeds of which were to go to the American Red Cross. R. Lindley Murray, a young chemical engineer, product of Stanford University and a well-known player, was persuaded to enter the tournament. Murray was working for a company which was engaged in making high explosives for the French government and he had doubts about the propriety of taking the time off for the tournament. Persuaded that it was his duty to play—as Williams, Johnston, and many other first-class players who would have assured the success of the tournament were in the service—Murray defeated Nat Niles in the final. A handsome sum was realized by the Red Cross for its war work.

The following year it was decided to carry on the regular championship, and Murray was

Maurice E. McLoughlin, often called the "California Comet," was a United States star just before World War I.

again importuned to enter. As his company was far behind schedule with orders it was filling for the United States government, Murray had a difficult time coming to a decision; when he finally decided to play, he had only eight days in which to get in shape. However, he defeated William Tatem Tilden, Jr., only then coming to the start of his wonderful career, and earned himself a bona fide national singles title and had the satisfaction of seeing the tournament net a goodly sum for the beneficiary—the Training Camp Activities Fund. Writing about it 13 years later, Murray said: "I believe holding those two tournaments was a very fine thing to do."

The USNLTA doubles championships were started in 1881 and were played at the same time as the men's singles. The first doubles championship at Newport in 1881 was played in the form of an "All-Comers'" tournament. Clarence M. Clark and F. W. Taylor were the winners of the title. The following year Richard D. Sears, the national singles champion, and his partner, Dr. James Dwight, seized the reins and won the title for three years in succession. Sears teamed with Joseph S. Clark for his fourth victory, but in 1886 the Sears-Dwight combination was resumed and functioned successfully for two more years, making five wins in all for this first famous doubles team.

In 1888 Valentine G. Hall and Oliver S. Campbell, the latter a future singles champion, won the title, and were followed in 1889 by Henry W. Slocum, Jr., and Howard Taylor. Hall joined forces with Clarence Hobart to capture the 1890 title; in that year a new method of doubles competition was inaugurated. That was the first time that men's singles and doubles tournaments were played separately. Tournaments were held in the East and the West, and the winners of these sectional meets then played off for the privilege of meeting the standing-out champions in the challenge round. In 1907, with the growth of tennis interest throughout the country, the sectional tournaments were increased to three. This number was further increased in subsequent years.

In 1891 Oliver S. Campbell joined up with a new partner, Robert P. Huntington, and two years' supremacy, added to the one he already had retired the second doubles trophy. The next outstanding doubles team was Clarence Hobart and Fred H. Hovey, who held the title for two successive years, this being the third time Hobart won the title.

The next doubles combination to win two years in succession was Leonard Ware and George P. Sheldon, Jr.—1897 and '98—their predecessors being Malcolm G. Chace and Robert D. Wrenn in 1895 and Carr B. Neel and Samuel Neel (the first brother combination to do this) in 1896. It was evident that continued doubles success depended in some measure upon continuous partnership between two players whose style of play supplemented each other. Such a combination was that of Holcombe Ward and Dwight F. Davis, which proved itself invincible to all challengers from 1899 through 1901. After a two years' interim, in which the title was won by the famous Doherty brothers of England, Ward found an equally congenial partner in Beals C. Wright and won the title for three years more, setting a record up to this point in the history of the event.

In 1907 one of the most famous doubles combinations of all time made its debut. Harold H. Hackett and Fred B. Alexander are legendary figures in the annals of tennis doubles and held the title undefeated for four successive years, from 1907 through 1910. They were followed after a year's interval when Raymond D. Little and Gustave Touchard were the champions by another outstanding partnership—Maurice McLoughlin and Thomas C. Bundy—both Pacific Coast players, who held the title for three straight years. Another Western team, William Johnston and Clarence J. Griffin, came into prominence in 1915 and won the event that year and repeated in 1916. In 1917 Fred Alexander returned to the courts and with Harold A. Throckmorton as his partner won the Patriotic Tournament of World War I.

The USNLTA's membership rolls increased from the 34 clubs in 1881 to 75 clubs and one association in 1890. (An association was a group of clubs in a geographic area. The USNLTA, fearing that these local associations might become independent and be a threat to their organization, urged them to join the national group.) Five years later, in 1895, there were 106 clubs and ten associations as members of the USNLTA. This early growth in membership indicated that tennis was spreading throughout the country. But a great drop in membership occurred after this year and by 1902 there were only 44 member clubs and tennis associations. This decline was attributed to several causes. For a short period of time several of the better players were serving their country in the Spanish-American War and consequently could not compete in tournaments or belong to clubs. Furthermore, the sport of golf was spreading rapidly in America, and many tennis players had changed to this game. Some critics felt that the lack of interest was due to the perfunctory reelection of officers in the USNLTA. However, in 1908 membership increased again to 115 clubs and sixteen associations. In 1971 the USLTA reported a membership of over 2,500 clubs affiliated with seventeen geographical associations.

In England during the early 1900's, Wimbledon legends were fast collecting. Yet it was in 1910 that the greatest to that date arose—Anthony F. Wilding of New Zealand. Nicknamed "little Hercules" at the age of two, his clean living, persistent training, and assiduous practice to eliminate weaknesses won him hosts of friends, admirers, and a wonderful reputation wherever he traveled. Tony Wilding began with a weak backhand . . . but he knew it. So, while at Cambridge, he badgered the local authorities to let him improvise a covered court in the Corn Exchange and there he and his friends practiced long hours after they had cleared away the remnants of the vegetable market before each session. Of course, all his work paid off since he won the singles at Wimbledon four times (1910 to 1913).

The International Lawn Tennis Federation was born in 1913, and in gratitude to England for the part she had played, the ILTF awarded to Wimbledon "in perpetuity" the championships of the world on grass, an honor which Wimbledon viewed with some misgivings and abandoned ten years later.

The year (1913) also brought to Wimbledon the "California Comet," Maurice McLoughlin, as well as the ticket "scalpers" who asked and received 10 pounds each for Centre Court tickets to view the McLoughlin-Wilding Challenge Round, won by Wilding, 8–6, 6–3, 10–8.

Tony Wilding of New Zealand (*left*) and Norman Brookes of Australia (*right*) were the stars of Wimbledon before World War I. Wilding was killed in action during the war.

Impending war did not discourage the organizers, and for the 1914 meeting the main stand was extended to accommodate a further 1,200 spectators. Norman E. Brookes of Australia—the man who had a service "with four different speeds"—beat Wilding in the Challenge Round. Less than one month later World War I closed the championships' gates for five terrible years. Thanks to the efforts of H. Wilson-Fox, president from 1915 to 1921, the club was kept going, and it fortunately proved possible to resume the event in 1919.

International Team Competitions

Of the many popular games played for pleasure or profit, few indeed are truly international in appeal. To Americans, baseball seems of world importance but although introduced in Canada, Japan, and some Central American and Caribbean countries, baseball remains American in its real interest. Cricket,

much older, is confined to the British spheres of influence, and golf in the main has flourished basically in the British-American orbit. Of team games, football of the variety we call soccer is really international, but of all outdoor games of skill for individual competitors, lawn tennis is the sole one in which men and women of all nations, races, creeds, and colors compete under the same rules not only on the courts of their own countries but on those of foreign fields.

To most players and followers of lawn tennis, international competition stems from the start of the Davis Cup matches in 1900. But individual Americans played in international lawn tennis competition as far back as 1883, when two American brothers, Clarence M. and Joseph S. Clark, went to the homeland of lawn tennis. There they promptly engaged the Renshaw brothers, then British champions in doubles, in a series of two matches, but lost. Remember, of course, that an Englishman, C. E. Woodhouse, won the first so-called "champion of America" event at Staten Island in 1880.

In 1884, '85, and '86 Dr. James Dwight played in England with fair success and was the first of a long line of American "greats" to play in the sacrosanct "Championships" at Wimbledon. R. D. Sears also competed in England in 1884, and R. L. Beeckman, later to become governor of Rhode Island and a supporter of our Nationals at Newport, played in tournaments in the early English season of 1886.

Doubtless disturbed by brash American invaders, E. G. Meers, rated tenth that year in Great Britain, appeared at our National Championships at Newport in 1889. This was the era, as previously noted, of the standing-out champion, and Meers went to the semi-finals of the All-Comers', where he lost to O. S. Campbell. Campbell, our champion from 1890 through 1892, returned Meers' visit in 1892 and played some excellent matches in the British Isles.

Then came an invader from another country on the American scene. Not to be outdone by a mere Englishman, M. F. Goodbody of Ireland arrived on our American lawn tennis stage in 1894 and won the All-Comers' national championship tournament but was beaten in the Challenge Round by Robert D. Wrenn, the standing-out champion. But in 1897 America faced a formidable triple threat with the appearance in our National Championships at Newport of Dr. W. V. Eaves,

H. S. Mahony, and H. A. Nisbet from Great Britain. In spite of being unfamiliar with American conditions, Dr. Eaves went to the Challenge Round in the singles where he lost to Bob Wrenn, the defending champion, and Mahony and Nisbet lost the doubles final to L. E. Ware and George P. Sheldon, Jr. Although Eaves, Mahony, and Nisbet were a team, it must be remembered that American and British players of that day were not official representatives of their countries. Until the establishment of the Davis Cup matches in 1900, there were no official national team meetings.

The Davis Cup story started on August 24, 1899, when four young Harvard men set out from New York on a trip to the Pacific Coast. Two Bostonians, Malcolm Whitman and Beals Wright (interscholastic champion who was to enter Harvard in the fall), joined with Holcombe Ward of Orange, N.J. The organizer was a tall, strong young man from St. Louis. His name was Dwight F. Davis. They were accompanied by George Wright of Boston. In California they opposed the two Hardy brothers, Sumner and Sam, and the two Whitney brothers, George and Robert, in the first East versus West contest. While on the coast the Eastern team made a trip to the Pacific Northwest and returned home via Canadian Pacific Railroad in time to enter their classes at Harvard late in September.

The success of their West Coast tour convinced Dwight Davis that an international competition would be of great benefit to the

(*left*) The first Davis Cup team (*left to right*) Malcolm Whitman, Dwight F. Davis, and Holcombe Ward and their prize. (*right*) Some thirty years later during USLTA Diamond Jubilee celebration they get together again.

game. With the approval of the USNLTA, Davis ordered a Boston silversmith firm to make up 217-troy ounces of sterling silver into a 13-inch high bowl. It was to be entitled the International Lawn Tennis Challenge Trophy. It became popularly known as the Davis Cup.

On February 21, 1900, the Cup was officially accepted. From the first, the Championship was thrown open to the world. England, under the nomer of the British Isles, sent a team of three players to the United States in August of 1900. "The Dauntless Three" the official publication of the English Lawn Tennis Association (LTA) dubbed the players, for though an occasional Englishman had visited our championships previously, America was considered a bit on the wild and wooly side to our British cousins. The three players were Arthur Gore, twice champion of England, H. Roper Barret, English doubles champion, and E. D. Black, champion of Scotland. Our team consisted of Dwight Davis, youthful donor of the Cup, Malcolm D. Whitman, the current singles champion, and Holcombe Ward, No. 7 in singles ranking but current doubles champion with Davis, who was to play only in the doubles. The matches were scheduled for the old Longwood Cricket Club in Boston.

The English players arrived in New York unescorted and unmet, and lacking anything better to do decided to go to Boston by way of Niagara Falls, of whose wonders they had heard from returned travelers. This little side trip caused some delay in their reaching Boston, much to the worriment of the mystified committee set to meet them in that city.

Conditions for play at Longwood did not meet with the approval of the visitors, and the fact that they received a sound beating at the hands of the American team did not make any softer their criticisms of the ground—"abominable"; the net—"a disgrace to civilized lawn tennis, held up by ropes which were continually sagging"; the balls—"They were awful—soft and mothery-looking—and when served with the American twist came at you like an animated egg plum."

But the English, you know, never say die. So in spite of or perhaps because of that 3–0 score they were back in 1902 for a second try at the bally thing. They fared a little better, 2

matches to our 3 at the Crescent Athletic Club, with Whitman and Larned for America in the singles and Ward and Davis in the doubles. England sent the great Doherty brothers, Reginald and Hugh, and Dr. Joshua Pimm.

The third time did it. Britain's Dohertys defeated America's Wrenns, Robert D. and George L., and William Larned, and the Cup was on its way, not to see its native shores again for nearly a decade and then after traveling all the way around the world. For, believe it or not, the USNLTA did not have cash in the till to send a team abroad in quest of the wandering trophy in 1904, and by the next year the competition had broadened.

Austria, Belgium, and France were the 1904 challengers; Britain defeated Belgium, who came through to the challenge round, 5–0. Public-spirited Americans raised the funds to send a team to Wimbledon in 1905. By this time the Antipodean giant had roused and stretched and another challenger was added to the field, a combination of Australia and New Zealand known as Australasia. The American team of Ward, by then U.S. singles champion, Larned, Wright, and Clothier managed to rout the Australasians—Anthony Wilding and A. Dunlop of New Zealand and the young Norman Brookes of Australia, destined to be the guiding star of Australian tennis for years. But they were not able to lift the Cup defended by the Dohertys and Sidney H. Smith, another great English racketman. England kept the trophy another year and then it was carried off, not by the United States but by the Australasians, Brookes and Wilding, whose prowess was to stand between it and all challengers until 1912.

America sent a team to Melbourne in 1908, one to Sydney in 1909, and one to Christchurch, New Zealand, in 1911. All returned empty-handed though some of the most stirring matches in Davis Cup history marked their attempt and failure. Brookes and Wilding were seemingly invincible on their home grounds. But in 1912, Wilding being absent from competition, a team from the British Isles cracked the Anzac defense by the narrow margin of 3–2. The Cup went back to England but was allowed to remain there for only one year. The number of challengers rose to seven in 1913. The United States was drawn against Australasia. The matches were

 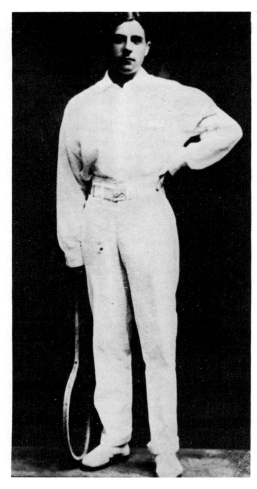

The famed Doherty brothers, Reginald (*left*) and Hugh (*right*).

played at the West Side Tennis Club, then at Broadway and 238th Street. Over 2,000 spectators were turned away for lack of seats. The United States launched a brand-new team: Maurice McLoughlin and R. Norris Williams II for singles, Harold Hackett and Raymond Little in the doubles. The Australian players were also new to international competition. They included S. N. Doust, A. B. Jones, and Horace Rice, neither Brookes nor Wilding making the trip. The United States won the tie and set sail for England, where they played first Germany and then Canada and at last were in the Challenge Round. There they defeated England 3–2, and again the Cup headed west across the Atlantic.

In 1914, on the eve of the World War, Brookes and Wilding journeyed to America, met our team in the Challenge Round at Forest Hills, and won 3–2 in one of the most stirring series of matches. The score of the singles in which McLoughlin defeated Brookes made a record at that time in which, during the first set, 32 games were played. There was a lapse of four years in the competition, during which many of the players fought in the war.

The Ladies Enter the Scene

On February 2, 1889, the United States National Lawn Tennis Association issued the following statement: "It was moved and seconded that the Association extend its protecting wing to the Lady Lawn Tennis players of the country—Carried."

When that action was taken, it meant that for the first time the ladies were to be taken seriously as tennis players. Tennis, of course, was played by women from the start, but their entry into competitive tournaments was delayed. Even in England, as late as 1879, after men's tournaments had been firmly established at Wimbledon, the offer of a member to present a Ladies' Cup was put aside, in spite of his protest that he "could not but think the members ungallant in passing by the ladies. They would, I think, arrive in time!"

Actually, it was not until 1884, seven years after the championships began, that Maud Watson became the first women's champion of Wimbledon by winning from an entry of 13 players. Whether due to the more gallant nature of the Irishman or the more aggressive tactics of the Irishwoman, the first annual championship tournament of the Fitzwilliam Club, second in point of establishment to Wimbledon, carried on its program for June 4, 1879, besides men's singles and doubles events, ladies' singles and mixed doubles. The latter was so much of an innovation that it was considered necessary to print an explanatory note on the program to the effect that this referred to "Doubles with a lady and gentleman as partners."

An old cut of this event shows the lady partner, albeit with wasplike waist and skirt to the ground, hopping nimbly about the court while her attendant gentleman, clad in skin-tight trousers, with a diminutive derby perched on his head, looks solicitously in her direction. It is also interesting to note that two prizes, one of £20 and the other of £5, were offered in the men's singles of this first Fitzwilliam tournament and that there were fifteen entries for the event, while there were seven entries for the ladies' singles and fourteen and nine respectively for the men's doubles and the mixed doubles.

The American tennis and cricket clubs which sprang up in the wake of those of Great Britain were quite conservative about featuring the ladies in their tournaments. The Seabright Club, one of the earliest established in this country, did not list mixed doubles in their first championship matches though there were women members of the club.

Even though it was a woman, Mary Outerbridge, who introduced tennis to the United States, the game like most sporting activities was at first taken up by the men. It was not considered proper, ladylike, or too wise, prior to the late 1800's, for females to indulge in vigorous physical activity. The courageous women who attempted to defy convention and participate in the same games as men were at first small in number and did so amidst much scorn and ridicule. On June 16, 1877, the *New York Daily Graphic* published some sketches of tennis on the lawn at the Staten Island Cricket Club. In this same issue of the *Graphic* there was a prophetic editorial entitled "Athletic Sports" which had, for its time, some extremely favorable comments concerning women and athletics. Some of its pertinent remarks are worthy of mention.

. . . A few years ago the delightful game of croquet was welcomed by ladies, and soon became the fashion. It led the way to other out of door sports for ladies, and last week we reported the formation of an athletic club for practice of archery and other field sports by ladies on Staten Island. The tendency is a good one and ought to be heartily encouraged. . . . The physical side of life for women as well as for men is beginning to receive the attention which is its due. . . . And athletic sports will become fashionable for ladies as well as for men . . . and many sports which a few years ago were considered unwomanly will doubtless be fashionable. . . .

However, in 1878, Adeline King Robinson, who played on the courts of the Staten Island Cricket Club, was the first of a long line of "net queens" to be hailed by the newspapers. These same papers described her style of play to be quite masculine in its aggressiveness and determination. While winning the club championship and being most important as a pioneer in women's tennis, Miss Robinson was never officially recognized as a national champion. In fact, the first Women's National Singles Championship was not held until 1887, and the scene was the Philadelphia Cricket Club. The contestants were mainly a group of Philadelphia girls who had been going out to the club for a number of years to play tennis with the boys after the serious business of the day, the cricket matches, were finished. After the girls had been coached for four or five years by the boys of the club, they began to be ambitious for real competition, something that meant more than the weekly set-to's among members of neighboring organizations.

Among the best local players was a quartet who called themselves the Big Four. They were Ellen Hansell, Bertha Townsend, Louise Allderdice, and Margaret Ballard, and they were the moving spirits in the national championship project. They labored for days writing invitions in longhand and sending them out to all the girl tennis players they knew. Milton Work, later a bridge expert, then a newspaper sports writer, and one of the men players who had coached the girls, interested himself in making contacts in New York, New Jersey, and New England.

When the great day arrived the girls were all ready, clad in long, full-skirted, tight-waisted gingham dresses with plenty of starched petticoats underneath and large top-heavy felt hats perched on their elaborate hairdos. The gallery was ready too, mostly loving relatives prepared to root for and coach their own girl. They stood grouped around the

The "Big Four of the Belmont Cricket Club of Philadelphia": (*left to right*) Bertha Townsend, Margaret Ballard, Louise Allderdice, and Ellen Hansell.

court, close enough to make themselves heard when they screamed, "Run to the net!" "Place it on her left!" "Don't dare lose this game!"

The players, armed with their funny "square-toed" rackets, swooped about the court, innocent of backhand or serve, hitting the low skimming balls over the sagging net. Most serves were underhanded, net play virtually unknown, chop strokes seemed to be held most in esteem, resulting in low bounces. But in spite of the style of play, seventeen-year-old Ellen F. Hansell won the first official Women's Singles championship of the United States and became the proud possessor of the trophy, a silver tennis girl bearing aloft a silver platter, the whole in the form of a small epergne.

Ellen Hansell lost her title the next year to another of the Big Four, Bertha Townsend who, being left-handed, had inadvertently discovered a new stroke, now known as the backhand. Bertha kept the title two years. It was in 1889, as previously stated, that the USNLTA took the women into its "protective" fold. When the Association sponsored the championship, it said that the silver tennis girl could be won outright only by a woman who captured the title three times. It was decided to credit Misses Hansell and Townsend victories toward the championship cup.

In 1890 the Women's National Doubles was added to the tournament, and an outsider, Ellen Roosevelt of New York, won the singles and shared doubles honors with her sister Grace. The following year Mabel Cahill, an Irish girl who was visiting in the United States, defeated Grace Roosevelt for the title and won the doubles with Mrs. W. Fellowes Morgan. Miss Cahill captured both events again the next year, with A. M. McKinley as her partner in the doubles, besides capturing the newly inaugurated mixed-doubles title with Clarence Hobart.

Aline Terry and Helen R. Helwig were the next two singles champions, each scoring a doubles title as well, but in the offing was Juliette P. Atkinson, one of the best-remembered of the women players of that era. Miss Atkinson, a tiny wiry girl who excelled in all outdoor activities of the day, came into the national tennis picture by winning the mixed doubles in 1894 with Edwin P. Fischer. This pair held the title for three years, and in the meanwhile Miss Atkinson had added the women's singles to her tennis honors as well as the 1894 and '95 doubles with Miss Helwig. Miss Atkinson was the first woman to retire a singles trophy by three times winning the title—'95, '97, '98—and the little silver tennis girl disappeared forever from the scene and a silver cup took her place. Miss Atkinson was doubles champion seven times in all, between 1894 and 1902, with various partners.

Another well-known player of the period was Elizabeth Moore, who was runner-up to Miss Atkinson in 1895 and defeated her for the title in 1896, when the two girls joined forces to win the doubles. Miss Moore won the singles title four times, from 1896 to 1905, was twice women's doubles champion, and won the mixed doubles twice with Wylie C. Grant.

One of Miss Moore's most formidable rivals was Marion Jones, the first of a long procession of West Coast players, who invaded the Eastern courts in 1899, won the singles twice, and the doubles and mixed doubles twice each, in the years between 1899 and 1902.

While women's tennis developed rather slowly and regionally in America during the 1890's, it was on the lawns of the homes in England that the female game really progressed. Among the first British women to excel at tennis were Charlotte "Lottie" Dod and Mrs. W. G. Hillyard (née Blanche Bingley). Miss Dod won the Wimbledon title five

May G. Sutton was the first American to win at Wimbledon.

Four of the better-known lady players at the turn of the century: (*left to right*) Helen Gilleandeau, Marie Wagner, Elizabeth Moore, and Grace Gilleandeau.

times between 1887 and 1893, and Mrs. Hillyard was champion six times during the period 1886 to 1900. An English official in 1898 wrote that "Miss Dod was by far the best lady player that the lawn tennis world has yet seen." It was her volleying powers, added to her fine base-line play, that gave her such prestige in her time. Mrs. Hillyard was noted for her excellent ground strokes and "the most indomitable resolution." Incidentally, Miss Dod was only 15 years old when she beat Blanche Bingley in the 1887 final with the loss of only two games, and her record of being the youngest winner at Wimbledon may see out the twentieth century since current International Lawn Tennis Federation rules forbid entry below the age of 16. Miss Dod was also an excellent golfer, winning the British Ladies Golf Championship in 1904.

Back in the United States, a West Coast girl, May G. Sutton, was the next great women's star. She won both the singles and doubles with her vigorous play. The following year Miss Sutton defeated Doris K. Douglas (afterward the famous Mrs. Lambert Chambers) at Wimbledon in 1905, thus becoming the first American ever to capture an English title. She again defeated her rival to win the

A section of the gallery at the 1908 Women's National Championships at the Philadelphia Cricket Club.

championships in 1907. It is interesting to note that twenty years from that time Miss Sutton, then for many years Mrs. Thomas Bundy, was still active in the game, being one of the 1925 Wightman Cup team. By the way, Mrs. Bundy was born in England, coming to California at an early age, and derived her inspiration from the 1899 tour of Dwight Davis and his Harvard classmates.

For the next three years the United States women's singles title was passed around among Helen Homans, Evelyn Sears, and Mrs. Maude Barger-Wallach. Miss Homans also won the doubles in 1905, with Carrie Neely, and Miss Sears was winner of the event in 1908 with Margaret Curtis.

The clothing worn by the women in those days seemed inappropriate to the rising quality of the game. Marie Wagner, American indoor titlist in 1908 and four times thereafter, once described the female attire this way: "No girl would appear unless upholstered with a corset, a starched petticoat, a starched skirt, heavily button-trimmed blouse, a starched shirtwaist with long sleeves and cuff links, a high collar and four-in-hand necktie, a belt with silver buckle, and sneakers with large silk bows."

Despite this handicap the women's game moved ahead at an astonishing pace as two other Californians followed Miss Sutton to fame. First came Hazel Hotchkiss, who in 1909, 1910, and 1911 did the "hat trick" on a national scale, winning the women's singles, doubles, and mixed-doubles championships three times in succession. In 1919 as Mrs.

Hazel H. Wightman, she again captured the singles title. In the meantime Mary K. Browne duplicated the record of Miss Hotchkiss by winning the USNLTA women's singles, doubles, and mixed-doubles titles in three successive years, 1912, 1913, and 1914.

In 1913 the ladies were given official ranking for the first time, and Mary Browne headed

Hazel Hotchkiss after she captured her third straight title in 1911.

the list. Two years later another great player came along to win the American Championship—Molla Bjurstedt. The women's cause received another big boost in France, where Suzanne Lenglen began her rise to fame. She showed by beautiful and consistent play what women's tennis could really produce. In her wake followed a flock of younger players, to give the ladies great popularity with the tennis public. But, like men's play, World War I put a stop to many major women's competitive tennis events.

Women in tennis had made great progress in the period from 1890 to 1917 and gained many followers. An interesting statement appeared in the July, 1894, issue of the *Queen of Fashion* in an article which stated that except for putting, golf was not a game for ladies. The writer continued by saying that "it was not as violent as tennis, which had been accepted."

At the annual meeting of the Association in 1899, enthusiastic comments were made about women in the game. The profound interest was felt to be a "natural result of increasing tendency on the part of women to enter athletics." A resolution was passed to direct clubs to sponsor events for women during the coming season. In 1902 the Association reported that one of the outstanding events of the season was the "increased play of women and increase of women's tournaments. Today very few tournaments are held without the inclusion of both sexes, thus indicating the Association's belief in the equal importance of men and women players."

As with most new movements certain personalities stand out in the public's mind at the time, and years later history credits them as the "trail blazers." Authorities give credit to a number of sportswomen for opening up vistas in athletic contests, but two tennis players are at the top of the list: Eleanora Sears and May Sutton Bundy. Many historians single out Miss Sears as the person who led

Mary K. Browne (*left*) and Molla Bjurstedt (*right*) were America's two leading players before World War I stopped tournament play.

the way for women in sports. In tennis she was national women's doubles titleholder in 1911, 1915, 1916, and 1917. In addition she was also an outstanding athlete in riflery, swimming, golf, and squash. Miss Sears received additional fame for her walking stints between Boston and distant points. Her contributions are keenly noted by Durant and Bettmann in *Pictorial History of American Sports:*

> At first the daring young woman horrified New England conservatives with her tomboyish activities. But she demonstrated that a woman could play men's games like a man without causing a revolution. She won her cause and was the prime liberator of women in sports.

THE GOLDEN ERA OF TENNIS AND BEYOND

The twenties have often been called "the Golden Age of Sport." All sports had great names in that era—baseball, Ty Cobb and Babe Ruth; golf, Walter Hagen and Bobby Jones; football, Red Grange and the Four Horsemen of Notre Dame; etc. Lawn tennis also had its great stars.

William M. Johnston, better known as

Lawn tennis stars in service during World War I: (*left to right*) Lt. Col. Dwight Davis, Maj. R. D. Wrenn, Maj. W. A. Larned, Capt. Watson Washburn, Capt. Norris Williams II, Capt. D. S. Walters, Lt. Dean Mathey, and Col. W. C. Johnson.

"Little Bill," won his second Men's Singles Championship in 1919, defeating a player who was to dominate world tennis for the next decade—William Tatem Tilden, Jr. Tilden's slow development into championship stature paralleled that of Larned, whose record of seven-times winner he was to equal. That is, until the lanky Philadelphian, better known as "Big Bill," reached the age of 28, he was just a so-so player. Practically all our past and present champions reached that level in their teens or early twenties. When Tilden was 26, he was a struggling chop-stroke artist, and not a very good one. He spent the better part of his youth as a fringe player. When he was 27 he reached the National Singles final and, as already stated, was beaten by "Little Bill" Johnston. "Big Bill's" backhand betrayed him. Johnston's forehand, the best in the world at that time, pulverized Tilden's backhand, which was a chop stroke.

Determined to become champion and real-

"Big Bill" Tilden and "Little Bill" Johnston with two USLTA officials looking over the awards before a meet.

izing he did not have the equipment, Tilden moved to Providence, where he played daily the entire winter on an indoor clay court. Hour after hour, day after day, and week after week, Tilden worked on his backhand until it became his strength. The following summer he won the United States Singles, handling Johnston's ferocious forehand so well that he broke "Little Bill's" heart. To the public's dismay, Johnston could never beat him again in an important match. In fact, Johnston was Tilden's opponent in the finals every year from 1920 to 1925, except in 1921, when Wallace F. Johnson was runner-up. "Big Bill" accomplished his seventh win in 1929.

Many authorities feel that no one has dominated a game such as William Tilden dominated tennis, especially in the 1920's. He was the number-one ranking player for ten consecutive years, 1920 to 1929, and he was the first American to win the men's singles championship at Wimbledon. He was a member of the Davis Cup team for eleven years, and during his amateur career won seventy American and International titles. Not only is he still referred to by many in tennis circles as the greatest player who ever lived, but he is also still referred to as the player who gave the USLTA (the "N" was dropped in 1920) the most difficulty. In almost every instance the differences between Tilden and the USLTA concerned the amateur code. As expressed by one writer, "No player has ever flouted the amateur rule with the persistence —and success—of Bill Tilden."

In the middle twenties it became apparent that Tilden was making considerable profit by being a tennis writer for several newspapers. The USLTA felt that these writings were a violation of the amateur code, which stated that a player was prohibited "from profiting directly or indirectly from the game." In 1924 the USLTA, on the recommendation of its Amateur Rule Committee, issued the order that it was no longer permissible for a player to write about tennis for any publication if he received compensation for doing so. This new application of the amateur code was quite a shock to the players who were also writers, especially to Tilden. He contended that he had been a writer before he achieved fame as a tennis player. Previously, most interpreted the amateur rule to mean that no player could receive money for teaching or playing tennis. Furthermore, until this edict of 1924, most of the best writings on lawn tennis were by the players, and they had been credited with considerably helping the growth of the game. After the pronouncement of this rule, there was such a bitter protest raised not only by the players but also by the press and some tennis officials that an important committee of seven was appointed on February 7, 1925, for the purpose of revising the amateur code with "special reference to the player-writer controversy." Grantland Rice, a member of the committee, commented on the meeting in his book, *The Tumult and the Shouting.* He mentioned that another member of the committee, Devereux Milburn, the polo star, stated that he had turned down a $5,000 offer to write on the international

When Tilden and Johnston met, there was always a full house, as shown above during the 1922 National Tennis Championships held at the Germantown Cricket Club.

Bill Tilden was "the" man tennis player of 1920, if not of all time.

polo matches. He felt it was not within the amateur code. It was a well-known fact that Tilden made about $25,000 one year for writing about tennis for the Philadelphia *Public Ledger* Syndicate. Rice's reply to Milburn's statement was, "It's a matter of taste, not amateurism."

The committee's recommendations were accepted and again, as has been evident with other revisions of the code, the new ruling was a compromise. The player was still allowed to profit financially by using his name as a by-line for newspaper articles, with some added restrictions. The ruling was stated in two sections:

1. A player was not allowed, "after February 1925, the use of his titles or statement of his reputation won on the tennis courts in connection with books, newspaper, magazine or other written articles, motion pictures of himself, lectures or radio talks, for which he is to receive any payment or compensation."

2. A player is not allowed to write "for pay or for a consideration, current newspaper articles covering a tournament or match in which he is entered as a competitor."

Furthermore, again on the recommendation of the committee, the USLTA indicated its leniency toward the rule by stating that a violation of this edict would not make the violator a professional but would only lead to his suspension for a certain length of time from the tournaments.

Consequently, the controversy seemed settled and all was relatively calm, although Tilden did write an article on a tournament he was in during the matches in the summer of 1925. The Executive Committee of the Association held a special meeting in New York City on August 1, 1925, and discussed whether Tilden should be suspended for violating the rule. The minutes of this meeting total 117 pages: it was decided to warn Tilden that the next time he violated the rule he would be suspended.

In 1928 an incident occurred that resulted in unfavorable publicity internationally for both the USLTA and Bill Tilden. During June of that year the Davis Cup team with Tilden as captain was competing in the championships at Wimbledon. While there, Tilden filed daily reports of the matches for the press. Naturally, the USLTA heard of these reports and felt compelled to take action. Two special meetings of the Executive Committee were held, on July 17 and August 24, to discuss the latest violation by Tilden. It was the culminating point of all his apparent disregard over the years for the amateur bylaws. The decision to suspend him was not lightly made and the Association was aware of the tremendous step it was taking in defense of its amateur principle.

Tilden's suspension was announced as the United States Davis Cup team was en route to play Italy for the right to challenge the cup holder, France. According to the historian Preston Slosson, the news of Tilden "drove election news, the assassination of Mexico's president-elect and a search for lost aviators in the Arctic off the front pages of the evening newspapers."

Even without Tilden the United States was able to defeat Italy in the matches. In view of the ensuing damage which was done to the dignity and reputation of the USLTA, it was

Tennis was popular in the 1920's as witnessed by the gathering in New York's Central Park for an exhibition between Vinny Richards and Bill Johnston.

unfortunate that the team did not lose to Italy and then the whole matter would never have arisen. As can be imagined the press had a heyday with the announcement, and many attacks were leveled at the USLTA. But the USLTA was determined to stick by its decision and remained adamant that its course of action was sound and just. Its intentions were sincere in trying to show that no one, not even the great Tilden, was above the rules or the spirit behind them. But the USLTA was forced to change its mind and the resulting image was not too complimentary. A brief

résumé of why it vacillated in its stand is necessary.

France never had the honor of being the host country for the challenge round of the Davis Cup until 1928. In honor of the occasion a new stadium had been erected. Not only was Tilden a great favorite with the French, but it was obvious that gate receipts would be affected if Tilden did not participate. International tension over the matter reached such proportions that the United States Ambassador, Myron T. Herrick, appealed to the USLTA through the United States State De-

Two of France's great players of the 1920's and '30's: Jean Borotra (*left*) and Henri Cochet (*right*).

Ted Husing, the famed radio sportscaster, interviews John Doeg after his 1930 victory, in the press box at Forest Hills.

partment for reconsideration of its ruling until after the Davis Cup matches in France. On the force of this diplomatic pressure the USLTA rescinded its ruling and allowed Tilden to play in the matches which we lost, and then suspended him again when he returned home. Even though his suspension lasted six months, the USLTA as a governing body was severely criticized over this matter for a long time.

Tilden was granted reinstatement on February 8, 1929, after the USLTA was reassured by him that he would abide by the rules. He turned professional after the 1930 season but not without once more causing a furor with the USLTA before he did so. To avoid another incident like the one that occurred in 1928, the USLTA had further stipulated that a member of a team could not write about matches. Tilden negotiated a contract for $3,000 to write about the 1930 Davis Cup matches. Finally, after much discussion between the Association and Tilden, he was allowed a dispensation whereby he could write reflective comments about the matches after they were completed.

Today the situation concerning player-

writers is strictly stated in the amateur code of the International Lawn Tennis Federation bylaws, which states that an amateur lawn tennis player is specifically prohibited from

. . . contributing under his own name to the Press, Broadcast or Television, in regard to and during the time of any tournament, match or competition in which he is entered as or is a competitor, except with the general previous consent of the National Association of the country concerned and under the direct control of the Chairman of the Committee or other authorized management of the event, to which the contribution relates. In no case may a player receive any pecuniary advantage.

During the decade following World War I the United States championships began to attract the cream of foreign players. René Lacoste captured the title in 1926, defeating his Davis Cup comrade and compatriot, Jean Borotra, in an all-French final. Lacoste won again the next year, and in 1928 the third of the "French Musketeers," Henri Cochet, became American Singles Champion.

Coincidentally, the Golden Era of Sports was the forerunner of another outstanding period in American history—the advent of radio. The new medium emerged from the throes of experiment to become a reality, and with its inception America became more and more sports-conscious. Tennis partook of the advantages afforded by radio broadcasting of sports events.

The years 1930–1932 saw the men's championships dominated by West Coast talent. In 1930 John H. Doeg, a nephew of the famous May Sutton Bundy, won the title in a match with Frank Shields. He was followed by young Elsworth Vines, in some ways the most remarkable player of them all. Vines ended a meteoric championship career in 1932 after wresting his second title from Cochet in an epic final.

In 1933 and 1934, Fred Perry, athletic and popular English Davis Cup star, won the title defeating Jack Crawford, Australian Davis Cup player, the first year and Wilmer Allison, American Davis Cup player, the second. Attempting his third win in 1935, Perry suffered a heavy fall in an early round match against

Allison, and the Texan went on to win the championship, defeating Sidney B. Wood in the finals. Perry completed his third win the following year by outplaying Don Budge, a red-headed young Californian, who was just then beginning a march to world championship.

Fully developed and seasoned by his experience in Davis Cup play and at Wimbledon, Budge won his first United States Singles Championship the next year by defeating Germany's Davis Cup ace, Baron Gottfried von Cramm. Budge's sterling qualities were proved the next year by his sweep of all the outstanding championships of the world (Australian, French, British, and American—now called "the grand slam") as well as his winning of his two singles matches and with Gene Mako of the doubles in the Davis Cup challenge round against England. Until his retirement from amateur play in 1939 he was undisputed world champion.

Robert L. Riggs won the title in 1939, was runner-up to Donald McNeill in 1940, and

Vincent Richards was one of the all-time great doubles players.

Ted Schroeder slips after making a difficult return to Bobby Riggs in the 1941 Nationals. Riggs went on to defeat Frank Kovacs in the final.

returned to first place in 1941 when he defeated Frank Kovacs in the final. With the onset of the war in 1942, championship competition was subject to the exigencies of military service. Frederick R. (Ted) Schroeder won the title that year while on the verge of being inducted into the service, winning in a doggedly fought five-set match from Frank A. Parker. The following year saw the Navy battling the Coast Guard when Lieutenant Joseph L. Hunt (who was killed during the war) of the Navy defeated Seaman John A. Kramer of the latter branch. The Army ruled the lawn tennis world in 1944 and '45 when Sergeant Frank Parker defeated William F. Talbert both years.

Men's Double Play After World War I

In the men's double play, the end of World War I meant the abolishment of the challenge round. Bill Tilden and Vincent Richards (then only 15) won the 1918 United States doubles crown. Two Australian Davis Cup stars proved themselves invincible in 1919, and the names of Norman E. Brookes and Gerald L. Patterson were engraved on the doubles trophy. Bill Johnston and Clarence

George Lott (*left*) and Lester Stoefen (*right*) were considered by many as one of the greatest doubles teams.

Griffin chalked up their third victory in 1920, and then Tilden came back for three years, with Richards as partner the first two and Brian Norton in 1923. 1924 marked the advent of the United States' second "brothers' doubles team," when Howard O. and Robert G. Kinsey defeated Patterson and Pat O'Hara Wood for the title. Richards and "Dick" Williams were champions for the next two years, and in 1927 Tilden made his fifth win of the title, this time with Frank Hunter.

In 1928 American tennis found that it had another highly talented doubles champion in the person of George M. Lott, Jr. Lott teamed with three different partners to win the title five times in the years from 1928 through 1934. John F. Hennessey was his first partner. There followed two years with John Doeg and then two with Lester Stoefen, Lott proving himself equally successful with each.

A famous Davis Cup doubles pair were the winners of the 1931 championship, when Wilmer Allison and John Van Ryn defeated Gregory Mangin and Berkeley Bell for the title. The team was beaten by Ellsworth Vines and Keith Gledhill in 1932 and did not win their second national doubles championship until 1935, although they were three times Wimbledon doubles champions between 1929 and 1931, and defeated the much younger combination of Don Budge and Gene Mako for the national title in 1935. Budge and Mako turned tables on the "veteran" combination of Allison and Van Ryn in 1936 and won their first national doubles.

Twice in the next three years the United States national doubles title was captured by visiting foreign teams. In 1937 Baron Gottfried von Cramm and Henner Henkel, German Davis Cup stars, defeated Budge and Mako and in 1939 there was an all-Australian final—Adrian Quist and John E. Bromwich defeated their Davis Cup teammates, Jack H. Crawford and Harry Hopman in a stirring match.

Both sides in World War II lost good tennis players, but two of the greatest killed in action were Joseph Hunt of the United States (*left*) and Henner Henkel of Germany (*right*).

In 1940 a brand-new youthful doubles team was crowned when Jack Kramer and Ted Schroeder, both from the Pacific Coast, brought their first year of partnership play to a successful climax. The young Californians fought their way to victory the following year but in 1942 Kramer did not compete and Schroeder joined forces with Sidney Wood. The pair came through to the final, where they were forced to yield to the pressure of Gardnar Mulloy, a lieutenant junior grade in the Navy, and William F. Talbert, teaming up for the first time in a national tournament. The Mulloy-Talbert team won again in 1945, but in the meantime Jack Kramer and Sergeant Frank Parker took the doubles crown in 1943, and Lieutenant Don McNeill and Bob Falkenburg took it in 1944.

Women's Play in the Golden Era of Sports

The golden twenties arrived early in the United States for women's tennis. It happened when a Norwegian masseuse came to America to practice her profession and play a little tennis. Molla Bjurstedt, later Mrs. Franklin I. Mallory, was the Norwegian champion for eight years. As previously stated, she won her first United States championship in 1915. Her contribution to women's tennis was a steady all-court game distinguished for its force and accuracy which won her seven national singles titles, a record equaled only by Helen Wills Moody. Mrs. Mallory also won the Patriotic Tournament during World War I, not strictly speaking a national championship. One of her most spectacular feats was the match against Suzanne Lenglen, in which the much-publicized visit of the French star to Forest Hills ended in her default to Mrs. Mallory. Another of Mrs. Mallory's outstanding victories was her defeat of Elizabeth "Bunny" Ryan in the 1926 final of the women's singles. Mrs. Mallory had stepped down from the championship three years before, and this victory, said to be one of the most hotly contested matches in the history of the championship, in which the final score of 4–6, 6–4, 9–7 tells the tale, was in the nature of a glorious comeback. In addition, Molla Mallory was also a fine doubles player. She won the women's doubles in 1916 and 1917 with

Helen Wills is considered by many the greatest woman player ever.

Eleanora Sears and the mixed doubles three times between 1917 and 1923, once with Irving C. Wright and twice with Tilden.

During the years 1897 to 1920 inclusive, the Women's Championships were played at the Philadelphia Cricket Club and, as the doubles and mixed doubles were added, they were played with the women's singles in a combined tournament. In 1921 the three events were transferred to the West Side Club at Forest Hills and played in August before the men's championships began. There in 1923 with the opening of the big tennis stadium a new woman star made her debut, and an amazed gallery saw sixteen-year-old Helen Newington Wills of California defeat

The famous Moody-Jacobs contest which Miss Jacobs won.

the reigning favorite, Mrs. Mallory. One of the most remarkable careers in the history of women's tennis had begun.

For three years "Little Miss Poker Face" remained invincible, defeating Mrs. Mallory in 1924 and Kathleen McKane, the English champion, in 1925. In 1926 Miss Wills did not compete and a fast and furious final, as just mentioned, was waged between Mrs. Mallory and Miss Ryan, which resulted in Mrs. Mallory's seventh and final win of the title. Miss Wills was back again in 1927 for three more successive years of supremacy but did not compete in 1930, when Betty Nuthall became the first English girl ever to win the American title. In 1931 Miss Wills, then Mrs. Moody, won the singles title for the seventh time, the only woman to reach the mark set by Mrs. Mallory. She had won her first national doubles in 1924 with Mrs. Wightman and the pair won again in 1928, and Miss Wills won the mixed doubles in 1924 with Vincent Richards. Thus, Miss Wills, as can be seen, overshadowed all other women players of the day, indeed perhaps of any day. Totally unspectacular in her style of play, steady and accurate to the point of genius, her victims were disposed of with a neatness and dispatch that brooked no opposition.

Incidentally, most tennis fans think of the great woman champion as Helen Wills since, as Helen Wills, she won the first six of her seven United States singles championships, played most of her Wightman Cup matches,

and was ranked No. 1 in the first five of the seven years she held that position. Only at Wimbledon did she win more singles titles as Mrs. Moody (five) than she did as Helen Wills (three). Her four French singles championships were equally divided, the first two being won as Helen Wills and the last two as Mrs. Moody. Helen and her first husband,

Fred Perry and Helen Jacobs ruled the lawn tennis world in the mid-1930's.

Betty Nuthall of Great Britain was the first non-American to win the Women's Singles title.

F. S. Moody, were divorced in 1937 and in 1939 she married Adrian Roark.

Her default to Helen Jacobs in 1933 was a seven-days' wonder and caused more argument than perhaps any other match ever played in the women's singles. Mrs. Moody had been confined to the hospital for several weeks before the tournament started, with an old back injury, but she managed to get through to the final where she was destined to meet her perennial rival and fellow Californian. Miss Jacobs was reported to be indisposed too and near collapse. But she had won her first title the previous year when Mrs. Moody did not compete and was determined to win again. She won the first set at 8–6. Mrs. Moody rallied and got the second 6–3. Miss Jacobs had 3 games to love in the

The first non-American finals for the Women's title occurred when Anita Lizana of Chile (*left*) and Jadwiga Jedrzejowska of Poland (*right*) met in 1937. Miss Lizana won.

Alice Marble was one of the finest women players.

In 1938 Alice Marble was back, and won the United States title. The next year saw her win the Wimbledon singles and doubles and mixed doubles as well as our own, a feat never equaled by any woman player to that date. Until she retired from amateur play at the end of 1940, Miss Marble was undisputed world champion. Her game perhaps illustrates better than that of any other woman the strides women's tennis made. Using the so-called American twist service, Alice volleyed and played the net like a man, earning her points outright and risking all to do so.

Alice Marble won the doubles 1937 to 1940 with Sarah Palfrey and the mixed doubles in 1936, 1939, and 1940. Mrs. Sarah Palfrey Cooke, who had won an enviable reputation as a doubles player, winning that event nine times in the years between 1930 and 1941, fulfilled a lifelong ambition by winning the singles title for the first time in 1941, defeating Pauline Betz. For the next

deciding chapter when Mrs. Moody walked over to the umpire's stand and said she was unable to finish.

Thus in possession of her second championship title, Miss Jacobs, one of the most popular of our champions, became the first since Mrs. Mallory to win for four successive years, and was prominent in the championship for five years more. Her defeat in the event came in 1936 when another California star, Alice Marble, making a tennis comeback after a long illness, started on the road to world championship. Miss Marble tried again the next year but found her strength unequal to the task, and Forest Hills was treated to its first all-foreign final in the championship. Diminutive Anita Lizana, South American star who had been attracting notice in the British and French championships, visited the United States that year. Also in the entry list was Pana Jadwiga Jedrzejowska, sturdy Polish woman champion. The final day saw the vigorous, romping Polish girl pitted against the dancing, dainty Latin-American. Senorita Lizana won the match 6–4, 6–2, mainly by her cleverly executed drop shots.

Mrs. Sarah Palfrey Cooke during the late 1930's and early 1940's won many events.

three years after that, however, Miss Betz won the title and was out to reach the four years' record of Miss Jacobs. But fate intervened in the person of Mrs. Cooke, who took her second singles title in 1945.

The European Golden Age of Tennis

In Europe the end of World War I was the dawn of the "big name" era, too. In 1919 the organizers of Wimbledon, acting with characteristic courage and energy, took up where matters had left off five years earlier, when the grim specter of World War I intervened and forced a temporary cessation of tennis's premier event for the duration.

Entries so numerous (128) that selection was considered; applications for tickets so numerous that the now-famous ballot had to be introduced—these were the first two signs that Wimbledon, despite the interruption of the war, was to escalate to greater popularity than ever before. And the signs proved right. As a reunion of players and patrons, the meeting was a remarkable success, and the final seal of greatness was applied by King George V and Queen Mary, who made two visits to the committee box. They became tennis addicts, and ever after until their deaths were frequent and keenly interested visitors to the championships.

World War I had taken its toll of the speed and skills of the older players, who had been at their peak prior to the hostilities, and the newcomers were sadly lacking in experience of any kind. Thus, the general standard of play suffered. The women's challenge round atoned for it all, however, as it produced probably the greatest women's final in the years between 1877 and 1972. It was between Dorothea Lambert Chambers, who had won the first of her seven singles titles 19 years earlier, and the stocky, swarthy, full-bosomed, but magnificently fleet and supple Suzanne Lenglen, just 20 years old.

By the time the French girl had reached the challenge round, Suzanne had completely captured the popular fancy, and 8,000 enthusiasts, including the King, Queen, and Princess Mary, filled the Centre Court accommodation to overflowing for their meeting. Age might have diminished Mrs. Lambert Chambers'

Suzanne Lenglen, one of the most outstanding women players.

speed marginally but she still remained a tremendous fighter. Down 1–4, then 3–5 in the first set, she did not surrender it until the 18th game. Undaunted she took the second set, and Suzanne appeared on the point of defaulting. Then, while Mrs. Lambert Chambers sat down quietly during a rather long interval, Suzanne fortified herself by swallowing some sugar soaked in cognac thrown to her by her father from the stand.

Suzanne raced to 4–1, but Mrs. Lambert Chambers fought back heroically and in an electric atmosphere reached 6–5, and 40–15, for double match point. Unflinchingly, Suzanne hit deep to the forehand and raced for the net. Alert to this move, Mrs. Lambert Chambers tossed back a lob that appeared to be beyond Suzanne's reach. Leaping desperately, Suzanne caught the ball near the frame and it just barely crawled over the net. Had she expected this lucky reply, Mrs. Lambert Chambers could scarcely have failed to reach the ball and score with a placement into Suzanne's unprotected court, but she was caught completely flat-footed by surprise.

Thus reprieved, Suzanne hit boldly down the line with a backhand, raising chalk with a clean winner that saved the second match point. Although the tension and superb tennis were maintained until the end, Suzanne was never again in serious danger of defeat before winning 10–8, 4–6, 9–7.

From that moment until 1926 and the sad misunderstanding with the committee which ended her Wimbledon career, Suzanne Lenglen was front-page news whatever she said, did, or wore. The cult of personality had indeed arrived at the All England Club.

It was augmented considerably in 1920 by the Wimbledon debut of "Big Bill" Tilden. The records show that others participated— in fact there were more than 128 entries for the men's singles so that selection and rejection became necessary—but so far as the press and crowds were concerned there were only two players at Wimbledon, Suzanne and Big Bill. Their popularity confirmed the long-time realization that the old Wimbledon was no longer large enough to accommodate these championships, and so new grounds were found in the lovely, tree-lined hollow at the foot of picturesque Church Road near Wimbledon Common. Thus, the last championships at Worple Road took place in 1921, with Suzanne Lenglen hitting the last ball on the old Centre Court—a lusty smash that all but bowled over Mrs. Peacock, one of her losing opponents in the women's doubles final. Mlle. Lenglen and Elizabeth Ryan were the winners.

Incidentally, Miss Ryan holds the most Wimbledon titles, having won 19 over a span of some 20 years. Her long string of victories included doubles and mixed doubles. Although she never captured the coveted singles championship, she did win the All-Comers in 1921 but lost to the great Suzanne Lenglen in the challenge round. Twice Miss Ryan was runner-up in the All-Comers. She won the women's doubles championship at Wimbledon 12 times, six with Mlle. Lenglen, twice with Mme. Mathieu, and once each with A. M. Morton, Mary K. Browne, P. Saunders, and Helen Wills Moody. Miss Ryan won the mixed-doubles title at Wimbledon seven times, three times with Randolph Lycett and once each with Francis T. Hunter, P. D. B. Spence, Jack H. Crawford, and E. Maier.

Kitty McKane, later Mrs. Godfree, was one of Great Britain's great women stars of the late 1920's.

The "new" Wimbledon, created by Captain Stanley Peach, was opened by King George V on June 26, 1922. The Centre Court capacity was around 14,750 and that of its main support, Court 1, 5,000. (By 1968, the Centre Court could "sardine" in about 14,990, while Court 1, where structural alterations were far simpler, had gained 2,000 in capacity.) The weather utterly failed the occasion and the tarpaulins were in constant use throughout the fortnight, play lasting until the third Monday.

The challenge round was abolished and Gerald Patterson, Australia, and Suzanne Lenglen, France, won the singles titles in the beautiful new setting, which was to add immeasurably to the Wimbledon legend.

Suzanne Lenglen's arrival in 1919 preceded by five years six years of domination by those immortal "French Musketeers" of tennis: Borotra, Brugnon, Cochet, and Lacoste. All but Brugnon won the singles twice and Brugnon took the men's doubles four times in all.

In the women's field, Suzanne was invincible, but England's Kitty McKane, later Mrs. Godfree, won twice in her absence. Yet Suzanne's true greatness can best be gathered from her performances in 1925, for she beat in succession Elizabeth Ryan, Mrs. A. E. Beamish, and the holder, Kitty McKane, in 36 straight games before thrashing Joan Fry, 6–2, 6–0, in the final. In the ten sets she played in singles, the incredible French girl dropped only five games!

Seeding was first introduced in 1924, the same year in which Helen Wills reached the final and held four points for a 5–1 final set lead before losing to the ever-tenacious Kitty McKane.

From the moment when the earliest surviving champion, P. F. Hadow (won in 1878), stepped on to the Centre Court to receive his commemorative medal from the hand of Queen Mary and the congratulations of King George V till the last strokes of the match which made an Englishman and his wife, Mr. and Mrs. L. A. Godfree, mixed-doubles champions, the "Jubilee Championships" (50th anniversary) of 1926 ran a course crammed with interest and excitement.

Fittingly, the King's son, the Duke of York, later King George VI, won the place that year in the men's doubles reserved in those days for the winners of the Royal Air Force Championship. His partner was Commander Louis Grieg, who later became chairman of the club

The first all-German final at Wimbledon occurred in 1931 when Cilli Aussem (*left*) met Hilda Krahwinkel (*right*). Miss Aussem won, but Miss Krahwinkel (as Mrs. Sperling) won many of Europe's leading titles.

and received a knighthood for his service to the crown. The following year, 1927, brought the strongest entry and the worst weather in Wimbledon's history, the last final carrying over until the third Tuesday. Those who believe in miracles received strong supporting evidence from the championship win of Henri Cochet that year; first he recovered from a two-set and 5–1 deficit against Tilden in the semifinal, and then survived six match points —on one of which most onlookers believed there was a double hit—before beating Jean Borotra in the final.

All previous attendance figures were broken in 1928, although it was not until 1932 that the total first exceeded 200,000 for the fortnight. (Thirty-five years later, in 1967, it reached 301,800, the record up to the present time.)

One of the most interesting matches occurred in the winter of 1926 at Cannes, France, when Helen Wills played Suzanne Lenglen in the final of the Carlton Club tournament. This was the only meeting of these two great champions. In this test on the French Riviera, the French star overcame her younger American opponent in two sets 6–3, 8–6. Miss Wills held leads of 3–1 and 5–4 in the second set. The match lasted one hour, according to the record.

Several months later in the French championships, the stage was set for another Lenglen-Wills encounter, but Miss Wills after two early-round matches suffered an attack of appendicitis and underwent an emergency operation. Mlle. Lenglen had no trouble in winning the French title for the sixth time. The year before the Cannes meeting, Suzanne had won her sixth, and last, championship at Wimbledon and Helen had won the third of her seven U.S. championships. In 1927, after Mlle. Lenglen had defaulted at Wimbledon and had become a professional, Miss Wills won the first of her eight record-breaking Wimbledon singles titles.

In 1930, Tilden possibly achieved the greatest-ever performance at Wimbledon by winning the men's title at the age of 38. A. W. Gore was older when he won in 1909 but in 1930 the entry abounded with names that have since become tennis legends. The United States took all five titles that year.

There was no men's singles final in 1931.

Ellsworth Vines was one of the most powerful players in the history of tennis.

Frank Shields, at the behest of the U.S. Davis Cup captain, had to scratch to his compatriot, Sidney Wood, because of a knee injury sustained when falling in the semifinal. Helen Wills was absent and, surprisingly, two German girls (Cilli Aussem, the winner, over Hilda Krahwinkel) contested the women's singles final for the first and only time in history.

Many who saw Ellsworth Vines demolish E. ("Booby") Maier of Spain, Jack Crawford of Australia, and Bunny Austin of Britain in the last three rounds of the 1932 Wimbledon are convinced that no man before or since has quite touched those heights—and that includes Vines himself. Everything was right. Vines was in superb form, there was a slight skin of wetness on the court which kept the ball at just the right height for Vines' no-margin-for-error flat, thunderbolt drives, and the three opponents were stylists who tended to bring the best out of those they were playing.

Vines' power was frightening. Old-time Wimbledon fans remember seeing one of his smashes hit a ball boy in the chest and knock him head over heels. Bunny Austin vowed the next morning that he never saw the service ace which ended the final. The lanky Californian's services were timed at 128 miles per hour, ap-

proximately the same or slightly faster than Pancho Gonzalez at his fastest. If Vines was great in victory, he was possibly even greater in defeat the following year, in 1933, when Jack Crawford played one of the greatest tactical finals ever, to win in the fifth set. Some feel this was the greatest men's final of all. Fighting like a demon, Vines held on to the finish and then not by a flicker showed the bitter disappointment he must have felt. Instead, he was the soul of generosity to Crawford, continuing a long line of United States sportsmanship that has always been a credit both to the country and to the spirit of Wimbledon.

From 1934 to 1936 British tennis came out of long doldrums. Fred Perry won the men's singles three years running during this period and Dorothy Round the women's singles twice. They were followed by Donald Budge in 1937 and 1938, Helen Wills Moody—inevitably—in 1938, and the brave Alice Marble in 1939 just before the war. To what heights would Alice have climbed but for World War II and the resulting interruption of Wimbledon from 1939 to 1945?

The Davis Cup Moves About in the Twenties and Thirties

On the international lawn tennis team scene, one year after the Armistice (1919) England sent a team to Sydney to challenge for the Davis Cup. The Australasians— Brookes, Gerald Patterson, and James O. Anderson—fought off the invaders, 4 matches to 1. But by 1920 two of America's greatest players, William Tilden II and William Johnston, had reached international stature. Together they set out for Auckland and after a titanic struggle with Brookes and Patterson returned triumphant with the precious trophy. Now the Cup remained in the land of its birth for six fat years, defended by the two iron men, "Big Bill" and "Little Bill," against the onslaughts of Japan in 1921, Australasia in 1922, '23, and '24, and France in 1925. In those five challenge rounds only two matches were lost by Americans, the first when Pat O'Hara Wood and Gerald Patterson defeated Tilden and Vincent Richards in the doubles in 1922, and the second the following year when Jim Anderson of Australia beat John-

President Harding meets with the 1921 United States Davis Cup team: (*left to right*) A. Y. Leach, F. S. Myrick (president of USLTA), Watson M. Washburn, Col. C. O. Sherrell (aide to the President), Samuel Hardy (captain of Davis Cup team), President Harding, Wallace F. Johnson, R. N. Williams II, William T. Tilden II, and C. Christian (Secretary to the President).

ston in singles. The doubles match of that 1923 challenge round still stands as one of the longest on record, with a score of 17–15, 11–13, 2–6, 6–3, 6–2 in favor of Tilden and Williams against Anderson and J. B. Hawes.

But 1926 was to see another shift in the possession of the trophy. The four French players, René Lacoste, Jean Borotra, Henri Cochet, and Jacques Brugnon, who had returned home in 1925 without having won a single match, had now reached the heights toward which they had been struggling. In the 1926 challenge round at the Germantown Cricket Club they defeated the American team 4–1, leaving them only the solace of the doubles, which Williams and Richards won from Cochet and Brugnon.

The tennis supremacy of the world now rested with France, where it was steadfastly defended against the challenge of the United States through 1930. At the Stade Roland Garros at Auteuil, the "French Musketeers" turned back the bid of the American players for the fourth successive year for possession of the Cup. In 1931 America could not even get into the challenge round. Great Britain was the challenger and was turned back by the still-dominant French. But Britain had a

champion maturing in the person of Frederick J. Perry, and France was not producing any new players of the stature of Cochet, Lacoste, and Borotra. Only one year was left of French dominance, 1932, when the French team defeated the American team of Vines, Allison, and Van Ryn, 3 matches to 2, with Vines winning from Cochet and Van Ryn and Allison salvaging the doubles from Cochet and Brugnon.

1933 saw Great Britain pick up the banner in a 3–2 victory over the French team. The British Isles were to enjoy the first period of tennis supremacy since World War I, and it was to last as long as Perry kept his place as world champion. Twice in succession the United States saw its team go down to defeat in the challenge round. In 1936 the Americans were beaten before they reached the challenge round by the Australian team of Adrian Quist and Jack Crawford, but the Australians were mowed down by the British in the challenge round.

In 1937 the tide of tennis turned once more. World champion Perry was no longer available for the defense of the Cup. Only Austin was left of Britain's top-flight defenders. In America, young Don Budge of the magic

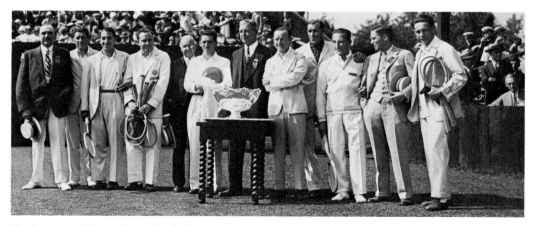

The French and United States Davis Cup teams played under the watchful eye of the donor of the cup.

backhand and blasting service had reached the peak, and with his doubles partner Gene Mako could be counted upon to put up a mighty battle. To this duet was added Frank Parker who, as it turned out, won the deciding match against England's Charles Hare before Budge won his second singles. America was once more in possession of the Cup, and the returning heroes were greeted with a Broadway parade.

Australia came through to the 1938 challenge round, which was staged at the Germantown Cricket Club, with Robert Riggs, Budge, and Mako representing the United States and Quist and John Bromwich carrying the Australian colors. It was a closely contested series, with Riggs unexpectedly defeating Quist but losing to Bromwich, Budge winning his two singles matches but losing in the doubles with Mako to the Australian pair.

In pre-World War II days, the Davis Cup team traveled by boat. The 1934 United States team of Frank Shields, L. R. Stoefen, and Sydney Wood practice aboard the S.S. *Paris*.

Australia, pinning its hope again on Quist and Bromwich, challenged in the American zone in 1939. Eliminating Yugoslavia in the interzone final, they again faced the United States team in the challenge round. The matches were held at the Merion Cricket Club at Haverford, Pa., in September of that year. The United States players were Riggs, then national singles champion, Frank Parker, and, for the doubles, the youthful team of Joseph R. Hunt and John A. Kramer. Riggs defeated Bromwich but lost to Quist, whom he had beaten the previous year. Parker defeated Quist but lost to Bromwich. America lost the deciding doubles match. Australia carried off the Cup—and kept it throughout another war.

The Start of the Wightman Cup

In 1922 Mrs. Hazel Hotchkiss Wightman presented to the USLTA a cup which was to promote better play and broader competition among women players. In the early stages of discussion of the new trophy, the idea was that it should be open to competition among women of all nations, similar to Davis Cup competition. But lack of high-ranking women players in any number in many tennis-playing countries and the difficulties in the way of a team of girls making trips to faraway points like Australia and the Orient narrowed the field, and the Wightman Cup went into competition in 1923 as a trophy for matches between women players of the United States and England. On February 6, 1926, the championship was officially relabeled by the USLTA as the "Women's Lawn Tennis Team Championship between Great Britain and the United States." This meant that no effort would be made to increase the number of competing countries. Also in 1926, it was stated that all regulations for the Wightman Cup would follow those governing Davis Cup play.

The first Wightman Cup matches played in the summer of 1923 marked the opening of the West Side Club Tennis Stadium at Forest Hills and resulted in a 7–0 victory for the American forces. It also set a pattern of procedure for the matches. Seven matches are played, five singles, four alternating the No. 1 and No. 2 players of each team and the fifth

between the two No. 3 players. The program is completed with two doubles matches.

The American lineup for the 1923 matches included Helen Wills, Mrs. Molla Mallory, and Eleanor Goss in singles, while Mrs. Wightman and Mrs. Goss carried one doubles assignment and Miss Wills and Mrs. Mallory the other. The English team featured the old-time favorites, K. McKane, Mrs. A. Clayton, Mrs. A. E. Beamish, and Mrs. B. C. Covell. With an almost identical personnel the following year, with the addition of Mrs. M. Jessup for America and Mrs. D. C. Sheppard-Barron and E. L. Colyer for the British, the English women reversed the score on their home grounds, winning the Cup 6–1. They held the trophy for the next year, the matches being played alternately at Wimbledon and Forest Hills. But in 1926 the Americans won it back at Wimbledon, and since then the English women while putting up a good show won only two more series in the seventeen played before World War II, 1928 and 1930, at Wimbledon.

Other Cup Competitions

In the 1920's and '30's the concept of the Davis and Wightman Cups led to a host of cup competitions in restricted areas and classes such as the Mitre Cup, the Prentice Cup, the King of Sweden's Cup, the Butler Cup, and doubtless many others less well known.

The Mitre Cup is the Davis Cup of South American lawn tennis and has stimulated development on that great continent. It was originated in 1920 by an Argentine sportsman whose family had given a President to Argentina and other members of which founded the great newspaper, *La Nacion*. Practically every South American player of note has appeared in this competition or in the Patino Cup play, which represents the South American Junior Championship.

The King of Sweden's Cup was endowed in 1936 by that loyal and royal player and patron of our game, King Gustav V of Sweden. It is the indoor version of the Davis Cup for Continental Europe and since its establishment has been held annually with the exception of the years of World War II.

Play for the Butler Cup, or more properly

The first United States (*top*) and British (*bottom*) Wightman Cup teams.

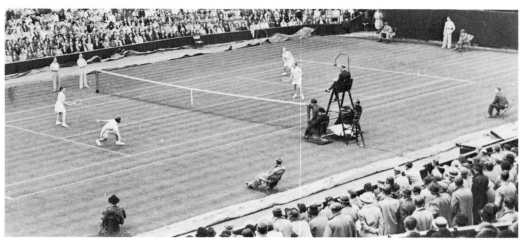

The deciding match of the 1936 Wightman Cup matches played at Wimbledon. Helen Jacobs (going for the ball) and Mrs. Sarah Palfrey Cooke defeated Kay Stammers and Freda Jones 1–6, 6–3, 7–5, and the United States retained the Cup 4 matches to 3.

Cups, was begun in the period between the Great Wars by the American George Butler, who was a regular winter resident of the French Riviera. The Cups are played for annually in varied classes, and interestingly one of the competitions is for men's doubles in which members of teams entered must be of identical nationality.

The Olympic Games and Tennis

Lawn tennis has at various times been a part of the Olympic Games. When the games were revived in 1896, tennis was not one of the events on the program. Olympic tennis events were first mentioned in the records of

In 1928, Bill Tilden and Wilbur Coen (nearest the camera) of the United States defeated Bunny Austin and Harold Kinsey of Great Britain in the Butler Cups final at Monte Carlo. The famed clubhouse and terraces of this beautiful tennis complex are in the background.

1900 games, but a resolution passed by the USNLTA stated that the Association would take no part in them. The United States, however, did compete in the 1904 Olympics held at St. Louis, Mo. Beals C. Wright—at that time United States doubles champion—won the singles and with E. W. Leonard the doubles. There were no other events.

Tennis was not on the games program in 1908, and the USNLTA did not send players in 1912, although it approved the entry of a United States player who competed on his own. The 1916 games were canceled owing to World War I. In 1920 the Olympic game dates and those of the United States National Championships were the same; the USLTA issued a request to the Belgian authorities to change the Olympic events to July. The Belgian Committee replied that they were unable to make such a change, and consequently the USLTA withdrew from the games. However, thirteen tennis nations did enter teams in the 1920 games.

After a lapse of 20 years the United States again entered a tennis team in the Olympics held in Paris in 1924. Twenty-seven other nations were represented in this last Olympic tennis competition. Four players were nominated by each nation for singles and two teams for the doubles. The events were men's and women's singles, doubles, and mixed doubles. The U.S. team which won all five events included Francis T. Hunter, Vincent Richards, Watson M. Washburn, and Richard Norris Williams; and Eleanor Goss, Mrs. Marion Zinderstein Jessup, Lillian Scharman, Edith Sigourney, Mrs. Hazel H. Wightman, and Helen N. Wills.

The final results:

Men's singles: Richards d. Henri Cochet (France) 6–4, 6–4, 5–7, 4–6, 6–2.

Men's doubles: Richards-Hunter d. Cochet–"Toto" Brugnon (France) 4–6, 6–2, 6–3, 2–6, 6–3.

Women's singles: Miss Wills d. Mlle. Diddie Vlasto (France) 6–2, 6–2.

Women's doubles: Miss Wills–Mrs. Wightman d. Mrs. Phyllis Covell–Kathleen McKane (Great Britain) 7–5, 8–6.

America's victorious Olympic tennis team: (*left to right, seated*) Edith Sigourney, Eleanor Goss, Mrs. Marion Zinderstein Jessup, Mrs. Hazel Wightman (captain), Helen Wills, and Lillian Scharman. (*standing*) Watson Washburn, Dr. Sumner Hardy (President of the California Lawn Tennis Association), Vincent Richards, Francis T. Hunter, Richard Norris Williams (captain), and Julian Myrick (Chairman of Davis Cup and International Committee of the United States Lawn Tennis Association).

Mixed doubles: Mrs. Wightman–Williams d. Mrs. Jessup–Richards 6–2, 6–3.

After the 1924 games, friction between the ILTF and the Olympic Committee arose, and in 1926 the ILTF reported to the Olympic Committee that tennis would be absent from future games unless these four demands by the Federation were met:

1. The ILTF to be granted one representative at least on the International Olympic Committee.
2. The ILTF to be allowed to cooperate in the technical and material organization of lawn tennis at the Olympic Games.
3. The definition of an amateur as adopted by the ILTF to be accepted so far as lawn tennis is concerned.
4. The holding of the Olympic Games in any one year not to cancel or supersede the holding during that year of any officially recognized lawn tennis championships or competitions and the Olympic Games not to be regarded as "a championship of the world in lawn tennis."

The Olympic Committee would not accept the demands, and tennis was eliminated from the program of events. In the ensuing years different countries suggested to the ILTF that perhaps a compromise could be reached, but the proposals were always turned down by the Federation.

Recently the tide has turned, and the USLTA and the ILTF have made enthusiastic pleas to be once again on the Olympic program. However, the Olympic Committee evidently is reluctant to have tennis as an event. The latest developments are perplexing and contradictory, but as anyone familiar with the International Olympic Committee knows, the International Olympic Committee is not prone to explain its actions.

Tennis, however, was added as an exhibition nonmedal sport at the 1968 Olympic Games in Mexico City. Although it still has not been formally accepted for Olympic competition, the exhibition series staged at these games may have represented a major stride in the right direction. Manuel Santana of Spain defeated Manuel Orantes, also of Spain, in the men's singles final during the exhibition. The scores were 2–6, 6–3, 3–6, 6–3, 6–4. The women's singles title went to Helga Niessen of West Germany who defeated Peaches Bartkowicz of the United States, 6–4, 6–2.

Other winners in the competition were: Rafael Osuna and Vicente Zarzua of Mexico, men's doubles; Helga Niessen and Edda Buding of West Germany, women's doubles; Herb FitzGibbon II and Julie Heldman of the United States, mixed doubles.

As previously stated, in 1913 delegates from the major tennis nations of the world, except for the United States, met in Paris and founded the International Lawn Tennis Federation (ILTF). Interestingly enough, the idea was suggested by an American, Duane Williams. He felt that since tennis was bound to spread throughout the world, it was necessary for the national associations to unite so that there would be uniformity in administration as well as in the rules of the game. He first spoke to the Secretary of the Swiss Lawn Tennis Association, who in turn spoke to Henry Wallet, president of the French Lawn Tennis Federation. Wallet was heartily in favor of the idea and convinced other nations of its feasibility.

It is necessary to trace the early development of the Federation as it related to the tennis picture in the United States to understand why the USNLTA would not join this international body for nine years. The purpose of the Federation was to increase international tennis, to make the laws of the game uniform throughout the world, and to hold world championships. At the first meeting the constitution and bylaws were established, and a world's championship grass tournament to be held annually was awarded to the British Isles (see page 18).

The USNLTA declined membership for several reasons. First of all, the Association felt that the Davis Cup matches were the epitome of international tennis supremacy and it did not wish to back any move that might take the place of Davis Cup play. Second, the constitution of the ILTF had a slightly stricter amateur code than did the USNLTA. This difference of opinion on the interpretation of an amateur, however, was a minor problem; the point of controversy centered on England holding an annual tournament entitled "World's Championship on Grass." Negotiations between the USNLTA and ILTF were held yearly on this question of membership. The results were nearly always the same. The USNLTA would not affiliate as long as the Federation's constitution gave a perpetual award of the "World's Championships" to any one country.

In 1923 it was resolved at the annual meeting of the USLTA that if the awarding of a world's championship by the ILTF was nullified from its constitution, the United States would become a member of this international group. In March of that same year the ILTF met and made some noteworthy decisions: It abolished the World's Championship from the constitution; it adopted international playing rules; and it recognized the national championships of Australia, England, France, and the United States as the four "big" events. Consequently, the USLTA became a member and, thus, with the United States in the ranks, the Federation was indeed the international body for lawn tennis.

Men's Play in America After World War II

In 1947 Jack Kramer won the United States singles title from Tom Brown, Jr., in straight sets. While Kramer repeated his win the next year, he had to come back after losing the first two sets to the wartime champion, Frank Parker. Kramer turned professional after this victory, and the following year a youngster out of southern California named Richard "Pancho" Gonzalez took over the throne and defended it in 1949 by defeating Ted Schroeder in one of the longest matches in the history of the championship—16–18, 2–6, 6–1, 6–2, 6–4.

Gonzalez divorced himself from the amateur ranks after winning his second title, and Arthur Larsen defeated Herbert Flam for the crown. Then, in 1951, the United States Singles Championship went to Australia, when Frank Sedgman—nicknamed "The Gentleman"—took the first of two titles. (No player has won three *amateur* men's singles titles since Fred Perry did in 1936. Actually, Sedgman was the first foreign player to take the title since that year.) Sedgman repeated in 1952 by defeating Gardnar Mulloy in straight sets.

The title came back to the United States in 1953 when Tony Trabert won it from fellow American, E. Victor Seixas, Jr. The next year

Tony Trabert (*left*) held the Men's Singles title in the United States in 1953 and 1955; Vic Seixas (*right*), the oldest first-time winner of the United States title, held it in 1954.

Seixas won the title by turning back the bid of Rex Hartwig to take the crown back to Australia. In 1955 Tony Trabert repeated his 1953 victory, defeating Australian Ken Rosewall in straight sets. The following year Rosewall beat his fellow countryman, Lewis Hoad, for the title and thus started a string of twelve years (1956 to 1967) in which the United States Men's Singles Championship left the country. Only in 1963 and 1967 did Americans, Frank Froehling III and Clark Graebner, even reach the finals. During that period Australians won ten championships— (Rosewall, 1956; Malcolm T. Anderson, 1957; Ashley T. Cooper, 1958; Neale Fraser, 1959 and 1960; Roy Emerson, 1961 and 1964; Rodney Laver, 1962; Fred Stolle, 1966; and John Newcombe, 1967). Only a Mexican (Rafael Osuna, 1963) and a Spaniard (Manuel Santana, 1965) broke the Australian string of victories.

In 1968 the *National* singles title came to the United States when Arthur Ashe defeated his countryman, Robert Lutz, in a five-set affair. It remained here with the victory by Stan Smith in 1969. In 1968 the USLTA championship became an open title, as discussed later in this section, and the National Championship was discontinued after 1969.

The United States men's doubles championship remained for the most part overseas during the postwar period. True, Gardnar Mulloy and William Talbert did capture the crown in 1946 and 1948, and Jack Kramer and Ted Schroeder won in 1947. But from 1949 to 1960, except in 1954 when Seixas and Trabert won it, the doubles title remained with foreign players. (In 1952 Seixas joined with an Australian, Mervyn Rose, to take the doubles championship.)

Charles McKinley and Dennis Ralston teamed to win the crown in 1961, 1963, and 1964, but the rest of the years it remained out of the United States. In 1968 Robert Lutz and Stan Smith brought it back.

After a lapse of Davis Cup competition for six years because of the war, the United States team, made up of Jack Kramer, Ted Schroeder, and Gardnar Mulloy, went as challenger to Australia in December of 1946 and came back with the Cup and a clean sweep. Again in 1947 the United States team, this time as defenders, defeated Australia 4 to 1

Darlene Hard of the United States and Neale Fraser of Australia captured the majority of the silverware at the 1960 Nationals. Miss Hard won the singles and doubles, while Fraser took the singles and mixed doubles.

at Forest Hills, with Jack Kramer and Ted Schroeder doing all the playing for the Americans. This was the first time since 1920 that the United States used only two men in Davis Cup challenge-round competition. It is interesting to note that, from 1946 through 1949, the United States was only defeated in doubles in challenge-round competition.

In 1950, however, the scene changed when Sedgman and McGregor teamed to give Australia supremacy. With Frank Sedgman and Ken McGregor as the backbone of the Australian team, the men from Australia retained the Davis Cup in 1951 and 1952, and even though the Australian aces were lured to professional tennis, Australia, with youngsters Lewis Hoad and Ken Rosewall, was able to retain the Cup again in 1953 by the score of three to two. In 1954 by the same score, with the excellent play of Tony Trabert and Vic Seixas, the United States recaptured the Cup. But the Aussies came right back with Hoad and Rosewall to snatch the bowl in 1955 and keep it until the U.S. stretched its boundaries to include Peru in 1958.

Then Peruvian Alex Olmedo, a resident student at Southern California whose homeland had no Davis Cup team, was allowed to stand for the U.S. He became the first man

The victorious 1958 United States Davis Cup team: (*left to right*) Bernard Bartzen, Alex Olmedo, Perry Jones (captain), Barry MacKay, and Earl Buchholz, Jr.

ever to score three points for America in a 3–2 victory—singles victories over Cooper and Anderson and a doubles triumph with Ham Richardson over Anderson and Fraser (Stan Smith did it again in 1969). Undaunted however, the Aussies were back a few months later with Laver, Fraser, and rookie Roy Emerson—to take the Cup back from Olmedo, Butch Buchholz, and Barry MacKay.

That shock sent the U.S. into a dive to the depths as in 1933, the last year Yanks had been excluded from the challenge round. For an unprecedented stretch of three years, losing twice to Italy and once to Mexico, the United States was quarantined from the challenge. The 1962 loss to Mexico was the heaviest blow, the first time we had been conquered by a nation from our part of the world. Neither Italy nor Mexico was able to disturb the Emerson-Fraser-Laver triumvirate in the challenges.

Then Denny Ralston and Chuck McKinley grew up, strong and mature enough to forget earlier defeats and behavior. Even so, with Chuck, 22, and Denny, 21, they were the youngest American victors since Don Budge, 22, and Frank Parker and Gene Mako, both 21, grabbed the Cup from Britain in 1937. Playing their first challenge round, the U.S.'s twenty-fifth against Australia, McKinley and Ralston returned the Cup, 3–2, McKinley stopping John Newcombe in the decisive match. But the Cup was quickly gone, pinched from Cleveland nine months later, 3–2, on Emerson's final match win over McKinley, to remain Down Under until December of 1968. In the next three years there were to be two new challengers—Spain, 1965 and 1967, and India, 1966—while America fell into another losing rut.

During this period occurred perhaps the greatest upset in any sport when those unknowns Miguel Olvera and Pancho Guzman propelled Ecuador past Arthur Ashe, Clark Graebner, Cliff Richey, and Marty Riessen, 3–2, in Guayaquil. Nobody can explain it yet, but it added spice to the already intriguing Cup flavor. Losses to Spain in 1965 and Brazil in 1966 did not make the United States feel any better.

Australia had no trouble in the challenge rounds as Emerson, Fred Stolle, John Newcombe, and Tony Roche carried the load. As they turned pro (Emerson after 10 challenge rounds, playing on a record eight winning teams), the Aussies became easy prey when the Americans Ashe, Graebner, Lutz, Smith, and Pasarell finally worked their way through to the final in December, 1968.

Now it was the Australians who were stunningly down and out. Their unapproached run of 25 consecutive challenge-round appearances, dating from 1938—during which they won 16 times—had been snapped. They were beaten 3–2 by Mexico in 1969 during the opening round. Since that time Australia has been eliminated in the early stages of zone play each year.

In 1969 and 1970, Ashe, Richey, Smith, and Lutz of the United States defeated Romania and West Germany, 5–0 and 5–0 respectively. After the 1971 Davis Cup finals, in which the United States defeated Romania 3–2, the challenge-round form of competition was dropped. Thus, after 1972 all nations had to compete in the zone elimination matches (see Section V).

Women's Play After the War

The latter part of the 1940's failed to produce any *great* woman champion. During the war years, as previously noted, Sarah Palfrey Cooke, an Easterner, and Pauline Betz, a Californian, led the field, Mrs. Cooke winning her second championship in 1945 and Miss Betz her fourth in 1946, after which they turned professional. Margaret Osborne du Pont, Louise Brough, Doris Hart, and Shirley Fry, sometimes referred to as "the big four," dominated the game at Forest Hills, Wimbledon, and in other countries wherever they competed, including France, England, South Africa, and Australia.

Then in 1951, Maureen ("Little Mo") Connolly from California, like Miss Sutton in 1904, took complete command, winning the first of three successive United States championships at Forest Hills before she had reached her seventeenth birthday. Miss Connolly was the second-youngest player to capture the title. Miss Sutton was only a few days younger when she won the championship

American women stars of late 1940's and early 1950's: (*left to right*) Mrs. Margaret Osborne du Pont, A. Louise Brough, Doris Hart, and Shirley Fry.

In her very short career, few, if any, tennis players have approached Maureen Connolly's record.

in 1904 and Miss Wills was almost a year older when she captured her first United States title in 1923.

On her first attempt at Wimbledon in 1952, Miss Connolly won the crown and successfully defended it in 1953 and 1954. In 1953 she also won the Australian, French, and United States titles, and so this little mistress of ground-stroke play became the first woman to hold the four major championships simultaneously—the grand slam. She sustained a leg injury while horseback riding which prevented her from defending her United States title in 1954. Later Miss Connolly, perhaps the only player of the immediate postwar era to rank with Suzanne Lenglen and Helen Wills Moody Roark and who was to die at a tragically young age, became a professional.

Doris Hart won the United States championship in 1954 and retained it in the follow-

ing year, when Louise Brough had recaptured the Wimbledon title after an interval of five years. Actually, Miss Brough collected 13 Wimbledon titles between 1948 and 1955. She won the singles four times, the doubles five times, with Margaret Osborne du Pont, and the mixed doubles four times, twice with John Bromwich, and once each with Tom P. Brown, Jr., and Eric Sturgess.

In 1956 Althea Gibson of New York became the first Negro player to win a major title when she won the premier clay-court title in the world—the French championship—at Paris. She was the dominating player for the next two seasons, notably by reason of her service power, winning both the Wimbledon and United States championships. The United States strength-in-depth weakened at this time, and the British trio of Angela Mortimer (1955), Shirley Bloomer (1957), and Christine Truman (1959) won the French championship, as did the Hungarian Suzy Kormoczy in 1958.

The first player to break the 13-year-old postwar United States women's monopoly of the Wimbledon and United States championship titles was Maria Esther Bueno, a slim, superb stylist from Brazil. She won both these championships in 1959 with artistic ease and retained her Wimbledon title in 1960. She, however, lost her American title to her doubles partner, Darlene R. Hard of California. Miss Hard had already won the French championship that year, and went on to retain her United States title in 1961 following the severe illness of Miss Bueno. In the season

Maria Bueno was the first non-American player to break the United States' monopoly on National and Wimbledon titles after World War II.

Mrs. Margaret Smith Court, with her Wimbledon win shown here, was the second woman to accomplish the Grand Slam.

One of the finest mixed-doubles teams was Billy Talbert and Mrs. Margaret Osborne du Pont.

of 1961, two British players won major championships: Ann Haydon took the French title and Angela Mortimer became the first British singles winner at Wimbledon for 24 years.

While the star of Australia's amateur men players began to wane, the prowess of their women players waxed and Margaret Smith, a player of rare physique and power, won the Australian championship in 1960 and retained it for the next three years. In 1962 Miss Smith took the French and United States championships but was thwarted at Wimbledon in the first round, the title eventually going to Karen Hantze Susman (United States). In 1963, Miss Smith lost her French title to her compatriot, Lesley Turner; became the first Australian woman ever to win Wimbledon; but lost her United States championship to Miss Bueno, who had recovered from the aftereffects of her severe attack of jaundice.

In 1964 and again in 1966, Miss Bueno won the United States title; Miss Smith won it in 1965. Mrs. Billie Jean King, three-time winner at Wimbledon, captured the women's crown in 1967, only to have Margaret Smith (now Mrs. Court) take it back for the next three years. Incidentally, Mrs. Court, in 1970, won the grand slam, equaling "Little Mo" Connolly's feat of 1953.

Wimbledon After World War II

In England, after World War II was over, a new battle—this time in tennis—was starting. Like the rest of the nation, Wimbledon

buckled into the war effort, and acting secretary Norah Cleather helped in the raising of pigs where courts had once been. Yet when the European fighting ended midway in 1945, very little time passed before two international encounters, celebrating victory, were staged on Court 1. Participants somehow delved into bottom drawers to rediscover whites, but shoes were a problem and at least one player was reduced to appearing in khaki gym shoes, service issue. Crowds turned out in abundance, and at least one WAAF officer was surprised to see the RAF officer from the office next door at her station walk out on the court, but it was that kind of a time in Britain. Bomb damage put a large section of the Centre Court out of action, but this was carefully roped off and other sections of the ground disguised with green canvas. Thus, when the championships were resumed in

Jack Kramer receives his award from the King and Queen in the Royal Box at Wimbledon after his 1947 victory.

1946, the intervening war years scarcely seemed real so far as tennis was concerned.

The general standard of play was somewhat lower than usual, but the crowds turned out in tens of thousands, closing the doors of the Centre Court on many occasions. Despite their lack of practice, the organizers did a magnificent job and the success of the fortnight exceeded all expectations.

Bobby Riggs and Alice Marble, the 1939 champions, had turned professional in the interim years. There were many notable absentees, among them Jean Borotra, whose entry had been refused for alleged cooperation with the Nazis. Jack Kramer, United States, and Dinny Pails, Australia, arrived with enviable reputations but both fell along the wayside. The men's title eventually went to Yvon Petra, the giant Frenchman. He defeated Geoff Brown of Australia in the final.

Kramer returned to capture the singles in 1947 and also won the doubles with fellow Californian Bob Falkenburg, and then forecast accurately that Falkenburg would win the singles in 1948. No singles winner has ever aroused more controversy than Falkenburg because of his long rests on the court each time he fell—and he fell many times during the fortnight. Two years later it was discovered he was suffering from a severe thyroid deficiency and that it had been little short of

a miracle he had won at all, rests or no rests.

"Lucky" Ted Schroeder came, saw, and conquered in 1949, after one of the most eventful passages in the history of Wimbledon. Down 2–5 in the fifth set to Gardnar Mulloy in the first round, he just pulled that one out. Then he saved several match points against Frank Sedgman and was taken to five sets both by Eric Sturgess and, in the final, by Jaroslav Drobny. His courage lives yet in the minds of all who saw him that one year he competed at the All England Club for the Championship.

Budge Patty succeeded Schroeder in 1950 and Dick Savitt took over from Patty in 1951. These were high days in United States power, for neither Patty nor Falkenburg ever played on a Davis Cup team for their country, although Falkenburg later represented Brazil.

Frank Sedgman won the men's singles in 1952. In 1930 Wilmer Allison had reached the final despite being omitted from the seedings. Kurt Nielsen repeated this feat in 1953 and then gave an encore in 1955, losing to Vic Seixas the first time and Tony Trabert the second.

In between, Jaroslav Drobny beat Ken Rosewall in 1954, so becoming champion 16 years after his first appearance in 1938. No winner before or since has enjoyed such sustained applause as when the popular, self-exiled Czech finally triumphed at long last.

The 1957 championships were nonvintage except for an astonishing final display by Lew Hoad against Ashley Cooper, who lasted only 57 minutes and collected a meager five games. A final-day visit by Queen Elizabeth II raised the championships to new importance. But the occasion was marred slightly by the sudden appearance on the Centre Court of a woman bearing a near-political banner; she was quickly escorted away by the referee, Colonel John Legg, who, in true Wimbledon fashion, skillfully mixed courtesy with a firmness that brooked no resistance from the demonstrator.

Sweden set up a "first" when Sven Davidson and Ulf Schmidt won the 1958 doubles title. And the ship scheduled to return them home lingered for them in mid-River Thames while they tore almost straight from the court to a waiting launch to catch it.

Hoad had turned professional less than 24 hours after completion of the 1957 championships and so began the era which culminated in the first "open" 11 years later.

Until then the tennis seen at Wimbledon equaled in standard anything produced by the professionals—more or less. The departure of Hoad meant he, Rosewall, Gonzalez, Sedg-man, and Segura were all in one camp. Early-round play at Wimbledon retained all the excitements of youth pitting its skills and enthusiasm against the experience of older players, but the second week from 1958 onward became something of a bore. This was not lost on the Wimbledon Management Committee, whose attitude was summarized ten years later by Chairman Herman David: "I like to think of Wimbledon as a beautiful frame into which we put the finest possible pictures each year." With the exception of Rodney Laver, who won in 1961 and 1962, the year of his first grand slam, the pictures were no longer "Rembrandt" in quality. Additionally, commercial, municipal, and national sponsorship in worldwide competition escalated demand for top amateur players, and the expenses they were able to command made use of the term "amateur" farcical and hypocritical.

The Wimbledon committee decided the time had come for bold leadership. A quietly convened special general meeting of club members resulted in only two votes going against a motion virtually giving the committee carte blanche to take whatever actions it felt necessary to bring honesty back into

Rod Laver winning his first of four Wimbledon titles. The Duchess of Kent made the presentation.

Chuck McKinley in 1963 was the most recent American to win a Men's Singles title at Wimbledon.

John Newcombe of Australia won the Men's title in 1967, 1970, and 1971.

tennis and to throw Wimbledon open once more to the best possible "pictures," no matter their color, creed, or artificial category.

The Professional and His Part in Lawn Tennis

It was beyond imagination in the early years of tennis in the United States that any aspect of professionals or professionalism would ever enter the game. The activity flourished in its traditional setting of exclusive estates and private clubs. It was strictly a game for the wealthy class, who had not only the leisure time for sports but had access to courts. Even those who engaged in the limited number of tournaments considered it more of a joyful social event, compared to the businesslike manner of later competition. Instruction for the most part was obtained through personal conversations and from printed tips in books and magazines.

When professionalism began to appear in some other sports, tennis still was an avocation participated in by simon-pure amateurs. But soon some professional players began to appear who were employed by clubs to provide practice for the members. In fact, even a 1910 book on tennis mentioned that there were no teaching professionals in the game. However, slowly as the game grew and its strokes and play became more intricate, professional teachers were needed. The lack of teachers was noted in a 1921 article which stated that it was doubtful "if there are twenty-five professional players and instructors of lawn tennis in the whole country." The need was increased with not only the addition of more member clubs in the USLTA, but clubs that had been exclusively for golf began to install tennis facilities. As the number of professional teachers increased, some unification seemed necessary by many of the early tennis instructors. Consequently, in 1927 a group met in New York and formed the Professional Lawn Tennis Association. The following notice was sent to all those who taught tennis.

For some time past there has been a very strong feeling among lawn tennis professionals that there is a need for some organization to protect and promote their interests and to assist them in obtaining a proper and recognized status in the tennis world. A meeting was accordingly held September 23 and it was decided to form an Association. This meeting was followed by others at which the following regulations were agreed upon:

An initiation fee of $10 will be charged all new members.

Dues are to be $5 annually.

An executive committee has been elected and a constitution adopted. It is the desire of this executive committee to have all tennis professionals of accepted standards become members of the Association. . . .

It is important to note the phrase "to assist them in obtaining a proper and recognized status in the tennis world." Even though it was recognized that these instructors were helping to promote the game, it was evident that they were considered as "outsiders" by those of the inner tennis circle. There is also substantial evidence that the PLTA might have been formed at this time to establish a definite differentiation between the professional teacher and the professional player, as touring professionals had just begun to emerge on the scene. Perhaps, since feeling toward professional players was not too favorable from officials of the USLTA, the teachers wanted to be sure that there was no question of where they stood as a group. It appears that the USLTA sensed the good faith and sound purpose of the PLTA but was wary that the professional player might detract from the amateur game. The Association attempted to assist the organization in its early years by giving it official recognition, but issued firm

resolutions concerning certain aspects of professional tennis. On March 17, 1928, the Executive Committee of the USLTA held lengthy discussions concerning professionals playing tournaments at member clubs. The matter had been brought to its attention because the Palm Beach Tennis Club had recently held a tournament just for professionals. Furthermore, the Longwood Cricket Club had requested permission to have pro-amateur exhibitions in conjunction with the forthcoming national championships. The previous year, 1927, the USLTA had passed a three-part resolution which in brief stated the following: It approved the PLTA, it frowned on recognizing individual promoters of professional matches and of professional and amateur matches, and it ruled that clubs must ask permission to hold matches open to professionals only or to both amateurs and professionals. Consequently, permission was denied to the Longwood Cricket Club, and a motion concerning exhibitions between professionals and amateurs at USLTA tournaments was tabled until a future meeting. The motion was eventually acted upon, and on February 13, 1931, the Executive Committee stated that "no exhibition matches between amateurs and professionals would be authorized." Later on a compromise was reached whereby they would be allowed under certain restrictions.

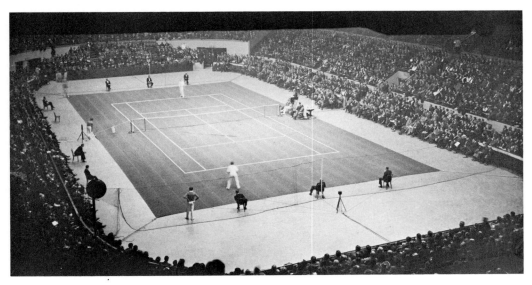

Madison Square Garden in New York was scene of the first United States professional exhibition in 1926.

Even though the Association gave its approval to the formation of the PLTA, there had never been a close relationship between the two groups until recently. The PLTA influence on the promotion of tennis has been rather negligible. First of all, it has been a loose-knit organization with rather casual standards and policies. Second, it has been somewhat ineffective, as many of the leading teachers and few of the playing professionals secured membership, evidently because it did not seem necessary. Yet, the ever-increasing growth of the game demanded more and more instructors who were qualified to teach effectively. Both the USLTA and the PLTA have been concerned over this matter, and just recently banded together to set up the United States Professional Tennis Registry. This Registry is a listing of all registered tennis teaching professionals in America. It was established "in order to improve the teaching standards of the game among the professionals and to make it possible for member clubs of the USLTA to deal with teaching professionals of recognized standing." Membership is based on meeting certain minimum requirements and successfully passing written and practical tests.

The type of professionals that created the most concern for the USLTA was the touring professional player. For a full understanding of the situation it is necessary to examine the historical development of players who openly played for monetary benefit. In 1926 Charles C. Pyle, an ingenious promotor, felt that there could be substantial financial returns from staging exhibition tennis matches between well-known players. He first convinced Suzanne Lenglen from France, the leading drawing card in the female ranks, to turn professional and join his troupe. Mary K. Browne, American champion from 1912 to 1914, was signed on as her opponent. He tried to enlist Tilden and William Johnston but they declined. However, he was able to persuade Vincent Richards to sign a contract. Richards was one of the top players in the United States at the time and his defection from the amateur ranks was a blow to the USLTA. Not only had it lost one of the leading gate attractions of the tournament circuit, but he was also one of the mainstays of the Davis Cup team. Perhaps, fearing repeat performances

in the future by the leading amateur stars, the Association omitted Richards from the 1926 rankings. Furthermore, it passed a resolution whereby "none who had accepted a professional contract could be ranked as an amateur." Pyle also contracted Paul Feret, a well-known player in France; Howard Kinsey, United States doubles titleholder in 1924; and Harvey Snodgrass, a teaching professional who had been a ranked amateur. The first in a long series of exhibitions was held at Madison Square Garden on October 9, 1926. This was the beginning of professional exhibition tennis in the United States, which as time went on had far-reaching effects on amateur tennis.

This first professional tour, although a novelty, was not too successful. Both Lenglen and Richards were so superior to their opponents that interest waned for lack of competition. The following statement appeared in *American Lawn Tennis* concerning the tour:

As to the future of professional tennis, it does seem that the outlook is dark. Unless the competitive element can be introduced into the professional game—by open tournaments or in some other way—the idea is sure to fail. Exhibition tennis is never much fun from the spectator's point of

The Czechoslovakian star Karel Koseluth was a big winner on the pro tour of the early 1930's.

view and can even be a pretty boring business.

The writer was rather prophetic, for Pyle's troupe split up after the first year because Lenglen refused to tour any more. Consequently, Richards and Kinsey tried to instill interest by staging a professional championship. It was not too successful, for Richards won easily and the teaching professionals were not any match for the exhibition players.

However, professional tours received new impetus in 1930 when Bill Tilden joined the professional ranks. He organized Tilden's Tennis Tours, Inc., and had some very successful years. He first toured the United States competing against Karel Koseluth and then had some fruitful matches in Europe. When he repeated his tour in the United States, the venture was not as successful. Similar to Pyle's first attempt, the public lost interest as Tilden had no opposition. He needed new opponents, and thus a new trend began to enter the professional picture. The object was to lure the top amateur players into the professional ranks. It had to be the top-named players, for attempts at lesser-known competitors had not proved successful. From 1937 on, when Fred Perry of England and Ellsworth Vines of the United States turned professional, there was a succession of stars who made the switch to the "play for pay" ranks, such as Don Budge, Alice Marble, Mary Hardwick, Bobby Riggs, Frank Kovacs, Pauline Betz, and Gussie Moran. But the player who really changed the professional picture was Jack Kramer, who turned professional in the late 1940's. He not only was the best in the professional class but he was also a fantastic promoter. He expanded to greater proportions what Tilden had started when he began to lure the top amateurs for his tours. Furthermore, Kramer did not just deal with American players but attracted foreigners as well. In succession he signed Pancho Gonzalez, Frank Sedgman, Ken McGregor, Pancho Segura, Tony Trabert, Rex Hartwig, Ken Rosewall, Lew Hoad, Alex Olmedo, and others. An interesting contrast is pointed out by Al Laney, famous tennis writer for the *New York Herald Tribune:*

In the period between World War I and the market crash, a period to which we usually apply the name Golden Age of Sport, no player who won either the Wimbledon or the US title became a professional. In the decade which followed World War II, 5 of the 7 winners of the US title and 3 others who won at Wimbledon turned professional.

As can be expected, this aspect of professionalism has caused great consternation in the USLTA. The Association does not deny that the loss of the big stars has had its effects. The situation is briefly summarized by remarks in a letter to Julian S. Myrick, former head of the USLTA, from the president in 1961, George Barnes:

I am convinced that in the days when there were no touring pros we were able to keep amateur players in the game long enough for them to become name players and draw large paying audiences. Gradually over the years the top amateurs are turning pro sooner and sooner and as a result, we have less and less opportunity to build up name players. This hurts the gate which has been used over the years to send our Davis and Wightman cup teams around the world and to build players and the game from the grass roots up.

Professional tennis has come a long way since 1926. You will note above that Rod Laver collected $35,000 for victory in the finals of the 1970 Tennis Champion Classic. In 1971 he received $170,000 for winning all fourteen matches in the 1971 Classic.

The income from our National Singles Championships has been gradually diminishing until the USLTA income in 1960, as you know, was nil. To rebuild our name players we need money, to get money we need more spectators, and to get more spectators we need name players. So it is ring-around-the-rosie! Which comes first, the spectators, the name players, or the money? . . .

The defection of so many top players from the amateur camp brought forth much discussion concerning the amateur code and, in particular, the possibilities of having open tournaments.

Open Tennis Tournaments

The beginning of professional exhibition matches was the actual beginning of consideration by the USLTA of open tournaments. Even though the very first exhibition was held at Madison Square Garden, it was natural that requests were made to hold some of the other matches at member clubs of the USLTA. The Association did not disapprove of these exhibitions but did want to have control over them. Consequently, in 1927, it passed a resolution whereby clubs wishing to have matches or tournaments open to professionals only or to both amateurs and professionals had to get permission from the USLTA. The resolution was a definite step to prevent any club from holding an open tournament until the Association decided the time was right to have one. However, during this era the leaders of the USLTA were in favor of this type of tournament but were just being very cautious concerning its introduction. The resolution was discussed at the annual meeting of 1928 by the president, Samuel H. Collom, and indicates the attitude of the governing body:

> The intention of the resolution was to recognize the same principle, in tennis, as does exist in golf. You have amateur championships and professional championships and eventually, as that develops, you will have open championships.

In 1930 the Germantown Cricket Club, which had suffered severe financial losses, appealed to the USLTA for permission to hold an open tournament in order to help its treasury. The Association gave its approval provided the ILTF had no objection. Accordingly, the USLTA proposed an amendment to Federation Rule 23, which at that time permitted amateur-professional matches when approved by a member association. The association proposed adding the words "and tournaments" after the word "matches" in order that member nations could hold open competitions. When the proposal came before the ILTF meeting, it received strong objections from Chevalier de Borman of Belgium, who was one of the founders of the Federation, with these words: "The day we open our gates to the professionals, all our points of view will change." The proposal was soundly defeated, with only the United States and Great Britain casting favorable votes. Consequently, permission was denied the Germantown Cricket Club, and the Association adopted a new resolution whereby "no further action be considered toward holding Open Tournaments until a different and more cooperative attitude on this proposal is adopted by ILTF."

In 1933 the Germantown Cricket Club again requested permission from the USLTA to hold an open championship. The president at the time, Louis J. Carruthers, was a lawyer by profession, and he had studied the Federation ruling very carefully. It is obvious that the Association did not wish to jeopardize its membership in the ILTF by violating the rules but it did want to hold an open tournament. Carruthers said that it was possible to have these types of championships for "there was nothing in Rule 23 which forbade the holding of an open tournament if the member nation wished to hold one." Therefore, again, Germantown Cricket Club was granted its request. Several months prior to the scheduled open event, the annual Federation meeting was held in England. The USLTA was represented by John MacVeagh, who was not a tennis official but the second secretary of the American Embassy in London. With such an important step being taken by the USLTA, it is difficult to understand why the Association did not send one of its officers to the meeting. An examination of the records provides no explanation for this course of action. Due to the publicity given by the press to the proposed open by the USLTA, the subject was debated at the Federation meeting. With no one to forcefully defend the Association's stand, persuasive arguments were presented against the position of the USLTA. A resolution was adopted whereby "neither Rule 23 nor any other Rule permits the holding of such tournaments."

In 1937 the USLTA was faced with a new problem. Without requesting permission, the Greenbrier Golf and Tennis Club held what it described as the "First U.S. Open Tennis Championship." Many professionals and six amateurs participated in the tournament. This situation was specifically prohibited by the Federation rule. The Association took drastic steps in order to prevent the staging of other such tournaments. It suspended the six amateurs and withdrew the membership of the Greenbrier Club in the USLTA.

The subject of open tournaments was revived in 1938, when the Lawn Tennis Association of India submitted a proposal to the ILTF whereby each Association would be allowed to hold one open tournament annually. The USLTA submitted an amendment to the Indian proposal which was a repetition of the Association's earlier resolution, namely, "that each nation should have the right to decide for itself if it wanted to hold an open tournament." However, the attitude of the Association toward the prospect of an open had definitely changed as evidenced by an attachment to the amendment. It stated that the USLTA "neither favors or disapproves of such a tournament at this time." The proposal was defeated by a 118 to 51 vote at the Federation meeting.

During World War II permission was granted by the Federation for the USLTA to hold exhibition matches between amateurs and professionals for the benefit of the Red Cross and other war charities. Otherwise, there were no more discussions or proposals concerning the possibility of open championships.

However, by 1957, the situation was ripe again for renewal of discussion concerning tournaments open to both amateurs and professional players. Most of the top players in the world had joined Jack Kramer's professional group, there was increasing evidence that the remaining top amateurs were making more money than ever from the game, and the press and the public were asking for open competition. At the suggestion of the Florida Lawn Tennis Association it was proposed at the 1957 annual meeting of the USLTA that the Association resubmit its amendment of 1938 to the Federation. But the USLTA action was to turn the matter over to committee.

By 1959 the ILTF was so concerned with the problems connected with the amateur code in the tennis world that a special committee was chosen to study the entire question of amateurism. The recommendations of the committee were greeted with both dismay and ecstasy by the lawn tennis associations, for there were extreme proposals in contrast to the traditional philosophy of amateur tennis. The recommendation that created the most discussion was a proposal offered by the Lawn Tennis Association of France to create a new class of player called "authorized" or "registered." Any amateur player over the age of sixteen could register as an "authorized player" whereby he could compete in amateur tournaments for cash prizes. The following explanation for the system was given by Jean Borotra of the French Lawn Tennis Association:

> The National Associations and the International Federation would control two categories of players: the amateurs . . . the registered players. . . . Both would be expected to respect the written and unwritten rules of the game, but only the former would observe its disinterested side. There would be no actual barrier between these categories, and the players could all take part in the same tournaments.
>
> This formula would completely solve the problem, because all the players so wishing would be allowed to "cash in" openly on their talent; the public would be able to see championships in which the best players could participate without exception; and the amateurs would remain as such and still not be cut off from first-class tennis.

The committee's other recommendation was to experiment with a limited number of open tennis championships in 1961.

The USLTA unanimously rejected the "authorized player" proposal, feeling it was just another name for professionals. Moreover, it threatened to withdraw the Davis Cup from competition if the Federation gave it sanction. The other proposal was approved by the Association with an amendment which gave each lawn tennis association the principle of self-determination.

The ILTF meeting was held in Paris in July, 1960, and action was taken on the two proposals. The "authorized player" motion received so much opposition that it was not even brought to a vote. As an alternative, another Special Committee of Amateurism was appointed and commanded to make a report at the annual meeting in 1962. The open tournament proposal was rejected by the close margin of five votes out of a total of 209.

Since approval of the motion appeared to be a foregone conclusion, the results of the voting demand some explanation. Even though the big tennis nations, such as United States, Australia, France, and Great Britain, were all in favor of open competition, it was the small nations whose total vote cast the die. As a group, they were not in favor of open tournaments, fearing that such events would detract from their amateur competitions. These small countries were doubtful that they could raise the finances necessary to attract players if open tournaments were allowed.

At the annual meeting of the USLTA in 1961 it was decided again to press the issue with the ILTF for an open. It submitted an amendment to the amateur rules to be voted upon at the 1961 Federation whereby

> . . . a Member Nation, in its own discretion, may sanction tournaments to be held within its jurisdiction open to both amateurs and professionals without loss of their amateur status to any amateurs competing therein with the consent of their own National Associations.

Although worded somewhat differently, the proposal was similar to every other United States recommendation, namely, that nations should be allowed to choose for themselves whether they wished to hold open tournaments. Furthermore, the Open Tennis Committee of the USLTA was instructed to formulate plans for the management of open tennis that "will be in the interest of amateur tennis." The Federation was also presented with a proposal from the British Lawn Tennis Association that Wimbledon be an open tournament in 1962 as an experiment.

The Federation meeting of 1961 was held in Stockholm, Sweden, and again the issue of open tournaments was the main topic on the agenda. This time no vote was taken but the question was postponed for another year. However, the delegates were asked to consider three possible proposals as a solution to the amateur problem. These proposals were recommended by the Special Committee on Amateurism and were as follows:

1. To abolish from the ILTF rules any references to "amateurs" and "professionals" as such, leaving to national associations' local autonomy to make their own rules.
2. To retain the present rules and organize a central ILTF "control" to insure compliance throughout the world.
3. To retain the present rules but to delegate to each national association the responsibility of defining allowable expenses and enforcing of the rules.

The vote on the proposals would be taken at the Federation meeting in 1962.

The ILTF meeting of 1962 was held in Paris in July. The main topics on the agenda were the aforementioned proposals and the open-tournament resolution. The proposal concerning elimination of the terms "amateur" and "professional" was defeated, as was the proposal concerning each Association establishing its own expense regulations. The third proposal concerning Federation control of the amateur rules received much discussion, and it was decided that further study was necessary before voting for or against its adoption. The request to have experimental open tournaments received 120 votes in favor and 100 votes were cast against the resolution. Since a two-thirds majority vote is necessary for implementation, the proposal was defeated. Furthermore, it was resolved that the open question could not be discussed again until 1964. Three of the leading tennis nations, Great Britain, France, and United States, voted for the motion. Joining Australia against the motion were Germany, Italy, Yugoslavia, and the Soviet Union and its satellites.

In 1964 USLTA reversed itself and went on record as adamantly opposed to open play and remained so—with the majority of the

ILTF—until Great Britain challenged the Federation with their famous declaration that "come hell or high water" they would conduct Wimbledon as an open championship. In addition, they would also end all distinction between amateurs and professionals, thus establishing a single class of competitors to be known simply as "players." As previously detailed, with typical British candor, the gentry declared that only in this way could tennis be rid of the shame of the "shamateur" and the secret payments of excessive "expense" money to so-called amateurs.

When the Council of the British Lawn Tennis Association voted on October 5, 1967, to recommend that Wimbledon be conducted as an open event, it was the declaration of war. Early that year the ILTF had overwhelmingly rejected the British proposal by a vote of 139 to 83.

Assuming, it seemed logically, that Federation members had expressed their desires, the management committee of the Federation declared on December 2 that it would suspend the British Lawn Tennis Association if it carried through its proposal. Immediately, panic buttons were pressed around the world. Tennis was shaken to its grass roots. A state of chaos and international anarchy was envisioned if the British, the bulwark of conservatism, stood to their guns while Federation members backed punitive action. The suspension of the British association would mean that its players would be beyond the pale in all amateur competition outside their country and that amateurs of other nations who played in an open Wimbledon would be disqualified from any Federation-recognized tournament. The Davis Cup was in jeopardy, along with the Wightman Cup.

The British refused to abandon their collision course. On December 14, the tennis "barons" of England voted by 295 to 5 to conduct the 1968 Wimbledon tournament as an open championship and further to abolish all distinction between amateur and professional. The effective date was set for April 22, 1968, when the hard-court championship at Bournemouth would be held as the first open event.

Reaction by the Federation management was swift and predictable. From Rome, on January 8, 1968, Giorgio di Stefani, Federation president, announced that the British Lawn Tennis Association would be suspended, effective April 22. Reaction among Federation members was equally swift, but not quite as predictable. There was deep concern among tennis executives all over the world. In the hierarchy of the USLTA, a deeply disturbing dilemma presented itself. It was in sympathy with the British proposal for open tennis, opposed to the English notion of eradicating all distinction between amateur and professional.

Robert J. Kelleher, USLTA president, and his aides had succeeded in leading the American tennis leaders back to the position the Association had held on open tennis in 1962. The USLTA president argued that open competition should be held within the framework of the International Federation, not in rebellion that would be so disruptive to amateur tennis and the program of the establishment. His thesis gained strength when it became obvious that leading players of the United States and other countries fully intended to play at Wimbledon, open or no.

A key portion of the USLTA campaign for compromise was the thinly veiled threat to the Federation to pull the United States out of the international body, but it was a threat Kelleher hoped would never materialize. Sup-

Many experts believe that if "open" tennis had come in the early 1950's Pancho Gonzalez would have been ranked as the world's greatest player.

Mrs. Billie Jean King of the United States won the Wimbledon in 1968.

Virginia Wade of Great Britain won the first United States Women's Open title.

port for the British stand gradually grew within the USLTA as Kelleher's forces explained the problem in American terms.

On February 3, 1968, at the USLTA annual meeting in Coronado, Calif., America took its strongest stand in favor of open tournaments, while still resoundingly rejecting the elimination of the distinction between amateur and professional. Kelleher, as the delegate from America, was empowered to pose the threat of Federation withdrawal if the Federation did not alter its stand on open tennis and permit home rule. The USLTA did not go so far as to grant permission for Americans to compete in a Wimbledon open held without Federation sanction, but nevertheless it was obvious that the United States would take a tough stand at a special meeting.

The British, meanwhile, had acquired other allies. Australia now endorsed both the open game and the proposition for a single class of player, yet affirmed its allegiance to the Federation, seeking change through legal and not rebellious methods.

Sweden became the initial sponsor for a special Federation meeting to avert chaos. Kelleher, working with the Swedish Associa-

tion, set up a conference in Paris for March 30 as a last chance for the Federation to sanction open play before the British made their move on April 22. The conclave in the Place de la Concorde on March 30 changed tennis for all time. Without a single dissenting voice, the Federation sanctioned open tournaments, to the number of 12 for 1968.

For the British, their victory was not a total one, for the Federation refused to end distinction between amateur and pro, voting for the "retention of the notion of amateurism in the rules of the ILTF, as its removal would indisputably weaken the ideal which the ILTF has the duty to protect and develop." However, the Federation, in the face of strong opposition from Kelleher, did make it possible for countries that wished to do so to set up a class of "registered" players who can profit by any amount they can command for competing in tournaments and still remain eligible for amateur events. Thus Jean Borotra's idea of 1960 was adopted.

The way was now clear for open tennis to become a reality, and it was at Bournemouth that the first historic confrontation took place. Rod Laver won the men's singles crown at the first Wimbledon Open, while Mrs. Billie Jean King won the women's title.

Many experts had felt that in open competition the pros would prove vastly superior to the amateurs. Yet the amateurs have served strident notice that they are not to be taken lightly. The brightest of the amateur stars have turned in some stunning upsets. For example, in the first United States Open Championship, Arthur Ashe, an amateur, defeated Tom Okker of the Netherlands, a registered player. The $6,000 women's award also went to a nonprofessional, but one who was "registered" for the prize money in her home country, Virginia Wade of Great Britain defeating Billie Jean King.

Open tennis has not solved completely the problems of amateur versus professional, contract pros versus registered player pros versus USLTA, etc. Time, however, will work out most of them. In the meantime, lawn tennis is increasing in popularity. As previously stated, because of an early start and convenient location, the championships at Wimbledon first received the great surge of international rivals. In 1971 the entry lists at Wimbledon included not only British players and those from the commonwealths and colonies, not only the American contingent, not only entrants from practically every Continental country even including some from behind the Iron Curtain, but also from Egypt, Indonesia, the Philippines, Iran, Argentina, Brazil, Colombia, and Uruguay.

At Paris, where until 1919 the competition was entirely homebred, we find the same international mélange plus visitors from Monaco and Israel. At Forest Hills, United States native talent is supplemented by Australian, British, Canadian, Bermudian, Danish, Swedish, Puerto Rican, Colombian, Argentinian, Ecuadorian, and Filipino players. Short of the Olympic Games, what other sport can boast such a United Nations of competitors?

During the postwar years American players of both sexes have campaigned in the British Isles, France, Germany, Belgium, Holland, Austria, Switzerland, Italy, Egypt, Israel, India, Japan, Pakistan, Indonesia, the Philippines, Canada, Mexico, most of the South American republics and in many of the Caribbean islands. They have been, to use an old but in this case true bromidic expression, "ambassadors of good will." Where the trips were not sponsored by the USLTA, American amateurs were the guests of individuals, clubs, lawn tennis associations, or the governments of the nations visited; our professionals were rewarded by the enthusiastic galleries who paid to see their great play.

In all these keen rivalries, there were few if any international crises. Conditions were generally peaceful and the closest approach to mayhem was a heavy frown at a supposedly erring ball boy, linesman, or umpire.

Perhaps here is something for a world ideologically and politically confused to ponder over. If all these international lawn tennis meetings were waged bloodlessly under the same rules for all, why should it not be possible for nations, which are merely collections of men, to solve their claims to glory or domination under similar set rules of fair play and good conduct? If players from the whole world, with all their varying backgrounds of race, color, and creeds both religious and political, can meet in amity to settle their rivalries, why cannot nations govern their international affairs similarly?

If we cannot arrive at some such solution for the problems of our world and, to paraphrase a wise man of ages ago, beat our weapons into tennis rackets, golf clubs, and fishing rods, man's present preoccupation with the development of unholy gadgets of destruction will result in the obliteration of all players of innocent games—even including our own of lawn tennis.

Arthur Ashe won both the United States Men's National and Open titles in 1968.

The professionals even have their own Davis Cup type of competition called the World Cup. Australia won it in 1970 and the United States in 1971. The key to the 1971 victory was the team of Arthur Ashe and Dennis Ralston winning over Australians Tony Roche and John Newcombe (*forecourt*).

SECTION II

Lawn Tennis Equipment

Before you can play tennis, there are certain "tools of the trade" that you will need. These include tennis balls, a racket, and suitable clothing. In addition you need a court to play on.

The Tennis Ball

The balls used in court tennis were, in the oldest times, made of strips of cloth rolled together and stitched with thread. Later, for a period, they were made of leather stuffed with wool, feathers, bran, and other materials. In fact, some of the manufacturers in France began using inferior materials, so that in 1480 an ordinance was passed by Louis XI prohibiting the making of tennis balls except in a certain manner, and threatening confiscation of all those made in any other way. There was a time when it was quite popular to stuff tennis balls with human hair. William Shakespeare, in his time, comments: ". . . the barber's man hath been seen with him; and the old ornament of his cheek hath already stuffed tennis balls."

The present type of lawn tennis ball was invented by John Heathcote, one of the most famous of British sportsmen. An interesting account of his invention appeared in the British publication *Spectator:*

In a very characteristic English country house there is preserved as an historical relic—it may become an heirloom—the first, the very first, covered lawn-tennis ball. It was invented within the family circle of

Mr. John Heathcote, for very many years champion of real tennis, a great player and a great sportsman. When the new game was invented (in the early 1870's) he found the uncovered ball over light—to a player of the court game it must have felt light indeed—and between the genius of himself and his wife the pattern of two globular strips of flannel, which would completely envelope a sphere, was worked out, and the flannel bandage applied. The invention was made public property.

Various improvements in lawn tennis balls, of course, have been made from this early time.

Specifications. For many years little effort was made to standardize the balls, but now the rules of lawn tennis not only specify their size and weight, but even go so far as to define their resilience with great accuracy. The International Lawn Tennis Federation has succeeded in standardizing the balls used throughout the world to such an extent that there is hardly any difference noticeable when players of one country play in the tournaments of others.

The official ILTF rules require that the ball

. . . shall have a uniform outer surface and shall be white in color. If there are any seams they shall be stitchless. The ball shall be more than 2½ inches (6.35 centimeters) and less than 2⅝ inches (6.67 centimeters) in diameter, and more than 2 ounces (56.7 grams) and less than 2 1/16 ounces (58.5 grams) in weight. The ball shall have a bound of more than 53 inches (135 centimeters) and less than 58 inches (147 centimeters) when dropped 100 inches (254 centimeters) upon a concrete base. The ball shall have a forward deformation (or change of shape) of more than .230 inch (.58 centimeter) and less than .290 inch (.74 centimeter) and a return deformation of more than .355 inch (.90 centimeter) and less than .425 inch (1.08 centimeters) at 18 pounds (8.165 kilograms) load. The two deformation figures shall be the averages of three individual readings along three axes of the ball and no two individual readings shall differ by more than .030 inch (.08 centimeter) in each case.

Tennis balls marked "Meets USLTA (ILTF) specifications" or "Approved by USLTA" are manufactured according to these specifications and should provide standard performance. Approved balls are clearly stamped. Other balls not approved by this organization might be of improper size and off weight, causing inaccurate flight and bounce.

How Balls Are Made. To produce tennis balls worthy of meeting USLTA or ILTF specifications, generally about sixteen manufacturing operations are involved.

Prior to the manufacture of the ball itself, the rubber mill room processes the crude or synthetic rubber into cylindrical slugs of solid rubber measuring about an inch in diameter and 1¼ inches long.

From the mill room the rubber slugs are sent to the tennis-ball department. Each slug is then placed in a press where it is molded to form a shell which will become one-half of a ball center. When taken from the press, each hemisphere has an unnecessary appendage called the flash—a lip around the entire edge of the section where a mate will be joined to form the whole center. The flash is removed by women operating cutting machines, after which the shell edges are buffed before receiving a coating of cement.

In preparing the shells for vulcanizing, the shells are placed into molds, the edges coated with cement, then two molds are set facing each other. Several sets of molds are arrayed in a line, then moved into a drum-shaped vulcanizer. Here, in addition to the vulcanizing itself, an important process occurs. So that a tennis ball will bounce properly when it lands on a tennis court, its center must contain the correct amount of air pressure—about 10 to 15 pounds. Air is therefore introduced into the vulcanizer and thus into the center of the balls. As the air pressure is applied, a ram within the vulcanizer squeezes each set of molds together as one unit. After the shells have been forced together within their molds —and stimultaneously inflated with air— actual curing in the vulcanizer takes place.

Withdrawn from the vulcanizer and removed from the molds, the now completely spherical balls are buffed at the flash line (or joint line) to remove any excess cement. The centers are next tumbled in a large drum in order to slightly rough up the entire surface for later application of cover cement. Then they are sent through a washer to a gauging bin, where they are measured to determine conformance within maximum and minimum limitations of size. Any centers found to be outside the official size limitations are rejected.

The rubber centers are next placed on a vertically rotating rack which dips the balls through a coating of cement. Removed from the rack after their cement bath, the centers are hung in a drying room to give the adhesive a "tackier" property. When dried to the proper degree, the centers are ready to receive their covers.

During these operations, other workers have been cutting out covers for tennis balls from huge rolls of nylon-dacron-wool fabric, using a knife-edged device shaped in the form of a cover panel. Nylon and dacron are used for strength and durability and wool for fluffiness.

The balls are now placed in a final mold in which the covers are "cured" to the ball. Upon completion of the curing, the balls are sent through a steamer, which brings out the fluffiness of the wool in the cover. Then the balls are forwarded on conveyors to inspectors who thoroughly examine each ball to make certain it meets a rigid standard of perfection for a tennis ball.

Following final inspection, brand names are stamped on each ball, utilizing a stencil which transfers the name to the cover. After stamping, three balls are pressure-packed in a can which is hermetically sealed to preserve the factory freshness of each ball.

An important new development in tennis balls is the so-called "pressureless" ball. Very special properties are necessary in the cores of such balls. The wall of the core must provide the required bounce and compression unaided by any internal pressure. This means in practical terms that the wall of the core must be thicker and yet the core must be no heavier than the weight of a normal pressurized core.

The main basic production techniques are similar to those for a conventional ball except that special molds (to give a thicker wall) are used for the core and no core inflation takes place. The nylon-dacron-wool cover used on the pressureless ball is about the same as that used on the conventional pressurized one.

The difference between pressureless and pressurized tennis balls can be detected by some players but not by others. In general, top-class players can detect a difference, due to the fact that they are particularly sensitive to the feel of the ball on the racket and its response to their stroke. Other players seem unable to distinguish between them. The major advantage of the pressureless ball appears to be increased storage and playing life. But, up to the present time, this new type of ball has not been acceptable in the higher levels of lawn tennis.

Buying and Caring for Balls. As previously stated the USLTA tests and approves balls that meet ILTF specifications. These are the ones you should purchase in most cases.

There are balls designed for special uses, too. For instance, so-called heavy-duty balls are covered with more felt or fuzz and are supposed to last longer on hard-surface courts. Other balls are made especially for clay and indoor composition courts, while still others are built specifically for better action on grass courts. There are even balls designed to give normal playing action at elevations above 5,000 feet.

At one time all tennis balls were white. Today, yellow and red balls are employed in "nonofficial" play at night and other times where high visibility is required. Thus, you can purchase tennis balls for almost any type of play.

No tennis ball will last for an indefinite period of time. Advanced players like to start a match with new balls, but they will use old balls for rallying or practicing on the backboard. Balls can be used for three to eight sets, although they are pretty well worn at the end of three sets on concrete. Most advanced players will use balls three to five sets. Balls that are older can be employed for backboard and service practice.

A tin of tennis balls will, of course, last the inexperienced player a longer time, but they should not be used when the felt covering is worn thin, or the fuzz is knocked off. This covering gives balls the necessary grip with the stringing at impact. As the felt wears, this grip is gradually lost, the bounce increases considerably, and the flight of the ball becomes more erratic. With this resultant loss of ball control, it becomes most difficult to make the proper tennis strokes and the game becomes less interesting. Also remember that once the pressure has escaped from the can, the balls will soon lose some of their bounce.

Since dampness and extreme temperature are the greatest enemies of tennis balls, never store them in locations where these conditions exist. Also do not play with balls that are wet or damp. After a day's play, a light brushing of the ball with a stiff brush will help rough up the nap, insuring more sets of accurate play.

The Tennis Racket

While the *Rules of Lawn Tennis* (Rule 3) give detailed specifications for the ball used in the game, there are no specifications for the racket or any description thereof in the rules. In the *Glossary of Technical Terms Used in the Game of Lawn Tennis,* published by USLTA and printed in Section VII, the racket is described as "the implement used to strike the ball."

In the playing rules, the first reference to the racket is in Rule 6, which reads in part as follows: "The server shall then project the ball by hand into the air in any direction and before it hits the ground strike it with his *racket* and the delivery shall be deemed to have been completed at the moment of the impact of the racket and the ball."

In the fifties there appeared in *American Lawn Tennis* magazine an editorial entitled "What Is a Racket?" For further enlightenment on this subject the editorial is reprinted in part:

> The appearance in an English tournament of a player using a racket in each hand occasioned surprise recently. Upon investigation, it was found that there is no rule forbidding such action. Some people think this strange. It is nothing of the kind. A player can use as many rackets, and as many kinds, as he desires; just as he may play with a racket in either his right or his left hand, or with both. He does not even have to use a racket, as the term is generally understood. He can use anything that by any stretch of the imagination can be described as a racket. Indeed, there have been cases where, as a special stunt, instead of a racket a barrel stave was used, and even a soda bottle.
>
> The laws, properly enough, are not concerned with the kind of racket used; it can be of any size or shape.
>
> Summed up, a player can use to hit the ball any implement that can be regarded as complying with the term racket. About the only thing that cannot legally be used to hit the ball is a player's hand or arm.

Although there are no *rule* standards, manufacturers have set racket-frame specifications that make them the same length and with the same size of head. Rackets, however, may vary in six other aspects: weight, balance, size of handle, frame material, flexibility, and type of strings.

Weight of the Racket. Racket-frame weights are classified light (12 to 12¾ ounces); medium (12¾ to 13½ ounces); and heavy (13½ to 14¾ ounces). A few especially designed rackets go into the extra-heavy class (above 14¾ ounces). These weight designations are determined by weighing on a scale without regard to balance. The strings of rackets weigh approximately ¾ ounce, but are *not* figured into the manufacturer's weight classification.

The difference between a light and a heavy frame is less than 3 ounces, but it will result in a great difference in playing characteristics. The proper racket weight, however, is largely a question of feel and individual preference. But remember that while you employ your muscles to start the stroke, it is the momentum (or weight) of the racket that gives the necessary follow-through. If the racket is too light, it is difficult to obtain a smooth follow-through and there will be a certain amount of unnecessary strain and wear on the racket

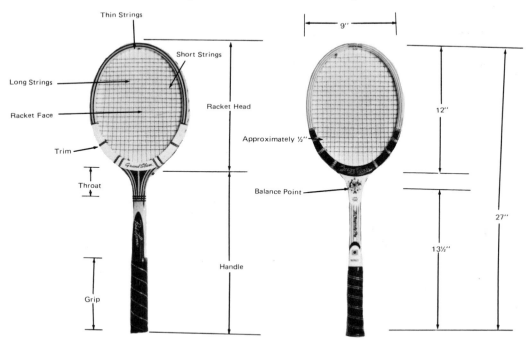

Parts and dimensions of a typical tennis racket.

as well as on arm muscles. On the other hand, a racket that is too heavy generally results in slow stroking and an unnatural tiredness of the playing arm. The following can be used as a guide to the range you should consider:

	Weight in Ounces
Children*	12 to 12¾
Junior girls	12½ to 13
Junior boys	12¾ to 13½
Women	12½ to 13¾
Men	13⅜ to 14½

* Small children may use a junior-size racket, which is 1 or 2 inches shorter than standard size, is lighter, and has a smaller handle. The racket head, however, is standard size.

Balance of the Racket. The weight of a tennis racket may be distributed in three ways: evenly; handle-heavy, or light in head and top; or head-heavy. Since the balance of a racket is seldom indicated, the player must determine the balance for himself.

The most common balancing point, or axis, you can use to determine a racket's balance is a finger. A ruler or straightedge, however, is much better. To determine the balance axis, the racket is supported on a straightedge and moved along until a position is found where it is balanced. This point should be marked with a felt-tipped pen. Next the racket length should be determined with a yardstick, and the distance from the bottom of the racket to the balance mark measured. For example, if the overall length of a tennis racket is 27 inches, and if the balance point is at 13½ inches from the bottom, the racket is said to be evenly, or well, balanced. If the balance axis is 14½ inches from the bottom, the

racket is said to be head-heavy by 1 inch; conversely, if the axis is 12½ inches from the bottom, the racket is said to be handle-heavy by 1 inch.

The majority of today's players prefer a racket that is either evenly balanced or slightly handle-heavy, or head-light. Except in the hands of an experienced player, the top-, or head-, heavy racket is hard to manipulate when volleying and has the tendency to permit an average player to swing through too fast on ground strokes.

Size of Handle. The size of the tennis racket's octagonally shaped handle (a few expert players prefer special shapes—round, square, or built up in some other fashion) usually depends on the size of your hand and fingers. *Standard* handle sizes vary, in ⅛-inch steps, from 4 to 5 inches (i.e., 4, 4⅛, 4¼, etc.). When the racket is gripped, the handle should feel quite comfortable with the fingers lightly spread around it. Many experts suggest the use of a handle which is large enough for the thumb of the hand to overlap the tip of the third finger. This is a matter of preference; some like a smaller handle and others select a larger one.

There are several types of racket-handle coverings, or, as they are more commonly called, grips, used today. While the selection of the grip is again a matter of individual preference, the leather covering is usually recommended. Perforations in the covering are desirable since they help to absorb perspiration moisture and prevent racket slippage.

Some of the leading players in the 1970's have the following preferences as to weight, balance, and handle size:

Player	Weight, ounces	Balance	Handle, inches
Rod Laver	14¼	Heavy handle	4⅝
Tony Roche	13⅝	Heavy handle	4⅝
Roy Emerson	14	Evenly balanced	4⅝
John Newcombe	14¼	Heavy head	4⅝
Margaret Court	13⅝	Evenly balanced	4⅝ (square built)
Lew Hoad	13⅜	Heavy handle	4¹¹⁄₁₆ tapering to 4⅜
Ilie Nastase	13½	Heavy handle	4⅝ tapering to 4⁷⁄₁₆
Tom Okker	13¼	Heavy handle	4⅝ tapering to 4½
Virginia Wade	13⅜	Heavy handle	4⁹⁄₁₆ tapering to 4⁷⁄₁₆
Sharon Walsh	13	Heavy handle	4⅝
Mary Ann Curtis	13½	Evenly balanced	4¾ rounded handle

Frame Material. The racket may be made from either wood or metal. Just before World War II, the laminated type of wood racket

frames started to replace the single bend construction. This change brought an end to the 150-year reign of the old frame, which

The three types of racket frames: (*left to right*) wood, aluminum, and stainless steel.

was steam-bent from one piece of stock to the desired shape of the finished product. With its varying degrees of resiliency, this single strip was no stronger than its weakest section and was susceptible to severe warping. To eliminate these defects, the modern laminated frame features 8 to 12 long, thin, individual strips which form the basic racket frame and run in a continuous length from the handle around the bow and back down the handle. A triangular throat wedge, inside and outside shoulder reinforcements, and the long handle wedge strengthen the racket to give maximum performance and wear at all stress points.

In all, as many as 18 pieces of wood are permanently bonded together to create a perfect union of all parts. The present-day laminated system neutralizes opposing stresses and strains and provides greatest resistance to splitting and warping while insuring symmetrically perfect shape and uniform performance.

To the well-known long-fiber woods of ash and hickory, which had always been used, have been added beech for strength and attractive grain, and maple for resiliency and lustrous finish. Other woods such as mahogany, sycamore, basswood, and bamboo are also used for more diversified and attractive appearances. It is in the careful selection of wood that the secret of lamination lies. The long, laminated strips are chosen from stock that is free from knots and flaws. They must have even grain running their entire length. All other wood assemblies are also free from any imperfections that could cause weakness, especially at points of greatest strain.

When the parts have been cut and selected, adhesive is applied and they are assembled in the bending jig, a process requiring only 45 seconds, so perfectly do all parts fit. The clamps are then tightened, and the complete bending jig is placed in a kiln at controlled heat and humidity conditions suitable to the adhesives used in the bonding operation. One of the greatest improvements of modern laminated construction has been achieved by technical advances in the bonding and gluing operation. Water-soluble animal glues have been replaced by insoluble synthetic-resin adhesives to make the wood joints and plies virtually weatherproof.

From the bending jig, the racket begins its course through the wood room, where it is planed, drilled, grooved, and shaped. Fiber faces also are applied during this stage to provide flexible reinforcement over critical glue joints of the throat and handle wedges. These fiber faces prevent lacquer cracks where the lacquer itself is not as flexible as the wood. It is at this point that the handles are built up to the desired size with basswood overlays, called flakes. Expert woodworkers complete the operation, giving the entire frame a cabinet finish.

Now the frame is ready for one of the most important operations in the whole fabrication of a top-quality racket: weighing and balancing. A ¾-inch hole is drilled 6 inches into the handle, into which is placed a high-gravity, leaded rubber plug. The weight and the positioning of the plug in the handle locates the balance point. This is the all-important operation that gives a racket that intangible quality of "feel" so eagerly sought by all players.

After weighing and balancing, the frames continue into the finishing department, where they receive three full spray coats of highest-quality clear lacquer. Between coats, decorative and identifying decals as well as the bindings are applied. After the finish coat, the grips are individually wrapped by skilled craftsmen.

Metal—both aluminum and steel—have been extremely popular in the last few years with better players. These players claim that a metal racket gives them added zip on their serves and volley; they say it provides more power on ground strokes with far less effort; and they claim it cures (or at least eases) the pain of tennis elbow (Section IV). They do admit, however, that some minor adjustments are necessary to get used to a metal racket, such as timing and the length of the backswing. Metal rackets are also more expensive than the wood types.

Metal rackets are manufactured in various ways and the exact techniques of bending and shaping of the steel and aluminum in racket shapes is still a trade secret. However, if you wish to purchase a metal racket—and this holds good for wood ones—buy from a reliable manufacturer and carefully examine the construction. Neatness in the making of the joints, fastening of the grip, etc., all show good workmanship as well as a good racket.

Remember that the racket you select should be a good one, although not necessarily expensive. There are many good, inexpensive rackets available at your local sporting goods dealer or tennis pro shop. Unfortunately, however, there are also inferior frames that can have a serious effect on your game. While these rackets may cost a little less originally, they will not hold their strings tight and will lose their shape in a comparatively short time.

Flexibility of the Racket. Although wood and metal (aluminum and steel) racket frames appear rigid enough when picked up in the hand, during play quite large stresses are set up in the frame, which result in a certain amount of flexing. This is not a drawback, since it is desirable that the racket frame shall "give" to some extent. However, there are some rackets that are noticeably stiffer than others.

Of the three frame materials, steel is the most flexible, while wood is the least. In most cases the more flexible a racket is, the greater the speed that can be obtained, since the less a ball is compressed when hit, the faster it will fly. But this greater speed is at the sacrifice of control. In other words the stiff racket permits better control of the ball when making a shot. Like the other points of selection, the amount of flexibility is largely a question of individual preference. Players must decide, based on their own experience, when to use a flexible racket and when to use a stiff one.

Type of Strings. Tennis strings today fall into two categories: gut and nylon.

Genuine gut strings are made from animal intestines. Although the name "cat-gut" is still occasionally heard, no cats are or ever were involved in the process. The raw material for the finest genuine gut tennis strings comes from young, healthy lambs. Hog gut is also used for tennis strings, but it does not have the resiliency of lamb gut.

As a rule, gut strings are preferred by tournament players because of somewhat greater resiliency. They have the disadvantage of considerably higher cost and susceptibility to damage by moisture. The moderately priced multi-ply nylon strings are impervious to moisture and possess playing qualities which can be recommended to the great majority of tennis players.

Strings are made in two thicknesses, 15 and 16 gauge. Sixteen gauge is the thinner string, which has greater resilience but wears through faster. Fifteen gauge, the thicker string, lasts longer but does not quite match the 16 gauge for resilience. For this reason 16 gauge is preferred for tournament play, while 15 gauge is best for the average player.

High-quality rackets should be purchased unstrung. This will permit a greater selection of frames as well as wider choice of type of string for the racket. Rackets may be strung with the desired tension on the strings. Prestrung rackets are usually not strung as tightly as good play requires; however, most prove satisfactory for beginners. Tensions between 55 and 65 pounds provide excellent playing characteristics.

Care of the Racket. Taking proper care of your tennis racket insures maximum life and top playing at all times. Even metal rackets, which do not warp like wood, require a little care.

When outdoors and not playing, keep the racket head covered in a waterproof case. Many of these cases or covers are made with a pocket for tennis balls, eliminating some extra carrying.

After you finish play, dry the grip off and check your racket to be certain that it is clean. Indoors, metal rackets can be kept in a case, but wooden ones should be kept in a press. A press is exactly what its name implies, a metal or wooden frame that slides over the racket head and then is secured tightly in place. The type with a centered lever arrangement is preferable to that with four corner screws, as it is not always possible to obtain equal tension on the frame with the latter. A press is essential to avoid warping of a wooden racket. Also always store the racket in a place that is at room temperature, never in a location where there is dampness or extreme heat.

Tennis Clothing

There is nothing in the *Rules of Lawn Tennis* that states you cannot romp around the court in pink tights or blue denim overalls. Traditionally, however, the basic principle of proper tennis dress is that *white is right*. While the custom of wearing white is more rigidly observed at some tennis clubs, resorts, and hotels than at others (most public parks and municipal courts usually have no restrictions on the color or type of clothing worn), it is always reassuring to know that in white you are right wherever you might play.

Actually, there are some practical reasons behind this old tennis tradition: white reflects, rather than absorbs, heat, thus aiding the player to stay cool. In addition, the uniform wearing of white is not distracting to other players, as bright colors might be.

Some other general suggestions for proper dress are that your outfit should be clean, neat, comfortable, and always within the bounds of good taste. Bathing suits, while frequently convenient, are usually frowned upon, and not always the most comfortable tennis dress in any case.

Shoes and Socks. Shoes can be considered the most important part of your tennis outfit. Flat-soled, heelless, canvas-topped or leather, white tennis sneakers or shoes are the accepted rule both for your own comfort and out of consideration for other players, since heeled or heavy shoes do not improve the surface of most types of courts. Be sure the pair you select are lightweight, durable, comfortable, well-fitting, and well-constructed with smoothly molded soles for skidproof traction. Do *not* substitute basketball or other sports shoes—you can easily find many brands made solely for tennis playing. Actually, many tennis shoes have a cushioned support arch and heel.

Have your shoes laced tightly enough for comfort and do not have any loose ends hanging about. After playing for the day, be sure to clear out any grit which has lodged in the soles, otherwise, you may have some problem the next time you play.

Socks are also important. White cotton or

Women's tennis clothes have changed greatly in the twentieth century: (*left to right*) early 1900's, 1920's, and 1970's.

thick woolen ones are the most absorbent and are most comfortable. Be sure that your socks do not have any holes since these could cause blisters. Also make certain that your socks are clean. Aside from the hygienic aspect, dirt is an abrasive substance and constant movement will make your feet sore. When playing on hard court surfaces, some players wear two pairs of socks.

Suggested Women's Outfits. The woman's outfit should have as few frills as possible. The most highly recommended (and often required for tournament play) is the typical one-piece tennis dress with abbreviated, pleated skirt. Sharkskin, piqué, poplin, nylon, polyester, cotton, and combinations of these materials are all good-looking, practical, and washable. Shorts and shirt or blouse combinations are also a good choice if you have the figure for the former. And that brings up another point. The clinging type of outfit that covers you like a coat of paint might do wonders for your physical form, but your tennis form will suffer. While your outfit should not "bag," it should be loose enough so that it does not bind your swing or otherwise cramp your style. Today, women's tennis outfits—both the dresses and shirt-and-shorts combinations— are so attractive that some women have been known to take up the game just to wear one.

While you might prefer to play bareheaded, a white peaked hat or tennis visor helps to keep the sun off your eyes and your hair in place. Remember that hair flopping all over the place is a distraction and hinders your vision. If you do not wear a hat, a hair ribbon will keep your hair under control.

"Flappy" jewelry also has a tendency to interfere with your play. It is better left in a safe place where it will not get lost or broken.

In cooler weather a white cardigan sweater is eminently correct and comfortable, either off court or on. As a matter of fact, a medium-weight sweater or jacket comes in handy after you finish playing in any weather. It will help keep you from catching a cold or stiffening up while cooling off after the match.

Suggested Men's Outfits. Although in cool climates, slacks of flannel or gabardine are still worn often, the usual attire for men, both in tournament and informal play, now consists of a white T-shirt, polo shirt, or sport shirt with a collar, and white tailored shorts of duck, cotton, nylon, or similar material. The standard undershirt is not correct on the court. Also you may be tempted in hot weather to tan your manly torso, to shed your shirt and play bare-chested. This is not a major sin but there are many places where it is considered more polite to "keep your shirt on." And the fact of the matter is you will probably be more comfortable anyhow with some kind of covering to absorb the perspiration. Remember that neatness is important in tennis—shirts hanging sloppily out of shorts are tabu.

The white peaked hat or tennis visor is again practical for shading the eyes. In cooler weather a white pullover sweater will come in very handy.

Knitted sweatbands are often worn by both ladies and men around their wrists to keep perspiration from running down their arms into their hands, making the racket slippery and difficult to hold. On hot days a band of some type of absorbent material worn around the forehead will prevent misting of the lenses in the case of players who wear glasses.

For male players, it is also important to wear an athletic supporter during a match. Like all sports, the activity in tennis places a physical strain on the body. An athletic supporter can help prevent a painful hernia and pulled groin muscles, particularly when one is chasing balls that require reaching and lunging.

In the racket or tennis bag that you take on court, it is a good idea to have a towel so that you can dry off between games. Other helpful items that you may have in that bag could include salt tablets to avoid cramps, safety pins for broken shoulder straps (for women), bandage for blisters and small cuts, rosin for gripping moist rackets, and so on. Maybe you do not have to have all these items, but if an emergency arises, it is nice to have them.

Practice Devices

Tennis requires as much practice as you can give it (see Section III). While practicing with a partner is ideal, a partner unfortunately cannot always be found. Here are several devices that may be employed to practice without another player.

Practice Board. Many tennis clubs, municipal courts, and playgrounds have back-boards to practice on. Building a practice board requires the construction of a backboard —wood or concrete is preferable—high enough to maintain a steady rhythm during a practice session. Here are instructions for building a typical practice board:

The framework is made of four 12-foot 4 by 4-inch hemlock posts which will be set 6 feet apart and 3 feet into the ground. The actual work on the board is done with the whole thing laid flat on the ground. The four posts are laid on the ground first and on top of these are laid the five 18-foot 2 by 4's flat side down and securely spiked on the posts, which makes them parallel to the ground. Every joint is painted before putting the pieces together so as to make the whole thing as weather- and waterproof as possible. On top of these is laid (as it lies on the ground) a floor of ordinary 3-inch matched fir flooring. Each edge of each board is painted also before it is laid so that when the assembly is finished, there is no joint that is exposed to the ele-ments. (Three-quarter-inch exterior-grade ply-wood can be substituted for the flooring if desired.) This makes a board which is 18 feet long and 9 feet high with the boards laid verti-cal. As the boards run this way, there is no piecing of the floor as the longest piece is only 9 feet long. The practice board is then raised into place and secured by using four 2 by 4 planks as braces. These braces are spiked to the top of the practice board and then to four 4 by 4-inch posts set 3 feet into the ground at the rear of the board to form a triangular support arrangement.

On top of this board is a headpiece which makes a sort of roof over the width of the board and forms a drip edge on the back side to prevent the water from running down the full height of the boards. Above all this is a screen of 2 by 4's which slants out over the front of the board at an angle of about 30 degrees from the perpendicular. The long pieces are 6 feet long and are extended down the back side to join the main 2 by 4 braces to which they are spiked. The top end is joined by another 2 by 4 spiked to the ends of the long pieces. While common poultry wire is often used on this type of board it usu-ally does not prove at all satisfactory, as the force of the balls which hit it broke through

it in a few days. Inasmuch as the width of the board is half the width of a tennis court, you can hang in place of the poultry wire an old net cut in half. One part of this was hung along the extreme outer edge of the frame and the other piece about halfway down the slant of the frame. As these are fastened only at top and on the extreme ends, there is enough "give" to it so that there is not the wear and tear on them that there was on the netting, which was stretched taut. On either side there are wings which extend for 12 feet and about 45 degrees. These are of the same construc-tion as the frame on top of the board itself, as netting, etc., soon gives way under the constant pounding of the balls.

The whole board is then painted a grass green. On this is painted a white line indicat-ing the proper position that the net takes on the court, that is, 3 feet high at the center and rising toward the edges. The playing surface should, of course, be the same as that on the courts themselves.

Rebound Net. The rebound net has several advantages over the fixed backboard. Its mobility and quiet are foremost among these, and in addition the net is adjustable to permit various types of rebound. The net is stretched over a well-braced frame which can be set up anywhere. Depending on the amount of use and outside exposure, the netting may have to be replaced possibly as often as each year. The rebound from such tension-strung netting is more like a ball struck by a racket than the rebound from a wood or concrete surface, and thus a player may better learn how to handle an opponent's "pace."

Ball-Throwing Machine. There are a num-ber of mechanical devices on the market for throwing tennis balls for practice purposes. All of these perform more or less on the cata-pult principle and are capable of various ad-justments for both speed and trajectory. A number of balls are placed in a storage rack and then fed individually into position to be hit by a wood or metal paddle toward the player. These electrically operated machines are readily moved around the surface of the court, and from the opposite side of a tennis net go far toward creating actual game condi-tions. Ball-throwing machines are of inestim-able value in clinics as well as in individual teaching and practicing.

Typical rebound net in action.

Rebound Ball. There are several automatic ball-return devices on the market. Several of them may be used in the home or in the backyard. For example, one of these rebound ball devices is a standard tennis ball on the end of an 8½-foot nylon cord attached to a 5-foot heavy rubber band. The end of the rubber is connected to a solid base. You stand a step behind the base and stroke out at the ball, in a similar manner as with the paddleball toy. The ball travels about 16 feet and rebounds to the front of the stand, where it can be restroked.

The use of the various practice devices—backboards, rebound nets, ball-throwing machines, and rebound balls—is fully discussed in Section III.

The Tennis Court

In brief the rules state that the court for the "singles game" shall be a rectangle 78 feet

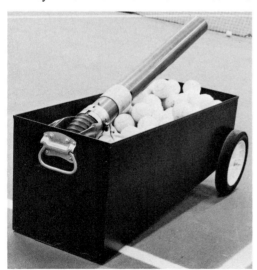

Two types of ball-throwing machines.

A rebound ball device such as this is ideal for home use.

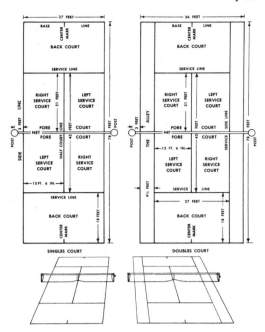

Diagram and dimensions of official singles and doubles courts.

long and 27 feet wide. It shall be divided across the middle by a net the ends of which shall be attached, or pass over, the tops of two posts, 3 feet 6 inches high, which shall stand 3 feet outside the court on each side. The height of the net shall be 3 feet at the center.

The lines bounding the ends and sides of the court shall respectively be called the "base lines" and the "side lines." On each side of the net, at a distance of 21 feet from it and parallel with it, shall be drawn the "service

The first tennis court in the United States is generally considered to be this one at Staten Island, New York, which was illustrated in the September 24, 1881, issue of *Harper's Weekly*.

lines." The space on each side of the net between the service line and the side lines shall be divided into two equal parts called the "service courts" by the "center service line." There are other details pertaining to the width of the lines, band on the net, etc.

Rule 31 relates to the "doubles game." For this game the court shall be 36 feet in width, there being an "alley" 4½ feet wide on each side of the court. The service courts stay the same for the doubles game. It will be seen that the posts in singles shall be 3 feet outside the singles court and in doubles 3 feet outside the doubles court.

But what happens when you play a singles game on a doubles court with the net posts set up for doubles, as they are on most club courts? The rules say nothing about this except that in Rule 20 of the ILTA a note under the rule mentions "if for the sake of convenience a doubles court is to be used for singles play, it should be equipped with singles posts for the purposes of the singles game." Where the posts can be easily moved, as in the National Championship on grass courts, the rule can be taken care of. On other courts singles or net sticks can be placed at the

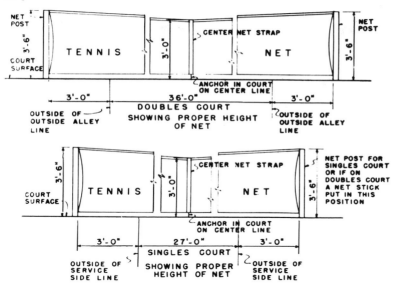

Proper net heights.

proper distance, raising the net a little over an inch at a point 3 feet outside the singles side lines. The exact measurement is 1.29 inches. But thousands of games and matches are played without these singles sticks with the result that the players have a lower net to play over for side-line shots.

How to Lay Out a Tennis Court. Most-accurate results are obtained if a tennis court is laid out by a civil engineer or competent surveyor using proper surveying instruments. However, if such services are not readily available, adequate accuracy can be obtained with the proper use of two good 50-foot tapes as indicated below.

It is desirable for courts to be laid out for both singles and doubles play. However, since the same lines—except for the side-line extensions for doubles play—are required for each, it is best to first lay out the singles court, establishing the lines shown in the accompanying diagram. Courts should be laid out with the long way north and south if possible. First establish the net or center line. This is done by driving a nail at point A, then a second nail—27 feet from A—at point B. Then take the two 50-foot tapes and attach their respective ends to the nails A and B. On the first, which will determine the side line A-E, measure off 39 feet and on the second, which will determine the diagonal B-E, measure off 47

feet 5¼ inches; pull taut in such directions that at these distances they meet at point E. Drive a nail at E. Then establish point D in a similar manner. (Note that the distance from E to D should be 27 feet—the same as from A to B.)

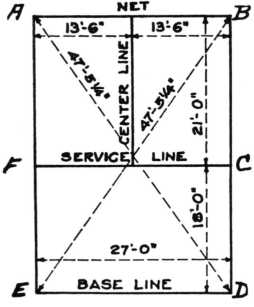

Method of laying out a tennis court.

Check this for accuracy before driving a nail at *D*. Point *F* (21 feet from *A*) and point *C* (21 feet from *B*) should then be established and nails driven at these points. This gives you the lower (or south) half of the court. The upper (or north) half is determined in a similar manner. This completes the boundaries for the singles court. The doubles-court boundaries are established by prolonging the base lines (from points *E* and *D* on lower half and similarly for the upper half) 4 feet 6 inches in each directon and joining the four new points to establish the side lines for the doubles court. (Note that the doubles court is actually 9 feet wider than the singles court, with side lines parallel to those of the singles court.)

Note the inside face of the net posts 3 feet outside the doubles side line and other details given. For championship play, the space behind the base line—i.e., between the base line and fence (or wire netting)—should be not less than 21 feet and the space between the side lines and the fence not less than 12 feet. Lines are a maximum of 2 inches in width, with the exception of the base line, which may vary from 2 to 4 inches, and the center line, which must be 2 inches in width.

For tournament play when a doubles court is used for a singles match, net sticks should be placed exactly 3 feet outside the service side line to support the top of the net at exactly 3 feet 6 inches above the court.

Court Material

There are almost as many different tennis-court surfaces as there are countries. However, for the purpose of the *Encyclopedia of Tennis,* we shall use general classifications.

First of all, it might be well to remark that well over 90 percent of the courts in the world are of clay, or of a surface so comparable to clay that they can be grouped under this heading. Throughout Europe, for example, one may look a long time before discovering any other type of outdoor court surface. The game was first played upon grass and, while the number of grass courts total but a fraction of the total number of clay courts, the great championships of the game are still competed for upon grass surfaces.

The United States Championships played at the West Side Tennis Club at Forest Hills, perhaps the most important championship after Wimbledon, is also played each year upon grass. That great tennis country, Australia, holds its championships upon grass. So, even though millions of tennis players never hit a ball upon a grass court, it is still the surface of the great championships. For the most part, grass courts are to be found in England, the eastern seaboard of the United States, and in Australia.

Cement courts are mostly in America and in the state of California particularly, where one must look long for a court other than cement. Other sections of America have their cement courts but not to the extent one finds in California.

Certain sections of Europe, notably Sweden, possess many indoor courts with a wood surface. And there has been a great increase in the number of indoor courts in the United States in recent years.

There can be no real understanding of the playing qualities of the various surfaces, or any intelligent approach to how best to play on the various surfaces, without an understanding of one all-important fact. Some court surfaces play "fast" and some play "slow." There persists a complete misunderstanding on the part of a great majority of players as to just what is meant by this. In what manner is it judged that a certain court possesses fast or slow playing qualities? What exactly is the gauge of measurement?

The speed of the game (is the court fast or slow?) is determined by the amount of time which elapses between the moment the ball meets the court the first time and the moment it hits, or would hit if allowed to bounce again, the court the second time. The length of that period of time between bounces is the time one has to reach and hit the ball. The longer this period of time, the slower the game and, conversely, the shorter this period of time, the faster the game. (The subject of how to "play" the various court surfaces is fully covered in Section III.)

Selection of Tennis-Court Surfaces. The selection of the tennis-court surface depends on a variety of factors. Among the factors to be considered are climate, the amount of money available for construction, upkeep and maintenance, the preference of the players who will be using the court; and the reputation, experience, and availability of the court installer. Other than grass, most porous surfaces (ones which permit water to filter through the surface) use some type of tape for lines rather than marking the lines daily. Tapes often affect a ball bounce differently than the rest of the surface and require maintenance; and if not properly maintained they create tripping hazards.

One of the main factors to be considered is the amount of supervision to be provided at the court location. The cushioned-type tennis-court surface and the fast-drying tennis-court surface, and other surfaces such as clay and grass, should never be constructed in an area where anyone except tennis players, wearing tennis shoes, is to be allowed. Should courts using these types of surfaces be constructed in an area where constant supervision is not provided, children with street shoes, bicycles, etc., could do a great amount of damage. In general, tennis courts with these surfaces are found in country clubs and tennis clubs, where supervision is provided constantly by someone, such as the tennis professional, who sees that the courts are properly cared for. These types of courts can also be installed in parks and in schools provided that the authorities in these places supply the supervision necessary to insure that the tennis surfaces are not abused.

Tennis courts to be constructed in areas such as parks or schools where supervision cannot be provided should have surfaces of the noncushioned type. This type of court, such as hot plant-mix asphalt, concrete, or job-mixed asphaltic composition, is sturdier and stronger and can take some abuse without damage.

Climate may affect choice of courts. Extreme heat may produce softening of certain surfaces, glare, heat radiation, or cracking of surface. Extreme cold and frost action may be more likely to damage certain surfaces unless specific precautions are taken by an experienced court builder and maintenance personnel.

The following is a discussion of the "pros" and "cons" for each surface, and these factors should be carefully considered in the selection of the tennis-court surface.

Grass Courts. It is on grass, perhaps, that the full range of tennis skill can best be employed. That is, grass courts in good condition provide one of the most luxurious of all surfaces. The U.S. championships and Wimbledon matches are held on grass. There is great resilience under foot, and grass lends itself to the largest variety and perfection of stroking of any surface. It is a cool, clean surface, free of dust and glare. Owing to climate and soil requirements, it cannot be grown everywhere. The installation costs are high, as is the daily care required to keep these courts in playable condition. Therefore if you are concerned about cost, consider something other than this most luxurious of surfaces.

It is essential that the installer be an expert in turf construction. The drainage lines and porous beds below the surface must be perfectly installed. Over this must be a minimum of 6 inches of specially prepared, tested, fertile soil. Specially selected grass seed must be expertly sown and maintained.

Daily care is a must with grass courts. They need watering, top dressing, fertilizing, mowing, and reseeding or sodding. The court needs moving periodically to rest the most abused grass. In addition, there is rolling, fungus control, aerification, grub and worm control, additions of chemicals, and brushing to properly maintain a grass court. Its high initial and maintenance cost, lack of uniform bounce when not in nearly perfect condition, relatively slow drying after a moderate rain, slipperiness when damp, discoloring of balls, and the need for experts to maintain the court are the major disadvantages. Remember that grass varies a great deal even at clubs in the same geographical area. Different types of grass combinations can be used. Some grass courts are kept close-cropped and are heavily rolled. Others are maintained in an entirely different manner because of differences in grass types. Local conditions such as the amount of rainfall, presence of certain fungi, or even the preference of groundsmen or club officials must be taken into consideration when selecting a grass surface. The differences between the courts at such world-famous clubs as Wimbledon's All England Club and Forest Hills' West Side Tennis Club are quite pronounced.

In most cases, however, grass courts are considered fast, since the ball does not rise appreciably from the surface and one has a minimum of time to reach the ball and execute the necessary stroke.

Clay Courts. These courts and so-called claylike surfaces are many times more numerous than all the other surfaces combined. From almost the beginning of tennis upon the continent, the standard or popular court has carried the name of its maker. What this "maker" produced was a gritty top dressing for a court. It was usually dark red in color, which made it most pleasant to the eye and which served as a fine background. This top dressing, or court surface, was quite porous and was applied on top of a carefully installed foundation which allowed quick drainage.

There are today many such top dressings on the market and they usually bear the name of the manufacturer. There are thousands of such courts in this country, and they fall definitely within our term of "clay" courts. In fact, the U.S. National Clay Court Championships are played upon these courts. Their advantage lies in the fact that they drain much more quickly than regular clay and, as a rule, the maintenance is much less than clay. They are seen more often in this country in a green color, while Europe prefers the dark red. Sometimes this top dressing mentioned is applied on top of a clay court in this country simply to add color to the court. As to real clay, the color and substance varies in different sections and so do the courts. Some clay courts are light in color and others quite dark. Some may be more dirt than clay.

Advantages of clay courts are that materials for construction are available in most parts of the country. They can be built with relatively inexperienced labor. With reasonable maintenance, one can have relatively uniform ball bounce. Repairs are rather inexpensive. Because the player can slide on this surface, it is easy on the feet and legs. Clay courts are the least expensive to construct.

One disadvantage of a clay court is that it may take a day to be playable after a moderately heavy rain. Depending on the color and nature of the clay, it also may stain the balls and create a glare in the player's eyes. Daily maintenance is required to keep the courts in reasonably playable condition. Painted lines must be marked freshly every day—or at least cleaned. If there are leaded or other types of lines, they can create irregular ball bounce or possible tripping hazards and they must be kept clean to be seen.

On clay surfaces, the ball usually bounces up higher than on grass, its forward speed slowed more by contact with the surface than in the case of grass, and one has much more time in which to reach the ball and make the necessary stroke. Of course, clay courts have many variations. An extreme example might be some sun-baked courts in the mid-United States as compared with a fast-drying type of court in France. The ball bounces high on sun-baked clay and, of course, much lower on the fast-drying type. The latter sometimes gives the impression that the ball is almost hanging in air so much does surface check bounce.

In the construction of the clay court today there is nationally used and constructed a clay-base composition installation. This construction utilizes the binding of clay and eliminates the slow drying properties of the clay material by introducing certain composition aggregates into the clay and surfacing over the clay. These courts, constructed in either red or green, afford excellent playing qualities and are at least 50 percent faster in drying than the old clay court. However, they still require maintenance, which should be given daily and which usually consists of dragging, watering, and rolling.

In recent years there has been an increased use of the fast-drying composition installation which usually is constructed in green and which affords a most excellent playing surface. This court features a porous cushion base over which is laid an approximate 1 to 1½ inches of fast-drying green composition surface (usually patented). This type of court dries off almost immediately after rains, therefore affording almost uninterrupted play during the season. However, it is put out of commission by frost action, and in the northern sections of the country usually has to be covered during the winter months to prevent deterioration of the surface. This fast-drying court presents very fine playing qualities and has great player acceptance. These courts are relatively expensive to construct because drainage through the surface and into the base is necessary and because of the problem of transporting surfacing materials from the sources of supply to the site of the installation.

Concrete and Asphalt Courts. For some years concrete courts were to be found only in California. Of recent years, court-construction companies have found that by far the greatest growth and demand, by percentage, has been with this type of court. Now they are found in all sections. There are several reasons for this. Perhaps one of the leading reasons is economics. Once a cement court is installed, the only upkeep is that of brushing the court clear of dirt and occasionally repainting the lines or restaining the surface. In these days of soaring labor costs, the maintenance problem has become no small item.

On concrete, the ball is not slowed appreciably by contact with the surface, but it bounces much higher than on grass. It is definitely a fast surface. In addition, one generally doesn't think of variations on concrete court surfaces. However, for some time two of California's biggest tournaments were played within a week of each other and upon courts which varied a great deal as to speed. The answer can be found in the method of finishing the concrete surface: a smooth-finished concrete as compared with a concrete finished with certain whorls, or a slight degree of coarseness, which to a certain extent may somewhat slow the bounce of the ball.

Concrete courts, while they present no great problem of maintenance, do present a problem of abrasiveness and rigidity which creates such undesirable features as shock to the feet and legs and wearing out of tennis shoes and tennis balls. In recent years, great strides have been made in so-called "all-weather," nonmaintenance types which fall within the concrete category but also include some added features. Each company seems to have its own name or names for these surfaces, but they are quite alike in that they have produced a solid-surfaced court with some "give" and spring.

By "all-weather" we mean that the surface of the court is ready for play whenever weather conditions permit. This means that play would only be interrupted during the actual periods of rain or snow on the court area. The "nonmaintenance" features of this court mean that the surface requires no daily maintenance, although there is a certain degree of refinishing required approximately every five to six years, depending upon the type of court installed and the location relative to climatic and weather conditions.

Most all-weather, nonmaintenance courts built today have a semiresilient to resilient surface and usually consist of asphalt compositions. These compositions consist of an asphalt mixture with mineral aggregate, fibers, cork, granules, asbestos, and other ingredients which tend to give a certain degree of resiliency to the court. This court usually presents a sealed surface, which means that all drainage is taken care of off the surface of the court and not through to the base of the construction. The surfaces vary from regular black finish to green compositions using asphalt and acrylic mixtures. There are also rubber-composition installations.

The all-weather, or so-called "hard," court affords the school, college, playground, municipality, and club a tennis-court surface which requires no daily maintenance, has excellent player acceptance, and for purpose of surface damage generally requires no supervision. These are definite assets, and because of the resiliency of the surface and the development of nondiscoloring rubberized finishes make these courts the most desirable and acceptable. The all-weather courts play very much the same as concrete.

Wood Courts. The use of wooden courts indoors, has, of course, been quite extensive in tennis-loving Sweden and, to a much lesser extent, in other countries where long and hard winters are the rule. These wooden courts vary too, but to a lesser extent than some of the other surfaces. Upon occasion, wooden courts may be found with canvas stretched over the surface.

Wood is the fastest of all court surfaces. The ball skids upon contact with the surface, remains low, and the player has the absolute minimum of time in which to react.

Other Surfaces. Currently, other surfaces are being tested and in some cases have been in use for some time, particularly abroad. One such imported material is sheet cork. This material requires a solid sub-base over which the sheet cork can be laid. Therefore the cost will be relatively high. At present, available information is not sufficient to evaluate the material.

Another "new" method of cushioned construction is the so-called asphalt-bound system. Favorable features of these especially designed asphalt courts are: superb playability, true ball bounce, true plane surface, nonabrasive surface which is easy on players as well as tennis balls and shoes, all-weather and all-year availability, nonglaring surface in a choice of many standard nonstaining colors, low pro-rated yearly maintenance cost, no daily upkeep, rapid drying after a rain, and a cushioned surface with sure footing and no skidding. These courts are used for championship play and are recommended for tennis clubs and varsity play where protection (fence and gates) is provided.

These courts require little maintenance. If the colored surface is the full acrylic system, a new top dressing may be required after four to six years. If the colored surface is not the full acrylic system, but asphalt emulsion and acrylic, a new top dressing may be required after three to six years. To keep the color vivid, the surface should be occasionally flushed with water and broomed to remove dust or dirt.

In the past few years a number of artificial or synthetic court surfaces have been placed on the market. There have been a number of carpetlike materials; grass-like surfaces; sheet plastics in a variety of colors, patterns, and thicknesses; and waffle-like plastic placed over a thin layer of foam rubber.

There are numerous other synthetic surfaces being manufactured in the United States. They play similar to grass, but because of their synthetic nature, they play more consistent than grass. The actual speed of the court, however, can be regulated by spraying the courts or shaving the fibers.

Many of these surfaces have been tried indoors and outdoors. Since all of these surfaces must be placed over a base, the court is only as true as the base. Also the cost is relatively high when the cost of the base is added to the cost of the synthetic surface. This type of surface might be considered when only the playing surface needs to be replaced and the base is in good condition. The advantages are pleasant colors, uniform bounce, easy maintenance, comfort for the feet, and easy replacement of worn places. But a number of synthetic court materials have been withdrawn from the market because of one or a number of problems, such as lack of durability, color stability, dimensional stability, quick-drying ability, or adherence to surface below, or the surface is too fast or too slow, seams pull apart, or it is too costly. Therefore it is recommended that the would-be purchaser of a synthetic surface check very thoroughly with a previous user of this same surface and that he play on it, particularly if it is to be used outdoors, and be sure the installer is willing to make repairs if necessary.

Actually, there are now available throughout the country tennis-court contractors who specialize in tennis-court construction, or who have an organization available to construct properly installed tennis courts. Anyone interested in the construction of a court whether for private use or for clubs, schools, colleges, municipalities, or parks departments would do well first to consult such an organization in order to obtain the benefit of its experience along this line. The United States Lawn Tennis Association will furnish a list of such contractors either local or those with a nationwide construction organization specializing in the installation, resurfacing, and reconstruction of tennis courts. In this way accurate and complete information can be obtained which will assist the prospective court owner in proper site selection, orientation, and construction procedure, and also help him to decide the type of court, surfacing, and equipment required for the particular installation.

Where to Play

In today's age of booming tennis popularity, there are few cities, towns, or villages where tennis courts are not available to the public either free of charge or for a nominal hourly rental. There are also many private tennis clubs throughout the United States. These clubs vary in size, services, activities, and costs. Some are informal groups which pool their resources to buy land and build courts, and provide only an old shed in which to store the nets and other gear. They seek new members to reduce individual costs or to get equipment that all can use. Then there are the huge, nonprofit organizations with million-dollar properties that include stadiums, swimming pools, and luxurious clubhouses.

Night tennis is increasing the popularity of the sport. Above is the installation at Stowe Stadium, Kalamazoo College, Kalamazoo, Michigan.

Membership in such tennis clubs is rather expensive and exclusive. For most beginners, however, it is best to get the feel of tennis first on public park and municipal courts or on private rental courts. Later after they learn the sport, they can join private tennis clubs, either large or small.

Locating a place to play in a town where you are a stranger is usually a relatively simple matter. Rental courts will probably be listed in the classified telephone directory. Local sporting-goods dealers frequently can supply further information. Or a phone call to the local YMCA or Junior Chamber of Commerce should give you the desired information. The latter organization, incidentally, has been responsible for developing both extensive new tennis facilities and widespread interest in the game in many areas throughout the country. If public tennis facilities are inadequate in your area, perhaps it might prove helpful to contact your local Junior Chamber of Commerce and enlist its support. A complete list of USLTA member clubs can be had by writing to USLTA.

Winter Tennis. The growth of winter ten-

Inflated building structures, such as this one of the courts of the DuPont Country Club in Wilmington, Del., have made winter tennis possible to many more players.

nis as a sport can be attributed to the new facilities, surfaces, and interest generated by playing year round. The new facilities include such devices as synthetic "bubbles," which can be blown up and used as coverings on outdoor courts during the winter.

The opportunities for winter tennis are improving. Owing to the limited facilities, many courts have been reserved in the past on a three- or four-month basis at prices few players can afford. As more facilities continue to be established and renovated for winter play, the fees will undoubtedly be reduced. When playing winter tennis, several points should be remembered:

1. Check the lights and background in the facility. Nothing can replace natural sunlight. Playing indoors can affect your serve, volley, and return of serve.
2. Check the surface. Is it faster or slower than the surface you normally play on outdoors? Adjust your game accordingly.
3. Give yourself sufficient warmup time to avoid injuries or pulled muscles.
4. Be on time for your game. Indoor courts are not as plentiful as outdoor facilities.
5. If you are changing from outdoors to indoors, approach your game gradually; do not expect too much the first time out.

Tennis Camps and Their Selection

A few years ago, the idea of a camp specializing in tennis was a radical concept. Today, the present popularity of the tennis camp is based on three ingredients: 1) top flight instruction and facilities; 2) readily available stiff competition; and 3) the fun and camaraderie of being together with others of the same age and interest for a period of time.

The tennis camp results are invariably impressive and parents are quick to recognize this, as well as their children's enthusiasm for the game and the camp. Today's youngsters want to specialize and are anxious to get away from the old-styled camp routine of riflery, swimming, canoeing, sailing, arts and crafts, and so forth. Teenagers get their fill of this type of hourly routine during the school year and cannot wait for the opportunity to channel their efforts into a single chosen field of endeavor whether it be tennis, golf, basketball, hockey, swimming, or music.

What should a parent look for in helping his child select a tennis camp? There are some who feel that the objective of the tennis camp should be to produce winners. We take exception to that viewpoint for it is obvious

Tennis at the Seventh Regiment Armory, New York—An artist's conception, *Harper's Weekly,* December 10, 1881.

Fine community tennis programs such as the one at Princeton, N.J., help to develop an interest in the game as well as many fine young players.

everyone cannot be a winner. Furthermore, there are more important objectives worth striving for. The young player will discover that through tennis he can expand such qualities as perseverance, courtesy, courage, and sportsmanship.

Tennis should develop not only a winning spirit, but control over one's body, mind, and emotions. The tennis camp should help campers discover these inner resources, in addition to acquiring to the fullest of their individual abilities a lifetime sport of challenge and enjoyment.

Tennis is reportedly the fastest growing sport in the country. This is primarily the result of today's youth who have been challenged by the game, and have seen the long-range value of acquiring an individual sport that they can play for the rest of their lives. Let us hope that the tennis camps can continue to play a leading role in assisting the youngsters on their long and enjoyable careers as lifetime tennis players. Here are some discernible factors parents should look for in selecting a tennis camp for their youngsters:

Age: Generally 12 to 16 years of age for a boarding camp, and from 8 to 18 years of age for a day camp when on a lesson basis, and only then if there is sufficient interest, attention span, strength, and ability to concentrate for the duration of the lesson.

Interest: It is essential that the youngster who plans to attend camp have a keen interest in learning the game rather than just playing. *Parents please* do not push a child into such highly specialized instruction, but rather wait for him to request the opportunity.

Coed: This is an individual preference. The youngsters understandably seem to favor the idea and it tends to produce a more enjoyable and socially rounded summer. The problems one associates with the coed situation can be realistically dealt with by experienced supervision.

Length: Camps range from one week to eight. We have tried three-, four-, and six-week sessions, and find that the four-week session is the most ideal from the standpoint of maximum learning and enjoyment, as well as family vacations. Any period less than two weeks has an extremely limited value, except for the most experienced players.

Staff: An extremely important factor, particularly if one holds by the educational theory of developing the whole child while at camp. There should be a good mix of Professional Lawn Tennis Association coaches and college or tournament players. An instructor to pupil ratio of 1 to 6–8, and an overstaff to camper ratio of 1 to 4–6 are advisable.

Facilities: These will vary widely between educational campuses, hotel-motel complexes, and large family homes. Accommodations tend to be luxurious by the old camp standards with two or more in a room having an adjoining bath. The really important factor is the camper-to-court ratio which should be 4–6 campers per tennis court. There should be adequate backboard space and other teaching aides. Particularly helpful are video-tape replay equipment or slow-motion movies, which, when used in conjunction with a film editor and viewer, permit the camper and his instructor to analyze on a frame-by-frame basis the individual problems before and after instruction.

Food: Tennis campers need the best of foods, and the camp should go to extremes to provide carefully balanced training meals of high-protein content. Campers prefer good plain food and plenty of it.

Supervision: Paramount to a productive summer is careful planning and thoughtful organization that leaves sufficient free time for bull sessions, summer reading, pick-up games of ping pong, volley ball, and so forth. Weekend trips to state and national tournaments, summer stock theater, polo or baseball games, as well as nearby points of interest provide welcome relief from the daily routine.

Other Activities: To balance out the high degree of physical activity during the day, many camps have an evening activity program ranging from such academically helpful courses as typing and speed-reading to guitar, musical theater, art or chess.

Instruction: The key to the success of tennis camps rests on both imaginative and productive instruction on as well as off the court. The program should follow four basic steps: 1) analyze and identify the specific problems of each camper; and 2) convince the camper, with the help of instant replay video tape or slow-motion stop-action movies, of his specific faults that need correction. At the same time, show films of proper stroking so as to give the camper a proper mental fix as to what he is to emulate; 3) arrange a four-hour-a-day instructional program best suited to the individual needs of each camper. Six to eight campers in a group under the full-time guidance of one instructor has proved most beneficial. The group and instructor come on a regular rotation basis before the professional master teachers who constantly oversee the whole program of instruction and drills; and 4) competitive play needs to be carefully arranged to minimize the tendency, when under pressure, to revert to familiar but improper habits. Competition should be varied and equally matched to produce best results. Davis Cup team-styled play and individual ladder play have proved more effective than elimination tournaments in this regard.

Tips for Parents

The great tennis controversy currently raging in the United States no longer concerns open tennis, the footfault rule, the Davis Cup captain, the next president of the USLTA or the financing of the National Championships. It is being fought over the role of the parent in the development of young tennis players. People are either "for" parents or "against" them; most of us are "for" the good ones and "against" the bad ones. If you are a mother or a father and you think you are encouraging your offspring, check the following DOs and DON'Ts to see if your conduct toward your child is irreproachable and tends to encourage his interest in the game:

1. If you play well, make yourself avail-

Tennis camp programs are one of the fastest ways for young people to learn the game.

able for your child as an opponent or a partner. Never coach him or offer him helpful hints. Leave this up to his pro.

2. When your son or daughter takes a lesson, do not sit on the sidelines and watch.

3. The only time you ever give pointers on strategy to your child is when he literally begs you to do so. Your comments then should be brief, encouraging, and to the point. If he asks you a vague question, such as "What did I do wrong?", do not answer him in detail; let it go with a brief commiseration and encouragement for the future.

4. Never watch your child (in practice or in a tournament) unless he specifically requests your presence. Do not call lines, applaud, berate the opponent, discuss the match with the umpire or expound on the match with fellow spectators. You are the epitome of the Silent Observer.

5. When your child enters a tournament, he is on his own. Do not go up to the tournament desk for any reason, unless your child wishes to introduce you to the committee. Do not comment on the seedings, the draw, the scheduling or the court assignments.

6. When people tell you how well your child is playing, you reply "Thank you," and let it go at that. Never go into the Department of Fuller Explanations, Expostulations or Exhortations, including such "modest" declamations as "We really don't care just how good he gets as long as he enjoys the game" or "We leave it all up to him because . . ."

7. When your child has lost, never ask "what happened?" or "what went wrong?" If

he wishes to tell you, he will and you should silently commiserate. He knows he can talk to you because you are interested and because he will not face either an inquisition, a lecture or a series of stories on matches *you* played.

8. If your child wants to play a tournament, give him every help you can in getting there. You do not fill out his entry blank but you do provide the entry fee. Never *suggest* that he enter a tournament.

9. Do not arrange practice games for your child but do help him get to the courts if he asks for help.

10. Display your child's trophies because you are proud of his achievements. If someone comments on them, thank them but do not then proceed to identify every cup and medal.

11. Be content about the amount of practice (or lack thereof) given to the game by your child. Forcing a youngster to practice will never make a champion. If you want a champion in the family, try to be one yourself; do not force your child to be one for you.

12. The only time to interfere is when your child has thrown his racket, screamed, yelled or otherwise behaved outrageously on the court.

13. Do not insist that your child train. This is up to him and perhaps he does not care as much about the game as you do.

14. If your child has a "bad year," simply encourage him and explain (once) that every great player has had a bad loss, a bad season or a bad year. These defeats are what make the champion.

15. When your child's forehand goes "off" or he chokes in a match or he gets stale, let him work it out for himself. If he is capable of playing in a tournament, he is capable of deciding what he is going to do with regard to his forehand, his choking or his staleness. If he requests your advice, ask him his solution before you give him your own. After all, you cannot hit the ball for him.

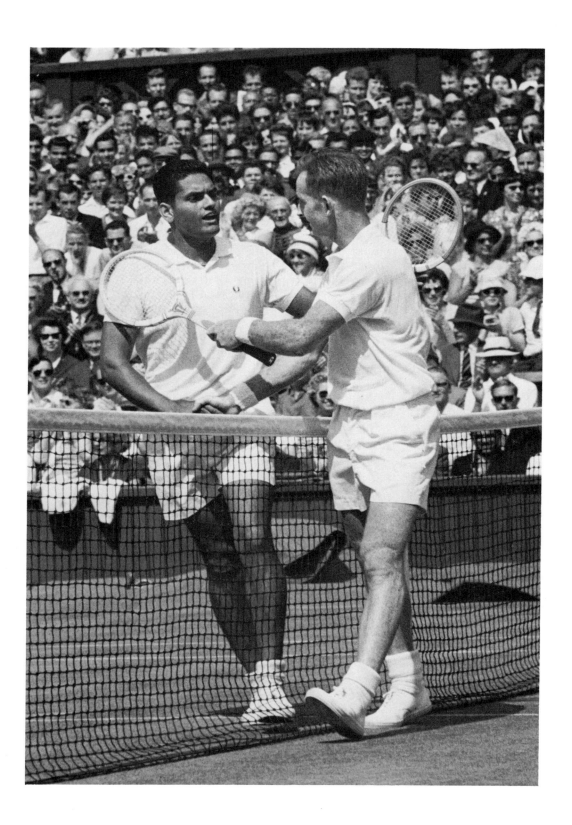

SECTION III

Principles of Lawn Tennis

FUNDAMENTALS OF TENNIS

Tennis is a basically simple game which involves opposing players who stroke the ball back and forth over a net into the court. Play continues until one of the players hits the ball out of the court, into the net, or does not stroke the ball before it bounces twice.

Play is started when one player (the server) stands behind the base line and to the right of the center mark and puts the ball in play by tossing it in the air and striking it with his racket so that it lands in the right service court on the opposite side of the net. This player has then "served" the ball to his opponent.

The opposing player (the receiver) must let the served ball bounce and then must hit it into his opponent's court, between the side lines, the base line, and the net. Balls are hit alternately until one of the players fails to return the ball into his opponent's court. After the service, balls can be played before they have bounced or on the first bounce. Points are scored according to the official United States Lawn Tennis Association rules (see Section IV). After the first point is completed, the server moves to the left of the center mark and serves into his opponent's left service court. Subsequently, he alternates service courts for every point. A designated number of points makes up a game; games make up a set, and sets, a match. (See *Scoring* on page 186.)

In doubles, two players on one side oppose two players on another side. The idea of the game, however, remains essentially the same as in singles. Players serve in turn in doubles, first a member of one team, then a member of the other team, and so on. However, players need not take turns hitting the ball after it is in play following a return of service.

As in all sports there are basic fundamentals. In tennis these are a good grip and proper tennis form. The latter includes the swing and hitting the ball, footwork, and timing.

Spinning to determine who serves first.

Three basic grips: (*left to right*) Eastern, Continental, and Western.

The Grip

The fundamentals of lawn tennis are affected more perhaps by the player's grip of the racket than anything else that is within his control. His playing position, his swing, the twist the ball receives, all depend on the grip he has on his racket when he hits the ball.

There has been controversy over the best methods of gripping the racket almost since the birth of the game. There have been three distinct schools, each of which has its merits, and beyond these a half dozen eccentric styles of holding the racket have earned more or less success. But while we find that certain methods of gripping have apparent advantages for certain strokes, they lose in other strokes as much or more than is gained. It is not practicable to change the hold for every stroke, so some set style must be adopted that gives the most advantage for all the strokes required.

A slight shifting, for instance, in the position of the hand gives a much better hold for the rolling backhand drive, but only for this stroke, and so it is available only for those players who use this stroke regularly. If this is adopted, then other strokes on the backhand side must be adapted to this hold or suffer in consequence.

There are three *major* different types of grips: the Eastern, the Continental, and the Western. The basic difference between the three is position of the palm of the hand. In the Western grip, the palm is under the han-

dle; in the Continental, it is over it; while in the Eastern, the palm is behind the handle.

Eastern Grip. This is the most popular grip today, being used by over 70 percent of American players. It is recommended by most experts for the novice. It is equally good for dealing with high, waist-high, or very low shots.

The Eastern grip is made by holding the racket at the throat with the left hand and extending it comfortably in front of you with the butt end of the handle toward your body. The face of the racket should be at right angles to the ground. Grasp the racket with the right hand so that the back knuckle of the thumb is directly on top of the racket, about an eighth of an inch to the left of center. This means that the V or wishbone formed between the forefinger and the thumb should be above the top plane of the handle. The butt of the racket should rest easily on the heel of the hand. The thumb is wrapped around the racket and the fingers extended comfortably along the handle. The palm of the hand should be against the back plane of the handle. This grip is often described as "shaking hands with the racket." A left-handed player should do the above procedure by holding the racket with the right hand and grasping it with the left.

The backhand grip can be obtained from the Eastern forehand grip by shifting the hand to the left (counterclockwise) about one quarter of a turn. This should bring the back knuckle of the first finger directly on top of the racket. Now, the V between the thumb and forefinger will come just at the inner edge of the handle and your thumb will point diagonally across the handle. By having part of the thumb behind the racket, this grip gives added support and control to the stroke. The change from the forehand to the backhand is made by using the left hand to help guide the racket. This can be accomplished while you are in the anticipatory position or during the backswing.

Continental Grip. For the Continental grip, the handle is rotated about an eighth of a turn (counterclockwise by right-handers, clockwise by left-handers) from the Eastern grip. Since the Continental grip is halfway between the Eastern forehand and backhand grips, it is good for either of these two basic ground strokes without the necessity of shifting the hand grip. It also facilitates making short cross-court shots and, in addition, is excellent for dealing with low bounces. However, unless your wrist is very strong, you will find it difficult to control high-bounding balls.

The Continental grip is made by standing the racket on one edge and then simply picking it up from that position. In so doing, the palm of the hand is virtually on top of the racket and the thumb extends across the front of the handle.

Many top Australian players use the Continental grip because of their emphasis on net play even in the beginning stages of learning. The no-change feature of the grip makes it especially suitable for the fast action required there, and doubtless many players have simply transferred their net grips into back-court play.

Western Grip. This grip is very good for dealing with high shots and suitable for waist-high balls, but is difficult to use on very low shots. In other words, it is not as good an all-around grip as the other two, and hence is the least used of the three.

The Western grip is obtained by laying the racket face down on the ground and then picking it up in the same manner as the Continental. This places the palm of the hand underneath the handle when the racket head is brought into a vertical or hitting position.

There is no general agreement as to precisely when the hand has left the range of the Eastern grip to become, let us say, a Continental or, if moved in the other direction, a Western. This is simply a matter of semantics. Actually, some players, over the years, have used variations or combinations of these grips and some have even used unorthodox ones. For example, Pancho Segura—who had one of the best forehand drives—used an unorthodox two-handed grip. Likewise, John Bromwich, the Australian great, used both hands on the handle for the backhand. A few players have used no backhand at all. They shifted the racket from right hand to left and played forehands on either side. Such a style has a major disadvantage when it comes to rapid net play.

Whether you use an Eastern, a Continental, or a Western grip, there is only one way to hold the racket—with firm fingers. The racket is your weapon and it must move the ball; if you hold it loosely, the ball will twist the racket in your hand and you will have no control.

Many players, when trying to grip the racket firmly, will tighten up the whole arm. The arm itself should be relaxed. All strokes (with the exception of the moment of impact on serve and overhead) are hit with a bent arm. On ground strokes, the arm wheels freely from shoulder and elbow on the backswing, and the arm is bent slightly on the hit. It becomes almost straight only on the follow-through. It becomes stiff only when one stretches wide for a ball almost out of reach. The arm is also bent on the volley, again the only exception being the side ball.

Learning to keep the fingers firm and the arm relaxed is a prerequisite to good tennis. At first the arm will always stiffen. It is like learning to pat your stomach with your left hand and rub your head with a circular motion with your right hand; in the beginning both hands will perform the same motion, and it takes concentration to make them act out different motions simultaneously.

The wrist should be as firm as the fingers. Beginners and intermediates should practice hitting the ball with a wrist that is absolutely locked during the hit. If the wrist is loose, the ball moves the racket instead of the racket moving the ball. Wrist and arm are practically one straight line on the backhand groundstroke and volley; wrist and arm form a 20-degree angle on forehand groundstroke and volley. The wrist snaps only on the service and overhead.

The player should be well past the intermediate stage before he ever tries to put wrist action into his ground strokes. When he has learned to stroke the ball well with firm fingers, locked wrist, and relaxed arm, he can introduce "wrist" shots into his game. The "wrist" movements are necessary for slice, drop shots, chops, and the angle or touch game; if they are acquired too soon, the player may never learn a solid set of ground strokes.

When wrist is introduced into a player's repertoire, he is at a stage when he understands that the wrist moves the ball, not the ball the wrist. To hit ground strokes with such an action, the wrist must be strong as iron and the timing must be perfect. It is not a shot for a beginner.

To rest the hand from the fatigue of constant tight gripping, relax the grip between the strokes, and if necessary help to carry the weight by resting the neck of the racket in the left hand between shots.

Always grip the racket by the very end; never shorten the grip. This is the hardest thing to impress on the beginner's mind, because he finds it more difficult to swing the racket at first with the full length of the handle, and he is very reluctant to do this, when the shorter grip gives him a quicker control and permits him to hit the ball with a jerky half swing. At first the beginner swings his racket only a foot or two in striking, making more of a push than a blow of his stroke, and this lets him delay striking until the last second, and the stroke seems easier to be made in this way. But the error of this method is that it depends on the strength of the player's arm for success, and this is the first great fallacy by which the novice is led into bad habits of play. The arm's strength has little to do with the good tennis stroke; it depends almost entirely on the momentum of the racket, and at the moment of impact little or no strength is exerted by the arm.

As in golf, the player "presses" as soon as he uses his muscles too much. The racket and the golf club really do the work required, and it is only necessary for the player to start them in the right direction, and increase their momentum and speed by the swing of the body and arm until they reach the maximum

when the ball is hit. He need only guide the racket or club, rather than push it along.

The length of the racket is increased by every inch of the handle that is extended beyond the gripping hand, so that its leverage and the power of its swing under momentum increase fast with this extension. As it is difficult to shift the grip after first habits are formed, it is doubly important to begin with the long grip, even though it seems more difficult at first.

The reluctance of most beginners to grip the handle by the extreme end comes from the difficulty of making a successful stroke with only a half swing and a long grip. The novice hesitates to make a full swing because he cannot calculate at first so far ahead where the ball is going to bound and how high and how deep it will jump up in front of him. He fears to draw his racket far back to make the stroke because he expects to make only a half swing.

The leather "button," or binding at the end of the handle helps to prevent the racket from slipping from the hand, and also warns the player, without his needing to look down, when his hand has reached the end of the handle. This leather end should rest against the fleshy part of the hand at the base of the thumb, and, if the full-length grip is cultivated, it will rest very comfortably there while in play.

The size of the handle is an important point. There is a tendency to have it too large. It should be of such diameter that it fills the hand but allows the fingers to work. If it is too large this is impossible. The smaller the handle the quicker is the work of hand and fingers. On the other hand, there is the principle that the handle should be large enough to act as a strut in the hand, and so keep the wrist firm. The best size, as previously stated in Section II, is that which makes the thumb and middle finger overlap to the extent of about an inch, not less in any case, but very little more.

Tennis Form

Good form in any sport is one of those elusive qualities that are hard to describe, and often harder to adopt. Briefly defined, good form, so far as it applies to lawn tennis, may be said to be the manner and method of playing which will produce in the hands of the average man the greatest percentage of success. It is that method of using the body, the arms, and the legs which gives the greatest freedom and the best ability to make successful strokes.

There have been many players and some experts who have won high honors despite bad form, and too often have these men been followed as models simply because it was thought that their success vindicated their methods. But this is an empty fallacy, for such a player may have certain mental or physical qualities that are entirely foreign to the average player. Abnormal length of arms or legs may affect his manner of swinging his racket or the position he assumes during play. The same methods adopted by a player of a different mold would not give the same results.

Three of the elements of good tennis form are sound strokes, perfect balance, and proper timing. A well-founded stroke gives the player the equipment to deal with the ball, good balance enables the player to hit with the full force of his weight and regain his ready position immediately thereafter, and fine timing allows the player to meet the ball at the right moment. There are other factors in the good player's repertoire—anticipation, footwork, stamina, a cool head, the will to win, strategy, and so on—but these are the refinements of match play and are developed as the player moves to higher levels. First the player must acquire good strokes, good balance, and good timing.

The Swing and Hitting the Ball. Whether you make a forehand or backhand, a lift or slice stroke, the general principles involved are much the same, and a thorough study of these will help the beginner a great deal.

Three distinct actions must be kept in mind, although they frequently all run into one with such rapidity that it is hard to separate them. First we have the back swing in preparation for the stroke; then the act of hitting the ball, and finally the follow-through.

To hit the ball properly, the eyes should be kept on the ball until it is hit, and in calling attention to this, it should be pointed out that "keeping the eye on the ball" means actually focusing the eyes on the ball as it approaches. A player should have a sense of bringing the focus in as the ball comes toward him. By so doing, the inside muscles of the eyes will become tired sooner, but the effort will be worthwhile. Most beginning players fail to do this and too often look through the ball. This means that as the ball leaves the opponent's racket the eyes are fixed on it but as it comes toward the player he does not bring the focus in with the advance of the ball. Most persons can unconsciously gauge with great accuracy their distance from an object on which the eyes are properly focused. Nothing will help you to hit the ball with the center of the racket as much as will this matter of focusing and, if a ball is not hit with the center of the racket, the shot is generally flubbed, or at least, is ineffective. Therefore, all through the stroke, be careful to keep your head down and your eye on the ball.

During play there are times when it is necessary to see where an opponent is, and to glance at the court and its boundary lines. Expert players also use a special *finesse* in the higher art of expert play, in which they look away from the ball just before they hit it, in order to more accurately direct a placed shot. But this kind of technique is not for beginners, and should be put aside entirely until the player is well on the road to expert skill.

Only by watching the ball constantly will it be possible to calculate the angle of its flight, the distance it will travel before striking, and how high and how far it will bound before you must hit it. The white ball in the sharp sunlight offers a fine mark and the eye can be focused on it no matter how fast it may fly through the air. Whether it is coming or going, so long as the play continues, it must be followed constantly to play well.

The anticipatory, or readiness, position should be somewhat crouching, with bent knees, shoulders thrown well forward, and the weight carried up on the toes. Ready to spring in any direction on the instant, the player in this position is wonderfully able to reach the return that may be placed in some other part of the court. He should always be ready to move quickly, and even when the ball comes directly toward him, he should jump forward in striking. The greatest power in making any stroke comes from leaning to meet the ball, which brings all the player's weight into the blow.

As soon as your opponent hits the ball you should as quickly as possible determine the direction of the ball, then determine whether you are going to receive it on the forehand or backhand. Immediately upon making this decision you should carry the racket back into position for the stroke, whether on forehand or backhand. In the event of an overhead smash, it is well to get the racket back and up in position well ahead of time.

The reasons for this precaution are very sound, as well as obvious. If the racket is in position to make the stroke when the ball reaches you, you can go through with the stroke easily, without hurrying, without jerking, and the stroke is more than likely to be well timed and sound. If you await the arrival of the ball before getting the racket in position, you must take the backswing and return to the point of contact with the ball so quickly that accuracy is very difficult. If you get your racket back as soon as your opponent hits the ball, you are more than likely to be able to handle the position of your feet. In running to receive the ball, at the same time get the racket back, or up in case of a smash, in position to make the stroke.

A good test to see if you are getting the racket back early enough in anticipation of the stroke and getting it back properly is in noting whether you have started for position on balls which your opponent has hit toward your court, but which have been stopped by the net. If you have started toward the correct position before the ball hits the net, you will know that you are anticipating reasonably well. If you have not started before the ball is netted, you will know that your anticipation is bad.

As soon as you know the ball is coming on your forehand or your backhand, swing your shoulders to the right or to the left, as the case may be, so that the shoulders are at right angle to the net. You should be able to tell whether the ball is going to be on the forehand or the backhand before the ball in flight is on your side of the net. If you swing your shoulders in time your feet will have the tendency to move more easily and to cooperate more smoothly so you may be in correct position for a proper stroke. Taking advantage of all the time available for getting into proper position assures you ample time to

make your shot unhurried. Shots made in a great hurry cannot consistently be good shots.

A full and free back swing is most essential. It is not necessary, as in golf, to wrap your arm and racket around your neck in order to get the full impetus necessary for a hard drive, but a stroke that starts only a foot or two back of the point of impact with the ball is unlikely to have any great power. In fact, the power of a tennis stroke depends almost entirely on the momentum of the racket, and this is gained largely by the swing that adds the weight of the body to the force. Little if any muscle is required to make a good stroke. The well-timed swing of the arm and racket, accelerated by body swing, and the all-important "follow-through" are what do the work. Not only is the swing of the body before the ball is hit needed to produce a good stroke, but it should be carried far beyond that point, following the ball long after it has left the racket. This follow-through, so much talked of in golf, is equally important in tennis, and the fastest strokes of expert players are the result of perfect timing to secure the maximum momentum in the racket, added to a full follow-through of the body weight.

A good player starts his windup when he runs. He does not wait until he gets to the ball. If he has to run wide on his forehand, he starts his semicircular (or straight-back) backswing immediately. By the time he has reached the ball, the racket has begun its forward motion. The only time a player can start his backswing after his feet are planted for the shot is against a soft hitter. The more pace the opponent has on his ball, the sooner the windup must begin.

Beginners invariably start their backswing after the ball has cleared the net; advanced players start as soon as the ball leaves the opponent's racket. Players in the intermediate category frequently show a tendency to be late either on forehand windup, backhand windup, or on the backswing when running for a short ball or drop shot.

A top player always looks ready because he starts his windup in plenty of time; a lesser player always looks rushed because he waits too long to begin the stroke.

At the back of its preliminary swing the racket must pause anyway and lose its momentum before starting forward, so that it can be checked for a slightly longer period if necessary, if you should unintentionally swing too early for the stroke. It is far better to err on this side than on the other, so it is a safe rule to keep swinging back earlier until you find you must noticeably check the racket before starting the forward swing for the stroke. This pause at the end of the backswing has an inclination to steady the stroke, but it can easily be exaggerated and it then has a tendency, particularly when marked, to expose the direction of the attack.

The total absence of any pause may result in hurrying the stroke too much, and the tendency to "snap" on the ball which follows this habit invariably results in a loss of control. If full time is not allowed and the forward swing is hurried, the slightest deviation of the ball from the expected flight will result in a bad stroke, as there is no time left to correct the swing to meet this shift.

At the end of the reach backward, it will be noticed that the arm swings naturally either upward or sidewise behind you. By all means, select the upward motion. This keeps the racket in the direct line of flight and avoids the side motion that is so apt to throw off the accuracy of the stroke as well as the body's poise during the forward stroke. It is also well to increase somewhat the arc of this circle in the backswing by turning slightly with the shoulders so that you have the longest reach possible without getting out of position for a free stroke. The shoulders at the end of the backswing should be parallel with the feet and the line of flight of the ball. The weight of the body, too, should be shifted full on the back foot and when making a strong stroke, it should be swung back as far as it is possible to preserve the balance.

If you find that you run well on either side but that you make too many errors when running in for short balls or drop shots, the fault may lie in the fact that you are not ready. Start your windup as you run forward. The backswing is not only completed but the racket should actually be moving forward when you reach the ball. Errors are corrected by exaggerations in the other direction. If you have been late on your windup, get your racket back the moment the ball leaves the opponent's racket, even if it makes you too early for the ball.

When the time is right to begin the forward swing, that is, to make the stroke, the body turns on the hips, the right shoulder comes forward, followed by the upper arm, and then the forearm; and finally just before the ball is hit, the wrist adds the snap of a whiplash to the blow and the full weight of the body shifts quickly forward from the backward to the forward foot, so that at the moment of impact all possible energy is concentrated in the blow.

Now comes the greatest difficulty that is found in the play of most players. They are inclined to stop here. The ball hit, they feel that is as far as they can control it, and they make no effort to follow through, recovering the balance as quickly as possible in the most convenient way. But this is all wrong. Just as in golf, the follow-through is most important, while it is true that after the ball has once left the racket, it is impossible to further affect its movements, the after swing of the player does affect the whole stroke most materially. It is impossible to make a true stroke without it, since any effort to cut short the swing infallibly affects the stroke itself and draws the racket away from its work before its maximum power has been exerted.

The racket should not only follow the ball itself just as far as you can normally reach, but you should also bend the whole body as far as the balance will allow to lengthen the swing of the arm. The entire body should be turned on the hips, the bent knees allowing it to move forward with the stroke and extend the swing of the racket. At the end of this following swing, the body should turn still further around, the shoulders pulling in, the arm and the wrist bending to allow the racket's impetus to be checked with a short swing like the *moulinet* of the swordsman.

For the most exaggerated ground strokes, the weight of the body is thrown so violently forward in the follow-through that the balance is frequently checked by carrying the back foot forward to a further advanced position. Indeed this style is not at all uncommon, and where well practiced it almost invariably increases the body swing, the follow-through, and the power of the stroke. It is an excellent habit to allow the weight to draw the back foot forward to a new position, and the habit of taking this forward step in making the stroke will add greatly to the vigor of the attack.

This method should be used sparingly when the player is well forward in his court, for if the weight is thrown too far forward when in the volleying position, it is easy to lose the balance forward and become exposed to an overhead attack by a lob before the balance can be recovered.

Now, through all these three motions of the stroke, one cardinal rule should always be kept in mind. Every motion should be as far as possible in the direct line of the ball's flight; every motion that is off this line tends to lessen or check the power of the stroke and to lessen its accuracy. Side motion of any kind only weakens the swing.

It is not an uncommon fault among beginners to see the player bend his body backward away from the ball, particularly in making the forehand ground stroke. This only serves to detract from the body swing by checking the forward motion of the weight. Swinging the racket across the face of the ball to exaggerate the cut checks the forward force of the stroke, and sometimes loses more in speed than it gains in the twist.

The more directly every motion can be kept in line with the flight intended for the ball, the more accurate will be the aim of the player and the more power there will be in the stroke. Side motions of the racket and arm are almost invariably lost power, and cause poor direction as well. The player who swings his racket across the path of the ball, rather than directly after it in the same plane, is generally wild in his returns and finds it difficult to control the ball as he should.

It is practically impossible to make a good stroke when the ball is played from close to the body. One should keep away from it in every direction. As it approaches, keep further back than you think necessary, and then jump forward to meet it, which gives the much-needed body weight in the stroke. Sidewise, also, never let the ball approach directly toward your body. Rather keep it off to one side and lean out to meet it, again using the balance of the body to add weight to the stroke. When a ball comes straight at you, step to one side or the other or your stroke will be ruined.

The elbow becomes bent and cramped when the ball gets in close to the player's body, and there is little or no power in a stroke made from such a position. If the ball bounds to the right or left of what was expected, the difference can be taken up by the bend of the elbow if well extended, but when cramped, all chance to correct the error in calculating the ball's flight is lost.

The idle arm should be used as a counterbalance. With it extended far out in the opposite direction from that carrying the racket, the balance can be preserved much better, and it also permits the player to lean farther out to meet the ball and to use his body weight in the stroke.

Watch a man run and you will see that whenever his right leg goes forward, his right arm swings back, and the same with the left. Without the arms swinging as counterbalances, it would not be possible for him to run nearly so fast, as the efforts of his legs would throw him off his balance with no help from the arm on the opposite side. It is the same thing in tennis, and the value of the idle arm as a counterbalance in fast play cannot be overestimated.

In all ground strokes, where a full swing is called for, and in most others, the player should turn his side toward the net when he makes the stroke. This gives a free swing for the racket and brings the feet into line so that the weight can be shifted from one to the other during the stroke to increase the body swing that is so necessary for speed. In stepping into this position, the player moves forward with one foot or backward with the other, according to whether the next ball is coming short or deep into his court.

Except while making a few volleys at the net, it is best to loosen up the joints so that the swing of the racket is not jerky. A pliable wrist is a great help, and the "flick" of the racket just before the ball is hit, by which experts add so much to their speed, all comes from the wrist. The more the whole arm from shoulder to wrist can be treated like a whiplash, the smoother and more powerful will be the stroke. The arm acts like a jointed rod, but the smoother the joints work, the better will be the stroke.

Another important point for the beginner to keep in mind is the necessity of preparing for the next stroke the instant the ball has been hit. Do not wait to see where your return is going before you start, but begin instantly to recover your balance and move to the best position for the next stroke. Anticipation of this kind is one of the greatest advantages an experienced player has over the novice.

Footwork. Footwork is the means of perfect weight control and balance, while timing is the transference of the player's weight into his stroke, thus giving "pace" to the ball. Actually good footwork is the secret of success in boxing, baseball, tennis, football, dancing, and many other sports, for by this medium the punch of the boxer, the carrying power of the batter, the pace of the tennis player, the distance of the punter, or the balance of the dancer is determined. There is a fraction of a second when ball and body are in such a juxtaposition that if the ball is struck then the speed and pace are increased over any other time of stroking. That is the moment when the weight of the body crosses the center of balance in a forward movement, and simultaneously the ball in its flight meets the racket. Only by this forward movement of striking the ball is it possible to acquire the maximum power. That is perfect timing.

Good footwork in tennis is as important as sound ground strokes or a big serve. Without the proper footwork, a player may find his weight moving backward or sideways rather than forward. He may plant his feet too late or too early, block himself from moving into the ball, or find himself glued to the ground when he should be taking a step forward or sideways. Good footwork can mean speed in reaching the ball, balance when meeting it, and power on the hit.

The basic requirements for proper tennis footwork are: (1) the weight should be on the balls of the feet rather than the heels; (2) the hop-skip motion should be used when necessary to wind up on the correct foot; and (3) the player should step toward the net with the left foot on the forehand and the right foot on the backhand.

When the player is in the ready position, his weight should be evenly distributed on the toes of both feet. He should feel "bouncy" rather than flatfooted. His feet are well spread and his knees are bent, but he is not leaning over so far that he loses his balance.

The "bouncier" he is, the more ready he is to move. When the ball leaves his opponent's racket, he makes his move: he pushes off with his left foot if he is moving toward his right (he lets his weight go onto the heel of his left foot, which is used as the "pusher"). If he does not have far to go, he simply skips sideways, with his body still facing the net. When a ball comes to his backhand, the action is reversed: he pushes off with his right foot to move toward his left. He skips toward balls that he can reach easily but runs toward balls that are wide or very short.

If the opponent hits a short ball that can be reached without difficulty, the player skips forward (the right foot on the forehand is always one step closer to the net than the left). If the ball comes directly to the player rather than to his side, he hop-skips one step toward the backhand so that he can play the ball naturally on his forehand.

The skip is used to prevent a player from getting glued to the ground, to make it easy for him to step toward the net with the proper foot, and to make last-minute adjustments if he misjudged the bounce. The run is always used instead of the skip to reach a difficult ball, but you will often see good players run toward the ball, then skip on the last step (if there is time) so that their footwork will be correct for the hit.

The proper footwork on the hit is neither the open stance with body facing the net nor the closed stance with left foot crossing toward the right alley (or right foot crossing toward the left alley).

The wide-open stance does not make it easy to put one's weight into the ball and the extreme closed stance prevents the weight from moving forward (it is, instead, moving sideways). Correct footwork is to step toward the net—with the left foot on the forehand and the right foot on the backhand. The stance is slightly open on the forehand, but the right side is toward the net on the backhand.

There are times when the player must use the wide-open or the extreme closed stance. One does not have time to adjust footwork against a cannonball serve (one simply turns the left shoulder toward the net on the forehand and the right shoulder toward the net on the backhand). Again, when one is running for a very wide ball, one may end up in an extreme closed stance. In the latter case, the shot cannot be an attacking one since the weight is moving in the wrong direction.

If you have been having problems with footwork, review the three basic requirements for the proper approach: (1) on your toes, (2) hop-skip whenever possible, (3) step toward the net with left foot on forehand and right foot on backhand. This may be the answer to bettering your balance and increasing your speed and your power.

Timing. A player with good timing knows when to commence his stroke so that he will meet the ball at the proper moment. A player with poor timing may plan to hit the ball slightly in front of him but may catch it behind him. The two factors which will enable the player to improve his timing are: a consideration of the stroke involved (a forehand is timed differently from a backhand) and very early preparation.

Even if a match is played on a perfect court with no bad bounces, and the opponent hits every ball with exactly the same amount of pace, the player still must adjust his timing to the particular stroke involved. The timing on a ground stroke is different from that on a volley, and the timing on an overhead is different from that on a serve. Forehands are hit a fraction of a second earlier than backhands. Often a player's timing will be "off" on his forehand but perfect on his backhand: occasionally he will have a good backhand day but his forehand will be "off." The stroke did not come apart suddenly: the timing did. The first stage of the cure is to recognize that the timing on forehands is different from that on backhands, that the timing on volleys is different from that on ground strokes.

In all strokes one must decide at what point one wishes to meet the ball. The serve should be hit to the side of and slightly in front of the body; volleys should be met 12 to 18 inches in front of the body; ground strokes should be met several inches in front of the body (for beginners) or several feet in front of the body (for advanced players). Once the desired point of contact is established, the stroke should be practiced until this contact is met with more and more regularity. The stroke gets grooved to meet the ball at a particular point.

The easiest way to develop good timing is to play a soft hitter. You are not being rushed and so you can always meet the ball at the point in front of you which you have decided is most desirable. The harder your opponent's pace, the more rapid your preparation must be. One must still try to meet the ball in front of the body, and so the windup must begin as soon as the opponent hits the ball. Never compromise when playing a hard hitter by taking the ball late; keep to the desired point of contact, which is in front of your body.

A change-of-pace artist may throw your timing off. His object is to prevent you from getting a rhythm: he will try to make you hit late by throwing in an occasional hard ball and to make you hit too early by giving you an occasional softer ball. Your own concentration will defeat his strategy of spins, cannonballs, and drop shots since you will be aware immediately of the change in his plan and you can alter your own preparation at once to adjust to the shot.

Awareness of early preparation, the desired point of contact, and your opponent's style will help you develop good timing. This "awareness," which allows you to make adjustments in your own game, will enable you to change from a slow court to a fast one, from soft balls to hard ones, and from ideal conditions to windy ones.

TENNIS STROKES

Tennis strokes can be divided into three categories: ground strokes, volleys, and service strokes.

Ground strokes are those you play after the ball has bounced on your side of the net and include the drive (forehand and backhand), the lob, the drop shot, the half volley, and the overhead smash.

The volley strokes are shots played when the ball is in flight, before it has bounced on your side of the net, and include horizontal volley (forehand and backhand), the overhead volley, the smash, the lob volley and the stop volley.

The basic forehand drive from the anticipatory position to the completed follow-through.

The service stroke is the one employed to put the ball in play during an actual game. Now let us take a closer look at each of these three categories of strokes.

Forehand Ground Strokes

The forehand drive "off the ground" is the commonest stroke in the game, so you should learn to make it before you go on to any other. It is the foundation both of attack and defense; and it must be thoroughly mastered if you are to become a good player.

It is the commonest stroke in the game because, first, the number of strokes off the ground is never less than 50 percent even when both players are volleyers by temperament, and rises to considerably over 90 percent when both players are base-liners; and second, because three-quarters of all these ground strokes are forehand strokes, owing to everybody's natural preference for, if possible, taking the ball forehanded rather than backhanded. The purpose of the forehand is to return a ball on the racket side of the body (the right side of a right-handed player or the left of a left-handed player) after it has bounced once. It should be used to keep the ball and the opponent deep in the opposite court. That is, a deep drive into your opponent's court gives you more time to reach the net and materially reduces the possibility of being successfully passed or lobbed. To accomplish this, a ball hit by the forehand drive must be placed near the top of the net (low), near the opponent's base line (deep), and should carry speed (flat or topspin). Fortunately, this most important stroke is the easiest and the most natural to learn.

To make a forehand stroke properly, it is most important to get into the proper position to hit the ball right. This means to run to a position in the court about 2 or 3 feet to the left of where the ball will come up from its bound. You should be well back of the spot where it hits the ground so as to allow room for the bound, and also to permit you to meet it as your weight is thrown forward or toward the ball itself. When this position is reached your left foot should be forward or toward the net and the right back of it nearly in direct line with the flight of the ball.

As the ball strikes the ground, your racket should start to move in the backswing, and should pass around behind your body and slightly upward, extended at the full reach of the arm. As previously stated, most beginners find it very difficult to start the backswing early enough, and a late start shortens the backswing and makes the stroke jerky and poorly executed, lacking power. In the forehand drive, the swing should be as continuous as possible, with no stopping of the racket at the end of the backswing, but a slight turn and an immediate forward swing without checking the headway of the racket. To pull back the racket only a foot or so, stop it to gauge the flight of the ball, and then start it forward to hit will never accomplish anything in tennis. The momentum of the racket must be kept up from the start back until long after the ball has been hit, for that is what gives the power to the stroke, not the strength in the arm.

The racket should act as simply an extension of the forearm, and be kept as far away from the body as possible. The upper arm, forearm, and racket all three act as a jointed rod that strikes like a flail, and if the wrist is added to the movement it becomes like a whiplash in its action, imparting a powerful blow. At all times avoid getting your elbow cramped up close to the body.

As the backswing is made the body should be turned or pivoted around on the hips, and both the shoulders and the hips turned to follow the racket back and make its swing easier. The weight should be evenly balanced between the two legs when the backswing is started, and then transferred back onto the right foot to carry the weight back evenly without losing balance.

As the ball starts to rise from the ground, the forward, or hitting, swing starts, and the unwinding of the backward coil reverses its first action. The hips turn first, then the shoulders, followed by the upper arm, forearm, and wrist as the racket sweeps forward to meet the ball. In this forward swing, the weight is again shifted back from the right foot to the even center when the ball is met, and then continued on until it ends entirely on the left foot.

The ball should be met at a height between the knee and waist and as nearly as possible opposite the center of the body. The racket must be guided so that the ball strikes the center of the strings of the racket, the nearer the center the better. Meeting the ball off center is likely to turn the racket in the hand, and always reduces the strength as well as the accuracy of the shot.

The head of the racket should be perpendicular to the ground at the moment when the ball is hit—that is, the top part of the frame should be no farther forward nor back than the lower part. This gives what is known as an "open" racket and the greatest accuracy and strength in the stroke. The handle of the racket should be very nearly parallel with the ground.

From the point of impact, there are three variations of the end of the stroke, all having their own uses and advantages, and the player can select any style he pleases, and vary the style of shot, if he can control several styles, for different results.

The Flat Forehand Drive. The ideal forehand drive is a flat drive which skims the net and yet is able to keep your opponent deep in his court. But flat drives are too difficult to control, especially on low bounces; for if the ball crosses the net higher than 6 inches or so above the net cord, it will land out of court. This margin of safety is too small. Topspin, on the other hand, enables you to drive the ball 2 or more feet above the net and also deep to your opponent's base line. Your margin of safety above the net is much greater than with the flat drive; and the forward downspin, aided by gravitation, pulls the ball downward within the court after it has crossed the net. You should therefore make fewer errors.

The term *flat* as it is used in tennis means a ball hit without spin. A ball hit *totally* without twist or spin would naturally travel in the same direction in which it starts until its momentum is spent and gravity alters its course. But it is almost impossible to hit a tennis ball without giving it some spinning motion. The strings of the racket cling very close to its rough surface, and the slightest motion of the racket that is off the straight line tends to wipe or brush them across the surface of the ball, and makes it revolve before it loses contact.

Topspin on the Forehand. Topspin enables a player to hit with more pace, depth, and control. A stroke without spin depends on gravity alone to bring the ball into court. Topspin makes a hard-hit ball dip after it clears the net comfortably; under the same circumstances, a flat ball would sail out. A stroke with topspin is the ideal passing shot since the spin pushes the ball down, thus forcing the volleyer to hit a low ball; a stroke with underspin is the most dangerous passing shot since the underspin causes the ball to rise, thus allowing the volleyer to hit down on a high ball.

In topspin (or overspin or loop), the top edge of the tennis ball is turning in the direction of the opponent while the bottom edge is moving away from him. In underspin (or backspin), the bottom edge of the ball is spinning toward the opponent. The topspin ball tends to drop to the ground faster than a ball without spin, while the underspin ball tends to hang in the air.

Topspin is achieved by the upward motion of the racket with respect to the ball. Therefore the racket must approach the ball from below ball level (this does not mean that the racket head should be dropped). A player can still take a high backswing if he so chooses, but he must then develop a circular or figure-8 swing so that his racket will be below ball level just before the hit. The racket face can be either slightly closed, absolutely perpendicular to the ground, or slightly open. However, if the face is too closed, the ball will go short or into the net; if the face is too open, the player will have to pull up sharply with his racket (use an enormous amount of topspin) to bring the ball into court.

The follow-through on a topspin shot must be higher than the level at which the ball is hit. In other words, the racket starts below ball level and ends above ball level. It is not necessary to roll the face of the racket over

after the ball has been hit. This action has no effect on the ball since the moment of impact is already over. Some players do roll the face of the racket over, but it is just a matter of personal idiosyncrasy—just as a big backswing or a small backswing are matters of personal idiosyncrasy.

Players with Eastern, Western, or Continental grips can hit topspin shots. The Continental grip is usually hit with a cocked wrist (the racket head points upward). Continental players who try topspin will pull up sharply with the arm as the ball is hit. The movement is therefore upward rather than forward, and this makes for a rather erratic action. In the Western style, the wrist is laid way back, the elbow is bent, and the racket ends up very high. The topspin is pronounced, but the grip makes it difficult to handle low balls because the wrist must be bent around so much. The Eastern grip is ideal for the topspin shot since it can be used on low, medium, or high balls. The wrist is laid back on the backswing but is firm at the moment of impact. Beginners and intermediates should use as little wrist action as possible since topspin with the Eastern grip can be achieved by racket trajectory alone (the racket starts below ball level and ends above ball level). Wrist action or wrist snap can be developed later by the good player who wants to add a little variety to his game.

The amount of topspin given to any shot depends to a degree on the hitting position of the ball. For example, a ball that is higher than the waist (which is higher than the net) requires less spin, and can be hit almost flat. But when a ball is lower than the waist (below the net), it requires some lifting. Where one has to lift, one is required to put something on the ball to bring it down again. Thus more topspin is required on a low shot than on a high one. To do this, the face of the racket must be kept slightly open (you must reconcile the angle of your racket face with the angle of your hitting), and you must start your stroke lower than where the ball will be hit. In other words, you use topspin in different degrees as the situation demands to control shots. This knowledge comes only by trial and error and plenty of practice.

Slice and Chop Strokes. There is still a third variation of making the forehand ground stroke with an underspin or backspin. The predominating feature of these is the under-spin on the ball that is imparted, for a slice stroke (sometimes called a *cut shot*) or chop stroke always makes the ball spin *backward* in a direction opposite to that used in the drop stroke. The spinning motion is against the flight of the ball through the air, the top moving backward and the bottom forward, which is again exactly opposite to what happens when the topspin is used.

All of these strokes are made by striking the ball with a glancing blow, the bottom edge of the racket being forward and the strings touching more of the under side of the ball than the top. In order to prevent such a blow underneath from lifting the ball up too high, the swing must be made with a downward angle. The racket starts high and ends low, very different from the drop stroke, and the head is dragged across the ball sharply while the strings are still in contact with its cover.

The chop stroke is used primarily as a defensive weapon to change the pace of the game, or against a player who does not like to run or to handle a stroke with spin. There are two distinct types of chop shots: the deep chop and the soft chop.

The deep chop, or underspin drive, is used as a change upon the topspin drive and is played from the same position on the court. This chop also is highly effective as a means of returning the wide-bounding American twist service. As a rule, you should restrict its use to only high-bounding balls where you have a straight angle down over the net. On low-bounding balls, those below the level of the net, this shot has the tendency to sail out of the court.

The soft chop shot (known also as the *dink* or *softie*) is used only when you are up close (never more than 5 feet from the net) and your opponent is playing deep. Then it is aimed to drop closely over the net and should be played on a cross-court angle. For if you play it straight down the court, nine out of ten times the shot will go too deep and be recovered. Therefore, you must angle the ball away from your opponent.

In making the chop stroke, the player crouches even more than in any of the other strokes, the bend from the hips forward being more pronounced. The racket is swung back slower than in the drop shot and not nearly

so far. Few of the slice-stroke players carry their rackets in the preliminary swing back farther than behind the shoulder. As the swing is shorter, it can be made later with greater accuracy than with the drop shot. This is the feature that generally appeals to beginners, the short swing, and many adopt the chop-stroke style at first and change afterward when they learn of its limitations. It is much wiser to begin with the other stroke and learn that properly to avoid the necessary change in style afterward.

The position of the feet for the chop stroke also is slightly different from the others, as the shorter swing does not depend so much on momentum, and the right foot is extended as a rule farther forward to steady the player as he strikes. This stroke is made off the right foot, while the drop stroke is made off both feet, the weight being pretty equally divided during the stroke. As the racket is brought sharply down to meet the ball, the shoulders straighten up a little to take some of the bend out of the elbow, but at no time in the stroke is the arm as straight as in the other strokes. There is an inclination to bend the elbow somewhat in making all chop strokes, and this bend is not fully straightened out with most players until the very end of the stroke.

When the ball is met, all of the body weight is suddenly exerted in the racket, the shoulders doing more than the hips, and the wrist adds to the "drag" of the racket across the ball to give it the necessary twist. As the stroke is finished, all of the weight is thrown over to the forward foot and the arm and racket end their swing with the downward thrust still further pronounced. The racket finishes out in front of the left knee, extended at the full length of the arm, and the shoulders turned around completely in their effort to check its swing without losing the balance.

The greatest difficulty the player has to overcome in using the chop stroke is its tendency to drive the ball out of court. In order to prevent this, the stroke must be played slower and with less power so it will not go too far, and this necessity robs the stroke of the virtue of speed that other strokes possess. As against this drawback, however, it must be conceded that the short backswing and the more constrained position permit greater accuracy, and as a rule chop-stroke players have a closer control of their slow returns than do drop-stroke players of their faster shots. The player can delay longer before striking, and this allows him to change his swing later if a bad bound or a change in the opponent's position makes it necessary.

On the other hand again, it is much easier for the opposing player to volley an undercut ball at the net than a drop shot, for its underspinning motion makes the ball twist downward and go away from his racket faster. The revolution of a top-spinning ball tends to make it leave a volleyer's racket slower and jump upward when volleyed. For this reason, the cut strokes are less effective against an opponent who is at the net ready to volley, and the drop strokes are the best against such an opponent. Conversely, the drop stroke is best against a net player and weakest against an opponent at the back of his court.

As has been previously mentioned, it is a distinct advantage to play the ball from as high in the air as possible, but the upward motion of the racket makes it difficult to do this when making a drop shot. The motion of the racket in the chop stroke just reverses this, being in the downward direction, so that these strokes can be played from a much higher bound than the others.

Often the disadvantage of the underspin which keeps the ball up in its flight can be overcome by striking it from a higher point and consequently closer to the net, which will sometimes take the volleyer by surprise and pass him with the slower ball this stroke affords, because it is played with more of a downward angle which allows it to travel nearly as fast as the other and still remain inside the court lines.

The slice, or side-twist shot, causes the ball to bounce low and to curve to the side on which the spin is applied. It can be hit either forehand or backhand and is good on low-bounding balls. Actually, the slice and chop are executed in exactly the same manner from the standpoint of grip, position, and stance. However, in the slice, instead of hitting down on the back of the ball, you hit down and to the outside of it, imparting under- and side-spin. When making the forward swing for a forehand slice, the racket, starting outside and above the ball, is brought down through the air at an angle almost 45 degrees to your left,

and as it moves in this almost forward-sideward diagonal path, the racket cuts across the bottom of the ball. This severe right-to-left cut causes the ball to curve to your right. For the backhand slice, the cut is from the left to your right, which causes the ball to rotate in the same direction and curve in its flight to your left. As you could expect, these strokes require strong wrist action, an open-face racket, and a follow-through that will extend naturally in the direction of the shot.

Some players succeed in using side twists with either a topspinning or an undercut ball. When hit with a horizontal racket these are only possible by advancing the wrist well ahead of the ball and drawing the racket in toward the body while in contact, which gives the ball an out twist as well as an underspin or a topspin according to whether the racket travels upward or downward when it meets the ball. These side twists are used most in the services, however, which are made with a racket that is more nearly perpendicular, and therefore allows the motion to be sidewise without interfering with the body swing, by the use of the wrist. This will be taken up later in this section under the heading of Services.

The backspinning shots, both of them, carry less speed than the flat-hit or the topspinning shot and are therefore more used for defense than for attack. But with any tennis stroke, do not try for speed in your drives until you have mastered the stroke. Remember, in tennis, science is often more important than strength. Do not try to "knock the cover off the ball," or "blast your opponent off the court." Placing the ball in the right spot at the right time is more important.

Actually, learning to drive a tennis ball fast is something like driving an automobile. You will come to grief if you drive at eighty miles per hour before you have learned to control the car at a speed of forty. Apply the same principle when learning to drive a tennis ball. If you are a beginner, do not drive too fast. As your control improves, gradually increase your speed. When you have so mastered the forehand stroke that you do not need to think about your footwork or your swing, then drive as fast as you like, provided you do not sacrifice control for speed, and provided further that increased speed warrants the increased risk. Therefore, as you develop your forehand, concentrate first on control. Power, speed, and deception will come naturally, if you learn first the fundamentals of control.

Backhand Ground Strokes

The backhand ground strokes are used to return balls which have bounced once on the court to the left of a right-handed player or to the right of a left-hander. Their importance cannot be overemphasized. The opportunity of playing the backhand drive should never be avoided by moving position to play the ball on your stronger and generally more reliable forehand. Such a practice not only reveals a major weakness to your opponent, but it also leaves an area of the court unprotected. In other words, one may prefer the forehand stroke and use it on every possible occasion, but no chain is stronger than its weakest link, and if there is a distinct weakness in the back-

The regular Eastern backhand grip.

hand play, the defense will be vulnerable whenever attacked by a "heady" player.

There is no question that the forehand stroke is the easier way to play the ball. It is the natural way, and the arm and elbow are less embarrassed when swinging the racket on the right side of the body than when they must be crossed over to reach a ball on the other side. That is, in forehand play, the backswing is clear of the body and the turn as the blow is delivered keeps the arm free, but in backhand play the arm must swing across the body, and the pushing muscles of the upper arm rather than those that pull are used in making the stroke. The grip of the hand too allows all the power to be *behind* the racket for a forehand shot, while on the other side the necessary grip forces the hand *above,* and in the Continental style, a little *ahead* of the racket, giving the effort more of a pull than a push. The shoulder is seldom behind the ball and the turning of the body for the follow-through is never so pronounced in backhand play, because the striking arm is already far advanced when the stroke begins and it is difficult to shift so that the ball can be followed as long as in forehand play.

The methods of gripping the racket, which vary distinctly for this stroke from all the others, have been fully covered earlier in this section, and the general elements of good form also bear strongly on this stroke. But in addition to these, there are a good many points which apply only to backhand strokes, which the beginner should study carefully before going deeper into the play.

As in the forehand stroke, there are the same options regarding the best way of hitting the ball and the exact amount of twist to put on it. One can play the ball nearly straight with little or no twist, by using a perfectly straight follow-through; he can put topspin on the ball and give it the same dropping tendency already recommended for the forehand stroke, or he can use a chop stroke that will make the ball spin backward in its flight through the air.

In the backhand stroke the proper stance and backswing should be coordinated even more closely than in the forehand. From the anticipatory or readiness position, with the right hand relaxed on the handle and the left lightly cradling the throat, you begin the back-

The basic backhand drive stroke from the anticipatory position to the completed follow-through.

swing of your body and racket immediately when the ball is seen to be coming toward your backhand.

Start the stroke by turning your right shoulder toward the net. This turning movement begins as the racket head starts swinging back at hip level. The left hand guides the racket back and the right hand makes a change to the backhand grip. With the racket still coming back, pivot to the left on the ball of your left foot. As the backswing nears its completion, the racket should be well back and behind you, knees flexed, the eyes and head forward, and the body and shoulders rotated away from the net. Actually, your body should be swung around to the left far enough so that your back is almost half turned to it. Watch the flight of the oncoming ball over your right shoulder and keep the racket head about the wrist at all times during the backswing. The weight of your body should

be on the back, or left foot. Thus, the pivot in the backhand stroke is much more emphatic than in the forehand drive. Many inexperienced players do not turn their bodies nearly enough; in consequence, the racket arm meets with resistance by not being able to swing past the body. If there is any doubt of the importance of the turn of the body, stand sideways facing the net and, without turning the body, see how far the racket can be taken back. Then try it again, but on this occasion turn your hips away from the net, and you will quickly find that your racket arm has a much smoother swing.

During the backswing, the racket's path can be either an almost horizontal flat arc kept at hip level on its trip back or it can be circular with its peak at about shoulder height and with the racket head tilted slightly backward. The flat-arc backswing, similar to the horizontal straight-back motion in the forehand stroke, is usually recommended for beginners. Once you have the footwork and timing mastered, you can use the circular backswing. But with either backswing, the left hand should be kept on the racket until you start the forward swing.

In the completed backswing position your weight is back on the rear foot, left knee loose and bent, right knee sagged; and you are looking over your right shoulder, eyes glued on the oncoming ball. Having "wound" yourself up into such a position, you must now reverse the action into and through the ball. Release the left hand from the throat of the racket, and swing the arm and racket toward the net in an almost flat arc in line with the oncoming ball or slightly below it. In the latter case, the racket head will help to give the ball its necessary topspin, but do not exaggerate the upward movement or too much spin will occur. As the racket comes closer to the point of impact, the weight of the body is gradually transferred to the front, right foot. Your wrist should be straight and your elbow kept slightly bent and close to your body until the ball has been hit.

The ball should be met at a point from 10 to 15 inches in advance of the right hip and the right hip should be drawn in. The mechanics of the backhand drive make it next to impossible to execute the shot consistently unless impact occurs before the ball reaches a point opposite the body. Actually, there is no feature in connection with the execution of any stroke in tennis as important as this. Also keep away from the ball. All too many players hit the ball with a backhand stroke too close to the body, which cramps the shot and results in less power and speed. Keeping away from the ball makes for free, confident, hard hitting, and will materially help to eliminate errors.

At the moment of impact, the complete momentum of your swing should have reached its maximum speed with the body turned into the ball by swinging the left shoulder well around. The weight of the body should now all be on the right foot. The right knee should be bent while the left knee should be sagged and turned inward, with the rear foot steadying your body for balance. Do not use any type of push-off action with this foot to

The two-handed backhand stroke of Franjo Puncec, Yugoslavian star of the 1930's (*left*). Some players like Peaches Bartkowicz (*right*) continue to use it today.

help the shot. Your grip should be gradually tightening on the racket handle so that at impact the wrist is firm or locked. Your arm should be straightened well out from the body as you swing through the ball.

While it is best to stroke a ball at waist level, your opponents do not always oblige by hitting the ball so that it bounces to this height. Therefore, you must learn to make the backhand swing at all levels. For a low shot, one below waist level, you follow the same procedure as for low forehand strokes. That is, you bend your knees so that you bring your waist level down to the level of the ball. Except for the bending of the knees, the backhand stroke is executed in the same manner as that used on a waist-level ball. For balls that have a very low bounce, those just off your shoe top, the hitting should be a little upward, with the racket face slightly tilted back. This open face will lift the ball to the proper height over the net. Remember that it is usually advantageous to hit the ball on the rise—at least it should be hit before it begins to fall. This means that your opponent will have less time to get into position and your shot may be concealed to a greater extent.

Topspin and Underspin. As stated earlier, topspin and backspin can be applied to backhand drives. The topspin backhand starts low and ends high; the underspin backhand starts high and ends low. In the topspin shot, the face of the racket is perpendicular to the ground at the moment of impact; in the underspin or slice shot, the racket face is open at the hit. That is, by rolling the racket backward

and allowing the racket to pass under the ball, a backspin is given, and we have an undercut that has a tendency to keep the ball up in the air long and make its bound low. It is a good stroke for straight sideline shots, when the distance to the base line or diagonally to where the ball would go out of court is so long that the stroke can be played fast without danger; but for cross-court shots it is generally difficult to play fast and hold in court. This stroke is easy to volley at the net, too, so that it is seldom as good a passing stroke against a volleyer. With the opponent at the base line, however, when only driving must be considered, it is very useful, because its slow "hop" is a mean, lifeless ball to handle off the ground.

For the chop and slice stroke, the racket should finish low, generally at about the height of the waist, but for the topspinning, rolling lift stroke, the racket's swing should end much higher, generally above the shoulder. The same principles of meeting the ball and imparting the twist apply as in the forehand stroke, and some experts get the same variations here by increasing their follow-through and imparting the twist with a turn of the wrist at the last moment before the ball leaves the racket.

As the player becomes better and the competition stiffer, he will find it more difficult to hit backhand topspin shots down the line. The ball is coming hard and deep, and if the player's preparation is the least bit late, he will err on the down-the-line. He therefore has two choices: to slice or to prepare earlier.

The forehand chop shot from the backswing to the completed follow-through.

The backhand slice stroke from the backswing to the completed follow-through.

The latter is the wiser decision although frequently he will slice for better control. But the backhand stroke without any twist at all, the straight hit ball, is perhaps more valuable for general play than either of the others. As in forehand drives, however, control is the most important consideration in your backhand stroke production. Uncontrolled speed loses more points than it wins; it is where you place the ball that counts.

Lobbing

The lob was, originally, almost entirely a defensive ground stroke. It consists of hitting the ball up high in the air, so that it will pass high over the head of your opponent if he is forward in the court, and drop far back by his base line. It was, and still is, of great use in getting yourself out of a disadvantageous position and giving you time to assume an advantageous one, or perhaps, only to give you breathing time, if you are being run about a great deal from one end to the other of your base line. Its two main objects are to drive your opponent away from the net and to enable you to get there yourself. To attain these objects, two kinds of lob are in use: the fast, comparatively low, one, which is played just over the top of your opponent's reach; and the high toss, which is intended to hit right at the back of his court. There is one essential common to both forms: they must be deep. You must aim to hit right on

his base line, or at most a foot inside it. A short lob is, or ought to be, fatal. The most useful lob is one to your opponent's backhand corner; but you should, of course, not always lob to the same place.

The development of the lob into an effective weapon of attack was introduced by American international players in the late 1920's. Actually, it is a valuable means of dislodging a volleyer from the net. No volleyer can stay at the net against a good lob, and there are very few players who can smash a deep lob, or, at any rate, who can go on doing so. Sooner or later the strain of watching—and hitting—the ball tells; the ball goes into the net, and the patient lobber gets his reward.

Like other ground strokes, lobs can be made either forehand or back. In addition, many of the same rules apply here as in the ground-stroke drives. The ball must not be taken in front of the body, nor with the wrong foot or shoulder forward. The body should be turned with the side toward the net to allow a full swing as in a good drive, and the same freedom of the arm and shoulder is required.

The lob is a slower stroke and much more deliberate than any other ground stroke. The backswing is shorter and the body motion in the actual stroke less pronounced, while the follow-through is very much reduced. The racket should be dropped with the head distinctly below the wrist, and the stroke has an upward swing that is absent in the other

The forehand lob stroke from the anticipatory position to the completed follow-through.

ground stroke. With the head of the racket hanging downward at an angle of 45 degrees, the same free sweep of the arm is made, with the ball well off to the side so that the shoulder can be brought into the stroke. The same grips are used as previously mentioned for ground-stroke drives.

The sweep of the racket must be long and smooth, not jerky like the stab of a chop stroke. The ball is met with even less impact than in other ground strokes and is swept away rather than hit with a sharp blow. The slower the stroke can be made, the better are the results likely to be. No other stroke in the game is made with such deliberate movements.

The most dangerous error for the beginner to counteract, however, is the desire to strike the ball from underneath and drive it straight upward in the air. On the contrary, the ball must be hit clearly from behind, with a for-ward sweep, the upward turn coming just before the racket meets the ball. The bevel of the face of the racket can be depended on almost as much as the upward swing to direct the ball high enough to pass over the opponent's head. Except when it is played for the purpose of gaining time to recover position in court or to get a resting spell when the player is hard pressed, a lob should not be driven any higher in the air than is necessary to keep clear of the opponent's reach. With the other man at the net ready to smash, which is generally his position when the lob is used, it is only necessary for the ball to pass a foot or two above the highest point he can reach by jumping, and the lower it can safely pass him the better. If only a little out of reach, the stroke will have a flatter trajectory, more forward motion on the ball, and will greatly reduce the other man's chances of turning and running back to make the return.

The backhand lob stroke from the start of the backswing to the completed follow-through.

The angle of the bound of a low lob also makes it much more difficult to return than a high straight ball. From every point of view then, it is desirable to keep lobbed balls as low as safe, and for this reason as much forward motion as possible should be put into the swing of the racket. If a purely upward swing is used for the lob, it will be difficult to avoid raising the ball unnecessarily high in the air, even when the low lob is very much to be desired.

For the backhand lob, the same general rules hold good as for the backhand drive. The body should be turned around so that the playing shoulder is toward the net and the feet are lined up almost in the direction that the ball is to be sent. As the upward swing of the racket requires it to start very low in the forward swing, the body should be bent somewhat away from the net and the left knee bends a little to let the shoulder drop.

With the racket turned slightly backward in the grip, as in the forehand lob, and the thumb extended behind its handle for support, the stroke is inclined to be even a little more upward in direction than the forehand lob. The ball should be met further forward than on the other side, and this makes it more difficult to swing as straight and still lift the ball as in the other stroke.

The finish of the stroke in both cases is in an upward direction, and the racket should be allowed to follow after the ball as long as possible. The body swing cannot be pronounced, as the forward motion is not long enough.

The elbow should be bent more than in the ground strokes, but the ball must be kept well clear of the body.

Even after a lob, it is necessary as in every other stroke of the game to recover position quickly and prepare at once for the next stroke no matter what it may be. It is as dangerous to stand and watch a lobbed ball sail through the air as it is to watch a drive until the opponent has returned it. In either case, you are very likely to be caught out of position and not ready for the next stroke.

Many a lob that was started with good intentions of being kept out of the antagonist's reach is ultimately smashed hard in return. Except for very low lobs that are well timed and well placed so as to catch the opponent so close to the net that he is unable to back away fast enough to volley them, the chances are very strong that any lobbed ball will be returned and will come back fast.

The stroke itself is of necessity slow enough to allow the other man in most cases time to reach it, and it only depends on how deep the lob has been placed whether it will be smashed or returned only moderately hard. In either case it behooves the lobber to hurry to his best defensive position immediately after every lob has been sent up.

As already explained, a short lob is like throwing the point away, but what constitutes a short lob is not quite so easy to state. Against the average player, any ball that will fall inside the service line should be considered a short lob, and most players will have long odds in favor of their being able to kill the ball, if they can smash from within 15 feet of the net. Some players are able to kill from even back of the service line, or at least to smash hard enough to keep the lobber in constant trouble unless he gets better length than this.

To be out of danger, safe from hard smashing, a lob should not fall more than 10 feet inside the base line of the court. Except when the opponent is caught "anchored" at the net and passed overhead with a low lob, any lobbed ball is defensive and the lobber can hardly expect to win, except through an error by his opponent, until he is able to turn the attack against him.

A deep lob will often drive the other man back far enough to open his court for a drive on the next play, and the lob therefore will often turn the attack against a volleyer unless he is very quick at recovering his position at the net again after each smash.

The lob is best used as a surprise stroke against a volleyer. To lob repeatedly to your antagonist often means that he will soon become used to the stroke and, preparing himself in position and swing, will shortly be able to smash successfully. If he is given a lob only occasionally, he will be less likely to handle them well and they are more likely to be successful.

When the server runs in constantly to the net and takes a position very close up to volley, it is often a good plan to lob regularly to dislodge him; and such a campaign will often break up his net attack, so that he is forced to give it up. When he does stop running in, however, that should be the signal to stop lobbing at once and go to driving at his feet.

Placing a lob generally increases its attacking power, and the backhand corner near the base line is almost invariably the best spot to aim for. It is doubly difficult to smash lobs over the backhand shoulder, so a lobbing attack in the backhand corner is always the hardest to meet.

The success of any lob, of course, does not depend on speed or hitting power but rather on the touch and feel of the racket in the lift of the ball. It should be so finely judged that it just misses the head of your opponent's racket when he jumps up to intercept it. Insufficient

height and distance render lobs ineffective. It is usually better to make the highest point of the ball loop closer to the net than to you (the lobber). Disguise the position of the racket almost to the moment of impact so that your opponent will not suspect the nature of the stroke. This deception is of the utmost importance, particularly when using the lob as an offensive weapon. If you betray your intentions before making the stroke, your opponent will have sufficient time to retreat near the base line and get ready for a countering return smash.

Volleying

The volley (both forehand and backhand) is the stroke used to hit the ball before it bounces. This stroke is employed chiefly when you are playing the net—the primary objective of an attacking player. It is often called a finishing shot because its principal purpose is to win the point and put an end to a rally.

Originally, all strokes in lawn tennis were made after the ball had bounded, and it was not until some years after the game had reached England from its native home in India that the idea of striking the ball in the air, "on the fly" as we used to say in baseball, came into vogue. But it was only a short time after this before the value of the new stroke was well appreciated. The famous Renshaw brothers, among the earliest English champions, introduced the volley stroke and revolutionized the early development of the game.

Two distinct advantages are offered by the volley, time and angle of attack. A ball hit in the air, particularly when close in toward the net, offers a much wider range of the antagonist's court for attack than when hit off the ground. In addition to this, much valuable time is gained by using the stroke, since the player on the other side has less time to anticipate the volleyed stroke than one played from the back of the court. This element of time is of far greater importance than is understood by most players. A tennis player forced to one side of his court to make a return requires a certain amount of time to recover a safe position in the center, from which he can reach any stroke that his adversary may deliver to him. If he is badly hurried, his stroke falters, and he suffers

The forehand volley stroke from the anticipatory position to the completed follow-through.

soon from fast breathing, which also hurts his play immediately. To keep an opponent in such a condition is to maintain a constant attack that keeps him on the defensive.

Primarily, then, the volleying position at the net is the best position for attack, and by the volleying position we mean anywhere in front of the service line, for it is next to impossible in fast play to hit a ball off the ground from in front of the service line. Now, two players cannot survive long with both at the net against each other because the closeness of their positions does not afford either time enough to anticipate the other's attack, and one or the other must lose at once. Hence, it is necessary that one of them must retire to the back of his court and assume the defensive when his adversary outgenerals him and gains the coveted net position. But you must not reason from this that it is always safe to make a dash for the net if the other

man has not anticipated you. On the contrary, a very dangerous attack can be maintained from the base line, and blindly rushing to the net is as short-sighted as camping indefinitely at the back of the court. There are correct principles which should be learned to show how and when it is safe to take the volleying position. This subject will be fully covered later in this section under position play.

Horizontal Volleying. There are two distinctly different types of volleys which have sharply defined lines to identify them. First, there are the volleys of a horizontal ball, one that is coming straight at the player, and generally pretty fast; and, second, the volleys of dropping balls, which are most often distinguished as smashes. There are several variations of these two basic types.

The correct horizontal-volleying position is from 6 to 15 feet back of the net, but it also has its own relation to the position of the ball as well. The volleyer should be directly opposite his opponent only if the ball is in the center of the court. The playing center is not always the middle of the net, for if the ball is far out to the right in your opponent's territory, your own court will be open to attack on the same side more than on the other, and you should move over a little more in that direction to protect yourself against the next stroke.

Having assumed the right position in court —whether by running up immediately after serving or by gradually working up during a long rally makes no difference—the actual position of the body differs somewhat from that assumed for ground strokes. The volleyer does not have time to change position from backhand to forehand volleys or vice versa, and he must be ready at all times to handle either kind of a ball. His position at the net therefore must be squared around more, his feet almost parallel with the net.

For the fastest kind of volleying, it is better to have the right foot extended slightly behind the left, but with the legs spread well apart and the weight carried low to give the player the advantage of an instant start in any direction. Not to keep one foot a little behind the other makes it slower to get started back for a lob, and the opponent can often catch a volleyer napping at the net and win an easy point by lobbing over his head, if the position of his feet does not guard him against such a surprise attack. To anticipate a sharp drive at either side, the volleyer must be ready to jump sidewise on the instant and the racket must be balanced in front of his body, as when waiting for the return of the service. The "splice," or "wedge," at the throat should be balanced in the left hand well out in front and the player will then be ready to shift it to either side without a second's hesitation to meet the ball. Bent knees and the weight carried up on the toes, as in the other strokes, are also essential to quick starting.

When the direction of the oncoming ball is known and the actual stroke starts, the racket is swung out on that side of the body and back with a short, quick swing that is less deliberate and more snappy than that used for the ground strokes. The backswing is shorter because there is *very* little follow-through required and less time to make it.

The racket is kept nearly horizontal, except when the ball comes higher or lower than the waist, and then, of course, its angle must be accommodated to the height of the ball.

The face of the racket should be beveled slightly backward to strike a glancing upward blow, but the amount of this angle depends largely on the height of the ball. For a low ball, which is below the level of the net when hit, the racket must be beveled enough to raise it back over the net, while balls that are met well above the height of the net require little or none of this cut, for the racket can meet them almost square. In other words, high volleys are hit downward; low volleys, which are to be hit up and over the net, are approached with an open racket face so that the underspin will carry the ball upward. The knees are slightly flexed on high volleys; the knees are bent deeply on low ones. High and low volleys are both hit in front of the body and the feet are comfortably apart. The racket head should never point downward but instead the volleyer gets down to the ball.

The stroke itself is much shorter and sharper than a ground stroke. There is less swing, both forward and backward, and there is less follow-through. The ball is met with an almost stiff wrist, the flexibility of the ground stroke not being required here. The short swing is more like a sweep than a blow, but the racket follows only a short distance, being quickly swung back into line and recovered in the former position for waiting, balanced in front of the player. The body should be swung forward slightly as the blow is struck, but the squared position makes it impossible to follow far after the ball without losing the balance. That is, the ball is merely pushed or punched, and the racket head is brought back with the elbow slightly bent and the wrist cocked. The racket head, both in the movement back and in the shot itself, should never be permitted to fall below the wrist, and the wrist should remain firm or locked throughout the entire stroke.

As a rule you should use the same grips for the forehand and backhand volleys as you do for the forehand and backhand drives. But efficient changing from the forehand grip to backhand and vice versa can be acquired only by practice and, when volleying, this change must be quick and automatic. For this reason, many players use the Continental grip—this can be used for either type of shot —because they find that they cannot change their grip from one to the other fast enough. When first starting to volley, however, it is generally best to use the two conventional grips. When you are more experienced you can then switch to the grip or grips that best suit your style of volleying. To volley successfully, you need very accurate timing and a strong wrist. If you think that your wrists are weak, choke up on the racket handle a little. While this is not necessary to perform the volley stroke, it may give you confidence when you first start using it.

It is always dangerous, of course, to stand too close to the net, and beginners who find it difficult to get back fast enough to smash lobs will do better to stand 3 or 4 feet back of the position from which they expect to volley, and then step forward to meet the ball when the time comes to make the stroke.

Stepping forward like this as you strike increases the power of any volley stroke, as well as acting as a safeguard against overhead attack by a lob.

Always take a volley shot as high as possible and direct the ball downward in order to place your opponent at the greatest possible disadvantage. This can be achieved by opening up the racket face so that the ball will bite the ground quicker and will not bounce up to any degree. The direction of your shot can also be controlled or angled (this is called an *angle volley*) off and away from an opponent by regulating the timing of your stroke. For a straight-down-the-middle shot, the ball should be hit just in front of your forward foot. If you wish the ball to angle to your left, punch it slightly earlier than you would for the shot straight down the court. To push the ball off to your right, time your punch a fraction later or hit the ball a little farther out from your left foot.

The backhand volley stroke from the anticipatory position to the completed follow-through.

As was stated earlier, little follow-through is needed in making most volley strokes and that which occurs is largely from the action of your wrist. Actually, when volleying close to the net on a hard-hit ball, all that is needed at impact is a tightening of your grip on the racket, letting the racket remain still. The resulting effect is the same as if the ball were to hit a solid wall. But it is very important that the ball strike the center of your racket so that it will have enough force to carry it back over the net.

When volleying a slow- or medium-speed ball, you can increase the length of your backswing and follow-through. This type of shot is called a *drive volley* and is made for a kill. In the drive volley, the racket head should not go much farther back than your right shoulder, but there should be a follow-through to give the shot speed. Contact should be made with an open-face racket, and the ball should be hit down. The wrist may be bent slightly as the racket is drawn back, but it should be a firm and locked impact. The racket shoulder should turn toward the net as the ball is punched over, and the extent of the follow-through is controlled by the locked wrist. Remember that the drive-volley shot can be compared with the close-in body punch or jab of a boxer—a compact punch with a great deal of power behind it.

You can control the direction or angle of a backhand volley by the positioning of your left foot and by regulating the point of impact. For a volley shot straight down the court, the point of impact should be well in front of the body. The left foot should be also parallel to the net and directly in back of the right. For a volley shot that you wish to angle off to your right, punch at the ball a little earlier than for the straight shot and at the same time the back foot should be brought forward. For a shot to your left, you should punch at the ball a fraction later (closer to your body) and the rear foot, if possible, should be a little farther back. The backhand drive volley is played in the same manner as for the forehand style except that the procedure is reversed.

Special effort should always be made to meet the ball at a point higher than the net whenever possible. A volley becomes more defensive than aggressive when struck from lower down, as in that case the ball must be lifted back over the net, and this robs it of its attacking power. Actually, the low volley, especially one just a few inches above the court, should be employed only when it is impossible to play the ball off the ground (after the bounce). Low volleying is a purely defensive weapon and, unless perfectly played, is rarely effective even as good defense since the stroke all too often results in a pop-up. This, of course, gives your opponent a chance for a kill.

Regarding the placing of volleys, everything depends on the position of the antagonist. First, the volley should always be deep back into the other court, unless a short stroke is certain to end the rally. To let the opponent reach the ball in close to you spells disaster every time, for the volleyer has very little time to prepare for his stroke under the most favorable conditions, and, if the opponent is close to him, this will be so short that he must often miss the stroke from lack of time to swing on the ball even though it comes straight at him.

The unexpected point is always the best attack against the opponent, but, other things being equal, the extreme left-hand corner is perhaps the most vulnerable spot. From that position it is most difficult to pass a volleyer at the net, and this offers the most profitable point for attack, as a rule.

But there are other considerations than power of attack. Often a volleyer himself is in trouble and needs defense. He may be hard pressed, jumping from side to side so fast that he is in imminent danger of being passed on the next play. Then the middle of the court is the safest place to direct a volley stroke. From the middle of the court, the opponent will find the angles for passing more difficult than from the sides, and a deep volley down the center of the court to near his base line is generally a safe return. The ball can be directed best with the swing of the arm, but the wrist also can be bent slightly and deflect the ball to one side or the other at will. Some good players swing the whole body around to place a ball across the court on the volley, but this style generally defeats its own object by showing the opponent which way the ball is going.

Smashing and Overhead Volleying. The distinction between overhead volleying, or smash-

How to smash.

ing, and the horizontal volley lies chiefly in the angle at which the ball is taken. For these strokes the ball is met higher up and driven downward. With the head of the racket above the arm and shoulder, ready to meet a dropping ball, the stroke is completely altered from that used in horizontal strokes, and even more closely resembles the blow of a woodsman's ax than the service.

There is much more freedom in this position, and a longer swing and follow-through are permitted. For the smash the player can put all his power in the stroke and hit the ball as hard as he is able. The horizontal volley is apt to be a cramped, punched stroke, while overhead the play is freedom itself.

The smash is primarily a killing stroke. It is intended to end the rally every time, and the player, if he is fairly close to the net, calculates, as a rule, that he will be able to kill the ball with that stroke. He does not expect another return and the smash is therefore played with great abandon. Some players even lose their balance at the end of the stroke and make little or no effort to recover position to be ready for another, in case the unexpected should happen and the adversary return the ball they intended to kill. These are poor tactics, however, and dangerous always.

The smash is a stroke that is properly used only on a lob, for no other return provides the dropping lifeless ball needed for its execution. On a short lob, that is, a ball that falls within 12 or 15 feet of the net, the risk of error is small, and even this risk decreases rapidly as the distance to the net is lessened. When within 10 feet of the net, it is always safe to hit the ball hard, and when so close as this it is seldom difficult to earn a clean ace by smashing the ball right "through" the other man.

The deeper the ball to be smashed, the more difficult it is to handle, the danger of missing increasing very rapidly, and when a lob drops back of the service line, it depends entirely on the individual skill of the player whether it's better to smash than to volley the return. To ease up on a smash generally results in ruining the stroke. If the full power and speed cannot be risked, it is generally better to change the stroke to a volley and wait for a better opening for the attempt to kill.

Making the smash requires the fullest action possible. The racket should start well behind the back with a full backswing, and come forward with rapidly increasing energy, striking the ball with a sharp impact. The entire body weight should be thrown into the blow, and there should be a full body swing and follow-through to add to the power of the stroke. No other stroke of the game is played so "wide open," for as this shot is expected to end the rally nine times out of ten, the attitude is one of finality that permits the player to literally throw himself at the ball regardless of what may follow.

The ball should always be met with an "open" racket, that is, with the full face of the stringing exposed, the face being at right angles to the direction of the ball, and it is essential that the ball should be struck in the center of the strings. Twist is almost unnecessary, although some players have an inclination to wrap the racket around the ball slightly, as in the service, and this has a tendency to keep the ball somewhat better under control.

The position of the player for a smash or an overhead volley is very important. He must be directly under the ball for a smash, and nearly as far forward for the volley. Nothing will ruin an otherwise good smash so quickly as to stand too far back for the ball. As in the service, this position is almost sure to bring it down into the net instead of over into the adversary's court.

For a hard smash, the player should stand so directly under the ball that, if he should miss it, the ball would fall on his head, but the whole body should be bent somewhat forward so the head would be slightly in front of the rest of the body. For a less severe volley, the ball can be slightly in front of the player's position, but under no circumstances should it be forward enough to make him reach out far for it. This is a fault that is almost certain to bring failure.

One of the most common mistakes of beginners is to try to smash every high ball that they can reach. The smash is a stroke that is used far more than is necessary, both because it wastes the player's strength and because it often entails an unnecessary risk. Hosts of overhead balls, even short lobs at the net, can be killed quite as effectually with a well-directed volley as by a smash, and this stroke results in many less errors.

It is a safe rule to remember, when you have a dropping ball to handle, that it should be smashed only when you feel certain that you will not miss the shot. If the player is off to one side of the court, even then it is not necessary, as a sharp volley to the other side will be just as effective and more easily made.

If the opponent is close to you, play the ball straight at him fast and he will have little or no chance of returning it, but if he is at the back of his court and ready for a ball in the center, smash to the edges if you feel sure of the stroke, or volley off to one side. As mentioned earlier, on a deep lob, the smash is almost always dangerous, and a deep volleyed return will generally give you another chance at the ball, with perhaps better chances for success on a shorter return. The player who takes few risks with deep lobs and patiently waits for an easy ball to kill generally wins out in the end, while the dashing swashbuckler who wants to bury every ball in the ground is always found among the losers.

In some cases, the overhead smash can be

The low forehand volley stroke from the anticipatory position to the point of impact.

a ground stroke. That is, it can be executed when a ball bounces high in the air. The mechanics of this smash is the same as the overhead volley smash just described.

The overhead volley of a horizontal ball calls for a full swing, a sharp impact with less twist than any other stroke of the game (unless it be the lob), and a medium follow-through. The success of the shot depends more on direction than the mere execution of the play. It is an easy stroke to make and not difficult to direct. If the adversary has left an opening, it should afford an ace on the next play, but if he is well covered up and the ball is over the center of the net, a deep volley into one corner will often open up the way for a clean ace on the next return. This stroke is so simple and affords so many chances to kill that the experienced player seldom offers his opponent such an opening.

Overhead volley strokes are made with much the same motions as the smash, except with less speed or abandon and with more caution to control the ball. That is, you will lessen the backswing, and stop the racket

behind the head, hitting with a slower motion. Sometimes a slight bevel on the face of the racket, to overcome the dropping angle of the ball, will lessen the danger of missing from far back in the court. Also the finish differs slightly. With the overhead volley, the racket is stopped out in front of the player, about opposite the waist as a rule, and it is quickly recovered at the finish to a safe position for the next stroke, no matter what may come. For the smash, remember that the racket is allowed to follow after the ball as far as it will go and generally ends close to the ground at the end of the swing.

The Lob Volley. The lob volley, in which the ball is pushed up over the head of your opponent at the net, is another very useful variant of the volley, especially in doubles. It is not, however, easy to play. It must obviously be made sufficiently high to be sure of being out of your opponent's reach, and at the same time sufficiently fast to make it impossible for him to get back in time to take it off the ground. Otherwise he gets an easy smash.

The low backhand volley stroke from the anticipatory position to the point of impact.

The forehand stop-volley stroke from the backswing to the completed follow-through.

Since this lob shot is usually played in much the same manner as the low volley shots (both forehand and backhand), all instructions for these strokes (see page 115) apply here. The only major difference is that in the case of the lob volley, the racket face is opened to a greater angle. You still need the same backspin to control the ball but there is little or no follow-through necessary. The weight should be on the forward foot at impact.

The Stop Volley. The stop volley (also called a *drop volley*) is another very effective form of the volley. It is a volley stroke, hit either forehand or backhand, in which the ball barely drops over the net. To execute it, you should be right up to the net. Hold your racket upright, and, just as the ball comes to it, move it either upward, with a dragging action, or downward, with a digging action. However fast the ball is coming to you it will drop quietly, very dead, just over the net.

Indeed, the harder your opponent's drive, the more effective the stop volley. Fingers and wrist, here again, must be very delicately employed. Actually, the stop volley's aim is to keep the ball away from your opponent. Its success depends on the deftness and delicacy of your touch. At impact, the wrist should be loose and flexible. The purpose is to stop the flight of the oncoming ball and to drop it just over the net with a minimum bounce. While it is a rather simple stroke and is fairly easy to perform, there is considerable danger that the return will either fail to clear the net or go too far over; in the latter case your opponent will return it and either pass or lob you, leaving you standing helpless at the net.

The Drop Shot. This shot closely resembles the stop volley, but it is a ground stroke (see page 103). While its execution is much the same, it is very much more difficult to make. It requires greater delicacy of touch than any

The forehand drop shot from the anticipatory position to the completed follow-through.

other stroke in tennis, and the faster the ball approaches the more difficult it is to make. Its success depends on your ability to hit the ball with considerable backspin and just enough forward motion to clear the net.

To accomplish this, the racket is held loosely and its forward motion results from a flick of the wrist. The face of the racket should be opened at an angle of 45 degrees or more from the vertical—the forward part of the rim being the lowest part of the racket face. The racket moves downward as well as forward, the downward motion being about equal to the forward motion. No follow-through is needed. The result of this stroke is a miniature lob with plenty of backspin. Because of the lower bounce, drop shots are much more effective on grass than on a hard or fast court.

A drop shot should be used only when made from a position inside the service line and a stop volley only when practically on

The forehand half-volley stroke from the anticipatory position to the completed follow-through.

The backhand half-volley stroke from the backswing to the completed follow-through.

top of the net; and in both cases only when your opponent is very deep or so hopelessly out of position that he has no chance whatsoever to retrieve the return. If he can reach and return either shot, you will both be so close to the net that your court will be wide open and the point very likely his. To be most effective, both the stop volley and drop shot should be disguised to resemble something else. For example, the stop volley should be masked as a drive volley, while the drop shot's preparation should be made to resemble that of a forehand or backhand drive.

The Half Volley. The half volley is, technically, also a ground stroke, the ball being hit when it has only risen an inch or two from the ground. It is usually a defensive stroke used either when you are caught out of position or against balls that bounce at your feet. As you have so little time in which to make the stroke, it is a rather difficult shot to play. The half volley may be hit either forehand or backhand.

The technique of the half-volley stroke (sometimes called a *pickup shot*) is very much the same as that for the low volley; that is, the same grip, same stance, and a short backswing are employed, with short follow-through. Since the ball is played near the ground and very soon after it has bounced, you should bend from the knees and waist to keep the wrist stiff and the racket head from hitting the ground. The ball should not be stroked but should merely be blocked by placing the head of the racket a foot or so behind the point at which you judge it will hit the ground; the momentum of the ball provides the power for the return. While on a

few occasions the racket face should be open as in a low volley, the majority of the time the ball should be hit with a closed-face racket. (This means the racket face is tilted forward at the top, producing a natural overspin or topspin.)

The closing of the racket face is not a wrist action, but rather it is a rolling over of the entire arm in the same manner as for the forehand drive. This rolling over is very important since if you do not do it, the ball will sail out of court, while if you just move your wrist, the ball will probably end up in the net. The impact point should be slightly ahead of your forward foot, but often you will be caught without time to place your body correctly. At these times the ball still is met out in front of the body, but to the side. Keep your head down as the racket follows through on its up-and-over course. This will steer the ball where you want it to go.

It is a most important consideration in lawn tennis to keep the eye on the ball until it has left the racket, and never to make strokes with the body too erect, the follow-through being better accomplished with a slight leaning of the body with the stroke. In the half volley, the follow-through is a quicker process than in ordinary ground strokes.

The Service Stroke

The service, as previously mentioned, is the stroke used in putting the ball in play. It is the only stroke in tennis in which the player has complete control over the ball—as well as the only shot made which the ability of your opponent does not affect. Thus, it is a wise player who takes full advantage of his serve. For instance, a good service immediately puts your opponent (the receiver) on the defensive by forcing him out of position or playing to his weakness. This gives you the opportunity to obtain the maximum benefit from the rest of your shots. Remember that if you always win your service games, you never will lose a set or a match.

There are, however, many varieties of the service stroke, and no two of the best players use *exactly* the same style of delivery. More than any other stroke of the game, the mechanics of this particular play are left almost entirely to the individuality of the player himself. It opens up a lot of possibilities for this service stroke, to be told simply that you may stand at almost any point you please behind the base line and hit a ball into the opposite court in any way you please, when you please.

One has time to wait and think out his motions before he hits the ball, and his originality has much more chance for play here than in the heat of battle where the action is much faster, with less time to think of the stroke. It is very evident that many players have put their minds on this problem and with varying results that have developed many kinds of deliveries. But in spite of this fact, there are three principal types of service: the slice; the American twist; and the flat serve, or cannonball. All three follow the same basic techniques of grip, stance, and delivery, but vary in how the racket head strikes the ball and in the follow-through.

The service stroke itself is usually a long, free, rhythmic swing in a continuous motion. It is similar, to a degree, to that of the overhead volley stroke. Like the other strokes of tennis, the service requisites are good footwork, smooth body action, and correct method of hitting the ball. All of the very good servers follow closely the same set of fundamentals.

The Grip. The grip for the service is again a matter of individual preference. Most experts, however, seem to prefer the Continental grip. But, for the beginner it is usually best to use the same grip that he uses for the forehand drive stroke. After he has learned to make his toss and delivery correctly, and has gotten his timing, he can try the Continental serving grip.

The major difference between the modified Continental serving grip and the basic Continental is that the fingers are spread out more, the forefinger extending up the handle like a trigger finger. This permits more flexibility of the wrist, which is necessary to impart the various spins employed in serving.

The Stance. In taking the proper readiness position for the service, the left foot should be forward and about 3 to 6 inches behind the base line. The angle of the left foot depends on the individual. Most professional tennis instructors believe that the best form is to place the toe so that a slight pivot in serving will bring the foot around to a position perpendicular to the net. The right foot should be 12 to 18 inches behind the left, depending on the height of the player, and approximately parallel to the base line. In this position, an imaginary line drawn across the toes of both feet should point in the direction the ball will travel; thus, for serving into the opponent's right service court, the left foot should be drawn back slightly from the right foot, and vice versa when serving into the left court. (This is a right-handed world, and left-handers, as usual, will have to adjust accordingly.)

To complete the readiness position for a serve, hold the racket out toward the net so that your wrist is at approximately chest level and the racket head is about level with the face. The left hand should hold the balls. Be sure that the stance is comfortable and the body is as relaxed as possible in a position that is sideways to the net. The left shoulder should be directed toward the court into which the service is to be made. The weight is evenly distributed on the toes at the beginning of the stroke. As the toss is made and the backswing started, the weight falls back on the right foot. The forward swing brings all the weight rhythmically into the ball and onto the toes of the left foot. This is exactly the same procedure that a pitcher goes through in throwing a baseball. The serve is a combined arm and body swing.

When serving, remember that you play the first point from the right of the center mark and serve the ball diagonally across the court to your left into the opponent's right service court. The next point is served from the left of the center mark into your opponent's left service court, and then alternately right and left until the game is finished. While the tennis rules say that you can stand anywhere between the center mark and side line, the base of all good servers is near the center mark. (About 1 to 3 feet to the side of it, behind the base line, of course, is a good distance for the beginner.) The server who stands at a distance from the center mark leaves too much of the court open into which the opponent can place the return of the service.

It is very important for a beginner to avoid the error of foot-faulting. The player must keep the left foot behind the base line. He must not swing his right foot over the line before he hits the ball. Many fine players have had great trouble breaking themselves of the foot-fault habit. A serve illegally delivered is just as much a fault according to the rules as a ball hit outside the service court. The causes of foot-faulting are much easier to correct at the time the serve is being learned than afterward.

The Ball Toss. To serve, the ball is tossed into the air and hit. But throwing the ball consistently in the same place and at the same height requires practice and, to make it even more difficult, you have to swing your racket at the same time. The ball is held in the fleshy parts of the fingers. It is customary to hold two balls—the second ready for use if the first service is a fault or a let. (Some players

The method of holding the balls for a serve.

even hold three balls.) This second ball should be held between the ring and little fingers and the lower fleshy part of the thumb. The other ball is held between the first two fingers and the thumb.

The ball should be released by opening the first two fingers and thumb when the arm is slightly above shoulder height. For better control of the ball, toss with relaxed fingers and thumb, not the palm, and let the hand follow through after it has been released. The upward motion of the arm should have sufficient momentum to send the ball above the right eye, high enough for a comfortable reach with a fully extended arm, and enough to enable you to hit it as it starts to drop. To establish that height for yourself, hold the racket straight up above your shoulder with your arm bent at the elbow only enough to be comfortable. Now, toss one ball up just to the top of the racket, so that, if allowed to fall to the ground, it hits just off the point of your forward toe. Remember that it is much better to toss the ball too high and be able to hit it as it falls, than to toss it too low and hit it with the edge of the racket or miss it altogether.

Practice the toss both for proper height and direction for a while without hitting the ball. To check the toss direction, place the racket on the ground directly in front of the left foot. Then as you toss the ball to the proper hitting height, let it drop to see if it drops directly on the face of the racket on the ground. Many beginners toss the ball either too far behind them or too far toward the net. In order to reach a ball in the latter case without falling forward, the player swings his leg around and the foot passes over the base line before impact. When the ball is too far behind, the smooth rhythm so necessary in a serve cannot be obtained, resulting in a poor stroke. Remember that if you do not think your toss is straight to the point where you want it, you do not have to hit the ball. You can allow it to fall, catch it, and start your toss again.

The Swing. You should start your toss and backswing at the same time. To accomplish this easily, the two hands should be close together at the start in a position in front of the waist. As the left hand goes up, the right takes the racket down and backward to a point where the arm is completely extended.

After the racket has reached this low ebb, it is brought up with increasing momentum to perform a loop behind the head. From this loop the forward swing is made and the ball is hit. That is, from the serving readiness position, swing the left arm downward against the left thigh and, at the same time, draw the right arm down so that the racket head swings close to the body, past the right knee, over the shoe tops, and then backward away from the net. As it passes the right leg, the wrist will turn outward naturally turning the racket over completely. (You can feel the natural turn outward in the bones of your forearm.) Also as the racket passes the right foot, transfer the weight to the rear (right) foot and raise the heel of the front (left) foot, keeping the toes of the front foot on the ground and the knee slightly bent.

The racket should continue to move backward and upward in a circular arc until its head is about shoulder high, behind you, and pointing away from the net. It is now that the elbow should be bent in almost a 45-degree angle, dropping the racket behind the shoulders in an almost back-scratching position. In this cocked position (the racket behind the back with its head pointing downward toward the ground), keep the elbow, forearm, and both shoulders in direct line with one an-another. This is the point in your swing that you release the ball upward. Remember that the important error to avoid in making the backswing is that of pausing during the procedure. The long swing is necessary to get the weight properly into the ball. Any break in the rhythm of the stroke defeats this purpose.

The upward movement of the left arm starts as the racket head passes the shoe tops. Be sure that the release is smooth—not a jerky pitch—and as the ball leaves the fingers, watch its upward flight very closely. While the ball is traveling upward and after the racket has made a small looping swing behind the back, the wrist and elbow are snapped upward into a fully extended position overhead with the wrist, arm, and racket in line as one long lever. The ball should be overhead and slightly toward the net side of the forward foot. The ball should be hit at arm's length above the head, so that even in the case of a short player, it can be brought down into the service court. At the moment of impact, the top of the racket should be closer to the net than the lower edge or throat. The degree of this angle depends on the individual player. Obviously a very tall man would probably strike the ball with a more pronounced tilt to his racket than a short one. The player must use his own sense of touch. If the majority of his serves tend to find the net, the angle is too abrupt. If the serves tend to have too much length, the reverse holds true.

Actually, beginners often strike the ball in front of the head or off to the side at a height opposite the face, but it is not possible to make a really good service without a higher position to strike from. Hitting too far forward will cause the ball to go into the net, as a rule, while a ball that is hit too far back will more often go out of court by traveling too far over the net.

The forward swing of the racket that makes the actual stroke must be started before the ball reaches the point at which you have calculated to hit it. The wrist begins the movement, starting the racket directly upward, and the elbow next straightens out its bend so that the arm and handle are extended to their full reach by the time the racket approaches the ball. Then the body and shoulder take up the work and the full force of the weight is added to the momentum of the racket so that it is traveling at top speed when the ball is met. Everything depends on great momentum in the racket in order to secure speed in the stroke. But the ball must not be met squarely with the racket, as many beginners are inclined to believe. The overhead service stroke is even more of a glancing blow than the drive ground strokes. The face of the racket should be turned in the hand so that the racket passes outside of the ball, the right edge of the frame, as it appears up in the air, being forward and the other side beveling sharply backward.

As the racket leaves the ball, all the weight of the server's body and all the power of his shoulders are brought to play, so that the ball gains great momentum from the stroke. The speed of the racket pulls the player ahead rapidly, and before the racket can be checked, he is generally forced to take a step forward, even if he does not start at once to run in to the net to volley the next return of the antagonist.

The end of the racket's swing should be far out in front of the left foot and slightly to the right of it—more or less to the right according to the amount of side motion the racket carried to give the ball the spinning motion. The racket should be allowed to swing forward until it nearly touches the ground, and it is a serious mistake that ruins the service to attempt to check the swing at a point much higher than this.

The follow-through is as important in the service as in the ground strokes, and it is with both shoulders and body weight in this last end of the swing that it is most useful. Without the necessary following of the racket, the ball loses both power and speed, and it also becomes more difficult to control its direction accurately.

The feet and legs play a very important function in the swing. The legs maintain your balance while the weight is being shifted first to the back foot and then to the front. The forward thrust of your body will cause your front heel to rise from the ground during the forward swing, and the right foot, once the ball has been struck, should follow it across the base line. Failure to move the right foot into the court during the follow-through handicaps you in recovering your balance in case of a quick return of your service. Also

The slice serve from the ready position to the completed follow-through.

allow the back foot to follow across the base line and into the court so that you can assume the anticipatory position from which you are ready to begin the next stroke. But, when moving your feet, be careful you do not foot-fault.

The swing of a serve should be a long, free, continuous rhythmic motion. Racket arm, ball arm, and body must all be carefully synchronized so that there are no stops or hitches in your swing. Power in the serve comes from your body, your arm, and your wrist—it is the only tennis stroke that employs wrist snap.

The Slice Service. The differences between the three major types of services—slice, flat, and twist—are the way the racket meets the ball at impact and the method of follow-through. The slice service is the simplest to learn and execute and the one that should first be mastered. The ball is tossed slightly to the right of the head and shoulder, and the racket is brought around the outside of the ball and

The flat, or cannonball, service from the ready position to the completed follow-through.

slightly over it. The racket face is beveled slightly to aid the swing in imparting the side spin that adds control and from which the service takes its name. The swing is down and across the body to the left, completing the act of applying the spin to the ball. That is, the racket passes over the upper right-hand surface of the ball as the ball is hit down upon in a right-to-left twist of the racket. The racket must be whipped into the ball with a sharp wrist snap and smooth follow-through. This type of service causes the ball to spin in a sideways direction when it leaves the racket. The sideways spin on the ball makes it curve to the left during its flight in much the same manner as a ball curves in when a pitcher throws it.

In hitting the slice service you rotate the racket slightly during the swing so that its frame is inclined diagonally toward the right side line. This permits your racket strings to hit the ball a glancing blow, cutting across from left to right to get a slight slice that causes the ball to curve downward in its flight. Let the racket follow through down across your body to the left.

The slice service is the easiest to learn, to control, and can be accomplished with the least effort, and most women and beginners use it because it is not too tiring and the ball has plenty of action. When properly controlled, the curve of the sliced ball is downward over the net and to the left, away from the receiver's forehand. This means that your opponent cannot attack or hit an aggressive return of your service. If the spin is too great, of course, the ball will curve out of the service court. But this can be easily compensated for by aiming as far to the right as necessary to adjust for the curve of your service. It does not require too much practice to determine how much curve you actually are getting on your service, and from that point all that is necessary is for you to control it by proper placement.

The Flat Service. The flat, or cannonball, service is a powerhouse delivery and is the one in which the ball blasts down into the receiver's court in an almost straight line. When properly placed, it is very difficult for the receiver to handle. But this serve is a very risky one to employ since it must clear the net cord by at most a few inches or it will land out of court. The margin of safety is very small. Therefore it should only be used occasionally on the first ball and then only by players of well above average height. Actually, the cannonball should be used as a mixer and sparingly. Let the sudden and unexpected blast of this flat serve be employed to catch your opponent off guard and perhaps worry him somewhat. But for most players, this serve is not a percentage shot, which means if you employ it too often you are going to lose your service somewhere along the line.

The flat service is much like the slice service except that the toss is more to the left, but still a bit to the right of the head, and the flat face of the racket is exposed to the ball, as the name of the service implies, rather than a beveled racket face as in the slice or twist service. The follow-through is to the left of the body, about the same as the slice service. This service should be used as a first service only and, if missed, followed by the safer slice or twist service for a second ball.

The Twist Service. The American twist service is the most difficult of all serves to learn, and is probably the toughest and most physically demanding shot in tennis. It definitely is not a service recommended for women. But, once learned, the twist is a good change of pace since the ball curves to the server's left, and bounces toward the receiver's backhand, or away from the direction in which it was curving. The flight of the ball describes a comparatively high arc, allowing the server ample time in which to get set for the return or to reach the net if he desires. This service is usually played to an opponent's backhand, and it is difficult to return effectively because of the excessive spin and the high bounce. This is accomplished by moving the racket upward and across the ball, imparting spin to it, which causes it to bounce high when it lands in the service court.

The American twist service is started the same as the other services, with the weight on the back foot, and the body sideways to the net. In tossing the ball, the body is turned more decidedly until the back is almost turned to the net, the feet remaining in position. The ball is tossed slightly further back and to the left. The weight is handled very much the same as in the other services. It is shifted from the back foot to the front foot. There is a

The twist service from the ready position to the completed follow-through.

greater arch in the back at the most backward point in the back swing. The racket is whipped up from its low position and comes across the inside and left of the ball, and up, imparting the twist to the shot. As the weight is shifted to the front foot, the racket comes through, starts in its downward motion, and finishes down and, in the case of a right hander, to the right of the body instead of to the left of the body as in the slice and flat services. This service has not the speed of the flat or slice service, as a rule, but carries much more spin. There should be much more wrist action in this service than the others, which aids in imparting the great spin necessary to an effective twist service.

Service Strategy. Two services of average speed for first and second delivery are much stronger than one terrific "swipe" and a weak "pop" second delivery. The man who keeps a good average fast pace on his first service has to make less shift in his method of hitting for the second and is less likely to double-fault. The practice of the first delivery also helps him to gauge his error and he is able to keep fair speed on the second ball with less danger of a double fault. In short, the extremely fast first ball is so radically different from an easy second delivery that it does not help the player in gauging his second delivery, and he consequently takes no chances playing close to the net or to the court lines, and makes such an easy service that the ball is frequently killed outright, and generally the attack is turned against him on the next stroke.

Now, having acquired a fairly fast overhead, twist delivery that is well under control, and a second delivery that is of the same style, but just a trifle slower and a trifle higher to be sure of clearing the net, every player should practice both until he is reasonably certain of avoiding the deadly pitfall of double faults. The next point is the control of the direction. This is of the utmost importance, and no style of service should be adopted that does not permit of the most perfect control.

The average player of little experience considers his duty done in serving when the ball is safely delivered into the opponent's court; he does not see the far greater possibilities of attack in placing the service. To be sure, the latitude for placing is small, but there is ample range to outwit the adversary in even the small space allowed, as his time is short in which to shift his position to meet the attack.

Before making the delivery, the position of the adversary should be carefully noted, and the position of his arm and racket to see whether he is anticipating a backhand or a forehand stroke. If you have studied your adversary or are familiar with his play, you may already know his favorite strokes and what his attitudes mean. If he is a better player of forehand than backhand strokes, naturally his weak spot will be on the other side, while the reverse will sometimes be the case. Possibly he will habitually lean in one direction or the other in anticipating the service, to be in position for the stroke he prefers, and this at once should give the signal to place the ball on the opposite side of the court.

When the server is running in to volley, new problems complicate the service that must be taken into consideration. If the receiver is weak on the backhand side, the server should consistently place the service to his backhand side until he finds that it is being anticipated. The receiver may run around the backhand attack to get the ball on his forehand, or he may anticipate this attack by bringing his racket over into position for this return so that he is able to handle it better. Then an occasional service placed to the other extreme edge of the court will bring him back into a normal receiving position again, or possibly win an ace outright by the very unexpectedness of the play.

If the opponent is found to select one direction regularly for his return from a given position, this in itself can be anticipated often with success. For instance, the receiver may cross-court five balls for every one that he plays down the line from a backhand return. In this case, it is well to serve to the backhand and watch for the cross-court return, leaning a little to that side of the center of the court at the risk of the unexpected line pass. Or the opposite may be the case, and can be anticipated similarly.

The center theory is perhaps of more value to the server than at any other point of the play. The most difficult problem the server has to solve is to get to the net safely in order to secure the volleying position. The center theory is more fully covered later in this section on position play, but so far as it refers to the service, it is the principle of placing the service in the center of the court (that is, in the corners of the service courts nearest the center of the whole court) in order to keep the opponent in the center of his court, directly in front of you as you stand at the middle of the net to volley. This shuts off his chances for fast side-line drives, because from the center any fast ball that will pass you must be aimed out of court and a slow ball will give you more time to reach it.

Adopting this center theory, which is most valuable in a volleying net attack, the server should stand all the time very close to the center of his base line to serve. By shifting a yard to the right or left he can serve into the left or right court, and still keep his delivery right down the center by placing each ball close to the dividing line of his opponent's service courts.

Against a right-handed player, this will

bring his backhand presented to the delivery always in the right court and his forehand in the left court. If his backhand is weak, this will make the right court the more productive and the left court always dangerous if his forehand stroke is severe. However, this attack can be varied whenever one finds an opponent is handling these deliveries in an embarrassing manner. If the left-court service is being pounded with a forehand drive that is too fast to handle, an occasional service far out to the adversary's backhand toward the extreme edge of the court will often catch him by surprise, and if it does not score a clean ace will embarrass his return in consequence so that an easy chance for a kill will result.

Often the backhand weakness of an antagonist will make it advisable to work on the center theory only in the right-hand court where it attacks his backhand, and to place the service far to the edge of the court regularly in the left court. In this case the path of the server in running in must be further to his right to cover the dangerous opening along his right side line, unless the opponent has shown a marked tendency to cross-court his backhand returns.

Always keep an opponent guessing and off balance. For example, the first serve may be to the opponent's backhand and the next to his forehand. By using such a strategy, you will play your opponent's strong stroke often enough to prevent him from covering up his weakness. This makes for larger openings on his weak side and permits possible aces, or shots that he cannot reach.

When placing a serve, generally make your opponent move to meet the ball. Occasionally, however, it may be good strategy to serve directly at him, thus throwing him off balance. When planning to play the point near your base line, place the ball near his side line to pull the opponent out of position, thus opening up his court for the return. Serve a flat, fast service only occasionally, as a surprise ace or to keep your opponent from edging in or over too much.

If planning to rush the net after serving the ball, a good forcing serve, one which will enable the server to get beyond his service line before the ball can be returned, is essential. The best serve of this type is one with plenty of spin, which insures control and re-

tards the ball sufficiently in its flight to enable the server to reach the net quickly with the least effort. Either a slice serve with some top-spin or an American twist will permit you to vary your placement, and if you can serve both, your service attack will be greatly strengthened by varying the direction of the break and the height of the bounce. Speaking of the height of the bounce, watch whether your opponent prefers high or low balls. If he handles low-bounding services well, give him a high-bounding American twist serve. If he prefers high-bounding balls, hit a well-placed sliced serve that will bounce low. Do not overdo this strategy and likewise do not rush the net after each serve. Again, keep him guessing.

Regardless of your strategy, serve from the same spot behind the base line. Do not stand close to the center mark one time, and then near the side line the next. Select one spot on either side of center mark (one for serving to the left service court and one for the right), and develop your serve from these spots. The best players generally stand pretty close to the center mark since that puts them in good defensive position for the opponent's return.

The Return of the Serve

The return of serve is the second most important stroke in tennis; only the serve takes priority. Basically it must have consistency, since you are bound to lose every game in which you receive if 50 percent of your returns are errors. Remember that the receiver of service is heavily handicapped by the rules of the game. He is forced to stand back and await the attack of the server. He is forbidden to volley the ball, and his first return must often be made under the disconcerting conditions of an opponent thundering up to the net behind a twisting service that makes the ball curve in the air and bound crooked. This advantage of the server over his opponent in the opening duel is responsible for the records which show that a very large proportion of all games in tournament tennis are won by the side having service.

In order to offset this advantage and to get the ball into general play so that the receiver may get back on even terms with his adversary, every ingenuity of the player must be

How a John Newcombe serve looks to his opponent.

brought into play. But at least he has one thing in his favor, for the server is limited closely in the area that he can use for placing the ball, so the receiver need not move far out of his waiting position in order to reach the ball. For these reasons it is as well, perhaps, to consider the first return as a play in itself and treat it separately from the other ground strokes of the game.

But every precaution must be used to anticipate the service. Even though the service court is small, it is no easy task to cover all of it, and the striker-out should be keyed up to the highest pitch for instant action. The anticipatory, or readiness, position requires the legs spread well apart, the body bent forward from the hips and carried up on the toes, while the racket should be balanced in front, with the idle hand braced against its "throat" so that it can help start the backswing in any direction that the approaching ball requires.

As the forehand is usually the strongest weapon of offense, it should be slightly favored by the receiver. In other words, he should stand a little bit to the left of the center of the service court. This means that the server has a smaller portion of court in which to find his opponent's weakest shot off the ground. It also allows the receiver to run around any slow serves to his backhand, take them on his forehand, and often make a good forcing return.

The distance at which the player stands from the service line to receive depends on several factors. The speed of the service, the amount of spin on the service, the intention of the receiver and the quickness of his reflexes, all have an important bearing on the issue. If the service is of average speed and the ability of the receiver about average, the best position is either on or slightly to either side of the base line.

Against a powerful straight service it is often well to back up slightly. This gives the receiver a little extra time to judge and handle the ball. A service that is sharply angled and carries lots of spin presents a different problem. The ball breaks away from the court and the player. The farther back the receiver stands, the greater amount of court he has to cover. Against this service it is best to stand in closer. If the receiver is keen to take the ball on the rise and make an offensive thrust off each serve, he must also be in closer. Some players prefer to set up a defense against powerful serves by standing in close and blocking the ball back. The reflexes of the individual are his own problem. The individual must experiment in order to estimate the quickness of his own reflexes. When these factors are added together, the receiver usually finds himself anywhere between the base line and a spot 3 or 4 feet in front of it.

Taking the ball on the rise in returning service is a dangerous practice. It is hard to perfect one's timing to master the return of service when there is less time to get properly set. To make matters more difficult, the receiver must line the ball up so that it is on his direct path to the net, as he is usually forced to advance to the net after such a return, in order to cover his court. He would otherwise be badly out of position. He must therefore have both a first-class net game and wonderful anticipation to use this style of taking the ball on the rise successfully.

There are several advantages to the procedure, including a certain psychological edge over the server. He feels that he must make harder and better-placed deliveries to maintain the offensive. A net-rushing server, for instance, is constantly hurrying to get in to the net to keep from having to handle shots at his feet.

On the other side of the picture, we find that this policy results in more errors and bad positions on the part of the receiver. Although often giving a player a brilliant attack, it can also result in the exact opposite, making for inconsistency. Most teaching professionals' advice is to take the ball at the top of the bounce until the return is consistent. Then possibly learn to play it on the rise occasionally for the psychological effect on the opponent, if for nothing else.

Most players use a safer method of delivery on their second serve. This may take the form either of less pace or a greater amount of spin. The receiver, therefore, has a better chance to take over the offensive on the easier second serve. If you move in closer, this usually will worry the server a little and enable you to get to the net quicker, should you succeed in making a forcing return.

When the serve is placed well out of the reach of the receiver, he is often forced into some mad scrambling to retrieve it. Some exponents of the game are in favor of a jump or lunge to cover the necessary distance. In most cases, however, it is best to keep both feet on the ground and run or slide and stretch to get the shot. When you lunge or jump, you are apt to destroy your sense of balance.

Actually, when considering the best method of handling a service, it is necessary to examine the matter in two different situations: first, when the server runs up to the net, and second, when he does not. Against the volleyer, who is fast on his feet and well settled in position to handle the first return, the receiver has four plays open to him. He can pass down the line, he can pass across the court, he can lob over the server's head to drive him back, or he can drive toward the adversary with a low dropping stroke that is kept close to the net or drops soon after crossing it so that it leaves no chance for a killing volley.

The pass down the line is always easier (for a right-handed player) in the right court, where his forehand drive can be brought into play. If the service is directed toward the edge of the court, this stroke will generally offer the best chance, for the cross-court pass is

then more difficult and the line more open for attack. For a player with a fine control of the backhand drive, the line pass is also open in the left court when the service comes toward the side.

But when the server works on the center theory, or, without that plan of action, keeps his service well centered, the line pass is not open for a fast ball, and is more difficult for a slow ball.

From the center of the court, the dropping ball is often the best attack against a good smasher to whom it is dangerous to lob. The cross-court shot can be played slow from the center to either side, but the receiver is always in trouble against a fast server who centers his service and closes the alleys to attack from a pass up the side lines.

Occasionally, a short cross-court pass will be found very useful from the outside edge across in front of the server as he runs up to volley. A return from a wide position allows a sharper angle and more speed because of the greater distance the ball must travel, and while difficult to execute, it is a most valuable attack for occasional use. This shot should not be played often because it will give the server an easy chance to kill if he is able to anticipate it and lean toward the cross-court position to intercept it. Your own position at the side of the court will make it impossible for you to defend against his volley and the court will be open to him; such a shot must win outright or not at all.

But another side of this stroke is its value as a surprise and to keep the volleyer in the center of the court. If the cross-court return of service is never used, an experienced server will find it easy to direct his attack to the far edge of your service court and lean toward the same side to intercept your attempts at passing along the side lines. Then it is that the cross-court shot is most valuable, and one or two successes with this stroke will bring him back to his correct position and give you an even chance once more for the line pass, unless he centers his service.

If you fail to find the necessary opening for any passing shot, a dropping ball down the center of the court will make the volleyer block the ball upward again over the net, if you succeed in making it low enough and drop quickly enough for the purpose. Your second shot may offer a better chance for a winning pass, and often does. At least it brings the striker back on more nearly even terms with the server if the latter does not make a very aggressive stroke from such a return of his service.

The lob is often a good answer to a difficult service, and varied with passing strokes or drop strokes at the feet of the server, it is doubly valuable. To lob regularly to a server is to court destruction, for he will soon be able to anticipate the shot and then only the deepest and straightest dropping balls will not be killed; even they are likely to be volleyed back so deep as to drive you out of court to handle them. But worked occasionally with the other variations, the lobbing return has a tendency to keep the server from coming in close, which opens up his position in turn for the dropping attack. Particularly is this valuable from the extreme left of the left service court, where the backhand is attacked, and the server is running up diagonally to meet the return. A lob diagonally to his backhand corner then will be very difficult for him to reach, and may make him turn and give you the attack.

Lobbing the service is generally better toward the end of a hard match, rather than at the start when the adversary is fresh and strong. When he begins to show signs of fatigue, particularly if you are stronger than he at the end, a lobbing attack generally produces good results. Perhaps the most dangerous lob of all for the server is one that is made with the same motion used in playing a passing stroke. It is quite possible to swing the arm forward as though to drive the ball, and turn it at the last instant and lob with the face of the racket beveled back. The server is almost certain to lunge forward, if this stroke is concealed well, in order to volley the next stroke, and he will then be caught off his balance for a probable ace.

The server who remains on the base line presents a different problem. The receiver has more of an opportunity to put the ball in play and to bide his time to go to the net. As a general rule, the return should be a deep, well-placed shot, usually to the weaker side of the server. In this way, he may be forced into making a shot which offers a better opportunity for a sally to the net than his service

did. Against a base-liner, as well, the returns must be varied; no set program is practical.

The best way to cope with a base-liner is either to attack from the net or draw him in to it. The former practice is usually considered best for most players but it often pays to refrain from becoming overanxious to attack. It is best to rally with your opponent until he makes a shot well inside the base line. The tactics must depend on the soundness of the server in the different departments. Sometimes, in the case of a player whose serve is less severe, it is better to try the forcing shot from the service return, as that is more apt to be an easier shot than would result from a base-line exchange.

Whatever method the receiver uses, he should remember to mix his shots, and confuse and surprise his opponent whenever possible. Make the server run, and by all means take the offensive away from him at every opportunity.

Changing and Correcting a Stroke

The only time to change a stroke is when it will not do the job. This is not something to be done lightly; no matter how grooved the new stroke becomes, you may lapse back into old habits as soon as the stroke is put under pressure. As a result, you may end up with a new stroke that is even worse than the old one.

The only reasons for altering a grooved stroke are: (1) you cannot be consistent with the old one; (2) you have no control with it; or (3) it lacks power. Since a change must be made, make the change as simple as possible. In the case of ground strokes, stick with your old grip. Do not throw away a Western forehand just because a group of Continental stylists regard it disparagingly, and do not switch from Continental to Eastern simply because the Eastern is the thing to do. It is reasonably easy to make a service or volley grip change; it is almost impossible for most players to make a successful forehand ground-stroke alteration.

The best way to change a stroke is to understand what you have been doing and why it has prevented you from hitting the ball in court consistently, with control or with power. If you do not understand where your stroke has failed you, the transformation will be that much harder. But if, for example, you can see that you have closed the face of your racket and that therefore too many balls have been netted, it will be easier to learn to open it. You do not then need a complete new stroke; you simply concentrate on an exaggerated "open" racket face.

Never change a stroke just because someone says it does not look right. Some of the greatest strokes in the game have been the most unorthodox. No one ever had a less classical backhand volley than Jean Borotra, but no one ever hit it better or harder. Do not change a topspin backhand to an undercut; a pretty but ineffectual one—unless your ideal is to look good while losing. The criterion for changing a stroke is: lack of consistency, control, or power.

Never change a natural sidespin forehand to topspin. You can, if you wish, add a topspin forehand to your repertoire. Never change an awkward but effective stroke to you can acquire underspin as an additional shot to your game. Do not throw all your strokes out the window because they are "different." If they are preventing you from improving, alter them only as necessary.

Take the case of the player who hits the ball with so much wrist action that his timing has to be perfect. If he has a good edge and if he practices regularly, the stroke may be eminently satisfactory for him. He should not change it simply because it is wristy. However, if he feels his timing will never be good enough to handle such a stroke with consistency, he can decide to eliminate some of the wrist and to hold the face of the racket on the ball a little longer. His own understanding of the situation makes it that much easier to handle the transformation.

The pro who automatically alters a pupil's strokes simply because he is not conforming to the pro's ideas is performing an action that boosts his own ego but does not necessarily help his pupil. With pupils who are not yet grooved, changes are easy, but with those who have played regularly for one or two years or more, any major alterations are traumatic and should only be made after long and careful deliberation. This is not to say a pro should not make any number of minor changes such as cutting down the backswing or follow-through, teaching better balance, the bending

of the knees, a wider stance, or hitting the ball on the top of the bounce, on the rise, or further in front of the body. The major changes on ground strokes are a different grip, windup, wrist action, and spin. When the position of arm and/or wrist and/or racket with regard to the ball is changed, the transformation must be major.

A player with a weak service or a tendency to double-fault should analyze what he has before throwing away the whole action. The fault may lie in the toss or in poor transference of weight. If the fewest possible changes are made, the player can accomplish them without too much difficulty. Adding slice to a serve is relatively easy; changing the entire windup is extremely difficult. It is not, "How much of my stroke can I toss out?" but, "How much can I retain?"

When a service is unsound in every department but the player is grooved in his serving, the changes should be made gradually. One cannot in one hour learn a new toss, transference of weight, windup, hit, and follow-through. At least two things will go wrong every time because with each serve the player must concentrate on five different ideas. If, therefore, the player can keep his old windup, no matter how strange it looks, he may be able to acquire a better serve by making only one or two changes—and there will be less likelihood of the whole action falling apart.

The beginners and the intermediates (and very often the advanced players) do not know what they want in the way of a stroke. Too often a player thinks he would like to "hit hard and look good," but when he starts playing in top tournament level, he wants a lot less and a lot more—he will skip the looks and much of the pace to go for steadiness and control. He finds that points are won on the other fellow's errors, that a classical game can be beaten by an unorthodox one, and that there is more to the game than just strokes.

Whether the new stroke means a complete overhaul of the old one or two adjustments only, the same formula is used in discarding past reflexes and learning new ones. First, the player must understand what he has been doing and more important, what he is now trying to do. He must be willing to give ample time to the learning process, he must not expect to acquire the new stroke in one day, one week, or one month, and he must never revert back to the old habit. In other words, he must be mentally attuned to the program.

Second, he must learn to perform the stroke (or that segment of the stroke which he is learning) without a ball—i.e., in front of a mirror or, if he has professional help, to the satisfaction of his coach. If he cannot execute the stroke well without a ball, how can he do it well with one? The beginner will work on one phase of the stroke only; the advanced player has a less difficult job, although "unlearning" can be as frustrating as learning.

Third, the player now tests his stroke with a ball, but in the simplest possible manner. If it is a forehand, he learns to play it by dropping a ball and then hitting it or by having a coach or friend "feed" him balls. Once the concept is firmly set in his mind, he can utilize the backboard to best advantage. He practices the stroke itself, with the emphasis not on getting the ball back or on hitting it hard but on memorizing a process.

Fourth, once the new stroke is firmly estab-lished, the player can rally with anyone or play sets against those players who will not "press" his newly acquired series of habits; the weaker the opposition, the more confidence he achieves in his new weapon and the less likely he is to revert to the old stroke.

Fifth, when the new stroke appears to "work" against lesser players, he can test it out against a better, more forceful caliber of opposition. But the player must have the right mental outlook; he is practicing and learning, and the emphasis should be on hitting the new stroke properly, not on winning.

Sixth, when the new stroke is an integral part of the player's repertoire, the intermediate or advanced player is ready to use it in tournaments. This can take anywhere from 3 months to 6 months, provided the player has been practicing regularly and conscientiously. The novice or beginner can also enter tournaments in his own classification; his game is far from polished, but when segments of his stroke are grooved, he also is ready to use them in competition.

COURT TACTICS AND STRATEGY

The game of lawn tennis combines the skill in execution of the shots with a good deal of thinking on the part of the player. This thinking has to do with where the ball should be hit, how it should be hit, and from what position in the court it should be played. Strokes are not sufficient, by themselves, to produce top-grade tennis. Many players possessing beautiful stroke production are constantly defeated by opponents who are distinctly inferior in this department. To enjoy the most success a player must arrive at a combination of good stroke production and good court tactics.

The subject of court tactics cannot be dismissed with a fixed set of rules and regulations. Instead, the player must consider the different possibilities and organize them as he sees fit. He must use standard strokes, but must vary the depth and pace of his shots in order to enjoy the most success. The game has progressed so much in the last decade that the player must be able to apply these fundamentals from any position in the court. For this reason, the all-court style of play is the only one that completely fills the bill. I would advise the young player to set this as his goal. A game built on base-line play or on net-rushing tactics alone can be broken up by an expert strategist. On the other hand, an all-court game keeps the opponent guessing.

Player Position and the Placement of the Ball

The very foundation of court tactics is to play a purposeful game. You should determine before each stroke whether you are going to try to win a point, or whether you are merely keeping the ball in play and returning a defensive stroke so as to get yourself in better position. Purposeless tennis is the cause of much grief. The player should not strive for a forcing shot or winner on every return. As a matter of fact, he should not strive for this unless and until he is able satisfactorily to get himself into position to reasonably expect a placement, or unless he is striving to pull his opponent out of position for a point shot later.

Perhaps the most important theory of purposeful position play was first laid down by Wilfred Balleley of England in the book which he wrote on the game in the 1890's, when he and his brother were at the height of their fame. This is: The part of the court which lies between the base line and the service line is "forbidden territory." You ought never to come to rest in it; it should only be used as a means either of getting up to the net from the base line, or of getting back behind the base line from the net. If you take up your position, either for attack or defense, in the "forbidden territory," it is long odds that you will lose the ace against an opponent of equal stroke-playing capability. Your opponent will either drive hard at your feet—the most difficult stroke of all to return —or, more probably, drive right past you so deep that you will be unable to get back in time to reach the ball; and even if you do, you will be trying to return it over a net from which you are running away—an almost hopeless endeavor. Against a better player you are never likely to win an ace at all in that position. Do not stop there. There are two purposeful places from which you should conduct your campaign. One is the volleying position—the position of attack—for which you should always be between the net and the service line, and as near the net as you can get. The other is the ground-stroke position— the position of defense—for which you should always be behind the base line. If you should be drawn into the "forbidden territory" to make a stroke, leave it instantly the stroke is made, to regain either the net or the base-line position, according to whether you see opportunity for attack or recognize that you must act on the defensive.

After the service has been delivered, the server may run in to volley the next return of his opponent, or he may stay back and wait to play it after the bound. The latter method is much the better until a considerable degree of skill has been gained. If one runs in, he must be prepared to jump very quickly to the right or the left to intercept a wide return, and he must be able to hit on the run, for there will be no time when volleying at the net to get set for the stroke or to deliberate long on which stroke to play.

But whether you decide to run in or stay back, remember the "forbidden territory"

rule just given: Go all the way in or stay all the way back. Do not hesitate half way in the matter, for nothing is more deadly than to be caught part of the way up toward the net and meet the ball at your feet. As was stated, this general rule applies to all strokes in the game. After each stroke that you have made, either stay back at the base line or run all the way in to within 10 or 15 feet of the net. Against an opponent who drives a swift ball, it is better to stay well behind the base line in awaiting the next return, for you can get better force in your stroke if you are moving forward to meet the ball when you hit it than if you stand still or move backward.

Expert players often stand 10 feet outside the court at the back awaiting the fast drives of their adversaries, and when they do run in to volley, go up to within 6 or 8 feet of the net. To be caught half-way back means that you must volley a dropping ball, which is much more difficult to play than one flying horizontally over the net, and you must also hit it harder and further in your volleyed return.

Sidewise also, one must be very careful not to be caught in the wrong position, as this will offer the adversary a fine opening to place the ball out of your reach with his next stroke. If you have to run over to one side of the court to make a stroke, you should immediately return to the center (of the base line, not of the whole court itself) to be ready for the next return no matter where it may be placed.

Establish a base of operations in your mind, and after each play return to this central base without waiting to watch the result of your shot. If you hesitate, the delay may prove fatal, and the next return be placed far to the other side before you will have time to recover and reach the ball.

If you are volleying at the net, there is the same necessity to return to the center of the court near the net and ready for the next volley. If smashing and drawn back for a lob, the instant it has been hit, you must return to the volleying position near the net or retire to the base line for defensive play, else the next ball may be driven at your feet and the point lost. The most difficult returns of all are those that must be made when the ball strikes close to the feet.

In any case, one must take into consideration the position of the adversary, for if he has been drawn off far to one side you will be in more danger of being "passed" on that side than the other, and the "playing center" will be a little away from the actual center of the court. At the net this is even more important than at the base line, but there too some allowance must be made for the adversary's position when he is hitting the ball. If the opponent is far off to your right, move a little over toward this side of the court, and vice versa if he is off at your left. This can easily be overdone, however, and tempts the other man to try a short cross-court passing shot that will be a sure winner if it is successful. The sharply angled return is more difficult to reach, and the difficulty is added to if you are caught standing off at one side of the court, particularly if you happen to be at the same side as the player.

The return of service is almost invariably made from one side or the other of the court, as the server is by law required to serve somewhat diagonally and often does exaggerate this to a sharp angle to draw you out of position. The instant this first stroke has been made, the player should run to the center of the court to await the next return, and here again the playing position should be planned in advance, either at the back of the court or at the net. There are few chances to take the net position, however, immediately after the first return.

If the server is running up behind his service to volley the first return, as is sometimes the case, it is dangerous to return far back of the base line, because from the net position it is quite possible for him to play a stop volley, as its bound is almost always low. With the opponent at the net, it is doubly important to keep well up on the toes and ready for an instant start.

You must use good judgment in going to the net; for no matter how good you may be at the volley and smash, your net attack will fail if you give your opponent a setup. If, for example, the drive which you follow in is soft, short, and high-bouncing, you will almost certainly be passed. If you drive a very fast, flat ball or if you start to run in from far behind your base line, you will not be able to get beyond your service line, and you will

then give your opponent an excellent opportunity to drive the ball at your feet, forcing you to half-volley or to low-volley, thus enabling him to pass you on his next return. As a general rule, follow in the return if driving from inside the base line; stay back when driving from behind your base line.

To reach a volleying position quickly and safely, it is generally wise to play a forcing stroke. Do not confuse an ace with a forcing stroke, however. If you get a setup or if your opponent is out of position, drive hard to a corner for an ace. But if he is in position, play a forcing shot: drive deep to the center of his court with some topspin, not too close to the net cord, and follow in without hesitation. The object here is not to win the point outright, as it would be with a clean ace, but to force the opponent to make a comparatively weak return which can be volleyed or smashed. By driving deep to the center of his court, the possibility of an opponent driving straight down the side line is eliminated and this forces him, if he drives, to drive within a narrower angle; thus you limit his choice of drives and reduce the amount of unprotected court you must cover. The topspin will sufficiently retard the flight of the ball to enable you to reach the net before the opponent has returned the ball.

As previously mentioned, if the opponent's drive is short, falling more than several feet within the base line, there is a chance to capture the net behind a forcing stroke. But when his drive lands within a foot or so of the base line, or when driven out of position, do not attempt to go in; for you will have to run too far to get beyond your own service line before your opponent has returned your drive. His deep drive has put you temporarily on the defensive and you should wait for a more favorable opportunity to go in. To attempt to win the point by an ace unless he is out of position is usually also a waste of effort. This is the time for patience, not for a wild, impetuous drive—the time for you to use your head and try to maneuver him out of position or force him to make the weak return which will enable you to seize the net on your next return.

As soon as you have returned the opponent's deep drive, hurry into the anticipatory position for your next shot. Do not wait to see where your return will land; do not stand still, assuming that you will make an ace or that your opponent will make an error. You should know where your opponent will logically play his shot and get in position to return that shot; at the same time keep in mind that he may play an illogical shot to an unexpected spot to catch you off guard.

If your opponent has hit a good shot or you have made an error in judgment and are off balance, try to make your return as deep as possible, but be sure to get that ball back into your opponent's court. If your opponent stays on the base line, do not be afraid to hit the ball with less speed, well above the net, and as deep as you can without making an error. He will not often force you after a deep return that has a high bounce. On the contrary, his return is likely to lose its sting or even become weak, permitting you to take the offensive.

Remember that it is necessary to anticipate in tennis. It is a bad move to wait until the ball has already covered a certain part of its trajectory before going to meet it. In such an event you must run faster or hurry your stroke, which results in loss of breath, increased fatigue, and greater opportunity for errors. Certain players never give the impression of running on the court, yet they are always in the right position. Others are constantly on the move, always darting at full speed, and are easily played out. The former know how to anticipate.

Anticipation demands a certain mental alertness and an instinctive understanding of the game. One must not start until the ball leaves the opponent's racket. To start exactly at that moment, the mind must have made its decision in advance, one must already have an idea where the shot will land. Thus one gains a fraction of a second, and all these fractions added together at the end of a match represent the extent of time during which you have set the cadence of the play.

One must not start too soon, for this would allow your stratagem to be discovered and turned against you. Neither must you start too late. The interval is very short—it is between the moment when the opponent is sufficiently set so as no longer to be able to change his stroke and the moment when the ball is hit.

It goes without saying that from the moment when anticipation becomes a natural part of your game, you must take account of it in your method of placing the ball. Let us call the "closed side" of the court that part to which the previous shot has drawn the opponent, that is to say, where he tends to stay momentarily, and the "open side" that part of the court which is least well protected. The most elementary tactic will lead you to play always toward the open side so as to put the opponent out of position in the easiest possible way. When you play twice in succession to the same side, that is, to the closed side on the second shot, you have attempted a deception. Between two players of equal strength and whose strokes have an equal speed, the side to aim for becomes a sort of game of "odd or even." The better psychologist ought to win.

The study of anticipation and deception includes a second step, false anticipation. A pretended start in one direction naturally incites the opponent to try a deceptive shot to the opposite side—which fails because the start was a false one.

There are two ways of making a deceptive shot, in depth or width. It is an error to believe that this tactic can only be applied on shots placed to right and left. A deceptive lob, over an opponent rushing for the net, is one of the most effective shots. Again, a very short drop shot to surprise a player retreating toward the base line almost always wins the point. For a deception attempted laterally it is a good thing to play short, shorter if possible than the first ball. A short cross-court shot is very effective especially if it is deceptive. It will be noticed that the more one imposes one's game on an opponent, the easier it is to anticipate. Indeed a superiority in tactics or in cadence reduces the opponent's means of reply and one's own problems are less complex.

To repeat, your position in the court must be governed chiefly by the position of the ball first, then by the position of the opponent, and finally by the known characteristics of his play. If your return has carried the ball far over to the right of the other man's court, your waiting position must be correspondingly to your own left to anticipate his next shot. Similarly, you must lean toward your own right when you have played the ball far out to the left side of your opponent's court.

The "Center Theory." Speaking generally, you are safer on sharp cross-court angles the farther you are from the net, and the more in danger the nearer you approach the net. Conversely, you are more or less safe in the net position according to how near the center of your opponent's court the ball is placed when he is ready to make his next return. This is the basis of what is known as the "center theory," and those who study it most closely find it one of the better means of strengthening their net attack. This theory, with or without its name, was used by "expert" players for a great number of years. James Dwight of the United States was one of the first to make it his style of play.

The "center theory" is this: A volleyer is in a better position to command the court and so maintain his position at the net if he volleys *down the middle of the court rather than to the sides.* If he volleys down the middle, his opponent must be in the middle of his court to return the ball. If his opponent is in the middle, he will have less chance to drive the ball past the volleyer on either side than if he were driving from a corner of his base line. Less chance, because, if driving from either corner, he can drive hard down the side line, for he has the full length of the court to keep his shot in court; but, if he is in the middle of the court, he cannot drive so hard to either side line as he can when driving straight down the side line, because of the danger of the ball going out of court owing to the angle at which it is traveling. Since he cannot drive so hard, the ball travels more slowly, and therefore the volleyer has more time to intercept it. The only hard drive that can be made from the middle of the base line is down the middle of the court; and this drive, however fast, is generally quite easily dealt with by a volleyer in position.

Both in attack and defense the man who has made a study of the "center theory" has a good pull over one who has not. In defense (in a base-line duel) when you yourself are playing from the base line and your opponent's backhand is not sufficiently weak to make it worthwhile to keep on hammering at it, you should keep the ball down the middle of the court and as deep as possible, because your opponent will find fewer chances of making a winning stroke from the middle

of his own base line, or of making a shot that will even drive you so far out of position that he will be safe in running up to the net. But if he does get to the net, remember that the "center theory" is temporarily useless. You must either lob or try to pass him. In attack, or rather as a means of preparing for attack, it is also most useful; for when you have driven your opponent, let us say, out to the side of his court at one corner, a deep drive down the middle will give you a straight instead of a slanting run in to the net, at the same time lessening the danger of being passed. Once settled safely at the net, the center theory is still a splendid defense of your position if you do not get the opportunity at once to end the play by killing the ball. There are many times when a man is volleying that he can return the ball but cannot kill it, and then the part of wisdom is to keep the other man from passing and wait for a better opening for the kill you are playing for. Again the center theory is needed, for the volley that does not kill is better in the center of the court so that the next return shall not turn the tables against you and put you on the defensive.

Thus, from every viewpoint then, the center theory is a help to defense and a greater help to safety while attacking. For the man who wants to throw all caution to the winds and rip and slash his way through all opposition, perhaps the better course is to adopt only the sharpest angles for all his strokes, but this opens him up to even greater dangers than he is hoping to ensnare his antagonist with, and unless he is very skillful at this style of game, the safer man on the other side of the net is likely to beat him. Remember that the net position enables the skillful volleyer to dominate the court, and thus it is worth some risk to gain that advantage. By going to the net you force your opponent to make errors by the very fact that if he fails to be accurate, he will give you an opportunity to win the point. This mental hazard is of very real value in a long, hard match. You must expect to be passed now and then; but do not let an occasional pass discourage you from continuing your attack.

If the other man tries to dislodge you from the net by lobbing, then you must get back quickly to smash, and if your smash is not an outright kill, you must return to the net position instantly. The slightest hesitation or delay after smashing a lob means that it will be too late to get up close again, and the next return will be at your feet. You will be forced to stay back in your court and the adversary may take that opportunity to take the net attack into his own hands.

When lobbing yourself, place your lobs far back. It is better to risk putting the ball out of court than to lob short. That is sure death and the moral effect of a smashed ace puts more confidence in the enemy. If there is any choice, it is better to lob to the backhand corner of the other man's court than to his forehand side. Few players can smash from the backhand side, for the stroke is much easier when made with the ball over the right shoulder. On the left side, the player is generally forced outside of the court to smash, and if he does not kill outright, then his court is wide open for the next return.

The lob is often the best defense against a good net player who gets in close, but it should be varied. If you lob too much, the other man will get used to handling that stroke and soon begin to kill it. On the other hand, watch for the first time he fails to follow up his smash quickly to the net and try to get the next return at his feet before he comes in close enough to volley. That is the turning point and often wins a long rally.

In smashing one of your opponent's lobs, select the part of his court that seems least covered, but if the ball is falling short so you are not far from the net when you hit it, the direction is not so important and sheer speed alone will generally kill. It is sometimes more effective to smash directly at the other man's feet, particularly if he is fairly close to you. He will hardly have time enough to get his racket into position to make a return from a hard smash right at him, and this is sometimes more embarrassing than a hard-hit ball a little way off, as it gives less room in which to swing the racket.

Depth and Net Clearance. Top players automatically know when depth is important and when it is necessary to hit a ball with a large margin of net clearance. But beginners and intermediates are confused: they try for depth at the wrong times, and they cannot judge the proper moment to aim for net clearance.

The two subjects must be taken together because one goes with the other. In order to hit a deep ball, one should clear the net by 2 to 8 feet. A ball that whistles past the tape will fall short, whereas a ball with a great deal of net clearance is much more likely to land near the base line.

Depth is important when the opponent is on the base line. A short ball (or one that skims the net) gives the opponent the opportunity to make a forcing shot and to take the net position. Therefore all efforts in base-line exchanges should be toward keeping the opponent pinned back. One only hits a short ball (a net skimmer) when the opponent has been worked out of position. A sharply angled short shot can then be a winner. When playing from the base line, there is another consideration other than depth. The idea is to force the opponent, but not to the point where forcing shots become errors, and to prevent the opposition from getting grooved. For this reason, base-line exchanges should clear the net by different margins—by 8 to 10 feet when one is retrieving a very deep ball, and by 2 to 3 feet when one is trying for added pace.

Depth is unimportant when the opponent is at net. Now one tries only to keep the ball low, for a high ball to a net man is a setup. The ball should clear the net by the narrow margin of 3 inches to a foot. If the ball is dropping quickly (falling short), the opponent will have to volley up, which is the aim of the defender.

There is a third consideration. Should one try for depth on return of serve against a net-rusher? A few servers come in so fast that they can make their first volley from inside the service line. The return against them should be low and short (a net-skimmer to prevent them from hitting down on volleys and a fast-dropping ball to force them to volley up). However, many big servers take their first volley at a point several feet behind the service line. The ideal riposte is a ball which will land at the server's feet. This means a certain amount of depth, but basically the ball must be dropping fast when it reaches the area immediately behind the service line. A ball with high net clearance (6 to 8 feet) will not drop fast enough, and it is therefore better to try for 2 feet clearance. This gives the receiver a safety margin while insuring a reasonably deep return. But whatever you do, do not stick to one pattern and always avoid a high return to the net man. Skim an occasional one from the base line in a back-court exchange, go for high, looping bouncers at other times which clear the net by 10 feet, and see how your change of pace will break up your opponent's rhythm and make your hard shots seem harder.

Playing on Different Surfaces

As was stated in Section II, there are many "lawn" tennis surfaces, and each and every one of them requires a different technique and strategy. For instance, the man who is trained on clay always has trouble his first year on grass. Clay players develop an accurate base-line game, and power on attack is not important. It is necessary instead to run down the ball, to keep it in court, to lob very high, and to get back into position. This steady, accurate clay-court champion is lost on grass, where the premium is on speed and attack at any cost.

Grass is a game of moving forward, forward, forward. A stab volley is liable to be a winner, whereas on clay the stab volley is almost a sure loser since the player gets passed on the return. One needs only a big serve and volley on grass; the ground strokes are far less important. Conversely, one need not have a big serve or volley on clay; ground strokes that have depth, consistency, and accuracy are all-important. Bad grass is the greatest equalizer, for a man with a big serve and stab volley has a chance against the champion who has not only a big serve and volley but good ground strokes as well. Games follow serve, and with a few bad breaks (rough bounces) against him, the champ is out.

As was stated in Section II, there are numerous synthetic court surfaces being used today. Most of these surfaces are made of acrylic fibers, rubber, or a synthetic plastic grass, and play about as fast as grass. Because of their synthetic nature, they play more consistent than grass, but the speed of the court can be regulated by spraying the courts or shaving the fibers.

The cement player has a wider choice of games. One can become good on cement with an attacking game, but this surface can also develop excellent retrievers. One can be a base-liner or a net-rusher, and one can win with a good serve or beat a big server with one's excellent ground strokes. Cement is much faster than clay and it has a truer bounce than grass, but the ball bounces high, which gives one a chance to retrieve it. The cement player is usually better rounded than the clay or grass devotee; he is more likely to have both good ground strokes and a good volley, and he realizes the importance of a big serve.

Aggressive cement players make the transition to grass faster than to clay; steady cement players adjust more quickly to clay. The average cement player is more aggressive than steady since speed pays off and so does a well-founded attack.

Grass is an unusual surface for training. Grass players have real trouble adjusting to clay and a certain amount of difficulty in responding to the high bounces on cement. Grass is not only fast, but a hard ball tends to slither away from the opponent. It is difficult to groove one's strokes on this surface.

Wood is like fast cement. The trouble is that most wood courts are not well lit, and this adds another dimension to the difficulties of learning the surface. A big serve is vital, but one does have a chance to get a good swing at the ball because the bounce is true. Scandinavian indoor courts are excellent because they are well lit. A cement or grass player can adjust to them very quickly.

Most professionals teach their pupils to hit ground strokes with their side to the net. As they hit the ball, the front leg is supposed to move into the shot, i.e., toward the net. This always holds true when there is plenty of time to get to a ball and the footing is sure. On clay, composition, or grass, the player moving toward a ball runs several steps less, then slides into the shot. This saves energy for the long matches and means that the player does not have to be in perfect position to hit a ball since he has to slide at the last minute.

The slide when running to the forehand side finds the player hitting with an open stance. If the player is right-handed, he plants his left foot and slides his right foot sideways to meet the ball. If he were to slide his left foot, he would be too twisted in relation to the net to effect a good shoulder turn and powerful shot.

Normally the foot slides 2 or 3 feet. When our right-handed friend changes directions and goes forward, it is his left foot that slides; the shot usually looks like a classical hard-surface forehand, with the left leg a little more extended than usual. This spreading of the feet when moving forward is very good since the player hits the ball more in front of his body and, consequently, gets more power. The open stance usually results in a more defensive shot than the closed stance unless there is a good weight shift at the last minute, since the weight is not being moved from back to front foot unless the shoulder comes through well. Therefore the open-stance forehand is seen more frequently on clay or composition courts than on grass since on the latter surface most players are always moving into net (as the player moves to net behind a ball, he generally turns his left shoulder in and the stance is seldom completely open).

There are few if any open-stance backhands that are satisfactory. In other words, a right-handed player cannot slide his left foot to meet a ball on his backhand side. He is then unable to turn his right shoulder because he is facing the net and it has already been turned. When he moves forward, his right foot also slides because he must keep his right shoulder toward the net until he makes contact with the ball and turns it.

Because footing is sure on cement and the surface is so hard, players changing to clay or grass are afraid to slide or fall. But sliding on clay or grass is necessary, and falling properly is seldom dangerous on grass. A last-minute flat-out lunge often wins a point. However, such acrobatic action should not be overdone unless the player would prefer to be a circus performer rather than a tennis star.

A great, aggressive champion can attack on clay and win; a great defensive champ can parry a grass attack and come out ahead. The real champion is good on all surfaces. Usually he adjusts his game to the court, attacking more on the fast and defending more on the slow.

Playing the Wind

One cannot always play under ideal conditions. Many times the court will be rough, the background glaring, the underfooting wet, the gallery noisy, the backstops too short, the lighting poor, or the wind hazardous. The winner will have the better mental attitude and the better plan, and he will be oblivious to outside distractions. He will welcome the challenge of poor conditions because he knows that he can surmount them better than his opponent. The loser will be distraught; it is one of the facts of tournament tennis that the man who trails is the man who complains, while the winner takes everything in stride.

There are three kinds of winds. It can blow against you on one side of the net so that your best shots go short, and with you on the other so that all your lobs sail out. It can blow from one side to the other so that anticipated forehands come into your backhand. Or, hardest of all to master, it can be gusty, sweeping the ball in any direction just as you are set for it.

If you look on the wind as a challenge, you have won half the battle. You are fighting an opponent and the elements, but so is he. If you recognize the fact that not only your best shots but his, too, will be only adequate on a windy day, you automatically have the edge. The chances are that his attitude will not be as good as yours.

Topspin is the master wind shot. When the wind is blowing behind you, only topspin will make the ball drop into court. Do not try for depth; try for pace with topspin. This is not only a good base-line weapon when the wind is with you, but it is an ideal passing shot. Use enormous quantities of backspin on your lobs to enable you to lob high and yet keep the ball in court. Slice all your serves to prevent them from sailing. On the other side of the net, you are fighting the wind. Slug a little more than your wont and the ball will still go in. Lob with twice the strength of your usual lob. On this side of the net, you can be a "steady slugger." Overhit your serve; the wind will bring it in.

When the wind is bringing forehands into your body, watch for the wild bounce. Hit every ball wide to the opponent's backhand. Lob only to his backhand. When you hit a forehand cross-court (or a backhand down the line), do not try for too sharp an angle or to hit too close to the line. Reverse the preceding when you change sides on the odd game.

Gusty winds are the most difficult to play.

Shorten the toss on your serve to prevent the wind from taking the ball away from you. (This, of course, necessitates a speedup in the service stroke.) Watch the ball like a hawk and be light on your feet so that you can play a ball that either moves away from or into you. Be conscious of the changes in the wind. When it lets up, revert to your normal game. When it is with you, use topspin; when it is against you, hit out.

Tennis Strategy and Psychology

Tennis strategy and psychology are closely connected. The psychological element wins or loses as many matches as stroke production. The game between two well-matched opponents becomes similar to a series of chess-like maneuvers, each player trying to outsmart the other. The ability of one player to excel the other in quickness of combining physical and mental reflexes usually decides the match. He who can immediately grasp and sense the right play during a rally stands the best chance to win. The element of surprise is of particular advantage; it can do more to break up the opponent's game than any other factor.

The first and obvious rule of good court strategy is: Place the ball where the opponent cannot reach it. The second half of that rule: Be right at the spot to which the opponent directs his return. It stands to reason, however, that if the opponent's game is equal to or better than your own, you can hardly expect to score with every shot. So be patient. Do not try to win a point with every stroke. Bide your time by keeping the ball in play until some hole in his court opens up through which you can drive a scoring ace. Be satisfied to lose at first if such losses point the way to a final win. Often by keeping the ball in play without attempting kills, you can get a little rest when driven hard, can conserve your strength for your own offensive attack and the crucial moments of the battle. When your own offense fails, fall back on a steady defensive campaign and let your opponent make the errors.

Placing shots is the first consideration. Pacing the shots is only secondary. Speed under control is an asset but it may prove a boomerang when up against a player who can absorb the pace and use speed to his own ends. Often it pays to soften your own game and make the other fellow manufacture the speed. You have less pace to deal with and he is likely to make more errors. If you use speed continually you are serving your opponent with a steady diet and he soon accustoms himself to it; whereas if you mix your pace, you disturb his stroking. It is confusing to have a ball hit your racket like a thunderbolt at one time and like a feather the next. Remember that you cannot rely alone on either speed or strategy for success. Rather, you must arrive at a combination of both factors.

You must consider what effect you seek. If your opponent is well off court, you can score a placement by hitting the ball with a slight amount of pace. An opponent who maintains good court position can only be dislodged by a more severe shot. A player should mix up his pace and hit no harder than will permit a good margin of safety on all shots. By that it is not meant that you should rely on a minimum amount of speed. You should hit the ball hard enough, but should not sacrifice safety for too much speed.

There are two ways of playing the game—to your own strength or to your opponent's weakness. If your forehand cross-court is your strength but your opponent's backhand is his weakness, do you hit your forehand cross-court or do you hit it down the line to the weak spot of the opposition? If your game is based on rushing the net after service and your opponent's game is based on superb passing shots, do you continue to attack or do you try to bring your opponent to net where he is least at home? If you like to hit hard from the base line and your opponent dreads only soft, high loops deep to his backhand, do you hit crisply each time or do you lift the ball soft and easy?

The true tennis artist can adjust his game to play his strength when the opportunity rises but to play to the weakness of the opponent as well. But analyzing the opponent is a fascinating process. When you know what his weakness is, you may not have the equipment to make use of your knowledge. As an example, you may be a base-liner who hits with reasonable force and accuracy but who does not quite have the power to deal with a steady, fast retriever. You win a number of points but you lose more than 50 percent of the games. You are far too unsure of your volley to attack regularly. Your opponent, on the record, is not as good as you but he beats you. Now here is a good solution: Your weakness (which you avoid and never hit) may be superior to his weakness, so try a net attack. Do not serve and come in. Wait for the short ball. Then drive it or chip it or sidespin it on your forehand deep to his backhand and come to net. He will probably hit up and you will actually learn confidence in a volley because the weakness is so apparent.

If he is a lefty, slice every short backhand you get deep down the line, and then close in at net. Again, your confidence in your volley will grow because his return is short. Playing an opponent's weakness will be your best chance to overcome what had heretofore been your weakness. It will also give you greater enjoyment for you will learn to think and improve instead of simply hitting by rote.

Before leaving the subject of playing to an opponent's weakness, here is an important point to remember: do so discriminately. Plans of this nature do not always succeed. The opponent may be adept at covering his weaknesses and cause you an anxious afternoon. Preconceived plans are fine but they should be made quite flexible. Some opponents will hit to certain spots time after time when finding themselves in particular positions in the court. It is well to study these methods and base your plans on an attempt to take advantage of them when you discover them. For instance, when playing a good base-liner, it is often good strategy to lure him to the net with the intent of passing him for the point, Since he is a base-liner by choice, he probably is weak at the net. To draw him in and away from his favorite base-line position with a shot that has to be played close to the net would be, in this case, a sound tactical move.

Keep in mind that you should always change a losing game and never change a winning one. However, too many players believe that there are only two strategies—hitting hard or soft-balling. Some of the suggestions below may help you to develop a "thinking" game in which you make the most of your strokes and of your opponent's weaknesses.

If you have been losing in a match in which base-line play has predominated, try coming to net more or pulling in your opponent. Increase your depth or try alternating long with short. See if stepping up the pace will help or if soft, high balls are more effective. Play one side repeatedly to probe for a weakness. Discover any weakness in your opponent's passing-shot game. If depth does not produce errors, perhaps change of pace will do it or, as an alternative, heavy spins.

If you have been losing while playing an attacking game, change your method of attack. Your approach shots may be short, you may be coming in on "nothing" balls, or you may be playing to your opponent's strength. Perhaps there is a forehand weakness in the opponent's passing shots, or he may be susceptible to an attack down the center. Possibly he is grooved to your approach, so mix them up.

If your opponent has been winning by a successful attack, try lobbing more (to the backhand). If you have been hitting your passing shots hard, try soft, dipping balls. He may have been outguessing you; do not hit cross-courts (or down-the-lines) exclusively. A counterattack may take the play away from him.

If your serve has not been an effective weapon, try hitting it harder or, if your first serve has not been going in, throw in your second serve first. If your opponent has been stepping around your serve to the backhand, try a wide slice to the forehand. If you have stayed back, vary your tactics by coming in. Change of pace can be as effective on the serve as it is on ground strokes if you use your head.

It is fairly easy to understand the reason for changing one's game when losing. The next step is to know at what time the change should take place if it becomes necessary. In three-set matches, the loss of the first set due to a single breakthrough service is no sign that your game may not prevail—stick to it. However, the loss of the first set plus another breakthrough or a lead against you of 3–1 or 4–2 is convincing enough to indicate that your game is a losing one—change. In a five-set match, it requires a bit more time to prove that your tactics may not be the winning ones. Actually, great care should be taken and careful study should be given to this change. In some cases, for instance, like the one mentioned above, when you are down 1 set and trailing 3–1 in the second, it would be foolish to change your game if, let us say, you had based your tactics on steady base-line play to exhaust your opponent in a three-set match, and he was beginning to show the strain of the long rallies imposed upon him. In that case, the 3–1 lead would be offset by the fact that in all probability the opponent could not physically hold the pace that had given him this lead. Be sure the time is at hand to change by a clear concise summary of the effect which your efforts are having upon your opponent's game as well as the score.

Next let us consider the importance of the various sets, games, and points in the course of a match. Many players of ability play each point to the limit from the first to the last of a match, with the idea that a point is a point wherever you can get it.

Nothing could be further from the truth— no two points are of exactly the same value, and the keenest players sense this, doling out their resources, mental and physical, so as to be able to give every effort to those points considered vital to success. This has been known as playing to the score.

First, in regard to sets. In a three-set match every effort should be bent on winning the initial set. The shorter the scheduled course of the match, the more important becomes the advantage of an early and definite lead. Up goes the confidence of the leader, off falls that of his opponent. In a five-set match, many players do not take the loss of the first set too seriously, but attempt to win two of the first three, with the second considered the most important. In games, the seventh game of the set is usually considered the most important, although the fifth to the seventh are always vital. With a lead of 3–1, the player should go all out in an attempt to get to 4–1, which usually means the set. To see the importance of this particular game, the fifth, let us say the server is 3–1 and fails to hold. The opponent needs then only to hold service to be level 3–all. (Another point to consider is the fact that a service break usually means the loss of a two-game lead and not just one.) Following the same reasoning, it can be seen that at 4–2, holding means 5–2, a good lead, while losing results in 4–3. It is true these

leads of two games appear large. They are. But it is here that every effort must be bent to hold and add to this lead instead of letting up.

Second, in regard to points. The third point of a game is usually the most important— closely followed in importance by the second. Usually these points spell the difference between 40–0 and 30–15, or between 30–0, a huge allowance, and 15–all. Do not risk too much at 30–0, just because you realize you lead. At 40–0 treat the point in the same manner. If you lose it for 40–15, take more of a chance here, then more carefully at 40–30. Play two of the points carefully to one more risky when holding a lead for the game. Trailing 0–40 or 15–40, take a chance. Coming up to 30–40, do not disregard the effort you have made and play more conservatively before hitting for the winner. Take your chances when you are way down; you will not be any worse off and you may score. On the top, with everything to lose, do not throw it away; await your opening.

When playing a better player, there is always a tendency to "press." Actually, pressing means trying too hard, overhitting, going for the big shots, and, often, playing jerkily. The solution to the problem lies in getting ready more quickly. The better player hits harder and/or deeper and/or attacks more. The lesser player feels his only ripostes are harder returns and outright winners on passing shots. But instead of increasing his pace (which results in more errors) or going for the shots with too little margin, he would do better to prepare more quickly. As soon as the ball leaves his opponent's racket he must make his move; before the ball bounces, his own racket is coming forward for the hit.

The harder the opponent hits, the earlier the windup must be. If one prepares in time and meets the ball in front of the body, one can utilize the opponent's speed. A player who cannot generate his own pace against a soft hitter will find he has "natural pace" if he can meet the ball solidly in front of him against a hard hitter.

The better the opponent, the more closely one must follow the ball. Lapses of concentration are not as dangerous when one is playing a weak opponent who does not force, but one can never take one's eye off the ball when one is up against a better player. This is particularly true against the net-rusher; one must look at the ball, not the opponent.

The time to try a new stroke or to increase one's pace or to change one's style is against a lesser player; one must stick with one's own equipment and forget experimentation against a better man. Do not go for "the big winners" when you are losing; use the pace that is natural to you, but prepare earlier. This does not mean you cannot work out a tactical plan, but overhitting should never be part of it.

You cannot compensate for a weakness in your own strokes by "blasting" the ball. If your opponent is murdering your relatively innocuous serve, the riposte is not to try to murder his relatively effective delivery. Neither is it to go for cannonballs on your first serve. You use what you have as effectively as you can; if your serve is relatively weak, you try for accuracy, depth, and spin— not for aces. If your opponent is forcing you on your weak side, you try for consistency, accuracy, and change of pace by preparing early; you do not go for the big winners. One avoids "pressing" by early preparation, intense concentration, and utilizing one's own equipment. One can still lose simply because the opponent is better, but there is a much better chance of getting into the match and of playing one's best if these three precepts are followed. You may still be overpowered, but you will be ready for many more balls and you will be "in" many more points.

It is often foolish to try to outlast an opponent in a marathon duel if the weather is excessively warm, unless the heat particularly favors you. Some players lose energy quickly in the heat, while others thrive on it. One must also consider side winds and back winds when choosing tactics. The ball may travel a considerable distance from its intended line of flight due to a strong wind, and the player must adjust his shots to these conditions of play. A player must try to avoid becoming upset during a match because of bad bounces, decisions, or other adverse conditions.

Exhaustion or excess physical strain is to be avoided whenever possible. It may cause the loss of that particular match or of matches to follow in the tournament. Try to relax completely between points to accomplish this end. Another important factor in this connection is to avoid running yourself out on unimportant points. It is easy to tear about the court to make unusual gets, and find yourself winded on the next two or three points to follow.

There are some players who are willing to waste time and points on shots that just will not click on that day. This is a foolish practice. Some other shot should be substituted to gain the necessary result if a favorite continues to fail to come off after a reasonable trial.

A player must decide whether to assume the offensive or to content himself with defensive methods. The latter are sometimes quite effective against an opponent using great speed, with a good percentage of accompanying errors. Try to size up the opponent and find which styles of play are most effective against him. It may be that he is weak against a net attack or a combination of short shots and lobs. If these weaknesses, or others, can be found, force the issue. On the other hand, if he is erratic and has trouble keeping the ball in play, rally with him and give him opportunities to make mistakes. By all means avoid playing the game of your adversary. If he wants speed, slow-ball him. If he wants to bring you into the net, change tactics and make him come in. Base your tactics on the style that upsets and surprises your rival most effectively.

The best base for an attacking style is the net position. This saves considerable time, distance, and energy, and is most disconcerting to an opponent. If you are planning to attack, do not hesitate to advance to the net at every opportunity. Another offensive method is to draw your opponent to the net in an attempt to pass or lob over him, or run him from the base line with a sharply angled return.

The best method of defense is to exchange shots from the base line to force your opponent into error. It is a safer base because it offers the maximum territory of the opponent's court as a target.

Deception and the element of surprise are also important. They consist of doing the unexpected and hitting the ball to the least obvious place. The opponent who expects a shot in his backhand corner is often the victim of a placement ace when a tantalizing drop shot floats over the net. The best way to worry an adversary is to keep him guessing as to what will come next. There is nothing that will wear the opponent out like making him chase into a far corner for an unexpected drive, or causing him to change his direction to go back after a ball in a corner that he has just left. Actually, in the game of tennis, deception can take two forms: (1) concealment of your stroke and the direction you are going to hit the ball; and (2) not letting your opponent know where you are going to be in the court. Disguise the stroke and the direction of the ball as much as possible. Also, by feinting with your body—by leaning to the left or right at the correct moment—it is sometimes possible to draw the shot of the opponent where you want it to come. In other words, create a false opening. The use of deception requires extra practice on your part, but it generally pays dividends.

Do not be afraid to take a chance. If you play all your shots safe, right down the middle of the court, your opponent will have no trouble with you because you are not giving him any. Try placing some of the shots inches from the side line or the base line. Try dropping them a foot over the net. Try fast, top-spin drives, those high, twisting lobs, those sudden rushes to the net. You may lose plenty of points in the process, but practice makes perfect, and you will soon find your shots dropping where you want them. Then you have a good tennis attack. Remember that one of the cardinal rules of all sport is never alter a winning combination. The same is true of tennis. If the tide is against you, you must take chances to gamble for possible victory. In such a case, change your game, change your strokes, pace, and method of attack. But never change a winning game unless you believe your adversary has discovered your plan of attack and has mustered an adequate defense against it.

Match Play. The difference between a game with friends and a tournament match is pressure. There is no way to simulate competitive play, and the only way to get tournament experience is simply by entering as many tournaments as possible and learning from one's errors. There is not enough tension in practice, and therefore the development of a player will be limited if he cannot compete against others under tournament conditions.

Tension produces fatigue. A player in good condition may get exhausted in the third game of the first set of a tournament match. Top players therefore try to avoid prematch exertions which do not pay off. They may practice hard in the morning or have a hit just before playing, but they do not sit in the sun, do gymnastics, swim, or drive until after the match is over.

Each player is an individual and each will have his own method of training which is best for him. However, none will change their routine just before a tournament. If a player regularly goes to bed at 11:00, he should not suddenly go to bed at 9:00. If he eats lightly before playing, he should not switch to heavy meals when he enters a tournament. The one addition to his routine is salt pills, since players are susceptible to cramps because of match strain.

A good competitor goes into a match with a plan. He does not change it after he loses one point or one game; he does not stick to it if he has been badly beaten in the first set. It is good to be flexible, to play more aggressively on a wet, fast court, to serve short and wide against a receiver who plays too far back, to lob more against a player with a shaky overhead stroke, to play steadily on a slow court but to switch to another tactic if the plan is not succeeding.

The mental attitude of the match player is a function of his own personality. He needs confidence in his own game but respect for his opponent's abilities as well. The unconfident player will tighten on his strokes or will resort to retrieving or overhitting as a desperation measure. The overconfident player expects his opponent to fall over as soon as he steps on the court.

The temperament of a player can win or lose for him. If he cannot control his anger when he errs on a big point, the match will slip away from him. Anger against an opponent can be just as hazardous. If one expects misbehavior or mistakes on the part of the opposition, the crowd, and an occasional linesman, one is only pleasantly surprised if all goes well. The old tournament hand is not upset by stalling or any of the other gambits of gamesmanship whose object is to make him lose control. He takes the calls as they come and he does not fly into a tantrum when a linesman or umpire proves to be fallible. He is too good a competitor to let a partisan crowd get under his skin; he welcomes the opportunity of demonstrating his skill and his poise under the worst of circumstances. However, he sticks to his guns when it is a question of the rules.

Among the "don'ts" of competitive play: Don't listen to advice from well-wishers, don't gulp water on the odd games (sip it), don't worry about lost points, don't run for a ball that is going out (it is the mark of a rabbit), don't think of what you will say to your opponent after you have won, don't count the gallery, don't let extraneous thoughts come into your mind, and don't rush yourself out of the match. Among the "do's": When the nervous strain is great, try deep breathing; when fatigue overwhelms you, stay on your toes; when your strokes fail you, go back to fundamentals; when you are down two sets to one and are playing badly, take the intermission; and when you win or lose the match, be gracious. More on the etiquette of tennis can be found in Section IV.

Practice. The player who moans and groans the least on the court is the one who is in the best shape for his ability—i.e., the man who practices the most and who gets the most out of his practice. He will have his bad days, but the hours he has spent on the court have shown him how to play when reflexes or strokes are not what they should be. Only a few devotees of the game can spend unlimited time on the courts, but it is not just the number of hours but how they are spent that count.

To the champion, who at one time spent five hours a day, seven days a week, learning the game, match play is far more important than practice. Two or three tough matches a week are all he needs, and if he is in the finals of each tournament, that is exactly what he will get—three easy early rounds and two or three real tests—until he comes to the major championships, where he can expect at least three or four hard matches. His worry is usually not whether he can get enough tough matches in the season but whether he will get over-tennised before the end of the year.

The lesser tournament player—the man who is nationally ranked but who is generally "out" by the quarter-finals—has a problem that is particular to himself. Why is he losing repeatedly to players ranked above him and how can he improve? Does he lack a tactical plan, is he overhitting, does he have a service weakness, is he too unaggressive, is his return of serve faulty, does he understand the surface? A player of this level must learn self-analysis, since all the good advice in the world will have far less meaning than the discovery of a fault by himself. Once he sees it, he can cure it with diligent, intelligent practice.

The poor tournament player who has the desire but lacks the weapons to achieve victory is the man who must practice the most. His weaknesses are many. He needs no less than two hours a day (often four or five) to reach his goal. He is the reasonably good college player who beats the local talent but whose aims are much higher. He is the first or second rounder on the grass-court circuit (although often his entry is not accepted). He wants to be a tournament player, but his failings are many. Nine times out of ten this player is not giving tennis enough time and his practice is haphazard. He does not work on the backboard, he does not practice his serve, he does not give it full effort when he plays practice sets, he will only work against certain players, he starts the season too late and he is afraid to enter the lesser tournaments. He will be a loser until all these defects are corrected.

The club or parks player has a much more limited time schedule, but he, too, can make vast improvements by regular workout periods used intelligently. He may have been playing twenty years or more, and if so probably is not looking for sensational victories. The most profitable method for him to improve is not by stroke changes, which are senseless for a grooved player, but by regularity of practice and self-study. Every time he skips a week his game will fluctuate, but he can get his occasional good days without so many bad ones by sticking to a twice-a-week schedule and by analyzing the game through looking, reading, and discussing. Analysis is infinite: does he fail to lob? is he taking the ball late? can he start sooner? is his first serve going in? is he watching the ball? is he drop-shotting enough or too often? etc.

The beginner and intermediate player should be on the court no less than twice a week (more often if he can) and should have professional help as well. Desire and concentration will make every practice session worthwhile and more enjoyable. These two factors will enable the player to absorb what the pro is telling him, and the regularity with which he practices will keep him from forgetting the newly acquired nuances of his game. The more hours of concentrated effort he can give to it, the faster he will improve.

No player can ever get better without working at the game. Practice aids are fully discussed in Section II.

Taking a Tennis Lesson

Skill in tennis develops more quickly from systematic, meaningful practice than from random hitting. True, you will improve through endless hours of casual rallying and play, but supervised practice under the watchful eye of a good instructor will be far more economical of your time and effort. Regardless of your present level of development, whether you are a beginner, intermediate, or advanced player, and whether you have played continually all winter long or are starting over again after a long layoff, taking lessons from a competent professional is the logical way to proceed. There are many good teachers scattered across the land. A description of the teaching-learning process as conducted by experienced tennis professionals is presented here.

Kinds of Lessons. Lessons can be classified as private (individual) or group (more than one person). For a private lesson, the pro works with only one person and the lessons run for a half to one hour. This is the most expensive of all lessons. The fee for group lessons, in which two or more people are taught at the same time, depends on the number in the group. In the case of large groups—twenty or thirty—the fee may be very small. Some pros offer a series of lessons, often ten, for less than the cost of that number of separate lessons. It is economical for the learner and it permits the pro to plan his teaching in a way that provides full coverage of all essential parts of the game. For these reasons, the best approach to the problem of learning is to contract for a full series of lessons regardless of whether you prefer group or individual instruction.

When talking with the pro, describe your tennis background and ask what length and spacing of lessons he suggests. He will probably ask some questions also. He will want to know your aim in tennis, how much you intend to practice, and how many lessons you plan to take. He will need to know your level of aspiration and your degree of commitment before he can plan your learning program.

The Teacher's Methods. Most experienced professionals use the *show-and-tell, watch-and-praise* method of teaching. In this plan the pro first demonstrates and describes the action to be learned. He tells you step-by-step what to do and how to do it, and he demonstrates slowly as he explains his moves. He points out the important parts of the stroke that you should work on and he tells you what to notice in his demonstration. He stresses cue words to direct action, and he explains the sequence of moves. Last, he demonstrates the end result, the immediate goal you are working for. He makes a few shots, showing the speed and trajectory he wants you to imitate.

He then lets you try to do what he has demonstrated and described. Probably he will first have you make several "dummy" swings at an imaginary ball: if you cannot make the proper swing at an imaginary ball, you certainly should not expect to make it at a real ball. While you are swinging, he analyzes your stroke. If he is a skilled teacher, he will first tell you what you are doing right. He will offer praise and encouragement to help "nail down" these good moves. At the same time he will try to build around them to correct mistakes you are making; he will describe, demonstrate, and possibly even guide you manually through your moves and positions in your swing.

When you swing reasonably well with consistency, he will let you move ahead. He may then take you to "fixed ball" practice in which you swing at a ball suspended on a cord or string. In this practice you will not have to time or judge the flight of a moving ball and so you will be able to focus all your attention on the mechanical act of swinging.

After you get the feel of hitting these stationary balls, you are ready to apply your stroke to a moving ball. For this practice, your pro will toss or hit softly to you, giving you the easiest kinds of balls to hit. He stands close to the net and feeds balls accurately enough to let you concentrate fully on your form; he will practically hit the racket for you. As you improve he will gradually move farther and farther from you and feed you more difficult balls to hit. If, at some point, play becomes too difficult for you—if you become confused and have to struggle to hit—he will realize he moved you too fast. He will take you backwards a step or two to review teaching points or to present new and different ones. Temporary way-stops such as these are often necessary. The pro will always have you hitting at balls appropriate for your level. In this way he hopes to move you along gradually. Eventually you will be able to rally with him from full length at your best speed.

Learning Takes Time. Do not be alarmed if the corrections suggested by the pro do not feel right immediately. A new grip or a new kind of swing may feel strange for a while. As you work on the changes, they will begin to feel more comfortable. Finally the corrections will have replaced the old faulty habits.

Kinds of Practice. Besides acting as a practice partner for you, your pro will tell you what kind of practice to do on your own. He may suggest "dummy" swing drills, possibly in front of a mirror where you can see your form. He may demonstrate how he wants you to practice against a background or a suitable substitute such as your garage door. He may want you to rally across the net with your friends or with someone he provides for that purpose. If so, he will explain the procedure for these.

Most pros consider this separate practice to be essential for learning. Their lessons are merely the starting point from which learning takes place. By demonstration, explanation, and hand guidance, they try to give the learner an understanding of good form. In addition, they provide the learner with some practice under conditions as near perfect as possible. But they all feel the important task of establishing good habits of form falls to the learner. When it is attained, it is due as much to proper practice away from the pro as it is to practice done directly under his supervision.

Understanding the Learning Process. If practice is to be efficient, it cannot be done carelessly. Learning to hit a tennis ball is not merely a matter of meaningless repetition until a habit is formed. It is a process of conscious effort by which you try to make changes and corrections. Working under the pro's directions, you try to do as he suggests. But you do not always do it right the first time and so you try again. You attempt to correct mistakes indicated by the pro, changing a part of the swing here or there and noting whether or not the change makes any difference in the end result.

In order to make these changes permanent, you must learn to respond to cues of "feel" resulting from the movement of your hands, your arms, and your legs. In order to arrive at a point where you can respond to these cues of feel without thinking about them— when you can do that, you have learned what it is you are practicing—you must first concentrate on and learn to react to other cues, mainly voice cues offered by your pro. The cues, of course, will be carefully selected by him, and will be in keeping with the method of stroking recommended by him. "Point to the top of the fence," for example, could be a valuable guide to you if you continue to turn the racket face over despite the pro's advice to finish with the racket face perpendicular to the ground. Usually the ability to feel the stroke consistently comes only after many repetitions of voice cues by the pro or after manual guidance by him or after the repetition of voice cues by the learner himself.

You may be able to speed the transition of voice cues to cues of feel by describing to yourself what it is you are trying to do. Even though the pro uses carefully chosen cues, they do not always mean the same thing to all learners. Some of his cues may not have registered with you. Putting the action into your own words often makes certain parts stand out more clearly, and often these parts will be the most important parts for you.

Putting it into your own words also calls attention to the difference between good and bad shots. Try to describe how it feels when you make a good shot or when the pro commends you for good form. Remember the description and carry it over into your private practice. Describe how it feels when you make a bad shot. This emphasizes errors and directs your attention to what should be avoided.

It may also help if you ask the pro to

describe how it feels to him when he strokes correctly. Ask about the sequence of his moves. Make him define his terms so you understand exactly what part of the stroke he is referring to. If his explanation sounds too complicated, tell him so and ask for a simpler explanation with emphasis on the parts that confuse you. Repeat the description as you try to imitate his stroke. Do not just look at what he is doing: talk about it.

This sequence of watching the pro demonstrate while he explains, after which you imitate and put the action into your own words, can be summed up to provide a useful guide to learning to play: *see it—hear it, say it—do it*. Follow this sequence in your lessons. In this way, you will be using several senses and you will be responding to several cues. This is the efficient way to learn.

When practicing on your own afterward, try not only to duplicate the right motion and movements described by the pro but also to eliminate all unnecessary movements. In other words, keep it simple. Do not confuse yourself by adding fancy flourishes and flashy moves. Concentrate on the essential parts pointed out by the pro. Think about your lessons when you are away from the pro. It may help if you write down what you remember about each lesson immediately afterward. Many pros do this, keeping a file catalog of each pupil so they can keep track of the work done in each lesson. But putting it down for yourself, in your own words, will help you see your problems and your objectives more clearly. Try to summarize the lesson in a clear and orderly way. If you can do so, the pro has done his job well. But you have only started to learn. You must continue to review his teaching points and to apply them in your practice. There are no short cuts or magic words, except good, hard practice. If you have learned what and how to practice, your money was well spent.

DOUBLES PLAY

The game for pairs differs greatly from the singles game that has just been discussed in detail. Not only is the court larger, and the number of players doubled, but the tactics are a great deal different. In singles play it is possible to score a great many points from the base line. In doubles, practically all of the scoring is done from the net position.

Doubles play also injects another element: teamwork. (Two players make up a team in doubles—both of the same sex or one of each. The latter is called *mixed* doubles.) In fact, the essential basis of good doubles play is good teamwork and complete sympathy between the partners. Two inferior players who "pull well" together will nearly always defeat a pair who are perhaps better individually, but whose play and demeanor is selfish and egotistical. Your aim should be to help your partner in every possible way, giving confidence and encouragement when things are going badly, and keeping a cool and determined head in the hour of victory. Because of your proximity and the fact that you are only two in a team, your mental outlook on the ensuing match inevitably reacts on your partner, and it is up to you to see that it is a helpful, optimistic aspect.

A double fault or a badly missed setup by you at a critical moment may do more harm to your side than the actual losing of one point, because it may quite unsettle your partner, who in his or her turn may also become erratic. A consistently bad return of service is one of the most demoralizing faults

Close cooperation is required in doubles play, and this 1970 Austrian championship team of Karen Krantzcke and Kerry Melville do it well.

from your colleague's point of view that you can have—because however steady he or she may be, the game cannot be won if you repeatedly miss your return. In singles you can make mistakes, go out for winners, try the most impossible shots, and you have only yourself to consider—but in a double your partner must be your first consideration—even as you should be his or hers. To combine well, you must know by instinct or by experience what your partner's movements are likely to be, so that you neither clash nor leave part of the court unprotected.

Whether you are pairing up for men's doubles, mixed doubles, or ladies' doubles, you should try to find a partner whose type of game fits in with your own. If you prefer the right court, it is no use starting a partnership with another right-court player. If you are inclined to be brilliant but erratic in your play, then choose a partner who is steady and imperturbable—one who will have a restraining influence on your impetuousness. But above all choose somebody with whom you can be in complete sympathy on the court—this is the most important point of all, if you are to have a successful and enjoyable career as a doubles pair.

As a general rule the stronger player should take the left court, because he or she is in a better position to take more of the game than when in the right court—the center-court balls being on his forehand. Also the even points—the second, fourth, etc., in a game—are more important than the odd—because on them depends the winning or losing of games. Hence the return of service of the player in the left court is of vital importance. Find out as soon as possible in which court you return the service the best, and then always play in it, and persevere with your returns until you bring them up to a very high degree of consistency. If you specialize in one court you should in time become quite expert. You may, of course, have to change your court to fit in with your different partners.

There are two distinct formations in the doubles game, either both up at the net, or one up and one back. (The former is called the *parallel formation,* while the latter is the *echelon formation.*) In these days when nearly everyone can volley, you generally see the former combination in action and it is cer-

Mrs. Carole Graebner prepares for a backhand stroke while Judy Tregart rushes to back her up.

tainly more effective and greater fun. Two good volleyers will as a rule beat a "one up and one back" partnership, except where the base-line player is *exceptionally* good.

The objective in doubles, as pointed out earlier, is to get to the net and hold that position successfully. The position should be just as close to the net as possible, with the knowledge that any lob must be covered. This closeness depends on the height of the player in question. The most effective shots against a pair at the net are the low, well-concealed lobs, and fast-dropping "loop-drives." Lobs are used to drive them away, while the drives may force them to volley up and allow you to challenge their position. Good care must be taken to defend against either of these shots when you yourself are in position at the net.

When serving, a slice or twist service enables you to reach the net immediately. The volley and smash permit you to stay there and win the point. Sharply angled volleys and smashes are brought into play because of the extra width of the doubles court and because of your position at the net to the right or left of the half-court line. But when the opponents are serving, a clean passing shot is extremely difficult unless you can maneuver them out of position, because each opponent has 9 feet less court to protect than in singles. To win the point capturing the net is usually necessary, and the best way to do that is either to lob or to play a short shot, usually cross-court, directly at your opponent's feet. So important is it for you to steal the net that you are warranted in taking risks in going to the net. Quick thinking, good judgment, and daring are at a premium in forcing the net from your opponents.

The official rules of doubles play are given in Section IV.

Service Strategy

In doubles, it is very difficult to break through service. One break may cost the set. In protecting the service, the position of the server's partner is important. He should station himself as far inside the court as possible, allowing himself only enough margin to be able to cover all but the last outside foot or two of the alley; shots in this space are the exception rather than the rule. (About 6 to 8 feet from the net and about 9 to 12 feet from the doubles side line is usually considered a good netman's position. He should, of course, face the receiver.) Next, he must be in as close as possible, giving himself enough room to be able to cover any lob. This position forces a cross-court return of service beyond the reach of the net player, or a defensive lob which may be dealt with summarily. If your opponents have been able to win points by hitting cross-court placements against the server or have been returning the service at his feet, his partner can eliminate this by standing near the center of the net on the same half of the court on which the server stands. This defensive shifting of position is called the *Australian formation,* and when employed the receiver cannot make a cross-court return without giving the net man a volley and therefore must play his return down the side line. It is a simple matter for the server to run to the net up through the vacant half of the court, covering the alley as he goes.

Since the server must get to the net as quickly as possible, the most successful service in doubles is the twist or slice with a medium-paced delivery. This should be placed to the weakest point in the receiver's game, with sufficient spin and pace to keep him from running around the shot. The server should place special emphasis on getting the first service in the court. By the use of medium pace he is able to control the serve better as well as to have more time to gain the net. However, many good doubles servers believe in throwing in an occasional fast service to give a change of pace. Actually, the serve should be of good length and varied, so that the receiver is kept guessing. The down-the-middle serve, of course, is always a good one in doubles since it will limit the angle at which the receiver can return the ball. When the service is across the court, the server's partner must be prepared for a shot possibly down his alley and should move slightly in that direction.

The purpose of the server is to get in to volley as high a shot as possible. He should try to avoid having to make low or half-volleys. No matter where he makes the first volley from, he should keep bearing in to the net. The center theory here works to better advantage. A good first volley down the center of the court draws one of the opposition, if not both, to that point, and may leave an opening for a placement in either corner. If a lob is put up, the server and partner must deal with it and recover the net position immediately. That is, as you run up to volley the return you will not have much time to think, but must make up your mind in a flash what you are going to do with the ball. Speaking broadly, there are two courses open to you. If the return is a good low dipping drive, which you will have to volley upward, send it back from whence it came because in that quarter it will be fairly safe, the opponent of necessity still being back. If the return is an easy volley, fairly high over the net, then go for a winner, by playing it downward at the opponent at the net, who at such close quarters has very little chance of returning it. The nearer you can get to the net before you have to volley the return, the easier the stroke, and the more chance of winning the point.

If you decide not to come in on your service at all, you must try with your next stroke to make an opening to enable you to join your partner. But always remember that the longer you stay back, the better opportunities you give your opponents for attacking from the net position.

Return-of-Service Strategy

A team that can return service well can do much to destroy a good doubles combination. A return of serve seldom wins the point outright, but it can set up a less forceful return or it can open up the court to the defenders. Basically, there are three possible returns, speaking directionally—the cross-court to the incoming server, the lob over the backhand of the net man, and the down-the-line in the net man's alley.

Of the three returns, the topspin cross-court drive is the safest return and should be used more frequently than the other two. The length of this drive should vary according to the movements of the server. Should the server follow up the service, then the return should be a dipping shot, aimed to bounce at his feet, giving a very difficult low volley. Another good return to the oncoming server is a sharply angled ball, low over the net, and towards the alley—this shot if accurately played will often win the point outright. It is far more effective to return a well-placed dipping ball at the advancing server than just to hit hard, because a good volleyer never minds a hard ball if it is high over the net. If, however, the server remains on the base line, then a good length drive, deep into the corner, will give you the opportunity to join your partner at the net and you will have gained the attacking position.

A successful lob is a very difficult stroke to play. It must be a good length, and well disguised, otherwise the opponents will see what your intention is and will have plenty of time to get back and "smash" it.

The drive straight down the side line is risky, but if brought to perfection will win many points outright. Even if it is not successful and you lose the point, it is well worth trying because you will have conveyed to your opponent the fact that you are thinking of the shot, and in consequence he will keep in position and allow more cross-court drives to pass unmolested. It should also be used occasionally if one of the opponents is inclined to poach (to take the shots that normally belong to his partner) and to keep him from edging too much over to the center, to "keep him in his place." If, however, your opponents adopt the so-called Australian formation when they are serving, your cross-court drive must be eliminated, and you must either drive straight down the side line or lob.

A good man in the receiver's court will alternate his returns, but his decisions will be based not on the shots themselves but on the talents of the opposition. Remember, too, that it is most important to keep the ball in play when you return the service. Inexperienced teams waste too many points in trying to drive hard for a clean ace. A short, low drive is much more important than speed. In fact, a drive with moderate speed is usually more difficult to volley than a fast return. A clean pass off the service is so difficult that your errors will probably more than offset your aces.

Do not allow the opponents' activities at the net to fluster you and put you off your aim. The tendency is to have one eye on the volleyer and one on the ball, and the result is fatal. Watch the ball and concentrate and make up your mind—but not obviously— what you are going to do, and unless the adversary moves before you have hit the ball, he or she will not be in time to intercept a good shot. And if the volleyer does move before you strike the ball, you have only to change your direction and push it quite gently straight down the side line to win the point.

The return of service resolves itself into a battle of wits between the receiver and the opponent at the net—the former trying to avoid the latter—and the latter endeavoring to intercept the drives of the former.

It is difficult to define the best position for you to take when your partner is receiving the service, but it generally depends on two things, the movements of the server and the general quality of your partner's return. When the server remains back you should certainly stand up at the net, because you are in the attacking position. Also if your partner has a good return of service you should stand close to the net irrespective of what the server is doing, as you may have an opportunity of intercepting the server's return. Only when your partner is having great difficulty with the service, and more often than not putting the ball on to the opponents' rackets, should you stand back, because under these circumstances your position at the net is useless,

Position is important in doubles play. Here Rex Hartwig backhands the ball back to the team of Tony Trabert and Vic Seixas, while Lew Hoad is ready for their return.

whereas if you are back you have a chance of picking up the opponents' volleys. If there is any doubt as to which position is better, the simplest thing is to ask your partner's opinion as to where you should stand while this particular service is in progress.

To return service well in doubles, one needs concentration to a superb degree, mental relaxation, anticipation to handle flat, hard serves, and a knowledge of service spins for control in returning slices and twists. The left-handed slice or the right-handed American twist will bounce, then move toward your left. The sooner you take slice or twist, the less effective they will be; therefore you stand in as much as possible for spin serves. The

later you take flat, hard serves, the less the forward pace on them; therefore you want to take them from behind the base line, particularly on a fast court. And so you stay on your toes in anticipation of moving forward for slices and twists or of jumping backward for flat cannonballs.

Strategy During Rallies

In volley, the first objective, when serving, is to force a weak return from your opponents or to draw them out of position—in either case, you can then volley or smash for the point. If, for example, either opponent is standing on or inside his base line, volley deep, directly at him and as near to his feet as possible, so as to force a comparatively weak return which you can kill. Or, if you volley deep to the center of their base line, you will draw at least one, possibly both, of your opponents to the center, which may give you an opportunity to volley to a corner for an ace. Or you may volley deep to one corner, drawing your opponents apart, and then volley or smash between them through the opening you have made.

The sharply angled cross-court volley to the alley is often effective for an ace, but if it fails, you will probably give your opponents a setup. The extra width of the doubles court and your position to the side of the half-court line provide wide angles and frequent chances to kill a ball by a short, sharp, wide volley; you should, however, volley to kill. The stop volley is often effective, especially on grass courts. Somewhat similar tactics apply to the smash as to the volley. Eventually, you may learn to kill a lob from almost any part of the court; but for the beginner a good general rule is to smash for a kill when you are near the service line, but not when you are near your base line. Do not let lobs drop, however, no matter how deep they may be, or you will lose the net position. If the lobbers run in, smash at their feet; if they stay back, smash deep; and in either case, get back into a volleying position quickly. Your partner should tell you if your opponents are following in their lobs; he should also watch the lob and if it is going out he should call.

Actually, an important matter about which you must have a definite understanding with your partner is the taking of lobs. Many points are lost on this score, not because the lobs are untakable—but because the partners muddle one another. Here again, so long as you understand each other, you can adopt what method you like, but as a general rule it is easier for the partner standing at the net to retrieve the deep lobs, when the server is running in. It is obviously easier to get off the mark quickly from a stationary position than to have to stop, turn, and retrace your steps. In fact it is almost impossible for the server, if he or she is concentrating on getting right up to the net as quickly as possible, to cope with the deep lobs that go over either head, and pitch within an inch of the base line. On

A lob to the backcourt can cause problems in doubles play.

the other hand, the player at the net has only to watch the receiver's racket carefully to anticipate the lob, and will then have plenty of time to take the necessary action. Here is another important reason why the server should maintain a strict rule with regard to following up the service. The partner at the net must know what the server's movements are going to be if he or she is to deal satisfactorily with the lobs. If the server is coming in, the net player must not poach—but must be ready to fly back and retrieve the lobs.

When both partners are up at the net, they will of course each retrieve their own lobs. During a rally if one has to run back, the other should move back as well, so as to be on a level. There are fewer "gaps" in the court when the partners are in line with one another.

Your reply to the deep lob (one that you cannot kill) must depend on the movements of your opponents. If they follow their lob up to the net—as they should—then your only chance is to send back a lob, high and deep, one that they cannot reach to smash and which gives you the opportunity of reaching the net position again. If, however, the opponents do not advance to the net when they have lobbed over your heads, then a good-length drive will give you a chance of reaching the net once more. But always remember that when either you or your partner has to lob, if it is not a good one, it will be "killed," and your best chance of picking up a "kill" is by taking up your position outside the base line.

With regard to the short lob which can be smashed, each player should be responsible for those in his or her court, and those in the center should be dealt with by the partner in the left court, because they fall on the forehand—whereas they are on the backhand of the right court player, and therefore almost impossible to "kill."

A short, low cross-cut drive should always be attempted if your opponents are slow in regaining the net after smashing one of your deep lobs. If this squeeze play is well executed and followed in without the slightest hesitation, you can steal the net from the servers. It is demoralizing for your opponents to have the net taken away from them in this manner, and you only need to bring it off a few times in one game to break through their service and win a commanding lead in the set. This is, of course, a risky play; unless your drive is low, you will lose the point. But it is so all-important for your team to capture the net and chances of winning the point from the back court are so much against you that it pays to take chances—not by driving blindly with all your strength, but by finesse.

The lob comes into its own in doubles and can occasionally turn defense into attack if its use is not abused. An effective attack sometimes is to alternate deep lobs and short drives, being constantly on your toes to follow in your short drive when possible. Persistent lobbing sometimes will break down all but the strongest attack. If one of your opponents is not too strong on smashing, you can sometimes steal the net by lobbing deep, preferably to his backhand, and following in. If your opponent lets your lob drop near his base line, take the net.

Poaching is often sound strategy in doubles. When you are serving, for example, your partner, from his net position, can often get a possible volley shot on a ball returned to your side of court, and in such a case, he should take it. Partners who have played together for a long time almost know instinctively when each will poach on the other, but

it is a good idea to call out or signal a poach whenever possible. Too much poaching, however, may ruin the game—as well as leave one side of the court open for the opponents to drive over a winning point. A good rule to follow is to poach only when you can execute a decisive stroke.

While shots down the center usually belong to the partner on whose forehand they come, there should be a prearranged understanding about this and certain other types of shots. In a quick encounter at the net, the partner who has just played the ball generally continues to finish the point if possible. He is warmed up and in close contact with the exchange. However, when this is the case the player not handling the shot or shots must move swiftly to cover any section of the court exposed by his partner's action.

In doubles, when all the players are volleying, many balls are taken which if left alone would go out. There is so little time for your partner to judge the pace and elevation of the ball that he or she has to volley, but you are in a better position and should call "out" clearly and distinctly. Again, if there is any doubt in your mind as to which of you is going to take a certain ball, a quick "yours" or "mine" will prevent you from hampering one another.

Doubles Tips

The game of doubles is much more than serve, return of serve, and volley. It is a game of skill, tactics, and headwork. Here are suggestions for good doubles:

1. The partner who is winning his serve more easily should start serving first in each set.
2. A lefty should serve on the sunny side since it is *not* the sunny side for him.
3. Lefties are generally better in the right court since it gives them an opportunity to poach off the forehand.
4. When in doubt, hit down the center.
5. Do not baby setups; hit them!
6. Lob frequently; drop-volley rarely; drop-shot never.
7. Vary your returns of serve and disguise them.
8. If you never poach, your opponents

need be less careful about their returns.

9. Never be angry with a partner who is passed when he poaches.

10. Do not moan or look unhappy when your partner misses.

11. When you have pulled the opponent wide to the backhand court, you and your partner should cover your forehand alley and the center, leaving your backhand alley open. The reverse holds true on a wide ball to the forehand court.

12. Play the weaker opponent and play his weakness.

13. Practice the doubles shots you do not know—except in a match.

14. When a lob goes over your head and your partner goes back for it, cross over quickly so that you are not both caught on the same side.

15. Show good manners: do not call shots on your opponent's side (unless asked), do not quick-serve, do not stall, and do not blame your partner if you lose.

Mixed Doubles

Mixed doubles is a branch of the game which calls for some principles very different from those used in either singles or men's doubles. The same methods of play that are used in other doubles do not often hold good and frequently cannot be brought into use because of the inequality of the two partners in this kind of a game. That is, the principle of the weaker link of a chain applies very strongly here, and it is very difficult to prevent the opposing players from selecting the woman on your side of the net for attack and by directing their strokes to her, to reduce the opposing strength to the level of the weaker player's game. To prevent this only one way seems practicable, and that is to get the woman up to the net at the first opportunity and then to direct your strokes, if you be the man partner, so as to support her in that position where she can be of the most value to her team.

The woman is usually more valuable to her side at the net and the man at the back of her court, unless he can work his way in and support his partner in the volleying position, when both might hold the attack safely to-gether. The difficulty is in getting the woman up to the net safely. When her man partner serves, there is no question but that her place is at the net, and she can take up her stand there before the ball is put into play. Similarly, when he is the receiver, she can take the same position safely and he can support her by his first return.

But when the woman serves and when she is the receiver, the man's place generally is at the middle of the base line to cover any return that the other side can make. For the dangerous run that the woman must make toward the net without being caught half way up with the ball at her feet, a strategic stroke must be made that will give her the needed time, and this is not always afforded by the return of the adversaries. If both of the opponents are back in their court, perhaps the safest way to secure the desired position is to drive deep into the woman's corner on the other side and have your partner run up behind this drive.

If the other woman is on the same side of the court as your partner, this can be done at the first opening, but if they are diagonally opposite, it is always safer to have her cross over to the side opposite her woman opponent, and then make the run to the net on the first deep drive into the woman's corner. If the woman on the other side is playing at the net, this chance is not open, and the next alternative is to lob deep over the woman's head and your partner can then run in under this lob unless the man on the other side is an exceptionally good smasher, when it might be dangerous to lob at all. However that may be, one of these two devices should be used and maneuvered for until your partner can reach the net safely, after which a new situation presents itself.

With the woman at the net, this tactical position is usually sound, and if the other woman has also reached the net, then it is a matter of better tennis on even terms or better strategy that ought to win. With the woman against you at the base line and your partner at the net, the odds are all in your favor, of course, so long as you can prevent the opposing woman from running in. Unless she be exceptionally clever at passing, a deep drive into her corner ought to let you follow it up safely, and with both yourself and your partner at the net together, victory is almost certain with the ball kept on the woman's side of the court, and about even if the opposing man gets a chance at the play.

With both women in the volleying position, the play between the two men generally is diagonally across the court, and it should be the aim of the clever player to keep his drives well over in front of his partner, so that from her position she will be able to cover as much territory as possible. To play to the other corner leaves the "open diagonal" of the court wide open and limits the partner's usefulness to covering a very small sector of the court.

When the opponent follows the same tactics and simply tries to outdrive you, a splendid variation is to work him far out to the outside of his court to meet a diagonal drive and then to lob deep and low over his partner's head and follow the play up to the net. The effect of this play is to bring the man on the other side directly behind his partner, leaving them doubled up and the other side of the court entirely unguarded.

If you follow this play up to the net quickly, the court will be wide open for a kill and nothing but a lob or a brilliant passing stroke will save the other side from losing. The greatest danger of this play is that the man opponent will be able to cross quickly enough to smash, but if the lob is low and well placed

to the side of the court, he will find it very difficult to get there in time, especially if he was far over to the other side before.

When volleying with all four at the net it is in most cases the best to aim at the woman, for she is likely to be not only less strong in the wrist for the return, but less able to keep up a series of short crisp shots. She may volley finely, but she has not the endurance of the man. Do not think, however, that she will be slower at chasing lobs or less reliable when dealing with them. She will not be so punishing overhead, but she will be as well, possibly better, able to deal with them after the bounce, and swifter to reach a good position for that purpose.

There are many other variations of play for mixed doubles, but success in this game depends largely on getting your woman partner up to the net, and keeping her there safely so her position covers as much of the court as possible. Naturally, the woman who volleys well is much the stronger partner, and to select one who volleys badly is to court defeat.

The service is a big advantage in mixed doubles, and the man should always serve first as he ought to win his own service game 70 percent of the time with evenly matched teams. The struggle usually develops around the winning of the games in which the women serve and both of the men are expected to win their own service games.

SECTION IV

Rules and Etiquette of Lawn Tennis

The United States Lawn Tennis Association—in this, its own "official" book—has been, of course, mentioned many times. Its early history was fully covered in Section I. Now let us take a look at the activities of the organization itself.

UNITED STATES LAWN TENNIS ASSOCIATION (USLTA)

The United States Lawn Tennis Association is a nationwide, noncommercial membership organization devoted to the development of tennis as a means of healthful recreation and physical fitness and to the maintenance of high standards of amateurism, fair play, and sportsmanship. The oldest amateur sport-governing body in the United States, it is a non-profit organization, consisting of seventeen geographical sectional associations, many of which contain district associations. Organization and promotional work for and through the over 2,000 affiliated clubs composing the National Association are directed by close to 700 officers and committeemen throughout the entire country. All such activities are conducted by elective or voluntary workers without remuneration, supervised from the various sectional headquarters or the National Executive Director's Office in New York City, which includes the only recompensed staff within the USLTA.

One of the main functions of the USLTA has been to establish or alter rules for the benefit of the sport and players. Most of the legislation concerning rules of the game occurred during the early years of the Association. Beginning with the first meeting, three rules were adopted which have not been changed over the years. The most important decree concerned the method of keeping score. The present system of counting was chosen and thus the old system of racquets scoring that was being used by some clubs was outlawed. The present dimension of 21 feet between the service line and the net was established as the official measurement for a tennis court. Also, to avoid disputes in tournaments, it was ruled that the decision of the umpire was to be final.

In the fall of 1881, the Association published a book of rules with some additional changes. The server was to stand with one foot behind the base line, although the other foot could be on or over the base line. A good service delivered when the receiver was not ready was not to count, a "let" on the service was no longer to be in play, the net and posts were not to be touched, and the ball was not to be volleyed before it passed the net. If the umpire wished, he could direct the players to change sides after every game, either throughout the match or in the deciding set. Court regulations were to the effect that the service court in doubles was to be reduced to the same size as in singles.

Other major rule changes occurred in 1891. A rest was provided for in a match, although it was only 7 minutes instead of the present period of 10 minutes. There was to be a referee for every tournament and an umpire for every match. By 1895 most of the rules of tennis were well established and these have lasted through the years. A few minor changes have been made since, which concern the action of the server. In 1898 it was ruled that the server must keep both feet behind the base line. In 1955 it was stated that while both feet must be behind the base line during service, one foot may swing over the line so long as it does not touch the ground before the ball is struck. The present USLTA tennis rules are given later in this section.

The United States Lawn Tennis Association not only formulates standard tennis rules but also sanctions national tournaments and the rules of organization. As previously stated in Section I, the first United States national tournament was held at Newport, R.I., in 1881. This contest included men's singles and men's doubles. Presently the national USLTA championships are: The USLTA Open Championship; United States Amateur Championship; United States Clay-court Championship; United States Hard-court Championship; United States Father-Son Championship; United States Mother-Daughter Championship; United States Husband-Wife Championship; United States 18, 16, 14, and 12-and-under championships; United States Interscholastic Championship; and National Collegiate Championship (men and women). In all veterans' championships, divisions are junior veterans 35 and up, senior 45 and over, senior 60; in women's competition, there is women's 35, senior, and senior 50. Greater detail on these tournaments is given in Section V. In 1971, over 10,000 tournaments were held throughout the United States under the auspices of the USLTA.

As the number of tournaments and players increased, it was necessary to make official regulations for the organization of tourna-ments. As was the case with the rules of the game, most of the laws were laid down during the early years of the Association. For instance, in 1884 the Bagnall-Wild system of draw was adopted for tournaments. This innovation eliminated "byes" after the first round. Prior to this, a new draw had been made after each round, and byes had occurred in any round. Also in 1884, a novel step was introduced to make tournaments fairer and more interesting. It was decided that the present champion of a tournament should not compete in the matches until the last day of the contest. This meant that the champion would "stand out" and defend his title against the winner among the other players. This system was used until 1912, when it was abolished in favor of the present system by which all contestants play throughout the tournament.

In 1885 the first official rankings of players were made, whereby the ten most skilled men in the country were rated in order of ability as shown by their tournament records. In 1910 the list grew to include 100 players but this proved to be too large a number and the next year the list was reduced to 35 players. These rankings have continued to be made each year, and at present approximately 35 players in each division and age group are ranked by the USLTA. More on ranking can be found in Section VI.

The USLTA in 1922 inaugurated "seeding a draw" for tournaments. Previously players had been placed in a draw at random and consequently the two best players often had to play against each other before the final round. The principle behind seeding was to place the best players in different sections of the draw so that they would not meet each other in the early rounds. Today seeding is done in all tournaments, whether local or national.

In 1922, after years of negotiations, the USLTA joined the International Lawn Tennis Federation (ILTF), which had been founded in 1913. Then, as today, this body encompassed all the lawn tennis associations in the world in an endeavor to provide standard regulations everywhere for the game of tennis. Thus, as a member of the Federation, the USLTA is an effective factor in supervision and changes of the worldwide playing rules, maintaining high standards in the production of tennis balls, rackets, and all other playing paraphernalia.

The USLTA is probably the most active and enthusiastic member of the International Federation in developing and expanding junior tennis in its many phases. Actually, the promotion of junior development is one of the most important programs in the United States Lawn Tennis Association. Clinics, a series of tournaments, and the encouragement of travel opportunities are among some of the benefits to be derived from junior development. The junior development program offers such opportunities as:

1. A summer tour and practice program on the Junior Davis Cup team, from which future Davis Cup players are selected.
2. The chance for international competition on the junior level in such top tournaments as the Orange Bowl Championships, held annually in Miami Beach, and the Sunshine Cup, or Junior Davis Cup, also held in Miami Beach, and the Junior Wightman Cup for girls.
3. A comprehensive group of national tournaments for players in the junior (18-and-under, 16, 14, and 12) divisions, in both girls' and boys' competition.
4. Clinics and instructional programs through various tournaments. Several leading tournaments in the U.S. donate part of their proceeds to junior development in underprivileged areas.
5. The chance for financial aid to deserving young players, who show a need and desire to improve themselves.
6. The formation of foundations in various states and by certain sectional associations to help deserving players meet the financial responsibility that goes with traveling to top tournaments.

Annual reports are submitted to the USLTA by a Junior Development Committee on the progress of programs. Interested parents should contact the USLTA National Executive Director's Office, 51 East 42 Street, New York, N.Y. 10017, or their sectional association for information on junior development programs available in their area.

In the beginning years of the Association, tennis was a young sport and only engaged in by a very small minority of the population. Consequently, the structure of the organization was simple and its problems were relatively few. Though a small group it had unchallenged authority as the national body for the game of tennis from its inception. It undertook projects that had far-reaching results, such as selection of a standard ball, adoption of a common method of scoring, issuance of standard rules, and so forth. It is important to keep in mind that in its first years the Association did not have on its membership rolls all those clubs playing tennis. Yet, as the game developed and the functions of the Association became more numerous, it became more of a necessity for a club to belong to the national body in order to receive certain privileges. The early years of the Association received these comments from J. Parmly Paret in his 1904 book on tennis:

> The USNLTA is the controlling body, but its membership includes only a small proportion of the tennis clubs of the country. There are many smaller sectional associations through the West, and some also in the East, few of which hold membership in the USNLTA. The policy of the National Association has not been aggressive, and no attempt is made to outlaw players who compete in tournaments under other auspices, or to insist on the enforcement of its laws outside of its own membership.

However, it should be pointed out that since the very first national tournament in 1881 many tournaments were open only to those players who belonged to clubs which had membership in the USLTA.

As tennis grew in popularity and the responsibilities of the Association toward the game became more numerous, it is natural that the organization itself became larger and more complex in order to carry out its functions. A brief examination of some of the developments and changes in structure illustrates this point.

The governing body within the USLTA has always been an Executive Committee. In 1881 the Executive Committee consisted of six people: President, Vice-President, Secretary-Treasurer, and three delegates. Furthermore,

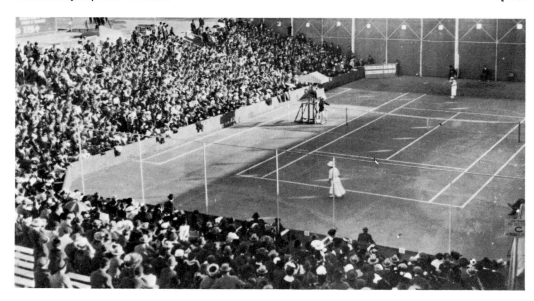

Resort areas were among the first to install tennis courts. Here is a partial view of the capacity audience watching the famous match between May Sutton and Molla Bjurstedt on the Hotel Virginia courts at Long Beach, Calif., in 1914. Miss Sutton was the winner.

it is recorded in its very first year that there were several committees, notably a Tournament Committee and a Prize Committee. Today the USLTA has an Executive Committee (numbering 42 people) which consists of the officers and delegates. In addition, there are 52 national committees. Each of the 17 sectional associations has a somewhat similar setup. Thus, it will be seen that several thousand tennis enthusiasts, many of them famous national and international champions of the past, voluntarily devote many thousand hours each year to coordinating and improving tennis playing conditions, and the maintenance of the high amateur standards which have always been the keynote of the game.

USLTA Sectional Associations

Here is a listing of the seventeen sectional associations of USLTA:

EASTERN—comprising the state of New York and those parts of Connecticut and New Jersey within 35 miles of New York City Hall.
FLORIDA—comprising the state of Florida.
HAWAII—comprising the state of Hawaii.
INTERMOUNTAIN—comprising the states of Colorado, that part of Idaho south of

More than ten million players, who annually tread the thousands of courts throughout the United States, benefit by this promotional work, whether they play on school, public park, small community, or famous club courts with many years of history and tradition back of them, such as the West Side Tennis Club, New York, the Los Angeles Club, Town and Country Club of Chicago, and the historic clubs along the Atlantic Coast, the birthplace of American tennis, such as Seabright, Longwood, Newport, Germantown, Merion, Chevy Chase, and others, where first the turf was marked with the introduction of the game in America in 1874.

the 45th parallel of latitude, Montana, Nevada (except for the counties of Washoe and Ormsby in the state of Nevada), Utah, Wyoming.
MIDDLE ATLANTIC—comprising District of Columbia and the states of Maryland, Virginia, and West Virginia, except the following counties therein: Boone, Cabell, Calhoun, Jackson, Kanawha, Lincoln, Logan, Mason, Mingo, Pleasants, Putnam, Ritchie, Roane, Wayne, Wirt and Wood.
MIDDLE STATES—comprising the states of New Jersey (except that part within 35

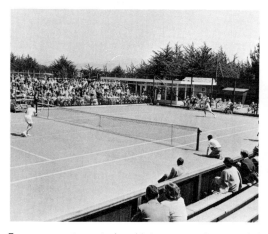

Famous resort courts in widely separated parts of the United States: (*top, left*) Arizona Inn, Tucson, Ariz.; (*top, right*) Spruce Point Inn, Boothbay, Me.; (*bottom, left*), Del Monte Lodge, Pebble Beach, Calif.; (*bottom, right*) Boca Raton Hotel and Club, Boca Raton, Fla.

miles of New York City Hall), Pennsylvania, Delaware.

MISSOURI VALLEY—comprising the states of Iowa, Kansas, Missouri, Nebraska, Oklahoma, that part of Illinois known as Rock Island County and that part of Illinois within a 30-mile radius of St. Louis City Hall.

NEW ENGLAND—comprising the states of Connecticut (except that part within 35 miles of New York City Hall), Maine, Massachusetts, New Hampshire, Rhode Island, Vermont.

NORTHERN CALIFORNIA—comprising the counties of Alameda, Alpine, Amador, Butte, Calaveras, Colusa, Contra Costa, Del Norte, El Dorado, Fresno, Glenn, Humboldt, Inyo, Kings, Lake, Lassen, Madera, Marin, Mariposa, Mendocino, Merced, Modoc, Mono, Monterey, Napa, Nevada, Placer, Plumas, Sacramento, San Benito, San Francisco, San Joaquin, San Mateo, Santa Clara, Santa Cruz, Shasta, Sierra, Siskiyou, Solano, Sonoma, Stanislaus, Sutter, Tehama, Trinity, Tulare, Tuolumne, Yolo and Yuba in the state of California, and the counties of Washoe and Ormsby in the state of Nevada.

NORTHWESTERN—comprising the states of Minnesota, North Dakota, South Dakota.

PACIFIC NORTHWEST, comprising the states of Oregon, Washington, and that part of Idaho north of the 45th parallel of latitude, and the province of British Columbia.

(*left*) Tennis courts on the island of Bermuda (Elbow Beach Surf Club) and (*right*) Nassau (Emerald Beach Plantation and Hotel).

PUERTO RICO—comprising Puerto Rico and U.S. Virgin Islands of St. Thomas, St. Croix and St. John.

SOUTHERN—comprising the states of Alabama, Arkansas, Georgia, Kentucky (except Boone, Campbell and Kenton Counties), Louisiana, Mississippi, North Carolina, South Carolina, Tennessee.

SOUTHERN CALIFORNIA—comprising the counties of Imperial, Kern, Los Angeles, Orange, Riverside, San Bernardino, San Diego, San Luis Obispo, Santa Barbara, Ventura.

SOUTHWESTERN—comprising the states of Arizona and New Mexico, together with El Paso County, Texas.

TEXAS—comprising the state of Texas, except El Paso County.

WESTERN—comprising the states of Illinois (except Rock Island County and that part of Illinois within a 30-mile radius of St. Louis City Hall), Indiana, Michigan, Ohio, Wisconsin, that portion of Kentucky included in the counties of Boone, Campbell and Kenton, and that portion of West Virginia included in the counties of Boone,

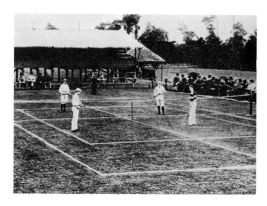

The Nationals at Newport in the 1880's and today at West Side Tennis Club in Forest Hills. There is some difference in the size of the crowd!

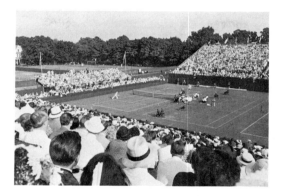

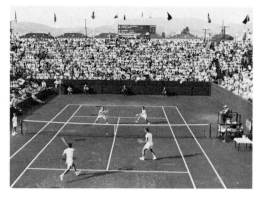
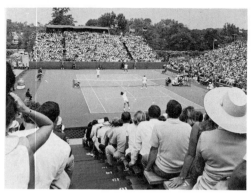

Three of the United States' most famous tennis stadiums: (*top*) Merion Cricket Club, Ardmore, Pa.; (*bottom, left*) Los Angeles Tennis Club, Los Angeles, Calif.; (*bottom, right*) The Harold T. Clark Courts, Cleveland Heights, Ohio.

Cabell, Calhoun, Jackson, Kanawha, Lincoln, Logan, Mason, Mingo, Pleasants, Putnam, Ritchie, Roane, Wayne, Wirt and Wood.

Since the addresses frequently change with the elections of new secretaries, addresses of these sectional associations as well as a list of clubs holding direct membership in the USLTA may be obtained by writing to the USLTA Executive Office, 51 East 42 Street, New York, New York 10017.

INTERNATIONAL LAWN TENNIS FEDERATION (ILTF)

The International Lawn Tennis Federation, which is located at Barons Court, London, W.14, Great Britain, is considered the governing body of world tennis. According to the rules of the ILTF, its objects are as follows:

1. To uphold the Rules of Lawn Tennis as at present adopted, and to make and maintain such alterations and additions thereto from time to time as may appear necessary or desirable.

2. To print and publish in the English language from time to time as occasion may require the official and decisive text of the Rules of Lawn Tennis.

3. To print and publish from time to time as occasion may require the official and decisive text of these Rules.

4. To check, and if necessary correct, the translation of the Rules of Lawn Tennis and interpretation of these Rules into any other language prior to the same being recognized as accurate by the Federation, such translation having

The new Madison Square Garden in New York plays host to many of the leading professional and open indoor matches.

pionships, tournaments open to all categories, and major tournaments open to amateurs and professionals.

8. To promote and encourage the teaching of lawn tennis.

9. To employ the funds of the Federation in such manner as shall be deemed expedient.

10. To strengthen the bonds of friendship between the existing associations and to encourage the formation of new associations.

11. To give associations by joint action a greater influence in their dealings with the governing bodies of other sports.

12. To enforce the observation of these rules in all national and international competitions.

13. To uphold the principles on which the Federation is founded and generally to take such measures as may appear expedient for advancing the interests of lawn tennis from an international point of view.

14. To preserve its independence in all matters concerning the game of lawn tennis without the intervention of any outside authority in its relations with its affiliated associations.

been first made by any nation or nations using such language and having been then submitted to the Federation for checking.

5. To recognize and uphold the regulations for the time being in force for the International Lawn Tennis Championships (Davis Cup and Federation Cup).

6. To award official lawn tennis championships recognized by the Federation.

7. To draw up a calendar of official cham-

Addresses of affiliated associations—those with voting rights in the ILTF—are as follows:

ALGERIA—Federation Algerienne de Lawn Tennis, 18 rue Dupuch, Algiers.

ARGENTINA—Asociacion Argentina de

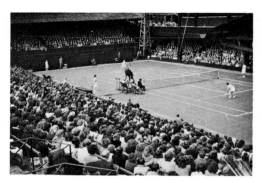

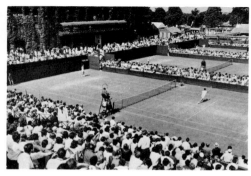

Wimbledon, headquarters of the All-England Club. (*left*) The famed Centre Court and (*right*) some of the 17 outer grass courts.

Tennis, Avenida Presidente Julio A. Roca, 546–7° Piso, Buenos Aires.

AUSTRALIA—L.T.A. of Australia, McKillop House, 23, McKillop Street, Melbourne, Victoria 3000.

AUSTRIA—Osterreichischer Tennisverband, Rustenschacherallee 1, 1020 Vienna.

BELGIUM—Federation Royale Belge de Lawn-Tennis, 164, Av. Louise, Brussels 5.

BOLIVIA—Federacion Boliviana de Lawn Tennis, Casilla No. 940, La Paz.

BRAZIL—Confederacao Brasileira de Tenis, Rua Anfilofio de Carvalho No. 29, Grupo 407/8—ZC—P. Centro, Rio de Janeiro.

BULGARIA—Bulgarian Lawn Tennis Federation, Boul. Tolboukhine, 18, Sofia.

BURMA—Burma Tennis Federation, Aungsan Stadium, Rangoon.

CANADA—Canadian Lawn Tennis Association, 333 River Rd. Vanier, Ontario, Kil 8139.

CEYLON—Ceylon L.T.A., 45 Edinburgh Crescent, Colombo 7.

CHILE—Federacion de Lawn Tennis de Chile, Casilla 1149, Santiago.

CHINA—All China Sports Federation, 3, Tai Yang Kung, Peking.

COLOMBIA—Asociacion Colombiana de Tennis, Apartado aereo 10.917, Bogota 1.

CUBA—Federacion Amateur Cubana de Lawn Tennis, Edificio "La Metropolitana" Apartamentos 810/811, Havana.

CZECHOSLOVAKIA—Ceskoslovenska Tenisova Asociace, Na Porici 12, Prague 3.

DENMARK—Dansk Lawn-Tennis Forbund, Vester Voldgade 11, 1552 Copenhagen V.

ECUADOR—Asociacion Ecuatoriana de Tennis, Box 1030, Guayaquil.

FINLAND—Suomen Tennisliitto, Box 25202, Helsinki 25.

FRANCE—Federation Française de Lawn Tennis, 15 rue de Teheran, Paris 8.

GERMAN DEMOCRATIC REPUBLIC— Deutscher Tennis-Verband der DDR, Storkower Strasse, 118, 1055, Berlin.

GERMAN FEDERAL REPUBLIC— Deutscher Tennis Bund, Bonnerstrasse, 12a, Hannover 3.

GREAT BRITAIN—The Lawn Tennis Association, Barons Court, West Kensington, London, W.14.

GREECE—Federation Hellenique de Lawn Tennis, 8 rue Omirou (133), Athens.

HUNGARY—Magyar Tenisz Szovetseg, Rosenberg Hold utca 1, Budapest V.

INDIA—All India L.T.A., 7/3, Asafali Road, New Delhi 1.

INDONESIA—Indonesian Lawn Tennis Association, Depora, Senejan-Djakarta.

IRAN—Iranian Tennis Federation, Sports Federations Joint Bureau, P.O. Box 11–1642, Teheran.

IRELAND—Irish L.T.A., 17, Leinster Road, Rathmines, Dublin.

ISRAEL—Israel Lawn Tennis Association, P.O. Box 20073, Tel Aviv.

ITALY—Federazione Italiana Tennis, Viale Tiziano 70, 00100 Rome.

JAMAICA—Jamaica L.T.A., 5 Port Royal Street, Kingston.

JAPAN—Japan Lawn Tennis Association, 1-1-1 Jinnan, Shibuya-ku, Tokyo.

KOREA—Korean L.T.A., Room 706, Sports Building, 19 Makyo-Dong, Chungku, Seoul.

LEBANON—Federation Libanaise de Lawn Tennis, Immeuble Assicurazioni Generali, Place de l'Etoile, B.P. 5798, Beirut.

LUXEMBOURG—Federation Luxembourgeoise de Tennis, 110, Val Ste. Croix, Luxembourg.

MALAYSIA—L.T.A. of Malaysie, No. 11, Jalan, 6/18, Petaling Jaya, Selangor.

MEXICO—Federacion Mexicana de Tenis A.C., Plaza de la Republica No. 43, Despacho 106, Mexico 1, D.F.

MONACO—Federation Monegasque de Lawn Tennis, 14, quai Antoine Ier, Monaco.

MOROCCO—Federation Royale Marocaine de Lawn-Tennis, Maison des Sports, Parc de la Ligue Arabe, Casablanca.

NETHERLANDS—Koninklijke Nederlandsche Lawn Tennis Bond, Box 5113, Amsterdam.

NEW ZEALAND—New Zealand L.T.A., G.P.O. Box 1645, Wellington, C.I.

NORWAY—Norges Tennisforbund, Kirkegt. 8, Oslo 1.

PAKISTAN—All Pakistan L.T.A., 106 Wazir Ali Road, Lahore.

PERU—Federacion Peruana de Lawn Tennis, Casilla 2243, Lima.

PHILIPPINES—Philippine Lawn Tennis Association, Box 4143, Manila.

POLAND—Polski Zwiazek Tenisowy, ul. Mysia 2, pokoj 541, Warsaw.

PORTUGAL—Federacao Portuguesa de Lawn Tennis, Rua do Arco do Cego, 90–6° Esq., Lisbon 1.

RUMANIA—Federatia Romana de Tenis, Vasile Conta 16, Bucharest.

SOUTH AFRICA—The South African Lawn Tennis Union, Box 2211, Johannesburg.

SPAIN—Real Federacion Española de Tenis, Via Augusta 109 bis, Barcelona 6.

SUDAN—Sudan Lawn Tennis Association, P.O. Box 1553, Khartoum.

SWEDEN—Svenska Tennisforbundet, Lidingovagen 75, S 115 37 Stockholm.

SWITZERLAND—Association Suisse de Tennis, Laubeggstrasse 70, 3000 Berne.

TAIWAN—Republic of China Tennis Association, 21 Lane 124, Sung Kiang Road, Taipei, Taiwan.

THAILAND—The Lawn Tennis Association of Thailand, c/o Sports Organization of Thailand, National Stadium, Bangkok.

TRINIDAD and TOBAGO—L.T.A. of Trinidad and Tobago, Red House, Lands & Surveys Dept., Port-of-Spain, Trinidad, W.I.

TUNIS—Federation Tunisienne de Lawn Tennis, 65 Avenue de la Liberté, Tunis.

TURKEY—Turkiye Tenis Federasyonu, Ulus Is Hani, Ankara.

UNITED ARAB REPUBLIC—L.T.A. of the United Arab Republic, 13, Sharia Kasr el Nil, Cairo.

U.S.A.—United States L.T.A., 51 East 42 Street (Suite 1008), New York, N.Y. 10017.

U.S.S.R.—Lawn Tennis Federation of the U.S.S.R., Skatertnyi pereulok 4, Moscow 69.

URUGUAY—Associacion Uruguaya de Lawn Tennis, Canelones 982, Montevideo.

VENEZUELA—Federacion Venezolana de Tennis, Altamira Tennis Club, Chacao, Edo. Miranda, Caracas.

VIET-NAM—Federation de Lawn Tennis du Viet-Nam, 135 Hai Ba Trung St., Saigon.

YUGOSLAVIA—Tenis Savez Yugoslavije, Terazije 35, Belgrade.

Addresses of associate members—those without voting rights in ILTF—are as follows:

AFGHANISTAN—Afghanistan L.T.A., c/o National Olympic Federation, Kabul.

BARBADOS—Barbados Lawn Tennis Association, Box 615c, Bridgetown.

CAMBODIA—Federation Cambodgienne de Tennis, 98, Vithei Dekcho Damdin, Phnom-Penh.

DAHOMEY—Federation Dahomeenne de Lawn-Tennis, Ecole Urbaine de Foun-Foun, Porto-Novo.

DUTCH ANTILLES—Nederlandsche Antilles Lawn-Tennis Bond, Laufferstraat 9, Curacao.

GHANA—Ghana L.T.A., Sports Council of Ghana, Box 1272, Accra.

GUATEMALA—Federacion Nacionale de Tenis, Apartado Postal 371, Ciudad de Guatemala.

GUYANA—Guyana Lawn Tennis Association, c/o J. W. Potter & Co., Ltd., 29 Main Street, P.O. Box 307, Georgetown.

HONG KONG—Hong Kong Lawn Tennis Association, 503 Realty Buildings, Des Voeux Road C, Hong Kong.

IRAQ—Iraqi Tennis Federation, c/o Baghdad Garrison, Karada Al-Sharkiya, Baghdad.

KENYA—Kenya L.T.A., Box 3184, Nairobi.

LIBERIA—Liberia Tennis Association, National Sports & Athletic Commission, P.O. Box 502, Broad Street, Monrovia.

LIBYA—Libyan Tennis Federation, c/o Libyan Olympic Committee, P.O. Box 879, Tripoli.

MADAGASCAR—Federation Malgache de Lawn-Tennis, B.P. 582, Tananarive.

MALAWI—Lawn Tennis Association of Malawi, P.O. Box 249, Blantyre.

MAURITIUS—Mauritius L.T.A., Rue Dr. Ferriere, Port-Louis.

NIGERIA—Nigeria Lawn Tennis Association, P.O. Box 145, Lagos.

PARAGUAY—Associacion Paraguaya de Lawn Tennis, Casilla Correo 26, Asuncion.

RHODESIA—The Rhodesia Lawn Tennis Association, P.O. Box 306, Bulawayo.

SAN MARINO—Federazione Sammarinese Tennis, 47031 Republic of San Marino.

SENEGAL—Federation Senegalaise de Lawn-Tennis, B.P. 510, Dakar.

SINGAPORE—Singapore Lawn Tennis Association, 15, Fort Canning Road, Singapore 6.

SURINAM—Surinaamse Tennis Bond, P.O. Box 1834, Paramaribo.

Two of Australia's larger stadiums: (*left*) Kooyong, Melbourne; (*right*) White City Courts, Sydney.

SYRIA—Syrian Tennis Federation, P.O. Box 421, Damascus.

TANZANIA—Tanganyika Lawn Tennis Association, P.O. Box 1750, Dar es Salaam.

TOGOLAND—Federation Togolaise de Lawn-Tennis, Lome.

UGANDA—Uganda L.T.A., P.O. Box 2107, Kampala.

RULES OF LAWN TENNIS

To *fully* understand the game of tennis you should know the rules. Although this may seem like a rather obvious suggestion, it sometimes is surprising how many players of long experience are still "sketchy" on the basic rules. A little understanding of the fundamentals may save considerable embarrassment both for yourself and those you play with. A knowledge of the rules will also help you to get the most fun possible out of the game and to apply your skill to the best advantage. Given below are the Official United States Lawn Tennis Association's *Rules of Lawn Tennis and Cases and Decisions:*

RULES OF LAWN TENNIS
and
CASES AND DECISIONS

EXPLANATORY NOTE

The appended Code of Rules, and Cases and Decisions is the Official Code of the International Lawn Tennis Federation, of which the United States Lawn Tennis Association is a member.

The Glossary of Terms is addenda adopted by the United States Lawn Tennis Association and is official in the United States only, although it in no way conflicts with the Code or international practice.

Italicized EXPLANATIONS, EXAMPLES and COMMENTS have been prepared by the USLTA Tennis Umpires Association to amplify and facilitate interpretation of the formal Code.

THE SINGLES GAME

RULE 1

Dimensions and Equipment

The Court shall be a rectangle, 78 feet long and 27 feet wide. It shall be divided across the middle by a net, suspended from a cord or metal cable of a maximum diameter of one-third of an inch, the ends of which shall be attached to, or pass over, the tops of two posts, 3 feet 6 inches high, the center of which shall be 3 feet outside the Court on each side. The height of the net shall be 3 feet at the center, where it shall be held down taut by a strap not more than 2 inches wide. There shall be a band covering the cord or metal cable and the top of the net not less than 2 inches nor more than 2½ inches in depth on each side. The lines bounding the ends and sides of the Court shall respectively be called the Baselines and the Side-lines. On each side of the net, at a distance of 21 feet from it and parallel with it, shall be drawn the Service-lines. The space on each side of the net between the service-line and the side-lines shall be divided into two equal parts called the service-courts by the center service-line. which must be 2 inches in width, drawn half-way between, and parallel with, the side-lines. Each base-line shall be bisected by an imaginary continuation of the center service-line to a line 4 inches in length and 2 inches in width called the center mark drawn inside the Court, at right angles to and in contact with such base-lines. All other lines shall not be less than 1 inch nor more than 2 inches ii. width, except the base-line, which may be 4 inches in width, and all measurements shall be made to the outside of the lines.

Note.—In the case of the International Lawn Tennis Championship (Davis Cup) or other Official Championships of the International Federation. there shall be a space behind each base-line of not less than 21 feet and at the sides of not less than 12 feet.

EXPLANATION OF RULE 1

The center of the posts in doubles should be 3 feet outside the doubles court.

The net should be 33 feet wide for a singles court, and 42 feet wide for a doubles court. It should touch the ground along its entire length and come flush to the posts at all points.

It is important to have a stick 3 feet, 6 inches long, with a notch cut in at the 3-foot mark for the purpose of measuring the height of the net at the posts and in the center. These measurements, as well as the measurements of the court itself, always should be made before starting to play an important match.

DIAGRAM AND DIMENSIONS OF TENNIS COURT

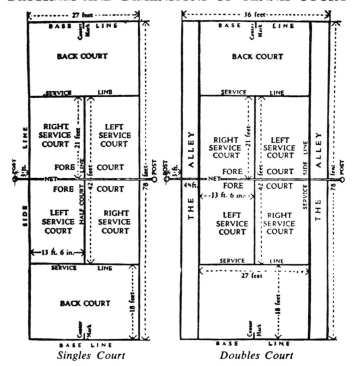

Singles Court   *Doubles Court*

RULE 2

Permanent Fixtures

The permanent fixtures of the Court shall include not only the net, posts, cord or metal cable, strap and band, but also, where there are any such, the back and side stops, the stands, fixed or movable seats and chairs around the Court, and their occupants, all other fixtures around and above the Court, and the Umpire, Net-cord Judge, Foot-fault Judge, Linesmen and Ball Boys when in their respective places.

RULE 3

Ball—Size, Weight and Bound

The ball shall have a uniform outer surface and shall be white in color. If there are any seams they shall be stitchless. The ball shall be more than two and a half inches and less than two and five-eighths inches in diameter, and more than two ounces and less than two and one-sixteenth ounces in weight. The ball shall have a bound of more than 53 inches and less than 58 inches when dropped 100 inches upon a concrete base. The ball shall have a forward deformation of more than .230 of an inch and less than .290 of an inch and a return deformation of more than .355 of an inch and less than .425 of an inch at 18 lb. load. The two deformation figures shall be the averages of three individual readings along three axes of the ball and no two individual readings shall differ by more than .030 of an inch in each case. All tests for bound, size and deformation shall be made in accordance with the Regulations in the Appendix hereto.

Note.—At the Annual General Meeting of the I.L.T.F. held on 12th July, 1967, it was agreed that for the time being non-pressurized balls and low-pressure balls may not be used in the International Lawn Tennis Championship (Davis Cup), unless mutually agreed by the two nations taking part in any particular event.

NOTE

"How often may the player have new balls?"

Generally the ball-change pattern is specified by the Referee before the match is started. According to Tournament Regulation 14 (g) the Umpire, subject to the approval of the Referee, may decide when new balls are required to insure fairness of playing conditions. In matches where there is no Umpire, the players should agree beforehand on this matter.

RULE 4

Server and Receiver

The Players shall stand on opposite sides of the net; the player who first delivers the ball shall be called the Server, and the other the Receiver.

Case 1. Does a player, attempting a stroke, lose the point if he crosses an imaginary line in the extension of the net, (a) before striking the ball (b) after striking the ball?

Decision. He does not lose the point in either case by crossing the imaginary line provided he does not enter the lines bounding his opponent's court. (Rule 18 (e).) In regard to hindrance, his opponent may ask for the decision of the umpire under Rules 19 and 23.

Case 2. The Server claims that the Receiver must stand within the lines bounding his court. Is this necessary?

Decision. No. The Receiver may stand wherever he pleases on his own side of the net.

RULE 5

Choice of Sides and Service

The choice of sides and the right to be Server or Receiver in the first game shall be decided by toss. The player winning the toss may choose, or require his opponent to choose:

(a) The right to be Server or Receiver, in which case the other player shall choose the side; or

(b) The side, in which case the other player shall choose the right to be Server or Receiver.

RULE 6

Delivery of Service

The service shall be delivered in the following manner. Immediately before commencing to serve, the Server shall stand with both feet at rest behind (i.e. farther from the net than) the base-line, and within the imaginary continuations of the center-mark and side-line. The Server shall then project the ball by hand into the air in any direction and before it hits the ground strike it with his racket, and the delivery shall be deemed to have been completed at the moment of the impact of the racket and the ball. A player with the use of only one arm may utilize his racket for the projection.

Case 1. May the Server in a singles game take his stand behind the portion of the base-line between the sidelines of the singles court and the doubles court?

Decision. No.

Case 2. If a player, when serving, throws up two or more balls instead of one, does he lose that service?

Decision. No. A let should be called, but if the umpire regards the action as deliberate he may take action under Rule 19.

Case 3. May a player serve underhand?

Decision. Yes. There is no restriction regarding the kind of service which may be used; that is, the player may use an underhand or overhand service at his discretion.

RULE 7
Foot Fault

The Server shall throughout the delivery of the service:

(a) Not change his position by walking or running.

(b) Not touch, with either foot, any area other than that behind the base-line within the imaginary extension of the center-mark and side-line.

Note.—The following interpretation of Rule 7 was approved by the International Federation on 9th July 1958:—

(a) The Server shall not, by slight movements of the feet which do not materially affect the location originally taken up by him, be deemed "to change his position by walking or running."

(b) The word "foot" means the extremity of the leg below the ankle.

COMMENT: This rule covers the most decisive stroke in the game, and there is no justification for its not being obeyed by players and enforced by officials. No tournament chairman has the right to request or attempt to instruct linesmen and/or umpires to disregard violations of it.

RULE 8
From Alternate Courts

(a) In delivering the service, the Server shall stand alternately behind the right and left Courts, beginning from the right in every game. If service from a wrong half of the Court occurs and is undetected, all play resulting from such wrong service or services shall stand, but the inaccuracy of the station shall be corrected immediately it is discovered.

(b) The ball served shall pass over the net and hit the ground within the Service Court which is diagonally opposite, or upon any line bounding such Court, before the Receiver returns it.

COMMENT: The Receiver is not allowed to volley a served ball; i.e., he must allow it to strike in his court first. (See Rule 16 (a).

EXPLANATION: In matches played without umpire or linesmen, it is customary for the Receiver to determine whether the service is good or a fault; indeed, each player makes the calls for all balls hit to his side of the net. (In doubles, the Receiver's partner makes the calls with respect to the service line.)

RULE 9
Faults

The Service is a fault:

(a) If the Server commit any breach of Rules 6, 7 or 8;

(b) If he miss the ball in attempting to strike it;

(c) If the ball served touch a permanent fixture (other than the net, strap or band) before it hits the ground.

Case 1. After throwing a ball up preparatory to serving, the Server decides not to strike at it and catches it instead. Is it a fault?

Decision. No.

Case 2. In serving in a singles game played on a doubles court with doubles and singles net posts, the ball hits a singles post and then hits the ground within the lines of the correct service court. Is this a fault or a let?

Decision. In serving it is a fault, because the singles post, the doubles post, and that portion of the net, strap or band between them are permanent fixtures. (Rules 2 and 9, and note to Rule 22.)

EXPLANATION: The significant point governing Case 2 is that the part of the net and band "outside" the singles sticks is not part of the net over which this singles match is being played. Thus such a serve is a fault under the provisions of article (c) above . . . By the same token, this would be a fault also if it were a singles game played with permanent posts in the singles position. (See Case 1 under Rule 22 for difference between "service" and "good return" with respect to a ball's hitting a net post.)

COMMENT: In doubles, if the Server's delivery hits his partner, the serve is a fault (not necessarily loss of point). See Rule 37.

RULE 10
Service After a Fault

After a fault (if it be the first fault) the Server shall serve again from behind the same half of the Court from which he served that fault, unless the service was from the wrong half, when, in accordance with Rule 8, the Server shall be entitled to one service only from behind the other half. A fault may not be claimed after the next service has been delivered.

Case 1. A player serves from a wrong court. He loses the point and then claims it was a fault because of his wrong station.

Decision. The point stands as played and the next service should be from the correct station according to the score.

Case 2. The point score being 15 all, the Server, by mistake, serves from the left-hand court. He wins the point. He then serves again from the right-hand court, delivering a fault. The mistake in station is then discovered. Is he entitled to the previous point? From which court should he next serve?

Decision. The previous point stands. The next service should be from the left-hand court, the score being 30/15, and the Server has served one fault.

RULE 11

Receiver Must Be Ready

The Server shall not serve until the Receiver is ready. If the latter attempt to return the service, he shall be deemed ready. If, however, the Receiver signify that he is not ready, he may not claim a fault because the ball does not hit the ground within the limits fixed for the service.

EXPLANATION OF RULE 11

The Server must wait until the Receiver is ready for the second service as well as the first, and if the Receiver claims to be not ready and does not make any effort to return a service, the Server may not claim the point, even though the service was good.

RULE 12

A Let

In all cases where a let has to be called under the rules, or to provide for an interruption to play, it shall have the following interpretations:

(a) When called solely in respect of a service, that one service only shall be replayed.

(b) When called under any other circumstance, the point shall be replayed.

Case 1. A service is interrupted by some cause outside those defined in Rule 13. Should the service only be re-played?

Decision. No, the whole point must be replayed.

EXPLANATION: The phrase "in respect of a service" in (a) means a let because a served ball has touched the net before landing in the proper court, OR because the Receiver was not ready . . . Case 1 refers to a second serve, and the decision means that if the interruption occurs during delivery of the second service, the Server gets two serves.

EXAMPLE: On a second service a Linesman calls "fault" and immediately corrects it (the Receiver meanwhile having let the ball go by). The Server is entitled to two serves, on this ground: The corrected call means that the Server had put the ball into play with a good serve, and once the ball is in play and a let is called, the point must be replayed . . . Note, however, that if the serve were an unmistakable ace — that is, the Umpire was sure the erroneous call had no part in the Receiver's inability to play the ball — the point should be declared for the Server.

Case 2. If a ball in play becomes broken, should a let be called?

Decision. Yes. (See Note after Rule 38.)

RULE 13

The service is a let

The service is a let:

(a) If the ball served touch the net, strap or band, and is otherwise good, or, after touching the net, strap or band, touch the Receiver or anything which he wears or carries before hitting the ground.

(b) If a service or a fault be delivered when the Receiver is not ready (see Rule 11).

COMMENT: A "let" called for the reason the Receiver had indicated he is not ready, if called on second service, does not annul a fault on first serve.

RULE 14

When Receiver Becomes Server

At the end of the first game the Receiver shall become the Server, and the Server Receiver; and so on alternately in all the subsequent games of a match. If a player serve out of turn, the player who ought to have served shall serve as soon as the mistake is discovered, but all points scored before such discovery shall be reckoned. If a game shall have been completed before such discovery, the order of service remains as altered. A fault served before such discovery shall not be reckoned.

RULE 15

Ball in Play Till Point Decided

A ball is in play from the moment at which it is delivered in service. Unless a fault or a let be called, it remains in play until the point is decided.

COMMENT: A point is not "decided" simply when, or because, a good shot has clearly passed a player, nor when an apparently bad shot passes over a baseline or sideline. An outgoing ball is still definitely "in play" until it actually strikes the ground, backstop or other fixture. The same applies to a good ball, bounding after it has landed in the proper court. A ball that becomes imbedded in the net is out of play.

Case 1. A ball is played into the net; the player on the other side, thinking that the ball is coming over, strikes at it and hits the net. Who loses the point?

Decision. If the player touched the net while the ball was still in play, he loses the point.

RULE 16

Server Wins Point

The Server wins the point:

(a) If the ball served, not being a let under Rule 13, touch the Receiver or anything which he wears or carries, before it hits the ground;

(b) If the Receiver otherwise loses the point as provided by Rule 18.

RULE 17

Receiver Wins Point

The Receiver wins the point:

(a) If the Server serve two consecutive faults;

(b) If the Server otherwise lose the point as provided by Rule 18.

RULE 18

Player Loses Point

A player loses the point if:

(a) He fail, before the ball in play has hit the ground twice consecutively, to return it directly over the net (except as provided in Rule 22(a) or (c)); or

(b) He return the ball in play so that it hits the ground, a permanent fixture, or other object, outside any of the lines which bound his opponent's Court (except as provided in Rule 22 (a) and (c)); or

(c) He volley the ball and fail to make a good return even when standing outside the Court; or

(d) He touch or strike the ball in play with his racket more than once in making a stroke; or

(e) He or his racket (in his hand or otherwise) or anything which he wears or carries touch the net, posts, cord or metal cable, strap or band, or the ground within his opponent's Court at any time while the ball is in play; or

(f) He volley the ball before it has passed the net; or

(g) The ball in play touch him or anything that he wears or carries, except his racket in his hand or hands; or

(h) He throws his racket at and hits the ball.

EXPLANATION: Referring to (d), a player may be deemed to have "touched the ball more than once" if the ball rests on his racket in such a way that the effect is more that of a "sling" or "throw" than a hit. (See "carry" and "double hit" in Glossary.)

In (g), note that this loss of point occurs regardless of whether the player is inside or outside the bounds of his court when the ball touches him.

Case 1. In delivering a first service which falls outside the proper court, the Server's racket slips out of his hand and flies into the net. Does he lose the point?

Decision. If his racket touches the net while the ball is in play, the Server loses the point. (Rule 18 (e).)

Case 2. In serving, the racket flies from the Server's hand and touches the net before the ball has touched the ground. Is this a fault, or does the player lose the point?

Decision. The Server loses the point because his racket touches the net while the ball is in play. (Rule 18 (e).)

Case 3. A and B are playing against C and D. A is serving to D. C touches the net before the ball touches the ground. A fault is then called because the service falls outside the service court. Do C and D lose the point?

Decision. The call "fault" is an erroneous one. C and D have already lost the point before "fault" could be called, because C touched the net while the ball was in play. (Rule 18 (e).)

Case 4. May a player jump over the net into his opponent's court while the ball is in play and not suffer penalty?

Decision. No; he loses the point. (Rule 18 (e).)

Case 5. A cuts the ball just over the net, and it returns to A's side. B, unable to reach the ball, throws his racket and hits the ball. Both racket and ball fall over the net on A's court. A returns the ball outside of B's court. Does B win or lose the point?

Decision. B loses the point. (Rule 18 (e) and (h).)

Case 6. A player standing outside the service court is struck by the service ball before it has touched the ground. Does he win or lose the point?

Decision. The player struck loses the point (Rule 18(g), except as provided under Rule 13 (a).)

Case 7. A player standing outside the court volleys the ball or catches it in his hand and claims the point because the ball was certainly going out of court.

Decision. In no circumstance can he claim the point;
(1) If he catches the ball he loses the point under Rule 18 (g).
(2) If he volleys it and makes a bad return he loses the point under Rule 18 (c).
(3) If he volleys it and makes a good return, the rally continues.

EXPLANATION: In Case 6 above, the exception referred to is that of a served ball that has touched the net en route into the Receiver's court; in that circumstance it is a let service, not loss of point. Such a let does not annul a previous (first service) fault; therefore if it occurs on second service, the Server has one serve coming.

EXAMPLE: Player has let racket go out of his hand clearly before racket hits ball, but the ball rebounds from his racket into proper court. This is not a good return; player loses point under Rule 18 (h).

COMMENT: The strokes referred to in (d) of Rule 18 are difficult to define and to rule on. Some are obvious, others are arguable. Most experienced umpires give the player the benefit of the doubt, but do call it a double-hit if there is even the suggestion of a "second push' or, as noted in the explanatory note for (d), the return seems to be more of a sling than a hit.

RULE 19

Player Hinders Opponent

If a player commits any act either deliberate or involuntary which, in the opinion of the Umpire, hinders his opponent in making a stroke, the Umpire shall in the first case award the point to the opponent, and in the second case order the point to be replayed.

Case 1. Is a player liable to a penalty if in making a stroke he touches his opponent?

Decision: No, unless the Umpire deems it necessary to take action under Rule 19.

Case 2. When a ball bounds back over the net, the player concerned may reach over the net in order to play the ball. What is the ruling if the player is hindered from doing this by his opponent?

Decision. In accordance with Rule 19, the Umpire may either award the point to the player hindered, or order the point to be replayed. (See also Rule 23.)

RULE 20

Ball Falling on Line—Good

A ball falling on a line is regarded as falling in the Court bounded by that line.

COMMENT:In matches played without umpire or linesmen, it is customary for each player to make the calls on all balls hit to his side of the net.

RULE 21

Ball Touching Permanent Fixture

If the ball in play touch a permanent fixture (other than the net, posts, cord or metal cable, strap or band) after it has hit the ground, the player who struck it wins the point; if before it hits the ground his opponent wins the point.

Case 1. A return hits the Umpire or his chair or stand. The player claims that the ball was going into court.

Decision. He loses the point.

Good Return   RULE 22

It is a good return:

(a) If the ball touch the net, posts, cord or metal cable, strap or band, provided that it passes over any of them and hits the ground within the Court; or

(b) If the ball, served or returned, hit the ground within the proper Court and rebound or be blown back over the net, and the player whose turn it is to strike reach over the net and play the ball, provided that neither he nor any part of his clothes or racket touch the net, posts, cord or metal cable, strap or band or the ground within his opponent's Court, and that the stroke be otherwise good; or

(c) If the ball be returned outside the post, either above or below the level of the top of the net, even though it touch the post, provided that it hits the ground within the proper Court; or

(d) If a player's racket pass over the net after he has returned the ball, provided the ball pass the net before being played and be properly returned; or

(e) If a player succeeded in returning the ball, served or in play, which strikes a ball lying in the Court.

Note.—If, for the sake of convenience, a doubles court be equipped with singles posts for the purpose of singles game, then the doubles posts and those portions of the net, cord or metal cable and band outside such singles posts shall be regarded as "permanent fixtures *other than* net, post, strap or band," and therefore *not* posts or parts of the net of that singles game.

A return that passes under the net cord between the singles and adjacent doubles post without touching either net cord, net or doubles post and falls within the area of play, is a good return. (But in doubles this would be a "through"— loss of point.)

Case 1. A ball going out of court hits a net post and falls within the lines of the opponent's court. Is the stroke good?

Decision. If a service; no, under Rule 9 (c). If other than a service; yes, under Rule 22 (a).

Case 2. Is it a good return if a player returns the ball holding his racket in both hands?

Decision. Yes.

Case 3. The Service, or ball in play, strikes a ball lying in the court. Is the point won or lost thereby?

Decision. No. Play must continue. If it is not clear to the Umpire that the right ball is returned a let should be called.

Case 4. May a player use more than one racket at any time during play?

Decision. No: the whole implication of the rules is singular.

Case 5. May a player request that a ball or balls lying in his opponent's court be removed?

Decision. Yes, but not while a ball is in play.

RULE 23

Interference

In case a player is hindered in making a stroke by anything not within his control except a permanent fixture of the Court, or except as provided for in Rule 19, the point shall be replayed.

Case 1. A spectator gets into the way of a player, who fails to return the ball. May the player then claim a let?

Decision. Yes, if in the Umpire's decision he was obstructed by circumstances beyond his control, but not if due to permanent fixtures of the Court or the arrangements of the ground.

Case 2. A player is interfered with as in Case No. 1, and the Umpire calls a let. The Server had previously served a fault. Has he the right to two services?

Decision. Yes: as the ball is in play, the point, not merely the stroke, must be replayed as the rule provides.

Case 3. May a player claim a let under Rule 23 because he thought his opponent was being hindered, and consequently did not expect the ball to be returned?

Decision. No.

Case 4. Is a stroke good when a ball in play hits another ball in the air?

Decision. A let should be called unless the other ball is in the air by the act of one of the players, in which case the Umpire will decide under Rule 19.

Case 5. If an Umpire or other judge erroneously calls "fault" or "out" and then corrects himself, which of the calls shall prevail?

Decision. A let must be called, unless, in the opinion of the Umpire, neither player is hindered in his game, in which case the corrected call shall prevail.

Case 6. If the first ball served—a fault—rebounds, interfering with the Receiver at the time of the second service, may the Receiver claim a let?

Decision. Yes. But if he had an opportunity to remove the ball from the court and negligently failed to do so, he may not claim a let.

Case 7. Is it a good stroke if the ball touches a stationary or moving object on the court?

Decision. It is a good stroke unless the stationary object came into court after the ball was put into play in which case a "let" must be called. If the ball in play strikes an object moving along or above the surface of the court a "let" must be called.

Case 8. What is the ruling if the first service is a fault, the second service correct, and it becomes necessary to call a let under the provision of Rule 23 or if the Umpire is unable to decide the point?

Decision. The fault shall be annulled and the whole point replayed.

COMMENT: See Rule 12 and Explanation thereto.

RULE 24

The Game

If a player wins his first point, the score is called *15* for that player; on winning his second point, the score is called *30* for that player; on winning his third point, the score is called *40* for that player, and the fourth point won by a player is scored *game* for that player except as below:

If both players have won three points, the score is called *deuce*; and the next point won by a player is called *advantage* for that player. If the same player wins the next point, he wins the game; if the other player wins the next point the score is again called *deuce*; and so on until a player wins the two points immediately following the score at deuce, when the game is scored for that player.

COMMENT: The word "love" is generally used in tennis for zero, or nothing, with respect to points, games, and sets. (Perhaps from the French l'oeuf, the egg.) In stating the score in points and games the Server's score is given first; in reporting the full score of a match the ultimate winner's score is given first throughout.

RULE 25

The Set

A player (or players) who first wins six games wins a set; except that he must win by a margin of two games over his opponent and where necessary a set shall be extended until this margin be achieved. NOTE: See Page

RULE 26

When Players Change Sides

The players shall change sides at the end of the first, third and every subsequent alternate game of each set, and at the end of each set unless the total number of games in such set be even, in which case the change is not made until the end of the first game of the next set.

RULE 27

Maximum Number of Sets

The maximum number of sets in a match shall be 5, or, where women take part, 3.

RULE 28

Rules Apply to Both Sexes

Except where otherwise stated, every reference in these Rules to the masculine includes the feminine gender.

RULE 29

Decisions of Umpire and Referee

In matches where an Umpire is appointed, his decision shall be final; but where a Referee is appointed, an appeal shall lie to him from the decision of an Umpire on a question of law, and in all such cases the decision of the Referee shall be final, except that in Davis Cup and Federation Cup matches the decision of a linesman can be changed by the Referee, or by the Umpire with the consent of the Referee.

The Referee, in his discretion, may at any time postpone a match on account of darkness or the condition of the ground or the weather. In any case of postponement the previous score and previous occupancy of Courts shall hold good, unless the Referee and the players unanimously agree otherwise.

RULE 30

Play shall be continuous from the first service till the match be concluded; provided that after the third set or when women take part, the second set, either player is entitled to a rest, which shall not exceed 10 minutes, or in countries situated between Latitude 15 degrees North and Latitude 15 degrees South, 45 minutes, and provided further that when necessitated by circumstances not within the control of the players, the Umpire may suspend play for such a period as he may consider necessary. If play be suspended and be not resumed until a later day the rest may be taken only after the third set (or when women take part the second set) of play on such later day, completion of an unfinished set being counted as one set. These provisions shall be strictly construed, and play shall never be suspended, delayed or interfered with for the purpose of enabling a player to recover his strength or his wind, or to receive instruction or advice.

The Umpire shall be the sole judge of such suspension, delay or interference, and after giving due warning he may disqualify the offender.

EXAMPLE: In a best-of-five-sets match, play is suspended because of darkness at one set all and 2-all in the third. Next day play is resumed, and after Player A wins the third set (10-8) he claims he is entitled to an intermission. He is not. Note that Rule 30 specifies the rest period may come after the third set of play on that day. In cases of prolonged delay, with resumption the same day, it is advisable to come to an agreement about any further rest periods before resuming play.

(a) Any nation is at liberty to modify the first provision of Rule 30, or omit it from its regulations governing tournaments, matches, or competitions held in its own country, other than the International Lawn Tennis Championships (Davis Cup and Federation Cup).

(b) When changing sides a maximum of one minute shall elapse from the cessation of the previous game to the time players are ready to begin the next game.

EXPLANATION: In Men's and Juniors' (males 18) events there is no rest period in a best-of-three-sets match, but in a best-of-five-sets match a 10-minute rest may be taken (must, if either side requests it) after the third set. It may not be taken any time before the third set or at any time after the fourth set has been started. It must be taken after the third set or not at all . . . Likewise, in best-of-three matches where a rest period is allowed, it must be taken after the second set or not at all.

All matches for Juniors shall be the best of three sets WITH NO REST PERIOD, except that in Tennis Center championships or Interscholastic, State and Sectional tournaments equivalent to Tennis Centers, and in National Junior championships, the FINAL ROUND may be best-of-five. If such final requires more than three sets to decide, a rest of 10 minutes after the third set is MANDATORY.

Matches for all players, both boys and girls, in the 16-, 14-, and 12-year classes shall be best-of-three-sets; 10-minute rest before the third set is MANDATORY.

The United States Lawn Tennis Association has approved a modification of the first provision in Rule 30 to provide after the second set in tournaments exclusively for Seniors 45, 55, and 60, as well as for Men's 35, and in tournaments for Fathers and Sons, either player or doubles team is entitled to a rest which shall not exceed ten minutes.

The players must be back on the court ten minutes after play has ceased.

Should a player, on account of physical unfitness or an unavoidable accident, not within his control, be unable to continue play, he must be defaulted.

"Stalling" is one of the hardest things to deal with. The rules say that play shall be continuous." An Umpire should determine whether the "stalling" is deliberate and for the purpose of gaining time. If he decides that it is, he should warn the player to stop his unfair practice. If this does not end it, he should then default him.

The Umpire has the power to suspend a match for such period as he may think necessary, if, in his judgment, the play is interfered with by circumstances beyond the players' control. Such circumstances might be the passing of an airplane, moving of spectators in the stands, etc.

Case 1. A player's clothing, footwear, or equipment becomes out of adjustment in such a way that it is impossible or undesirable for him to play on. May play be suspended while the maladjustment is rectified?

Decision. If this occurs in circumstances not within the control of the player, of which circumstances the Umpire is the sole judge, a suspension may be allowed.

Case 2. If, owing to an accident, a player is unable to continue immediately, is there any limit to the time during which play may be suspended?

Decision. No allowance may be made for natural loss of physical condition. Consideration may be given by the Umpire for accidental loss of physical ability or condition.

COMMENT: *Case 2 refers to an important distinction that should be made between a temporary disability caused by an accident during play, and disability caused by fatigue (cramps, for example). Not even momentary "rest" — other than the normal toweling-off pause at changeover — is allowed for recovery from "natural loss of physical condition."*

Case 3. During a doubles game, may one of the partners leave the court while the remaining partner keeps the ball in play?

Decision. Yes, so long as the Umpire is satisfied that play is continuous within the meaning of the rules, and that there is no conflict with Rules 33 and 34.

COMMENT: *When a player competes in an event designated as for players of a bracket whose rules as to intermissions and length of match are geared to a different physical status, the player cannot ask for allowances based on his or her age, or her sex. For example, a female competing in an intercollegiate (men's) varsity team match would not be entitled to claim a rest period in a best-of-three-sets match unless that were the condition under which the team competition was normally held. . . . A corollary of this is that it is strongly recommended that, because of health considerations, young persons not be entered in divisions of a tournament above their own bracket, if the higher bracket has more demanding rules as to rest periods and length of matches . . . It is recommended that in high school matches a rest period be allowed in all cases, whether or not girls are playing.*

NOTE: When a match is resumed following an interruption necessitated by weather conditions, it is allowable for the players to engage in a "re-warm-up" period. It may be of the same duration as the warm-up allowed at the start of the match; may be done using the balls that were in play at the time of the interruption, and the time for the next ball change shall not be affected by this.

THE DOUBLES GAME

RULE 31

The above Rules shall apply to the Doubles Game except as below.

RULE 32

Dimension of Court

For the Doubles Game, the Court shall be 36 feet in width, i.e., 4½ feet wider on each side than the Court for the Singles Game, and those portions of the singles side-lines which lie between the two service-lines shall be called the service-side-lines. In other respects, the Court shall be similar to that described in Rule 1, but the portions of the singles side-lines between the base-line and service-line on each side of the net may be omitted if desired.

Case 1. In doubles the Server claims the right to stand at the corner of the court as marked by the doubles side line. Is the foregoing correct or is it necessary that the Server stand within the limits of the center mark and the singles side line?

Decision. The Server has the right to stand anywhere between the center mark and the doubles side lines.

RULE 33

Order of Service

The order of serving shall be decided at the beginning of each set as follows:

The pair who have to serve in the first game of each set shall decide which partner shall do so and the opposing pair shall decide similarly for the second game. The partner of the player who served in the first game shall serve in the third; the partner of the player who served in the second game shall serve in the fourth, and so on in the same order in all the subsequent games of a set.

Case 1. In doubles, one player does not appear in time to play, and his partner claims to be allowed to play single-handed against the opposing players. May he do so?
Decision. No.

EXPLANATION: It is not required that the order of service, as between partners, carry over from one set to the next. Each team is allowed to decide which partner shall serve first for it, in each set. This same option applies with respect to the order of receiving service.

RULE 34

Order of Receiving

The order of receiving the service shall be decided at the beginning of each set as follows:

The pair who have to receive the service in the first game shall decide which partner shall receive the first service, and that partner shall continue to receive the first service in every odd game throughout that set. The opposing pair shall likewise decide which parner shall receive the first service in the second game and that partner shall continue to receive the first service in every even game throughout that set. Partners shall receive the service alternately throughout each game.

EXPLANATION OF RULE 34

The receiving formation of a doubles team may not be changed during a set; only at the start of a new set. Partners must receive throughout each set on the same sides of the court which they originally select when the set begins. The first Server is not required to receive in the right court; he may select either side, but must hold this to the end of the set.

Case 1. Is it allowable in doubles for the Server's partner to stand in a position that obstructs the view of the Receiver?
Decision. Yes. The Server's partner may take any position on his side of the net in or out of the court that he wishes.

RULE 35

Service Out of Turn

If a partner serve out of his turn, the partner who ought to have served shall serve as soon as the mistake is discovered, but all points scored, and any faults served before such discovery shall be reckoned. If a game shall have been completed before such discovery the order of service remains as altered.

RULE 36

Error in Order of Receiving

If during a game the order of receiving the service is changed by the receivers it shall remain as altered until the end of the game in which the mistake is discovered, but the partners shall resume their original order of receiving in the next game of that set in which they are receivers of the service.

RULE 37

Ball Touching Server's Partner Is Fault

The service is a fault as provided for by Rule 9, or if the ball served touch the Server's partner or anything he wears or carries; but if the ball served touch the partner of the Receiver or anything which he wears or carries, not being a let under Rule 13 (a), before it hits the ground, the Server wins the point.

RULE 38

Ball Struck Alternately

The ball shall be struck alternately by one or other player of the opposing pairs, and if a player touches the ball in play with his racket in contravention of this Rule, his opponents win the point.

EXPLANATION: This means that, in the course of making one return, only one member of a doubles team may hit the ball. If both of them hit the ball, either simultaneously or consecutively, it is an illegal return. The partners themselves do not have to "alternate" in making returns. (Mere clashing of rackets does not make a return illegal, if it is clear that only one racket touched the ball.)

NOTE concerning Case 2 of Rule 12: The USLTA Umpires Committee has authorized this interpretation of that Case: A ball shall be regarded as having become "broken" if, in the opinion of the Umpire, it is found to have lost compression to the point of being unfit for further play, or unfit for any reason, and there is any likelihood that this deficiency had an effect on the preceding point.

Should any point arise upon which you find it difficult to give a decision or on which you are in doubt as to the proper ruling, immediately write, giving full details, to John Stahr, U.S.T.L.A. Umpires Committee, 65 Briar Cliff Rd., Larchmont, N. Y. 10538, and full instructions and explanations will be sent you.

APPENDIX

Regulations for Making Tests Specified
in Rule 3

1.   Unless otherwise specified, all tests shall be made at a temperature of approximately 68 degrees Fahrenheit and any ball tested shall be at that temperature throughout when the test is commenced.

2.   Unless otherwise specified the limits are for a test conducted in an atmospheric pressure resulting in a barometric reading of approximately 29.95 inches.

3.   Other climatic standards may be fixed for localities where the average temperature and/or average barometric pressure at which the game is being played differ materially from 68 degrees Fehrenheit and 29.95 inches respectively.

Applications for such adjusted standards may be made by any National Association to the International Lawn Tennis Federation and if approved shall be adopted for such localities.

A table of such adjusted standards shall be added to the Appendix from time to time as they may be adopted.

4.   In all tests for diameter a ring gauge shall be used, consisting of a metal plate, preferably non-corrosive, of a uniform thickness of one-eighth of an inch, in which there are two circular openings 2.575 inches and 2.675 inches in diameter respectively. The inner surface of the gauge shall have a convex profile with a radius of one-sixteenth of an inch. The ball shall not drop through the smaller opening by its own weight and shall drop through the larger opening by its own weight.

5.   In all tests for deformation conducted under Rule 3, the machine designed by Percy Herbert Stevens and patented in Great Britain under Patent No. 230,250, together with the subsequent additions and improvements thereto, shall be employed, or such other machine which is approved by a National Association and gives equivalent readings to the Stevens machine.

6.   Immediately before any ball is tested, it shall be dropped four times from a height of one hundred inches onto a concrete base.

7.   To ascertain the deformation of any ball, three readings shall be taken—one each of three diameters at right angles to one another—so chosen that initially neither platen of the machine shall be in contact with any part of the cover seam. The average of these three readings shall be the deformation reading.

8.   After the ball has been placed in position, the contact weight applied, the beam brought to the pointer level, the pointers set at zero, and the test weight placed on the beam, the pressure shall then be applied to the ball by turning the hand wheel at a uniform speed, and exactly five seconds shall elapse from the instant the beam leaves its seat until it is brought to the pointed level, whereupon the turning shall cease and the reading shall be taken.

SCORING

Shortly after Major Wingfield received his patent for a game called "Sphairistike" in 1874, suggestions for improvement were proffered and a number were adopted. The name was changed to lawn tennis, the hourglass court was transformed into a rectangle, the net measurement was altered from 7 feet to 3 feet, and lawn tennis enthusiasts began to play not only on lawns but on dirt, clay, cement, and even boards. The original fan-shaped racket became oval and the ball was improved by welding the seams. After the first few years changes in the rules were extremely rare, and for the most part they were concerned with the definition of a foot fault.

But suggestions never stopped pouring in for more alterations. Twenty years ago Gardnar Mulloy proposed that the scoring be changed from "love," "15," "30," and "40" to "0," "1," "2," and "3." Cleveland's Jack March experimented with a 21-point table tennis scoring which he used in his World Pro Championships. As the game got faster, tennis players recommended that (1) only one serve be allowed, (2) the balls be softened, and (3) servers be required to stand 3 feet behind the base line. Jack Kramer, then the promoter of the pro tour, introduced the "3-bounce" rule, which restricted the server from volleying until the third return, and the pro set, in which the preliminary tour match was reduced to one long set. Then James H. Van Alen, a devotee of the short match, appeared on the scene, and has dedicated much time to the promulgation of the Van Alen Simplified Scoring System (VASSS). VASSS offered several new styles of scoring—a 31-point game, a 21-point game, and a no-ad set of otherwise regular scoring—plus a "one-serve" rule and an alternative serving requirement of standing 3 feet behind the base line. VASSS was used in the Consolation event at the Newport Invitation and in the Newport Pro Championships. Eventually it spread to other Consolation tournaments and even to college matches. However, neither the Jack March, the Jack Kramer, nor the James Van Alen system received ILTF approval, and so any matches played under these rules were not considered for ranking purposes. Nevertheless, the pro set and VASSS continued to grow in popularity; in the summer of 1970 the Eastern Grass Court Championships at Orange used pro sets in the early rounds when rain delayed play, and the 1969 U.S. Open ran a Consolation event along VASSS lines.

In 1968 the Middle States section of the USLTA adopted a sudden-death rule to prevent marathon matches. When the set score reached 5-all, only one more game was played. Van Alen considered that this was unfair to the receiver and he therefore proposed a VASSS sudden-death tie-breaker of 9 points which is described later in this section.

The pros adopted a sudden-death play-off in their 1970 $10,000 Classic. Some 14,000 spectators at Madison Square Garden watched Pancho Gonzalez win a tie-breaker set against Rod Laver. The Philadelphia Open also utilized a sudden-death system which was a variation of the VASSS tie-breaker. At 6-all in games, the players alternated serves until one of them reached 7 points. If the score got to 6 points all, play continued until one of them won by 2 points. There were small confusions since serve changed with every point, and occasionally a player forgot whether he or she was to serve in the forehand or the backhand court. Still it was tremendously exciting, and players and spectators would flock into the auditorium from the lounges, locker rooms, and dining areas whenever the word was passed that a sudden-death tie-breaker was about to begin.

The sudden-death system used by Philadelphia was, unfortunately, specifically prohibited by International Lawn Tennis Federation (ILTF) rules. The Philadelphia promoters were notified by the USLTA at the end of the first day's play that the tie-breaker rule must be abandoned. The promoters, however, continued to use sudden-death, and as a consequence the ILTF fined the USLTA $500.

The ILTF earlier in the summer of 1970 approved a nine-point sudden-death tie-breaker sequence for use experimentally in several major tournaments, of which the United States Open was the largest and most prestigious. In 1971 the USLTA authorized use of the 7-out-of-12 as well as the 5-out-of-9 point method as permitted options for any tournament wishing to use the tie-breaker. However, only one designated method is to be used for all events of a given tournament. This will not preclude use of conventional scoring in singles and a specified tie-breaker method in doubles. However, it will not be proper to use the 5-out-of-9 point system in singles and the 7-out-of-12 point system in doubles. The intention is to be open-minded but to minimize confusion in a given tournament.

Conventional Scoring System

Although tennis scoring seems to have its basis more in tradition than in practical mathematics, once mastered it is a relatively simple system. There are four units of scoring: point, game, set, and match. The *point* is the smallest unit of scoring.

Scoring the Game. If a player wins his first point, his score is 15; on winning his second point, his score is 30; on winning his third point, his score is 40; on winning his fourth point he has won the game. The exception to this is when each player has scored three points (40–40); the score is then called *deuce*. The next point after deuce is called *advantage*. If the player with the advantage scores the following point, he wins the game. However, if the other player wins the following point, the score again becomes deuce. This continues until a player wins the two points immediately following a score at deuce; then the game is scored for that player. A score of zero is called *love*.

To avoid any misunderstandings it is considered good practice for the server to call the point score for confirmation at the end of every point played. In so doing, it is standard for the server to call his own score first. For example, if the server should lose the first point of the game, he would call the score, "love–15." Should he win the first point, he would call the score "15–love." When the score is even (15–15, 30–30), it is called *all* or *up*. For example, the server would call the score "15–all," "30–all." If the score is tied at 40–40, the call is "deuce." When the server has the advantage, he calls "server's advantage," or "ad in"; when the receiver has it, the call is "receiver's advantage," or "ad out."

Scoring the Set. The player who first wins six games wins a *set*. If each player won five games, however, the score is called *games all*, and the next game won is scored *advantage* game for that player. If the same player wins the next game, he wins the set. However, if his opponent wins the next game, the score is again called games all, and so on until a player wins two games more than his opponent. Set scores may range from 6–0 to any combination of numbers (6–2, 6–4, 7–5, 12–10, 17–15, etc.).

The score in games should be called by the server at the end of each game, or whenever the players change sides of the court. Players should do this at the end of the first, third, and every subsequent alternate game of each

set, and at the end of each set unless the total number of games in such a set be even, in which case the change is not made until the end of the first game of the next set. The change of sides is intended to equalize such factors as sun and wind.

Scoring the Match. A match consists of the best two out of three sets although in national tournament competition (men only) it is the best three out of five sets. While cards vary slightly in arrangement, a typical one is reproduced here. It shows that in the first game the score ran, and would have been called: "15–love, 30–love, 30–15, 40–15, 40–30, game Mr. A." In the second game it was: "love–15, 15–all, 15–30, 30–all, 40–30, deuce, advantage B, deuce, advantage A, deuce, advantage B, game Mr. B."

In recent years a number of members of the Tennis Umpires Association have adopted some extra touches to (1) aid themselves in

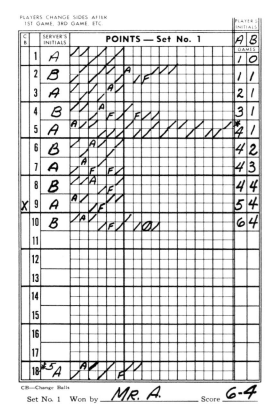

Typical tennis score card.

keeping track of things, and (2) provide more information for the contestants, their coaches or pros, the sports writers, or anyone interested. Here is an excerpt from a typical card of this kind:

The "3:48/4:20" figures show the starting and finishing times for the set. The placing of the server's initials shows from which end of the court (from umpire's viewpoint) the serve is delivered: quite useful, especially in doubles, or in case of intermission or interruption. The letters in the point-score boxes stand for: A—an ace; P—a placement; O—an out; N—netted ball, or one that fails to reach the net; F—double fault; H—player hit by ball in play. (The large X in the left margin calls attention quickly to the fact that this game was a break-through service.) Further refinements could include: a minus sign after an A or a P, to designate a serve or shot that is "all but" an outright ace or placement; Pl—placement scored on a lob; Pd—placement via drop shot; Pn—placement, but thanks to a net cord!

The heavy lines at the bottom of the game box (Game 9, right) on both the server's initial side and the running-score side are a means of avoiding the embarrassment of overlooking a ball change. The lines mean you change balls *after* that game.

It should be made clear that there is nothing mandatory about the codified type of score-keeping shown in the illustration at right. Any umpire is entitled to make his scorecard as simple or as complicated as suits his inclinations, and many will possibly prefer to make some variations on the symbols shown here. The principle, though, is sound. At least the recording of the starting and finishing times is very much to be recommended; and markings that make possible a recapitulation of—at least—the service aces and double faults often prove very useful.

Nine-Point Tie-Breaker Game

The nine-point sudden-death tie-breaker is in effect any time a set reaches 6-all in games. Hence, no set can be longer than 13 games. Here is how the tie-breaker sequence operates:

Singles. When the score reaches 6-all in games, a set will be decided by a best-of-nine-

Method of scoring in nine-point tie-breaker game.

points sequence. The player who began serving the set, and thus would serve the thirteenth game (call him Player A), leads off. He serves one point from the right court and one from the left court. Then the serve goes across the net to Player B, who serves two points in the same order. After four points, they exchange sides, and Player A serves two more points. Then (if necessary), Player B serves the last three points. If they reach 4–4 in points, Player A may receive serve from either the right or left court, whichever he chooses (this is an innovation for the U.S. Open; in other tournaments Player B has had his option of serving from either court). Thus, in sudden-death the first server, Player A, serves points 1, 2, 5, and 6, while Player B serves points 3, 4, 7, 8, and 9. Obviously, in the nine-point sequence, the game can end on points 5, 6, 7, 8, or 9.

The score of a sudden-death set is recorded as 7–6. When the sequence is completed, the players change sides and the second server of the tie-breaker game (that is, Player B) begins serving the next set.

At the beginning of a match the spin of a racket (see Section II) determines the server, as is traditional. But at the beginning of the third set of a best-of-three sets match (or the fifth set of a best-of-five match), the players spin a racket to determine the server again.

Doubles. In doubles, the sudden-death sequence is also best-of-nine points. The team that began serving the set also leads off in sudden-death. Either player may be designated to serve points 1 and 2. Let's say team AB is playing team CD. Team AB serves first, having started serving the set. They decide that A should serve points 1 and 2. He does, from the right court and then from the left court. The serve goes to the other side of the net and team CD decides that C will serve points 3 and 4. He does, and the teams change sides. B then serves points 5 and 6 and, if necessary, D serves points 7, 8, and 9. On point 9, team AB chooses the court from which they want D to serve.

Twelve-Point Tie-Breaker Game

The twelve-point sudden-death tie-breaker is preferred by the professional players and operates as follows:

Singles. When a set reaches 6-all Player A who would serve in normal rotation serves the first two points (right and left); B serves points 3 and 4 (right and left); A serves points 5 and 6 (right and left); the players change sides; Player B serves points 7 and 8; A serves 9 and 10; B serves 11 and 12. If either player wins 7 points, he wins the set 7 games to 6.

Upon completion of the tie-breaker game the player who served the last full game of the prior set serves the first game of the next set. After completion of that game the players change sides. If the tie-breaker game reaches 6 points all, the players change sides for 4 points and change every 4 points thereafter. The service shall alternate on every point. If either player establishes a margin of 2 points, the tie-breaker game and the set are concluded.

Doubles. The format for singles shall apply, and the service order shall continue during the tie-breaker game notwithstanding the circumstance that a player may serve in part from the end where he has not served during the body of the set.

In the 12-point game, it should be noted that service changes every two points and a change of sides occurs after the first six points of the tie-breaker game. This is in accordance with the procedure adopted by World Championship Tennis after consultation with the top professionals associated with that organization. WCT has announced it will invoke the tie-breaker at 5 games all, but USLTA will adhere to the 6–6 level for the present, regardless of the tie-breaker system being used. The only complexity presented by the 7-out-of-12-point system arises in the occasional situation where the score reaches 6 points all. The WCT officials have indicated an intention to play successive 12-point sequences until one player or team wins 7 points. USLTA is anxious to cooperate in uniform scoring methods, but in this instance the subcommittee feels that successive sequences of such length may defeat the purpose of achieving reasonable time control on matches. Accordingly, in USLTA-sanctioned tournaments, when the tie-breaker game reaches 6 points all, service is to alternate on every point until one player achieves a margin of 2 points and thereby wins the game and the set. The players or teams are to change sides at 6 points all and then after every 4 points (i.e., after points 12,

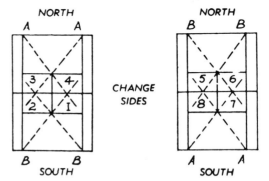

Tie-breaker diagram for the VASSS system. If tied at 4–4, A has the right to receive the 9th and final point either right or left.

16, 20, etc.). No rest is permitted on these changes.

Uniformity of rules worldwide has been a strong point for tennis, and the ILTF has now asked all of the national associations to join in the search for a generally acceptable tie-breaker method. Among the methods presently being tried in Europe is the single-traditional-game approach, to be scored 15-30-40-deuce-advantage. Service changes on every point, but the players do not change sides after selecting service and side by a racket toss at the start of the tie-breaker game. For the present, USLTA has not sanctioned this method, in consideration of the sun and wind factors in the decisive game.

VASSS (Van Alen Simplified Scoring System)

While all USLTA rules apply except in scoring, there are two sets of VASSS rules as follows:

Rules of VASSS "No-Ad." This method permits accurate scheduling of tennis matches since the length of the game is fairly well controlled. It operates as follows:

1. The *advantage point* is eliminated in the game, and the *advantage game* in the set.
2. The first to win 4 points, 1-2-3-4 (not 15-30-40) wins the game, the first to win 6 games wins the set. However, where time is a factor, the set may be reduced from 6 to either 5 or 4 games. If the score is tied (5 games all) the 9-point tie-breaker decides the set. Maximum number of points 79, playing time 25 to 30 minutes.

Rules of VASSS "Single Point." This method permits an efficient way to handicap accurately and consists of the following:

1. It is scored as in table tennis—1-2-3-4. . . .
2. The serve changes from A to B every 5 points (5, 10, 15, . . .). This 5-point sequence is called a "hand." Serve also changes at the end of the set.
3. The first point in each "hand" (1, 6, 11, 16, . . .) is served into the right, or forehand, court.
4. Sides are changed on the odd 5-point "hand" (5, 15, and 25).

5. The official set is fixed at 31 points. But where time is at a premium, 21 points may be used.
6. If there is no umpire the server is required to *call score loud and clear* after each point.
7. The winner of the set must lead by at least 2 points (31–29). Maximum number of points 69, playing time 25 to 30 minutes.

Nine-Point VASSS Tie-Breaker Rule. In the event the score is tied in "no-ad" at 5 games all or in "single point" at 30 points all, he who would normally serve the eleventh game in "no-ad" or the sixty-first point in "single point" shall serve points 1, 2, 5, 6, of the 5-out-of-9-point tie-breaker. Sides shall be changed after the first 4 points. The receiver in the tie-breaker game shall serve points 3 and 4, 7 and 8, and if the score shall reach 4 points all, he serves the ninth point into either the right or left court. Each player shall serve 2 points in succession, right-left, 1 and 2, 3 and 4, etc. At the end of the tie-breaker game the receiver in the first set (he who served points 3, 4, 7, 8, and 9 of the tie-breaker) shall commence serving in the second set. In the event the score is again tied in the second set, 5 games all, or 30 points all respectively, he shall serve points 1, 2, 5, and 6 of the tie-breaker game, etc., etc. If the sets are tied 1 set all in a 3-set match or 2 sets all in a 5-set match, the players shall spin the racket again for choice of service or side in the final set. The advantage enjoyed by Player B who serves the ninth point, providing the score is tied at 4–4, is offset by the fact that his opponent, Player A, serves 4 out of the first 6 points, namely, 1, 2, 5, and 6, and the fact that the ninth point may never be reached.

In doubles, the same player on team A serves points 1 and 2, his partner 5 and 6. On team B the same player serves points 3 and 4 and his partner points 7, 8, and 9. Each player shall serve from the side from which he served during the preceding games in the set.

In regular VASSS play, a match may be either 2 sets or 4 sets with the 9-point tie-breaker to decide the winner if sets are divided, or the regular 2 out of 3 or 3 out of 5 set match formula may be used.

Handicapping in Lawn Tennis

In early court tennis games, handicapping was by means of what was known as a "bisque." This was equivalent to a stroke (point as we say in the United States) claimed at pleasure by the recipient subject to certain limitations as to when it could not be taken. It is uncertain when this was introduced into the game but it was probably about the end of the fourteenth century.

Early lawn tennis rules also called for the using of the bisque. In 1888 a movement was made in England toward the abolition of the bisque and the substitution of a system of handicapping by means of fractions of fifteen. A committee was appointed and reported that the value of a bisque was not ascertainable and that it would be for the best interests of the game that the bisque should be discarded. The quarter system was recommended and finally adopted in 1890.

Even this was not entirely satisfactory, and finally in 1894 the method of handicapping by sixths of 15 was adopted. In the case of received odds this works out as follows:

In each series of six games,

- 1/6 of 15, one point received in the 2nd game of the series
- 2/6 of 15, one point received in the 2nd and 4th games
- 3/6 of 15, one point received in the 2nd, 4th, and 6th games
- 4/6 of 15, one point received in the 2nd, 4th, 5th, and 6th games
- 5/6 of 15, one point received in the 2nd, 3rd, 4th, 5th, and 6th games

A handicap of 15 (i.e., 6/6 of 15) would be one point in each game of the set.

For example, a player receiving four-sixths of fifteen receives nothing in the first and third games, and fifteen in the second, fourth, fifth, and sixth games of a set. In the next and every succeeding six games of a set the odds recur in the same order. At the start of a new set, of course, you start again with a new series of six games.

With a handicap over fifteen, one point per game is added to the handicap shown above. For example, with a handicap of 15 4/6, the player would receive 15 in the first game, 30 in the second game, 15 in the third, 30 in the fourth, fifth, and sixth games, repeating this order in each series of six games until the set is ended.

When the sixth system was devised, complex handicap tables were formulated. But the tables and mathematics required to figure out the proper handicap between two players was far too complicated and unwieldy. Unfortunately, the so-called "official" system, as well as some of the peculiar rules otherwise affecting handicapping, have prevented handicap tennis tournaments from being overly popular in the United States. The inability of the average player or official to understand and apply the handicap tables is the principal drawback.

In actual practice, most clubs which have handicap tournaments deviate from the official system in that they compute the differentials by direct subtraction. For most practical purposes, there seems to be little objection to this procedure other than its lack of official sanction.

Other handicap systems can be employed such as by either spotting a player a certain number of points per game, say one point, or the first point (15); or a certain number of games per set, if the difference in level between the players is noticeably great. Other handicaps can be used by moving the service line 3 feet further back to give the opponent more time to return serve, or by allowing the weaker player more serves per game in an effort to help him hold service and thus stay in the match.

VASSS Handicap Rules. Handicaps are not as effective in the conventional scoring system as they are when using the VASSS single-point method described earlier in this section. On March 2, 1968, Gene Scott, a top-ranking male tennis player, beat Billie Jean King, the then No. 1 women's player in the United States, 21–17, in a tennis match at the Long Island indoor tennis tournament in Old Brookville, N.Y. Scott spotted Mrs. King 10 points in a 21-point set played under VASSS scoring rules. On the basis of this, 10 points in a 21-point game would be a suitable man-to-woman ratio, while the man-to-man handicap would be lower, ranging anywhere from 1 to 10—again depending on the quality level of the players established in earlier matches.

In the VASSS handicap system, play proceeds as if the points of the handicap had actually been played. For example:

(a) Handicap 2 points: Server commences, serving point 3 into right, or forehand, court. Service and side both change after 3 points (2 + 3 = 5).

(b) Handicap 6 points: Server commences serving point 7 into the left, or backhand, court. Service changes after 4 points (6 + 4 = 10). Sides are changed after 9 points (6 + 9 = 15).

The giver of the handicap shall have the choice of service and side in the opening set, choice of service only in subsequent sets. At the conclusion of the set players do not change sides.

To estimate handicap points to be received at 30–30 in the nine-point tie-breaker, the following should be used:

First to third points, no points handicap; fourth to seventh points, 1-point handicap; eighth to fourteenth points, 2-point handicap; fifteenth to twenty-first points, 3-point handicap; twenty-second to thirtieth points, 4-point handicap.

In the nine-point tie-breaker handicap, points shall be considered as if already played. Examples: 1-point handicap, A shall serve point 2 into left, or backhand, court. 2-point handicap, B shall serve point 3 into right, or forehand, court.

Par Tennis

Par tennis is a new game developed by Dan Sullivan, the pro and part owner of The Racquet Club in St. Petersburg, Fla. The game follows the same idea of conventional tennis except that the scoring system and playing procedures are different.

In par tennis, Sullivan starts a certain number of players on a specific number of courts, say ten playing on five courts, or eight on four courts. Each of the players plays a 10-point match and the lowest number of errors in each game wins. Each player meets every other player in his group once. After these players finish, Sullivan puts another ten on the courts and the same procedure is followed.

To establish a total of 18 matches in a day, or the figure that will correspond to a round of 18 holes in golf, Sullivan repeats the procedure, either rotating his groups or playing the same ten in the round-robin.

At the end of a weekend, the players have played 36 matches, or if the tournament is over three or four days, they can play 72 matches. Par is considered four errors per 10-point match or 72 for an 18-match series, similar to the par 72 of many golf courses. Thus, if a player finishes all of his 18 matches with only three errors, he is deemed to have scored 3 under par, or 69 for the tournament. Naturally, the player with the lowest score wins. Sullivan has clocked his groups and figures that it takes 80 minutes for all 10 players to complete a round. The scoring system can be revised so that the highest number of points, rather than fewest errors, are used to determine a winner.

The par system is particularly effective for club tournaments or events that may entice players to participate knowing they will not be eliminated in the first round, since each player will complete an entire 18-, 36-, 54-, or 72-match series, or whatever figure is established for the tennis tournament.

COMPETITION AND TOURNAMENTS

One of the best ways to improve your game of tennis, and to gain experience, is by playing against a variety of opponents, especially those who are better at the game than yourself. It is a well-known fact that if you play with people whose game is more advanced than your own, you will gradually improve, until you reach their standard, and conversely, if you consistently play with weaker players, your standard of play will deteriorate. Therefore, it is up to you to get as much play as you can against those who excel at the game, always remembering that an occasional game with weaker players will help them on, and should do you no harm. It is not an easy matter for the "rabbit"—a term that was commonly used at one time to describe a beginner or weak player—to obtain practice against the more advanced exponents, because they hardly like to suggest a game themselves, and the "stars" perhaps do not think of fixing one up. Remember that all tennis champions were in the "rabbit" class at the very beginning of their careers.

Types of Tournaments

There are various types of tournaments held during the tennis year. They are generally classified as follows:

1. *Surface.* National championships are held in the United States on grass, clay, hard court, and indoors. The actual locations of these tournaments are determined by the United States Lawn Tennis Association.

2. *Categories.* Each tournament is broken down into playing categories: men's singles, women's singles, men's doubles, women's doubles, senior singles, mixed doubles, junior veterans, boys' singles, etc.

3. *Age.* National junior championships are held in the United States in age groups. The age breakdown is 18, 16, 14, and 12 and under, in singles and doubles, and for boys and girls; in addition to general men's and women's groups, there are junior veterans (35 and up) and seniors (45 and up).

4. *Section.* Each section of the United States has its own state and sectional championships. These tournaments, besides being broken down into surfaces if more than one type of surface is used in the section, are further defined by divisions (men's singles, women's singles, junior singles, etc.).

5. *Open.* These are tournaments in which amateur and professional players are allowed to compete. The concept of open tennis is not new. As early as the 1930's, promoters were discussing the blending of amateur and professional. But not until 1968 did open tennis become a reality; when it did, it surpassed even the dreams of its early proponents.

A complete listing of national USLTA championships, including winners and qualifications, is given in Section V.

USLTA Amateur-Player Ruling

At its Annual Meeting February 8, 1969, the USLTA amended Article III of its Constitution to create new definitions of categories for players under its jurisdiction, as follows:

Section 1: The following categories of tennis players are recognized as within the jurisdiction of the USLTA:
  a. Amateurs
  b. Players

Section 2: Any tennis player is an *Amateur* who does not receive and has not received, directly or indirectly, pecuniary advantage by the playing, teaching, demonstrating or pursuit of the game, except as expressly permitted by the USLTA.

An *Amateur* will not be deemed to have received pecuniary advantage by reason of: (1) Being reimbursed for reasonable expenses actually incurred by him in connection with his participation in a tournament, match or exhibition, or (2) being the recipient of a scholarship or other benefits authorized by his school (high school, college or university) which does not affect his eligibility as a tennis player for such school.

Section 3: Any tennis player who is still eligible to play in any age category under 19 years of age will be permitted to participate in a tournament, match or exhibition only if he is in good standing under amateur regulations.

Section 4: All other tennis players who accept the authority of, and who are in good standing with the USLTA shall be designated as *Players*.

Section 5: Both *Amateurs* and *Players* shall play only in tournaments, matches or exhibitions which are sanctioned or approved by the USLTA, and both *Amateur* and *Player* may compete in all such sanctions; provided, that *Players* may not participate in tournaments, matches or exhibitions expressly limited to *Amateurs*.

Essentially what these rules do is this: They divide USLTA tennis players into two basic categories:

1. Those who play tennis for the love of the game and for its healthful recreational benefits, i.e., the *Amateur* who derives no pecuniary advantage from the game.
2. Those who play tennis to earn money therefrom, i.e., the nonamateur, designated, *Player*.

The new rules do not attempt to regulate the touring professionals who are under contract to the promoters, except to recognize that such touring professionals may play in ILTF-sanctioned open tournaments.

A *Player* is eligible to play in all the events for which an amateur is eligible except for tournaments for amateurs only. A *Player*:

> May be given this status only after reaching the age of 19 years.
> May receive any total of living and traveling expenses.
> May receive prize money without limit.

Further effects of the new rules are to permit:

> The sanction by USLTA of tournaments (other than ILTF approved opens) at which prize money is offered for which *Players* may compete.
> The sanction of USLTA tournaments for amateurs only.

Enrollment in the USLTA. Any person can enroll in the USLTA and all players, officials, committee members, patrons, spectators, and commentators regardless of age or degree of skill can be a part of this nationwide organization through the Enrollment Program. Each receives a numbered identification card which entitles him to apply for entry in USLTA-sanctioned tournaments anywhere, to have his record considered for ranking, and to be placed on the official mailing list. It is a positive requirement for participants under USLTA tournament regulations; a privilege for enthusiasts. The fees are $6 (including subscription to the Official Magazine) for adult enrollees (21 years of age and over) and $2 for junior enrollees (under 21 years of age). Juniors who subscribe to the magazine pay another $2, total fee $4. Life Enrollment fee is $100, which is tax deductible. Checks for $100 should be made out to National Tennis Education Fund, and sent to 51 East 42 Street, New York, N.Y. 10017.

One half of every enrollment fee goes right back to the section in which it was collected for promotion and conduct of tennis in that area.

All tournament entry blanks should provide a line for the applicant's current enrollment number. If he has none, an application must be filled out; the appropriate fee must be paid and a receipt given prior to his first match. All cards are issued by USLTA, 51 East 42 Street, New York, N.Y. 10017. Information on the enrollment program can also be had at this address.

USLTA Championship Tournament Regulations

Each USLTA Championship Committee is authorized to select from its own membership a subcommittee to pass upon the qualifications of the applicants for entry, to make the draw, and determine the seeding, in accordance with USLTA Tournament Regulations and such Committee shall select the referee of the event.

In addition to meeting the requirements stated in the following regulations, every applicant for entry in a USLTA Championship (or other event sanctioned by the USLTA) must qualify as an amateur and meet other eligibility requirements as set forth in the Constitution, By-Laws and Standing Orders of the USLTA.

Entries for all USLTA Championship events shall close on a published date at least five (5) days prior to the beginning of play. The Committee in charge of each Championship shall have the power to include other players for proper reasons, prior to the making of the draw.

Entries shall be considered from players in good standing, belonging to clubs affiliated with the USLTA or the recognized association of a foreign country; from players of schools and colleges who are otherwise eligible; and from such other players as are acceptable to the Committee.

Entries should be made through the Secretary of the player's club or through the properly constituted authorities of the player's school or college and, in the case of foreign entrants, through the National Association of the player's country.

All players who wish to have their entries considered for the National Championships must submit their complete tournament records from October of last year to the date of filing entry in the current year. This information should cover dates, location and scores of all matches played in sanctioned tournaments, domestic and foreign. Give singles data if entering singles; doubles data if entering doubles.

The USLTA Committee in charge of each Championship shall have authority to exercise its judgment in accepting or rejecting entries. In the case of domestic entries, lack of membership in a club affiliated with the USLTA shall be sufficient reason for rejection. The foregoing rules are supplemented by the following special limitations for certain Championships.

USLTA Men's and Women's Singles Championships

1. Players are eligible for consideration whose entries are acceptable to the Committee by reason of unusual promise of skill in the case of young players, or the recommendation of the player's Sectional Associations.

2. Each duly accredited Sectional Association shall be entitled to have accepted the entry of either its first or second ranked player.

3. The first four United States seeded men and the first four United States seeded women players in the Singles Championships shall be entitled to receive a daily expense allowance not in excess of the amount which, under existing regulations, may be received as a per diem allowance under Standing Order IV (8) nor shall such expense be allowed seeded players who are residents of the city or its immediate environs where the Championships are held.

USLTA Men's and Women's Doubles Championships

If applicants are otherwise qualified, the following entries shall be accepted:

1. Members of the team which won the current Sectional Doubles Championship. If the winners cannot compete, the runners-up may take their places. If neither the winners nor the runners-up can compete, the Sectional Association may in its discretion appoint one of the semi-finalist teams to take their places, it being intended that each duly accredited Sectional Association shall be entitled to a Doubles Championship entry.

2. In the case of the Men's Doubles Championship the winning team of the two No. 1 teams in the Army, Navy, Air Force and Marine Corps Leech Cup Matches of the current year.

3. The first two United States seeded men's teams and the first two United States seeded women's teams shall be entitled to receive a daily expense allowance not in excess of the amount which, under existing regulations, may be received as a per diem allowance under Standing Order IV (8) nor such expense be allowed seeded players who are residents of the city or its immediate environs where the Championships are held.

USLTA Mixed Doubles Championship

The USLTA Mixed Doubles Championship is restricted to 48 teams.

USLTA Men's 35 Championships (Singles and Doubles)

The USLTA Men's 35 Championships in Singles and Doubles are open to men 35 years of age or who become 35 years of age during the year of competition.

USLTA Husband and Wife Championship

The USLTA Husband and Wife Championship is to be held annually and is restricted to approximately 32 teams.

USLTA Men Seniors' Championships (Singles and Doubles)

1. The USLTA Seniors' Championships in Singles and Doubles are open to men 45 years of age or who become 45 years of age during the year of competition.

(a) The Seniors' Singles Championship is restricted to 64 players and the Seniors' Doubles Championship to approximately 32 teams.

2. The USLTA Seniors' 50, 55, 60, 65 & 70 Championships in Singles and Doubles are open to men 50, 55, 60, 65 & 70 years of age or who become 50, 55, 60, 65 & 70 years of age respectively during the year of competition.

USLTA Women's 35 Championships (Singles and Doubles)

The USLTA Women's Championships in Singles and Doubles are open to women of 35 years of age or who become 35 years of age during the year of competition.

USLTA Women Seniors' Championships (Singles and Doubles)

The USLTA Women Seniors' Championships in Singles and Doubles are open to women of 40 years of age or who become 40 years of age during the year of competition.

USLTA Women Seniors' 50 Championships (Singles and Doubles)

The USLTA Women Seniors' 50 Championships in Singles and Doubles are open to women of 50 years of age or who become 50 years of age during the year of competition.

USLTA Father and Son Championship

The USLTA Father and Son Championship is to be held annually and is restricted to approximately 32 teams composed of father and son of blood relationship, or son adopted by order or judgment of a court of competent jurisdiction.

USLTA Mother and Daughter Championship

The USLTA Mother and Daughter Championship is to be held annually and is restricted to approximately 32 teams composed of mother and daughter of blood relationship, or daughter adopted by order or judgment of a court of competent jurisdiction.

USLTA Indoor Championships

The USLTA Indoor Championships are subject to the entry and management rules and regulations for the corresponding outdoor events.

USLTA Interscholastic Championships

1. The competition shall be known as "The USLTA Interscholastic Tennis Championships."

2. Such championships shall be played annually, the time and place to be determined by a standing committee of the USLTA (par. 8).

3. To be eligible to compete a player must be the semi-finalist in a qualifying interscholastic tournament which must be held in the United States by or under the direction of a college, university, school or USLTA Sectional Association, hereinafter referred to as the "Holder."

4. Notice of intention to hold a qualifying tournament shall be filed prior to the event by the Holder with the Executive Secretary, USLTA, 51 East 42nd St., New York, N.Y. 10017. Written approval of the Executive Office of the USLTA must be obtained before any qualifying tournament may be scheduled.

5. The Holder shall admit to competition, under such rules and limitations as the Holder may prescribe, students certified by a responsible school official to have been in good standing at a preparatory school or high school located within the United States, or within any foreign country, during the current school year.

Entries shall not be accepted from high schools affiliated with the National Federation of State High School Athletic Associations, unless such entries have been approved by the Federation.

A semi-finalist in Singles and/or Doubles in any preceding qualifying tournament held during the currently qualifying period shall not be eligible for re-entry in a succeeding qualifying tournament for the current championships.

6. The Holder shall immediately communicate the results of all matches to the Executive Secretary, USLTA, and the Chairman of the Interscholastic Tennis Tournament Committee of the institution holding the championship event, and such communication shall in every case include the home address of the semi-finalists in each completed competition, together with the certificates of responsible school officials as to such semi-finalists, as required by par. 5 above.

7. The Holder shall be permitted to charge an entry fee to such Qualifying Tournaments to provide whatever revenue may be necessary to cover the purchase of balls and other tournament expenses. Neither the USLTA nor its Sectional Associations shall be liable for financial deficits arising from the operations of a Qualifying Tournament.

8. A standing committee of the USLTA shall promote and be responsible for the championship competitions. Such committee shall have power to accept entry of outstanding schoolboy players who actually had no opportunity to attend a Qualifying Tournament, and who are recommended by Sectional Associations or by individuals whose opinions should carry weight. Although a player may qualify in all respects and be eligible to enter a championship competition, the Championship Committee shall have full power in its discretion to reject any entry or limit the number of entries. The Committee shall, from its membership if practicable, appoint a Referee and an Assistant Referee for the USLTA Interscholastic Championships, Singles and Doubles. The Committee shall select a date when entries will close.

9. All matches in the Championship competitions shall consist of best two of three sets in all rounds excepting the final round which may consist of best of five sets.

10. Entry to qualifying Doubles competitions shall be limited to teams nominated as such by individual schools, and members of a doubles team must be schoolmates representing the same school. Qualifiers in

Doubles may be permitted at the discretion of the Committee, to play in both Singles and Doubles.

11. Points for the team score shall be awarded for each event (singles and doubles) on the following basis:

1 point for each match won. In the case of a bye or a default in the first round no point shall be awarded unless the player or double team shall win the next round match, in which case 2 points shall be awarded, one for the bye or default and one for the next round match win.

12. No school may enter more than four singles players and two doubles teams.

USLTA Junior Davis Cup Sectional Team Championship

1. The event shall be known as the USLTA Junior Davis Cup Sectional Team Championships.

2. This event will be held annually.

3. The competition is open to teams representing each of the Sections comprising the United States Lawn Tennis Association. Each of said sections shall be represented by one team which shall consist of male players only.

4. Membership on each Sectional Team shall be by arbitrary selection of the section and the Junior Davis Cup Chairman in each section shall select the sectional team for his own section; the president of each section shall act in case his section does not have a sectional Chairman. The method of selection for membership on the sectional team may be as each section elects, either on the basis of ranking lists, center tournaments, regional center playoffs, inter-city Junior Davis Cup matches, tournaments, elimination try-outs, round-robins, character, sportsmanship and availability, or any combination of these factors.

5. Players selected for membership on each Sectional Team must be permanent residents of their respective sections. Each team member shall not have reached his 21st birthday as of the first day of January of the year of the tournament and each player is required to possess a current annual USLTA enrollment card.

6. The number of players on a Sectional Team shall be a maximum of four. (Maximum two singles players and one doubles team for scoring purposes.)

7. The referee of the tournament shall be the National Chairman of the Junior Davis Cup Committee of the USLTA or the person designated as referee by him.

8. All matches shall be played under the laws and rules of lawn tennis as sanctioned and interpreted by the USLTA. The tournament shall consist of both singles and doubles play. Points shall be earned in both singles and doubles as follows: Winner—5 points; Finalists—4 points; Semi-finalists—3 points; Quarter-finalists—2 points. A consolation tournament for singles only shall be conducted at the same time and place as the tournament herein provided and first-round losers shall automatically be entered in the consolation round and shall play in it. Points in the consolation round shall be at one-half the value of the main tournament. The Sectional Team scoring the most points in the main tournament plus the points earned by its players in the consolation event, shall be declared the winner of the event. In case of ties, the two Sectional Teams earning the same number of points shall be declared co-holders of the place earned by their point scores.

USLTA Women's National Collegiate Tennis Championship

Eligibility requirements for the Women's National Collegiate Championship and all Sectional Championships shall be as follows: (exception Point 5)

1. Any woman student who is presently enrolled as a full-time undergraduate student in a university, college, or junior college, and is approved by her college as meeting its academic requirements, shall be eligible. An undergraduate student is defined as one who has not received the B.A. degree or its equivalent.

2. A student may participate in a tournament held during the summer provided she was enrolled for the semester or quarter preceding the tournament. (Exception: Seniors graduating any time during the school year prior to the tournament may participate.)

3. Transfer students are immediately eligible for participation following enrollment in the institution.

4. A student may participate no more than four times.

5. Entries shall be limited to four players from each college. Two doubles teams, all of whom may play singles. Doubles teams shall consist of players

from the same college.

Note: Singles players may also play Doubles. Exception: Sectional Championships may determine their own regulations in regard to the number of entries in Singles and Doubles play.

6. All participants shall be of amateur standing as defined by USLTA. There shall be no scholarship or financial assistance specifically designated for women athletes. This does not preclude women who participate in Inter-Collegiate Athletic Programs from holding scholarships or grants-in-aid obtained through the normal scholarship programs of the institution (player's school).

7. Each participant in the Women's National Collegiate Championship and in all Sectional Championships shall be an individual member of USLTA.

8. All participants shall be certified by the chairman of the Department of Physical Education for Women of their respective institutions.

9. The responsibility for the health status of students shall be assumed by the respective institutions.

Regulations for USLTA Junior, Boys' 16, 14 & 12, Girls' 18, 16, 14 & 12 Chps., and Girls' Intersectional Team Matches

1. Age Limit Eligibility—The following are the correct USLTA titles for age classifications and they should be used at all times:

Junior refers to 18 and under boys.
Girls' 18 refers to 18 and under girls.
Boys' 16 refers to 16 and under boys.
Girls' 16 refers to 16 and under girls.
Boys' 14 refers to 14 and under boys.
Girls' 14 refers to 14 and under girls.
Boys' 12 refers to 12 and under boys.
Girls' 12 refers to 12 and under girls.

Junior Championship tournaments shall be open only to players who have not reached their eighteenth birthday before January 1st in the year of competition but who have reached their sixteenth birthday before January 1st in that year. Any player winning the Boys' 16 Championships shall be eligible to compete in the Junior Championships the following year even though still eligible for the Boys' 16 Championships; however, he cannot play in both.

Boys' 16, Boys' 14, Boys' 12 and Girls' 18, Girls' 16, Girls' 14 and Girls' 12 tourna-ments shall be open to players in these divisions who have not reached the maximum age limit before January 1st in the year of competition.

An individual or doubles team holding a USLTA Championship title in any of the age divisions may compete for a subsequent similar title without further qualification while remaining within the age limit of such age division and winners (singles and doubles) of a lower age division in their final year of age limitation in their respective age divisions shall be eligible to play in the next higher age division the following year without further qualification for all USLTA Championships played under these regulations.

2. Duration of Matches—Matches for Boys' 14, Boys' 12, Girls' 16, Girls' 14 and Girls' 12 shall be the best of three sets and there shall be a ten-minute rest period after the second set. Matches for Boys' 16 and Girls' 18 shall be the best of three sets, but at the request of any player a rest period of ten minutes may be taken at the conclusion of the second set. Matches for Juniors shall be the best of three sets, except in the final round of a USLTA Championship tournament when at the discretion of the referee the best of five sets may be required to decide the winner. When such a final round of competition requires more than three sets, there shall be a ten-minute rest period after the third set.

3. Qualifying Tournaments—Sectional, State, District, Tennis Center Tournaments and sanctioned State Jaycee (Championship) Tournaments shall be qualifying tournaments for the USLTA Junior, Boys' 16, Boys' 14, Boys' 12, Girls' 18, Girls' 16, Girls' 14 and Girls' 12 Championships.

From these qualifying tournaments the USLTA Sectional Associations will select players and alternates whose legal residence must be in that section to represent such section. These players must be qualified and be recommended by their respective sections. A Sectional Association may, at its discretion, waive the necessity of local qualifications for players who were ranked nationally the preceding year and who are still playing in the same age division during the current year. The Girls' 18 players selected to represent their sections in the "Girls' Intersectional Team Matches" played prior to the Girls' 18 USLTA Championships shall be accepted for entry in said Girls' 18 Championships and also any girls who have played in the Girls' 16 USLTA Championships and who have been recommended by the Girls' 16 USLTA Championship Committee. In the event an applicant is denied the right to participate in a qualifying tournament in his or her own section, the USLTA Championships Chairmen may accept such entry at their discretion.

A. Sanction for qualifying tournaments must be obtained by application to the Executive Secretary, USLTA, 51 E. 42nd St., New York, N.Y. 10017, or by application to a Sectional Association where such Sectional Association compiles its own schedules.

B. Registration—Qualifying Tournament Committees shall accept as entrants only those who present a USLTA Enrollment Card with their entry fee and also an "age identification card" if the player's home Sectional Association requires such a card.

Sectional Associations or District Associations may at their discretion issue "age identification cards" and charge a fee therefore. If a fee is charged the fee shall not exceed One Dollar ($1.00) per card or Fifty Cents (50¢) for duplicating issuance of card.

C. It shall be the duty of the Qualifying Tournament Committee to properly publicize the tournament and to report the results promptly to a designated Sectional official.

D. This designated Sectional official shall list those qualified or eligible players in their proper order, whenever specified for the limitation of a USLTA Championship.

E. Any Junior, Boy 16, Boy 14, Boy 12, Girl 18, Girl 16, Girl 14, or Girl 12 who qualified in either singles or doubles is eligible for selection by his or her Sectional Association for either or both events in the applicable USLTA Championship.

(1) Junior, Boys' 16, Boys' 14 and Boys 12 finalists in qualifying tournaments shall be eligible for selection by their respective Sectional Associations for the USLTA Championships in their respective classes.

(2) Semi-finalists in Girls' 18, Girls' 16, Girls' 14 and Girls' 12

District, Sectional and State qualifying tournaments shall be eligible for selection by their respective Sectional Association for the USLTA Championships for which they were able to qualify. Finalists in Tennis Center qualifying tournaments shall be eligible for selection by their respective Sectional Association for the USLTA Championships of the same age group in which they have qualified.

F. Tennis Center Tournaments will be held in the cities listed herein which have been designated as Tennis Centers.

(1) Tennis Centers—(see list of Tennis Centers on pages 203–204).

(2) Entry to Tennis Center Championships shall be restricted to residents of the section wherein such Tennis Centers are located unless the Sectional Association designates other limitations within that section.

(3) A Sectional Association shall be authorized to rule that no player who has previously qualified for the USLTA Junior, Boys' 16, Boys' 14, Boys' 12, Girls' 18, Girls' 16, Girls' 14 and Girls' 12 Championships through any one of the two qualifying methods or tournaments shall be permitted to enter another qualifying Tennis Center Tournament during the same calendar year.

G. The USLTA will present gold and silver medalettes to properly registered winners and runners-up of qualifying tournaments upon application in accordance with the rulings below.

(1) These tournaments must be completed after January 1st at least two weeks prior to the date of the beginning of the USLTA Championships of the current year in the classification specified.

(2) These tournaments shall have had not less than eight bona fide entries in singles and not less than four bona fide teams in doubles in each classification.

(3) The Chairman of the Junior Tennis Programs Committee shall have the authority to use his discretion and judgment to the extent

that he may authorize the award of tennis center medalettes to winners and runners-up in qualifying tournaments which began in time to finish prior to two weeks before the USLTA Championship but which, because of weather conditions or other unusual circumstances, were not completed as originally scheduled.

(4) The Chairman of the Sectional Junior Programs Committee shall apply to the Executive Secretary of the USLTA, through the Secretary of the Sectional Association, before May 1st, for the required number of medalettes for the current year.

(a) The medalettes will be sent to the Secretary of the Sectional Association who will see that they reach the committee of the qualifying tournament before the completion of the event.

(b) A certification that medalettes have been distributed in accordance with USLTA regulations shall be sent in with the report of the qualifying tournament's results to the Secretary of the Sectional Association who shall then forward it to the Executive Secretary of the USLTA.

4. Entries for all USLTA Junior, Boys' 16, Boys' 14, Boys' 12, Girls' 18, Girls' 16, Girls' 14 and Girls' 12 Championships must be in the hands of the Championships Committee fourteen days prior to the dates scheduled for the beginning of play. Each entry must be accompanied by an entry fee of not less than Two Dollars ($2.00) nor more than Six Dollars ($6.00) for each single entry and not less than Three Dollars ($3.00) nor more than Eight Dollars ($8.00) for each doubles team entry. The fees are to be set forth on the entry blanks and the entry blanks to USLTA Championships shall bear the signature of the officer of the Sectional Association who recommends the player for play in the Championship. (These entry fee rates shall not be construed as applying to or for the USLTA Junior, Boys' 16, Girls' 18 or Girls' 16 Indoor Championships.)

A. Each USLTA Junior Championships Committee shall accept as entrants only those players whose ages qualify them according to the age limit eligibility regulations.

B. Any Boy 16 eligible to compete in the USLTA Junior and Boys' 16 Championships may compete in the Boys' 16 class only.

C. No Junior, Boy 16, Boy 14, Boy 12, Girl 18, Girl 16, Girl 14 or Girl 12 shall be permitted to enter a USLTA Championship unless he or she shall have first been officially registered in the office of the Sectional (or District) Association in which the player lives and also possesses a USLTA identification card.

D. Quarter-finalists in the USLTA Girls' 16 Championships or players who have been recommended by the USLTA Girls' 16, Girls' 14 or Girls' 12 Committee shall be eligible for the USLTA Girls' 18 Championships.

5. No players shall be eligible to compete for the Singles or Doubles Championships except those qualifying under the foregoing regulations; but the Championship Committee may accept the entries of foreign players who do not qualify under these regulations and who are within the established age limits, and the Championship Committee may, at its discretion, accept the entry of any Junior, Boy 16, Boy 14, Boy 12, Girl 18, Girl 16, Girl 14 or Girl 12 whose record in its judgment warrants; provided such entrant has the endorsement of his or her Sectional Association.

A. Each Sectional Association shall name a qualified official, one who is thoroughly familiar with the playing record of the boys and juniors in his Section, who shall send to the Chairman of each of the following Championship Committees, namely, Junior and Boys' 16, and Boys' 14 and 12, a list of the qualified players whose entries are recommended by said Sectional Association.

B. Each Sectional Association shall name a qualified official, preferably a woman, one who is thoroughly familiar with the playing record of the girls in her Section, who shall send to the Chairman of each of the following Championship Committees, namely, Girls' 18, Girls' 16, and Girls' 14 and 12, a list of the qualified players whose entries are recommended by said Sectional Association.

6. These Annual USLTA Championship tournaments shall be held upon courts of

the type of surface selected by the respective Championship Committee with the approval of the USLTA Junior Tennis Development Committee.

7. The Championships Committee of the USLTA Junior and Boys' 16 Championships may require:

A. Entrants to report not later than a full day preceding start of play;

B. That entrants be requested not to play in Men's Tournament Events the week preceding the USLTA Junior and Boys' 16 Championships;

C. That all members of USLTA holding Junior and Boys' 16 Tournaments during the week preceding the. USLTA Junior and Boys' 16 Championships be requested to complete such tournaments at least two full days before the opening of the USLTA Junior and Boys' 16 Championships.

8. The number of entries in the USLTA Junior Championship shall be limited to one hundred twenty-eight with eight alternates and the number of entries in the USLTA Boys' 16 Championship shall be limited to 128 with eight alternates, provided, however, that the Chairman of the Championships Committee may, at his discretion, from time to time, or at any time, enlarge the aforesaid quotas, the entries to be distributed equitably among the sections, as set forth in the following paragraph, subject to acceptance by the USLTA Junior and Boys' 16 Championships Committee. In the event of cancellation for any cause, the alternates may be placed in the draw. In the event of no cancellations, the alternates will be permitted to play doubles.

The minimum allocation of entries to each section shall be based upon the ratio that the total number of its enrolled Juniors bear to the total number of enrolled Juniors in the entire USLTA; said ratio to be multiplied by one hundred twenty to determine the minimum allocation for Juniors; and the ratio determined as aforesaid to be multiplied by 120 to determine the minimum allocation for Boys' 16 (16 & under). Enrollment as aforesaid shall be based upon the aggregate totals in each section and the cumulative totals throughout the USLTA, as at December 31st in each preceding calendar year, commencing· in 1961. The term "enrolled juniors" shall be construed to mean all boys and girls who will not reach or pass their nineteenth birthday during the calendar year of their enrollment. The final decision as to the number of entries, their acceptance and all other matters pertaining to these Championships, will rest within the discretion of the USLTA Junior and Boys' 16 Championships Committee.

Each player will send his entry to the Championship Committee in the usual way.

9. The USLTA Girls' 18 and Girls' 16 Championships shall each have a draw of ninety-six if that number of qualified entrants are received by the Championship Committee.

A. The Sectional official in charge of reporting the list of qualified players shall have the responsibility of listing and ranking said qualified players in the order in which the Sectional official believes that their records place them.

(1) Preference in listing shall be shown to players who have qualified in tournaments in the following order: Sectional, State, State Jaycees, District and Tennis Center.

(2) The complete records of all players shall be included with the list.

B. The USLTA Girls' 18 Championship Committee shall accept at least six girls from each Sectional Association who are recommended by their respective Sectional Association.

C. The remainder of the draw shall be filled by qualified players from Sectional Associations already represented and by foreign entries.

D. The Sectional official may change the order of his qualified players at any time until the entry closes, and this order must be retained unless additional data is received by the Championship Committee when it may change the order.

E. Entry blanks for the USLTA Girls' 18 Championship shall be sent to the Presidents of the Sectional Associations with the request that the blanks be forwarded to the Sectional official in charge for distribution to the players.

(1) The players shall fill out the blanks and return them to their Sectional Association accompanied by their entry fees.

(2) The Sectional Association

shall check all entry blanks to see that the individual membership numbers are listed and that each blank has a complete and correct record.

(3) The Sectional Association shall send in the previously mentioned list of qualified players promptly and then send in the entry blanks and fees to the USLTA Girls' 18 Championship Committee before the entry closes.

10. The draws for the Junior, Boys' 16, Boys' 14, Boys' 12, Girls' 18, Girls' 16, Girls' 14 and Girls' 12 Championships are to be made so as to avoid, if possible, the presence in the same quarter of more than one of the first four players representing the same Sectional Association.

Tennis Center Designations as of December 31, 1971

The following cities listed by Sectional Associations have been designated as tennis centers:

Alaska—Anchorage.

Hawaii—Honolulu.

Puerto Rico—Piedras.

EASTERN

Connecticut—Stamford.

New Jersey—Arlington, East Orange, Glen Ridge, Hackensack, Hoboken, Maplewood, Montclair, Orange, Short Hills, Westfield.

New York—Albany, Andes, Ardsley-on-Hudson, Bayside, Binghamton, Bronxville, Brooklyn, Buffalo, Elmira, Garden City, Great Neck, L.I., Great Kills, S.I., Hartsdale, Jackson Heights, L.I., Mamaroneck, New Rochelle, New York City, North Tarrytown, Rochester, Scarsdale, Syracuse, Schenectady, Tannersville, Utica, Woodmere, L.I., Yonkers.

FLORIDA

Florida—Coral Gables, Daytona Beach, Delray Beach, Ft. Lauderdale, Fort Walton Beach, Hollywood, Jacksonville, Lakeland, Miami, Miami Beach, Ocala, Orlando, Sarasota, St. Petersburg, Tampa.

INTERMOUNTAIN

Colorado—Denver, Ft. Collins, Pueblo, Colorado Springs.

Idaho—Boise.

Montana—Butte, Billings, Great Falls, Missoula.

Nevada—Las Vegas.

Utah—Lehi, Salt Lake City, Ogden.

MIDDLE ATLANTIC

D.C.—Washington.

Maryland—Baltimore, Bethesda–Chevy Chase, Cumberland, Hagerstown, Salisbury.

Virginia—Arlington County, Charlottsville, Hilton Village, Lynchburg, Norfolk, Richmond.

West Virginia—Alderson, Beckley, Bluefield, Princeton, Wheeling.

MIDDLE STATES

Delaware—Wilmington, New Castle.

New Jersey—Haddonfield, Ocean City, Woodbury, Princeton, Lawrenceville, Trenton.

Pennsylvania—Allentown, Altoona, Bethlehem, Cynwyd, Drexel Hills, Erie, Harrisburg, Haverford, Lancaster, Norristown, North Philadelphia, Philadelphia, Pittsburgh, Reading, Scranton, Williamsport, Huntington Valley, Bloomsburg, Wyomissing, Eagles Mere, Narbeth, Hershey, Carnegie, York.

MISSOURI VALLEY

Iowa—Ames, Burlington, Cedar Rapids, Keokuk, Des Moines, Red Oak.

Kansas—Arkansas City, Winfield.

Missouri—Kansas City, St. Louis.

NEW ENGLAND

Connecticut—Bridgeport, Hamden, Hartford, New Haven, Westport.

Maine—Portland, York.

Massachusetts—Boston, Osterville, Quincy, Springfield, Wianno, Winchester, Worcester.

New Hampshire—Concord, Hanover, Portsmouth, Rye Beach.

Rhode Island—Newport, Providence.

Vermont—Brattleboro, Burlington.

NORTH CALIFORNIA

California—Fresno, Monterey, Sacramento, San Francisco.

Nevada—Reno.

NORTHWESTERN

Minnesota—Duluth, Minneapolis, Rochester, St. Paul.

North Dakota—Fargo.

South Dakota—Sioux Falls.

PACIFIC NORTHWEST

British Columbia—Duncan, Vancouver, Victoria.

Oregon—Eugene, Portland, Klamath Falls, Corvallis.

Washington—Bellingham, Bremerton, Burien, Everett, Hoquiam, Seattle, Spokane, Tacoma, Wenatchee, Yakima.

SOUTHERN

Arkansas—Little Rock.

Alabama—Anniston, Birmingham, Huntsville, Mobile.

Georgia—Atlanta, Augusta, Columbus, Macon, Rome, Savannah.

Kentucky—Louisville.

Louisiana—New Orleans, Shreveport.

Mississippi—Jackson.

North Carolina—Asheville, Chapel Hill, Charlotte, Goldsboro, Greensboro, Raleigh.

South Carolina—Belton, Charleston, Clinton, Columbia, Greenville.

Tennessee—Chattanooga, Knoxville, Memphis, Nashville, Sewanee.

SOUTHERN CALIFORNIA

California—La Jolla, Los Angeles, San Diego.

SOUTHWESTERN

Arizona—Phoenix, Tucson.

New Mexico—Albuquerque.

Texas—El Paso.

TEXAS

Texas—Austin, Beaumont, Brownsville, Corpus Christi, Dallas, Fort Worth, Galveston, Greenville, Houston, San Antonio, Tyler, Waco, Wichita Falls.

WESTERN

Illinois—Aurora, Chicago, Danville, Decatur, Dixon, Evanston, Fox River Valley, Hinsdale, Joliet, North Shore, Oak Park, Pekin, Peoria, Quincy, Rockford, South Chicago, Urbana, West Suburban Chicago.

Indiana—Bloomington, Calumet, Culver, Elkhart, Evansville, Fort Wayne, Hammond, Gary, Goshen, Indianapolis, La Porte, Mishawaka, New Paris, Plymouth, South Bend, Terre Haute.

Michigan—Allen Park, Ann Arbor, Battle Creek, Bay City, Berrien Springs, Birmingham, Bloomfield Hills, Highland Park, Dearborn, Detroit, East Detroit, Flint, Grand Haven, Grand Rapids, Grosse Pointe, Holland, Hubbell, Iron Mountain, Kalamazoo, Lansing, Marquette, Midland, Monroe, Muskegon, Niles, Pontiac, Saginaw, St. Joseph, South Haven, Traverse City, Trenton, Wyandotte.

Ohio—Akron, Cincinnati, Cleveland, Columbus, Dayton, Hamilton, Lakeside, Lima, Mt. Vernon, Middletown, Newark, Springfield, Toledo, Youngstown.

W. Virginia—Charleston, Huntington, Parkersburg.

Wisconsin—Appleton, Ashland, -Beaver Dam, Chippewa Falls, Delafield, Eau Claire, Green Bay, Janesville, Kenosha, La Crosse, Madison, Manitowoc, Menasha, Milwaukee, Milwaukee Suburbs, Oshkosh, Platteville, Rhinelander, Stevens Point, Superior, Waukesha, Wausau, Wauwatosa.

The administrative Committee may, in its discretion, add to the number of centers.

How to Make the Draw

The USLTA, as previously stated, employs the Bagnall-Wild system of making a drawing. The object of this method of drawing is to place the byes, if any, in the first round, both for convenience and still more because a bye is of less value in the first round than later in the tournament.

By the method used for making the draw of a tournament during the early days of the game, it was possible for a player to have a bye in the semifinal round; he could then rest and watch two players hammering away at each other for hours to decide which should meet him in the final. The Bagnall-Wild system precluded that by placing all the byes, if any, in the first round, so that in subsequent rounds the number of players in each round would be a power of 2; after each round the number of players remaining would be half as many as in the preceding round.

When the total number of entries is 2, or a power of 2 (4, 8, 16, 32, 64, and so on), then all the names can be written down in a single column, and two of the players will meet in the finals. It is when the total is not a power of 2 that difficulties arise. It is then necessary to so arrange the first round that the number of players thereafter will equal a power of 2. This is done by placing a certain proportion of players in the second round without having played a match in the first round. These are the byes and have one less match to play than the other competitors.

In making the draw, first determine the number of byes by subtracting the total number of entries from the next higher power of 2. For example, if you have 41 entries you subtract 41 from the next higher power of 2, which is 64. This leaves 23 byes, 11 of which should be placed in the upper half of the draw and 12 at the bottom. This leaves 18 players in the first round, and after these men have played, 9 of them will be advanced to the second round, in line with the 23 byes. We now have 23 plus 9, or 32 players in the second round, and as 32 is a power of 2, there will be no byes during the remainder of the tournament, and only two men can meet in the final round.

G. A. Bagnall-Wild was the secretary and treasurer of the Bath Lawn Tennis Club of England and delegate to the meeting of secretaries that used to be convened annually by the All England Club in the early days of the game in England. Early in 1883 a meeting to discuss the formation of a Lawn Tennis Association was held in London, but the result was inconclusive. A proposal was made and carried that a conference should be held with the All England Club on the subject. That club, in declining the conference, offered to institute an annual meeting of secretaries of clubs with power to arrange fixtures and to discuss matters affecting the game; and a second meeting for the discussion of the question of an association turned down the project by a very small majority. The offer of the All England Club was then accepted, and thenceforth until 1888 a meeting of lawn tennis representatives was annually held under the presidency of the secretary of the All England Club.

Bagnall-Wild first brought his system before the delegates' meeting in the winter of 1883, but he was not allowed to move its adoption on the ground that he had failed to give due notice of his intention to do so. However, in the winter of 1884 Bagnall-Wild got his system adopted with the difference that whereas he put the byes at the bottom, the All England Club decided to draw matches and byes alternately, putting the surplus, if any, of byes or matches at the bottom. The top and bottom method of drawing byes was adopted in England in 1886. As mentioned earlier, the USNLTA Executive Committee adopted the Bagnall-Wild system of drawing in 1884, at its meeting on July 7. It took quite a number of years for the top and bottom method, when adopted, to become the general

practice, and the draws in even the championships were very much mixed up until about the year 1890.

Even today the theory does not seem to be understood by some tournament committees, and from time to time some weird methods of drawings are to be seen. In recent years the method of making the draw has been further complicated by various systems of seeding and placing of entries. Some seeding was done in the championship held at Newport in 1895 and again in 1896; but not thereafter until the present seeding regulations were adopted on February 4, 1922.

In the Senior championships the committees are authorized to "place" the same number of players in the draw as they are allowed to seed. In the Girls' USLTA championship the normal procedure is to place players of high rank from the same Sectional Associations in different quarters of the draw. In competitions between nations, states, cities, clubs, colleges, schools, and similar bodies, when the competition is really between such bodies and not between the players as individuals, the players may be placed in such manner as agreed upon by the management of the competition.

Seeding the Draw

In order to prevent the best players from meeting each other during the early rounds of a tournament, it is common practice to place, or seed, them in the draw. Seeding is usually determined by ranking, record, and reputation. When seeding the draw, three principal points should be kept in mind:

1. USLTA Tournament Regulations stipulate that, in a sanctioned tournament, not more than 1 player in every 4 may be seeded. Note that this stipulation is permissive, not mandatory. In many tournaments the tournament committee may feel that less liberal seeding is preferable. (Obviously, the further down the line one goes in selecting seeds, the more difficult the judgments.) There is no minimum specified. One in eight is the most usual pattern.

2. Every seeded position is drawn by lot. You draw to determine whether No. 1 goes on the very top, or the very bottom; then No. 2 gets the opposite position. The same principle is followed for the rest of the seeds. (Note that each seeded player drawn to a

spot in the lower half of the draw is placed on the bottom line of whatever segment he draws.)

3. USLTA Tournament Regulations make no provision for showing seeded players any special consideration in "giving" them first-round byes (where there is a less than full bracket). Thus, in a tournament with 27 entries the byes would be opposite Seeds 1 and 2—on Lines 2 and 31—and also on Lines 4 and 29, and Line 27. This would mean that Seeds 3 and 4 would not get byes, while the players who happen to be drawn to Lines 3, 28, and 30 would get them. But in club, league, and invitation tournaments the tournament committee has the option of distributing byes among seeded players (in case of a less than full bracket).

Where the Seeds Go. Here are how the seeds should be placed in the draw:

For a 16-player draw, with two seeds: One goes on line 1, the other on line 16. Decide by drawing.

For a 32-player draw, with four seeds: Seeds 1 and 2 draw for lines 1 and 32, seeds 3 and 4 draw for lines 9 and 24.

For a 64-player draw, with eight seeds: Seeds 1 and 2 draw for lines 1 and 64; seeds 3 and 4 draw for lines 17 and 48; seeds 5, 6, 7, and 8 draw for lines 9, 56, 25, and 40.

For a 128-player draw, with 16 seeds (two 64-line draw sheets, Upper and Lower): Seeds 1 and 2 draw for lines U–1 and L–64 (or 128).* Seeds 3 and 4 draw for lines U–33 and L–32 (96). Seeds 5, 6, 7, and 8 draw for lines U–17, L–48 (112), U–49, and L–16 (80). Seeds 9, 10, 11, 12, 13, 14, 15, and 16 draw for lines U–9, L–56 (120), U–25, L–40 (104), U–41, L–24 (88), U–57, and L–8 (72).

If your number of entries is only a few over the number for an even bracket—say, 37—

* Numbers in parentheses apply if you have re-numbered the second sheet 65 to 128.

1. Seed 1 or 2
2.   Bye
3.
4.   Bye
5. Seed 5, 6, 7 or 8
6.
7.
8.
9. Seed 3 or 4
10.
11.
12.
13. Seed 7, 8, 5, or 6
14.
15.
16.
17.
18.
19.
20. Seed 8, 5, 6 or 7
21.
22.
23.
24. Seed 4 or 3
25.
26.
27.   Bye
28. Seed 6, 7, 8 or 5
29.   Bye
30.
31.   Bye
32. Seed 2 or 1

A 32-place draw sheet ready for a tournament with 27 entries.

you might find it less confusing to "build up" from a 32-line sheet than to "build down" from 64. To do this you start at the middle and create two-line (two-player) pairings at each of several lines until you have provided as many lines as you have players. When doing it this way, remember that if you have an uneven number of these "extra" matches to chart, the top half of the draw gets the odd one (just the opposite of the disposition of the odd bye).

The Rest of the Draw. Once you have filled in the lines to be occupied by seeded players, and marked those lines that represent byes, the rest of the draw is filled in by drawing the names of all the rest of the competitors and writing them on the remaining unoccupied lines, in the order in which they are drawn.

When this drawing procedure operates to bring together, for their first match, players of the same family, same school or college, or same foreign country, the tournament committee may, at its discretion, place the second player so drawn in the same relative position in the next quarter of the draw. (This is in accord with the procedure followed in making the draw for USLTA National Championships.)

"Foreign" Seeds. In recent years there has been a strong trend away from having separate seeding lists for "foreign" and domestic players—along with a trend toward minimizing the total number of seeds. However, in some situations it may be deemed desirable to have such separate lists.

Procedure: (1) The domestic seeds should be only half as many as the total seeds planned; (2) draw these domestic seeds according to the pattern indicated above, and insert the names on the lines to which they are drawn; (3) the No. 1 foreign seed is then placed at the opposite end of the same half of the draw as the No. 2 domestic seed, while, conversely, the No. 2 foreign seed is placed at the opposite end of the half to which the No. 1 domestic seed was drawn; (4) foreign seeds Nos. 3 and 4 are drawn by lot and placed in the two quarters that do not already have foreign seeds 1 and 2, the one drawn to the top half going to the bottom line of the first quarter, the other one going to the top line of the fourth quarter.

For example, in a 64 draw, with 4 domestic seeds and 4 foreign seeds, assume that the No. 1 domestic seed is drawn for line 1 on the draw sheet. Domestic seed No. 2 would be on line 64, and domestic Nos. 3 and 4 would be drawn for lines 17 and 48. Then foreign seed No. 1 would go on line 33, and foreign seed No. 2 would go on line 32 . . . and foreigns 3 and 4 would be drawn for lines 16 and 49. This would mean that each of the eight 8-line segments would have a seeded player, alternating, top to bottom, between domestic and foreign.

Obviously, it is desirable, for simplicity's sake, to have an even number of seeded positions. However, if an odd number of players is to be seeded, the determination of which half of the draw gets the "extra" seed should be made by lot.

Rankings. Most local, sectional, and national tennis associations issue an annual list of rankings for players in each division. Rankings are based solely on tournament won-lost records for that year. Generally, a player must compete in a specific number of sanctioned tournaments before being eligible for a ranking.

Other Types of Competitions

There are several different types of competitive events that can be used by tennis clubs and similar groups to provide stimulating competition. The most popular types of events are: single elimination, double elimination, consolation, handicap, move-up move-down, round-robin, pyramid, and ladder. The first five of these competitions are generally used to determine a champion and runner-up, and when the tournament is to be of short duration.

The round-robin tournament requires a great deal of time but is used to give each member of a group an opportunity to play every other member. Frequently it is used early in a course to determine the positions of the players on a challenge ladder or pyramid.

The ladder and pyramid events are used to maintain a flexible or changing ranking list over a prolonged time period. The handicap tournament can be used as a single elimination, double elimination, consolation, or round-robin event.

Single Elimination Tournament. The simplest type of tournament is the single elimina-

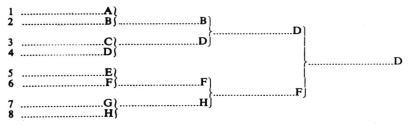

Diagram of a single elimination tournament.

tion tournament, in which the winner of each match advances in the tournament and the loser is eliminated. As the name implies, one loss eliminates a player; no provision is made for an off day or bad luck occurring to a player. This type of draw is most convenient with a large number of contestants and only a short time available for play.

If all players are of equal ability or their ability is unknown, all names are placed in a hat and drawn blindly for positions on the draw sheet. The first name drawn is placed on the first line of the draw, the second name drawn is placed on the second line, and so on, assuming, of course, that proper provision has been made for the number of byes required. The single elimination tournament type is used in all USLTA events, but the method of drawing and seeding is as described earlier.

Double Elimination Tournament. The double elimination tournament, in which a player must lose twice before he is eliminated, is superior to the single elimination tournament when a small number of contestants is involved (less than eight) for it makes allowances for players having off days. Byes are given for less than eight players. If more than eight players are entered, two separate tournaments can be held and the winners can meet for the championship.

Consolation Tournament. The consolation tournament is generally used only when the number of entries is eight or sixteen. Here, the losers in the first round of play compete with each other for the consolation title. First-round winners advance to the right and compete for the championship.

Round-Robin Tournament. In a round-robin tournament, each player plays every other player once, and the final standing is determined on a percentage basis.

For an even number of players: Assign each player a number. Schedule matches according to the following (for eight entries):

1–8	1–7	1–6	1–5	1–4	1–3	1–2
2–7	8–6	7–5	6–4	5–3	4–2	3–8
3–6	2–5	8–4	7–3	6–2	5–8	4–7
4–5	3–4	2–3	8–2	7–8	6–7	5–6

Note that number 1 remains stationary and the other numbers revolve around it in a counterclockwise direction.

For an odd number of players: Assign each player a number. Schedule matches according to the following (for nine entries):

9	8	7	6	5	4	3	2	1
1–8	9–7	8–6	7–5	6–4	5–3	4–2	3–1	2–9
2–7	1–6	9–5	8–4	7–3	6–2	5–1	4–9	3–8
3–6	2–5	1–4	9–3	8–2	7–1	6–9	5–8	4–7
4–5	3–4	2–3	1–2	9–1	8–9	7–8	6–7	5–6

Note that all figures revolve, and one player has a bye in each round.

Handicap Tournament. The handicap tournament can be run as a single or double elimination, consolation, or round-robin event. Handicaps can be determined as previously discussed or in such other manner as decided by the club. The best player gets the lowest handicap, the most inferior player gets the highest handicap.

Move-Up Move-Down Tournament. In this type of tournament the players move up a court (from court 5 to 4 to 3, etc.) when they win. Each player strives to reach court 1 and to remain there throughout the tournament. It provides much fun in a group situation.

Players are paired as opponents and assigned to numbered courts. All start play on a signal from the tournament chairman. After some arbitrary length of time, play is halted. The number of games won by each player is then recorded. The winner on each court "moves up" to the next lower-numbered court. The loser on each court "moves down" one court. The winner on court 1 can go nowhere, so he stays there; the loser on the last court also stays on that court (the highest-numbered court). Another round is played, after which changes in position are again made. In doubles, players change partners after they change courts.

Ladder Tournament. In a ladder tournament, players are listed according to ability or ranking, with the best player at the top of the list. Competition is arranged by challenge, and a player is allowed to challenge either of the two players above him on the ladder. If the challenger wins, he changes places with the loser on the ladder. If the challenged player wins, he is allowed to challenge someone above him before he must accept another challenge. All challenges must be accepted and played before a definitely agreed time. Specific rules should be posted concerning the ladder tournament in order to avoid disputes and to keep the tournament running smoothly. This type of tournament is ideal for maintaining a continuous ranking of players over a long period of time.

Pyramid Tournament. The pyramid tournament, like the ladder tournament just described, maintains continuous, prolonged competition. It allows for more challenging and participating and can include a larger number of participants than the ladder tournament.

After the original drawings are made, any player may challenge any other player in the same horizontal row. If he wins, he can challenge any player in the row above him. When a player loses to someone on the row below him, he changes places with the winner. Again, as in the ladder tournament, clear, concise, and specific rules should be posted with the challenge board in order to avoid disputes about challenge matches.

The VASSS round-robin score sheet.

VASSS Round-Robin Medal Play. This round-robin tournament follows the same basic schedule as given earlier for conventional round-robin play except that VASSS Single-Point system of scoring is employed. In addition, a round-robin in this VASSS-type tournament may be any multiple of 20 (40, 60, 80) total points of one 31-point set. The winner shall receive a 5-point bonus for the win, plus the unplayed points in the set (e.g.: A player wins 31–10, his score for that round will be $31 + 5 + 20 = 56$ points). The winner of the tournament is the player with the most points at the end of the round-robin schedule.

Individual handicaps are estimated against scratch for the number of points in a round, as decided by the tournament committee. A tournament doubles-team handicap is the sum of the individual players' handicaps.

Team Matches

Here are some general guidelines regarding formats for team matches:

Any scholastic, college, industrial, or club league is entitled to choose its own format for the matches. The larger universities usually play six singles and three doubles, and individuals are allowed to compete in both.

A popular format for industrial leagues, clubs, high schools, and smaller colleges is four singles, three doubles. Many have found that the scheduling is easier, and the playing opportunities better distributed, if players are confined to playing either singles or doubles, but not both.

Singles matches always are first on the schedule. The scoring is simple: each match, whether singles or doubles, counts one point; a tie counts a half point for each side.

First Aid on the Courts

During a tournament—or actually any other time during a game—an accident may occur that requires first aid. Here is some general information that may help should any of the following situations occur:

SCRATCHES, BLISTERS: Clean wounds thoroughly before applying medicine or bandages. For blisters, cease playing immediately in order to avoid aggravation (wear two pairs of socks to avoid blisters).

BLEEDING: Do not wash wound. Press down on bleeding point, wrap with handkerchief, piece of shirt, towel, etc. If bleeding won't stop, apply pressure above wound, or make tourniquet, tie around limb with half knot, place stick over it; tie another knot over stick and twist. Be sure to loosen frequently. Send for doctor.

TWISTED ANKLES, CRAMPS: Stay off ailing legs and seek immediate medical attention. With cramps, sit down and rub affected area toward heart; do not resume activity without medical approval.

BROKEN BONE: Whether simple or compound, do *not* move victim. Send for doctor. Make victim lie still.

ARTIFICIAL RESPIRATION: If victim is not breathing, apply mouth-to-mouth breathing at once. Lay victim on back. Clear mouth and throat. Tilt head back. Pull chin up. Pull jaws forward with thumb. Place mouth over victim's, pinch victim's nostrils, take deep breath, blow hard enough to make victim's chest rise. Remove mouth, let victim's chest fall. Repeat at rate of 12 breaths a minute (20 for children) until victim breathes naturally.

LIGHTNING: If victim is not breathing, apply mouth-to-mouth breathing. Send for doctor. Make victim comfortable.

FAINTING: Have victim sit with head between knees or lie down with head lower than feet. Sprinkle water on face. Do not give stimulant. Send for doctor.

HEART ATTACK: Send for doctor. Make victim comfortable. Loosen tight clothing. Keep victim warm. Do not give stimulant. Suggest slow, deep breaths.

SUN STROKE: Lay victim on back in shade with head slightly elevated. Cool head and body with water. Rub arms and legs toward heart. Send for doctor.

TENNIS ELBOW: One of the most discussed but still medically vague problems on the court is the "tennis elbow." Thousands of players complain annually of pains in the elbow area around the arm, and doctors offer consoling words of wisdom without any real cure. A tennis elbow can be detected by pain, throbbing, or stiffness in the area on top of and around the elbow of your rack hand. Generally, the tennis elbow is a result of (1) overworking the arm with too much tennis in too short a period of time; (2) a gradual age level, where the player is not physically able to participate as freely as he formerly did; or (3) racket strung too tightly puts undue pressure back into the elbow.

Doctors say the best remedy for the tennis elbow is rest. Painkillers and aspirin may be a temporary answer, but they may lead to more serious problems. With rest, doctors may be able to restore the elbow to normalcy and a gradual program of tennis can be incorporated. Continually overworking the arm may lead to complications in the shoulder and other areas of the body. Heat treatments, massages and whirlpools, are other means of relaxing the arm and relieving some of the pain, off the court.

Other medical ailments such as "trick knees," stiff wrists, or stiff shoulders require more delicate handling. Many players with knee problems find doubles an easier outlet than singles. They also play more on clay courts than cement or hard courts because the sliding eases the stop-and-start irregularities.

It is only safe to say that a player's health is more important than winning or losing; for without it, the player never gets the chance to even walk on the court.

DUTIES AND JURISDICTIONS OF OFFICIALS

Umpires and linesmen have been a familiar sight on the courts since the earliest annals of the sport. An old photograph of one of the early Wimbledon tournaments shows the umpire in a gray top hat seated in a chair raised on a table near the net, and linesmen in their positions opposite the lines. Evidently it was found this early that men to call the score and judge the lines relieved the players, added to the enjoyment of the gallery, and insured fairness of play for any match. Actually, it is the duty of every player to become an efficient umpire or linesman, and although it is rather an irksome task, a really good official is much admired and is of great value to the game of lawn tennis. Even if as a player you have not studied the rules of the game, as an umpire it is essential that you should know them. It is amazing what a number of obscure and unique points arise at different times, questions which the umpire has to decide. If, however, you are uncertain of some technicality, you should refer the matter to the referee, whose decision shall be final.

When playing in an open tournament, you must always be ready to do your share of umpiring, and there are often occasions in ordinary club tournaments and matches when umpires and linesmen are badly needed. The only time when it is not advisable to take on a match is if you yourself are due to play immediately afterward. Officiating is apt to tire your eyes and sitting in one position for a long time stiffens your muscles, so avoid umpiring just before you are going to play.

Duties of Referee, Umpire, and Linesman

By far the question most often asked of a tennis official—usually by a spectator who has just watched a close match that might have been decided by one questionable call—is: Can the umpire overrule a linesman's call?

The answer is no. But let us not just drop it there. Good, experienced umpires—and good, experienced linesmen—know the rest of the answer, the practical solution in those unhappy instances where, as they say, "Everybody knew it was out, but. . . ."

In such a situation it is possible for the umpire to help avoid an injustice. If the umpire is sure the call was erroneous he can refrain from repeating the linesman's call as he normally would, and this, coupled with a quietly inquiring look, gives the linesman a cue and an opportunity to volunteer either a "correction" or a "not sure." Thereupon the umpire can make the amended call or call a let, whichever in his discretion is the fairest solution. The above refers, of course, to calls based on matters of fact, not on interpretations of the rules. If, for instance, a linesman calls a foot fault for "hopping" (no longer prohibited), it is within the umpire's province to reverse such a call (and to make sure all his linesmen know all the rules!).

There are three basic group officials involved in the play of lawn tennis, and their duties are as follows:

Referee. The referee is *ex officio* a member of the tournament committee. He should be present at the making of the draw, and should be on the premises at all times that tournament play is going on. If he must be absent he must appoint a *pro tem* referee. Any time the referee plays in or officiates in a tournament match, he must appoint a *pro tem* referee.

The referee shall have power to appoint and remove umpires and linesmen, to assign courts, and decide starting times for matches. He shall decide any point of law (but not a question of fact) which an umpire may be unable to decide—or which may be referred to him on appeal from the decision of an umpire.

Generally the referee—in cooperation with the tournament chairman—decides such matters as the number of games between ball changes, and the number of balls per change, and whether or not spikes will be permitted.

It is the referee's decision as to whether any match, once started, shall be postponed because of weather conditions—rain, darkness, etc. Note this distinction: An umpire may *suspend* play—as in the event of rain—but actual *postponement* may be ordered only by the referee.

The referee has the authority to declare a competitor defaulted for failure to be ready when his match is called. Usually such a default is declared after consultation between the referee and the tournament committee, but the referee is the ultimate authority. USLTA tournament regulations provide that the umpire may default a player who, in the opinion of the umpire, deliberately ignores and/or refuses to follow his directions with respect to the player's conduct in a match. Discerning umpires make a distinction between the words "default" and "retired" in recording the outcome of a match. The former term is applicable in cases of a player's failing to appear for a match, or of being defaulted for misconduct, whereas once a match has been started and a player is unable to continue because of illness or other cause, the outcome should show the actual score so far as the match progressed, followed by "retired." The situations could logically be reported this way: (1) player failed to appear—"John Doe *won from* Richard Roe by default"; (2) player defaulted for misconduct —"John Doe *defeated* Richard Roe, 3–3, default"; (3) player unable to continue— "John Doe *defeated* Richard Roe, 6–4, 3–3, retired."

There is a fundamental distinction to be made between the roles of the referee and the tournament committee chairman: The referee is primarily responsible for judgment decisions regarding fairness of conditions of actual play, whereas the tournament committee's responsibility is primarily that of seeing to it that proper and adequate physical facilities are available for the conduct of the tournament.

In the matter of equipment for the umpires' chairs, the referee and the umpires themselves have the primary responsibility—the referee first, the umpires as a "check." Here is a basic list of equipment with which the umpires' chairs should be stocked:

Towels
Salt tablets
Mercurochrome or iodine
Smelling salts
Wrist sweat bands
Water and cups
Aspirin
Rosin or sawdust
Rubber bands
Safety pins
Adhesive bandages
Adhesive tape
Scissors
Yardsticks and singles sticks

Score cards are also, basically, the responsibility of the referee, but the responsibility for obtaining them and preparing them, with names and descriptions for particular matches, is usually delegated to a chairman of umpires.

Umpire. The umpire has general oversight of the conduct of a match. Primarily this entails making optimum disposition of the linesmen that are available; introducing the players; keeping the running score on his score card and calling it after each point, game, and set (and at other times when requested by a competitor). Other specific duties of the umpire are:

1. To ascertain that the net be the right height before the start of play, and to measure and adjust the net after each set or at other suitable intervals.

2. To repeat "out" or "fault" calls of linesmen (or make those calls himself with respect to lines for which he has assumed responsibility, in a match not fully staffed with linesmen).

3. To see that the competitors change sides at the proper times, and serve and receive in proper rotation.

4. To see that play is resumed promptly at the expiration of time allowed for a rest period.

5. To see that play is "continuous" within the generally accepted meaning of the term. The rules now have a time limit of 60 seconds on court changes. This means the players should be "in position and ready to resume play" within 60 seconds.

6. To suspend play (subject to confirmation by the referee) when weather or other conditions make this advisable.

7. To request the presence of the referee when confronted with a question of tournament procedure on which he, the umpire, does not have authority (for example, the question of whether a competitor shall be allowed to put on spikes).

8. To complete the score card, sign it, and deliver it, at the conclusion of the match, to the authorized person or desk.

A competitor who wishes to have a linesman removed must make such a request to the umpire in charge of the match, and it is the umpire's decision whether the request shall be referred to the referee for decision. If the competitor's request is that the umpire himself be removed, it must be communicated to the referee for decision. In either case it is generally desirable that no such request bring about an interruption of play—and the umpire has the authority to decide whether there shall be any suspension while the request is relayed to the referee. The latter should give full consideration to the known and assumed reasons for the requested removal—and act only if they are well founded, not simply on a competitor's objection.

As for the umpire's procedure, most persons learn tennis umpiring techniques largely by following the examples of established officials. For those who have little or no opportunity to do this—and as a check list for even those who have had some experience—here follows a set of recommended procedures:

Upon getting your assignment and score card, make sure you understand the basic facts about the match, such as name of the tournament, division (men's, women's, singles, doubles, etc.), the round, best of ? sets, correct names and residences of the contestants, and the ball change. All of this should be on your score card when it is handed to you, but if it is not, you should write it in. Be sure you have two eraser-equipped pencils in good working order.

When you go onto the court (preferably accompanying the contestants, although that is not always possible), check these matters first: height of the net; singles sticks properly placed—or removed, as the case may be; adequate supply of balls; other equipment for the umpire's chair.

If there are linesmen who have been assigned to your match but have not been given specific line assignments, it is your function to deploy them in the way that gives you best coverage, considering the nature of the contest, the setting, the type of court, and the known capabilities of the available linesmen. Have the players spin for choice of service or court, etc., then mark that part of your score card accordingly, noting at least the first ball change.

If there are ball boys, be sure they understand the players' preferences regarding clearing balls on missed first services, or any special arrangements that need to be made. Also that they understand about quickly moving all balls to the server's end of the court. Make sure you know how each player prefers to have his name pronounced. If there is a warmup time limit indicated, "inviting" the players to take their practice serves is a polite way of reminding them it's about time to get started. Allow about 45 seconds for this.

While there is no requirement that every person umpiring a tennis match must use exactly the same phrases in given situations, it is true that over the years a well-standardized pattern of announcements has evolved through pursuit of the "A-B-C" ideal of Accuracy, Brevity, and Clarity—plus another C,

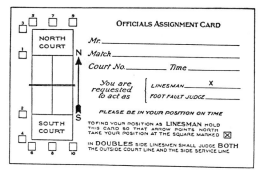

A typical official's assignment card.

Courtesy. Here is the way it goes:

Starting the match: "Ladies and gentlemen, your attention, please. This is a third-round match in the Eastern Grass Court Championships, men's singles. On my right (or, in the court nearer the boxes), from Denmark, Mr. Torben Ulrich; on my left (or, in the far court), from Evanston, Illinois, Mr. Martin Riessen. . . . This will be the best of three sets. Mr. Ulrich won the toss and elected to receive, so Mr. Riessen will serve first." (Glance to see that all linesmen are ready) "Ready? Play!" (Announce each player as he serves for the first time: "Mr. Ulrich serving.")

Always use Mr. and Miss or Mrs. in introductions, and in the call at the conclusion of a game, set, or match: "Games, Mr. Smith." However, it is not necessary to use the "Mr." when calling advantage points for male players; often it occurs so repetitiously in a long deuced game as to be tiresome. "Advantage, Smith" suffices. But always use the player's name on these calls, not such terms as striker, or server, or receiver, or "advantage in" or "advantage out." (In doubles, because of the awkwardness of calling both partners' names on every advantage point, most experienced umpires use the server's name for all advantage-point calls for that side, and sort of "divide up" the identifications of the receiving side, being in part guided by the action that gave the receivers their advantage.)

Call games as follows: "Game, Mr. Smith; he wins the first game." In sets other than the first set, make it "Game, Mr. Smith; leads three games to two, first set." Or "Game, Mr. Jones. Three games to two, Mr. Smith leads, first set." . . . "Game, Mr. Jones; games are three-all, first set."

Note: In the game mentioned above where Mr. Jones won the game but nevertheless still trailed in the score, there is a full-stop period after the name Jones. *Then* the score is given, and then Mr. Smith's name occurs. This sequence is used to avoid the slight confusion that might result if one phrase ended in "Mr. Jones" and the next one started with "Mr. Smith."

Call sets as follows: "Game and third set, Mr. Smith, seven games to five. Mr. Jones leads in sets, two to one."

Note: It is desirable for the umpire to be alert to game points and set points—and of course match point—and that he make his call promptly when those points are concluded. Delay (except to allow applause to subside) gives rise to lack of confidence in the official. But *do not ever* announce that an upcoming point is "set point" or "match point."

In matches where players take an intermission, it is the umpire's responsibility to see that they are back on the court ready to resume play at the specified time. At resumption of play the umpire's announcement is: "With Mr. Jones leading, two sets to one, Mr. Smith will serve first in the fourth set . . . Ready? Play!"

Linesman. It is the duty of a linesman to decide every question of fact regarding the line to which he is assigned. Primarily this means making the decision as to whether any ball falling near that line is good or out . . . but questions regarding foot faulting also will present themselves to base-linesmen, and occasionally also to center service-linesmen and side-linesmen.

The linesman's only cries are "out" and "fault," the latter being the call on any served ball that clears the net but falls outside any of the service-box lines. Use of hand signals, in moderation, can be helpful in supplementing voice calls—but beware of starting a hand signal "too soon," lest you decide, a split second later, that the ball was not out, after all!

The calls of the linesman must be prompt, loud, and decisive. He should make an audible call on every ball that is "out" on his line, even those that go flying many feet beyond the line. That is because, properly, the umpire cannot make an "out" call on any line that is covered by a linesman unless he gets a call from that linesman or gets a signal from the linesman that he was "unsighted" and unable to make a decision. Never call a ball "out" until the ball has actually struck. The call on an out ball is "out"—not "outside."

If a linesman, in his effort to make his call quickly, calls a ball "out" and then instantly realizes it was good, he must immediately get the attention of the umpire and indicate a correction. The umpire will take it from there. If the umpire calls the score or makes a call at variance with the linesman's decision— possibly through failure to hear a call—the linesman should call the umpire's attention to the error.

Linesmen calling the side lines should be alert to the probability that they will have to stand, moving a few feet "outside" their chair's position, in order to get an unobstructed view of services coming toward that side line. The linesman has the obligation also of being alert to the possibility of his being called upon for an opinion on an occasional ball falling near a line not "his own," and should give his opinion—only when asked— and only if he is positive about the ball.

The linesman should quickly inform the umpire by signal (both hands in front of eyes) or voice if for any reason he is unable to make a call on a ball falling near his line. . . . It is *not* a linesman's duty to catch (or try to catch), or to retrieve, any ball. Do not be a ball boy.

Although white is the traditional color of clothing for tennis players, it is not desirable in the garments of linesmen.

Net Umpire. In important matches such as the finals and semifinals of a major tournament, a net-cord umpire is added. The net-cord umpire usually keeps one hand on the net cord to ascertain service lets by touch. It is the duty of the net umpire to:

1. Keep his own score card as a double check on the chair umpire.
2. Measure the net before the start of the match and at changeover games at the start of each set (and at other times when in his judgment and that of the umpire it would be advisable).
3. Make sure the umpire knows any time

a served ball touches the net in passing.

4. Call attention to any instance where a player or anything he wears or carries touches the net while the ball is still in play, or where the ball in play touches a player or anything he wears or carries, other than his racket held in his hand or hands.

5. Help the umpire keep track of ball changes, etc.

6. When requested by the umpire, be responsible for calling "not up." (This should be the sole responsibility of either the umpire or the net umpire. Whose responsibility it is should be clearly understood before the match starts.)

Foot-Fault Judge. The foot-fault judge is seldom used today. In most tournaments the calling of infractions of the foot-fault rule is left to the linesmen—primarily the base-linesman, although it is possible for players to violate the center mark and side line, also, and when this happens the linesmen on center service and the side line make the call. However, in some events it is deemed desirable to have a separate foot-fault judge. The purpose of this, originating in earlier times, when there was more of an element of "interpretation" involved in judging whether a foot fault was committed, is to insure that interpretation is the same at each end of the court. To a lesser extent, this still is the purpose, so a match should have only one foot-fault judge, if it has any.

The foot-fault judge has a chair at either end of the court. If the physical layout permits, it may be desirable for these chairs to be at the opposite end of each base line from the chairs of the base-linesmen. Regardless of which side his chairs are on, the foot-fault judge should remember that he "changes on the even" instead of the odd—and should make his move quickly so that the players never have to wait for him.

The Tennis Umpires' Association

The Tennis Umpires' Association is an organized group which furnishes officials of training and experience for tournament tennis. The early judges were generally men intimately connected with the tournament; the linesmen were almost always players, and the umpire was perhaps some official of the home club conducting the event. They were picked up in haphazard fashion by an overworked referee if they could be persuaded to serve. But, because of the supply of such individuals being limited, only the very important matches were ever graced by their presence.

These conditions, with only minor improvements, existed down to the last ten years. As more men became interested, the available candidates for umpires and linesmen increased; but with the growth of the game, tournaments advanced in entries, so that it was still unusual to find any but feature matches properly umpired and lined. This was true of the championships, for even here where tennis enthusiasts gathered in numbers, the supply of umpires and linesmen by no means equaled the demand. Some of these old umpires were just as good as we have today. No one could umpire a match better and be heard more clearly by the gallery than Fred S. Mansfield, the dean of umpires, who for many years handled the principal events at Newport and Longwood. Unfortunately, there were not many like him and good linesmen were even more scarce, for it developed that judging the lines was not the easy job that it would seem and that some men were very much more accurate than others.

Finally the demand became insistent. Players who had enjoyed the benefit of an umpire wanted one whenever a match seemed likely to be close, and they wanted an experienced umpire and competent linesmen, for careless ones were worse than useless. About this time the singles championship was moved from the Newport Casino to the West Side Tennis Club at Forest Hills and the men of the club determined that this feature of the tournament could be improved. They selected E. C. Conlin, who had had experience in a Davis Cup Challenge Round, to handle the umpiring, and to him is largely due the credit of inaugurating a Tennis Umpires' Association. Other men had suggested such an organization but his energy put it into being. He planned a national body of umpires and for their training conceived the idea of an umpires' manual which gave not only the rules and regulations but complete instructions for umpires and their handling of situations during tournaments, as well as many hints on the management of tournaments and the tennis spectators.

The original idea was to have an integral organization with chapters in all tennis centers, but after trial it was found better to affiliate with USLTA. The Association still exists, but now as a committee of USLTA, although the old name is retained. The parent body does the secretarial work, keeps the umpires' lists, and takes care of the expenses, such as printing the manual and tournament stationery.

Once started, the idea grew rapidly and has spread over all of the important tennis centers of the United States and has even invaded foreign countries. All of the championships in this country are played under its regulations and its work has made for the smooth running of these prominent events as well as innumerable smaller tournaments.

The average spectator little realizes the detail that applies to the selecting of the best man for officiating at championship matches. A very brief outline may be interesting. All of the umpires in adjacent tennis sections are called upon, through the mailing list, to serve in the tournament and the applications are listed on a card system. From this card list,

daily before the play starts, men are assigned for every match, and a card is given each man designating the match, number of the court, the time, and his exact position. This removes all confusion; the men know their positions and take them when the players go to the court.

A fully staffed tennis match requires the services of an umpire and ten or eleven linesmen. For these duties it is not necessary to have been an ex-regional or national tennis champion. The job is available to anyone with good eyesight who either knows or is ready to learn the rules of lawn tennis, and who has the ability to make accurate and instantaneous decisions as to the outcome of a match.

Applicants for these positions must pass a written test and serve as an umpire or linesman in a "friendly" match under the guidance of a member of the Tennis Umpire's Association. After these and a final test, the aspirants are accepted to sectional membership and are given their cards in the Tennis Umpire's Association. Any match held under the sanction of USLTA is open for holders of these cards to serve as umpire or linesman. They are entitled to present themselves or be invited. For information, write the USLTA at their New York office.

TENNIS ETIQUETTE

Good sportsmanship, good manners, and the generally accepted customs that constitute the social graces of court play are the lifeblood of tennis. While it is true that tennis is a competitive game and can be a tough and grueling sport, it is one in which the niceties are cherished. The majority of the tennis matches that you will participate in, at least until you reach tournament status, will be friendly get-togethers where the fun of playing is as important as winning.

Many of the manners and customs of the game are not included in the official rules given earlier in this section. They have come about from the experience of players through the years and are now considered as part of the game of tennis. Since some of the suggestions contained herein may seem obvious to the veteran player, it should be pointed out

that one of the basic objectives of the following "Twelve Unwritten Rules of Good Courtmanship" is to start the *beginner* off in the right direction. By learning these rules you and your fellow players will be able to realize the fullest measure of sporting pleasure from the game.

Twelve Unwritten Rules of Good Courtmanship

The following twelve are reprinted here by courtesy of Ashaway Products, Inc.:

1. PROPER ATTITUDE. Your attitude toward the game can add to or detract considerably from both your own and your fellow players' enjoyment of it. Enthusiasm, naturally, is always a plus factor. Even if you are "stuck" with an opponent you outclass completely, it's

in poor taste to act bored and superior. The good sport will maintain his interest and offer encouragement whenever possible. In general, it is traditional in tennis to praise good shots or plays made either by a doubles partner or an opponent. However, this *can* be overdone —to the point where it no longer seems sincere or is open to misinterpretation. For example, should you serve an obvious ace and follow it up with a too vehement "Nice try," it really turns into praise for your own shot.

As in any other sport, knowing how to lose in tennis is also an accomplishment. The alibi artist and the Jonah whose "game is way, way off today" can quickly and unfairly take the edge off a hard-won victory. It is not necessary to hurdle across the net to do it, but a sincere word of congratulation for the winner, and the trite but traditional "Nice game" for the loser always add to the general good feeling.

Before you play, greet your opponent, or opponents, in a friendly manner and introduce yourself. Spin your racquet or toss a coin to decide choice of side or serve. Rally to warm up and then ask if your opponent wishes to take any practice serves before starting the match. "First one in" should not be used to start a match.

All of your equipment, incidentally, should be kept in good condition—so you will not be tempted to use it as an alibi, and also because it means far more enjoyment from your game.

2. KNOW THE RULES. To avoid embarrassment to yourself and to those with whom you play, learn and know the official rules of the game. While you do not need to know all the finer points involved in the rules, you should learn the basic ones. This speeds up play and allows more time for concentration on improving your game.

3. DRESS THE PART. White is comfortable and sharp—to wear it on the court marks you as right for the occasion. It has been the standard tennis attire for years, so to look your best, white is right. (More details on dressing the part can be found in Section II.)

4. MEET YOUR MATCH. No matter how you play or with whom you play, any kind of tennis is better than no tennis at all. However, everyone enjoys it more if opponents are at least somewhere near the same level of playing ability.

In club play, it is standard practice to try to improve your ranking by challenging opponents several notches up the ladder. An eager beginner, on the other hand, would be way out of line to try to set up a match with the club champion. However, if the champ himself suggests the match, that is something else again, and by all means hop to it. In fact if you consider yourself among the better players in a tennis group, it is good practice to invite a match with a lesser opponent now and then to avoid the tag of snob.

The doubles game quite frequently offers the ideal situation in that it makes it easier to distribute the talent evenly on both sides of the court.

5. AVOID STALLING. Because a faster tennis game is more fun to play, and also, since wearing down an opponent is a legitimate and frequently used tennis strategy, it is considered bad form to stall for a breather during a match. While it is hardly necessary to sprint around the court retrieving balls for the server, it is not considered good form to be a "creeper" either. You should get back into position for receiving the next serve as soon as possible after a point is completed.

Because it helps to keep play moving, it is the receiver's duty after each point has been played to retrieve all balls on his side of the court so that the server has two or three in hand to start each serve with. This eliminates delay in case of a let and helps the server zero in.

6. CALLING SERVES. In lieu of an umpire it falls upon the receiver of the service to plainly call close serves either good or out. And, in the case of doubt, it is, of course, good tennis manners to give your opponent the benefit of the call. Strictly speaking, the receiver really should not touch any service which does not fall good. However, in most friendly games it has become accepted practice to stop bad serves with the racket to keep balls off adjoining courts and reduce mileage rolled up in chasing them. Return balls directly to the server when he is waiting to serve.

In case of any delayed or misunderstood call, or any circumstance outside of normal play which throws the server off his balance, it is customary for the *receiver* to offer replay of the point. Lets should also be clearly called in accordance with the official rules.

Unless your match has the benefit of an umpire, it is the responsibility of the server to call the score after each point. Do not wrangle over decisions or behave like a spoiled child.

During a rally, you are the linesman (in lieu of an official linesman) for all balls that land on your side of the net. Do not call the good balls, just the outs. Again, if any question arises, replay the point. Also, offer to replay the point if during a rally there is interference caused by a ball rolling on your court from an adjoining one or by a piece of paper blowing around.

7. REPLAY OF FAST SERVICE. Before delivering the service, it is the responsibility of the server to be sure the receiver is ready—and to offer replay of the service if any doubt exists. This is worthy of special note by players who are in the habit of delivering a fast second serve right on top of a first-service fault.

When receiving, do not return the ball unless the serve was good and you intended to play the point.

8. CROSSING COURTS. When one of your balls wanders over into an adjoining court where play is in progress, never attempt to retrieve it during play. Even though you might not interfere with the action itself, your presence is distracting. Wait until the point is completed; then retrieve the ball quickly, or if it is convenient to a player on the other court, ask for it with a polite, "Thank you!"

In the same regard, if a ball from another court turns up on yours, it is proper for you to return it at the first break in your own play.

To avoid confusion on crowded public courts, if balls are not already marked it is a good idea to do so by inking on some identifying symbol.

9. OTHERS ARE WAITING. On crowded club and public courts where others are waiting to play, it is both thoughtless and selfish to hog a court. Unless you have hired a court for a specific period of time, it is considered proper to vacate it upon completion of the set.

When the players waiting outnumber the courts available, it is often an easy and polite solution to suggest a doubles match so that more players may participate. Practice outside the playing area—not on the side lines between courts.

Another sacrifice you may be called upon to make at times is to forego the pleasures of play completely when courts are wet and soft. Although this does not apply, of course, to concrete and some composition courts, wet-weather play on other types of surfaces will chew them up considerably and spoil the fun.

10. DON'T ARGUE. If an umpire and linesman have been assigned to your match, show them consideration and treat them with courtesy. In every match, you and your opponent will probably believe that one or more inaccurate decisions have been made; but as a general rule the linesman is in a better position than you are to make close decisions.

When you get a questionable decision, do not bang the ball against the backstop or high in the air or show your irritation in any other way. Accept all decisions in a sportsmanlike manner. This ability to take it is a test of your sportsmanship.

11. CONTROL YOUR TEMPER. Keep your temper under control; do not allow things to distract or annoy you. Keep your mind concentrated on the game. Keep on fighting until the last point has been scored, whether you are winning or losing. Remember that self-control is one of the most important attributes of sportsmanship and successful play. Shake hands with your opponent and thank him for the match.

12. SIDE-LINE ETIQUETTE. While you are waiting for a court, it is not hard at all to make a nuisance of yourself. Loud conversation, shouting to someone down the line, bouncing balls, or jumping around at the side of the court will all help to distract the players. Also, kibitzing a match with uninvited umpiring, or unasked advice, no matter how expert it might be, will win you few tennis friends.

On the other hand, you can sometimes be quite helpful while you are watching or waiting. It is a nice gesture, for example, for a spectator to chase balls hit out of the court so that play can continue without interruption.

Another thing to remember is that when you are walking to your court to start your match you should never walk behind another match while play is in progress. Even at a distance you can be a distraction. And it is not any major sacrifice to wait a moment or two until the point is completed.

Etiquette for the Gallery

When you are a spectator at a tennis match, you are one of the "gallery" which has assembled to see good tennis played. There are well-defined (although unwritten) laws of conduct for the gallery, which are as binding upon them as the laws of tennis are upon the players and officials. Only by your cooperation in observing these unwritten laws can the perfect playing conditions be secured which make for the successful conduct of a tournament and your enjoyment of the matches you witness.

The spirit of good sportsmanship and correct behavior that tennis demands on the court is no less important on the part of the gallery. Whenever tournaments are played and there is promise of keen competition between players, onlookers will be found on the side lines. The tennis audience has always been supposed to be a discreet and refined one. There are correct times for applause if a shot or rally has been particularly brilliant. No one boos the umpire or hurls pop bottles. Tennis has thrills for the onlookers, but no noisy thrills. It is with this in mind that the following suggestions are made:

A moving background is the most disturbing condition that a player can experience; it makes perfect play of the ball next to impossible. For this reason you should not move about when opposite the end of a court, except when it is absolutely necessary to do so.

If you are in a stand that faces more than one court, do not move from one match to the other while the play is on; it is fatal to good play. If you want to watch the other match, wait until a set is finished before moving.

Do not applaud or give vocal expression of your feelings while a rally is on, but wait until the point has been played out and then applaud all you want to.

Do not applaud errors; by that is meant that your approval should be given to good strokes only. Do not applaud a shot that goes out of court or into the net, even if it gives a point to the player you want to win.

Do not coach the players. Never call "good," "out," "let it go," "hit it," etc., because thereby you are influencing a player's judgment, which is a factor in the outcome of the match. Coaching interferes with the fair playing of a match and may become extremely disconcerting by causing doubt as to whether some particular call came from a spectator or was an official's decision.

Never talk to an umpire, linesman, or player while a match is in progress.

If you do not agree with the decisions as they are given, withhold your disapproval; remember that the linesmen and umpires are in a better position to judge the play than you are and that the committee has selected the most competent men available for these duties.

Do not throw a stray ball into the court while play is on; wait until a stroke is finished and then roll it in.

Refrain from talking loudly while a match is on, as a player hears you and frequently takes it as a call from a linesman and does not play a good ball.

Under no circumstances walk or stand so near a court that you obstruct a contestant; this is inexcusable.

Do not walk or stand on the playing surface of a court before or after a match, as the heels of your shoes make holes in the surface that cause the ball to take bad bounds when a match is played.

Just before a match, do not try to renew an old acquaintanceship or express your wishes for victory to a player. Leave him alone; he has enough on his mind at that time. See him after the match; he has more time then and you will find him more cordial.

If you have to bring a dog with you, see that he watches the match from the side lines. All players are fond of dogs—after the match.

Know your neighbors at a tennis match before you criticize a player—friends and relatives frequently attend.

Read and know the rules; it will add to your enjoyment of the matches.

And last, do what you can to help the committee, for they are working for your pleasure. While the etiquette of the gallery at tennis may seem conservative, it is based on sane and logical reasons. Tennis is a conservative and dignified sport. The etiquette of both gallery and court conforms to the spirit of the game.

SECTION V

Results of Major Tournaments and Lawn Tennis Championships

USLTA Champions—Men's Singles

National champions of the United States Lawn Tennis Association were provided for when that body was organized, May 21, 1881. Prior to that time so-called national championships had been held, in some cases several being contested in one year, but conditions varied at each tournament and the implements and equipment of the game had not become standardized. The first championship of the United States under uniform conditions, open to all comers and sanctioned by the National Association, was held at The Casino, Newport, R.I., in August, 1881, and for 34 years without interruption the championship was held there. From 1915 to 1920 the West Side Tennis Club staged the tournament at Forest Hills, N.Y., and from 1921 to 1923 it was held at the Germantown Cricket Club, Philadelphia. In 1924, after the completion of the West Side Tennis Club Stadium, the championship returned to Forest Hills, and since then has been held there. Championships have been held each year since 1881 with the exception of 1917. In that year and only in that year Patriotic Tournaments were sanctioned by the National Association, because of the participation of the United States in World War I. The challenge round was instituted in 1884 and abandoned after the 1911 championship. During those years the champion "stood out"—in other words did not play through the tournament—eventually meeting the winner of the All Comers' in a challenge round for the championship.

Year	Winner	Runner-up	Score
1881	R. D. Sears	W. E. Glyn	6–0, 6–3, 6–2
1882	R. D. Sears	C. M. Clark	6–1, 6–4, 6–0
1883	R. D. Sears	J. Dwight	6–2, 6–0, 9–7
1884	R. D. Sears	H. A. Taylor	6–0, 1–6, 6–0, 6–2
1885	R. D. Sears	G. M. Brinley	6–3, 4–6, 6–0, 6–3
1886	R. D. Sears	R. L. Beeckman	4–6, 6–1, 6–3, 6–4
1887	R. D. Sears	H. W. Slocum, Jr.	6–1, 6–3, 6–2
1888*	H. W. Slocum, Jr.	H. A. Taylor	6–4, 6–1, 6–0
1889	H. W. Slocum, Jr.	Q. A. Shaw	6–3, 6–1, 4–6, 6–2
1890	O. S. Campbell	H. W. Slocum, Jr.	6–2, 4–6, 6–3, 6–1
1891	O. S. Campbell	C. Hobart	2–5, 7–5, 7–9, 6–1, 6–2
1892	O. S. Campbell	F. H. Hovey	7–5, 3–6, 6–3, 7–5
1893*	R. D. Wrenn	F. H. Hovey	6–4, 3–6, 6–4, 6–4
1894	R. D. Wrenn	M. F. Goodbody	6–8, 6–1, 6–4, 6–4

* No challenge round played.

USLTA Champions—Men's Singles (*cont.*)

Year	Winner	Runner-up	Score
1895	F. H. Hovey	R. D. Wrenn	6–3, 6–2, 6–4
1896	R. D. Wrenn	F. H. Hovey	7–5, 3–6, 6–0, 1–6, 6–1
1897	R. D. Wrenn	W. V. Eaves	4–6, 8–6, 6–3, 2–6, 6–2
1898*	M. D. Whitman	D. F. Davis	3–6, 6–2, 6–2, 6–1
1899	M. D. Whitman	J. P. Paret	6–1, 6–2, 3–6, 7–5
1900	M. D. Whitman	W. A. Larned	6–4, 6–1, 6–2, 6–2
1901*	W. A. Larned	B. C. Wright	6–2, 6–8, 6–4, 6–4
1902	W. A. Larned	R. F. Doherty	4–6, 6–2, 6–4, 8–6
1903	H. L. Doherty	W. A. Larned	6–0, 6–3, 10–8
1904*	Holcombe Ward	W. J. Clothier	10–8, 6–4, 9–7
1905	B. C. Wright	Holcombe Ward	6–2, 6–1, 11–9
1906	W. J. Clothier	B. C. Wright	6–3, 6–0, 6–4
1907*	W. A. Larned	Robert LeRoy	6–2, 6–2, 6–4
1908	W. A. Larned	B. C. Wright	6–1, 6–2, 8–6
1909	W. A. Larned	W. J. Clothier	6–1, 6–2, 5–7, 1–6, 6–1
1910	W. A. Larned	T. C. Bundy	6–1, 5–7, 6–0, 6–8, 6–1
1911	W. A. Larned	M. E. McLoughlin	6–4, 6–4, 6–2
1912†	M. E. McLoughlin	Wallace F. Johnson	3–6, 2–6, 6–2, 6–4, 6–2
1913	M. E. McLoughlin	R. N. Williams	6–4, 5–7, 6–3, 6–1
1914	R. N. Williams	M. E. McLoughlin	6–3, 8–6, 10–8
1915	Wm. M. Johnston	M. E. McLoughlin	1–6, 6–0, 7–5, 10–8
1916	R. N. Williams	Wm. M. Johnston	4–6, 6–4, 0–6, 6–2, 6–4
1917‡	R. L. Murray	N. W. Niles	5–7, 8–6, 6–3, 6–3
1918	R. L. Murray	Wm. T. Tilden II	6–3, 6–1, 7–5
1919	Wm. M. Johnston	Wm. T. Tilden II	6–4, 6–4, 6–3
1920	Wm. T. Tilden II	Wm. M. Johnston	6–1, 1–6, 7–5, 5–7, 6–3
1921	Wm. T. Tilden II	Wallace F. Johnson	6–1, 6–3, 6–1
1922	Wm. T. Tilden II	Wm. M. Johnston	4–6, 3–6, 6–2, 6–3, 6–4
1923	Wm. T. Tilden II	Wm. M. Johnston	6–4, 6–1, 6–4
1924	Wm. T. Tilden II	Wm. M. Johnston	6–1, 9–7, 6–2
1925	Wm. T. Tilden II	Wm. M. Johnston	4–6, 11–9, 6–3, 4–6, 6–3
1926	Jean René Lacoste	Jean Borotra	6–4, 6–0, 6–4
1927	Jean René Lacoste	Wm. T. Tilden II	11–9, 6–3, 11–9
1928	Henri Cochet	Francis T. Hunter	4–6, 6–4, 3–6, 7–5, 6–3
1929	Wm. T. Tilden II	Francis T. Hunter	3–6, 6–3, 4–6, 6–2, 6–4
1930	John H. Doeg	Francis X. Shields	10–8, 1–6, 6–4, 16–14
1931	H. Ellsworth Vines, Jr.	George M. Lott, Jr.	7–9, 6–3, 9–7, 7–5
1932	H. Ellsworth Vines, Jr.	Henri Cochet	6–4, 6–4, 6–4
1933	Frederick J. Perry	John H. Crawford	6–3, 11–13, 4–6, 6–0, 6–1
1934	Frederick J. Perry	Wilmer L. Allison	6–4, 6–3, 3–6, 1–6, 8–6
1935	Wilmer L. Allison	Sidney B. Wood	6–2, 6–2, 6–3
1936	Fred Perry	J. Donald Budge	2–6, 6–2, 8–6, 1–6, 10–8
1937	J. Donald Budge	Baron G. von Cramm	6–1, 7–9, 6–1, 3–6, 6–1
1938	J. Donald Budge	C. Gene Mako	6–3, 6–8, 6–2, 6–1
1939	Robert Riggs	S. Welby Van Horn	6–4, 6–2, 6–4
1940	Donald McNeill	Robert L. Riggs	4–6, 6–8, 6–3, 6–3, 7–5
1941	Robert L. Riggs	Francis Kovacs II	5–7, 6–1, 6–3, 6–3
1942	Frederick R. Schroeder, Jr.	Frank Parker	8–6, 7–5, 3–6, 4–6, 6–2
1943	Lt. Joseph R. Hunt	Seaman John A. Kramer	6–3, 6–8, 10–8, 6–0
1944	Sgt. Frank A. Parker	William F. Talbert	6–4, 3–6, 6–3, 6–3
1945	Sgt. Frank A. Parker	William F. Talbert	14–12, 6–1, 6–2
1946	John A. Kramer	Tom Brown, Jr.	9–7, 6–3, 6–0
1947	John A. Kramer	Frank A. Parker	4–6, 2–6, 6–1, 6–0, 6–3
1948	Richard A. Gonzalez	Eric W. Sturgess	6–2, 6–3, 14–12
1949	Richard A. Gonzalez	Frederick R. Schroeder, Jr.	16–18, 2–6, 6–1, 6–2, 6–4
1950	Arthur Larsen	Herbert Flam	6–3, 4–6, 5–7, 6–4, 6–3
1951	Frank Sedgman	E. Victor Seixas, Jr.	6–4, 6–1, 6–1
1952	Frank Sedgman	Gardnar Mulloy	6–1, 6–2, 6–3
1953	Tony Trabert	E. Victor Seixas, Jr.	6–3, 6–2, 6–3

* No challenge round played.
† Challenge round abolished.
‡ National Patriotic Tournament.

(*above*) Rod Laver with the USLTA Open Trophy, which he won in 1969.

(*left*) Frank Sedgman was the first of a long line of Australians who won the Men's Singles National Championship after World War II.

Year	Winner	Runner-up	Score
1954	E. Victor Seixas, Jr.	Rex Hartwig	3–6, 6–2, 6–4, 6–4
1955	Tony Trabert	Ken Rosewall	9–7, 6–3, 6–3
1956	Kenneth Rosewall	Lewis Hoad	4–6, 6–2, 6–3, 6–3
1957	Malcolm J. Anderson	Ashley J. Cooper	10–8, 7–5, 6–4
1958	Ashley J. Cooper	Malcolm J. Anderson	6–2, 3–6, 4–6, 10–8, 8–6
1959	Neale Fraser	Alejandro Olmedo	6–3, 5–7, 6–2, 6–4
1960	Neale Fraser	Rodney Laver	6–4, 6–4, 9–7
1961	Roy Emerson	Rodney Laver	7–5, 6–3, 6–2
1962	Rodney Laver	Roy Emerson	6–2, 6–4, 5–7, 6–4
1963	Rafael Osuna	Frank Froehling III	7–5, 6–4, 6–2
1964	Roy Emerson	Fred Stolle	6–4, 6–1, 6–4
1965	Manuel Santana	Clif Drysdale	6–2, 7–9, 7–5, 6–1
1966	Fred Stolle	John Newcombe	4–6, 12–10, 6–3, 6–4
1967	John Newcombe	Clark Graebner	6–4, 6–4, 8–6
1968	Arthur Ashe	Robert Lutz	4–6, 6–3, 8–10, 6–0, 6–4
1969	Stanley R. Smith	Robert Lutz	9–7, 6–3, 6–1

USLTA OPEN CHAMPIONS—MEN'S SINGLES

Year	Winner	Runner-up	Score
1968	Arthur Ashe	Tom Okker	14–12, 5–7, 6–3, 3–6, 6–3
1969	Rod Laver	Tony Roche	7–9, 6–1, 6–3, 6–2
1970	Ken Rosewall	Tony Roche	2–6, 6–4, 7–6, 6–3
1971	Stanley R. Smith	Jan Kodes	3–6, 6–3, 6–2, 7–6

USLTA AMATEUR CHAMPIONS—MEN'S SINGLES

Year	Winner	Runner-up	Score
1969	George Seewagen	Zan Guerry	9–7, 6–3, 1–6, 6–2, 6–4
1970	Haroon Rahim	John Gardner	6–3, 6–4, 1–6, 11–13, 6–4
1971	not held		

USLTA Champions—Men's Doubles

Prior to 1890 the national doubles championship was played in conjunction with the singles tournament. From 1890 to 1906 tournaments were held in the East and West, and the sectional winners at these meets then played off for the privilege of meeting the standing-out champions in the challenge round. In 1907 there were three sections competing in preliminary doubles, and this number was increased in subsequent years. In 1917 a play-through Patriotic Tournament was held, as no championships were sanctioned that year. The 1918 championship meet was also a play-through tournament, the sectional and preliminary doubles and the challenge round having been done away with. In 1919 the plan of qualifying sectional winners was restored, although an exception was made in the case of the Australian teams, which were on a visit to the United States at that time, and the last challenge round in national doubles was played that year. Since 1920 there have been few changes in the conditions that now prevail. The mixed-doubles championship was contested in conjunction with the women's national tournament until 1921, after which it was added to the men's doubles competition. In 1935 the Women's Doubles Championship was added to the Doubles Championship Tournament, and the Mixed Doubles Championship was added to the Singles Championship Tournament.

Year	Winners	Runners-up
1881	C. M. Clark and F. W. Taylor	A. Van Rensselaer and A. E. Newbold
1882	R. D. Sears and J. Dwight	W. Nightingale and G. M. Smith
1883	R. D. Sears and J. Dwight	A. Van Rensselaer and A. E. Newbold
1884	R. D. Sears and J. Dwight	A. Van Rensselaer and W. V. R. Berry
1885	R. D. Sears and J. S. Clark	H. W. Slocum, Jr. and W. P. Knapp
1886	R. D. Sears and J. Dwight	H. A. Taylor and G. M. Brinley
1887	R. D. Sears and J. Dwight	H. A. Taylor and H. W. Slocum, Jr.
1888	O. S. Campbell and V. G. Hall	C. Hobart and E. P. MacMullen
1889	H. W. Slocum, Jr. and H. A. Taylor	V. G. Hall and O. S. Campbell
1890	V. G. Hall and C. Hobart	J. W. Carver and J. A. Ryerson
1891	O S. Campbell and Robt. Huntington, Jr.	V. G. Hall and Clarence Hobart
1892	O. S. Campbell and Robt. P. Huntington, Jr.	V. G. Hall and Edward L. Hall
1893	Clarence Hobart and Fred H. Hovey	O. S. Campbell and Robt. P. Huntington, Jr.
1894	Clarence Hobart and Fred H. Hovey	C. B. Neel and Samuel R. Neel
1895	M. G. Chace and R. D. Wrenn	J. Howland and A. E. Foote
1896	Carr B. Neel and Samuel R. Neel	Robert D. Wrenn and M. G. Chace
1897	Leo E. Ware and Geo. P. Sheldon, Jr.	Harold S. Mahony and H. A. Nisbet
1898	Leo E. Ware and Geo. P. Sheldon, Jr.	Holcombe Ward and Dwight F. Davis
1899	Holcombe Ward and Dwight F. Davis	Leo E. Ware and Geo. P. Sheldon, Jr.
1900	Holcombe Ward and Dwight F. Davis	Fred B. Alexander and Raymond D. Little
1901	Holcombe Ward and Dwight F. Davis	Leo E. Ware and Beals C. Wright
1902	Reginald F. Doherty and Hugh L. Doherty	Holcombe Ward and Dwight F. Davis
1903	Reginald F. Doherty and Hugh L. Doherty	Kreigh Collins and L. Harry Waidner
1904	Holcombe Ward and Beals C. Wright	Kreigh Collins and Raymond D. Little
1905	Holcombe Ward and Beals C. Wright	Fred B. Alexander and Harold H. Hackett
1906	Holcombe Ward and Beals C. Wright	Fred B. Alexander and Harold H. Hackett

The National Doubles Championships were held at the Longwood Courts near Boston for many years.

Year	Winners	Runners-up
1907	Fred B. Alexander and Harold H. Hackett	William A. Larned and William J. Clothier
1908	Fred B. Alexander and Harold H. Hackett	Raymond D. Little and Beals C. Wright
1909	Fred B. Alexander and Harold H. Hackett	Maurice E. McLoughlin and George J. Janes
1910	Fred B. Alexander and Harold H. Hackett	Thos. C. Bundy and Trowbridge W. Hendrick
1911	Raymond D. Little and Gustave F. Touchard	Fred B. Alexander and Harold H. Hackett
1912	Maurice E. McLoughlin and Thos. C. Bundy	Raymond D. Little and Gustave F. Touchard
1913	Maurice E. McLoughlin and Thos. C. Bundy	John R. Strachan and Clarence J. Griffin
1914	Maurice E. McLoughlin and Thos. C. Bundy	George M. Church and Dean Mathey
1915	William M. Johnston and Clarence J. Griffin	Maurice E. McLoughlin and Thos. C. Bundy
1916	William M. Johnston and Clarence J. Griffin	Maurice E. McLoughlin and Ward Dawson
1917*	Fred B. Alexander and Harold A. Throckmorton	Harry C. Johnson and Irving C. Wright
1918	William T. Tilden II and Vincent Richards	Fred B. Alexander and Beals C. Wright
1919	Norman E. Brookes and Gerald Patterson	William T. Tilden, II and Vincent Richards
1920	William M. Johnston and Clarence J. Griffin	Willis F. Davis and Roland E. Roberts
1921	William T. Tilden II and Vincent Richards	R. N. Williams, II and W. M. Washburn
1922	William T. Tilden II and Vincent Richards	Gerald L. Patterson and Pat O'Hara Wood
1923	William T. Tilden II and Brian I. C. Norton	R. N. Williams II and W. M. Washburn
1924	Howard Kinsey and Robert Kinsey	Gerald L. Patterson and Pat O'Hara Wood
1925	R. Norris Williams II and Vincent Richards	Gerald Patterson and John B. Hawkes
1926	R. N. Williams II and Vincent Richards	Wm. T. Tilden, II and Alfred H. Chapin, Jr.
1927	Wm. T. Tilden II and Francis T. Hunter	Wm. M. Johnston and R. Norris Williams, Jr.
1928	George M. Lott, Jr. and John Hennessey	Gerald L. Patterson and John B. Hawkes

* National Patriotic Tournament.

USLTA Champions—Men's Doubles (cont.)

Year	Winners	Runners-up
1929	George M. Lott, Jr. and John H. Doeg	Berkeley Bell and Lewis N. White
1930	George M. Lott, Jr. and John H. Doeg	John Van Ryn and Wilmer Allison
1931	Wilmer Allison and John Van Ryn	Gregory Mangin and Berkeley Bell
1932	H. Ellsworth Vines and Keith Gledhill	Wilmer Allison and John Van Ryn
1933	George M. Lott, Jr. and Lester R. Stoefen	Francis X. Shields and Frank A. Parker
1934	George M. Lott, Jr. and Lester R. Stoefen	Wilmer L. Allison and John Van Ryn
1935	Wilmer L. Allison and John Van Ryn	J. Donald Budge and C. Gene Mako
1936	J. Donald Budge and C. Gene Mako	Wilmer L. Allison and John Van Ryn
1937	Baron G. von Cramm and Henner Henkel	J. Donald Budge and C. Gene Mako
1938	J. Donald Budge and C. Gene Mako	Adrian K. Quist and John Bromwich
1939	Adrian K. Quist and John Bromwich	John A. Crawford and Harry C. Hopman
1940	John A. Kramer and Frederick T. Schroeder, Jr.	Gardnar Mulloy and Henry J. Prussoff
1941	John A. Kramer and Frederick T. Schroeder, Jr.	Wayne Sabin and Gardnar Mulloy
1942	Lt. Gardnar Mulloy and William Talbert	Frederick Schroeder, Jr. and Sidney B. Wood, Jr.
1943	J. A. Kramer and Frank A. Parker	William Talbert and David Freeman
1944	Lt. W. Donald McNeill and Robert Falkenburg	William Talbert and Francisco Segura
1945	Lt. Gardnar Mulloy and William Talbert	Robert Falkenburg and Jack Tuero
1946	Gardnar Mulloy and William Talbert	Donald McNeill and Frank Guernsey
1947	John A. Kramer and Frederick T. Schroeder, Jr.	William Talbert and William Sidwell
1948	Gardnar Mulloy and William Talbert	Frank A. Parker and Frederick T. Schroeder, Jr.
1949	John Bromwich and William Sidwell	Frank Sedgman and George Worthington
1950	John Bromwich and Frank Sedgman	William Talbert and Gardnar Mulloy
1951	Kenneth McGregor and Frank Sedgman	Don Candy and Mervyn Rose
1952	Mervyn Rose and E. Victor Seixas, Jr.	Kenneth McGregor and Frank Sedgman
1953	Rex Hartwig and Mervyn Rose	Gardnar Mulloy and William F. Talbert
1954	E. Victor Seixas, Jr. and Tony Trabert	Lewis Hoad and Ken Rosewall
1955	Kosei Kamo and Atsushi Miyagi	Gerald Moss and William Quillian
1956	Lewis Hoad and Kenneth Rosewall	Hamilton Richardson and E. Victor Seixas, Jr.
1957	Ashley J. Cooper and Neale Fraser	Gardnar Mulloy and Budge Patty
1958	Alex Olmedo and Hamilton Richardson	Sam Giammalva and Barry MacKay
1959	Neale Fraser and Roy Emerson	Alex Olmedo and Earl Buchholz, Jr.
1960	Neale Fraser and Roy Emerson	Rod Laver and Bob Mark
1961	Charles McKinley and Dennis Ralston	Rafael Osuna and Antonio Palafox
1962	Rafael Osuna and Antonio Palafox	Charles McKinley and Dennis Ralston
1963	Charles McKinley and Dennis Ralston	Rafael Osuna and Antonio Palafox
1964	Charles McKinley and Dennis Ralston	Graham Stilwell and Mike Sangster
1965	Roy Emerson and Fred Stolle	Frank Froehling III and Charles Pasarell
1966	Roy Emerson and Fred Stolle	Clark Graebner and Dennis Ralston
1967	John Newcombe and Tony Roche	William Bowrey and Owen Davidson
1968	Robert Lutz and Stan Smith	Robert Hewitt and Ray Moore
1969	Richard Crealy and Alan Stone	William Bowrey and Charles Pasarell

USLTA OPEN CHAMPIONS—MEN'S DOUBLES

Year	Champions	Runners-up
1968	Robert Lutz and Stan Smith	Arthur Ashe and Andres Gimeno
1969	Ken Rosewall and Fred Stolle	Charles Pasarell and Dennis Ralston
1970	Pierre Barthes and Nicki Pilic	Roy Emerson and Rod Laver
1971	John Newcombe and Roger Taylor	Stan Smith and Erik Van Dillen

USLTA AMATEUR CHAMPIONS—MEN'S DOUBLES

Year	Champions	Runners-up
1969	Tom Leonard and Erik Van Dillen	Robert McKinley and Richard Stockton
1970	Robert McKinley and Richard Stockton	Haroon Rahim and Jeff Borowiak
1971	not held	

(*left*) Vinny Richards and Norris Williams II won the doubles title in 1925 and 1926.

(*below*) Molla Bjurstedt playing Eleanor Goss in 1918 for the Women's National Championship. Miss Bjurstedt won 6–4, 6–3, for one of seven titles.

USLTA Champions—Women's Singles

The national women's championships were held at the Philadelphia Cricket Club from 1887 to 1920 inclusive. Since 1921 they have been held at Forest Hills. Originally the mixed doubles and women's doubles were played in connection with the Women's Singles Championship Tournament. In 1921 the mixed doubles and in 1935 the women's doubles were transferred and made part of the National Doubles Championship program. From 1942 to 1945 inclusive the women's doubles and since 1942 the mixed doubles were played in connection with the men's championships at Forest Hills.

USLTA Champions—Women's Singles (*cont.*)

Year	Winner	Runner-up	Score
1887	Ellen Hansell	Laura Knight	6–1, 6–0
1888	Bertha B. Townsend	Marion Wright	6–2, 6–2
1889	Bertha B. Townsend	Louise D. Voorhees	7–5, 6–2
1890	Ellen C. Roosevelt	Grace W. Roosevelt	6–3, 6–1
1891	Mabel Cahill	Elizabeth Moore	6–3, 7–5
1892	Mabel Cahill	Bessie Moore	
1893	Aline Terry	Mabel Cahill	default
1894	Helen Helwig	Aline Terry	7–5, 3–6, 6–0, 3–6, 6–3
1895	Juliette P. Atkinson	Helen Helwig	6–4, 6–2, 6–1
1896	Elizabeth Moore	Juliette Atkinson	6–4, 4–6, 6–3, 6–2
1897	Juliette Atkinson	Bessie Moore	6–3, 6–3, 4–6, 3–6, 6–3
1898	Juliette Atkinson	Marion Jones	6–3, 5–7, 6–4, 2–6, 7–5
1899	Marion Jones	Juliette Atkinson	default
1900	Myrtle McAteer	Marion Jones	default
1901	Elizabeth Moore	Myrtle McAteer	6–4, 3–6, 7–5, 2–6, 6–2
1902	Marion Jones	Elizabeth Moore	6–1, 1–0, default
1903	Elizabeth Moore	Marion Jones	7–5, 8–6
1904	May Sutton	Elizabeth Moore	6–1, 6–2
1905	Elizabeth Moore	Helen Homans	6–4, 5–7, 6–1
1906	Helen Homans	Elizabeth Moore	default
1907	Evelyn Sears	Carrie Neelie	6–3, 6–2
1908	Mrs. Maud Barger-Wallach	Evelyn Sears	6–2, 1–6, 6–3
1909	Hazel Hotchkiss	Mrs. Barger-Wallach	6–0, 6–1
1910	Hazel Hotchkiss	Louise Hamond	6–4, 6–2
1911	Hazel Hotchkiss	Florence Sutton	8–10, 6–1, 9–7
1912	Mary K. Browne	Eleanora Sears	6–4, 6–2
1913	Mary K. Browne	Dorothy Green	6–2, 7–5
1914	Mary K. Browne	Marie Wagner	6–2, 1–6, 6–1
1915	Molla Bjurstedt	Mrs. H. Wightman	4–6, 6–2, 6–0
1916	Molla Bjurstedt	Mrs. E. Raymond	6–0, 6–1
1917*	Molla Bjurstedt	Marion Vanderhoef	4–6, 6–0, 6–2
1918	Molla Bjurstedt	Eleanor E. Goss	6–4, 6–3
1919	Mrs. H. Wightman	Marion Zinderstein	6–1, 6–2
1920	Mrs. M. Mallory	Marion Zinderstein	6–3, 6–1
1921	Mrs. M. Mallory	Mary K. Browne	4–6, 6–4, 6–2
1922	Mrs. M. Mallory	Helen Wills	6–3, 6–1
1923	Helen Wills	Mrs. M. Mallory	6–2, 6–1
1924	Helen Wills	Mrs. M. Mallory	6–1, 6–2
1925	Helen Wills	Kathleen McKane	3–6, 6–0, 6–2
1926	Mrs. M. Mallory	Elizabeth Ryan	4–6, 6–4, 9–7
1927	Helen Wills	Betty Nuthall	6–1, 6–4
1928	Helen Wills	Helen H. Jacobs	6–2, 6–1
1929	Helen Wills	Mrs. M. Watson	6–4, 6–2
1930	Betty Nuthall	Mrs. L. A. Harper	6–4, 6–1
1931	Mrs. Helen Wills Moody	Mrs. E. B. Whittingstall	6–4, 6–1
1932	Helen H. Jacobs	Carolin A. Babcock	6–2, 6–2
1933	Helen H. Jacobs	Mrs. Helen Wills Moody	8–6, 3–6, 3–0, default
1934	Helen H. Jacobs	Sarah H. Palfrey	6–1, 6–4
1935	Helen H. Jacobs	Mrs. Sarah P. Fabyan	6–1, 6–4
1936	Alice Marble	Helen H. Jacobs	4–6, 6–3, 6–2
1937	Anita Lizana	Jadwiga Jedrzejowska	6–4, 6–2
1938	Alice Marble	Nancy Wynne	6–0, 6–3
1939	Alice Marble	Helen H. Jacobs	6–0, 8–10, 6–4
1940	Alice Marble	Helen H. Jacobs	6–2, 6–3
1941	Mrs. Sarah Palfrey Cooke	Pauline Betz	6–1, 6–4
1942	Pauline Betz	A. Louise Brough	4–6, 6–1, 6–4
1943	Pauline Betz	A. Louise Brough	6–3, 5–7, 6–3
1944	Pauline Betz	Margaret Osborne	6–3, 8–6
1945	Mrs. Sarah P. Cooke	Pauline Betz	3–6, 8–6, 6–4
1946	Pauline Betz	Mrs. Patricia Canning	11–9, 6–3
1947	A. Louise Brough	Margaret Osborne	8–6, 4–6, 6–1

* National Patriotic Tournament.

Year	Winner	Runner-up	Score
1948	Mrs. Margaret Osborne du Pont	A. Louise Brough	4–6, 6–4, 15–13
1949	Mrs. Margaret Osborne du Pont	Doris Hart	6–4, 6–1
1950	Mrs. Margaret Osborne du Pont	Doris Hart	6–3, 6–3
1951	Maureen Connolly	Shirley Fry	6–3, 1–6, 6–4
1952	Maureen Connolly	Doris Hart	6–3, 7–5
1953	Maureen Connolly	Doris Hart	6–2, 6–4
1954	Doris Hart	A. Louise Brough	6–8, 6–1, 8–6
1955	Doris Hart	Patricia Ward	6–4, 6–2
1956	Shirley J. Fry	Althea Gibson	6–3, 6–4
1957	Althea Gibson	A. Louise Brough	6–3, 6–2
1958	Althea Gibson	Darlene Hard	3–6, 6–1, 6–2
1959	Maria E. Bueno	Christine Truman	6–1, 6–4
1960	Darlene R. Hard	Maria E. Bueno	6–4, 10–12, 6–4
1961	Darlene R. Hard	Ann Haydon	6–3, 6–4
1962	Margaret Smith	Darlene Hard	9–7, 6–4
1963	Maria E. Bueno	Margaret Smith	7–5, 6–4
1964	Maria E. Bueno	Mrs. Carole C. Graebner	6–1, 6–0
1965	Margaret Smith	Billie Jean Moffitt	8–6, 7–5
1966	Maria E. Bueno	Nancy Richey	6–3, 6–1
1967	Mrs. Billie Jean King	Mrs. Ann H. Jones	11–9, 6–4
1968	Mrs. Margaret S. Court	Maria E. Bueno	6–2, 6–2
1969	Mrs. Margaret S. Court	Virginia Wade	4–6, 6–3, 6–0

USLTA OPEN CHAMPIONS—WOMEN'S SINGLES

Year	Winner	Runner-up	Score
1968	Virginia Wade	Mrs. Billie Jean King	6–4, 6–2
1969	Mrs. Margaret S. Court	Nancy Richey	6–2, 6–2
1970	Mrs. Margaret S. Court	Rosemary Casals	6–2, 2–6, 6–1
1971	Mrs. Billie Jean King	Rosemary Casals	6–4, 7–6

USLTA AMATEUR CHAMPIONS—WOMEN'S SINGLES

Year	Winner	Runner-up	Score
1969	Linda Tuero	Gwyneth Thomas	4–6, 6–1, 6–2
1970	Eliza Pande	Sharon Walsh	3–6, 9–7, 6–2
1971	not held		

USLTA CHAMPIONS—WOMEN'S DOUBLES

1890	Ellen C. Roosevelt and Grace W. Roosevelt	
1891	Mabel E. Cahill and Mrs. W. Fellowes Morgan	
1892	Mabel E. Cahill and A. M. McKinley	
1893	Aline M. Terry and Hattie Butler	
1894	Helen R. Helwig and Juliette P. Atkinson	
1895	Helen R. Helwig and Juliette P. Atkinson	
1896	Elisabeth H. Moore and Juliette P. Atkinson	
1897	Juliette P. Atkinson and Kathleen Atkinson	
1898	Juliette P. Atkinson and Kathleen Atkinson	
1899	Jane W. Craven and Myrtle McAteer	
1900	Edith Parker and Hallie Champlin	
1901	Juliette P. Atkinson and Myrtle McAteer	
1902	Juliette P. Atkinson and Marion Jones	
1903	Elisabeth H. Moore and Carrie B. Neely	
1904	May G. Sutton and Miriam Hall	
1905	Helen Homans and Carrie B. Neely	
1906	Mrs. L. S. Coe and Mrs. D. S. Platt	
1907	Marie Weimer and Carrie B. Neely	
1908	Evelyn Sears and Margaret Curtis	

1909	Hazel V. Hotchkiss and Edith E. Rotch
1910	Hazel V. Hotchkiss and Edith E. Rotch
1911	Hazel V. Hotchkiss and Eleonora Sears
1912	Dorothy Green and Mary K. Browne
1913	Mary K. Browne and Mrs. R. H. Williams
1914	Mary K. Browne and Mrs. R. H. Williams
1915	Mrs. Hazel Hotchkiss Wightman and Eleonora Sears
1916	Molla Bjurstedt and Eleonora Sears
1917*	Molla Bjurstedt and Eleonora Sears
1918	Marion Zinderstein and Eleanor Goss
1919	Marion Zinderstein and Eleanor Goss
1920	Marion Zinderstein and Eleanor Goss
1921	Mary K. Browne and Mrs. R. H. Williams
1922	Mrs. Marion Zinderstein Jessup and Helen N. Wills
1923	Kathleen McKane and Mrs. B. C. Covell
1924	Mrs. Hazel Hotchkiss Wightman and Helen N. Wills

* National Patriotic Tournament.

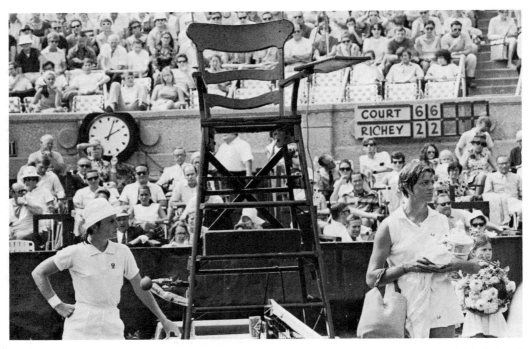

The result of the 1969 Open Championship can be seen on the scoreboard. Mrs. Court (*right*) defeated Miss Richey (*left*) 6–2, 6–2.

USLTA Champions—Women's Doubles (cont.)

1925	Mary K. Browne and Helen N. Wills
1926	Elizabeth Ryan and Eleanor Goss
1927	Mrs. Kathleen McKane Godfree and Ermyntrude Harvey
1928	Mrs. Hazel Hotchkiss Wightman and Helen N. Wills
1929	Mrs. Phoebe Watson and Mrs. L. R. C. Michell
1930	Betty Nuthall and Sarah Palfrey
1931	Betty Nuthall and Mrs. Eileen Bennett Whittingstall
1932	Helen Jacobs and Sarah Palfrey
1933	Betty Nuthall and Freda James
1934	Helen Jacobs and Sarah Palfrey
1935	Helen Jacobs and Mrs. Sarah Palfrey Fabyan
1936	Mrs. Marjorie Gladman Van Ryn and Carolin Babcock
1937	Mrs. Sarah Palfrey Fabyan and Alice Marble
1938	Mrs. Sarah Palfrey Fabyan and Alice Marble
1939	Mrs. Sarah Palfrey Fabyan and Alice Marble
1940	Mrs. Sarah Palfrey Fabyan and Alice Marble
1941	Mrs. Sarah Palfrey Cooke and Margaret E. Osborne
1942	A. Louise Brough and Margaret E. Osborne
1943	A. Louise Brough and Margaret E. Osborne
1944	A. Louise Brough and Margaret E. Osborne
1945	A. Louise Brough and Margaret E. Osborne
1946	A. Louise Brough and Margaret E. Osborne
1947	A. Louise Brough and Margaret E. Osborne
1948	A. Louise Brough and Mrs. Margaret Osborne du Pont
1949	A. Louise Brough and Margaret Osborne du Pont

1950	A. Louise Brough and Mrs. Margaret Osborne du Pont
1951	Shirley Fry and Doris Hart
1952	Shirley Fry and Doris Hart
1953	Shirley Fry and Doris Hart
1954	Shirley Fry and Doris Hart
1955	A. Louise Brough and Mrs. Margaret Osborne du Pont
1956	A. Louise Brough and Mrs. Margaret Osborne du Pont
1957	A. Louise Brough and Mrs. Margaret Osborne du Pont
1958	Jeanne M. Arth and Darlene R. Hard
1959	Jeanne M. Arth and Darlene R. Hard
1960	Maria E. Bueno and Darlene R. Hard
1961	Darlene R. Hard and Lesley Turner
1962	Darlene R. Hard and Maria E. Bueno
1963	Robyn Ebbern and Margaret Smith
1964	Billie Jean Moffitt and Mrs. Karen H. Susman
1965	Mrs. Carole Caldwell Graebner and Nancy Richey
1966	Maria E. Bueno and Nancy Richey
1967	Rosemary Casals and Mrs. Billie Jean King
1968	Maria E. Bueno and Mrs. Margaret S. Court
1969	Mrs. Margaret S. Court and Virginia Wade

USLTA OPEN CHAMPIONS—WOMEN'S DOUBLES

1968	Maria E. Bueno and Mrs. Margaret S. Court
1969	Françoise Durr and Darlene Hard
1970	Mrs. Margaret S. Court and Judy Dalton
1971	Rosemary Casals and Judy Dalton

USLTA AMATEUR CHAMPIONS—WOMEN'S DOUBLES

1969 Emilie Burrer and Pam Richmond
1970 Gail Hansen and Sharon Walsh
1971 not held

USLTA CHAMPIONS—MIXED DOUBLES

1892 Mabel E. Cahill and Clarence Hobart
1893 Ellen C. Roosevelt and Clarence Hobart
1894 Juliette P. Atkinson and Edwin P. Fischer
1895 Juliette P. Atkinson and Edwin P. Fischer
1896 Juliette P. Atkinson and Edwin P. Fischer
1897 Laura Henson and D. L. Magruder
1898 Carrie B. Neely and Edwin P. Fischer
1899 Elizabeth J. Rastall and Albert L. Hoskins
1900 Margaret Hunnewell and Alfred Codman
1901 Marion Jones and Raymond D. Little
1902 Elizabeth H. Moore and Wylie C. Grant
1903 Helen Chapman and Harry F. Allen
1904 Elisabeth H. Moore and Wylie C. Grant
1905 Mr. and Mrs. Clarence Hobart
1906 Sarah Coffin and Edward B. Dewhurst
1907 May Sayres and Wallace F. Johnson
1908 Edith E. Rotch and Nathaniel W. Niles
1909 Hazel V. Hotchkiss and Wallace F. Johnson
1910 Hazel V. Hotchkiss and Joseph R. Carpenter, Jr.
1911 Hazel V. Hotchkiss and Wallace F. Johnson
1912 Mary K. Browne and R. N. Williams II
1913 Mary K. Browne and William T. Tilden II
1914 Mary K. Browne and William T. Tilden II
1915 Mrs. Hazel Hotchkiss Wightman and Harry C. Johnson
1916 Eleonora Sears and Willis E. Davis
1917* Molla Bjurstedt and Irving C. Wright
1918 Mrs. Hazel Hotchkiss Wightman and Irving C. Wright
1919 Marion Zinderstein and Vincent Richards
1920 Mrs. Hazel Hotchkiss Wightman and Wallace F. Johnson
1921 Mary K. Browne and William Johnston
1922 Mrs. Molla Bjurstedt Mallory and William T. Tilden II
1923 Mrs. Molla Bjurstedt Mallory and William T. Tilden II
1924 Helen N. Wills and Vincent Richards
1925 Kathleen McKane and John B. Hawkes
1926 Elizabeth Ryan and Jean Borotra
1927 Eileen Bennett and Henri Cochet
1928 Helen N. Wills and John B. Hawkes
1929 Betty Nuthall and George M. Lott, Jr.
1930 Edith Cross and Wilmer L. Allison
1931 Betty Nuthall and George M. Lott, Jr.
1932 Sarah Palfrey and Frederick Perry
1933 Elizabeth Ryan and H. Ellsworth Vines, Jr.
1934 Helen H. Jacobs and George M. Lott, Jr.
1935 Mrs. Sarah Palfrey Fabyan and Enrique Maier
1936 Alice Marble and C. Gene Mako
1937 Mrs. Sarah Palfrey Fabyan and J. Donald Budge
1938 Alice Marble and J. Donald Budge
1939 Alice Marble and Harry C. Hopman

* National Patriotic Tournament.

1940 Alice Marble and Robert L. Riggs
1941 Mrs. Sarah Palfrey Cooke and John A. Kramer
1942 A. Louise Brough and Frederick R. Schroeder, Jr.
1943 Margaret Osborne and William F. Talbert
1944 Margaret Osborne and William F. Talbert
1945 Margaret Osborne and William F. Talbert
1946 Margaret Osborne and William F. Talbert
1947 A. Louise Brough and John Bromwich
1948 A. Louise Brough and Thomas P. Brown, Jr.
1949 A. Louise Brough and Eric Sturgess
1950 Mrs. Margaret Osborne du Pont and Kenneth McGregor
1951 Doris Hart and Frank Sedgman
1952 Doris Hart and Frank Sedgman
1953 Doris Hart and E. Victor Seixas, Jr.
1954 Doris Hart and E. Victor Seixas, Jr.
1955 Doris Hart and E. Victor Seixas, Jr.
1956 Mrs. Margaret Osborne du Pont and Kenneth Rosewall
1957 Althea Gibson and Kurt Nielsen
1958 Mrs. Margaret Osborne du Pont and Neale Fraser
1959 Mrs. Margaret Osborne du Pont and Neale Fraser
1960 Mrs. Margaret Osborne du Pont and Neale Fraser
1961 Margaret Smith and Robert Mark
1962 Margaret Smith and Fred Stolle
1963 Margaret Smith and Ken Fletcher
1964 Margaret Smith and John Newcombe
1965 Margaret Smith and Fred Stolle
1966 Mrs. Donna Floyd Fales and Owen Davidson
1967 Mrs. Billie Jean King and Owen Davidson
1968 Mary Ann Eisel and Peter Curtis
1969 Patti Hogan and Paul Sullivan

USLTA OPEN CHAMPIONS—MIXED DOUBLES

1969 Mrs. Margaret S. Court and Martin Riessen
1970 Mrs. Margaret S. Court and Martin Riessen
1971 Mrs. Billie Jean King and Owen Davidson

USLTA AMATEUR CHAMPIONS—MIXED DOUBLES

1969 Pam Richmond and Jacquin Loyo-Mayo
1970–71 not held

USLTA CHAMPIONS—JUNIOR SINGLES

1916 Harold A. Throckmorton
1917 Charles S. Garland
1918 Harold L. Taylor
1919 Vincent Richards
1920 Vincent Richards
1921 Vincent Richards
1922 Arnold W. Jones
1923 George M. Lott, Jr.
1924 George M. Lott, Jr.
1925 Cranston M. Holman
1926 John Doeg
1927 Francis X. Shields
1928 Francis X. Shields
1929 Keith Gledhill
1930 Wilmer Hines

Dennis Ralston won the USLTA Junior Singles title on his way to Davis Cup fame.

USLTA Champions—Junior Singles (cont.)

1931	Jack Lynch
1932	Frank Parker
1933	Donald Budge
1934	C. Gene Mako
1935	Robert Riggs
1936	Julius Heldman
1937	Joseph R. Hunt
1938	David Freeman
1939	Frederick R. Schroeder, Jr.
1940	Robert D. Carrothers, Jr.
1941	J. Edward (Budge) Patty
1942	J. Edward (Budge) Patty
1943	Robert Falkenburg
1944	Robert Falkenburg
1945	Herbert Flam
1946	Herbert Flam
1947	Herbert Behrens
1948	Gilbert A. Bogley
1949	Gilbert A. Bogley
1950	Hamilton Richardson
1951	Ted Rogers
1952	Jack Frost
1953	John Lesch
1954	Gerald Moss
1955	Esteban Reyes
1956	Rodney Laver
1957	Alan Roberts
1958	Earl Buchholz, Jr.
1959	Dennis Ralston
1960	William Lenoir
1961	Charles Pasarell
1962	Mike Belkin
1963	Cliff Richey
1964	Stanley R. Smith
1965	Robert Lutz
1966	Stephen Avoyer
1967	Jeff Borowiak
1968	Robert McKinley
1969	Erik Van Dillen
1970	Brian Gottfried
1971	Raul Ramirez

USLTA CHAMPIONS—JUNIOR DOUBLES

1918	Vincent Richards and Harold L. Taylor
1919	Frank T. Anderson and J. Cecil Donaldson
1920	Harold Godshall and Robert Hinckley
1921	Arnold W. Jones and William W. Ingraham
1922	Arnold W. Jones and William W. Ingraham
1923	George M. Lott, Jr. and Julius Sagalowsky
1924	George M. Lott, Jr. and Thomas McGlinn
1925	Malcolm T. Hill and Henry L. Johnson, Jr.
1926	Berkeley Bell and James Quick
1927	C. Alphonso Smith and Edward Jacobs
1928	Francis X. Shields and W. Barry Wood
1929	Ellsworth Vines and Keith Gledhill
1930	Wilmer Hines and Judge L. Beaver
1931	Kendall Cram and Judge L. Beaver
1932	Jack Lynch and C. Gene Mako
1933	C. Gene Mako and Ben Dey
1934	C. Gene Mako and Lawrence Nelson
1935	Robert Riggs and Joseph R. Hunt
1936	Joseph R. Hunt and Julius Heldman
1937	Joseph R. Hunt and John Moreno, Jr.
1938	David Freeman and S. Welby Van Horn
1939	John A. Kramer and C. E. Olewine
1940	R. D. Carrothers, Jr. and D. C. Woodbury
1941	James A. Evert and Robert Smidl
1942	J. E. (Budge) Patty and Robert Falkenburg
1943	Robert Falkenburg and James Brink
1944	Robert Falkenburg and John Shea
1945	Herbert Flam and Hugh Stewart
1946	Herbert Flam and Hugh Stewart
1947	Herbert Behrens and Richard Mouledous
1948	Richard Mouledous and Keston Deimling
1949	Gilbert A. Bogley and Richard Squires
1950	Whitney Reed and Norman Peterson
1951	Donald Flye and William Quillian
1952	Francisco Contreras and Sam Giammalva
1953	Jon Douglas and Myron Franks
1954	Earl Baumgardner and Gerald Moss
1955	Gregory Grant and Juan Jose
1956	Rodney Laver and James Shaffer
1957	Robert H. R. Delgado and Allen Fox
1958	Earl Buchholz, Jr. and Charles McKinley
1959	Charles McKinley and Martin Riessen
1960	William Lenoir and Frank Froehling
1961	Charles Pasarell and Clark Graebner
1962	Jackie Cooper and Martin Schad
1963	Jack Jackson and John Pickens
1964	Dean Penero and Jeff Brown
1965	Marcelo Lara and Jasjit Singh
1966	Alberto Carrero and Stanley Pasarell
1967	Zan Guerry and Tony Ortiz
1968	Robert McKinley and F. D. Robbins
1969	Richard Stockton and Erik Van Dillen
1970	Brian Gottfried and Alex Mayer, Jr.
1971	James Delaney and Chip Fisher

USLTA CHAMPIONS—JUNIOR SINGLES (GRASS)

1966   James Rombeau
1967   Mike Estep
1968   F. D. Robbins
1969–71   not held

USLTA CHAMPIONS—JUNIOR DOUBLES (GRASS)

1966   Stephen Avoyer and James Rombeau
1967   Mike Estep and Zan Guerry
1968   Robert McKinley and F. D. Robbins
1969–71   not held

USLTA CHAMPIONS—BOYS' 16 SINGLES

1962   Clifford Richey
1963   Bill Harris
1964   Alberto Carrero
1965   Zan Guerry
1966   Erik Van Dillen
1967   Richard Stockton
1968   Jimmy Connors
1969   James Hagey
1970   Fred De Jesus
1971   William Martin

USLTA CHAMPIONS—BOYS' 16 DOUBLES

1962   James Hobson and Steven Tidball
1963   Roy Barth and Robert Lutz
1964   William Davidson and James Rombeau
1965   Mike Estep and George Taylor
1966   Richard Stockton and Erik Van Dillen
1967   Mike Machette and Richard Stockton
1968   James Hagey and Robert Kreiss
1969   James Delaney and Chip Fisher
1970   Fred DeJesus and John Whitlinger
1971   William Martin and Trey Waltke

USLTA CHAMPIONS—BOYS' 14 SINGLES

1962   Alberto Carrero
1963   Zan Guerry
1964   Mac Claflin
1965   Richard Stockton
1966   Randall Thomas
1967   Bob Kreiss
1968   Fred DeJesus
1969   William Martin
1970   William Martin
1971   Ben McKown

USLTA CHAMPIONS—BOYS' 14 DOUBLES

1962   Zan Guerry and Richard Howell
1963   Zan Guerry and George Taylor
1964   Richard Stockton and George Taylor
1965   Richard Stockton and Erik Van Dillen
1966   Jimmy Connors and Brian Gottfried
1967   Fred DeJesus and Jake Warde
1968   Fred DeJesus and Jake Warde
1969   Mark Joffey and Chris Sylvan

1970   Earl Hassler and Eugene Mayer
1971   Gary Taxman and Percy Wright

USLTA CHAMPIONS—BOYS' 12 SINGLES

1962   Richard Stockton
1963   Richard Stockton
1964   Brian Gottfried
1965   Jake Warde
1966   Jake Warde
1967   Eugene Mayer
1968   Eugene Mayer
1969   Ben McKown
1970   Juan Farrow
1971   Teddy Staren

USLTA CHAMPIONS—BOYS' 12 DOUBLES

1962   Rick Devereaux and Richard Stockton
1963   Brian Gottfried and Richard Stockton
1964   Brian Gottfried and James Connors
1965   James Hagey and Paul Lockwood
1966   Fred DeJesus and Jake Warde
1967   David Bohrnstedt and Dave Sherbeck
1968   Billy Martin and Eugene Mayer
1969   Pem Guerry and Howard Schoenfield
1970   Juan Farrow and Chip Hooper
1971   Teddy Staren and Dave Pelisek

USLTA CHAMPIONS—GIRLS' 18 SINGLES

1918   Katherine Porter
1919   Katherine Gardner
1920   Louise Dixon
1921   Helen N. Wills
1922   Helen N. Wills
1923   Helen Hooker
1924   Helen Jacobs
1925   Helen Jacobs
1926   Louise McFarland
1927   Marjorie Gladman
1928   Sarah Palfrey
1929   Sarah Palfrey
1930   Sarah Palfrey
1931   Ruby Bishop

Helen Wills winning her first Girls' Championship in 1921.

USLTA Champions—Girls' 18 Singles (*cont.*)

1932	Helen Fulton
1933	Bonnie Miller
1934	Helen Pedersen
1935	Patricia Henry
1936	Margaret Osborne
1937	Barbara Winslow
1938	Helen I. Bernhard
1939	Helen I. Bernhard
1940	A. Louise Brough
1941	A. Louise Brough
1942	Doris Hart
1943	Doris Hart
1944	Shirley J. Fry
1945	Shirley J. Fry
1946	Helen Pastall
1947	Nancy Chaffee
1948	Beverly J. Baker
1949	Maureen Connolly
1950	Maureen Connolly
1951	Anita Kanter
1952	Julia Ann Sampson
1953	Mary Ann Ellenberger
1954	Barbara N. Breit
1955	Barbara N. Breit
1956	Miriam Arnold
1957	Karen J. Hantze
1958	Sally M. Moore
1959	Karen J. Hantze
1960	Karen J. Hantze
1961	Victoria Palmer
1962	Victoria Palmer
1963	Julie Heldman
1964	Mary Ann Eisel
1965	Jane Bartkowicz
1966	Jane Bartkowicz
1967	Jane Bartkowicz
1968	Kristy Pigeon
1969	Sharon Walsh
1970	Sharon Walsh
1971	Chris Evert

USLTA CHAMPIONS—GIRLS' 18 DOUBLES

1919	Elizabeth Warren and Penelope Anderson
1920	Virginia L. Carpenter and Helen Sewell
1921	Virginia L. Carpenter and Ceres Baker
1922	Helen N. Wills and Helen Hooker
1923	Helen Hooker and Elizabeth Hilleary
1924	Frances Curtis and Margaret P. Palfrey
1925	Marjorie Morrill and Louise Slocum
1926	Mianne Palfrey and Sarah Palfrey
1927	Marjorie Gladman and Jo Cruickshank
1928	Mianne Palfrey and Sarah Palfrey
1929	Mianne Palfrey and Sarah Palfrey
1930	Helen Marlow and Mercedes Marlow
1931	Alice Marble and Bonnie Miller
1932	Gracyn Wheeler and Katharine Winthrop
1933	Bonnie Miller and Frances Herron
1934	May Hope Doeg and Priscilla Merwin
1935	Hope Knowles and Patricia Cumming
1936	Margaret Osborne and Elinor Dawson
1937	Helen Bernhard and Patricia Cumming
1938	Margaret Jessee and Joan Bigler
1939	Patricia Canning and Marguerita Madden

1940	Doris Hart and Neillie Sheer
1941	A. Louise Brough and Gertrude A. Moran
1942	M. R. Donnelly and Barbara A. Brooke
1943	Doris Hart and Shirley J. Fry
1944	Margaret Varner and Jean E. Doyle
1945	Margaret Varner and Jean E. Doyle
1946	Barbara Wilkins and Mary Cunningham
1947	Nancy Chaffee and Beverly J. Baker
1948	Beverly J. Baker and Marjorie McCord
1949	Maureen Connolly and Lee Van Keuren
1950	Maureen Connolly and Patricia Zellmer
1951	Elaine Lewicki and Bonnie MacKay
1952	Mary Ann Ellenberger and Linda Mitchell
1953	Nancy Dwyer and Mary Ann Ellenberger
1954	Barbara N. Breit and Darlene Hard
1955	Barbara N. Breit and Diane Wootton
1956	Mary Ann Mitchell and Rosa Maria Reyes
1957	Sally M. Moore and Helene J. Weill
1958	Karen J. Hantze and Helene J. Weill
1959	Karen J. Hantze and Kathy Chabot
1960	Karen J. Hantze and Kathy Chabot
1961	Victoria Palmer and Judy Alvarez
1962	Jane Albert and Mary Arfaras
1963	Jane Albert and Stephanie DeFina
1964	Mary Ann Eisel and Wendy Overton
1965	Jane Bartkowicz and Valerie Ziegenfuss
1966	Jane Bartkowicz and Valerie Ziegenfuss
1967	Jane Bartkowicz and Valerie Ziegenfuss
1968	Kristy Pigeon and Denise Carter
1969	Gail Hansen and Patty Ann Reese
1970	Nancy Ornstein and Kris Kemmer
1971	Janet Newburg and Eliza Pande

USLTA CHAMPIONS—GIRLS' 16 SINGLES

1962	Kathy Blake
1963	Jane Bartkowicz
1964	Jane Bartkowicz
1965	Jane Bartkowicz
1966	Linda Tuero

The 1964 Girls' 16 Champions (*left to right*), Paulette Verzin, Mary Hardwick Hare (former British star), Patsy Rippy, and Jane "Peaches" Bartkowicz. Peaches defeated Patsy for the singles; Patsy and Paulette won the doubles title. Miss Bartkowicz was generally considered United States' best girl champion in the 1960's.

1967	Kristy Kemmer
1968	Janet Newberry
1969	Eliza Pande
1970	Chris Evert
1971	Laurie Fleming

USLTA CHAMPIONS—GIRLS' 16 DOUBLES

1962	Stephanie DeFina and Jean Danilovich
1963	Rosemary Casals and Pixie Lamm
1964	Paulette Verzin and Patsy Rippy
1965	Jane Bartkowicz and Valerie Ziegenfuss
1966	Connie Capozzi and Linda Tuero
1967	Gail Hansen and Patty Ann Reese
1968	Kris Kemmer and Janet Newberry
1969	Susan Epstein and Chris Evert
1970	Barbara Downs and Ann Kiyomura
1971	Carrie Fleming and Susan Mehmedbasich

USLTA CHAMPIONS—GIRLS' 14 SINGLES

1962	Jane Bartkowicz
1963	Jane Bartkowicz
1964	Linda Tuero
1965	Connie Capozzi
1966	Patty Ann Reese
1967	Karin Benson
1968	Chris Evert
1969	Laurie Fleming
1970	Marita Redondo
1971	Jeanne Evert

USLTA CHAMPIONS—GIRLS' 14 DOUBLES

1962	Paulette Verzin and Patsy Rippy
1963	Jane Bartkowicz and Ginger Pfeiffer
1964	Patricia Montano and Kristy Pigeon
1965	Marjorie Gengler and Alice deRochemont
1966	Karin Benson and Marcelyn Louie
1967	Whitney Grant and Janet Newberry
1968	Chris Evert and Susan Epstein
1969	Ann Kiyomura and Susan Kraft
1970	Marita Redondo and Gretchen Galt
1971	Jeanne Evert and Judy Gfroerer

USLTA CHAMPIONS—GIRLS' 12 SINGLES

1962	Connie Capozzi
1963	Connie Capozzi
1964	Patty Ann Reese
1965	Marcelyn Louie
1966	Christine Bartkowicz
1967	Ann Kiyomura
1968	Marna Louie
1969	Jeanne Evert
1970	Lynn Epstein
1971	Sherry Acker

USLTA CHAMPIONS—GIRLS' 12 DOUBLES

1962	Jane Lawson and Connie Capozzi
1963	Connie Capozzi and Gene Shapiro
1964	Marcelyn Louie and Karin Benson
1965	Karin Benson and Marcelyn Louie
1966	Susan Epstein and Chrissie Evert

1967	Lisa Barry and Laurie Jo Fleming
1968	Kathy May and Gretchen Galt
1969	Judy Gfroerer and Jeanne Evert
1970	Susan Wright and Susan Hagey
1971	Sherry Acker and Lea Antonoplis

USLTA CHAMPIONS—FATHER AND SON

1918	Alfred H. Chapin and Alfred H. Chapin, Jr.
1919	Fred G. Anderson and Fred C. Anderson
1920	Fred G. Anderson and Fred C. Anderson
1921	Fred G. Anderson and Fred C. Anderson
1922	J. D. E. Jones and Arnold W. Jones
1923	Joseph W. Wear and W. Potter Wear
1924	Alfred H. Chapin and Alfred H. Chapin, Jr.
1925	J. D. E. Jones and Arnold W. Jones
1926	Donald M. Hill and Malcolm T. Hill
1927	John Barton and Horace Barton
1928	J. D. E. Jones and Arnold W. Jones
1929	J. D. E. Jones and Arnold W. Jones
1930	J. D. E. Jones and Arnold W. Jones
1931	J. D. E. Jones and Arnold W. Jones
1932	J. D. E. Jones and Arnold W. Jones
1933	R. N. Watt and M. Laird Watt
1934	R. N. Watt and M. Laird Watt
1935	Wm. J. Clothier and Wm. J. Clothier II
1936	Wm. J. Clothier and Wm. J. Clothier II
1937	R. N. Watt and M. Laird Watt
1938	F. J. Sulloway and A. W. Sulloway
1939	R. B. Mulloy and Gardnar Mulloy
1940	L. R. Gay and F. R. Gay
1941	R. B. Mulloy and Gardnar Mulloy
1942	R. B. Mulloy and Lt. (j. g.) Gardnar Mulloy
1943–45	not held
1946	Arthur Nielsen and Arthur Nielsen, Jr.
1947	G. Diehl Mateer and G. Diehl Mateer, Jr.
1948	Arthur Nielsen and Arthur Nielsen, Jr.
1949	G. Diehl Mateer and G. Diehl Mateer, Jr.
1950	G. Diehl Mateer and G. Diehl Mateer, Jr.
1951	G. Diehl Mateer and G. Diehl Mateer, Jr.
1952	Karl Kamrath and Karl Kamrath, Jr.
1953	Roger Richardson and Hamilton Richardson
1954	Roger Richardson and Hamilton Richardson
1955	J. Andrew Crane and Michael Crane
1956	Sidney Wood, Jr. and Sidney Wood III
1957	Harry Hoffmann and Harry Hoffmann, Jr.
1958	Harry Hoffmann and Harry Hoffmann, Jr.
1959	F. A. Froehling, Jr. and F. A. Froehling III
1960	Harry Hoffmann and Harry Hoffmann, Jr.
1961	H. William Bond and William Bond
1962	F. A. Froehling, Jr. and F. A. Froehling III
1963	F. A. Froehling, Jr. and F. A. Froehling III
1964	Robert Ralston and Dennis Ralston
1965	F. A. Froehling, Jr. and F. A. Froehling III
1966	Chauncey D. Steele, Jr. and C. D. Steele III
1967	Leslie FitzGibbon and Herbert FitzGibbon
1968	Chauncey D. Steele, Jr. and C. D. Steele III
1969	Chauncey D. Steele, Jr. and C. D. Steele III
1970	Chauncey D. Steele, Jr. and C. D. Steele III
1971	Frederick McNair III and Frederick McNair IV

USLTA CHAMPIONS—MEN SENIORS' SINGLES

1918	Ross Burchard
1919	Clarence Hobart

USLTA Champions—Men Seniors' Singles (cont.)

1920	William A. Campbell
1921	Philip B. Hawk
1922	Philip B. Hawk
1923	Philip B. Hawk
1924	Craig Biddle
1925	Alfred J. Cawse
1926	Alfred J. Cawse
1927	Alfred J. Cawse
1928	Henry H. Bassford
1929	Clarence M. Charest
1930	Henry H. Bassford
1931	Fred C. Baggs
1932	Clarence M. Charest
1933	Clarence M. Charest
1934	Raymond B. Bidwell
1935	Raymond B. Bidwell
1936	Raymond B. Bidwell
1937	Cedric A. Major
1938	Henry H. Bassford
1939	Percy W. Guilford
1940	Watson Washburn
1941	Arthur W. Macpherson
1942	William L. Nassau
1943	not held
1944	J. Gilbert Hall
1945	J. Gilbert Hall
1946	J. Gilbert Hall
1947	J. Gilbert Hall
1948	J. Gilbert Hall
1949	J. Gilbert Hall
1950	J. Gilbert Hall
1951	Harold T. MacGuffin
1952	Harry Hopman
1953	William A. Maxwell
1954	David L. Freed
1955	R. Philip Hanna
1956	Bryan M. Grant, Jr.
1957	Bryan M. Grant, Jr.
1958	Gardnar Mulloy
1959	J. Hal Surface, Jr.
1960	Gardnar Mulloy
1961	Gardnar Mulloy
1962	Gardnar Mulloy
1963	Gardnar Mulloy
1964	Gardnar Mulloy
1965	Robert V. Sherman
1966	Jaroslav Drobny
1967	Jaroslav Drobny
1968	Gardnar Mulloy
1969	Robert Riggs
1970	Torsten Johansson
1971	Torsten Johansson

USLTA CHAMPIONS—MEN SENIORS' DOUBLES

1921	J. D. E. Jones and Arthur Ingraham
1922	Holcombe Ward and Dwight F. Davis
1923	A. Wallis Myers and Samuel Hardy
1924	Walter L. Pate and Samuel Hardy
1925	Walter L. Pate and Samuel Hardy
1926	Albert J. Gore and Claude J. Butlin
1927	Fred C. Baggs and Dr. William Rosenbaum
1928	Irving C. Wright and Harry C. Johnson
1929	Fred C. Baggs and Dr. William Rosenbaum
1930	S. Jarvis Adams and Henry H. Bassford
1931	Fred C. Baggs and Dr. William Rosenbaum
1932	S. Jarvis Adams and Henry H. Bassford
1933	G. P. Gardner, Jr. and Richard Bishop
1934	Fred C. Baggs and Dr. William Rosenbaum
1935	Raymond B. Bidwell and Richard Bishop
1936	William Clothier and Dwight F. Davis
1937	Lawrence A. Baker and John G. McKay
1938	Dr. William Rosenbaum and Fred C. Baggs
1939	Dr. G. Colket Caner and Cornelius C. Felton
1940	Watson Washburn and Hugh Kelleher
1941	Jacques Brugnon and Meade Woodson
1942	W. M. Washburn and A. W. Macpherson
1943	not held
1944	Watson Washburn and A. W. Macpherson
1945	J. Gilbert Hall and Sidney Adelstein
1946	J. Gilbert Hall and Sidney Adelstein
1947	J. Gilbert Hall and Sidney Adelstein
1948	Mel Gallagher and John Woodall
1949	Wilmer Allison and J. Gilbert Hall
1950	Wilmer Allison and J. Gilbert Hall
1951	Sidney Adelstein and Bernard Clinton
1952	Pierre Harang and Harry Hopman
1953	Edward Chandler and Gerald Stratford
1954	Edward Chandler and Gerald Stratford
1955	Edward Chandler and Gerald Stratford
1956	Jean Borotra and Harry Hopman
1957	Edward Jacobs and C. Alphonso Smith
1958	Leonard Prosser and J. Hal Surface, Jr.
1959	Harry Hoffmann and W. E. Hester, Jr.
1960	Jean Borotra and Adrian Quist
1961	Clifford Sutter and Ernest Sutter

Billy Talbert and Gardnar Mulloy won the National Doubles in 1945, 1946, and 1948. They teamed up again in 1963, 1964, 1965, and 1967 to win the Seniors' Doubles.

1962   Gardnar Mulloy and Mike McLaney
1963   Gardnar Mulloy and William F. Talbert
1964   Gardnar Mulloy and William F. Talbert
1965   Gardnar Mulloy and William F. Talbert
1966   Robert J. Freedman and Robert V. Sherman
1967   Gardnar Mulloy and William F. Talbert
1968   Ellis Slack and Richard C. Sorlien
1969   Gardnar Mulloy and Robert Riggs
1970   Gary Hippenstiel and Chauncey Steele, Jr.
1971   Lennart Bergelin and Torsten Johansson

USLTA OPEN CHAMPIONS—MEN SENIORS' DOUBLES

1968   Torsten Johansson and Gardnar Mulloy
1969   Emery Neale and Robert Riggs
1970   L. Straight Clark and E. Victor Seixas
1971   L. Straight Clark and E. Victor Seixas

USLTA AMATEUR GRASS COURT CHAMPIONS—MEN'S SINGLES

1970   Haroon Rahim
1971   John Gardner

USLTA AMATEUR GRASS COURT CHAMPIONS—MEN'S DOUBLES

1970   Robert McKinley and Richard Stockton
1971   Gene Scott and Vitas Gerulaitis

USLTA AMATEUR GRASS COURT CHAMPIONS—WOMEN'S SINGLES

1970   Eliza Pande
1971   Marita Redondo

USLTA AMATEUR GRASS COURT CHAMPIONS—WOMEN'S DOUBLES

1970   Gail Hansen and Sharon Walsh
1971   Pam Farmer and Janice Metcalf

USLTA GRASS COURT CHAMPIONS—MEN SENIORS' 55 SINGLES

1965   Bryan M. Grant
1966   Bryan M. Grant
1967   Bryan M. Grant
1968   Bryan M. Grant
1969   Gardnar Mulloy
1970   Chauncey D. Steele, Jr.
1971   Chauncey D. Steele, Jr.

USLTA GRASS COURT CHAMPIONS—MEN SENIORS' 55 DOUBLES

1965   Charles Brooke and C. Alphonso Smith
1966   Clayton Burewell and N. E. Powel
1967   N. E. Powel and Len Prosser
1968   Tom Bird and Bryan M. Grant
1969   Gardnar Mulloy and C. Alphonso Smith
1970   Chauncey D. Steele, Jr. and Frank Thompson
1971   Chauncey D. Steele, Jr. and Frank Thompson

USLTA GRASS COURT CHAMPIONS—MEN SENIORS' 60 SINGLES

1968   Bernard Clinton

1969   C. Alphonso Smith
1970   Leonard Prosser
1971   N. E. Powel

USLTA GRASS COURT CHAMPIONS—MEN SENIORS' 60 DOUBLES

1968   Monte Ganger and Crawford Christopher
1969   C. Alphonso Smith and Edward Tarangioli
1970   Charles Brooke and Leonard Prosser
1971   N. E. Powel and Leonard Prosser

USLTA GRASS COURT CHAMPIONS—MEN SENIORS' 65 SINGLES

1969   Bernard Clinton
1970   Edward Chandler
1971   Frank Goeltz

USLTA GRASS COURT CHAMPIONS—MEN SENIORS' 65 DOUBLES

1969   Bernard Clinton and Ted Wellman
1970   Edward Chandler and Ted Wellman
1971   Frank Goeltz and Kahl Spriggs

USLTA GRASS COURT CHAMPIONS—MEN SENIORS' 70 SINGLES

1970   Frank G. Roberts
1971   Reul Ritz

USLTA GRASS COURT CHAMPIONS—MEN SENIORS' 70 DOUBLES

1970   Frank G. Roberts and Farham Warriner
1971   Richard Dole and DeWitt Redgrave

USLTA GRASS COURT CHAMPIONS—WOMEN SENIORS' SINGLES

1938   Mrs. William V. Hester
1939   Mrs. Walter Blumenthal
1940   Mrs. Gretl Dupont
1941   Mrs. William V. Hester
1942   Mrs. Gretl Dupont
1943   not held
1944   Mrs. Philip Theopold
1945   Mrs. Gretl Dupont
1946   Mrs. Philip Theopold
1947   Mrs. Alice Wanee
1948   Mrs. Muriel Bostwick
1949   Mrs. Richard Buck
1950   Mrs. Richard Buck
1951   Mrs. Richard Buck
1952   Mrs. Richard Buck
1953   Mrs. Richard Buck
1954   Mrs. Nell Hopman
1955   Mrs. Nell Hopman
1956   Mrs. Richard Buck
1957   Mrs. Richard Buck
1958   Mrs. Richard Buck
1959   Mrs. Merceina Parker
1960   Mrs. Charlotte Lee
1961   Kay Hubbell

USLTA Grass Court Champions—Women Seniors' Singles (*cont.*)

1962	Kay Hubbell
1963	Mrs. Baba M. Lewis
1964	Mrs. Dorothy B. Cheney
1965	Mrs. Lucille Davidson
1966	Mrs. Betty R. Pratt
1967	Mrs. Dorothy B. Cheney
1968	Mrs. Betty R. Pratt
1969	Mrs. Betty R. Pratt
1970	Mrs. Nancy Neeld
1971	Mrs. Betty R. Pratt

USLTA GRASS COURT CHAMPIONS—WOMEN SENIORS' DOUBLES

1938	Mrs. Elizabeth B. Corbiere and Mrs. Henry R. Guild
1939	Eleanora R. Sears and Mme. Sylvia Henrotin
1940	Mrs. Hazel Hotchkiss Wightman and Mrs. Edith Sigourney
1941	Mrs. Hazel Hotchkiss Wightman and Mrs. Edith Sigourney
1942	Mrs. Hazel Hotchkiss Wightman and Mrs. Molly T. Fremont-Smith
1943	not held
1944	Mrs. Hazel Hotchkiss Wightman and Mrs. Edith Sigourney
1945	Mrs. Philip Theopold and Mrs. John B. Pierce
1946	Mrs. Hazel Hotchkiss Wightman and Mrs. Edith Sigourney
1947	Mrs. Hazel Hotchkiss Wightman and Mrs. Edith Sigourney
1948	Mrs. Hazel Hotchkiss Wightman and Mrs. Marion Zinderstein Jessup
1949	Mrs. Hazel Hotchkiss Wightman and Mrs. Richard Buck
1950	Mrs. Hazel H. Wightman and Mrs. Richard Buck
1951	Mrs. Richard Buck and Mrs. Edward Pinkhan
1952	Mrs. Richard Buck and Mrs. Hazel H. Wightman
1953	Mrs. Richard Buck and Mrs. Nell Hopman
1954	Mrs. Nell Hopman and Mrs. Hazel Wightman
1955	Mrs. Richard Buck and Mrs. Q. A. Shaw McKean
1956	Mrs. Walter Mahony and Mrs. Clarence Warner
1957	Mrs. Richard Buck and Mrs. Q. A. Shaw McKean
1958	Mrs. Richard Buck and Mrs. Q. A. Shaw McKean
1959	Mrs. Richard Buck and Mrs. Q. A. Shaw McKean
1960	Mrs. Richard Buck and Mrs. Q. A. Shaw McKean
1961	Mrs. Richard Buck and Mrs. Q. A. Shaw McKean
1962	Mrs. Richard Buck and Mrs. Q. A. Shaw McKean
1963	Mrs. Charlotte M. Lee and Katharine Hubbell
1964	Mrs. Richard Buck and Mrs. Q. A. Shaw McKean
1965	Katharine Hubbell and Mrs. Charlotte Lee
1966	Mrs. Baba M. Lewis and Mrs. Betty R. Pratt
1967	Mrs. Shirley F. Irwin and Mrs. Betty R. Pratt
1968	Mrs. Gloria E. Dillenbeck and Mrs. Betty R. Pratt
1969	Mrs. Dorothy B. Cheney and Mrs. June E. Gray
1970	Mrs. Nancy Neeld and Mrs. Betty R. Pratt
1971	Mrs. Nancy Neeld and Mrs. Betty R. Pratt

USLTA CHAMPIONS—MOTHER AND DAUGHTER

1967	Mrs. F. A. C. Vosters and Gretchen
1968	Mrs. F. A. C. Vosters and Gretchen
1969	Mrs. F. A. C. Vosters and Gretchen
1970	Mrs. F. A. C. Vosters and Gretchen
1971	Mrs. F. A. C. Vosters and Gretchen

USLTA INDOOR CHAMPIONS—MEN'S SINGLES

1898	Leo Ware
1899	not held
1900	J. Appleton Allen
1901	Holcombe Ward
1902	J. Parmly Paret
1903	Wylie C. Grant
1904	Wylie C. Grant
1905	Edward B. Dewhurst
1906	Wylie C. Grant
1907	Theodore R. Pell
1908	Wylie C. Grant
1909	Theodore R. Pell
1910	Gustave F. Touchard
1911	Theodore R. Pell
1912	Wylie C. Grant
1913	Gustave F. Touchard
1914	Gustave F. Touchard
1915	Gustave F. Touchard
1916	R. Lindley Murray
1917	S. Howard Voshell
1918	S. Howard Voshell
1919	Vincent Richards
1920	William T. Tilden II
1921	Frank T. Anderson
1922	Francis T. Hunter
1923	Vincent Richards
1924	Vincent Richards
1925	Jean Borotra
1926	Jean René Lacoste
1927	Jean Borotra
1928	William Aydelotte
1929	Jean Borotra
1930	Francis T. Hunter
1931	Jean Borotra
1932	Gregory S. Mangin
1933	Gregory S. Mangin
1934	Lester R. Stoefen
1935	Gregory S. Mangin
1936	Gregory S. Mangin
1937	Frank Parker
1938	Donald McNeill
1939	Wayne Sabin
1940	Robert L. Riggs
1941	Frank L. Kovacs II
1942–45	not held
1946	Francisco Segura
1947	John A. Kramer
1948	William F. Talbert
1949	Richard A. Gonzalez
1950	Donald McNeill

1951	William F. Talbert
1952	Richard Savitt
1953	Arthur D. Larsen
1954	Sven Davidson
1955	Tony Trabert
1956	Ulf Schmidt
1957	Kurt Nielsen
1958	Richard Savitt
1959	Alejandro Olmedo
1960	Barry MacKay
1961	Richard Savitt
1962	Charles R. McKinley
1963	R. Dennis Ralston
1964	Charles R. McKinley
1965	Jan Erik Lundquist
1966	Charles Pasarell
1967	Charles Pasarell
1968	Cliff Richey
1969*	Stan Smith
1970	Stan Smith
1970*	Ilie Nastase
1971	Ilie Nastase
1971*	Clark Graebner

USLTA INDOOR CHAMPIONS—MEN'S DOUBLES

1900	Calhoun Cragin and J. P. Paret
1901	Calhoun Cragin and O. M. Bostwick
1902	W. C. Grant and R. LeRoy

* Open champions.

1903	W. C. Grant and R. LeRoy
1904	W. C. Grant and R. LeRoy
1905	T. R. Pell and H. F. Allen
1906	H. H. Hackett and F. B. Alexander
1907	H. H. Hackett and F. B. Alexander
1908	H. H. Hackett and F. B. Alexander
1909	W. C. Grant and T. R. Pell
1910	G. F. Touchard and C. R. Gardner
1911	F. B. Alexander and T. R. Pell
1912	F. B. Alexander and T. R. Pell
1913	W. C. Grant and G. C. Shafer
1914	W. C. Grant and G. C. Shafer
1915	G. F. Touchard and W. M. Washburn
1916	A. M. Lovibond and W. Rosenbaum
1917	F. B. Alexander and W. Rosenbaum
1918	G. C. Shafer and K. Smith
1919	W. T. Tilden II and V. Richards
1920	W. T. Tilden II and V. Richards
1921	V. Richards and S. H. Voshell
1922	F. T. Anderson and S. H. Voshell
1923	V. Richards and F. T. Hunter
1924	V. Richards and F. T. Hunter
1925	J. Borotra and A. W. Asthalter
1926	W. T. Tilden II and F. C. Anderson
1927	J. Borotra and J. Brugnon
1928	W. Aydelotte and P. G. Rockafellow
1929	W. T. Tilden II and F. T. Hunter
1930	P. G. Rockafellow and M. Cutler

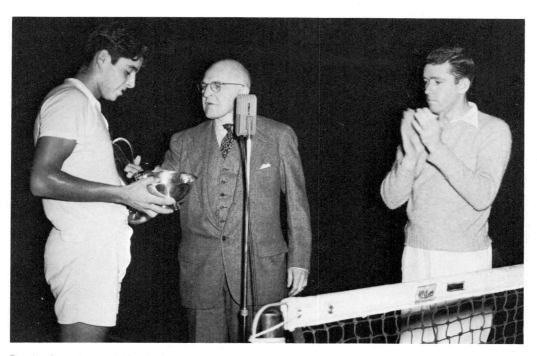

Pancho Gonzalez receiving the Indoor Championship trophy from Walter Merrill Hall, chairman of the USLTA Indoor Championships Committee, while Billy Talbert, runner-up for the title, which he won in 1948, applauds the new champion.

USLTA Indoor Champions—Men's Doubles (cont.)

1931	J. Borotra and C. Boussus
1932	G. M. Lott, Jr. and J. Van Ryn
1933	C. Cutter and E. McCauliff
1934	G. M. Lott, Jr. and L. R. Stoefen
1935	G. S. Mangin and B. Bell
1936	K. Schroder and J. G. Hall
1937	F. A. Parker and G. S. Mangin
1938	F. J. Bowden and J. Pitman
1939	E. McCauliff and C. Sutter
1940	R. L. Riggs and E. T. Cooke
1941	W. D. McNeill and F. D. Guernsey, Jr.
1942–45	not held
1946	W. D. McNeill and F. D. Guernsey, Jr.
1947	J. A. Kramer and R. Falkenburg
1948	J. Borotra and M. Bernard
1949	W. F. Talbert and W. D. McNeill
1950	W. F. Talbert and W. D. McNeill
1951	W. F. Talbert and W. D. McNeill
1952	W. F. Talbert and W. D. McNeill
1953	A. D. Larsen and K. Nielsen
1954	W. F. Talbert and T. Trabert
1955	E. V. Seixas, Jr. and T. Trabert
1956	S. Giammalva and E. V. Seixas, Jr.
1957	G. Golden and B. MacKay
1958	G. Golden and B. MacKay
1959	B. MacKay and A. Olmedo
1960	Andres Gimeno and Manuel Santana
1961	C. R. Crawford and R. Holmberg
1962	R. Laver and C. R. McKinley
1963	C. R. McKinley and R. D. Ralston
1964	Manuel Santana and Jose Luis Arilla
1965	C. R. McKinley and R. D. Ralston
1966	Robert Lutz and Stan Smith
1967	Arthur Ashe and Charles Pasarell
1968	Thomas Koch and Tom Okker
1969*	Robert Lutz and Stan Smith
1970	Arthur Ashe and Stan Smith
1970*	Arthur Ashe and Stan Smith
1971	Ilie Nastase and Ion Tiriac
1971*	Juan Gisbert and Manuel Orantes

* Open champions.

Mrs. Marion Zinderstein Jessup won many USLTA titles in the 1920's.

USLTA INDOOR CHAMPIONS—WOMEN'S SINGLES

1907	Elisabeth H. Moore
1908	Marie Wagner
1909	Marie Wagner
1910	Mrs. Frederick G. Schmitz
1911	Marie Wagner
1912	not held
1913	Marie Wagner
1914	Marie Wagner
1915	Molla Bjurstedt
1916	Molla Bjurstedt
1917	Marie Wagner
1918	Molla Bjurstedt
1919	Mrs. Hazel Hotchkiss Wightman
1920	Helen Pollak
1921	Mrs. Molla Bjurstedt Mallory
1922	Mrs. Molla Bjurstedt Mallory
1923	Mrs. Benjamin E. Cole II
1924	Mrs. Marion Zinderstein Jessup
1925	Mrs. Marion Zinderstein Jessup
1926	Elizabeth Ryan
1927	Mrs. Hazel Hotchkiss Wightman
1928	Edith Sigourney
1929	Margaret Blake
1930	Mianne Palfrey
1931	Marjorie Sachs
1932	Marjorie Morrill
1933	Dorance Chase
1934	Norma Taubele
1935	Jane Sharp
1936	Mrs. Marjorie Gladman Van Ryn
1937	Mme. Sylvia Henrotin
1938	Virginia Hollinger
1939	Pauline M. Betz
1940	Mrs. Sarah Palfrey Fabyan
1941	Pauline M. Betz
1942	Mrs. Patricia Canning Todd
1943	Pauline M. Betz
1944	Katharine Winthrop
1945	Mrs. Helen Pedersen Rihbany
1946	Mrs. Helen Pedersen Rihbany
1947	Pauline M. Betz
1948	Mrs. Patricia Canning Todd
1949	Gertrude Moran
1950	Nancy Chaffee
1951	Nancy Chaffee
1952	Mrs. Nancy Chaffee Kiner
1953	Mrs. Thelma Long
1954	Mrs. Dorothy W. Levine
1955	Katharine Hubbell
1956	Lois Felix
1957	Mrs. Dorothy W. Levine
1958	Nancy O'Connell
1959	Lois Felix
1960	Carole Wright
1961	Janet Hopps
1962	Carole Wright
1963	Carol Hanks
1964	Mary Ann Eisel
1965	Nancy Richey
1966	Mrs. Billie Jean King
1967	Mrs. Billie Jean King
1968	Mrs. Billie Jean King

1969   Mrs. M. A. E. Curtis
1970   Mrs. M. A. E. Curtis
1971   Mrs. Billie Jean King

USLTA INDOOR CHAMPIONS—WOMEN'S DOUBLES

1908   Mrs. Helen Helwig Pouch and Elisabeth H. Moore
1909   Elisabeth H. Moore and Erna Marcus
1910   Marie Wagner and Clara Kutroff
1911   Elizabeth C. Bunce and Barbara Fleming
1912   not held
1913   Marie Wagner and Clara Kutroff
1914   Mrs. S. F. Weaver and Clare Cassel
1915   Mrs. Helen Homans McLean and Mrs. S. F. Weaver
1916   Molla Bjurstedt and Marie Wagner
1917   Marie Wagner and Margaret T. Taylor
1918   Eleanor Goss and Mrs. S. F. Weaver
1919   Mrs. Hazel Hotchkiss Wightman and Marion Zinderstein
1920   Mrs. L. Gouverneur Morris and Helene Pollak
1921   Mrs. Hazel Hotchkiss Wightman and Marion Zinderstein
1922   Mrs. Frank Godfrey and Mrs. Marion Zinderstein Jessup
1923   Mrs. Benjamin E. Cole II and Mrs. Frank Godfrey
1924   Mrs. Hazel Hotchkiss Wightman and Mrs. Marion Zinderstein Jessup
1925   Mrs. William Endicott and Mrs. J. Dallas Corbiere
1926   Elizabeth Ryan and Mary K. Browne
1927   Mrs. Hazel Hotchkiss Wightman and Mrs. Marion Zinderstein Jessup
1928   Mrs. Hazel Hotchkiss Wightman and Sarah Palfrey
1929   Mrs. Hazel Hotchkiss Wightman and Sarah Palfrey
1930   Mrs. Hazel Hotchkiss Wightman and Sarah Palfrey
1931   Mrs. Hazel Hotchkiss Wightman and Sarah Palfrey
1932   Marjorie Morrill and Mrs. Marjorie Gladman Van Ryn
1933   Mrs. Hazel Hotchkiss Wightman and Sarah Palfrey
1934   Norma Taubele and Jane Sharp
1935   Mrs. Dorothy Andrus and Mme. Sylvia Henrotin
1936   Mrs. Dorothy Andrus and Mme. Sylvia Henrotin
1937   Mrs. Dorothy Andrus and Mme. Sylvia Henrotin
1938   Mrs. Virginia Rice Johnson and Katharine Winthrop
1939   Norma Taubele and Grace Surber
1940   Mrs. Gracyn Wheeler Kelleher and Norma Taubele
1941   Pauline M. Betz and Dorothy M. Bundy
1942   Katharine Winthrop and Mrs. Virginia Rice Johnson
1943   Pauline M. Betz and Mrs. Hazel H. Wightman

1944   Katharine Winthrop and Mrs. Virginia Rice Johnson
1945   Katharine Winthrop and Mrs. Virginia Rice Johnson
1946   Mrs. Helen Petersen Rihbany and Ruth Carter
1947   Doris Hart and Barbara Scofield
1948   Doris Hart and Barbara Scofield
1949   Gertrude Moran and Mrs. Marjorie Gladman Buck
1950   Nancy Chaffee and Mrs. Marjorie Gladman Buck
1951   Mrs. Marjorie Gladman Buck and Nancy Chaffee
1952   Mrs. Nancy Chaffee Kiner and Mrs. Patricia Canning Todd
1953   Mrs. Thelma Long and Mrs. Barbara Scofield Davidson
1954   Mrs. Dorothy W. Levine and Mrs. Barbara W. Ward
1955   Ruth Jeffery and Katharine Hubbell
1956   Lois Felix and Katharine Hubbell
1957   Mrs. Dorothy W. Levine and Nancy O'Connell
1958   Carol Hanks and Nancy O'Connell
1959   Lois Felix and Katharine Hubbell
1960   Mrs. Marjorie Gladman Buck and Ruth Jeffery
1961   Janet Hopps and Katharine Hubbell
1962   Belmar Gunderson and Ruth Jeffery
1963   Carol Hanks and Mary Ann Eisel
1964   Mary Ann Eisel and Kay Hubbell
1965   Mrs. Carol Hanks Aucamp and Mrs. Mary Ann Eisel
1966   Rosemary Casals and Mrs. Billie Jean King
1967   Mrs. Carol H. Aucamp and Mary Ann Eisel
1968   Mrs. Billie Jean King and Rosemary Casals
1969   Mary Ann E. Curtis and Valerie Ziegenfuss
1970   Nancy Richey and Peaches Bartkowicz
1971   Mrs. Billie Jean King and Rosemary Casals

USLTA INDOOR CHAMPIONS—MIXED DOUBLES

1921   Mrs. M. Bjurstedt Mallory and William T. Tilden II
1922   Mrs. M. Bjurstedt Mallory and William T. Tilden II
1923   Mrs. H. Hotchkiss Wightman and Burnham N. Dell
1924   Mrs. H. Hotchkiss Wightman and William T. Tilden II
1925   Mrs. M. Zinderstein Jessup and Karl S. Pfaffman
1926   Mrs. H. Hotchkiss Wightman and G. Peabody Gardner, Jr.
1927   Mrs. H. Hotchkiss Wightman and G. Peabody Gardner, Jr.
1928   Mrs. H. Hotchkiss Wightman and Henry L. Johnson, Jr.
1929   Margaret Blake and Richard Harte
1930   Margaret Blake and Richard Harte
1931   Sarah Palfrey and Lawrence B. Rice
1932   Marjorie Morrill and G. Colket Caner
1933   Sarah Palfrey and G. Holmes Perkins
1934   Norma Taubele and Frank J. Bowden
1935   Jane Sharp and Gregory S. Mangin
1936   Mrs. Sylvia Henrotin and Kalle Schroder
1937   Mrs. Sylvia Henrotin and Frank J. Bowden

USLTA Indoor Champions—Mixed Doubles (cont.)

1938   Norma Taubele and Frank J. Bowden
1939   Pauline M. Betz and Wayne Sabin
1940   Pauline M. Betz and Robert L. Riggs
1941   Pauline M. Betz and Albert H. Stitt
1942   Katharine Winthrop and Albert H. Stitt
1943   Pauline M. Betz and Albert H. Stitt
1944   Judy Atterbury and Albert H. Stitt
1945   Mrs. Norma T. Barber and Robert Stewart
1946   Mrs. Helen Pedersen Rihbany and Geo. W.
         Mandell
1947   Doris Hart and William F. Talbert
1948   Doris Hart and William F. Talbert
1949   Gertrude Moran and Richard Gonzalez
1950   Nancy Chaffee and Budge Patty
1951   Beverly Baker and Straight Clark
1952–53   not held
1954   Lois Felix and Winslow Blanchard
1955   Ruth Jeffery and Wallace McIntyre
1956   Ruth Jeffery and Dever Hobbs
1957   Mildred Thornton and Dr. Donald Manchester
1958   Mildred Thornton and Dr. Donald Manchester
1959   Mrs. Mildred Thornton Johnson and
         Dr. Donald Manchester
1960   Lois Felix and Dr. Donald Manchester
1961   Janet Hopps and Arthur (Bud) Collins
1962   Carole Wright and Chauncey D. Steele, Jr.
1963   Carol Hanks and Chauncey D. Steele III
1964   Belmar Gunderson and Chauncey D. Steele III
1965   Mary Ann Eisel and Chauncey D. Steele III
1966   Mrs. Billie Jean King and Paul Sullivan
1967   Mrs. Billie Jean King and Paul Sullivan
1968   Mary Ann Eisel and Chauncey D. Steele III
1969–71   not held

USLTA INDOOR CHAMPIONS—JUNIOR SINGLES

1915   Elliott H. Binzen
1916   Elliott H. Binzen
1917   E. H. Hendrickson
1918   Vincent Richards
1919   Vincent Richards
1920   Vincent Richards
1921   Edgar F. Dawson
1922   John F. W. Whitbeck
1923   Kenneth Appel
1924   Horace G. Orser
1925   Julius Seligson
1926   Julius Seligson
1927   Francis X. Shields
1928   Richard Murphy
1929   William Jacobs
1930   Mark Hecht
1931   Mark Hecht
1932   Mark Hecht
1933   Frank Parker
1934   Gilbert A. Hunt
1935   Alfred L. Jarvis, Jr.
1936   Donald McNeill
1937   Joseph Fishbach
1938   Joseph Fishbach
1939   William Umstaedter
1940   James Evert
1941–44   not held
1945   Sidney Schwartz
1946   Leonard Steiner

1947   Sidney Schwartz
1948   Tony Trabert
1949   Jerry DeWitts
1950   Hamilton Richardson
1951   Samuel Giammalva
1952   Samuel Giammalva
1953   Albert E. Harum, Jr.
1954   Alphonse Holtman
1955   Ronald Holmberg
1956   Earl Buchholz, Jr.
1957   Charles McKinley
1958   Charles McKinley
1959   Charles McKinley
1960   Arthur Ashe, Jr.
1961   Arthur Ashe, Jr.
1962   Gary Rieser
1963   Cliff Richey
1964   Frank Conner
1965   Armistead Neely
1966   Jeff Borowiak
1967   Don Lutz
1968   Robert McKinley
1969   Roscoe Tanner
1970   Brian Gottfried
1971   James Delaney

USLTA INDOOR CHAMPIONS—JUNIOR DOUBLES

1915   James Weber and R. C. Rand
1916   Willard Botsford and R. C. Haines
1917   Gerald B. Emerson and Herman F. Dornheim
1918   Frank T. Anderson and H. B. Kaltenbach
1919   Vincent Richards and Frank T. Anderson
1920   Vincent Richards and P. S. McHugh
1921   Jerome Lang and Edgar F. Dawson
1922   Kenneth Appel and John Van Ryn
1923   Malcolm T. Hill and Henry L. Johnson, Jr.
1924   Malcolm T. Hill and Henry L. Johnson, Jr.
1925   Malcolm T. Hill and Henry L. Johnson, Jr.
1926   Malcolm T. Hill and Henry L. Johnson, Jr.
1927   Francis X. Shields and Julius Seligson
1928   Richard Murphy and Samuel P. Hayes, Jr.
1929   Richard Downing and S. E. Davenport
1930   Kendal H. Cram and Frank M. Shore
1931   Bernard Friedman and Lester Kabacoff
1932   Giles Verstraten and John Nogrady
1933   Gilbert A. Hunt and Sumner Rodman
1934   Gilbert A. Hunt and Charles Mattmann
1935   Melvin L. Lapman and Marvin Kantrowitz
1936   Charles T. Mattmann and Peter Lauck
1937   Robert A. Low and Marvin Kantrowitz
1938   Joseph Fishbach and Dave Johnsen
1939   Richard E. Shipp and Fred V. Krais, Jr.
1940   James Evert and Richard J. Bender
1941–44   not held
1945   Richard Savitt and Leonard L. Steiner
1946   Pvt. Hugh Steward and Alex Hetzeck
1947   Sidney Schwartz and Alex Hetzeck
1948   Tony Trabert and Dixon Osburn
1949   Jerry DeWitts and Jack Turpin
1950   Hamilton Richardson and Bob Sierra
1951   Edward Daily and Samuel Giammalva
1952   Samuel Giammalva and Richard Schuette
1953   Mike Green and Richard Schuette
1954   David Harum and Wayne Pearce

1955	Arthur Andrews and Crawford Henry
1956	Earl Buchholz, Jr. and C. Edward Sledge
1957	Earl Buchholz, Jr. and Charles McKinley
1958	Charles McKinley and Raymond Senkowski
1959	Charles McKinley and Cliff Buchholz
1960	Frank Froehling III and Butch Newman
1961	Cliff Buchholz and Butch Newman
1962	B. H. Brown and Gary Rieser
1963	B. H. Brown and Gary Rieser
1964	John Good and Brian Marcus
1965	Richard Dell and George Turner
1966	Jeff Borowiak and Mike Estep
1967	John Fort and Don Lutz
1968	Robert McKinley and Richard Stockton
1969	Brian Gottfried and Richard Stockton
1970	Brian Gottfried and Alex Mayer, Jr.
1971	James Delaney and John Whitlinger

USLTA INDOOR CHAMPIONS—BOYS' 16 SINGLES

1962	Cliff Richey
1963	Chuck Brainard
1964	Jasjit Singh
1965	Jeff Borowiak
1966	George Taylor
1967	Richard Stockton
1968	Robert Kreiss
1969	John Whitlinger
1970	John Whitlinger
1971	Kenneth Walts

USLTA INDOOR CHAMPIONS—BOYS' 16 DOUBLES

1962	Cliff Brown and Steve Stockton
1963	Chuck Brainard and John Towner
1964	Leo Estopare and Dan Oram
1965	Bob Alloo and Leo Estopare
1966	Robin Sandage and Jack Hughes
1967	Mike Machette and Richard Stockton
1968	Timmy Connors and Brian Gottfried
1969	Randall Schneider and Brian Teacher
1970	William Martin and Patrick Dupre
1971	William Martin and Trey Waltke

USLTA Indoor Champions—Girls' 18 Singles

The USLTA Indoor Girls' Championships were held in the late winter or early spring from the time of the first tournament in 1920 (with the exception of three years, 1921, 1922, and 1923, when the tournament was not held) up to and including 1930.

Instead of holding the next tournament in the spring of 1931 as customary, the tournament was held in December, 1930, during the Christmas holidays. Thus, two tournaments were held in the same year. Since and including 1930, the Indoor Girls' Championships have been held regularly in December. In 1969 the tournament was held Thanksgiving weekend.

1920	Martha Bayard
1921–23	not held
1924	Elizabeth Hilleary
1925	Alice C. Francis
1926	Marjorie Morrill
1927	Sarah Palfrey
1928	Sarah Palfrey
1929	Mianne Palfrey
1930	Katharine Winthrop
1930	Sarah Palfrey
1931	Katharine Winthrop
1932	Helen Grawn
1933	Millicent Hirsh
1934	Virginia Hollinger
1935	Virginia Hollinger
1936	Helen Bernhard
1937	Helen Bernhard
1938	Marguerita Madden
1939	Marguerita Madden
1940	Dorothy Wightman
1941	Lillian Lopaus
1942	Lillian Lopaus
1943	Shirley J. Fry
1944	Barbara Wilkins
1945	Barbara Wilkins
1946	Barbara Wilkins
1947	Laura Lou Jahn
1948	Laura Lou Jahn
1949	Elaine Lewicki
1950	Edith Ann Sullivan
1951	Elaine Lewicki
1952	Mary Slaughter
1953	June Stack
1954	June Stack
1955	Nancy O'Connell
1956	Nancy O'Connell
1957	Nancy O'Connell
1958	Bonnie Mencher
1959	Justina Bricka
1960	Sue Behlmar
1961	Alice B. Christer
1962	Yale Stockwell
1963	Yale Stockwell
1964	Carolyn Clarke
1965	Vicky Rogers
1966	Judy Dixon
1967	Andrea Voikos
1968	Andrea Voikos
1969	Linda Rupert
1970	Andrea Voikos
1971	Susan Stap

USLTA INDOOR CHAMPIONS—GIRLS' 18 DOUBLES

1926	Marjorie Morrill and Lee Palfrey
1927	Mianne Palfrey and Sarah Palfrey
1928	Mianne Palfrey and Sarah Palfrey
1929	Mianne Palfrey and Sarah Palfrey
1930	Hilda Boehm and Helen Boehm
1930	Sarah Palfrey and Joanna Palfrey
1931	Katharine Winthrop and Helen Jones

**USLTA Indoor Champions—Girls' 18
Doubles (cont.)**

1932	Louise Harding and Marion Wood
1933	Millicent Hirsh and Helen Grawn
1934	Virginia Hollinger and Helen Bernhard
1935	Virginia Hollinger and Helen Bernhard
1936	Helen Bernhard and Virginia Kollinger
1937	Helen Bernhard and Dorothy Wightman
1938	Helen Bernhard and Dorothy Wightman
1939	Marguerita Madden and Dorothy Wightman
1940	Lillian Lopaus and Betty Rosenquest
1941	Lillian Lopaus and Betty Rosenquest
1942	Judy Atterbury and Norma Meister
1943	Shirley J. Fry and Norma Meister
1944	Mary DeYoung and Jean Pipes
1945	Sylvia Knowles and Nina Irwin
1946	Barbara Wilkins and Anne Wofford
1947	Laura Lou Jahn and Adrienne Goldberg
1948	Laura Jahn and Mrs. A. Goldbert Ayares
1949	Elaine Lewicki and Edith Ann Sullivan
1950	Elaine Lewicki and Bonnie MacKay
1951	Susan Bralower and Elaine Lewicki
1952	Belmar Gunderson and Mary Slaughter
1953	Patricia Sullivan and Carroll Wendell
1954	Lorraine Jake and June Stack
1955	Virginia Connolly and Nancy O'Connell
1956	Donna Floyd and Nancy O'Connell
1957	Nancy O'Connell and Virginia Hesse
1958	Susan Behlmar and Bonnie Mencher
1959	Justina Bricka and Susan Behlmar
1960	Susan Behlmar and Heidi Lincoln
1961	Virginia Gilbane and Joanne Swanson
1962	Duane Horan and Joanne Swanson
1963	Yale Stockwell and Roberta Zimman
1964	Carolyn Clarke and Susan Mabrey
1965	Carolyn Clarke and Charlotte Atwater
1966	Evelyn Haase and Bonnie Logan
1967	Connie Capozzi and Marjorie Gengler
1968–69	not held
1970	Karin Benson and Andrea Voikos
1971	Claude Smith and Andrea Voikos

**USLTA INDOOR CHAMPIONS—GIRLS' 16
SINGLES**

1962	Yale Stockwell
1963	Marilyn Aschner
1964	Carolyn Clarke
1965	Vicki Rogers
1966	Andrea Voikos
1967	Andrea Voikos
1968	Andrea Voikos
1969	Clare Schmoyer
1970	Susan Pritula
1971	Gretchen Galt

**USLTA INDOOR CHAMPIONS—GIRLS' 16
DOUBLES**

1962	Debbie King and Gery Wolf
1963–64	not held
1965	Hannabeth Jackson and Jade Schiffman
1966–69	not held
1970	Una Keyes and Claudia Smith
1971	Nancy Anderson and Leslie Vyce

**USLTA INDOOR CHAMPIONS—MEN SENIORS'
SINGLES**

1951	Karl Hodge
1952	Willard Roeder
1953	John E. Sisson
1954	not held
1955	R. Philip Hanna
1956	Reginald S. Weir
1957	Reginald S. Weir
1958	Gardnar Mulloy
1959	Reginald S. Weir
1960	Gardnar Mulloy
1961	C. D. Steele, Jr.
1962	George H. Ball
1963	Gardnar Mulloy
1964	Julius Heldman
1965	Julius Heldman
1966	Robert Galloway
1967	Emery Neale
1968	Robert Sherman
1969	Robert Sherman
1970	Robert Sherman
1971	Ed Doane

**USLTA INDOOR CHAMPIONS—MEN SENIORS'
DOUBLES**

1951	Monte Ganger and Karl Hodge
1952	John English and Willard Roeder
1953	John E. Sisson and Arthur LeVan Zerbe
1954	not held
1955	Edwards Jacobs and C. Alphonso Smith
1956	R. Berkeley Bell and R. Philip Hanna
1957	R. Berkeley Bell and R. Philip Hanna
1958	R. Berkeley Bell and Edgar B. Nye
1959	Gardnar Mulloy and M. H. Robineau
1960	Robert Hagey and Frank A. Thompson, Jr.
1961	George H. Ball and Reginald Weir
1962	George H. Ball and Reginald Weir
1963	Gardnar Mulloy and William Talbert
1964	George MacCall and Al Martini
1965	Randolph Gregson and Frank Thompson
1966	Robert Galloway and Robert Hagey
1967	Samuel Lee and Emery Neale
1968	Robert Freedman and Robert Sherman
1969	Emery Neale and Robert Sherman
1970	Butch Krikorian and Joseph Woolfson
1971	Robert Sherman and Richard Metteer

**USLTA INDOOR CHAMPIONS—MEN'S 35
SINGLES**

1967	Mike Oberlander
1968	Vladmir Petrovic
1969	S. L. Shafner
1970	Dell Sylvia
1971	Jim Ladin

**USLTA INDOOR CHAMPIONS—MEN'S 35
DOUBLES**

1967	Eldon Rowe and Don White

1968   Whitney Reed and Steven Voydat
1969   Ollie Gresham and S. L. Shafner
1970   John Been and Richard Schuette
1971   Sam Park and Ed. Kauder

USLTA INDOOR CHAMPIONS—MEN SENIORS' 55 SINGLES

1966   Bryan M. Grant
1967   Robert Shepherd
1968   Bill Lurie
1969   Chauncey Steele, Jr.
1970   Chauncey Steele, Jr.
1971   William Smith

USLTA INDOOR CHAMPIONS—MEN SENIORS' 55 DOUBLES

1966   N. E. Powel and Len Prosser
1967   N. E. Powel and Len Prosser
1968   Gardnar Mulloy and C. Alphonso Smith
1969   Bitsy Grant and Henry Crawford
1970   Len Prosser and Henry Crawford
1971   Robin Hippenstiel and Verne Hughes

USLTA INDOOR CHAMPIONS—MEN SENIORS' 60 SINGLES

1967   Kenneth Beer
1968   Kenneth Beer
1969   C. Alphonso Smith
1970   Len Prosser
1971   N. E. Powel

USLTA INDOOR CHAMPIONS—MEN SENIORS' 60 DOUBLES

1967   Robert Abnot and Les Wanee
1968   Edward G. Chandler and Gerald Stratford
1969   Edward Chandler and Gerald Statford
1970   Len Prosser and Charles Brooke
1971   Len Prosser and N. E. Powel

USLTA INDOOR CHAMPIONS—MEN SENIORS' 65 SINGLES

1968   Carl Busch
1969   Ken Beer
1970   Tom Sherburne
1971   Frank Goeltz

USLTA INDOOR CHAMPIONS—MEN SENIORS' 65 DOUBLES

1968   Carl Busch and Joe Ciano
1969   Joe Ciano and Carl Busch
1970   Edward Chandler and Gerald Statford
1971   Frank Goeltz and Ted Wellman

USLTA INDOOR CHAMPIONS—MEN SENIORS' 70 SINGLES

1970   Frank G. Roberts
1971   Joseph T. Ciano

USLTA INDOOR CHAMPIONS—MEN SENIORS' 70 DOUBLES

1970   Frank G. Roberts and Bryan Hamlin
1971   Joseph T. Ciano and Clarke Kaye

USLTA INDOOR CHAMPIONS—WOMEN SENIORS' SINGLES

1970   Mrs. June E. Gay
1971   Dodo Cheney

USLTA INDOOR CHAMPIONS—WOMEN SENIORS' DOUBLES

1970   Mrs. June E. Gay and Rhoda Herron
1971   Barbara Hultgren and S. Fuller

USLTA INDOOR CHAMPIONS—SENIORS' MIXED DOUBLES

1969   C. Alphonso Smith and Sarah Danzig
1970   Kitty Prince and Charles Brooke
1971   Dodo Cheney and C. Alphonso Smith

USLTA HARD COURT CHAMPIONS—MEN'S SINGLES

1948   Frederick R. Schroeder, Jr.
1949   Frederick R. Schroeder, Jr.
1950   Arthur Larsen
1951   Frederick R. Schroeder, Jr.
1952   Arthur Larsen
1953   Tony Trabert
1954   Gilbert J. Shea
1955   Herbert Flam
1956   Alejandro Olmedo
1957   Thomas P. Brown, Jr.
1958   Thomas P. Brown, Jr.
1959   Ramanathan Krishnan
1960   Whitney Reed
1961   Allen E. Fox
1962   Rafael Osuna
1963   Arthur Ashe
1964   Dennis Ralston
1965   Dennis Ralston
1966   Stan Smith
1967   Stan Smith
1968   Stan Smith
1969   Clark Graebner
1970   not held
1971   Robert Lutz

USLTA HARD COURT CHAMPIONS—MEN'S DOUBLES

1948   F. R. Schroeder, Jr. and E. Victor Seixas, Jr.
1949   Frederick R. Schroeder, Jr. and Eric Sturgess
1950   Thomas P. Brown, Jr. and Tony Trabert
1951   Jerry DeWitts and Harry Likas
1952   Thomas P. Brown, Jr. and Arthur D. Larsen

USLTA Hard Court Champions—Men's Doubles (cont.)

1953 Thomas P. Brown, Jr. and Tony Trabert
1954 William Crosby and Robert T. Perez
1955 Early Baumgardner and Hugh Stewart
1956 Noel Brown and Gilbert J. Shea
1957 Myron J. Franks and Alejandro Olmedo
1958 Noel Brown and Hugh Stewart
1959 Ramanathan Krishnan and Hugh Stewart
1960 Chris Crawford and Whitney Reed
1961 Wm. Hoogs, Jr. and James McManus
1962 Ramsey Earnhart and Rafael Osuna
1963 William Bond and Tom Edlefsen
1964 Dennis Ralston and William Bond
1965 Tom Edlefsen and Dennis Ralston
1966 Robert Lutz and Stan Smith
1967 Jim McManus and Jim Osborne
1968 Richard Leach and Rafael Osuna
1969 Robert Lutz and Erik Van Dillen
1970 not held
1971 Jim McManus and Jim Osborne

USLTA HARD COURT CHAMPIONS—WOMEN'S SINGLES

1948 Gertrude Moran
1949 Doris Hart
1950 Mrs. Patricia C. Todd
1951 Mrs. Patricia C. Todd
1952 Mrs. Mary A. Prentiss
1953 Anita Kanter
1954 Mrs. Beverly B. Fleitz
1955 Miriam Arnold
1956 Mrs. Nancy C. Kiner
1957 Mrs. Beverly B. Fleitz

Among her many titles, Rosemary Casals holds the 1965 Hardcourt championship.

1958 Mrs. Beverly B. Fleitz
1959 Sandra Reynolds
1960 Katherine D. Chabot
1961 Nancy Richey
1962 Carol Hanks
1963 Darlene Hard
1964 Kathy Harter
1965 Rosemary Casals
1966 Mrs. Billie J. King
1967 Jane Bartkowicz
1968 Maryna Godwin
1969 Eliza Pande
1970 not held
1971 not held

USLTA HARD COURT CHAMPIONS—WOMEN'S DOUBLES

1948 A. Louise Brough and Mrs. M. O. du Pont
1949 Mrs. Virginia Kovacs and Gertrude Moran
1950 Mrs. Pat Todd and Barbara Scofield
1951 Anita Kanter and Julia Sampson
1952 Mrs. M. Arnold Prentiss and Julia Sampson
1953 Barbara Lum and Doris Popple
1954 Mrs. Dorothy B. Cheney and Darlene R. Hard
1955 Mrs. Gracyn W. Kelleher and Mrs. Patricia C. Todd
1956 Mrs. Nancy C. Kiner and Mrs. Patricia C. Todd
1957 Mrs. Beverly B. Fleitz and Mrs. Patricia C. Todd
1958 Sally M. Moore and Gwyneth Thomas
1959 Sandra Reynolds and Renée Schuurman
1960 Carole A. Caldwell and Katherine D. Chabot
1961 Mrs. D. H. Knode and Mrs. M. A. Prentiss
1962 Marilyn Montgomery and Mrs. J. Hopps Adkisson
1963 Darlene Hard and Paulette Verzin
1964 Mimi Arnold and Barbara Benigni
1965 Kathy Harter and Sue Shrader
1966 Rosemary Casals and Mrs. Billie J. M. King
1967 Stephanie Grant and Valerie Ziegenfuss
1968 Patti Hogan and Maryna Godwin
1969 Pam Austin and Tam O'Shaugnessy
1970 not held
1971 not held

USLTA HARD COURT CHAMPIONS—MIXED DOUBLES

1948 Mrs. M. Osborne du Pont and Thomas P. Brown, Jr.
1949 Doris Hart and Eric Sturgess
1950 Mrs. Magda Rurac and Arnold Beisser
1951 Anita Kanter and Whitney Reed
1952 Julia Ann Sampson and Hugh Stewart
1953 not held
1954 Mrs. Patricia C. Todd and William Crosby
1955 Mrs. Patricia C. Todd and Gardnar Mulloy
1956 Mrs. Patricia C. Todd and Gardnar Mulloy
1957 Sally M. Moore and Michael G. Davies
1958 Sally M. Moore and Hugh Stewart
1959 Sandra Reynolds and Whitney Reed
1960 Carole A. Caldwell and Chris Crawford
1961 Mrs. M. A. Prentiss and Richard Leach
1962 Carol Hanks and James McManus
1963 Darlene Hard and Hugh Stewart

1964 not held
1965 not held
1966 Rosemary Casals and Ian Crookenden
1967 Kristy Pigeon and William Demas
1968 Mrs. Dorothy Cheney and Richard Leach
1969 Sharon Walsh and Mike Machette
1970 not held
1971 not held

USLTA HARD COURT CHAMPIONS—JUNIOR SINGLES

1946 Hugh Stewart
1947 Lorne Main
1948 Jerry DeWitts
1949 Hamilton Richardson
1950 Fred Hagist
1951 Herschel Hyde
1952 Mike Franks
1953 Franklin Johnson
1954 Dale Junta
1955 Gregory Grant
1956 Roger Werksman
1957 Joseph Cowley
1958 Thomas Edlefsen
1959 Dennis Ralston
1960 Paul Palmer
1961 Gary Rose
1962 Jerry Cromwell
1963 Gary Rose
1964 Stan Smith
1965 Stephen Avoyer
1966 Stephen Avoyer
1967 Jeff Borowiak
1968 F. D. Robbins
1969 Roscoe Tanner
1970 Jim Connors
1971 Raul Ramirez

USLTA HARD COURT CHAMPIONS—JUNIOR DOUBLES

1946 Hugh Stewart and Vincent Schneider
1947 Matt Murphy and Jerry DeWitts
1948 Jerry DeWitts and Ernest duBray
1949 Robert Perry and Reynolds McCabe
1950 Norman Peterson and Jacque Grigry
1951 Herschel Hyde and Cliff Mayne
1952 John Lesch and Alan Call
1953 Brooke Grant and Franklin Johnson
1954 Earl Baumgardner and Dick Peters
1955 Edward Atkinson and Robert Delgado
1956 Chris Crawford and George Stoesser
1957 Michael Crane and Rudy Hernando
1958 Michael Crane and Michael Farrel
1959 Dennis Ralston and Ramsey Earnhart
1960 Paul Palmer and Henry Kamakana
1961 Rodney Kop and James Osborne
1962 Jeff Brown and Dean Penero
1963 John Tidball and Steve Tidball
1964 Jim Hobson and Steve Tidball
1965 Marcelo Lara and Jasjit Singh
1966 Stephen Avoyer and Don Lutz
1967 Jeff Borowiak and Erik Van Dillen
1968 Richard Stockton and Erik Van Dillen

1969 Brian Gotfried and Roscoe Tanner
1970 Jim Connors and Bob Kreiss
1971 James Hagey and Raul Ramirez

USLTA HARD COURT CHAMPIONS—BOYS' 16 SINGLES

1962 Jeff Brown
1963 Carlos Carriedo
1964 Jim Rombeau
1965 Zan Guerry
1966 Erik Van Dillen
1967 Mike Kreiss
1968 Brian Gottfried
1969 Chico Hagey
1970 John Whitlinger
1971 William Martin

USLTA HARD COURT CHAMPIONS—BOYS' 16 DOUBLES

1962 Jeff Brown and Dean Penero
1963 Roy Barth and Robert Lutz
1964 Jim Rombeau and Jim Davidson
1965 Zan Guerry and Don Lutz
1966 Richard Bohrnstedt and Randy Verdieck
1967 Jeff Austin and Tim Ott
1968 Jim Connors and Brian Gottfried
1969 John Burrman and Jeff Cowan
1970 Steve Mott and Brian Teacher
1971 Steward Keller and Bruce Nichols

USLTA HARD COURT CHAMPIONS—BOYS' 14 SINGLES

1962 Steve Turpin
1963 Don Lutz
1964 Richard Bohrnstedt
1965 Erik Van Dillen
1966 Randy Thomas
1967 Bob Kreiss
1968 Jake Warde
1969 Bruce Nichols
1970 Tom Kreiss
1971 Matt Mitchell

USLTA HARD COURT CHAMPIONS—BOYS' 14 DOUBLES

1962 Stephen Fiske and James Rombeau
1963 Mac Claflin and Paul Marienthal
1964 Bud Bioun and Rick Ellsworth
1965 Clyde LeBaron and Dan Chadbourne
1966 James Hagey and Kent Woodard
1967 James Hagey and Bob Kreiss
1968 Stephen Mott and Bruce Nichols
1969 William Maze and Michael Nissley
1970 Drew Sweet and Ferdi Taygen
1971 Don Paulsen and Walter Redondo

USLTA HARD COURT CHAMPIONS—BOYS' 12 SINGLES

1962 Mac Claflin
1963 Erik Van Dillen

USLTA Hard Court Champions—Boys' 12 Singles (cont.)

1964	Randall Thomas
1965	Jake Warde
1966	Jake Warde
1967	Ken Walts
1968	William Maze
1969	Howard Schoenfield
1970	Walter Redondo
1971	Jeff Robbins

USLTA HARD COURT CHAMPIONS—BOYS' 12 DOUBLES

1962	Mac Claflin and Erik Van Dillen
1963	Barry Laing and Ronnie Marston
1964	Steve Derian and James Hagey
1965	James Hagey and Jake Warde
1966	Dave Sherbeck and Brian Teacher
1967	William Maze and Dave Sherbeck
1968	Tom Kreiss and William Maze
1969	Matt Mitchell and Jeff Robinson
1970	Don Paulsen and Walter Redondo
1971	James Curley and Eliot Teltscher

USLTA HARD COURT CHAMPIONS—GIRLS' 18 SINGLES

1922	Carolyn Swartz
1923	Avery Follett
1924	Edith Cross
1925	Dorothea Swartz
1926	Dorothea Swartz
1927	Louise McFarland
1928	Dorothy Weisel
1929	Charlotte Miller
1930	Helen Marlowe
1931	Alice Marble
1932	Gracyn Wheeler
1933	Claire Buckner
1934	Gussie Raegener
1935	Margaret Osborne
1936	Eleanor Dawson
1937	Margaret Jessee
1938	Patricia Canning
1939	Patricia Canning
1940	Shirley Catton
1941	Barbara Krase
1942	Shirley Catton
1943	Dorothy Head
1944	E. Louise Snow
1945	Nancy Chaffee
1946	Helen Pastall
1947	Beverly Baker
1948	Laura Lou Jahn
1949	Anita Kanter
1950	Diane Kostial
1951	Mary Ann Eilenberger
1952	Patricia Naud
1953	Patricia Naud
1954	Barbara Benigni
1955	Mary Ann Mitchell
1956	Sally M. Moore
1957	Sally M. Moore
1958	Barbara Benigni
1959	Victoria Palmer
1960	Victoria Palmer
1961	Jean Danilovich
1962	Jane Albert
1963	Kathy Harter
1964	Rosemary Casals
1965	Rosemary Casals
1966	Pixie Lamm
1967	Roylee Bailey
1968	Denise Carter
1969	Marcelyn Louie
1970	Eliza Pande
1971	Laurie Tenney

USLTA HARD COURT CHAMPIONS—GIRLS' 18 DOUBLES

1927	Betty Fitch and Margaret Smith
1928	Violet Doeg and Doris Doeg
1929	Ida Cross and Alice Marble
1930	Marian Hunt and Alice Marble
1931	Katherine Wood and Gracyn Wheeler
1932	Bonnie Miller and May Doeg
1933	Gussie Raegener and Margaret Osborne
1934	Margaret Osborne and Gussie Raegener
1935	Jane Stanton and Patricia Henry
1936	Janet Hartzell and Patsy Hiller
1937	Patricia Canning and Barbara Duncan
1938	Patricia Canning and Barbara Duncan
1939	Daphne Buckell and Dorothy Buckell
1940	Helen Gurley and Dorothy Head
1941	Barbara Krase and Shirley Catton
1942	Dorothy Head and Barbara Scofield
1943	Dorothy Head and Barbara Scofield
1944	E. Louise Snow and Jean E. Doyle
1945	Nancy Chaffee and Margaret Varner
1946	Nancy Chaffee and Katherine Smith
1947	Beverly Baker and Marjorie McCord
1948	Marjorie McCord and Bea Springer
1949	Mariane Hertel and Mihan Rumwell
1950	Gertrude Beall and Joan Merciadis
1951	Mary Ann Eilenberger and Linda Mitchell
1952	Jacquelyn Halleck and Lynn Wall
1953	Pat Naud and Mardel Railey
1954	Elspeth Bennett and Lynn Wall
1955	Audrey Arnold and Linda Vail
1956	Barbara Benigni and Mary Thompson
1957	Barbara Benigni and Farel Footman
1958	Barbara Benigni and Farel Footman
1959	Barbara Browning and Pam Davis
1960	Victoria Palmer and Laurie Callaway
1961	Jan Conroy and Andria Miller
1962	Rosemary Casals and Gloria Segerquist
1963	Kathy Harter and Kathy Blake
1964	Rosemary Casals and Toni Alford
1965	Lynne Abbes and Valerie Ziegenfuss
1966	Lynne Abbes and Valerie Ziegenfuss
1967	Gail Hansen and Debbie John
1968	Denise Carter and Pam Richmond
1969	Ann Lebedeff and Tam O'Shaugnessy
1970	Janet Newberry and Eliza Pande
1971	Ann Kiyomura and Jane Stratton

USLTA HARD COURT CHAMPIONS—GIRLS' 16 SINGLES

1962	Jane Albert
1963	Lynne Abbes

1964 Lynne Abbes
1965 Peggy Michel
1966 Kristy Pigeon
1967 Marcelyn Louie
1968 Marcelyn Louie
1969 Eliza Pande
1970 Ann Kiyomura
1971 Laurie Tenney

USLTA HARD COURT CHAMPIONS—GIRLS' 16
DOUBLES

1962 Kathleen Blake and Kathy Harter
1963 Margaret Fredericks and Wendy Overton
1964 Paulette Verzin and Robyn Berrey
1965 Stephanie Grant and Lea Trumbull
1966 Kris Kemmer and Ann Lebedeff
1967 Patty Reese and Cindy Thomas
1968 Whitney Grant and Karen Demmer
1969 Barbara Downs and Ann Kiyomura
1970 Barbara Downs and Ann Kiyomura
1971 Vicki Jensen and Kathy May

USLTA HARD COURT CHAMPIONS—GIRLS' 14
SINGLES

1962 Rosemary Casals
1963 Lynne Abbes
1964 Pam Teeguarden
1965 Pam Teeguarden
1966 Kris Kemmer
1967 Marcelyn Louie
1968 Barbara Downs
1969 Ann Kiyomura
1970 Vickie Jensen
1971 Susan Mehmedbasich

USLTA HARD COURT CHAMPIONS—GIRLS' 14
DOUBLES

1962 Kristen Stewart and Pixie Lamm
1963 Patti Hogan and Margaret Michel
1964 Stephanie Grant and Lea Trumbull
1965 Gaye Harris and Teresa Thomas
1966 Marcelyn Louie and Karin Benson
1967 Whitney Grant and Janet Newberry
1968 Ann Kiyomura and Janet Thomas
1969 Kathy May and Gretchen Galt
1970 Kathy May and Vickie Jensen
1971 Susan Mehmedbasich and Susan Zaro

USLTA HARD COURT CHAMPIONS—GIRLS' 12
SINGLES

1962 Pamela Teeguarden
1963 Gail Hansen
1964 Marcelyn Louie
1965 Marcelyn Louie
1966 Barbara Downs
1967 Ann Kiyomura
1968 Kathy May
1969 Susan Mehmedbasich
1970 Tobin Tenney
1971 Lea Antonopolis

USLTA HARD COURT CHAMPIONS—GIRLS' 12
DOUBLES

1962 Pamela Teeguarden and Jane Miller
1963 Karin Benson and Cindy Bridges
1964 Marcelyn Louie and Karin Benson
1965 Whitney Grant and Marcelyn Louie
1966 Anita May and Lori Sherbeck
1967 Sue Boyle and Ann Kiyomura
1968 Gretchen Galt and Kathy May
1969 Susan Mehmedbasich and Susan Zaro
1970 Susan Hagey and Susan Wight
1971 Dana Gilbert and Moreen Lorie

USLTA HARD COURT CHAMPIONS—FATHER
AND SON

1959 Guadalupe and Robert Delgado
1960 H. William and William Bond
1961 H. William and William Bond
1962 Robert and R. Dennis Ralston
1963 H. William and William Bond
1964 Frank A. Jr. and Frank A. Froehling III
1965 George and Steven Meyerson
1966 H. William and William Bond
1967 H. William and William Bond
1968 Glenn E. and Gary Hippenstiel
1969 W. E. and William Canning
1970 Robert and James Hagey
1971 Robert and James Hagey

USLTA HARD COURT CHAMPIONS—MEN
SENIORS' SINGLES

1948 John Murio
1949 John Murio
1950 George Rice
1951 not held
1952 Mel Dranga
1953 William A. Maxwell
1954 John E. Sisson
1955 Edgar D. Yeomans
1956 John E. Sisson
1957 Edgar D. Yeomans
1958 Gardnar Mulloy
1959 J. Hal Surface, Jr.
1960 William Lurie
1961 William Lurie
1962 C. D. Steele, Jr.
1963 Gardnar Mulloy
1964 Robert L. Galloway
1965 Robert V. Sherman
1966 Emery W. Neale
1967 Emery W. Neale
1968 Emery W. Neale
1969 Thomas Brown, Jr.
1970 Thomas Brown, Jr.
1971 Robert L. Riggs

USLTA HARD COURT CHAMPIONS—MEN
SENIORS' DOUBLES

1948 Earl Ehlers and Eli H. Bashor
1949 William Catton and Edwin McCord
1950 George Rice and Herschel Hyde

USLTA Hard Court Champions—Men Seniors' Doubles (cont.)

1951	not held
1952	James Hodgkins and Edward Leonard
1953	Mel Gallagher and William A. Maxwell
1954	Alan Herrington and John E. Sisson
1955	Alan Herrington and John E. Sisson
1956	Alan Herrington and John E. Sisson
1957	Edward G. Chandler and Gerald Stratford
1958	Robert J. Kelleher and Elbert R. Lewis
1959	Robert J. Kelleher and Elbert R. Lewis
1960	Robert J. Kelleher and Elbert R. Lewis
1961	H. William Bond and C. D. Steele, Jr.
1962	Robert J. Kelleher and Elbert R. Lewis
1963	Gardnar Mulloy and Alphonso Smith
1964	George MacCall and Al Martini
1965	Robert J. Freedman and Robert V. Sherman
1966	Emery Neale and Chauncey D. Steele, Jr.
1967	Robert L. Galloway and David E. Martin
1968	Robert L. Galloway and David E. Martin
1969	Emery Neale and Robert L. Riggs
1970	Sam Match and Robert L. Riggs
1971	Ron Dunas and Pancho Segura

USLTA HARD COURT CHAMPIONS—WOMEN SENIORS' SINGLES

1953	Mrs. Marion Raful
1954	Mrs. Gracyn W. Kelleher
1955	Mrs. Gracyn W. Kelleher
1956	Mrs. Mary A. Prentiss
1957	Mrs. Dorothy B. Cheney
1958	Mrs. Dorothy B. Cheney
1959	Mrs. Dorothy B. Cheney
1960	Mrs. Dorothy B. Cheney
1961	Mrs. Dorothy B. Cheney
1962	Mrs. Dorothy B. Cheney
1963	Mrs. Dorothy B. Cheney
1964	Mrs. Dorothy B. Cheney
1965	Mrs. Dorothy B. Cheney
1966	Mrs. Dorothy B. Cheney
1967	Mrs. Dorothy B. Cheney
1968	Mrs. Dorothy B. Cheney
1969	Mrs. Dorothy B. Cheney
1970	Mrs. Nancy A. Neeld
1971	Mrs. Barbara Weigandt

USLTA HARD COURT CHAMPIONS—WOMEN SENIORS' DOUBLES

1953	Dorothy DeVries and Florence D. Nebauer
1954	Mrs. Gracyn W. Kelleher and Mrs. Marion Raful
1955	Mrs. Gracyn W. Kelleher and Mrs. Gretl Dupont
1956	Mrs. Gracyn W. Kelleher and Mrs. Estelle Kristenson
1957	Mrs. Dorothy B. Cheney and Mrs. Janet Robbins
1958	Mrs. Gracyn W. Kelleher and Mrs. Mary Arnold Prentiss
1959	Mrs. Gracyn W. Kelleher and Mrs. Mary Arnold Prentiss
1960	Mrs. Gracyn W. Kelleher and Mrs. Mary Arnold Prentiss
1961	Mrs. Gracyn W. Kelleher and Mrs. Mary Arnold Prentiss
1962	Mrs. Gracyn W. Kelleher and Mrs. Mary Arnold Prentiss
1963	Mrs. Dorothy B. Cheney and Mrs. Mary Arnold Prentiss
1964	Mrs. Dorothy B. Cheney and Mrs. Helen McDowell
1965	Mrs. Dorothy B. Cheney and Mrs. Helen McDowell
1966	Mrs. Gracyn W. Kelleher and Mrs. Mary Arnold Prentiss
1967	Mrs. Gracyn W. Kelleher and Mrs. Mary Arnold Prentiss
1968	Mrs. Dorothy B. Cheney and Mrs. June E. Gay
1969	Mrs. Dorothy B. Cheney and Mrs. June E. Gay
1970	Mrs. Gracyn W. Kelleher and Mrs. Mary Arnold Prentiss
1971	Mrs. Louise B. Clapp and Mrs. Barbara G. Weigandt

USLTA HARD COURT CHAMPIONS—SENIORS' MIXED DOUBLES

1955	Mrs. Gracyn Kelleher and A. D. Herrington
1956	Mrs. Mary A. Prentiss and Joseph T. Ciano
1957	Mrs. Gracyn W. Kelleher and Jack Tidball
1958	Mr. and Mrs. Robert J. Kelleher
1959	Mrs. Janet Robbins and Clifford Robbins
1960	Mr. and Mrs. Robert J. Kelleher
1961	Mrs. Helen Watanabe and Verne Guertin
1962	Mrs. Mary A. Prentiss and Len Prosser
1963	Mrs. Corky Olerich and William Smith
1964	Mr. and Mrs. Robert J. Kelleher
1965	Mrs. Corky Olerich and Al Martini
1966	Mrs. Corky Olerich and Ralph E. Wyer
1967	Mrs. Phylis Adler and Merwin Miller
1968	Mrs. Dorothy B. Cheney and Vern Hughes
1969	Mrs. Dorothy B. Cheney and David Martin
1970	Mrs. A. Dalton and B. Press
1971	Mrs. Dorothy B. Cheney and Robert L. Riggs

USLTA HARD COURT CHAMPIONS—MEN'S 35 SINGLES

1959	Joseph Woolfson
1960	Joseph Woolfson
1961	Butch Krikorian
1962	Emery Neale
1963	Hugh Stewart
1964	Vladimir Petrovic
1965	Hugh Stewart
1966	Vladimir Petrovic
1967	Don Gale
1968	Clif Mayne
1969	Jacques Grigry
1970	Clif Mayne
1971	Don Kierbow

USLTA HARD COURT CHAMPIONS—MEN'S 35 DOUBLES

1959	Jack Bowker and John Williams
1960	Merwin Miller and George MacCall
1961	George MacCall and Merwin Miller
1962	George MacCall and Al Martini
1963	Emery Neale and Merwin Miller
1964	Clint Arbuckle and Joe Woolfson

1965   Don Gale and Butch Krikorian
1966   Merill Ehmke and Milt Richardson
1967   Hugh Ditzler and Ed Kauder
1968   Don Gale and Butch Krikorian
1969   Ed Kauder and Jerry Dewitts
1970   Hugh Ditzler and Clif Mayne
1971   Don Kierbow and Whitney Reed

USLTA HARD COURT CHAMPIONS—MEN SENIORS' 50 SINGLES

1968   Charles Lass
1969   Ed Doane
1970   Robert Sherman
1971   Robert Sherman

USLTA HARD COURT CHAMPIONS—MEN SENIORS' 50 DOUBLES

1968   Ed Doane and Len Prosser
1969   Bob Galloway and Bob Hagey
1970   Merwin Miller and Don White
1971   Glenn Hippenstiel and Milt Richardson

USLTA HARD COURT CHAMPIONS—MEN SENIORS' 55 SINGLES

1964   C. Alphonso Smith
1965   C. Alphonso Smith
1966   Jack Staton
1967   N. E. Powel
1968   Eugene Short
1969   William Smith
1970   William Smith
1971   William Smith

USLTA HARD COURT CHAMPIONS—MEN SENIORS' 55 DOUBLES

1964   C. Alphonso Smith and Eddie Jacobs
1965   Clayton Burwell and C. Alphonso Smith
1966   Charles Brooke and Len Prosser
1967   N. E. Powel and Len Prosser
1968   Len Prosser and Vern Hughes
1969   Len Prosser and Vern Hughes
1970   Len Prosser and Vern Hughes
1971   G. Hippenstiel and Vern Hughes

USLTA HARD COURT CHAMPIONS—MEN SENIORS' 60 SINGLES

1966   Les Wanee
1967   Monte Ganger
1968   Kenneth Beer
1969   C. Alphonso Smith
1970   Jack Staton
1971   Francis Manis

USLTA HARD COURT CHAMPIONS—MEN SENIORS' 60 DOUBLES

1966   Bernard Clinton and Monte Granger
1967   Bernard Clinton and Monte Granger
1968   Bernard Clinton and Monte Granger
1969   Marshall Christopher and Monte Granger

1970   Charles Brooke and Jack Staton
1971   H. Hoff and Herschel Hyde

USLTA HARD COURT CHAMPIONS—MEN SENIORS' 65 SINGLES

1970   Ken Beer
1971   Bud Goltz

USLTA HARD COURT CHAMPIONS—MEN SENIORS' 65 DOUBLES

1970   M. Hawks and W. Westbrook
1971   Les Wanee and Stanley Maloney

USLTA HARD COURT CHAMPIONS—MEN SENIORS' 70 SINGLES

1970   Steve Graves
1971   Joseph T. Ciano

USLTA HARD COURT CHAMPIONS—MEN SENIORS' 70 DOUBLES

1970   Frank Roberts and Carl Busch
1971   Joseph T. Ciano and Clarke Kaye

USLTA HARD COURT CHAMPIONS—WOMEN'S 35 SINGLES

1970   Evelyn Hansen
1971   Diana Gai

USLTA HARD COURT CHAMPIONS—WOMEN'S 35 DOUBLES

1970   Charlene Grafton and Anita Kappe
1971   Mary A. Prentiss and Evelyn Houseman

USLTA HARD COURT CHAMPIONS—WOMEN SENIORS' 50 SINGLES

1970   Pat Yeomans
1971   Dodo Cheney

USLTA HARD COURT CHAMPIONS—WOMEN SENIORS' 50 DOUBLES

1970   Ruby Bixler and Pat Yeomans
1971   S. Fuller and Pat Mahoney

USLTA CLAY COURT CHAMPIONS—MEN'S SINGLES

1910   Melville H. Long
1911   Walter T. Hayes
1912   R. Norris Williams II
1913   John R. Strachan
1914   Clarence J. Griffin
1915   R. Norris Williams II
1916   Willis E. Davis
1917   Samuel Hardy
1918   William T. Tilden II

Emmett Paré was the 1929 National Clay Court Singles Champion.

USLTA Clay Court Champions—Men's Singles (*cont.*)

1919	William Johnston
1920	Roland Roberts
1921	Walter T. Hayes
1922	William T. Tilden II
1923	William T. Tilden II
1924	William T. Tilden II
1925	William T. Tilden II
1926	William T. Tilden II
1927	William T. Tilden II
1928	not held
1929	Emmett Paré
1930	Bryan M. Grant, Jr.
1931	H. Ellsworth Vines, Jr.
1932	George M. Lott, Jr.
1933	Frank Parker
1934	Bryan M. Grant, Jr.
1935	Bryan M. Grant, Jr.
1936	Robert L. Riggs
1937	Robert L. Riggs
1938	Robert L. Riggs
1939	Frank A. Parker
1940	Donald McNeill
1941	Frank A. Parker
1942	Seymour Greenberg
1943	Seymour Greenberg
1944	Francisco Segura
1945	William F. Talbert
1946	Frank A. Parker
1947	Frank A. Parker
1948	Richard A. Gonzalez
1949	Richard A. Gonzalez
1950	Herbert Flam
1951	Tony Trabert
1952	Arthur Larsen
1953	E. Victor Seixas, Jr.
1954	Bernard Bartzen
1955	Tony Trabert
1956	Herbert Flam
1957	E. Victor Seixas, Jr.
1958	Bernard Bartzen
1959	Bernard Bartzen
1960	Barry MacKay
1961	Bernard Bartzen
1962	Charles R. McKinley
1963	Charles R. McKinley
1964	Dennis Ralston
1965	Dennis Ralston
1966	Cliff Richey
1967	Arthur Ashe
1968	Clark Graebner
1969	Zeljko Franulovic
1970*	Cliff Richey
1971*	Zeljko Franulovic

USLTA CLAY COURT CHAMPIONS—MEN'S DOUBLES

1910	Fred G. Anderson and Walter T. Hayes
1911	J. Horner Winston and Hugh C. Whitehead
1912	Harold H. Hackett and W. Merrill Hall
1913	John R. Strachan and Clarence J. Griffin
1914	Nat Browne and Claude Wayne
1915	George M. Church and Dean Mathey
1916	George M. Church and Dean Mathey
1917	Charles S. Garland and Samuel Hardy
1918	Charles S. Garland and Samuel Hardy
1919	William Johnston and Samuel Hardy
1920	Vincent Richards and Roland Roberts
1921	Clifton B. Herd and Walter T. Hayes
1922	Ralph H. Burdick and Fred Bastian
1923	Howard Kinsey and Robert Kinsey
1924	Howard Kinsey and Robert Kinsey
1925	Harvey Snodgrass and Walter Wesbrook
1926	Lewis N. White and Louis Thalheimer
1927	John Hennessey and Lucien E. Williams
1928	not held
1929	J. Gilbert Hall and Frederic Mercur
1930	J. Gilbert Hall and Frederic Mercur
1931	H. Ellsworth Vines, Jr. and Keith Gledhill
1932	George M. Lott, Jr. and Bryan M. Grant, Jr.
1933	Jack Tidball and C. Gene Mako
1934	J. Donald Budge and C. Gene Mako
1935	J. Gilbert Hall and Berkeley Bell
1936	Robert L. Riggs and Wayne Sabin
1937	John McDiarmid and Eugene McCauliff

* Open champions.

1938	Joseph R. Hunt and Lewis Wetherell
1939	Frank Parker and C. Gene Mako
1940	Robert Harman and Robert C. Peacock
1941	John A. Kramer and F. R. Schroeder, Jr.
1942	William F. Talbert and William Reedy
1943	Earl Cochell and Robert Kimbrell
1944	Francisco Segura and William F. Talbert
1945	Francisco Segura and William F. Talbert
1946	William F. Talbert and Gardnar Mulloy
1947	Frederick R. Schroeder, Jr. and Jack Tuero
1948	Samuel Match and Tom Chambers
1949	E. Victor Seixas, Jr. and Samuel Match
1950	Herbert Flam and Arthur Larsen
1951	Hamilton Richardson and Tony Trabert
1952	Grant Golden and Arthur Larsen
1953	Bernard Bartzen and Grant Golden
1954	E. Victor Seixas, Jr. and Tony Trabert
1955	Hamilton Richardson and Tony Trabert
1956	Francisco Contreras and Alejandro Olmedo
1957	Ashley J. Cooper and Neale Fraser
1958	Samuel Giammalva and Barry MacKay
1959	Bernard Bartzen and Grant Golden
1960	Bob Hewitt and Martin Mulligan
1961	Charles McKinley and Dennis Ralston
1962	Ramsey Earnhart and Martin Riessen
1963	Clark Graebner and Martin Riessen
1964	Charles McKinley and Dennis Ralston
1965	Clark Graebner and Martin Riessen
1966	Clark Graebner and Dennis Ralston
1967	Clark Graebner and Martin Riessen
1968	Robert Lutz and Stan Smith
1969	Bill Bowrey and Clark Graebner
1970†	Arthur Ashe and Clark Graebner
1971†	Jan Kodes and Zeljko Franulovic

USLTA CLAY COURT CHAMPIONS—WOMEN'S SINGLES

1912	May Sutton
1913	not held
1914	Mary K. Brown
1915	Molla Bjurstedt
1916	Molla Bjurstedt
1917*	Ruth Sanders
1918	Carrie B. Neely
1919	Corinne Gould
1920	Marion Zinderstein
1921	Mrs. B. E. Cole
1922	Mrs. Lois Moyes Bickle
1923	Mayme MacDonald
1924–39	not held
1940	Alice Marble
1941	Pauline M. Betz
1942	not held
1943	Pauline M. Betz
1944	Dorothy M. Bundy
1945	Mrs. S. Palfrey Cooke
1946	Barbara Krase
1947	Mrs. Mary A. Prentiss
1948	Mrs. Magda Rurac
1949	Mrs. Magda Rurac
1950	Doris Hart
1951	Dorothy Head

* Patriotic Tournament without championship.
† Open champions.

1952	Anita Kanter
1953	Maureen Connolly
1954	Maureen Connolly
1955	Mrs. Dorothy H. Knode
1956	Shirley J. Fry
1957	Althea Gibson
1958	Mrs. Dorothy H. Knode
1959	Sally M. Moore
1960	Mrs. Dorothy H. Knode
1961	Edda Buding
1962	Donna Floyd
1963	Nancy Richey
1964	Nancy Richey
1965	Nancy Richey
1966	Nancy Richey
1967	Nancy Richey
1968	Nancy Richey
1969	Mrs. Gail S. Chanfreau
1970†	Linda Tuero
1971†	Mrs. Billie J. King

USLTA CLAY COURT CHAMPIONS—WOMEN'S DOUBLES

1914	Mary K. Brown and Mrs. Robert Williams
1915–16	not held
1917	Mrs. Charles Gregg and Ruth Sanders
1918	Bobbie Esch and Mrs. Ralph Fields
1919	Carrie Neely and Katherine Voorhees
1920	Eleanor Tennant and Florence Ballin
1921	not held
1922	Leslie Bancroft and Mrs. Frank Godfrey
1923	Edith Sigourney and Mrs. Ream Leachman
1924–39	not held
1940	Alice Marble and Mary Arnold
1941	Mrs. Jane S. Gallagher and Barbara Bradley
1942	not held
1943	Pauline M. Betz and Nancy Corbett
1944	Pauline M. Betz and Doris Hart
1945	Pauline M. Betz and Doris Hart
1946	Shirley Fry and Mrs. Mary Arnold Prentiss
1947	Mrs. Mary A. Prentiss and Gertrude Moran
1948–49	not held
1950	Shirley Fry and Doris Hart
1951	Mrs. Magda Rurac and Mrs. Pat C. Todd
1952	Mrs. Lucille Davidson and Doris Popple
1953	Anita Kanter and Mrs. Thelma Long
1954	Maureen Connolly and Doris Hart
1955	Mrs. Dorothy H. Knode and Janet Hopps
1956	Shirley J. Fry and Mrs. Dorothy H. Knode
1957	Althea Gibson and Darlene R. Hard
1958	Karol Fageros and Mrs. Dorothy H. Knode
1959	Sandra Reynolds and Renée Schuurman
1960	Darlene R. Hard and Billie Jean Moffitt
1961	Justina Bricka and Carol Hanks
1962	Darlene Hard and Susan Behlmar
1963	Maria Bueno and Darlene Hard
1964	Mrs. Carole C. Graebner and Nancy Richey
1965	Mrs. Carole C. Graebner and Nancy Richey
1966	Karen Krantzcke and Kerry Melville
1967	Karen Krantzcke and Kerry Melville
1968	Nancy Richey and Valerie Ziegenfuss
1969	Mrs. L. T. Bowrey and Mrs. G. S. Chanfreau

USLTA Clay Court Champions—Women's Doubles (cont.)

1970* Rosemary Casals and Mrs. G. S. Chanfreau
1971* Mrs. Billie J. King and Judy Dalton

USLTA AMATEUR CLAY COURT CHAMPIONS—MEN'S SINGLES

1970 Roscoe Tanner
1971 Harold Solomon

USLTA AMATEUR CLAY COURT CHAMPIONS—MEN'S DOUBLES

1970 Lito Alvarez and Modesta Vasquez
1971 Alex Mayer and Roscoe Tanner

USLTA AMATEUR CLAY COURT CHAMPIONS—WOMEN'S SINGLES

1970 Linda Tuero
1971 Janice Metcalf

USLTA AMATEUR CLAY COURT CHAMPIONS—WOMEN'S DOUBLES

1970 Pam Austin and Margaret Cooper
1971 Pam Farmer and Janice Metcalf

USLTA CLAY COURT CHAMPIONS—JUNIOR SINGLES

1923 George Lott
1924–66 not held
1967 Zan Guerry
1968 Bill Colson
1969 Danny Birchmore
1970 Harold Solomon
1971 John Whitlinger

USLTA CLAY COURT CHAMPIONS—JUNIOR DOUBLES

1967 Jeff Borowiak and Erik Van Dillen
1968 Paul Gerken and Ron Cornell
1969 Brian Gottfried and Roscoe Tanner
1970 John Whitlinger and Gary Groslimond
1971 not held

USLTA CLAY COURT CHAMPIONS—BOYS' 16 SINGLES

1967 Woody Blocher
1968 Gery Groslimond
1969 Fred DeJesus
1970 John Whitlinger
1971 William Martin

USLTA CLAY COURT CHAMPIONS—BOYS' 16 DOUBLES

1967 Woody Blocher and Richard Stockton
1968 Emilio Montano and Larry Loeb
1969 Fred DeJesus and John Whitlinger
1970 Gray King and Patrick Dupree
1971 Horace Reid and William Martin

* Open champions.

USLTA CLAY COURT CHAMPIONS—GIRLS' 18 SINGLES

1967 Linda Tuero
1968 Linda Tuero
1969 Kristen Kemmer
1970 Sue Stap
1971 Sue Stap

USLTA CLAY COURT CHAMPIONS—GIRLS' 18 DOUBLES

1967 Carol Hunter and Ginger Pfeiffer
1968 Whitney Grant and Kristen Kemmer
1969 Whitney Grant and Kristen Kemmer
1970 Nancy Ornstein and Kristen Kemmer
1971 Sandy Stap and Sue Stap

USLTA CLAY COURT CHAMPIONS—FATHER AND SON

1949 Kirk Reid, Sr. and Kirk Reid, Jr.
1950 Edward Kaiser and Donald Kaiser
1951 Everett Hicks and David Hicks
1952 Cecil Powless and John Powless
1953 Bernard Leightheiser and Bernard Leightheiser, Jr.
1954 Harry Hoffmann and Harry Hoffmann, Jr.
1955 Clarence E. Sledge and Clarence E. Sledge, Jr.
1956 Clarence E. Sledge and Clarence E. Sledge, Jr.
1957 Cecil Powless and John Powless
1958 Cecil Powless and John Powless
1959 Frank Froehling, Jr. and Frank Froehling III
1960 Ward Parker and Jimmy Parker
1961 Hugh Lynch, Jr. and Hugh Lynch III
1962 Ward Parker and Jim Parker
1963 Chauncey D. Steele, Jr. and Chauncey D. Steele III
1964 Harry Hoffmann and Harry Hoffmann, Jr.
1965 Fred McNair III and Fred McNair IV
1966 Alex Guerry and Zan Guerry
1967 Fred McNair III and Fred McNair IV
1968 Fred McNair III and Fred McNair IV
1969 Glenn Hippenstiel and Gary Hippenstiel
1970 Fred McNair III and Fred McNair IV
1971 Alex Guerry and Zan Guerry

USLTA CLAY COURT CHAMPIONS—MEN'S 35 SINGLES

1964 Tony Vincent
1965 Tony Vincent
1966 Tony Vincent
1967 Bob Barker
1968 Tony Vincent
1969 Gardnar Mulloy
1970 Paul Cranis
1971 King Van Nostrand

USLTA CLAY COURT CHAMPIONS—MEN'S 35 DOUBLES

1964 Tom Falkenburg and Nolan Touchstone

1965   Bill Tully and King Lambert
1966   Gardnar Mulloy and Tony Vincent
1967   Bob Barker and Bill Tully
1968   Sidney Schwartz and Tony Vincent
1969   Sidney Schwartz and Tony Vincent
1970   Paul Cranis and Ed Rubinoff
1971   Paul Cranis and Hamilton Richardson

USLTA CLAY COURT CHAMPIONS—MEN SENIORS' SINGLES

1946   Karl Hodge
1947   William L. Nassau
1948   Fritz Mercur
1949   L. F. Kruger
1950   Larry Simmons
1951   Mel Dranga
1952   Mel Dranga
1953   Knute Krassenstein
1954   Jack Staton
1955   Bryan M. Grant, Jr.
1956   Bryan M. Grant, Jr.
1957   Harry R. Hoffmann
1958   Gardnar Mulloy
1959   Bryan M. Grant, Jr.
1960   Bryan M. Grant, Jr.
1961   Bryan M. Grant, Jr.
1962   Chauncey D. Steele, Jr.
1963   Bryan M. Grant, Jr.
1964   Julius Heldman
1965   Robert V. Sherman
1966   George Ball
1967   Lou Schopfer
1968   Robert V. Sherman
1969   Lou Schopfer
1970   Gustavo Palafox
1971   Gustavo Palafox

USLTA CLAY COURT CHAMPIONS—MEN SENIORS' DOUBLES

1946   Kirk Reid and Martin Tressel
1947   Karl Hodge and Martin Tressel
1948   Fritz Mercur and Percy Kynaston
1949   William L. Nassau and L. F. Kruger
1950   John Woodall and W. F. Widen
1951   Bernard Clinton and John Hoff
1952   Bernard Clinton and John Hoff
1953   Sidney Adelstein and Victor Heuser
1954   John Dorr and Monte L. Ganger
1955   Mal C. Courts and Bryan M. Grant, Jr.
1956   David L. Freed and Leonard Prosser
1957   W. E. Hester, Jr. and Alex Wellford
1958   Len Prosser and Hal Surface
1959   C. Alphonso Smith and Hugh Lynch
1960   Bryan M. Grant, Jr. and Larry Shippey
1961   Bryan M. Grant, Jr. and Larry Shippey
1962   Bryan M. Grant, Jr. and Larry Shippey
1963   Bryan M. Grant, Jr. and Larry Shippey
1964   Frank Thompson and Randy Gregson
1965   Bryan M. Grant, Jr. and Larry Shippey
1966   Bryan M. Grant, Jr. and Larry Shippey
1967   Fred McNair III and Richard Sorlien
1968   Glenn Hippenstiel and Joseph Woolfson
1969   George Druliner and Bob Stuckert

1970   Jay Freedman and Gustavo Palafox
1971   Robert L. Riggs and Tony Vincent

USLTA CLAY COURT CHAMPIONS—MEN SENIORS' 50 SINGLES

1968   Gardnar Mulloy
1969   Gardnar Mulloy
1970   Robert L. Riggs
1971   Robert L. Riggs

USLTA CLAY COURT CHAMPIONS—MEN SENIORS' 50 DOUBLES

1968   Tom Bird and Bryan M. Grant, Jr.
1969   Bryan M. Grant, Jr. and Jack Rogers
1970   Robert L. Riggs and Chauncey D. Steele, Jr.
1971   Tom Bird and Henry Crawford

USLTA CLAY COURT CHAMPIONS—MEN SENIORS' 55 SINGLES

1964   C. Alphonso Smith
1965   Bryan M. Grant, Jr.
1966   Bryan M. Grant, Jr.
1967   Bryan M. Grant, Jr.
1968   Bryan M. Grant, Jr.
1969   Bryan M. Grant, Jr.
1970   Gardnar Mulloy
1971   Harry Hoffmann

USLTA CLAY COURT CHAMPIONS—MEN SENIORS' 55 DOUBLES

1964   Jack Staton and Jim Hodgkins
1965   Charles Brooke and Alphonso Smith
1966   Clayton Burwell and N. E. Powel
1967   W. E. Hester and Harry Hoffmann
1968   Gardnar Mulloy and C. Alphonso Smith
1969   Len Prosser and Harry Crawford
1970   Tom Bird and Larry Shippey
1971   Charles Swanson and Howard Sprague

USLTA CLAY COURT CHAMPIONS—MEN SENIORS' 60 SINGLES

1967   Ike Macy
1968   Emil Johnson
1969   Jack Staton
1970   Gene Short
1971   Bryan M. Grant, Jr.

USLTA CLAY COURT CHAMPIONS—MEN SENIORS' 60 DOUBLES

1967   Dave Freeborn and Monte Ganger
1968   Bernard Clinton and Monte Ganger
1969   Frank Goeltz and C. Alphonso Smith
1970   Frank Goeltz and C. Alphonso Smith
1971   Frank Goeltz and C. Alphonso Smith

USLTA CLAY COURT CHAMPIONS—MEN SENIORS' 65 SINGLES

1968   A. L. Enloe
1969   Bernard Clinton

USLTA Clay Court Champions—Men Seniors' 65 Singles (cont.)

1970	Tom Sherbourne
1971	Frank Goeltz

USLTA CLAY COURT CHAMPIONS—MEN SENIORS' 65 DOUBLES

1968	A. L. Enloe and Hobart Wrobbel
1969	A. L. Enloe and Bernard Clinton
1970	A. L. Enloe and Thomas Marshall
1971	Frank Goeltz and Ted Wellman

USLTA INTERSCHOLASTIC CHAMPIONS—MEN'S SINGLES

1891	R. D. Wrenn
1892	M. G. Chace
1893	C. R. Budlong
1894	W. C. Parker
1895	L. F. Ware
1896	Rex Fincke
1897	Rex Fincke
1898	B. C. Wright
1899	B. C. Wright
1900	B. C. Wright
1901	E. P. Larned
1902	H. H. Whitman
1903	K. H. Behr
1904	N. W. Niles
1905	N. W. Niles
1906	J. A. Ross
1907	W. F. Johnson
1908	Dean Mathey
1909	M. E. McLoughlin
1910	E. H. Whitney
1911	Geo. M. Church
1912	C. B. Herd
1913	G. C. Caner
1914	Leonard Beekman
1915	H. A. Throckmorton
1916–22	not held
1923	John F. W. Whitbeck
1924	Horace Orser
1925–35	not held
1936	Robert A. Low
1937	William Gillespie
1938	John A. Kramer
1939	Charles E. Olewine
1940	Robert D. Carrothers, Jr.
1941	E. Victor Seixas, Jr.
1942	Robert Falkenburg
1943	Charles W. Oliver
1944	Bernard Bartzen
1945	Herbert Flam
1946	Hugh Stewart
1947	Herbert Behrens
1948	Gilbert A. Bogley
1949	Keston Deimling
1950	Hamilton Richardson
1951	Herbert Browne
1952	Edward Rubinoff
1953	Mike Green
1954	Gregory Grant
1955	Crawford Henry
1956	Clarence Edward Sledge, Jr.
1957	Earl Buchholz, Jr.
1958	Raymond Senkowski
1959	William Lenoir
1960	William Lenoir
1961	Arthur Ashe
1962	Jackie Cooper
1963	Mike Belkin
1964	Bob Goeltz
1965	Bob Goeltz
1966	Bob Goeltz
1967	Zan Guerry
1968	Charles Owens
1969	Fred McNair
1970	Harold Solomon
1971	John Whitlinger

USLTA INTERSCHOLASTIC CHAMPIONS—MEN'S DOUBLES

1936	Robert A. Low and Henry H. Daniels
1937	M. C. Hooper and Bob Patterson
1938	Don Buffington and Wm. Gillespie
1939	Bill McMurry and Carl Mitchell
1940	E. Victor Seixas, Jr. and William T. Vogt
1941	Blair Hawley and John Moses
1942	Robert Falkenburg and Thomas Falkenburg
1943	Macdonald Mathey and Dean W. Mathey
1944	Macdonald Mathey and Dean W. Mathey
1945	F. Burton Smith and Dean W. Mathey
1946	Macdonald Mathey and Dean W. Mathey
1947	Herbert Behrens and George King
1948	Gilbert A. Bogley and Jack Yates
1949	Charles Atherton and Edward Dailey
1950	Gilmore Rothrock and Roger Young
1951	Tim Coss and Ted Rogers
1952	Gerald Moss and Edward Rubinoff
1953	David Harum and Edward White
1954	Jeffrey Arnold and Robert Macy
1955	Robert Macy and John Skogstad
1956	Richard Ogden and Edward Simmons
1957	Gerald Dubie and Raymond Senkowski
1958	Frank Froehling III and John Karabasz
1959	Frank Froehling III and John Karabasz
1960	William Lenoir and Hal Lowe
1961	Jackie Cooper and Martin Schad
1962	Jackie Cooper and Martin Schad
1963	Linn Foss and Richard Dell
1964	Bob Goeltz and Richard Dell
1965	Bob Goeltz and Richard Dell
1966	Mac Claflin and Bill Monan
1967	Zan Guerry and Tony Oritz
1968	Mac Claflin and Bill Colson
1969	Roscoe Tanner and David Dick
1970	Joe Garcia and David Dick
1971	William Brock and Hunt Harris

USLTA WOMEN'S COLLEGIATE CHAMPIONS—SINGLES

1958	Darlene R. Hard	Pomona
1959	Donna Floyd	William & Mary College
1960	Linda Vail	Oakland City College
1961	Tory Ann Fretz	Occidental College
1962	Roberta Alison	U. of Alabama
1963	Roberta Alison	U. of Alabama

1964	Jane Albert	Stanford		1968	Emilie Burrer	Trinity University
1965	Mimi Henreid	UCLA		1969	Emilie Burrer	Trinity University
1966	Cecilia Martinez	San Francisco State		1970	Laura DuPont	North Carolina
1967	Patsy Rippy	Odessa Junior College		1971	Pam Richmond	Arizona State

USLTA WOMEN'S COLLEGIATE CHAMPIONS—DOUBLES

1958	Sue Metzger and	St. Mary's Notre Dame
	Erika Puetz	Webster
1959	Joyce Pniewski and	Mich. State Univ.
	Phyllis Saganski	Mich. State Univ.
1960	Susan Butt and	Univ. of British Columbia
	Linda Vail	Oakland City College
1961	Tory Ann Fretz and	Occidental College
	Mary Sherar	Yakima Valley Jr. College
1962	Linda Yeomans and	Stanford
	Carol Hanks	Stanford
1963	Roberta Alison and	Univ. of Alabama
	Justina Bricka	Washington (Mo.) Univ.
1964	Connie Jaster and	California State at Los Angeles
	Carol Loop	California State at Los Angeles
1965	Nancy Falkenberg and	Mary Baldwin College
	Cynthia Goeltz	Mary Baldwin College
1966	Yale Stockwell and	USC
	Libby Weiss	USC
1967	Jane Albert and	Stanford
	Julie Anthony	Stanford
1968	Emilie Burrer and	Trinity University
	Becky Vest	Trinity University
1969	Emilie Burrer and	Trinity University
	Becky Vest	Trinity University
1970	Pam Farmer and	Odossa Junior College
	Connie Capozzi	Odossa Junior College
1971	Pam Richmond and	Arizona State
	Peggy Michel	Arizona State

NATIONAL INTERCOLLEGIATE CHAMPIONS—MEN'S SINGLES

1883	H. A. Taylor (fall)	Harvard		1907	G. P. Gardner, Jr.	Harvard
1883	J. S. Clark (spring)	Harvard		1908	Nat W. Niles	Harvard
1884	W. P. Knapp	Yale		1909	W. F. Johnson	U. of Penn.
1885	W. P. Knapp	Yale		1910	R. A. Holden, Jr.	Yale
1886	G. M. Brinley	Trinity		1911	E. H. Whitney	Harvard
1887	P. S. Sears	Harvard		1912	G. M. Church	Princeton
1888	P. S. Sears	Harvard		1913	Richard N. Williams II	Harvard
1889	R. P. Huntington, Jr.	Yale		1914	G. M. Church	Princeton
1890	F. H. Hovey	Harvard		1915	R. N. Williams II	Harvard
1891	F. H. Hovey	Harvard		1916	G. Colket Caner	Harvard
1892	W. A. Larned	Cornell		1917–18	not held	
1893	M. G. Chace	Brown		1919	C. S. Garland	Yale
1894	M. G. Chace	Yale		1920	L. M. Banks	Yale
1895	M. G. Chace	Yale		1921	Philip Neer	Stanford
1896	M. D. Whitman	Harvard		1922	Lucien E. Williams	Yale
1897	S. G. Thomson	Princeton		1923	Carl H. Fischer	Phila. Osteo.
1898	L. E. Ware	Harvard		1924	Wallace Scott	U. of Wash.
1899	Dwight Davis	Harvard		1925	E. G. Chandler	California
1900	R. D. Little	Princeton		1926	E. G. Chandler	California
1901	Fred B. Alexander	Princeton		1927	Wilmer Allison	Texas
1902	William J. Clothier	Harvard		1928	Julius Seligson	Lehigh
1903	E. B. Dewhurst	U. of Penn.		1929	Berkeley Bell	Texas
1904	Robert LeRoy	Columbia		1930	Clifford Sutter	Tulane
1905	E. B. Dewhurst	U. of Penn.		1931	Keith Gledhill	Stanford
1906	Robert LeRoy	Columbia		1932	Clifford Sutter	Tulane

**National Intercollegiate Champions—Men's
Singles (cont.)**

1933	Jack Tidball	U. of Cal., L.A.
1934	C. Gene Mako	U. of So. Cal.
1935	Wilbur Hess	Rice Institute
1936	Ernest Sutter	Tulane
1937	Ernest Sutter	Tulane
1938	Frank D. Guernsey	Rice Institute
1939	Frank D. Guernsey	Rice Institute
1940	Donald McNeill	Kenyon College
1941	Joseph R. Hunt	U.S. Naval Acad.
1942	Frederick R. Schroeder, Jr.	Stanford
1943	Francisco Segura	Univ. of Miami
1944	Francisco Segura	Univ. of Miami
1945	Francisco Segura	Univ. of Miami
1946	Robert Falkenburg	U. of So. Cal.
1947	Gardnar Larned	Wm. & Mary
1948	Harry E. Likas	U. San Francisco
1949	Jack Tuero	Tulane
1950	Herbert Flam	U. of Cal., L.A.
1951	Tony Trabert	Univ. of Cincinnati
1952	Hugh Stewart	U. of So. Cal.
1953	Hamilton Richardson	Tulane
1954	Hamilton Richardson	Tulane
1955	Jose Aguero	Tulane
1956	Alejandro Olmedo	U. of So. Cal.
1957	Barry MacKay	U. of Mich.
1958	Alejandro Olmedo	U. of So. Cal.
1959	Whitney Reed	San Jose State College
1960	Larry Nagler	U. of Cal., L.A.
1961	Allen Fox	U. of Cal., L.A.
1962	Rafael Osuna	U. of So. Cal.
1963	Dennis Ralston	U. of So. Cal.
1964	Dennis Ralston	U. of So. Cal.
1965	Arthur Ashe	U. of Cal., L.A.
1966	Charles Pasarell	U. of Cal., L.A.
1967	Robert Lutz	U. of So. Cal.
1968	Stanley Smith	U. of So. Cal.

Francisco (Pancho) Segura while at the University of Miami won the National Intercollegiate Championship three years in a row (1943–45). The only other player to do this was M. G. Chace (1893–95) while at Brown and Yale.

1969	Joaquin Loyo-Mayo	U. of So. Cal.
1970	Jeff Borowiak	U. of Cal., L.A.
1971	Jim Connors	U. of Cal., L.A.

NATIONAL INTERCOLLEGIATE CHAMPIONS—MEN'S DOUBLES

1883	J. S. Clark and H. A. Taylor (spring)	Harvard
1883	H. A. Taylor and R. E. Presbrey (fall)	Harvard
1884	W. P. Knapp and W. V. S. Thorne	Yale
1885	W. P. Knapp and A. L. Shipman	Yale
1886	W. P. Knapp and W. L. Thacher	Yale
1887	P. S. Sears and Q. A. Shaw, Jr.	Harvard
1888	V. G. Hall and O. S. Campbell	Columbia
1889	O. S. Campbell and A. E. Wright	Columbia
1890	Q. A. Shaw, Jr. and S. T. Chase	Harvard
1891	F. H. Hovey and R. D. Wrenn	Harvard
1892	R. D. Wrenn and F. B. Winslow	Harvard
1893	M G. Chace and C. R. Budlong	Brown
1894	M. G. Chace and A. E. Foote	Yale
1895	M. G. Chace and A. E. Foote	Yale
1896	L. E. Ware and W. M. Scudder	Harvard
1897	L. E. Ware and M. D. Whitman	Harvard
1898	L. E. Ware and M. D. Whitman	Harvard
1899	Holcombe Ward and D. F. Davis	Harvard
1900	F. B. Alexander and R. D. Little	Princeton
1901	H. A. Plummer and S. L. Russell	Yale
1902	W. J. Clothier and E. W. Leonard	Harvard
1903	B. Colston and E. Clapp	Yale
1904	K. H. Behr and G. Bodman	Yale
1905	E. B. Dewhurst and H. B. Register	Pennsylvania

Year	Players	School
1906	E. B. Wells and A. Spaulding	Yale
1907	N. W. Niles and A. S. Dabney	Harvard
1908	H. M. Tilden and A. Thayer	Pennsylvania
1909	W. F. Johnson and A. Thayer	Pennsylvania
1910	D. Mathey and B. N. Dell	Princeton
1911	D. Mathey and C. T. Butler	Princeton
1912	G. M. Church and W. H. Mace	Princeton
1913	W. M. Washburn and J. J. Armstrong	Harvard
1914	R. N. Williams II and Richard Harte	Harvard
1915	R. N. Williams II and Richard Harte	Harvard
1916	G. C. Caner and Richard Harte	Harvard
1917–18	not held	
1919	C. S. Garland and K. N. Hawkes	Yale
1920	A. Wilder and L. Wiley	Yale
1921	J. B. Fenno, Jr. and E. W. Feibleman	Harvard
1922	James Davies and Philip Neer	Stanford
1923	L. N. White and Louis Thalheimer	Texas
1924	L. N. White and Louis Thalheimer	Texas
1925	Gervais Hills and Gerald Stratford	California
1926	E. G. Chandler and Tom Stow	California
1927	John Van Ryn and Kenneth Appel	Princeton
1928	Ralph McElvenny and Alan Herrington	Stanford
1929	Benjamin Gorchakoff and Arthur Kussman	Occidental
1930	Dolf Muehleisen and Robert Muench	California
1931	Bruce Barnes and Karl Kamrath	U. of Texas
1932	Keith Gledhill and Joseph Coughlin	Stanford
1933	Joseph Coughlin and Sam Lee	Stanford
1934	C. Gene Mako and G. Philip Castlen	U. of So. Cal.
1935	Paul Newton and Richard Bennett	California
1936	W. Bennet Dey and Wm. Seward	Stanford
1937	Richard Bennett and Paul Newton	California
1938	Joseph R. Hunt and Lewis Wetherell	U. of So. Cal.
1939	Douglas Imhoff and Robert Peacock	California
1940	Laurence A. Dee and James Wade	Stanford
1941	Charles E. Olewine and Charles H. Mattmann	U. of So. Cal.
1942	Frederick R. Schroeder, Jr. and Laurence Dee	Stanford
1943	John Hickmann and Walter Driver	Univ. of Texas
1944	John Hickman and Felix Kelley	Univ. of Texas
1945	Francisco (Pancho) Segura and Tom Burke	Univ. of Miami
1946	Robert Falkenburg and Tom Falkenburg	U. of So. Cal.
1947	Sam Match and Bobby Curtis	Rice Institute
1948	Fred Kovaleski and Bernard Bartzen	Wm. & Mary
1949	Jim Brink and Fred Fisher	U. of Wash.
1950	Herbert Flam and Gene Garrett	U. of Cal., L.A.
1951	Earl Cochell and Hugh Stewart	U. of So. Cal.
1952	Hugh Ditzler and Clifton Mayne	Univ. of Calif.
1953	Lawrence Huebner and Robert Perry	U. of Cal., L.A.
1954	Ronald Livingston and Robert Perry	U. of Cal., L.A.
1955	Francisco Contreras and Joaquin Reyes	Univ. So. Calif.
1956	Francisco Contreras and Alejandro Olmedo	Univ. So. Calif.
1957	Crawford Henry and Ronald Holmberg	Tulane
1958	Edward Atkinson and Alejandro Olmedo	Univ. So. Calif.
1959	Ronald Holmberg and Crawford Henry	Tulane
1960	Larry Nagler and Allen Fox	U. of Cal., L.A.
1961	Rafael Osuna and Ramsey Earnhart	U. of So. Cal.
1962	Rafael Osuna and Ramsey Earnhart	U. of So. Cal.
1963	Rafael Osuna and Dennis Ralston	U. of So. Cal.
1964	William Bond and Dennis Ralston	U. of So. Cal.
1965	Arthur Ashe and Ian Crookenden	U. of Cal., L.A.
1966	Ian Crookenden and Charles Pasarell	U. of Cal., L.A.
1967	Robert Lutz and Stan Smith	U. of So. Cal.
1968	Robert Lutz and Stan Smith	U. of So. Cal.
1969	Joaquin Loyo-Mayo and Marcella Lara	U. of So. Cal.
1970	Pat Cramer and Luis Garcia	U. of Miami
1971	Jeff Borowiak and Haroon Rahim	U. of Cal., L.A.

COLLEGES WINNING INTERCOLLEGIATE CHAMPIONSHIPS—MEN'S SINGLES

Brown, 1893
Columbia, 1904–1906
Cornell, 1892
Harvard, 1883 (Spring), 1883 (Fall), 1887, 1888, 1890, 1891, 1896, 1898, 1899, 1902, 1907, 1908, 1911, 1913, 1915, 1916
Kenyon, 1940
Lehigh, 1928
Philadelphia College of Osteopathy, 1923
Princeton, 1897, 1900, 1901, 1912, 1914
Rice Institute, 1935, 1938, 1939
San Jose State College, 1959
Stanford, 1921, 1931, 1942
Texas, 1927, 1929
Trinity, 1886
Tulane, 1930, 1932, 1936, 1937, 1949, 1953–1955
University of California, 1925, 1926
University of California (L.A.), 1933, 1950, 1960, 1961, 1965, 1966, 1970, 1971
University of Cincinnati, 1951
University of Miami, 1943–1945
University of Michigan, 1951
University of Pennsylvania, 1903, 1905, 1909
University of San Francisco, 1948
University of Southern California, 1934, 1946, 1952, 1956, 1958, 1962–1964, 1967–1969
University of Washington, 1924
U.S. Naval Academy, 1941
William & Mary, 1947
Yale, 1884, 1885, 1889, 1894, 1895, 1910, 1919, 1920, 1922

One of many Intercollegiate Champions who went on to greater heights in both tennis and learning was Rhodes scholar Hamilton Richardson.

WINNERS OF BOTH INTERCOLLEGIATE CHAMPIONSHIPS AND NATIONAL SINGLES
(Men's Singles)

	Intercollegiate	National
F. H. Hovey	1890, 1891	1895
William A. Larned	1892	1901, 1902, 1907–1911
Malcolm D. Whitman	1896	1898, 1899, 1900
William J. Clothier	1902	1906
Richard N. Williams II	1913, 1915	1914, 1916
Wilmer L. Allison	1927	1935
W. Donald McNeill	1940	1940
Joseph R. Hunt	1941	1943
Frederick R. Schroeder, Jr.	1942	1942
Tony Trabert	1951	1953, 1955
Rafael Osuna	1962	1963
Arthur Ashe	1965	1968, 1968*
Stanley Smith	1968	1969, 1971*

NATIONAL PUBLIC PARKS CHAMPIONS—MEN'S SINGLES

1923	Cranston W. Holman	1927	Theodore R. Drewes
1924	Theodore R. Drewes	1928	George J. Jennings, Jr.
1925	Theodore R. Drewes	1929	George J. Jennings, Jr.
1926	Theodore R. Drewes	1930	George J. Jennings, Jr.

* USLTA Open.

The outstanding University of Southern California team of Stan Smith (*left*) and Bob Lutz (*right*) won the Intercollegiate doubles title in 1967 and 1968. In the latter year, they also won the United States Open and National doubles crown as well as helping the United States to win the Davis Cup.

1931	George J. Jennings, Jr.
1932	Arnold Simons
1933	Arnold Simons
1934	Barnard Welsh
1935	Barnard Welsh
1936	Lewis Wetherell
1937	Lewis Wetherell
1938	Willis Anderson
1939	Willis Anderson
1940	Richard McKee
1941	Willis Anderson
1942–45	not held
1946	Richard Hainline
1947	Fred Kovaleski
1948	Willis Anderson
1949	Myron McNamara
1950	Clyde Hippenstiel
1951	Wade Herren
1952	Linn Rockwood
1953	Clyde Hippenstiel
1954	Clyde Hippenstiel
1955	Clyde Hippenstiel
1956	Linn Rockwood
1957	Linn Rockwood
1958	Noel Brown
1959	Alan Tong
1960	John Evans
1961	Gardnar Mulloy
1962	Fred Drilling
1963	Gerald Dubie
1964	Bob Potthast
1965	David Reed
1966	Rod Susman
1967	Rod Susman
1968	Gary Johnson
1969	William Tym
1970	Larry Paker
1971	Mike Anderson

NATIONAL PUBLIC PARKS CHAMPIONS—MEN'S DOUBLES

1923	Elmer Schwartz and Ted Heuerman
1924	Frank Regan and Cranston W. Holman
1925	Charles Lejeck and Leo Lejeck
1926	Gabriel Lavine and Gus Amsterdam
1927	Ralph Rice and George J. Jennings, Jr.
1928	Ralph Rice and George J. Jennings, Jr.
1929	G. J. Jennings, Jr. and Robert B. Considine
1930	George J. Jennings, Jr. and Jack DeLara
1931	George J. Jennings, Jr. and Gordon L. Braudt
1932	Gordon L. Braudt and Carl Ireneus
1933	William Schommer and Charles Britzius
1934	William Schommer and Charles Britzius
1935	Barnard Welsh and Ralph McElvenny
1936	Ted Drewes and Robert Norton
1937	Willis Anderson and Ronald Lubin
1938	Elbert R. Lewis and Willis Anderson
1939	Julius Heldman and Willis Anderson
1940	Willis Anderson and Jerry Crowther
1941	Dr. W. F. Widen and Ed Olson
1942–45	not held
1946	Willis Anderson and Geo. Druliner
1947	Fred Kovaleski and Gene Russell
1948	Nolan McQuown and Myron McNamara
1949	Myron McNamara and Nolan McQuown
1950	Bobby Curtis and Clayton Benham
1951	Thomas Chambers and Clyde Hippenstiel
1952	Nolan McQuown and Roy McQuown
1953	Nolan McQuown and Roy McQuown
1954	Thomas Chambers and Clyde Hippenstiel
1955	Glenn Basset and Clyde Hippenstiel
1956	Ralph Dudgeon and Allen Schmidt
1957	Wayne Pearce and Linn Rockwood
1958	Noel Brown and Ramsey Earnhart
1959	George MacCall and Marsh Miller
1960	Mickey Schad and Roddy McNerney
1961	Ed Foster and Don Schmidt
1962	Dick Horwitz and Jerry Johnson
1963	Gary Russell and Wayne Collett
1964	Bob Potthast and Dick Leach
1965	Gary Johnson and David Reed
1966	Jerry Johnson and Jim Parker
1967	Jerry Johnson and Rod Susman
1968	Bob Kreiss and Mike Kreiss
1969	Jerry Van Linge and Ed Grubb
1970	Larry Paker and Paul Tobin
1971	Robert Hetherington and Charles Garfinkel

NATIONAL PUBLIC PARKS CHAMPIONS— WOMEN'S SINGLES

1930	Mrs. Virginia B. Bueker
1931	Mary Z. McHale
1932	Helen Germaine
1933	Ruth Bailey
1934	Mrs. Ruth Bailey Prosser
1935	Elizabeth Deike
1936	Elizabeth Deike
1937	Mary Arnold
1938	Catherine Malcolm
1939	Marta M. Barnett

National Public Parks Champions—Women's Singles (cont.)

1940	Helen Germaine
1941	Muriel Magnuson
1942–45	not held
1946	Beverly J. Baker
1947	Mrs. Mary Arnold Prentiss
1948	Mrs. Mary Arnold Prentiss
1949	Mrs. Lucile Davidson
1950	Mrs. Mary Arnold Prentiss
1951	Mrs. Mary Arnold Prentiss
1952	Mrs. Mary Arnold Prentiss
1953	Mrs. Mary Arnold Prentiss
1954	Mrs. Mary Arnold Prentiss
1955	June Stack
1956	Mrs. Mary Arnold Prentiss
1957	Mrs. Mary Arnold Prentiss
1958	Mrs. Mary Arnold Prentiss
1959	Joyce Pniewski
1960	Joan Johnson
1961	Joan Johnson
1962	Joan Johnson
1963	Jane Bartkowicz
1964	Mimi Arnold
1965	Susan Dykes
1966	Eileen Rahlens
1967	Pat Cody
1968	Mrs. Janie Albert Freeman
1969	Alice Tym
1970	Joan Johnson
1971	Pat Cody

NATIONAL PUBLIC PARKS CHAMPIONS— WOMEN'S DOUBLES

1930	Ethel Haas and Elizabeth Kaiser
1931	Mary Zita McHale and Mary McQuiston
1932	Mrs. V. B. Ducker and Mrs. A. Linderman
1933	Mrs. Ruth Prosser and Mrs. Ella Felbinger
1934	Helen Rose and Mrs. Andree Russell
1935	Constance O'Donovan and Esther Politzer
1936	Edna Smith and Irene David
1937	Mary Arnold and Mrs. Gertrude Dockstader
1938	Mrs. Gertrude Dockstader and Mary Arnold
1939	Marta Barnett and Mrs. Catherine Sample
1940	Mrs. Merceina Parker and Frances Jacobson
1941	Muriel Magnuson and Beverly Pawlak
1942–45	not held
1946	Mrs. Wilma Smith and Mrs. Merceina Parker
1947	Mrs. Mary Prentiss and Mrs. June Crow
1948	Mrs. Mary Prentiss and Mrs. Alice Wanee
1949	Mrs. Nora Prosser and Mrs. Lucile Davidson
1950	Mrs. Nora Prosser and Mrs. Lucile Davidson
1951	Mrs. Lucile Davidson and Mrs. Nora Prosser
1952	Joan Johnson and Mary Hernando
1953	Joan Johnson and Mary Hernando
1954	Joan Johnson and Geralyn Shepard
1955	Mrs. Mary Prentiss and Barbara Talmadge
1956	Muriel Cooper and Joan Warner
1957	Joan Johnson and Geralyn Shepard
1958	Joan Johnson and Geralyn Shepard
1959	Winnie McCoy and Pat Moseley
1960	Winnie McCoy and Pat Moseley
1961	Joan Johnson and Geralyn Shepard
1962	Joan Johnson and Geralyn Shepard
1963	Joan Johnson and Geralyn Shepard

1964	Joan Johnson and Geralyn Shepard
1965	Marilyn Mueller and Lydia Weiberg
1966	Pat Cody and Barbara Grubb
1967	Marilyn Mueller and Lydia Wieberg
1968	Evelyn Houseman and Carol Schneider
1969	Pat Cody and Vicki Smouse
1970	Mrs. Mary A. Prentiss and Lenny Yee
1971	Mrs. Mary A. Prentiss and Pat Cody

NATIONAL PUBLIC PARKS CHAMPIONS— MIXED DOUBLES

1961	Geralyn Shepard and Sam Plancia
1962	Joan Johnson and Barry Pelton
1963	Joan Johnson and Gary Russell
1964	Betsy Roberti and Ed Kauder
1965	Mary A. Prentiss and Gary Johnson
1966	Eileen Rahlens and Gary Johnson
1967	Mrs. Karne H. Susman and Rod Susman
1968	Janie Freeman and Sam Plancia
1969	Pat Cody and Mike Baer
1970	Joan Johnson and Charles Pate
1971	Suzanne Gray and Ross Helft

NATIONAL PUBLIC PARKS CHAMPIONS— JUNIOR SINGLES

1948	Oscar Johnson
1949	Allen Cleveland
1950	James Reed
1951	Richard Doss
1952	Robert Jacobs
1953	not held
1954	Alex Olmedo
1955	Forrest Stewart
1956	Richard Leach
1957	Norman Karns
1958	Marcus Carriedo
1959	Marcus Carriedo
1960	Eltinge Brown
1961	Doug Sykes
1962	Joe Huey
1963	Edward Grubb
1964	Brian Cheney
1965	Ron Teeguarden
1966	Maurice Poirier
1967	Dale Fritz
1968	Gualberto Escudero
1969	Dan Lambert
1970	Grant Smith
1971	Banno Nunna

NATIONAL PUBLIC PARKS CHAMPIONS— JUNIOR DOUBLES

1961	Rodney Kop and Antonio Sison
1962	Dennis Law and Steve Rosen
1963	Ed Grubb and Robert Eisenberg
1964	Brian Cheney and Erick Baer
1965	Joel Ostroff and John Levin
1966	Rich Westphaln and Maurice Poirier
1967	Jim Logan and Bill Long
1968	Chuck Nachand and Paul Vodak
1969	D. Lambert and P. Lambert
1970	D. Lambert and P. Lambert
1971	not held

NATIONAL PUBLIC PARKS CHAMPIONS—
BOYS' 16 SINGLES

1962   Ron Willens
1963   Jim Rombeau
1964   Brian Parrott
1965   Robert Hill
1966   Mike Tesman
1967   Jim Armstrong
1968   Jeff Cowan
1969   Chris Kane
1970   Nick Saviano
1971   Mike Greenberg

NATIONAL PUBLIC PARKS CHAMPIONS—
BOYS' 16 DOUBLES

1962   Ron Willens and Rick Reed
1963   Lowell Chatburn and Brad Cornell
1964   Erich Wise and Richard Dauben
1965   Robert Hill and Jim Logan
1966   Jeff Austin and Mike Shires
1967   Jim Armstrong and Richard Ley
1968   Tom McArdle and Paul Novacek
1969   John Bennett and Chris Kane
1970   Steve Hahn and Nick Saviano
1971   not held

NATIONAL PUBLIC PARKS CHAMPIONS—
BOYS' 14 SINGLES

1962   Tom Leonard
1963   Richard Bohrnstedt
1964   Christopher Chapin
1965   Steve Derian
1966   Steve Derian
1967   Jim McNairy
1968   Ted Hagey
1969   Michael Nissky
1970   Michael Edles
1971   Alan Winkler

NATIONAL PUBLIC PARKS CHAMPIONS—
BOYS' 12 SINGLES

1965   James Hagey
1966   Joe Edles
1967   Michael Nissley
1968   Richard Grant
1969   Piya Moranon
1970   Ron Hightower
1971   Adam Cioth

NATIONAL PUBLIC PARKS CHAMPIONS—
GIRLS' 18 SINGLES

1948   Julie Sampson
1949   Anita Kanter
1950   Anita Kanter
1951   Mary Ann Eilenberger
1952   Darlene Hard
1953   not held
1954   Lorna Raymond
1955   Karen Hantze

1956   Patricia Cushman
1957   Carol Ann Loop
1958   Judy Minna
1959   Judy Minna
1960   Annette Stoesser
1961   Andria Miller
1962   Penny Myrell
1963   Jean Inez
1964   Barbara Strong
1965   Mary Anna Poiset
1966   Mary Anna Poiset
1967   Jane Richardson
1968   Gloria Pananides
1969   Gale Litton
1970   Rill Culver
1971   Sue Ince

NATIONAL PUBLIC PARKS CHAMPIONS—
GIRLS' 18 DOUBLES

1961   Andria Miller and Jane Conrol
1962   Karen Haase and Penny Myrell
1963   Cynthia Raymond and Linda Cushing
1964   Pam Teeguarden and Peggy Michel
1965   Cathy Apple and Stephanie Berger
1966   Sheryl Jorgenson and Cynde Haffner
1967   Debbie Brown and Jane Richardson
1968   Gloria Pananides and Dawn Crossen
1969   Diane Miller and Mary Miller
1970   Kevan Dignam and J. Wright
1971   not held

NATIONAL PUBLIC PARKS CHAMPIONS—
GIRLS' 16 SINGLES

1962   Sherrie Pruitt
1963   Robyn Berrey
1964   Valerie Ziegenfuss
1965   Diane Driscall
1966   Sharon Guthrie
1967   Janice Metcalf
1968   Christine Cheney
1969   Joy Schwikers
1970   Gloria Thomas
1971   Terry Holladay

NATIONAL PUBLIC PARKS CHAMPIONS—
GIRLS' 16 DOUBLES

1962   Jean Inez and Patti Hogan
1963   Kathy Apple and Robyn Berrey
1964   Valerie Ziegenfuss and Ann Chaboudy
1965   Mary Poiset and Ann Chaboudy
1966   Sharon Guthrie and Pam Austin
1967   Wendy Appleby and Christine Cheney
1968   Molly Tyson and Tracy Macnair
1969   Jill Schwikert and Joy Schwikert
1970   Gloria Thomas and Diane Desfor
1971   not held

NATIONAL PUBLIC PARKS CHAMPIONS—
GIRLS' 14 SINGLES

1962   Kristen Stewart
1963   Patti Hogan

National Public Parks Champions—Girls' 14 Singles *(cont.)*

1964	Betty Ann Grubb
1965	Ann Lebedeff
1966	Janet Newberry
1967	Lori Sherbeck
1968	Diane Desfor
1969	Lindsay Morse
1970	Tina Tsumas
1971	Susan Hagey

NATIONAL PUBLIC PARKS CHAMPIONS— GIRLS' 12 SINGLES

1965	Janet Newberry
1966	Abbe Wise
1967	Gretchen Gelt
1968	Marita Redondo
1969	Kimberly Nilsson
1970	Lea Antonopolis
1971	Judi Jacobi

NATIONAL PUBLIC PARKS CHAMPIONS— MEN'S 35 SINGLES

1969	Alan Schwartz
1970	Alan Schwartz
1971	Melvin Lewis

NATIONAL PUBLIC PARKS CHAMPIONS— MEN'S 35 DOUBLES

1969	Seymour Greenberg and Alan Schwartz
1970	John Foreman and Alan Schwartz
1971	Melvin Lewis and Larry Ross

NATIONAL PUBLIC PARKS CHAMPIONS— MEN SENIORS' SINGLES

1959	Ed di Leone
1960	Ed di Leone
1961	Norman MacDonald
1962	Alex Swetka

1963	Ed di Leone
1964	William Smith
1965	William Lurie
1966	Bob Weinstock
1967	Bob Galloway
1968	Dave Martin
1969	Seymour Greenberg
1970	Bob Thompson
1971	Chris Scott

NATIONAL PUBLIC PARKS CHAMPIONS— MEN SENIORS' DOUBLES

1961	Gardnar Mulloy and Homer Shoop
1962	Ed di Leone and Courtney Bock
1963	Courtney Bock and Ed di Leone
1964	Francis Gay and Robert Hill
1965	Courtney Bock and Ed di Leone
1966	Harry Burrus and Bob Weinstock
1967	Bob Galloway and Dave Martin
1968	Bob Galloway and Dave Martin
1969	George Lott and Sam Fields
1970	Dick McFarland and Bob Thompson
1971	Dick McFarland and Bob Thompson

NATIONAL PUBLIC PARKS CHAMPIONS— WOMEN SENIORS' SINGLES

1964	Mrs. Mary Arnold Prentiss
1965	not held
1966	Mrs. Merceina Parker
1967	not held
1968	Mrs. Mary Arnold Prentiss
1969	Marilyn Mueller
1970	Joan Johnson
1971	Mrs. Mary Arnold Prentiss

NATIONAL PUBLIC PARKS CHAMPIONS— WOMEN SENIORS' DOUBLES

1964	Mrs. Mary Arnold Prentiss and Gertie Irish
1965	not held
1966	Muriel Cooper and Jean Warner
1967	not held
1968	Phyllis Adler and Carol Schneider
1969	Marilyn Mueller and Jane Pratt
1970	Joan Johnson and J. Prentiss
1971	Phyllis Yambrack and Alphonzice Edwards

Church Cup

The Church Cup was donated by George Myers Church in 1918 for competition between teams of men representing Boston, New York, and Philadelphia, and it continued that format until 1932. In 1946 the competing teams represented three Sectional Associations, New England, Eastern, and Middle States. In 1947 the Middle Atlantic Section was admitted to the competition. The record of previous Church Cup matches is as follows:

Date	No. of Teams	Winner	Runner-up	Score
1918	3	New York	Philadelphia	6–3
1919	3	Boston	Philadelphia	6–3
1920	3	New York	Boston	5–3
1921	3	New York	Philadelphia	6–2
1922	not held			

Church Cup (cont.)

Date	No. of Teams	Winner	Runner-up	Score
1923	3	New York	Philadelphia	6–3
1924	3	New York and Philadelphia tied		2–2
1925	3	Boston	New York	5–4
1926	3	Philadelphia	New York	6–3
1927	3	Philadelphia	New York	5–4
1928	3	Boston	Philadelphia	5–4
1929	3	New York	Philadelphia	7–2
1930	3	New York	Philadelphia	6–3
1931	3	New York	Boston	7–2
1932	3	New York	Philadelphia	7–2
1933–45	not held			
1946	3	Eastern	Middle States	5–4
1947	4	Middle Atlantic	New England	5½–3½
1948	4	Middle States	Eastern	7–2
1949	4	Eastern	Middle States	6–2
1950	4	Middle States	New England	7–2
1951	not held			
1952	4	New England	Middle States	6–3
1953	4	Middle States	Eastern	6–3
1954	4	Eastern	Middle States	6–3
1955	4	Middle States	New England	7–1
1956	4	Middle States	Middle Atlantic	6–3
1957	4	Eastern	Middle Atlantic	5–4
1958	4	Middle States	Eastern	5–4
1959	4	Middle States	Eastern	5–2
1960	4	Middle Atlantic	New England	5–4
1961	4	Middle States	Eastern	5–4
1962	4	Middle States	Middle Atlantic	9–0
1963	4	Middle States	Eastern	5–4
1964	4	Eastern	New England	8–1
1965	4	Eastern	Middle Atlantic	5–2
1966	4	Middle Atlantic	New England	7–2
1967	4	Middle Atlantic	Middle States	6–3
1968	4	Middle States	Middle Atlantic	5–4
1969	4	New England	Eastern	5–4
1970	4	New England	Eastern	5–4
1971	4	New England	Eastern	5–4

Note: When 3 teams participated the runner-up listed was one of the finalists on the second day of play.

Sears Cup

The Sears Cup, named in honor of Eleanora Sears—a great woman player of early 1900's —is the women's counterpart of the Church Cup. It started in 1927, but unlike the men's trophy it has had a continuous life. The record of previous Sears Cup matches is as follows:

Date	No. of Teams	Winner	Runner-up	Score
1927	3	New England	Eastern	5–2
1928	4	New England	Eastern	9–0
1929	4	New England	Eastern	5–4
1930	4	New England	Eastern	6–3
1931	4	New England	Eastern	6–3
1932	4	Eastern	Middle States	7–2
1933	3	New England	Eastern	5–4
1934	4	Eastern	Middle States	7–2
1935	4	Eastern	New England	6–3
1936	3	Eastern	Middle States	5–4

Sears Cup (cont.)

Date	No. of Teams	Winner	Runner-up	Score
1937	4	New England	Eastern	6–3
1938	4	Eastern	New England	7–2
1939	4	New England	Eastern	5–4
1940	4	Eastern	New England	5–4
1941	3	New England	Eastern	8–1
1942	3	Eastern	Middle States	9–0
1943	2	Eastern	Middle States	8–1
1944	3	Eastern	New England	7–2
1945	3	Eastern	Middle States	9–0
1946	3	Eastern	Middle Atlantic	8–1
1947	4	Eastern	New England	6–3
1948	4	Middle States	New England	6–3
1949	4	Eastern	New England	8–1
1950	4	Eastern	New England	5–2
1951	3	New England	Middle States	5–4
1952	4	New England	Eastern	6–3
1953	4	Middle States	New England	9–0
1954	4	New England	Eastern	6–3
1955	4	Middle States	New England	6–3
1956	4	New England	Middle States	6–3
1957	4	Middle States	New England	7–2
1958	4	New England	Middle States	6–3
1959	4	Middle States	New England	5–0
1960	4	Middle States	Middle Atlantic	9–0
1961	3	Middle States	Middle Atlantic	7–2
1962	4	New England	Middle Atlantic	6–3
1963	4	Middle States	Middle Atlantic	8–1
1964	4	Middle States	Middle Atlantic	6–3
1965	4	Middle States	New England	6–1
1966	4	Eastern	New England	5–4
1967	4	Middle States	Eastern	6–3
1968	4	Middle Atlantic	Eastern	5–4
1969	3	Middle States	Middle Atlantic	6–3
1970	4	Eastern	Middle Atlantic	5–4
1971	4	Middle States	Eastern	7–2

Note: When 3 teams participated the runner-up listed was one of the finalists on the second day of play.

UNITED STATES TITLE MATCHES, LEADING EVENTS (1965–1971)

1965 Season

U.S. INDOOR, at Salisbury, Md.: Jan-Erik Lundquist (Sweden), d. Denny Ralston, 4–6, 13–11, 6–4, 11–9; at Boston: Nancy Richey d. Carol Hanks Aucamp, 6–3, 6–2.

DIXIE, at Tampa: Manolo Santana (Spain) d. Lundquist, 6–3, 8–6, 6–0; Tory Fretz d. Judy Alvarez Campbell, 6–2, 6–1.

GOOD NEIGHBOR, at Miami Beach: Ralston d. Tom Koch (Brazil), 3–6, 6–3, 7–5, 6–2; Margaret Smith (Australia), d. Lesley Turner (Australia), 6–2, 8–6.

THUNDERBIRD, at Phoenix: Chuck McKinley d. Arthur Ashe, 8–10, 6–4, 10–8; Justina Bricka d. Jane Albert, 6–2, 6–4.

CARIBE HILTON, at San Juan, P.R.: Santana d. Ralston, 6–4, 6–1; N. Richey d. Smith, 6–8, 6–4, 9–7.

MASTER, at St. Petersburg: Ram Krishman (India), d. Mike Belkin, 4–6, 6–1, 6–4, 6–3; N. Richey d. Smith, 6–3, 6–2.

RIVER OAKS, at Houston: Krishman d. Cliff Richey, 6–4, 2–6, 6–4, 6–3.

SOUTHERN CALIFORNIA, at Los Angeles: Ralston d. Ashe, 8–6, 6–2; Billie Jean Moffitt King d. Kathy Harter, 6–3, 6–1.

CALIFORNIA STATE, at Portola Valley: Ralston d. McKinley, 4–6, 6–1, 6–2, 6–3; King d. Rosemary Casals, 6–2, 8–6.

U.S. HARD COURT, at Sacramento: Ralston d. Ham Richardson, 6–4, 4–6, 6–1, 6–4; Casals

d. Harter, 6–4, 4–6, 6–2.

WESTERN, at Milwaukee: C. Richey d. Marty Riessen, 5–7, 6–4, 6–3, 6–3; N. Richey d. Carole Caldwell Graebner, 6–1, 6–0.

U.S. CLAY COURT, at Chicago: Ralston d. C. Richey, 6–4, 4–6, 6–4, 6–3; N. Richey d. Julie Heldman, 5–7, 6–3, 9–7.

PENNSYLVANIA, at Philadelphia: Charles Pasarell d. Roy Emerson (Australia), 6–4, 1–6, 6–3, 6–4; King d. Carole Graebner, 6–1, 6–2.

EASTERN, at South Orange, N.J.: Fred Stolle (Australia), d. Emerson, 6–3, 2–6, 6–4, 6–4; King d. Albert, 7–5, 6–3.

PIPING ROCK, at Locust Valley, N.Y.: Mary Ann Eisel d. Harter, 4–6, 6–2, 6–2.

MEADOW CLUB, at Southampton, N.Y.: McKinley d. Gene Scott, 3–6, 6–3, 8–6, 10–8.

BALTIMORE INVITATION, at Baltimore: Stolle d. Lew Gerrard (New Zealand), 6–3, 6–3, 6–4.

NEWPORT CASINO, at Newport, R.I.: Emerson d. Stolle, 6–3, 6–4, 6–3.

ESSEX, at Manchester, Mass.: King d. Aucamp, 6–2, 10–8.

NASSAU, at Glen Cove, N.Y.: Emerson d. McKinley, 6–4, 11–9, 7–5.

U.S., at Forest Hills: Santana d. Cliff Drysdale (South Africa), 6–2, 7–9, 7–5, 6–1; Smith d. King, 8–6, 7–5.

PACIFIC COAST, at Berkeley: Riessen d. Ralston, 5–7, 3–6, 6–1, 6–4, 8–6; Judy Tegart (Australia), d. Casals, 6–4, 3–6, 7–5.

PACIFIC SOUTHWEST, at Los Angeles: Ralston d. Ashe, 6–4, 6–3; Carole Graebner d. Fretz, 6–4, 6–4.

COLONIAL, at Ft. Worth: Ashe d. Stolle, 6–3, 6–4.

1966 Season

U.S. INDOOR, at Salisbury, Md.: Charles Pasarell d. Ronald Holmberg, 12–10, 10–8, 8–6; at Boston: Billie Jean Moffitt King d. Mary Ann Eisel, 6–0, 6–2.

DIXIE, at Tampa: Cliff Drysdale (South Africa) d. Boro Jovanovic (Yugoslavia), 6–2, 6–4, 6–4; Elena Subirats (Mexico) d. Alice Luthy Tym, 6–1, 8–6.

THUNDERBIRD, at Phoenix: Arthur Ashe d. Jim Osborne, 3–6, 6–3, 6–2; King d. Eisel, 6–3, 6–2.

CARIBE HILTON, at San Juan: Ashe d. Cliff Richey, 6–3, 6–4, 6–3; Norma Baylon

(Argentina) d. Eisel, 6–3, 7–5.

MASTERS, at St. Petersburg: Nik Pilic (Yugoslavia) d. Cliff Richey, 9–7, 7–5, 8–6; Nancy Richey d. Betty Stove (Netherlands), 6–2, 6–2.

RIVER OAKS, at Houston: Marty Mulligan (Australia) d. Pilic, 6–2, 3–6, 6–4, 0–6, 4–5, default.

SOUTHERN CALIFORNIA, at Los Angeles: Ashe d. Stan Smith, 6–4, 6–2; King d. Tory Fretz, 6–3, 10–8.

CALIFORNIA STATE, at Portola Valley: Allen Fox d. Bobby Siska, 9–7, 13–11, 6–4; Rosemary Casals d. Lynn Abbes, 6–1, 11–9.

CHARLOTTE INVITATION, at Charlotte, N.C.: Holmberg d. Frank Froehling III, 6–4, 6–3; Eisel d. Donna Floyd Fales, 6–2, 3–6, 7–5.

U.S. HARD COURT, at LaJolla, Calif.: Smith d. Ian Crookenden (New Zealand), 6–4, 6–1; King d. Patti Hogan, 7–5, 6–0.

WESTERN, at Indianapolis: Cliff Richey d. Ralston, 6–1, 1–6, 6–1, 6–2; Nancy Richey d. Peachy Kellmeyer, 6–0, 6–1.

U.S. CLAY, at Milwaukee: Cliff Richey d. Froehling, 13–11, 6–1, 6–3; Nancy Richey d. Stephanie DeFina, 6–2, 6–2.

PENNSYLVANIA GRASS, at Philadelphia: Clark Graebner d. Smith, 6–3, 6–4, 6–3; Karen Krantzcke (Australia) d. Peaches Bartkowicz, 6–1, 6–2.

EASTERN GRASS, at South Orange, N.J.: Tony Roche (Australia) d. Graebner, 6–4, 6–4, 6–3; Fales d. Casals, 5–7, 6–3, 6–0.

PIPING ROCK, at Locust Valley, L.I.: King d. Krantzcke, 6–2, 6–0.

MIDDLE STATES GRASS, at Philadelphia: Fales d. Mimi Arnold, 6–0, 6–3.

NASSAU BOWL, at Glen Cove, L.I.: Gene Scott d. Ray Moore (South Africa), 0–6, 6–3, 6–4, 6–4.

MIDDLE ATLANTIC GRASS, at Baltimore: Mark Cox (England) d. Jim McManus, 6–3, 6–2, 6–3; Virginia Wade (England) d. Bartkowicz, 6–4, 6–2.

MEADOW CLUB, at Southampton, N.Y.: Roche d. Graham Stilwell (England), 6–3, 5–7, 7–5, 6–4.

ESSEX COUNTY, at Manchester, Mass.: Maria Bueno (Brazil) d. Françoise Durr (France), 6–4, 6–8, 6–1.

NEWPORT CASINO, at Newport, R.I.: Ralston d. Cliff Richey, 14–12, 11–9, 8–6.

U.S. CHAMPIONSHIPS, at Forest Hills: Fred

Stolle (Australia) d. John Newcombe (Australia), 4–6, 12–10, 6–3, 6–4; Bueno d. Nancy Richey, 6–3, 6–1.

PACIFIC SOUTHWEST, at Los Angeles: Allen Fox d. Roy Emerson (Australia), 6–3, 6–3; Bueno d. Hogan, 6–2, 6–2.

PACIFIC COAST, at San Francisco: Stolle d. Pasarell, 6–4, 2–6, 6–4; Bueno d. Casals, 6–4, 2–6, 6–1.

1967 Season

NEW ENGLAND INDOOR, at Salem, Mass.: Mary Ann Eisel d. Billie Jean Moffitt King, 6–4, 5–7, 11–9.

NATIONAL INDOOR, at Salisbury, Md.: Charles Pasarell d. Arthur Ashe, 13–11, 6–2, 2–6, 9–7; Ashe and Pasarell d. Bobby Wilson and Roger Taylor (both England), 2–6, 6–3, 8–6.

NATIONAL INDOOR, at Boston: Billie Jean Moffitt King d. Trudy Groenman (Netherlands), 6–1, 6–0; Carol Hanks Aucamp and Mary Ann Eisel d. Judy Dixon and King, 6–4, 1–6, 6–2.

DIXIE, at Tampa, Fla.: Istvan Gulyas (Hungary) d. Cliff Drysdale (South Africa), 3–6, 6–1, 2–6, 7–5, 2–0, def. Patrice Beust and Daniel Contet (both France) d. Mark Cox (England) and Taylor, 6–4, 6–4. Ann Haydon Jones, England, d. Françoise Durr, France, 6–4, 8–6. Virginia Wade (England) and Jones d. Betty Stove (Netherlands) and Groenman, 5–7, 7–5, 6–3.

PACIFIC COAST MEN'S DOUBLES, at LaJolla, Calif.: Stan Smith and Bob Lutz d. Clark Graebner and Marty Riessen, 14–12, 9–7, 6–0.

THUNDERBIRD, at Phoenix: Smith d. Allen Fox, 7–5, 6–3. Smith and Lutz d. Joaquin Loyo-Mayo (Mexico) and Riessen, 12–10, 10–8. Nancy Richey d. Aucamp, 6–1, 6–4. Patti Hogan and Peggy Michel d. Donna Floyd Fales and Richey, 7–5, 6–4.

MASTERS, at St. Petersburg, Fla.: Fox d. Niki Pilic (Yugoslavia), 6–3, 3–6, 6–4, 4–6, 6–2. Zeljiko Franulovic (Yugoslavia) and Pilic d. Juan Gisbert and José Gisbert (both Spain), 8–6 (one set, by agreement). Jones d. Jan Lehane O'Neill (Australia), 6–4, 1–6, 6–3. Eisel and Jones d. Betty Rosenquest Pratt and Fales, 6–4, 1–6, 6–3.

DALLAS INVITATION, at Dallas: Tony Roche (Australia) d. Ron Holmberg, 4–6, 10–8, 6–2, 14–12. John Newcombe (Australia) and Roche d. Ron Barnes (Brazil) and Ham Richardson, 4–6, 7–5, 8–6.

RIVER OAKS, at Houston: Newcombe d. Roche, 6–2, 7–5, 6–3. Rafe Osuna (Mexico) and Barnes d. Vicente Zarazue (Mexico) and Eduardo Guell, 5–7, 6–2, 10–8, 6–4.

CARIBE HILTON, at San Juan, P.R.: Roche d. Pasarell, 6–2, 6–4. Roche and Newcombe d. Edison Mandarino and Tom Koch (both Brazil), 6–2, 1–6, 6–2. Jones d. Wade, 7–5, 6–1. Jones and Wade d. Durr and O'Neill, 6–3, 6–4.

SOUTHERN CALIFORNIA, at Los Angeles: Smith d. Fox, 7–5, 13–11. Jim McManus and Jim Osborne d. Smith and Lutz, 6–4, 6–2. Tony Fretz d. Dorothy Bundy Cheney, 9–7, def. Hogan and Michel d. Pam Teeguarden and Valerie Ziegenfuss, 6–1, 2–6, 6–2.

CALIFORNIA STATE, at Portola Valley: Roche d. Newcombe, 6–3, 6–2, 8–6. Newcombe and Roche d. Fox and Holmberg, 6–3, 6–2, 3–6, 6–4. King d. Rosemary Casals, 6–1, 6–3. King and Casals d. Lynn Abbes and Jane Albert, 6–1, 6–2.

CHARLOTTE INVITATION, at Charlotte, N.C.: Holmberg d. Vic Seixas, 6–4, 6–2. Richardson and Seixas d. Mike Green and Frank Froehling, 6–1, 6–4. King d. Peaches Bartkowicz, 6–1, 6–2. Peachy Kellmeyer and Bartkowicz d. Aucamp and Eisel, 7–5, 7–5.

ATLANTA INVITATION, at Atlanta: Riessen d. Cliff Richey, 7–5, 6–2, 6–4. Riessen and Richey d. Ashe and Pasarell, 4–6, 6–3, 11–9. Bartkowicz d. Aucamp, 6–2, 6–4.

SOUTHERN, at Birmingham: Herb FitzGibbon d. John Powless, 6–2, 6–1. Bill Cullen and FitzGibbon d. Chris Bovett (England) and Tom Mozur, 6–3, 5–7, 6–4. Roberta Alison Baumgardner d. Raymonde Jones, 6–2, 6–1. Linda Tuero and Baumgardner d. Sue Sterrett and R. Jones, 6–3, 6–3.

U.S. HARD COURT, at Sacramento: Smith d. Gary Rose, 6–4, 6–3. McManus and Osborne d. Bill Demas and Smith, 6–8, 6–3, 6–4. Bartkowicz d. Ziegenfuss, 6–4, 6–4. Stephanie Grant and Ziegenfuss d. Sue Shrader and Bartkowicz, 8–6, 9–7.

WESTERN, at Indianapolis: Mike Belkin (Canada) d. Pancho Guzman (Ecuador), 3–6, 6–3, 6–1, 6–2. Riessen and Graebner d. Miguel Olvera (Ecuador) and Guzman 6–1,

6–0. Nancy Richey d. Kerry Melville (Australia), 6–4, 6–0. Carole Caldwell Graebner and Richey d. Karen Krantzcke (Australia) and Melville, 6–4, 6–1.

TRI-STATE, at Cincinnati: Loyo-Mayo d. Jaime Fillol (Chile), 8–6, 6–1. Jasjit Singh (India) and Bill Brown d. Dick Knight and Tom Gorman, 6–1, 9–7. Bartkowicz d. Patsy Rippy, 6–4, 6–1. Bartkowicz and Rippy d. Marilyn Aschner and Pixie Lamm, 6–4, 6–1.

TENNESSEE VALLEY, at Chattanooga: Fillol d. Loyo-Mayo, 6–4, 4–6, 7–5. Mozur and Bovett d. Armistead Neely and Chuck Darley, 6–4, 7–5. Tuero d. Bonnie Logan, 6–1, 6–2. Laura DuPont and Tuero d. Betty Robinson and Green, 6–3, 6–1.

U.S. CLAY COURT, at Milwaukee: Ashe d. Riessen, 4–6, 6–3, 6–1, 7–5. Graebner and Riessen d. Brian Tobin and John Brown (both Australia), 6–2, 6–3, 6–4. Nancy Richey d. Casals, 6–2, 6–3. Melville and Krantzcke d. King and Casals, 6–4, 6–1.

PENNSYLVANIA GRASS, at Philadelphia: Drysdale d. Graebner, 3–6, 3–6, 11–9, 6–1, 7–5. Graebner and Riessen d. Bill Bowrey and Owen Davidson (both Australia), 6–2, 9–11, 7–5. Eisel d. Carole Graebner, 6–1, 6–3. Melville and Krantzcke d. Stephanie DeFina and Fretz, 6–3, 6–1.

EASTERN GRASS, at South Orange, N.J.: Riessen d. Graebner, 18–16, 6–2, 6–1. Bowrey and Davidson d. Graebner and Riessen, 6–4, 9–7. King d. Kathy Harter, 4–6, 6–2, 6–3. King and Casals d. Eisel and Fales, 6–3, 13–15, 6–4.

NASSAU BOWL, at Glen Cove, N.Y.: Newcombe d. Roche, 3–6, 6–3, 6–4, 12–10. Newcombe and Roche d. Lutz and Smith, 7–5, 9–7.

MEADOW INVITATION, at Southampton, N.Y.: Davidson d. Ray Ruffels (Australia) 6–4, 7–5, 6–4. Marcelo Lara (Mexico) and Loyo-Mayo d. Len Schloss and Mozur, 6–3, 6–4, 21–19.

MIDDLE STATES GRASS: Abbel d. Hogan, 5–7, 6–4, 6–1. Hogan and Michel d. Abbes and Fales, 6–4, 1–6, 12–10.

ESSEX COUNTY, at Manchester, Mass.: King d. Melville, 8–6, 6–1. Lesley Turner (Australia) and Wade d. Eisel and Fales, 6–4, 6–2.

NEWPORT CASINO, at Newport, R.I.: Bowrey d. Davidson, 6–4, 6–2, 6–2. Bowrey and Davidson d. Ruffels and Tobin, 6–3, 6–4.

U.S. CHAMPIONSHIPS, singles, at Forest Hills: Newcombe d. Graebner, 6–4, 6–4, 8–6. King d. Jones, 11–9, 6–4. Doubles, at Longwood: Newcombe and Roche d. Bowrey and Davidson, 6–8, 9–7, 6–3, 6–3. King and Casals d. Eisel and Fales, 4–6, 6–3, 6–4.

PACIFIC SOUTHWEST, at Los Angeles: Roy Emerson (Australia) d. Riessen, 12–14, 6–3, 6–4. Bob Hewitt (South Africa) and Emerson d. Lutz and Smith, 8–6, 15–17, 6–3. King d. Casals, 6–0, 6–4. King and Casals d. Carole Graebner and Ziegenfuss, 5–7, 6–3, 6–2.

PACIFIC COAST, at Berkeley, Calif.: Passarell d. Cliff Richey, 7–5, 8–6. Graebner and Riessen d. Ray Moore (South Africa) and Hewitt, 6–4, 12–10. Durr d. Carole Graebner, 6–3, 6–3. Casals and King d. Judy Tegart (Australia) and Durr, 6–3, 6–4.

1968 Season

SUGAR BOWL, at New Orleans: Arthur Ashe d. Niki Pilic (Yugoslavia), 5–7, 6–10, 6–3, 11–9, 6–3.

PITTSBURGH INDOOR, at Pittsburgh: Mark Cox (England) d. Bob Lutz, 6–4, 2–6, 7–5; Stan Smith and Lutz d. Ron Holmberg and Cox, 6–3, 7–5.

PHILADELPHIA INDOOR, at Philadelphia: Manolo Santana (Spain) d. Jan Leschly (Denmark), 8–6, 6–3; Charles Pasarell and Arthur d. Torben Ulrich (Denmark) and Tom Koch (Brazil), 6–3, 12–10.

MACON INDOOR, at Macon, Ga.: Leschly d. Mike Sangster (England), 6–3, 6–4, 5–7, 6–4.

NEW ENGLAND WOMEN'S INDOOR, at Salem, Mass.: Billie Jean Moffitt King d. Mary Ann Eisel, 6–3, 6–4; Rosemary Casals and King d. Kathy Harter and Eisel, 16–14, 6–3.

NATIONAL INDOOR, Men, at Salisbury, Md.: Cliff Richey d. Clark Graebner, 6–4, 6–4, 6–4; Okker and Koch d. Smith and Lutz, 6–3, 10–12, 8–6. Women, at Winchester, Mass.: King d. Rosemary Casals, 6–3, 9–7. King and Casals d. Kathy Harter and Eisel, 6–2, 6–2.

MADISON SQUARE GARDEN INTERNATIONAL, at New York City: Ashe d. Roy Emerson (Australia), 6–4, 6–4, 7–5. Nancy Richey d. Judy Tegart (Australia), 7–5, 7–5.

DIXIE, at Tampa, Fla.: Santana d. Istvan Gulyas (Hungary), 6–4, 7–5, 6–4; Ray Ruffels (Australia) and Cox d. Zeljko Franulovic (Yugoslavia) and Gulyas, 6–1, 6–4. Helga Niessen (Germany) d. Tegart, 2–6, 6–4, 6–1;

Faye Urban (Canada) and Niessen d. Valerie Ziegenfuss and Tegart, 6–2, 6–2.

PACIFIC COAST DOUBLES, at LaJolla, Calif.: Smith and Lutz d. Ashe and Emerson, 7–5, 7–5, 6–4.

THUNDERBIRD, at Phoenix: Smith d. Lutz, 4–6, 6–2, 6–1; Smith-Lutz d. Joaquin Loyo-Mayo and Marcelo Lara (both Mexico), 6–2, 22–20. Patti Hogan d. Tory Fretz, 6–2, 6–4; Eisel-Harter d. Peggy Michel and Hogan, 13–11, 6–2.

MASTERS, at St. Petersburg, Fla.: Mike Belkin (Canada) d. Jaime Fillol (Chile), 2–6, 6–0, 7–5; Pat Cramer (South Africa) and Fillol d. Allen Fox and Belkin, 6–1, 6–4. Nancy Richey d. Lesley Turner Bowrey (Australia), 7–5, 6–0; Richey-Bowrey d. Ingrid Lofdahl (Sweden) and Stephanie DeFina, 7–5, 7–5.

DALLAS INVITATION, at Dallas: Ray Moore (South Africa) d. Alan Stone (Australia), 4–6, 12–10, 6–3; Maryna Godwin (South Africa) d. Julie Heldman, 7–9, 6–3, 6–4.

RIVER OAKS, at Houston: Cliff Richey d. Boro Jovanovic (Yugoslavia), 6–4, 6–1, 6–0; Rafe Osuna (Mexico) and Loyo-Mayo d. Richey-Graebner, 6–4, 2–6, 7–5, 7–5; Nancy Richey d. Peaches Bartkowicz, 6–1, 6–1; Esme Emanuel (South Africa) and Harter d. Linda Tuero and Bartkowicz, 6–2, 9–7.

CARIBE HILTON, at San Juan, P.R.: Cox d. Fox, 6–2, 6–1, 4–6, 2–6, 6–2; Bill Bowrey (Australia) and Ruffels d. Sangster and Cox, 6–3, 4–6, 13–11. Nancy Richey d. Harter, 6–3, 6–4; Richey and Ziegenfuss d. Bartkowicz and Tuero, 6–4, 6–4.

SOUTHERN CALIFORNIA, at Los Angeles: Smith d. Dick Leach, 6–3, 6–4; Smith and Lutz d. Jim Osborne and Jim McManus, 6–3, 7–5. Hogan d. Fretz, 6–2, 8–6; Stephanie Grant and Debby Pruitt d. Janet Newberry and Hogan, 6–3, 6–1.

BUCCANEER DAYS, at Corpus Christi, Tex.: Peter van Lingen (South Africa) d. Ruffels, 4–6, 7–5, 6–1; Pancho Guzman (Ecuador) and Ruffels d. Jim Parker and Ron Fisher, 6–0, 6–3. Emilie Burrer d. Mary Lowdon, 2–6, 9–7, 6–3; Becky Vest and Burrer d. Lovie Beard and Lowdon, 6–1, 6–3.

CHARLOTTE INVITATION, at Charlotte, N.C.: Ashe d. Ron Holmberg, 6–2, 6–4; Ashe and Holmberg d. Vic Seixas and Bowrey, 6–3, 6–3. Tegart d. DeFina, 7–5, 3–6, 7–5; Lesley

Bowrey and Tegart d. Eisel and DeFina, 6–4, 6–2.

ATLANTA INVITATION, at Atlanta: Bill Bowrey d. Holmberg, 6–0, 7–5; Holmberg and Ruffles won over Bowrey-Ruffles, default. DeFina d. Tuero, 6–4, 8–10, 6–2; Tegart and Lesley Bowrey d. DeFina and Emanuel, 8–2 (pro set).

OJAI VALLEY, at Ojai, Calif.: Loyo-Mayo d. Jim Hobson, 6–4, 6–4; Bob Potthast and Leach d. Lara and Loyo-Mayo, 13–11, 8–6. Betty Grubb d. Pixie Lamm, 6–4, 6–2; Pam Teeguarden and Michel d. Grubb and Lamm, 8–6, 7–5.

CALIFORNIA, at Portola Valley, Calif.: McManus d. Jeff Borowiak, 6–2, 6–3, 6–1; Don Jacobus and McManus d. Erik Van Dillen and Bob Hill, 8–6, 6–4, 6–3. Denise Carter d. Kristy Pigeon, 6–8, 9–7, 6–1; Cecilia Martinez and Pigeon d. Sharon Russell and Gail Hansen, 6–2, 6–2.

TULSA INVITATION, at Tulsa: Van Lingen d. Loyo-Mayo, 7–5, 6–2; Ham Richardson and Fillol d. Vicente Zarazua (Mexico) and Loyo-Mayo, 7–5, 6–3.

CENTRAL CALIFORNIA, at Sacramento: Graebner d. Smith, 10–8, 6–4, 6–2; Smith and Lutz d. Pasarell and Ashe, 6–3, 4–6, 6–3; Carter d. Roylee Bailey, 7–5, 6–3.

BLUE AND GRAY, at Montgomery, Ala.: Loyo-Mayo d. Zarazua, 6–1, 6–1; Zarazua and Loyo-Mayo d. John Pickens and Butch Seewagen, 6–3, 3–6, 6–3. Tuero d. Burrer, 6–0, 6–4; Burrer and Tuero d. Lulu Gongora (Mexico) and Mary McLean, 6–2, 6–2.

SOUTHERN, at Birmingham: Van Lingen d. Zan Guerry, 6–2, 6–4; Van Lingen and Loyo-Mayo d. Rudy Hernando and Bob Conti, 9–7, 6–3. Tuero d. Gongora, 6–0, 6–0; Olga Palafox (Mexico) and Debby Wells d. Gongora and McLean, 6–2, 6–4.

TRI-STATE, at Cincinnati: Bill Harris d. Tom Gorman, 3–6, 6–2, 6–2; Bill Brown-Ron Goldman d. Loyo-Mayo and Fillol, 10–8, 6–3. Tuero d. Tory Fretz, 6–1, 6–2; Burrer and Tuero d. Carol Gay and Michel, 6–2, 6–3.

WESTERN, at Indianapolis: Fillol d. Cliff Richey, 6–1, 7–5, 6–2; Smith and Lutz d. Osborne-McManus, 6–4, 6–2. Nancy Richey d. DeFina, 6–3, 6–2. Fretz-DeFina d. Laura Roussow (South Africa) and Godwin, 8–6, 6–2.

NATIONAL CLAY COURT, at Milwaukee: Graebner d. Smith, 6–3, 7–5, 6–0; Smith-Lutz

d. Marty Riessen and Tom Mozur, 3–6, 6–2, 6–4, 6–2; Nancy Richey d. Tuero, 6–3, 6–3; Richey and Ziegenfuss d. DeFina and Bartkowicz, 6–0, 6–2.

MIDDLE STATES GRASS, at Philadelphia: Pigeon d. Martinez, 3–6, 6–1, 6–2; Pigeon and Martinez d. Tina Lyman and Carter, 9–7, 6–1.

PENNSYLVANIA GRASS, at Philadelphia: Ashe d. Riessen, 6–2, 6–3, 6–3; Ashe-Riessen divided final with Pasarell and Graebner, 2 sets each, 9–7 10–8, 2–6, 28–30, Ashe and Riessen winning first two. Pigeon d. Vicky Rogers, 9–7, 6–0; Eisel-Ziegenfuss d. Karen Krantzcke and Helen Gourlay (both Australia), 6–3, 6–3.

EASTERN GRASS, at South Orange, N.J.: Pasarell d. Graebner, 3–6, 4–6, 6–2, 6–3, 6–4; Graebner-Pasarell led Smith-Lutz, 6–4, 10–10, final not completed. Eisel d. Pigeon, 3–6, 6–1, 6–2; Eisel and Ziegenfuss d. Fretz and Rogers, 8–6, 8–6.

MEADOW CLUB, at Southampton, N.Y.: Holmberg d. Gene Scott, 6–4, 1–6, 6–3, 13–11; Hewitt and Moore d. Paul Sullivan and Chauncey Steele III, 6–2, 6–3.

PIPING ROCK, at Locust Valley, N.Y.: Eisel d. Krantzcke, 3–6, 16–14, 8–6; Eisel and Krantzcke d. Hogan and Michel, 6–0, 6–3.

BALTIMORE GRASS, at Baltimore: Hewitt d. Colin Stubs, Australia, 6–1, 6–4; Hewitt and Holmberg d. Patricio Cornejo (Chile) and Fillol, 6–4, 7–5. Eisel d. Harter, 6–2, 7–5; Krantzcke and Gourlay d. Eisel and Ziegenfuss, 3–6, 6–3, retired.

ESSEX COUNTY, at Manchester, Mass.: Maria Bueno, Brazil d. Mrs. Margaret Smith Court, Australia, 7–5, 3–6, 6–3; Bueno and Court d. Hogan and Michel, 6–1, 6–2.

NATIONAL AMATEUR CHAMPIONSHIPS, at Longwood, Boston: Ashe d. Lutz, 4–6, 8–6, 8–10, 6–0, 6–4; Smith-Lutz d. Hewitt and Moore, 6–4, 6–4, 9–7. Court d. Bueno, 6–2, 6–2; Court-Bueno d. Virginia Wade and Mrs. Joyce Barclay Williams, both England, 6–3, 7–5.

U.S. OPEN CHAMPIONSHIPS, at West Side, Forest Hills, N.Y.: Ashe d. Okker, 14–12, 5–7, 6–3, 3–6, 6–3; Smith and Lutz d. Andres Gimeno (Spain) and Ashe, 11–9, 6–1, 7–5; Wade d. King, 6–4, 6–2; Court and Bueno d. King and Casals, 4–6, 9–7, 8–6.

HEART OF AMERICA, at Kansas City, Mo.: Parker d. Ingo Buding, Germany, 6–8, 3–6,

6–0, 6–4, 6–4; Rod Susman and Parker d. McKenna and van Lingen, 6–2, 6–2. Heldman d. Laura Roussow (South Africa), 4–6, 6–2, 7–5; Heldman and Harter d. Godwin and Roussow, 6–4, 1–6, 6–0.

PENSACOLA INVITATION, at Pensacola, Fla.: Armistead Neely d. Fillol, 5–7, 16–14, 6–2; Tom Edlefsen and Neely d. Alan Stone, Australia, Stubs, 6–2, 6–3. Tuero d. DeFina, 9–7, 6–4; Tuero and DeFina d. Charlotte Grafton and Wendy McCloskey, 6–2, 6–2.

PACIFIC SOUTHWEST OPEN, at Los Angeles: Rod Laver (Australia) d. Ken Rosewall (Australia), 4–6, 6–0, 6–0; Fred Stolle (Australia) and Rosewall d. Cliff Drysdale, South Africa, and Roger Taylor, England, 7–5, 6–1. Casals d. Bueno, 6–4, 6–1; Mrs. Ann Haydon Jones, England, and Françoise Durr, France, d. Casals and Bueno, 6–3, 6–2.

PACIFIC COAST, at Berkeley, Calif.: Smith d. McManus, 10–8, 6–1; Smith and Lutz d. McManus and Osborne, 10–8, 11–9. Court d. Bueno, 6–4, 7–5; Court and Bueno d. Godwin and Emanuel, 6–2, 6–4.

NATIONAL HARD COURT, at LaJolla, Calif.: Smith d. Barth, 9–7, 6–1; Osuna and Leach d. Lara and Loyo-Mayo, 4–6, 8–6, 8–6. Godwin d. Janet Newberry, 6–3, 8–6; Godwin and Hogan d. Mrs. Jane Albert Freeman and Ziegenfuss, 6–2, 6–2.

1969 Season

SUGAR BOWL, 1968, at New Orleans: Cliff Richey d. Ron Holmberg, 6–4, 6–4, 4–6, 8–6; Jim McManus and Holmberg d. Tom Edlefsen and Richey, 6–1, 1–6, 6–2.

OMAHA INDOOR, at Omaha, Neb.: Cliff Richey d. Joaquin Loyo-Mayo (Mexico) 6–4, 6–2.

RICHMOND INDOOR, at Richmond, Va.: Clark Graebner d. Tom Koch, Brazil, 6–3, 10–12, 9–7; Cliff Richey and Graebner d. Torben Ulrich, Denmark, and Koch, 5–7, 9–7, 7–5.

PITTSBURGH INDOOR, at Pittsburgh, Pa.: Jan Kodes (Czechoslovakia) d. Herb FitzGibbon, 8–6, 6–1.

BUFFALO INDOOR, at Buffalo, N.Y.: Clark Graebner d. Mark Cox, England, 2–6, 9–7, 8–6; Tom Edlefsen and Cox d. Chuck McKinley and Graebner, 10–8, 6–3.

MACON INDOOR, at Macon, Ga.: Manolo Orantes (Spain) d. Mark Cox, 10–8, 7–5, 4–6, 10–8; Jan Kukal and Jan Kodes (both

U.S. Title Matches, Leading Events, 1969 (cont.)
Czechoslovakia) d. Peter Curtis and Cox (both England), 13–11, 10–8.

CITY OF MIAMI, at Miami, Fla.: Jaime Fillol (Chile) d. Pancho Guzman (Ecuador), 13–11, 5–7, 9–7; Gardnar Mulloy and Ed Rubinoff d. Nick Kalogeropoulos (Greece) and Guzman, 6–4, 6–4. Stephanie DeFina d. Suzanna Peterson (Brazil), 6–1, 6–2.

AUSTIN SMITH, at Ft. Lauderdale, Fla.: Pat Cramer (South Africa) d. Jaime Fillol, 6–2, 11–9; Luis Garcia (Mexico) and Cramer d. Frank Tutvin and Mike Belkin (both Canada), 6–4, 9–7. Stephanie DeFina d. Mary Ann Eisel, 6–3, 7–5; DeFina and Eisel d. Susan Epstein and Chris Evert, 6–1, 6–3.

FREED INVITATION, at Salt Lake City: Jim McManus d. Tom Gorman, 6–3, 6–3; Jim Osborne and McManus d. Steve Tidball and Roy Barth, 4–6, 6–3, 14–12.

NEW YORK STATE INDOOR, at New Rochelle, N.Y.: Clark Graebner d. Charlie Pasarell, 6–2, 6–2; Ned Weld and Steve Stockton d. Jaime Subirats (Mexico) and Butch Seewagen, 6–2, 7–5.

PHILADELPHIA OPEN, at Spectrum, Philadelphia: Rod Laver (Australia) d. Tony Roche (Australia), 7–5, 6–4, 6–4. Marty Riessen and Tom Okker (Netherlands) d. John Newcombe (Australia) and Roche, 8–6, 6–4.

MADISON SQUARE GARDEN OPEN, at New York City: Andres Gimeno (Spain) d. Arthur Ashe, 6–1, 6–2, 3–6, 6–8, 9–7.

NEW ENGLAND INDOOR, at Longmeadow, Mass.: Mary Ann Eisel d. Esme Emanuel (South Africa), 7–5, 6–2; Valerie Ziegenfuss and Eisel d. Kristy Pigeon and Stephanie DeFina, 6–2, 6–2.

NATIONAL INDOOR, MEN, at Salisbury, Md.: Stan Smith d. Ismail El Shafei (Egypt), 6–3, 6–8, 6–4, 6–4; Bob Lutz and Smith d. Ron Holmberg and Charlie Pasarell, 7–9, 8–6, 6–4. Women, at Winchester, Mass.: Mary Ann Eisel d. Stephanie DeFina, 6–3, 4–6, 6–2. Valerie Ziegenfuss and Eisel d. Peggy Michel and Patti Hogan, 6–1, 6–3.

THUNDERBIRD, at Phoenix, Ariz.: Cliff Richey d. Manolo Santana (Spain), 6–4, 6–4; Roy Barth and Steve Tidball d. Jim Osborne and Richey, 10–8, 9–7. Nancy Richey d. Patti Hogan, 6–2, 6–0; Peggy Michel and Hogan d. Cecilia Martinez and Esme Emanuel, 3–6, 6–3, 6–1.

PACIFIC COAST DOUBLES, at LaJolla, Calif.: Roy Barth and Steve Tidball d. Marcelo Lara and Joaquin Loyo-Mayo (both Mexico), 6–4, 6–3, 4–6, 8–10, 10–8.

STATION WLOD INTERNATIONAL, at Ft. Lauderdale, Fla.: Julie Heldman d. Virginia Wade (England), 6–1, 6–4; Mrs. Margaret Smith Court and Judy Tegart (both Australia) d. Karen Krantzcke (Australia) and Wade, 6–3, 3–6, 6–3.

MASTERS INVITATION, at St. Petersburg, Fla.: Zeliko Franulovic, Yugoslavia d. Jaime Fillol, 6–4, 6–2, 6–4; Ilie Nastase (Romania) and Franulovic d. Edison Mandarino (Brazil) and Mike Belkin, 6–4, 9–7. Kerry McIville (Australia) d. Mrs. Lesley Turner Bowrey (Australia), 6–4, 6–3; Bowrey-Melville d. Valerie Ziegenfuss and Mary Ann Eisel Curtis, 6–4, 7–5.

CARIBE HILTON INVITATION, at San Juan, P.R.: Arthur Ashe d. Charlie Pasarell, 5–7, 5–7, 6–0, 6–4, 6–3; Phil Dent and John Alexander (both Australia) d. Peter Curtis and Mark Cox, 6–3, 6–3; Margaret Court d. Julie Heldman, 6–4, 7–5; Karen Krantzcke and Kerry Melville d. Valerie Ziegenfuss and Mary Ann Eisel, 6–4, 7–5.

TIDEWATER INTERNATIONAL, at Norfolk, Va.: Hans Plotz (Germany) d. Jan Kukal, 6–4, 7–5; Geoff Battrick (England) and Milan Holocck (Czechoslovakia) d. Ray Ruffels and Bill Bowrey (both Australia), 6–4, 6–4.

CHARLOTTE INVITATION, at Charlotte, N.C.: Mark Cox d. Jan Kodes, 13–11, 6–2; John Alexander and Phil Dent d. Niki Spear and Zeljko Franulovic (both Yugoslavia), 3–6, 6–4, 6–2; Margaret Court d. Judy Tegart, 6–1, 6–1; Court and Tegart d. Lesley Bowrey and Mary Ann Eisel, 6–4, 6–2.

RIVER OAKS INVITATION, at Houston: Zeljko Franulovic d. Rafe Osuna (Mexico), 7–5, 6–3, 6–2; Clark Graebner and Osuna d. Stan Smith and Tom Edlefsen, 6–4, 6–4. Margaret Court d. Judy Tegart, 3–6, 7–5, 6–1; Court-Tegart d. Kerry Melville and Karen Krantzcke, 6–4, 6–3.

OJAI VALLEY, at Ojai, Calif.: Haround Rahim (Pakistan) d. Jeff Borowski, 4–6, 6–1, 9–7; Dick Leach and Bob Potthast d. Steve Cornell and Ron Cornell, 6–1, 6–3. Betty Ann Grubb d. Denise Carter, 3–6, 6–2, 6–3; Peggy Michel and Carter d. Mrs. Janie Albert Freeman and Kris Kemmer, 3–6, 6–2, 6–0.

JACKSONVILLE INVITATION, at Jacksonville, Fla.: Pancho Guzman d. Mike Belkin, 6–4, 6–2; Sven Ginman (Sweden) and Pat Cramer d. Bob Marcher (Brazil) and Herb Rapp, 6–1, 6–4. Judy Alvarez d. Wendy Overton, 7–5, 2–6, 6–1.

DALLAS INVITATION, at Dallas: Stan Smith d. Tom Koch, 6–3, 6–4: Tom Edlefsen and Smith d. John Alexander and Phil Dent, 7–9, 6–3, 6–4.

SOUTHERN CALIFORNIA, at Los Angeles: Stan Smith d. Bob Lutz, 6–3, 6–4; Alex Olmedo and Smith d. Bill Bond and Dick Leach, 6–3, 6–3. Janet Newberry d. Valerie Ziegenfuss, 6–2, 6–4; Barbara Green Weigandt and Louise Brough Clapp d. Tam O'Shaughnessy and Ann Lebedeff, 7–5, 6–4.

CALIFORNIA STATE, at Portola Valley: Erik Van Dillen d. Paul Gerken, 6–3, 6–4, 6–2; Jim McManus and Jim Osborne d. Don Kierbow and Henry Kamakana, 6–2, 6–4, 6–1. Denise Carter d. Gail Hansen, 6–4, 6–3; Kristy Pigeon and Carter d. Cecilia Martinez and Esme Emanuel, 10–8, 2–6, 6–0.

NORTHERN CALIFORNIA, at San Francisco: Tom Brown d. Erik Van Dillen, 6–4, 6–8, 7–9, 8–6, 6–1; Gene Cantin and Corky McInhardt d. Larry Dodge and Whitney Reed, 6–3, 6–1. Marcelyn Louie d. Farel Footman, 6–2, 9–7.

GLENWOOD MANOR INVITATION, at Overland Park, Kans.: Clark Graebner d. Tom Edlefsen, 6–4, 3–6, 6–3; Bob Potthast and Dick Leach d. Mike Davies and Rod Susman, 6–4, 6–8, 6–2. Betty Ann Grubb d. Mrs. Karen Hantze Susman, 6–4, 6–2; Carol Hanks Aucamp and Susman d. Cecilia Martinez and Esme Emanuel, 6–4, 10–8.

ATLANTA INVITATION, at Atlanta: Tom Koch d. Bill Bowrey, 6–3, 6–2; Ray Ruffels and Bowrey d. Edison Mandarino and Koch, 15–13, 8–6. Nancy Richey d. Linda Tuero, 7–5, 6–2.

WASHINGTON STAR INVITATION, at Washington, D.C.: Tom Koch d. Arthur Ashe, 7–5, 9–7, 4–6, 2–6, 6–4; Pat Cornejo and Jaime Fillol (both Chile) d. Bob Jutz and Stan Smith, 4–6, 6–1, 6–4.

NATIONAL AMATEUR, at Rochester, N.Y.: Butch Seewagen d. Zan Guerry, 9–7, 6–8, 1–6, 6–2, 6–4; Tom Leonard and Erik Van Dillen d. Bob McKinley and Dick Stockton, 6–4, 7–5, 6–3. Linda Tuero d. Gwyneth Thomas, 4–6, 6–1, 6–2; Emilie Burrer and

Pam Richmond d. Pat Cody and Tuero, 5–7, 9–7, 6–3.

WESTERN CHAMPIONSHIPS, at Cincinnati: Cliff Richey d. Allan Stone (Australia), 6–1, 6–2; Bob Lutz and Stan Smith d. Arthur Ashe and Charlie Pasarell, 6–3, 6–4. Lesley Bowrey d. Mme. Gail Sheriff Chanfreau (Australia), 7–5, 10–10, default; Kerry Harris, Australia and Valerie Ziegenfuss d. Pam Richmond and Emilie Burrer, 6–3, 9–7.

TULSA INVITATION, at Tulsa: Tom Koch d. Vicente Zarazue (Mexico), 6–2, 8–6; Humphrey Hose (Venezuela) and Zarazue d. Peter van Lingen (South Africa) and Jeff Borowiak, 5–7, 8–6, 6–4. Betty Ann Grubb d. Vicky Rogers, 6–1, 6–1; Esme Emanuel and Cecelia Martinez d. Connie Capozzi and Rogers, 7–5, 6–3.

NATIONAL HARD COURT, at Sacramento: Clark Graebner d. Erik Van Dillen, 6–4, 3–6, 4–6, 6–0, 7–5; Bob Lutz and Van Dillen d. Joaquin Loyo-Mayo and Marcelo Lara, 6–3, 5–7, 8–6. Liza Pande d. Kris Kemmer, 7–5, 6–4; Pam Austin and Tam O'Shaughnessy d. Cathie Anderson and Barbara Downs, 6–4, 6–1.

TENNESSEE VALLEY, at Chattanooga: Joaquin Loyo-Mayo d. Zan Guerry, 7–5, 6–8, 6–1; Humphrey Hose and Steve Faulk d. Mike Estep and Guerry, 6–3, 6–2. Linda Tuero d. Fiorella Bonicelli (Peru), 6–2, 6–0; Laura DuPont and Zoe Mills d. Pat Hickman and L. Weber, 6–2, 3–6, 6–1.

SOUTHERNS, at Birmingham: Turner Howard d. Jamie Pressly, 6–2, 6–3; Jiri Medonos (Czechoslovakia) and Steve Faulk d. Paul Gerken and F. D. Robbins, 3–6, 6–3, 6–2. Connie Capozzi d. Tish Adams, 6–1, 6–2; Laura DuPont and Zoe Mills d. Gwenda Adams and Tish Adams, 6–1, 6–2.

ALABAMA CHAMPIONSHIPS, at Mobile: Mike Belikin d. Peter van Lingen, 6–3, 9–11, 6–3; Jiri Medonos and van Lingen d. Roscoe Tanner and Raz Reid, 6–1, 13–15, 6–4. Emilie Burrer d. Peggy Moore, 6–4, 8–6; Becky Vest and Burrer d. Ann Moore and Peggy Moore, 7–5, 6–4.

NATIONAL CLAY COURT, at Indianapolis: Zeljko Franulovic d. Arthur Ashe, 8–6, 6–3, 6–4; Clark Graebner and Bill Bowrey d. Allan Stone and Dick Crealy (both Australia), 6–4, 4–6, 6–4. Gail Chanfreau d. Linda Tuero, 6–2, 6–2; Lesley Bowrey and Chanfreau d. Emilie Burrer and Tuero, 6–0, 10–8.

EASTERN GRASS, at South Orange, N.J.: Stan Smith d. Clark Graebner, 6–1, 6–4, 6–4; Bob Lutz and Smith d. Arthur Ashe and Graebner, 6–3, 9–7. Patti Hogan d. Kristy Pigeon, 3–6, 6–3, 6–4; Mrs. Mary Ann Eisel Curtis and Valerie Ziegenfuss d. Peggy Michel and Hogan, 6–4, 6–4.

MEADOW CLUB INVITATION, at Southampton, N.Y.: Clark Graebner d. Bob Lutz, 6–2, 6–2, 6–4; Graebner and Lutz d. Onny Parun (New Zealand) and Allan Stone, 7–5, 7–5.

PIPING ROCK INVITATION, at Locust Valley, N.Y.: Margaret Court d. Betty Ann Grubb, 6–1, 6–3; Kerry Harris and Court d. Peggy Michel and Patti Hogan, 8–6, 6–4.

PENNSYLVANIA GRASS, at Philadelphia: Cliff Richey d. Bob Carmichael (Australia), 6–4, 7–9, 6–2, 6–4; Jim Osborne and Bill Bowrey d. Dick Crealy and Allan Stone, 6–4, 6–3. Margaret Court d. Virginia Wade, 6–4, 6–4. Court and Wade d. Lesley Hunt (Australia) and Gail Chanfreau, 6–3, 6–0.

NATIONAL CHAMPIONSHIPS, at Longwood, Boston: Stan Smith d. Bob Lutz, 9–7, 6–3, 6–1; Allan Stone and Dick Crealy d. Bill Bowrey and Charlie Pasarell, 9–11, 6–3, 7–5. Margaret Court d. Virginia Wade, 4–6, 6–3, 6–0; Court and Wade d. Mary Ann Curtis and Valerie Ziegenfuss, 6–1, 6–3.

U.S. OPEN, at West Side Tennis Club, Forest Hills, N.Y.: Rod Laver d. Tony Roche, 7–9, 6–1, 6–2; Ken Rosewall and Fred Stolle d. Denny Ralston and Charlie Pasarell, 2–6, 7–5, 13–11, 6–3. Margaret Court d. Nancy Richey, 6–2, 6–2; Françoise Durr, France, and Darlene Hard d. Virginia Wade and Court, 0–6, 6–3, 6–4.

PACIFIC SOUTHWEST OPEN, at Los Angeles: Pancho Gonzalez d. Cliff Richey, 6–0, 7–5; Ron Holmberg and Gonzalez d. Jim Osborne and Jim McManus, 6–2, 6–3; Rosie Casals and King d. Françoise Durr and Jones, 6–8, 8–6, 11–9.

NORTHWEST INVITATION, at Minneapolis: Tom Edlefsen d. Mike Davies, 6–0, 6–3; Ned Neely and Crawford Henry d. Chuck McKinley and Edlefsen, 9–7, 7–5.

HEART OF AMERICA, at Kansas City: Gerald Battrick d. Bill Bowrey, 6–3, 6–4; Mark Cox and Bowery d. Graham Stilwell and Battrick, 16–14, 6–4. Lesley Bowrey d. Kerry Harris,

8–6, 4–6, 7–5; Bowrey-Harris d. Jennifer Waterman and Brozman, 6–1, 6–1.

PACIFIC COAST CHAMPIONSHIPS, at Berkeley: Stan Smith d. Cliff Richey, 6–2, 6–2; Tom Koch and Smith d. Terry Addison and Ray Keldie, 6–1, 6–3. Margaret Court d. Winnie Shaw (Scotland), 6–4, 5–7, 6–0; Lesley Hunt and Court d. Kerry Harris and Shaw, 6–3, 6–4.

LA COSTA INVITATION, at Carlsbad, Calif.: Bob Carmichael d. Tom Edlefsen, 7–5, 6–3; Ray Keldie and Terry Addison d. Roy Barth and Steve Tidball, 6–4, 3–6, 20–18. Julie Holdman d. Peaches Bartkowicz, 6–3, 7–5; Heldman and Bartkowicz d. Winnie Shaw and Valerie Ziegenfuss, 6–4, 6–1.

SUGAR BOWL: Cliff Richey d. Jim Osborne, 6–4, 6–4, 6–2; Roy Barth and Osborne d. Tom Mozur and Steve Faulk, 6–2, 6–4.

HOWARD HUGHES OPEN, at Las Vegas: Pancho Gonzalez d. Arthur Ashe, 6–0, 6–2, 6–4. Nancy Richey d. Billie Jean King, 2–6, 6–4, 6–1.

1970 Season

FLORIDA STATE, at Orlando, Fla.: Frank Froehling d. Mike Belkin, Canada, 6–2, 6–3, 6–4; Brian Parrot and Pancho Guzman (Ecuador) d. Froehling and Waters, 6–4, 3–6, 7–5. Stephanie Johnson d. Mona Schallau, 6–2, 6–1; Margie Cooper and Schallau d. Betty Pratt and Johnson, 6–4, 6–4.

AUSTIN SMITH, at Ft. Lauderdale, Fla.: Cliff Richey d. Clark Graebner, 6–3, 7–5; Frank Froehling and Graebner d. Gardnar Mulloy and Billy Higgins, 6–4, 5–7, 6–3. Chris Evert d. Laurie Fleming, 6–1, 6–0; Stephanie Johnson and Kathy Thornbrough d. Peachy Kellmeyer and Astrid Suurbeek (Netherlands), 9–7, 3–6, 6–3.

MARCH OF DIMES, San Diego: Roy Berth d. Tito Vasquez (Argentina), 6–1, 6–1; Barth and Vasquez d. Bill Brown and Dick Leach, 6–3, 7–9, 6–4. Nancy Ornstein d. Janet Newberry, 3–6, 6–4, 7–5; Patti Hogan and Laurie Tenney d. Chris Mattson and Newberry, 8–6, 9–7.

PHILADELPHIA INTERNATIONAL OPEN, Philadelphia, Pa.: Rod Laver (Australia) d. Tony Roche (Australia), 6–3, 7–6, 6–2; Ilie Nastase and Ion Tiriac (both Romania) d.

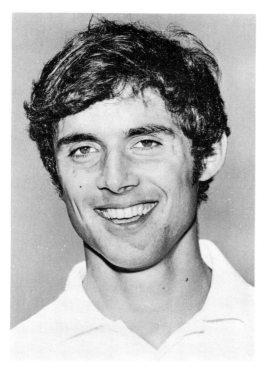

Four promising young men American players: (*top, left to right*) Tom Gorman and Erik Van Dillen. (*bottom, left to right*) Jeff Borowiak and James Connors.

U.S. Title Matches, Leading Events, 1970 (cont.)
Arthur Ashe and Dennis Ralston, 6–4, 6–3.
Margaret Court (Australia) d. Billie Jean
King, 6–3, 7–6.

FIDELITY INDOOR, at Richmond, Va.:
Arthur Ashe d. Stan Smith, 6–2, 13–11;
Charlie Pasarell and Ashe d. Jim McManus
and Smith, 9–7, 6–2.

NEW ENGLAND WOMEN'S INDOOR CHAMPION-
SHIPS, at Agawam, Mass.: Mary Ann Curtis
d. Pam Teeguarden, 4–6, 6–2, 7–5; Valerie
Ziegenfuss and Curtis d. Patti Hogan and
Peggy Michel, 6–3, 6–4.

NATIONAL INDOOR OPEN, at Salisbury, Md.:
Ilie Nastase d. Cliff Richey, 6–8, 3–6, 6–4,
9–7, 6–0; Arthur Ashe and Stan Smith d.
Onny Parun and Brian Fairlie (both New
Zealand), 6–4, 7–5.

NATIONAL WOMEN'S INDOOR, at Winchester,
Mass.: Mary Ann Curtis d. Patti Hogan, 7–5,
3–6, 6–4; Nancy Richey and Peaches Bartkowicz d. Valerie Ziegenfuss and Curtis, 8–6,
6–4.

EASTERN INDOOR, at Hackensack, N.J.:
Herb FitzGibbon d. Peter Fishbach, 13–11,
7–5, 6–0.

BUFFALO INDOOR, at Buffalo, N.Y.: Clark
Graebner d. Bob Lutz, 6–4, 3–6, 9–7;
Graebner and Gene Scott d. Bob McKinley
and Dick Stockton, 4–6, 7–5, 7–5.

VANDERBILT INDOOR, at New York City:
Margaret Court d. Virginia Wade (England),
6–3, 6–3.

MIDLAND INDOOR, at Omaha: Stan Smith
d. Jim Osborne, 6–2, 7–5, 6–3; Bob Lutz and
Smith d. Ion Tiriac and Ilie Nastase, 6–4, 6–4.

WORLD CUP, at Boston, Mass.: Australia
5, U.S. 2; Cliff Richey d. John Newcombe,
6–4, 3–6, 6–4; Fred Stolle d. Arthur Ashe,
6–3, 6–2; Newcombe d. Stan Smith, 7–5, 6–3;
Newcombe and Stolle d. Ashe and Clark
Graebner, 8–6, 4–6, 10–8; Richey d. Stolle,
4–6, 6–2, 6–4; Newcombe d. Smith, 6–3, 6–3;
Newcombe and Stolle d. Ashe and Smith, 6–3,
2–6, 7–5.

MAUREEN CONNOLLY MEMORIAL INDOOR, at
Dallas, Tex.: Margaret Court d. Billie Jean
King, 1–6, 6–3, 11–9; Rosie Casals and King
d. Patti Hogan and Mary Ann Curtis, 10–8,
6–3.

GREATER JACKSONVILLE INVITATION, at
Jacksonville, Fla.: Arthur Ashe d. Brian
Fairlie, 6–3, 4–6, 6–3; Ray Keldie (Australia)

and Hans Ploetz (Germany) d. Roy Barth
and Chauncey Steele III, 9–7, 6–4. Nancy
Richey d. Valerie Ziegenfuss, 6–1, 6–3.

CARIBE HILTON INVITATION, at San Juan,
P.R.: Arthur Ashe d. Cliff Richey, 6–4, 6–3,
1–6, 6–3; Terry Addison and Bob Carmichael
(both Australia) d. Charlie Pasarell and Ashe,
3–6, 8–6, 6–3. Peaches Bartkowicz d. Valerie
Ziegenfuss, 6–1, 6–4; Mary Ann Curtis and
Patti Hogan d. Stephanie Johnson and Bartkowicz, 6–3, 5–7, 6–0.

MACON INDOOR, at Macon, Ga.: Cliff
Richey d. Arthur Ashe, 3–6, 6–3, 8–6; Terry
Addison and Bob Carmichael d. Ion Tiriac
and Ilie Nastase, 14–16, 6–4, 8–6.

WLOD INVITATION, at Ft. Lauderdale, Fla.:
Nancy Richey d. Peaches Bartkowicz, 6–3,
6–1; Bartkowicz and Richey d. Kathy Harter
and Patti Hogan 6–2, 6–1.

RIVER OAKS INVITATION, at Houston, Tex.:
Clark Graebner d. Cliff Richey, 2–6, 6–3, 5–7,
6–3, 6–2; Terry Addison and Bob Carmichael
d. Manolo Santana (Spain) and Graebner,
6–4, 8–6.

NATIONAL INDOOR (independent pros only),
at Hampton, Va.: Stan Smith d. Tomas Kock,
6–3, 6–2, 7–5; Arthur Ashe and Smith d. Ilie
Nastase and Ion Tiriac, 15–13, 6–3.

PACIFIC COAST DOUBLES, at LaJolla, Calif.:
Marcelo Lara (Mexico) and Erik Van Dillen
d. Roy Barth and Steve Tidball, 6–4, 6–4, 7–5.

MASTERS, at St. Petersburg, Fla.: Jan
Kodes (Czechoslovakia) d. Joaquin Loyo-
Mayo (Mexico), 6–3, 6–3, 6–3; Szabolcs Bar-
anyi and Peter Szoke (both Hungary) d. Steve
Beeland and Armistead Neely, 6–4, 7–5.
Nancy Richey d. Judy Alvarez, 6–0, 6–1;
Mary Ann Curtis and Valerie Ziegenfuss d.
Kerry Harris (Australia) and Stephanie John-
son, 6–4, 6–4.

CAROLINAS SPRING INVITATION, at Charlotte,
N.C.: Cliff Richey d. Bob Carmichael, 6–4,
6–4; Manolo Santana and Clark Graebner d.
Jim McManus and Jim Osborne, 6–2, 8–6.
Nancy Richey d. Alena Palmeova (Czechoslo-
vakia), 6–0, 6–0; Ada Bakker (Netherlands)
and Richey d. Eva Lundquist (Sweden) and
Kathy Harter, 6–3, 4–6, 6–4.

CALIFORNIA STATE, at Portola Valley, Calif.:
Barry Mackay d. Allen Fox, 6–7, 7–6, 2–6,
7–6, 7–6; Dick Leach and Bob Potthast d. Rob
Rippner and Roscoe Tanner, 7–6, 6–4, 6–4.
Liza Pande d. Sharon Walsh 6–2, 6–3; Hansen

Four promising young lady American players: (*top, left to right*) Valerie Ziegenfuss, Chris Evert. (*bottom, left to right*) Patti Hogan and Kristy Pigeon.

U.S. Title Matches, Leading Events, 1970 (cont.)
and Walsh d. Barbara Downs and Lynn
Rolley, 6–3, 6–1.

CENTRAL CALIFORNIA, at Sacramento, Calif.:
Arthur Ashe d. Barry MacKay, 6–4, 6–2,
3–6, 10–8; Bob Lutz and Ashe d. Jim Osborne
and Jim McManus, 5–7, 6–3, 6–4. Nancy
Richey d. Denise Carter, 10–8, 2–6, 6–3;
Valerie Ziegenfuss and Richey d. Kristy
Pigeon and Carter, 6–2, 6–2.

OJAI VALLEY, at Ojai, Calif.: Jeff Austin d.
Jimmy Connors, 3–6, 8–6, 6–3; Doug Smith
and Austin d. Jim Rombeau and Terry Neu-
decker, 3–6, 6–4, 7–5. Janet Newberry d.
Sharon Walsh, 4–6, 6–3, 6–2; Gail Hansen
and Walsh d. Liza Pande and Newberry, 6–4,
4–6, 6–3.

SOUTHERN CALIFORNIA, at Los Angeles,
Calif.: Erik Van Dillen d. Allen Fox, 6–2,
6–1; Marcelo Lara and Van Dillen d. Fern-
ando Gentil (Brazil) and Dick Bohrnstedt,
6–2, 8–6. Janet Newberry d. Kris Kemmer,
6–3, 6–3; Nancy Ornstein and Kemmer d.
Ann Lebedeff and Tam O'Shaughnessy, 6–4,
6–4.

KANSAS CITY INVITATION, at Kansas City,
Mo.: Arthur Ashe d. Clark Graebner, 7–6,
6–1; Bob Lutz and Ashe d. Terry Addison
and Graebner, 6–4, 6–4. Kristy Pigeon d.
Denise Carter, 6–1, 1–6, 6–1; Mary Ann
Curtis and Stephanie Johnson d. Peaches Bartkowicz and Valerie Ziegenfuss, 4–6, 6–3, 6–3.

ATLANTA INVITATION, at Atlanta, Ga.: Cliff
Richey d. Frank Froehling, 6–2, 6–2; Turner
Howard and Len Schloss d. Crawford Henry
and John Skogstad, 6–4, 7–5.

GREEN ISLAND INVITATION, at Columbia,
Ga.: Clark Graebner d. Gene Scott, 6–3, 6–3.

TULSA INVITATION, at Tulsa, Okla.: Brian
Fairlie d. Tom Edlefsen, 6–2, 4–6, 6–1; Bob
McKinley and Dick Stockton d. Onny Parun
and Fairlie, 6–4, 6–3. Stephanie Johnson d.
Janet Newberry, 6–1, 6–4; Linda Tuero and
Johnson d. Kathy Kraft and Newberry, 6–0,
6–3.

BLUE AND GREY, at Montgomery, Ala.:
Peter Van Lingen (South Africa) d. Paul
Gerken, 11–9, 4–6, 6–3; Vincente Zarazue
and Marcelo Lara (both Mexico) d. Mike
Machetto and Gerken, 10–8 (1 set). Laura
DuPont d. Kathy Kraft, 6–1, 6–2.

NATIONAL AMATEUR CHAMPIONSHIPS, at
Rochester, N.Y.: Roscoe Tanner d. Haroon

Rahim (Pakistan), 3–6, 2–6, 6–1, 6–4, 10–8;
Lito Alvarez and Tito Vasquez (both Argen-
tina) d. Bob McKinley and Dick Stockton,
2–6, 6–1, 6–4, 2–6, 6–4. Linda Tuero d.
Laura DuPont, 7–5, 6–3; Pam Austin and
Margie Cooper d. Ann Lebedeff and Marjorie
Gengler, 2–6, 6–3, 7–5.

*WASHINGTON STAR INTERNATIONAL, at
Washington, D.C.: Cliff Richey d. Arthur
Ashe, 7–5, 6–2, 6–1; Bob Hewitt and Frew
McMillan (both South Africa) d. Ion Tiriac
and Ilie Nastase, 7–5, 6–0.

TENNESSEE VALLEY, at Chattanooga, Tenn.:
Paul Gerken d. Jeff Borowiak, 6–2, 11–9;
John Gardner (Australia) and Zan Guerry d.
Bob Goeltz and Fred McNair, 7–5, 6–3. Linda
Tuero d. Becky Vest, 6–2, 6–3; Vicky Smouse
and Tuero d. Linda Wert and Missie Weber,
5–7, 6–1, 6–2.

SOUTHERNS, at Birmingham, Ala.: Zan
Guerry d. Charlie Owens, 6–3, 6–3; Tom
Mozur and Turner Howard d. Bobby Siska
and Steve Stefanki, 8–6, 3–6, 6–4. Linda
Tuero d. Roberta Baumgardner, 6–1, 7–5;
Sue Eastman and Baumgardner d. Sue Vinton
and Linda Wert, 6–1, 6–0.

*WESTERN OPEN, at Cincinnati, Ohio: Ken
Rosewall (Australia) d. Cliff Richey, 7–9,
9–7, 8–6; Ilie Nastase and Ion Tiriac d. Bob
Hewitt and Frew McMillan, 6–3, 6–4. Rosie
Casals d. Nancy Richey, 6–3, 6–3; Gail Chan-
freau (France) and Casals d. Helen Gourlay
(Australia) and Pat Walkden (Rhodesia),
12–10, 6–1.

*NATIONAL CLAY COURT OPEN, at Indianap-
olis, Ind.: Cliff Richey d. Stan Smith 6–2,
10–8, 3–6, 6–1; Arthur Ashe and Clark
Graebner d. Ion Tiriac and Ilie Nastase, 2–6,
6–4, 6–4. Linda Tuero d. Gail Chanfreau,
7–5, 6–1; Rosie Casals and Chanfreau d.
Helen Gourlay and Pat Walkden, 6–2, 6–2.

*LOUISVILLE OPEN, at Louisville, Ky.: Rod
Laver d. John Newcombe (Australia), 6–3,
6–3; Tony Roche and Newcombe d. Roy
Emerson (Australia) and Laver, 8–6, 5–7,
6–4.

*U.S. PRO CHAMPIONSHIPS, at Boston, Mass.:
Tony Roche d. Rod Laver, 3–6, 6–4, 1–6,
6–2, 6–2; Roy Emerson and Laver d. Torben
Ulrich (Denmark) and Ismail El Shafei
(Egypt), 6–1, 7–6.

BUCKEYE CHAMPIONSHIPS, at Grove City,
Ohio: Bob Lutz d. Tom Gorman, 6–4, 1–6,

* Asterisks throughout major U.S. tournaments indicate Pepsi Grand Prix tournaments. See page 454.

7–5, 6–1; Stan Smith and Lutz d. Ray Ruffels (Australia) and Gorman, 6–2, 8–6.

NATIONAL AMATEUR GRASS COURT CHAMPIONSHIPS: Men, at Southampton, N.Y.: Haroon Rahim d. John Gardner, 6–3, 6–4, 1–6, 11–13, 6–4; Bob McKinley and Dick Stockton d. Jeff Borowiak and Rahim, 4–6, 6–3, 6–4. Women, at Wilmington, Dela.: Liza Pande d. Sharon Walsh, 3–6, 9–7, 6–2; Gail Hansen and Walsh d. Janet Newberry and Pande, 6–3, 7–5.

*PENNSYLVANIA LAWN TENNIS CHAMPIONSHIPS, at Philadelphia, Pa.: Ray Ruffels d. Jaime Fillol (Chile), 6–2, 7–6, 6–3; Bill Bowrey (Australia) and Ruffels d. Jim McManus and Jim Osborne, 3–6, 6–2, 7–5. Margaret Court d. Pat Walkden, 6–1, 6–0; Françoise Durr and Gail Chanfreau (both France) d. Mary Ann Curtis and Valerie Ziegenfuss, 6–3, 6–2.

*MARLBORO OPEN, South Orange, N.J.: Rod Laver d. Bob Carmichael, 6–4, 6–2, 6–2; Pat Cornejo and Jaime Fillol (both Chile) d. Andres Gimeno (Spain) and Laver, 3–6, 7–6, 7–6. Kerry Melville (Australia) d. Patti Hogan, 7–6, 6–4; Virginia Wade and Rosie Casals d. Françoise Durr and Gail Chanfreau, 6–3, 6–4.

*U.S. OPEN, at Forest Hills, N.Y.: Ken Rosewall d. Tony Roche, 2–6, 6–4, 7–6, 6–3; Nikki Pilic (Yugoslavia) and Pierre Barthes (France) d. Rod Laver and Roy Emerson, 6–3, 7–6, 4–6, 7–6. Margaret Court d. Rosie Casals, 6–2, 2–6, 6–1; Judy Dalton (Australia) and Court d. Virginia Wade and Casals, 6–3, 6–4.

*PACIFIC SOUTHWEST OPEN, at Los Angeles, Calif.: Rod Laver d. John Newcombe, 9–7, 4–6, 6–4, 7–6; Tom Okker (Netherlands) and Marty Riessen d. Bob Lutz and Stan Smith, 7–6, 6–2. Sharon Walsh d. Lesley Hunt (Australia), 6–3, 6–2; Janet Newberry and Walsh d. Esme Emanuel (South Africa) and Cecilia Martinez, 6–3, 6–4.

*PACIFIC COAST OPEN, at Berkeley, Calif.: Arthur Ashe d. Cliff Richey, 6–4, 6–2, 6–4; Bob Lutz and Stan Smith d. Roy Barth and Tom Gorman, 6–2, 7–5, 4–6, 6–2. Nancy Richey d. Rosie Casals, 7–6, 6–4; Kristy Pigeon and Lesley Hunt d. Patti Hogan and Judy Dalton, 6–2, 6–3.

PENSACOLA INTERNATIONAL, at Pensacola, Fla.: Dick Crealy (Australia) d. Bob Car-

michael, 6–7, 7–5, retired; Allan Stone (Australia) and Crealy d. Richard Russell (Jamaica) and Len Schloss, 3–6, 6–4, 2–0, retired. Lesley Hunt d. Pat Walkden, 6–2, 7–5; Helen Gourlay and Walkden d. Stephanie Johnson and Hunt, 6–2, 7–5.

HEART OF AMERICA, at Kansas City, Mo.: Rain prevented completion of tournament. Frank Froehling and Jim Osborne shared singles title. Bob Alloo and Jim Parker shared doubles with John Cooper (Australia) and Terry Addison. Valerie Ziegenfuss d. Corinne Molesworth (England), 6–0, 6–2; Mary Ann Curtis and Ziegenfuss shared doubles with Esme Emanuel and Cecelia Martinez.

CAROLINAS AUTUMN INVITATION, at Charlotte, N.C.: Cliff Richey d. Erik Van Dillen, 6–3, 7–6; Stan Smith and Bob Lutz d. Van Dillen and Richey, 10–4 (1 pro set). Nancy Richey d. Chris Evert (amateur) 6–4, 6–1; Margaret Court and Virginia Wade d. Françoise Durr and Richey, 10–1 (1 pro set).

*THUNDERBIRD OPEN, at Phoenix, Ariz.: Stan Smith d. Jim Osborne, 7–5, 6–7, 6–1; Dick Crealy and Ray Ruffels d. Jan Kodes and Charlie Pasarell, 7–6, 6–3.

VIRGINIA SLIMS HOUSTON, at Houston, Tex.: Rosie Casals d. Judy Dalton, 5–7, 6–1, 7–5.

VIRGINIA SLIMS RICHMOND, at Richmond, Va.: Billie Jean King d. Nancy Richey, 6–3, 6–3; Rosie Casals and King d. Mary Ann Curtis and Valerie Ziegenfuss, 6–4, 6–4.

1971 Season

BUDDY PONTIAC INTERNATIONAL, at Washington, D.C.: Jaime Fillol (Chile) d. Thomaz Koch (Brazil), 6–1, 3–6, 6–4, 6–7, 6–4.

FIDELITY INVITATIONAL, at Richmond, Va.: Ilie Nastase (Romania) d. Arthur Ashe, 3–6, 6–2, 6–4; Ashe and Dennis Ralston d. John Newcombe (Australia) and Ken Rosewall (Australia), 7–6, 3–6, 7–6.

CLEAN AIR TENNIS CLASSIC, at New York City: Ilie Nastase d. Clark Graebner, 6–2, 5–7, 6–4, 7–5; Manuel Orantes (Spain) and Juan Gisbert (Spain) d. Haroon Rahim (Pakistan) and Jim Connors, 7–6, 6–2.

NATIONAL INDOOR OPEN CHAMPIONSHIP, at Salisburg, Md.: Clark Graebner d. Cliff Richey, 2–6, 7–6, 10–6, 7–6, 6–0; Manuel Orantes and Juan Gisbert d. Graebner and Thomaz Koch, 6–3, 4–6, 7–6.

U.S. Title Matches, Leading Events, 1971 (cont.)

NATIONAL AMATEUR INDOOR CHAMPIONSHIP, at Salt Lake City: Roscoe Tanner d. Jeff Borowiak, 7–6, 7–6; Tanner and Sandy Mayer d. Borowiak and Lito Alvariz (Argentina), 6–7, 6–2, 6–3.

SOUTH FLORIDA CHAMPIONSHIP, at West Palm Beach: Frank Froehling d. Pat Cramer (South Africa), 6–3, 6–2; Eduardo Zuleta (Ecuador) and Miguel Olevera (Ecuador) d. Robie Smith and Steve Turner, 6–3, 6–4; Christiane Spinoza (France) d. Bunny Smith, 6–1, 6–2.

CITY OF MIAMI CHAMPIONSHIPS, at Miami: Eddie Dibbs d. Dan Blechinger, 6–1, 6–4; Pat Cramer and Rodney Mandelstam (South Africa) d. Eduardo Zuleta and Miguel Olevera, 6–3, 6–3.

MACON INVITATION, at Macon, Ga.: Zeljko Franulovic (Yugoslavia) d. Ilie Nastase, 6–4, 7–5, 5–7, 3–6, 7–6; Clark Graebner and Thomaz Koch d. Franulovic and Boro Jovanovic (Czechoslovakia), 6–3, 7–6.

UNITED STATES NATIONAL INDOORS CHAMPIONSHIP, at Hampton, Va.: Ilie Nastase d. Clark Graebner, 7–5, 6–4, 7–6; Nastase and Ion Tiriac (Romania) d. Graebner and Thomaz Koch, 6–4, 4–6, 7–5.

CARIBE HILTON INVITATION, at San Juan, P.R.: Stan Smith d. Cliff Richey, 6–3, 6–3; Smith and Eric Van Dillen d. Onny Parun (New Zealand) and Nicki Spear (Yugoslavia), 6–2, 6–2; Ann Jones (Great Britain) d. Nancy Richey Gunter, 6–4, 6–4; Françoise Durr and Jones d. Karen Krantzcke (Australia) and Kerry Melville (Australia), 7–6, 6–3.

RIVER OAKS INVITATION, at Houston: Cliff Richey d. Clark Graebner, 6–1, 6–2, 6–2; Onny Parun and Milan Holecek (Czechoslovakia) d. Frank Froehling and Tom Edlefsen, 7–5, 6–1.

CAROLINAS' INTERNATIONAL TENNIS OPEN, at Charlotte, N.C.: Arthur Ashe d. Stan Smith, 6–3, 6–3; Marty Riessen and Tony Roche (Australia) d. Ashe and Dennis Ralston, 6–2, 6–2; Chris Evert d. Laura DuPont, 6–2, 6–0; Evert and Sue Stop d. Liza Pande and Janet Newberry, 6–3, 1–6, 6–3.

JACKSONVILLE INTERNATIONAL CHAMPIONSHIP, at Jacksonville: Tom Edlefsen d. Clark Graebner, 7–5, 4–6, 6–3; Graebner and Edlefsen d. Onny Parun and Milan Holecek, 6–4, 6–3.

PENSACOLA INTERNATIONAL CHAMPIONSHIP, at Pensacola, Fla.: Milan Holecek d. Nicki Spear, 4–6, 6–3, 6–3; Terry Addison (Australia), and Ray Keldie (Australia) d. Tom Edlefsen and Frank Froehling, 6–4, 6–4.

NATIONAL INTERCOLLEGIATE CHAMPIONSHIP, at South Bend, Ind.: Jim Connors (USLA) d. Roscoe Tanner (Stanford), 6–3, 4–6, 6–4, 6–4; Jeff Borowiak and Haroon Rahim (UCLA) d. Dick Stockton and Bob McKinley (Trinity), 7–6, 7–6.

NATIONAL WOMEN'S COLLEGIATE CHAMPIONSHIP, at Las Cruces, New Mexico: Pam Richmond (Arizona State) d. Peggy Michel (Arizona State), 6–2, 6–1; Michel and Richmond d. Margie Cooper and Mona Schallau (Rollins), 6–2, 6–4.

*TANGLEWOOD CLASSIC, at Clemmons, N.C.: Jaime Fillol d. Zeljko Franulovic, 4–6, 6–4, 7–6; Jim Osborne and Jim McManus d. Jim Connors and Jeff Austin, 6–2, 6–4.

*NATIONAL AMATEUR CLAY COURTS at Chattanooga, Tenn.: Harold Solomon d. Charles Owens, 6–2, 2–6, 6–2, 6–4; Roscoe Tanner and Sandy Mayer d. Jeff Austin and Fred McNair, 3–6, 6–4, 6–4, 5–7, 6–2.

TULSA TENNIS CLUB INVITATION, at Tulsa, Okla.: Harold Solomon d. Zan Guerry, 3–6, 6–3, 6–4; Bob McKinley and Dick Stockton d. Jim Osborne and Pancho Guzman (Ecuador), 4–6, 6–2, 6–4; Chris Evert d. Mary Ann Curtis, 6–0, 6–3; Curtis and Karin Benson d. Evert and Jeanne Evert, 2–6, 7–5, 7–5.

NATIONAL AMATEUR GRASS COURT CHAMPIONSHIP, at Southampton, N.Y.: John Gardner d. Raul Ramirez (Mexico), 1–6, 4–6, 6–3, 7–5, 6–4; Gene Scott and Vitos Geruloitis d. Brian Teacher and Steve Mott, 6–4, 6–3.

* PENNSYLVANIA LAWN TENNIS CHAMPIONSHIPS, at Haverford, Pa.: Clark Graebner d. Dick Stockton, 6–2, 6–4, 6–7, 7–5; Jim Osborne and Graebner d. Bob McKinley and Stockton, 7–6, 6–3; Liza Pande d. Lesley Bowrey, 0–6, 6–2, 6–3; Bowrey and Helen Gourlay d. Laura DuPont and Marjorie Gengler, 5–7, 6–1, 6–1.

*BUCKEYE CHAMPIONSHIPS, at Grove City, Ohio: Tom Gorman d. Jim Connors, 6–7, 7–6, 4–6, 7–6, 6–3; Jim McManus and Jim Osborne d. Jim Connors and Roscoe Tanner, 4–6, 7–5, 6–2.

NATIONAL CLAY COURT CHAMPIONSHIPS, at Indianapolis, Ind.: Zeljko Franulovic d. Cliff

Richey, 6–3, 6–4, 0–6, 6–3; Jan Kodes and Franulovic d. Clark Graebner and Eric Van Dillen, 7–6, 5–7, 6–3; Billie Jean King d. Linda Tuero, 6–4, 7–5; King and Judy Dalton d. Julie Heldman and Tuero, 6–1, 6–2.

*WESTERN CHAMPIONSHIPS, at Cincinnati, Ohio: Stan Smith d. Juan Gisbert, 7–6, 6–3; Smith and Eric Van Dillen d. Roscoe Tanner and Sandy Mayer, 6–4, 6–4; Virginia Wade (Great Britain) d. Linda Tuero, 6–3, 6–3; Helen Gourlay and Kerry Harris d. Gail Chanfreau and Winnie Shaw, 6–4, 6–4.

*UNITED STATES OPEN CHAMPIONSHIP, at Forest Hills, N.Y.: Stan Smith d. Van Kodes, 3–6, 6–3, 6–2, 7–6; John Newcombe and Roger Taylor d. Smith and Eric Van Dillen, 6–7, 6–3, 7–6, 4–6, 5–3 (joint tie break); Billie Jean King d. Rosemary Casals, 6–4, 7–6; Casals and Judy Dalton d. Gail Chanfreau and Françoise Durr, 6–3, 6–3; King and Owen Davidson d. Betty Stove and Rob Maud, 6–3, 7–5.

*EASTERN GRASS COURT OPEN, at South Orange, N.J.: Clark Graebner d. Pierre Barthes, 6–3, 6–4, 6–4; Bob Carmichael and Thomas Leonard d. Erik van Dillen and Graebner, 6–4, 4–6, 6–4; Chris Evert d. Helen Gourlay, 6–3, 6–0.

*U.S. NATIONAL HARD COURT CHAMPIONSHIP, at Sacramento, Calif.: Robert Lutz d. Alex Olmedo, 6–3, 6–4, 6–3; Jim Osborne and Jim McManus d. Robert Maud and Frew McMillan, 7–6, 6–2.

USLTA AMATEUR CLAY COURT CHAMPIONSHIPS, at Chattanooga, Tenn.: Harold Solomon d. Charles Owens, 6–2, 2–6, 6–2, 6–4; Roscoe Tanner and Alex Mayer d. Fred McNair and Jeff Austin, 3–6, 6–4, 6–4, 5–7, 6–2; Janice Metcalf d. Laura DuPont, 3–6, 6–3, 6–4; Pam Farmer and Metcalf d. Pat Bostrom and DuPont, 6–1, 6–3.

USLTA WOMEN'S AMATEUR GRASS COURT CHAMPIONSHIP, at Wilmington, Dela.: Marita Redondo d. Barbara Downs, 6–0, 6–3; Pam Farmer and Janice Metcalf d. Sandy Stap and Sue Stap, 6–3, 6–2.

*PACIFIC SOUTHWEST OPEN CHAMPIONSHIPS, at Los Angeles, Calif.: Richard Gonzalez d. Jimmy Connors, 2–6, 6–3, 6–3; John Alexander and Philip Dent d. Frank Froehling and Clark Graebner 7–6, 6–4; Billie Jean King and Rosemary Casals d. Françoise Durr and Judy Dalton, 2–6, 7–5, 7–6.

Althea Gibson was the first ATA Champion to win the National title.

*REDWOOD BANK CHAMPIONSHIP, at Berkeley, Calif.: Rod Laver d. Ken Rosewall, 6–4, 6–4, 7–6; Roy Emerson and Laver d. Fred Stolle and Rosewall, 6–3, 6–3; Marcelyn Louie d. Barbara Downs, 7–5, 6–3; Cathie Anderson and Downs d. Kate Latham and Laurie Tenney, def.

American Tennis Association Champions

In 1916 the American Tennis Association, the governing body for black players, was formed, and singles championships for men and women were held in 1917, with other divisions—juniors, doubles, veterans, etc., constantly being added as in USLTA play. Several players in the ATA have made notable records in the sport. Dr. Reginald Weir earned high Eastern rankings in the USLTA, and, in 1956, he won the national senior's indoor championship to become the first member of his race to win a USLTA championship. Since that time, Althea Gibson and Arthur Ashe, Jr.—both former ATA singles champions—have won United States National Championships. Here are the winners of the ATA's major divisions:

ATA MEN'S SINGLES CHAMPIONS

1917	Tally Holmes
1918	Tally Holmes
1919	Sylvester Smith
1920	B. M. Clark
1921	Tally Holmes
1922	Edgar G. Brown
1923	Edgar G. Brown
1924	Tally Holmes
1925	Theodore Thompson
1926	Eyre Saitch
1927	Theodore Thompson
1928	Edgar G. Brown
1929	Edgar G. Brown
1930	Douglas Turner
1931	Reginald Weir
1932	Reginald Weir
1933	Reginald Weir
1934	Nathaniel Jackson
1935	Franklin Jackson
1936	Lloyd Scott
1937	Reginald Weir
1938	Franklin Jackson
1939	Jimmie McDaniel
1940	Jimmie McDaniel
1941	Jimmie McDaniel
1942	Reginald Weir
1943	not held
1944	Lloyd Scott
1945	Lloyd Scott
1946	Jimmie McDaniel
1947	George Stewart
1948	George Stewart
1949	unfinished*
1950	Oscar Johnson
1951	George Stewart
1952	George Stewart
1953	George Stewart
1954	Earthna Jacquet
1955	Robert Ryland
1956	Robert Ryland
1957	George Stewart
1958	Wilbert Davis
1959	Wilbert Davis
1960	Arthur Ashe, Jr.
1961	Arthur Ashe, Jr.
1962	Arthur Ashe, Jr.
1963	Wilbert Davis
1964	George Stewart
1965	Luis Glass
1966	Wilbert Davis
1967	Wilbert Davis
1968	Robert Binns
1969	Marty Gool
1970	Gene Fluri
1971	John Wilkerson

* Reginald Weir and Harold Mitchell were finalists. The score stood at two (2) sets all, Mitchell leading in the fifth set 1–0, when due to heavy rain they were unable to resume play.

ATA MEN'S DOUBLES CHAMPIONS

1917	Tally Holmes and Sylvester Smith
1918	D. Monroe and Percy Richardson
1921	Tally Holmes and Sylvester Smith
1922	Tally Holmes and Sylvester Smith
1923	J. L. McGriff, Sr. and E. D. Downing
1924	Tally Holmes and Theodore Thompson
1925	Tally Holmes and Theodore Thompson
1926	Eyre Saitch and Theodore Thompson
1927	Tally Holmes and Theodore Thompson
1928	Eyre Saitch and Sylvester Smith
1929	Eyre Saitch and Sylvester Smith
1930	J. L. McGriff, Sr. and E. D. Downing
1931	Nathaniel Jackson and Franklin Jackson
1932	Richard Hudlin and Douglas Turner
1933	Nathaniel Jackson and Franklin Jackson
1934	Nathaniel Jackson and Franklin Jackson
1935	Nathaniel Jackson and Franklin Jackson
1936	Nathaniel Jackson and Franklin Jackson
1937	James Stocks and Thomas Walker
1938	Nathaniel Jackson and Franklin Jackson
1939	Jimmie McDaniel and Richard Cohen
1940	Clifford Russell and Howard Minnis
1941	Jimmie McDaniel and Richard Cohen
1942	Clifford Russell and Howard Minnis
1943	not held
1944	Ronald Fieulleteau and Howard Minnis
1945	Lloyd Scott and Louis Graves
1946	Jimmie McDaniel and James L. Stocks
1947	John Chandler and Harold Mitchell
1948	George Stewart and Hubert Eaton
1949	George Stewart and Hubert Eaton
1950	James Stocks and Oscar Johnson
1951	George Stewart and Hubert Eaton
1952	Jimmie McDaniel and Eartha Jacquet
1953	unfinished
1954	Eartha Jacquet and Wilbert Davis
1955	Clyde Freeman and Harold Freeman
1956	George Stewart and Hubert Eaton
1957	George Stewart and John Chandler
1958	Wilbur Jenkins and Thomas Calhoun
1959	Joe Pierce and Shaw Emmons
1960	Wilbur Jenkins and Thomas Calhoun
1961	Arthur Ashe and Ronald Charity
1962	Wilbert Davis and Robert Davis
1963	Howard Minnis and William Monroe
1964	Luis Glass and Lenward Simpson
1965	Luis Glass and Lenward Simpson
1966	John Mudd and Arthur Carrington
1967	John Mudd and Arthur Carrington
1968	Marty Gool and Gregory Morton
1969	Marty Gool and Gregory Morton
1970	Gene Fluri and Tom Fluri
1971	William Heinbecker and Jerry Johnson

ATA WOMEN'S SINGLES CHAMPIONS

1917	Lucy Slowe
1918	M. Rae
1919	M. Rae
1920	M. Rae
1921	Lucy Slowe
1922	Isadore Channels

1923	Isadore Channels		1936	Ora Washington and Lulu Ballard
1924	Isadore Channels		1937	Bertha Isaacs and Lilyan Spencer
1925	Lulu Ballard		1938	Margaret Peters and Roumania Peters
1926	Isadore Channels		1939	Margaret Peters and Roumania Peters
1927	Lulu Ballard		1940	Margaret Peters and Roumania Peters
1928	Lulu Ballard		1941	Margaret Peters and Roumania Peters
1929	Ora Washington		1942	Lillian Van Buren and Flora Lomax
1930	Ora Washington		1943	not held
1931	Ora Washington		1944	Margaret Peters and Roumania Peters
1932	Ora Washington		1945	Margaret Peters and Roumania Peters
1933	Ora Washington		1946	Margaret Peters and Roumania Peters
1934	Ora Washington		1947	Margaret Peters and Roumania Peters
1935	Ora Washington		1948	Margaret Peters and Roumania Peters
1936	Lulu Ballard		1949	Margaret Peters and Roumania Peters
1937	Ora Washington		1950	Margaret Peters and Roumania Peters
1938	Mrs. Flora Lomax		1951	Margaret Peters and Roumania Peters
1939	Mrs. Flora Lomax		1952	Margaret Peters and Roumania Peters
1940	Mrs. Agnes Lawson		1953	Margaret Peters and Roumania Peters
1941	Mrs. Flora Lomax		1954	Evelyn George and Ivy C. Ransey
1942	Mrs. Flora Lomax		1955	Eva F. Bracy and Mary E. Fine
1943	not held		1956	Angela Imala and Lorraine Williams
1944	Roumania Peters		1957	Eva F. Bracy and Mary E. Fine
1945	Mrs. Kathryn Irvis		1958	Eva F. Bracy and Mary E. Fine
1946	Roumania Peters		1959	Marlene Everson and Darnella Everson
1947	Althea Gibson		1960	Bessie A. Stockard and Carolyn Williams
1948	Althea Gibson		1961	Carloyn Williams and Marreline Faggett
1949	Althea Gibson		1962	Mimi Kanarek and Carolyn Liguori
1950	Althea Gibson		1963	Mimi Fry and Ginger Pfiefer
1951	Althea Gibson		1964	Sylvia Hooks and Bonnie Logan
1952	Althea Gibson		1965	Jean Eichardson and Helen Watanabe
1953	Althea Gibson		1966	Bonnie Logan and Bessie Stockard
1954	Althea Gibson		1967	Sylvia Hooks and Bessie Stockard
1955	Althea Gibson		1968	Ann Koeger and Bessie Stockard
1956	Althea Gibson		1969	T. Rueter and S. Beauchamp
1957	Gwendolyn McEvans		1970	T. Rueter and S. Beauchamp
1958	Mary E. Fine		1971	Pamela Stienmetz and Bunny Wall
1959	Gwendolyn McEvans			
1960	Mimi Kanarek			
1961	Carolyn Williams			**ATA MIXED-DOUBLES CHAMPIONS**
1962	Carolyn Liguori			
1963	Ginger Pfiefer		1924	Nellie Nicholson and B. M. Rhetta
1964	Helen Watanabe		1925	C. O. Seames and L. C. Downing
1965	Helen Watanabe		1926	E. Robinson and E. Cole
1966	Bonnie Logan		1927	Blanche Winston and Louis Jones
1967	Doris Harrison		1928	Blanche Winston and W. A. Kean
1968	Dorothy Kornegay		1929	Anita Gant and O. B. Williams
1969	Dorothy Kornegay		1930	Anita Gant and O. B. Williams
1970	Dorothy Kornegay		1931	Anne Roberts and Theodore Thompson
1971	Alphonda Edwards		1932	Martha Davis and Henry Williams
			1933	Emma Leonard and C. O. Hilton
			1934	Emma Leonard and C. O. Hilton
	ATA WOMEN'S DOUBLES CHAMPIONS		1935	not held
			1936	not held
1924	Isadore Channels and Emma Leonard		1937	Flora Lomax and William H. Hall
1925	Ora Washington and Lulu Ballard		1938	Lulu Ballard and Gerald Norman, Jr.
1926	Ora Washington and Lulu Ballard		1939	Ora Washington and Sylvester Smith
1927	Ora Washington and Lulu Ballard		1940	Flora Lomax and William H. Hall
1928	Ora Washington and Lulu Ballard		1941	Eoline Thornton and Harold Mitchell
1929	Ora Washington and Lulu Ballard		1942	Kathryn Jones and William E. Jones
1930	Ora Washington and Blanche Winston		1943	not held
1931	Ora Washington and Blanche Winston		1944	Lillian Van Buren and Delbert Russell
1932	Ora Washington and Lulu Ballard		1945	Lillian Van Buren and Delbert Russell
1933	Ora Washington and Anita Gant		1946	Ora Washington and George Stewart
1934	Ora Washington and Lulu Ballard		1947	Ora Washington and George Stewart
1935	Ora Washington and Lulu Ballard		1948	Althea Gibson and R. Walter Johnson

Mike Davies (*left*) and Sam Giammalva (*right*) were consistently outstanding pro players in the 1960's. At the right, Giammalva is receiving his award from the great teaching professional Bill Lufler.

ATA Mixed-Doubles Champions (*cont.*)

1949	Althea Gibson and R. Walter Johnson
1950	Althea Gibson and R. Walter Johnson
1951	Mary Etta Fine and Leo Fine
1952	Althea Gibson and R. Walter Johnson
1953	Althea Gibson and R. Walter Johnson
1954	Althea Gibson and R. Walter Johnson
1955	Althea Gibson and R. Walter Johnson
1956	G. McEvans and W. A. Campbell
1957	Doris Harrison and Ernie Ingram
1958	Gwen McEvans and Clyde Freeman
1959	Gwen McEvans and Clyde Freeman
1960	Elaine Busch and George Stewart
1961	Mimi Kanarek and Ernest Ingram
1962	Mimi Kanarek and Ernest Ingram
1963	Lucy McEvans and Charles Berry
1964	Bessie Stockard and Charles Berry
1965	Sylvia Hooks and William Morton, Jr.
1966	Sylvia Hooks and William Morton, Jr.
1967	Bonnie Logan and Lenward Simpson
1968	Bonnie Logan and Lenward Simpson
1969	Bonnie Logan and Lenward Simpson
1970	Bonnie Logan and Lenward Simpson
1971	Beverly Hassel and Alberto Loney

USPTA NATIONAL PROFESSIONAL CHAMPIONS

The first National Professional Championships were held in America under the leadership of the Professional Lawn Tennis Association of the United States. In the 1930's this group joined with United States Professional Lawn Tennis Association (see page 60) in sponsoring the Championship. In 1970 USPLTA decided to drop the word "Lawn" from their name and became United States Professional Tennis Association (USPTA). Here are the winners of the National Professional Championships since their start in 1927:

USPTA NATIONAL MEN'S SINGLES CHAMPIONS

1927	Vincent Richards
1928	Vincent Richards
1929	Karel Kozeluh
1930	Vincent Richards
1931	William T. Tilden II
1932	Karel Kozeluh
1933	Vincent Richards
1934	Hans Nusslein
1935	William T. Tilden II
1936	Joseph Whalen
1937	Karel Kozeluh
1938	Frederick J. Perry
1939	H. Ellsworth Vines
1940	J. Donald Budge
1941	Frederick J. Perry
1942	J. Donald Budge
1943	Bruce Barnes
1944	not held
1945	Welby Van Horn
1946	Robert L. Riggs
1947	Robert L. Riggs
1948	Jack Kramer
1949	Robert L. Riggs

1950   Francisco Segura
1951   Francisco Segura
1952–1961   not held
1962   Bernard J. Bartzen
1963   Bernard J. Bartzen
1964   Samuel A. Giammalva
1965   Michael Davies
1966   Francisco Segura
1967   Samuel A. Giammalva
1968   not held
1969   Billy Higgins
1970   Samuel A. Giammalva
1971   Billy Higgins

USPTA NATIONAL MEN'S DOUBLES CHAMPIONS

1929   Vincent Richards and Karel Kozeluh
1930   Vincent Richards and Howard O. Kinsey
1931   Vincent Richards and Howard O. Kinsey
1932   William T. Tilden II and Bruce Barnes
1933   Vincent Richards and Charles M. Wood
1934   Bruce Barnes and Emmeth Pare
1935   George M. Lott, Jr. and Lester Stoefen
1936   Charles M. Wood and Harold Blauer
1937   Vincent Richards and George M. Lott, Jr.
1938   Vincent Richards and Frederick J. Perry
1939   Bruce Barnes and Keith Gledhill
1940   J. Donald Budge and Frederick J. Perry
1941   J. Donald Budge and Frederick J. Perry
1942   J. Donald Budge and Robert L. Riggs
1943   Bruce Barnes and Gene Mako
1944   not held

Vincent Richards and Bill Tilden won their first doubles title in 1918 when Richards was only 15. Here they are shown after winning their last major title—USPTA Doubles Championship—in 1945.

1945   Vincent Richards and William T. Tilden II
1946   Frank L. Kovacs and Frederick J. Perry
1947   J. Donald Budge and Robert L. Riggs
1948   Jack Kramer and Francisco Segura
1949   J. Donald Budge and Frank L. Kovacs
1950   Welby Van Horn and Frank L. Kovacs
1951   Francisco Segura and Richard Gonzalez
1952–1961   not held
1962   Samuel A. Giammalva and Eugene Gerrett
1963–1964   not held
1965   Michael Davies and Allan Quay
1966   Francisco Segura and Michael Davies
1967   Samuel A. Giammalva and Jason Morton
1968   not held
1969   Richard N. Leach and Robert A. Potthast
1970   Richard N. Leach and Robert A. Potthast
1971   Ramsey Earhart and Walter Johnson

USPTA INTERSECTIONAL MEN'S TEAM—MATCH CHAMPIONS

1964   Eastern
1965   New England
1966   New England
1967   Florida
1968   Midwest
1969   Florida
1970   Florida
1971   Florida

USPTA NATIONAL MEN SENIORS' OVER-35 SINGLES CHAMPIONS

1967   Juan F. Weiss
1968   not held
1969   Ben Press
1970   Robert A. Potthast
1971   Jason Morton

USPTA NATIONAL MEN SENIORS' OVER-35 DOUBLES CHAMPIONS

1967   Juan F. Weiss and Emilio Posada
1968   not held
1969   Ben Press and Alex Gordon
1970   Ed Kauder and Hal H. Miller
1971   Jason Morton and James Schmidt

USPTA NATIONAL MEN'S OVER-55 SINGLES CHAMPIONS

1967   Leonard Hartman
1968   not held
1969   Frank M. Goeltz
1970   not held
1971   John Faunce

USPTA NATIONAL MEN'S OVER-55 DOUBLES CHAMPIONS

1967   Leonard Hartman and William C. Lufler
1968–69   not held
1970   Garnet W. Glenney and William Millikan
1971   Garnet W. Glenney and William Millikan

USPTA NATIONAL MEN'S OVER-45 SINGLES CHAMPIONS

1970 Gustavo Palafox
1971 Ben Press

USPTA NATIONAL MEN'S OVER-45 DOUBLES CHAMPIONS

1970 Gustavo Palafox and Juan F. Weiss
1971 Ben Press and Alex Gordon

UNITED STATES PROFESSIONAL TOURNAMENTS (1967–1971)

1967 Season

NEW YORK PRO TOURNAMENT, at New York, N.Y.: Rod Laver (Australia) d. Pancho Gonzalez (U.S.), 7–5, 14–16, 7–5, 6–2; Gonzalez and Dennis Ralston (U.S.) d. Laver and Fred Stolle (Australia), 7–5, 3–6, 6–3.

SAN JUAN TENNIS CLASSIC, at San Juan, P.R.: Laver d. Andres Gimeno (Spain), 6–4, 3–6, 6–3; Laver and Stolle d. Butch Buchholz (U.S.) and Mike Davies (Great Britain), 6–3, 6–4.

PRO TOURNAMENT OF FLORIDA, at Orlando, Fla.: Laver d. Gonzalez, 6–4, 2–6, 6–0; Laver and Stolle d. Pierre Barthes (France) and Gimeno, 4–6, 7–5, 6–1.

PLANTERS' PRO CHALLENGE CUP, at Miami Beach, Fla.: Laver d. Gimeno, 6–3, 6–3; Laver and Stolle d. Gonzalez and Ralston, 6–4, 3–6, 6–4.

BOSTON PRO TOURNAMENT, at Boston, Mass.: Laver d. Ken Rosewall, 6–4, 6–0.

ENGLISH PRO CHALLENGE, Wembley, England: Rosewall d. Ralston, 6–4, 6–2.

PARIS PRO TOURNAMENT, Paris, France: Laver d. Rosewall, 6–10, 10–8, 10–8.

BIRMINGHAM PRO CLASSIC, Birmingham, Ala.: Gonzalez d. Alan Mills, 6–4, 6–2; Sammy Giammalva and Crawford Henry d. Buchholz and Wade Herren, 6–4, 2–6, 6–3.

PACIFIC INTERNATIONAL PRO TOURNAMENT, at San Diego, Calif.: Buchholz d. Davies, 6–2, 7–5; Laver and Stolle d. Buchholz and Davies, 10–5.

LOS ANGELES PRO TOURNAMENT, at Los Angeles, Calif.: Rosewall d. Laver, 6–2, 2–6, 7–5.

PACIFIC COAST PRO TOURNAMENT, at Berkeley, Calif.: Rosewall d. Laver, 4–6, 6–3, 8–6.

MADISON SQUARE GARDEN PROS, at New York, N.Y.: Laver d. Rosewall, 6–4, 6–4.

U.S. PRO HARD COURT CHAMPIONSHIP, at St. Louis, Mo.: Rosewall d. Gimeno, 6–3, 6–4.

INTERNATIONAL CUP, at Newport, Calif.: Rosewall d. Laver, 6–3, 6–3.

WORLD PRO CHAMPIONSHIP, at Oklahoma City, Okla.: Laver d. Rosewall, 6–2, 3–6, 6–4; Rosewall and Ralston d. Laver and Stolle, 10–8.

UNITED STATES PRO CHAMPIONSHIPS, at Brookline, Mass.: Laver d. Gimeno, 4–6, 6–4, 6–3, 7–5.

BINGHAMTON PRO CHAMPIONSHIPS, at Binghamton, N.Y.: Laver d. Gimeno, 6–1, 6–3.

BUCKEYE PRO CHAMPIONSHIP, at Cincinnati, Ohio: Gimeno d. Rosewall, 6–4, 6–3.

PRO ROUND-ROBIN, at Newport, R.I.: Laver (overall winner).

WIMBLEDON PRO CHAMPIONSHIPS, at London, England: Laver d. Rosewall, 6–2, 6–2, 12–10; Gimeno and Gonzalez d. Laver and Stolle, 6–4, 14–12.

MASTERS TOURNAMENT, at Binghamton, N.Y.: Laver d. Gimeno, 6–2, 7–5, 6–4; Barthes and Gimeno d. Laver and Stolle, 6–3, 6–4.

COLONIAL PRO INVITATION, at Forth Worth, Texas: Laver d. Ralston, 8–6, 6–0; Laver and Stolle d. Pancho Sequra (Ecuador) and Alex Almedo (Peru), 4–6, 6–2, 6–2.

MARSEILLES PRO, at Marseilles, France: Barthes d. Stolle, 2–6, 9–7, 11–9; Gimeno and Barthes d. Stolle and Barry McKay (U.S.), 8–5.

PARIS PROS, at Paris, France: Laver d. Gimeno, 6–4, 8–6, 4–6, 6–2; Barthes and Gimeno d. Laver and Stolle, 6–3, 6–4.

FRESNO PROS, at Fresno, Calif.: Ralston d. Olmedo, 7–5, 6–2; Ralston and Ian Crookenden d. Olmedo and Hugh Stewart, 6–3, 6–1.

WEMBLEY PRO CHAMPIONSHIP, at London, England: Laver d. Rosewall, 2–6, 6–1, 1–6, 8–6, 6–2.

PRAGUE PROFESSIONALS, at Prague, Czechoslovakia: Ralston d. Laver, 7–5, 6–1.

1968 Season

PRO MIAMI INVITATION, at Miami, Fla.: Butch Buchholz (U.S.) d. Tony Roche (Australia), 31–22, 31–26; Roger Taylor (Great Britain) and Cliff Drysdale (South Africa) d. John Newcombe (Australia) and Tony Roche (Australia), 31–26, 31–25 (VASSS scoring).

SOUTH AMERICAN PRO CHAMPIONSHIP, at

Buenos Aires: Rod Laver (Australia) d. Pancho Gonzalez (U.S.), 7–5, 5–7, 6–4.

SAN DIEGO PRO INVITATIONAL, at San Diego, Calif.: Buchholz d. Dennis Ralston (U.S.), 31–21, 31–15.

LOS ALTOS HILLS PRO INVITATIONAL, at Los Altos Hills, Calif.: Nicki Pilic (Yugoslavia) d. Ralston, 31–26, 31–25; Butch Buchholz and Ralston d. Newcombe and Roche, 31–27, 31–28.

BAKERSFIELD PRO CLASSIC, at Bakersfield, Calif.: Newcombe d. Drysdale, 31–12, 31–22; Ralston and Taylor d. Pilic and Roche, 31–25, 31–28.

FRESNO PRO CLASSIC, at Fresno, Calif.: Buchholz d. Roche, 31–23, 31–29; Taylor and Drysdale d. Newcombe and Roche, 31–28, 31–30.

EVANSVILLE TENNIS CLASSIC, at Evansville, Ind.: Newcombe d. Pilic, 31–17, 31–17.

BURGER KING PRO CHALLENGE CUP, at Hollywood, Fla.: Roy Emerson (Australia) d. Ken Rosewall (Australia), 6–1, 6–1; Emerson and Laver d. Gonzalez and Rosewall, 6–3, 6–4.

BOGOTA PRO CHAMPIONSHIP, at Bogota, Colombia: Andres Gimeno (Spain) d. Gonzalez, 7–5, 6–8, 7–5; Laver and Fred Stolle (Australia) d. Gimeno and Gonzalez, 10–5.

PRO CANNES, at Cannes, France: Gimeno d. Stolle, 6–4, 2–6, 7–5; Billie Jean King (U.S.) d. Rosemary Casals (U.S.), 10–6.

WEMBLEY CLASSIC, at Wembley, England: Laver d. Rosewall, 6–3, 10–8.

FRENCH PROFESSIONALS, at Paris, France: Rosewall d. Gimeno, 6–3, 6–4; King d. Ann Jones (Great Britain), 9–7, 6–4.

WEMBLEY CLASSIC, at Wembley, England: Laver d. Rosewall, 6–1, 6–0; King d. Jones, 4–6, 9–7, 7–5.

MADISON SQUARE GARDEN PROS, at New York City: Laver d. Rosewall, 4–6, 6–3, 9–7, 6–4; Jones d. King, 6–4, 6–4.

TWIN CITIES TENNIS CLASSIC, at Minneapolis, Minn.: Buchholz d. Pilic, 31–22, 31–25; Newcombe and Roche d. Ralston and Buchholz, 31–24, 20–31, 5–4.

BUFFALO PROS, at Buffalo, N.Y.: Buchholz d. Ralston 31–26, 31–22.

BALTIMORE TENNIS CLASSIC, at Baltimore, Md.: Ralston d. Roche, 6–0, 6–4; Drysdale

and Taylor d. Pierre Barthes (France) and Pilc, 7–5, 6–3.

FRENCH PROFESSIONAL CLASSIC, at Paris, France: Laver d. Newcombe, 6–2, 6–2, 6–3; Emerson and Laver d. Rosewall and Stolle, 1–6, 3–6, 11–9, 6–3, 6–2.

CANNES PRO CLASSIC, at Cannes, France: Newcombe d. Riessen, 7–5, 6–2.

MASTERS TOURNAMENT, at Binghampton, N.Y.: Gimeno d. Stolle, 6–4, 6–1; Laver and Stolle d. Emerson and Gimeno, 3–6, 6–3, 6–4; King d. Casals, 10–8, 6–4.

COLONIAL PRO INVITATION, at Fort Worth, Texas: Rosewall d. Gimeno, 6–4, 6–3; Jones d. King, 6–1, 6–2.

NEWPORT PROS, at Newport, R.I.: Riessen d. Drysdale, 21–10, 9–21, 21–19.

U.S. PRO CHAMPIONSHIP, at Boston, Mass.: Laver d. Newcombe, 6–4, 6–4, 9–7.

MIDLAND PROS, at Midland, Texas: Gonzalez d. Emerson, 7–5, 6–3.

SOUTH TEXAS PROS, at Corpus Christi, Texas: Laver d. Gimeno, 6–2, 6–4.

TRANSVAAL PRO CLASSIC, at Pretoria, South Africa: Newcombe d. Roche, 11–9, 4–6, 6–3.

JOHANNESBURG PROS, at Johannesburg, South Africa: Roche d. Buchholz, 6–2, 9–7.

DURBAN PROS, at Durban, South Africa: Newcombe d. Roche, 6–3, 6–4.

EAST LONDON PROS, at East London, South Africa: Newcombe d. Drysdale, 10–6.

PORT ELIZABETH PROS, at Port Elizabeth, South Africa: Taylor d. Roche, 10–8.

KIMBERLEY PROS, at Kimberley, South Africa: Newcombe d. Roche, 10–6.

WEMBLEY PROFESSIONAL CHAMPIONSHIP, at London, England: Rosewall d. Newcombe, 6–4, 4–6, 7–5, 6–4; Newcombe and Roche d. Gonzalez and Gimeno, 6–4, 9–7.

MADISON SQUARE GARDEN PROS, at New York City: Roche d. Gonzales, 6–4, 6–3.

1969 Season

HOLLYWOOD PRO, at Hollywood, Fla.: Tony Roche d. Rod Laver, 6–3, 9–7, 6–4; John Newcombe and Roche d. Dennis Ralston and Butch Buchholz, 6–4, 6–2.

OAKLAND PRO, at Oakland, Calif.: Roche d. Laver, 4–6, 6–4, 11–9.

LOS ANGELES PRO, at Los Angeles: Laver d. Marty Riessen, 6–4, 10–8; Roy Emerson and Laver d. Newcombe and Roche, 6–3, 5–7, 6–2.

U.S. Pro Tournaments, 1967–1971 (cont.)

MADISON SQUARE GARDEN PRO, at New York City: Laver d. Emerson, 6–2, 4–6, 6–1.

WEMBLY PRO, at London: Laver d. Ken Rosewall, 8–6, 6–0.

NETHERLANDS PRO, at Amsterdam: Tom Okker d. Andres Gimeno, 6–4, 6–3.

U.S. PRO CHAMPIONSHIPS, at Longwood, Boston: Laver d. Newcombe, 7–5, 6–2, 4–6, 6–1; Laver and Gonzalez d. Newcombe and Roche, 6–4, 5–7, 6–4.

MASTERS PRO, at Binghampton, N.Y.: Laver d. Gonzalez, 6–1, 6–2; Billie Jean King d. Ann Jones, 10–8, 3–6, 6–4.

AUSTRIAN PRO, at Portschach, Austria: Emerson d. Cliff Drysdale, 6–3, 3–6, 6–3.

COLONIAL PRO, at Fort Worth, Texas: Laver d. Rosewall, 6–3, 6–2.

1970 Season

DALLAS MORNING NEWS, at Dallas: Andres Gimeno d. Roy Emerson, 6–2, 6–3, 6–2; Warren Jacques and Emerson d. Ken Rosewall and Fred Stolle, 6–4, 6–8, 6–4.

ATLANTA PRO, at Atlanta: Tom Okker d. Dennis Ralston, 6–4, 10–8, 6–2; Marty Riessen and Okker d. Emerson and Pancho Segura, 7–5, 4–6, 6–4.

ROTHMAN'S ALBERT HALL, at London: Riessen d. Rosewall, 6–4, 6–2; Okker and Riessen d. Owen Davidson and Rod Laver, 6–3, 13–11, 9–11, 2–6, 7–5.

FORT WORTH NATIONAL INVITATION, at Fort Worth, Texas: Laver d. Emerson, 6–3, 7–5; Laver and Emerson d. Ray Moore and John Newcombe, 6–2, 6–2.

MIDLAND PRO, at Midland, Texas: Roger Taylor d. Newcombe, 2–6, 7–6, 6–1; Newcombe and Davidson d. Mark Cox and Graham Stilwell, 7–6, 6–4.

TUCSON CLASSIC, at Tucson: Riessen d. Emerson, 6–1, 6–4; Pancho Gonzalez and Emerson d. Ralston and Riessen, 7–6, 6–4.

HOWARD HUGHES INVITATION, at Las Vegas: Gonzalez d. Laver, 6–1, 7–5, 5–7, 6–3; Laver and Emerson d. Cliff Drysdale and Taylor, 8–6, 8–6.

RAWLINGS CLASSIC, at St. Louis: Laver d. Rosewall, 6–1, 6–4; Newcombe and Gimeno d. Emerson and Laver, 6–4, 6–2.

ROTHMAN'S PRO, at Vancouver, B.C.: Laver d. Emerson, 6–2, 6–1, 6–2; Emerson and Laver d. Nikki Pilic and Pierre Barthes, 6–1, 6–4, 6–3.

HALL OF FAME PRO, at Newport, R.I.: Riessen won VASSS round robin with 5–1 record.

MOROCCAN CHAMPIONSHIPS, at Casablanca: Newcombe d. Gimeno, 6–4, 6–4, 6–4; Cox and Stillwell d. Taylor and Riessen, 6–4, 6–4.

1971 Season

TENNIS CHAMPIONS CLASSIC (Finals), at New York City: Rod Laver d. Tom Okker, 7–5, 6–2, 6–1.

PHILADELPHIA INDOOR OPEN, at Philadelphia: John Newcombe d. Rod Laver, 7–6, 7–6, 6–4.

SPORTFACE INTERNATIONAL, at Chicago: John Newcombe d. Arthur Ashe, 4–6, 7–6, 6–2, 6–3; Tom Okker and Marty Riessen d. Newcombe and Tony Roche, 7–6, 4–6, 7–6.

AVENTURA TENNIS CLASSIC, at Miami: Cliff Drysdale d. Rod Laver, 6–2, 6–4, 3–6, 6–4; John Newcombe and Tony Roche d. Roy Emerson and Laver, 7–6, 7–6.

FIRST NATIONAL TENNIS CLASSIC, at Louisville: Tom Okker d. Cliff Drysdale, 3–6, 6–4, 6–1.

RAWLINGS TENNIS CLASSIC, at Dallas: John Newcombe d. Arthur Ashe, 7–6, 6–4; Tom Okker and Marty Riessen d. Bob Lutz and Charlie Pasarell, 6–3, 6–4.

UNITED STATES PROFESSIONAL CHAMPIONSHIP, at Longwood, Mass.: Ken Rosewall d. Cliff Drysdale, 6–4, 6–3, 6–0; Roy Emerson and Rod Laver d. Tom Okker and Marty Riessen, 6–4, 6–4.

COLONIAL PROFESSIONAL CHAMPIONSHIP, at Fort Worth: Rod Laver d. Marty Riessen, 2–6, 6–4, 3–6, 7–5, 6–3.

SEA PINES PROS, at Hilton Head Island, S.C.: Rod Laver d. John Newcombe, 6–2, 6–4.

WCT CHAMPIONSHIP, at Dallas, Texas: Ken Rosewall d. Rod Laver, 6–4, 1–6, 7–6, 7–6.

Women's Pro Tour (1971)

BRITISH MOTOR CARS INVITATIONAL, at San Francisco: Billie Jean King d. Nancy Richey Gunter, 64, 6–4; King and Rosemary Casals d. Ann Jones and Françoise Durr, 6–4, 6–7, 6–1.

BILLIE JEAN KING INVITATIONAL, at Long Beach, Calif.: Billie Jean King d. Rosemary

Casals, 6–1, 6–2; King and Casals d. Ann Jones and Françoise Durr, 7–5, 6–3.

VIRGINIA SLIMS INVITATIONAL OF MILWAUKEE, at Milwaukee: Billie Jean King d. Rosemary Casals, 6–3, 6–2; King and Casals d. Ann Jones and Françoise Durr, 6–3, 1–6, 6–2.

VIRGINIA SLIMS INVITATIONAL OF OKLAHOMA, at Oklahoma City: Billie Jean King d. Rosemary Casals, 1–6, 7–6, 6–4; King and Casals d. Mary Ann Curtis and Valerie Ziegenfuss, 6–7, 6–0, 7–5.

VIRGINIA SLIMS INVITATIONAL, at Chattanooga: Billie Jean King d. Ann Jones, 6–4, 6–1; King and Rosemary Casals d. Ann Jones and Françoise Durr, 6–4, 7–5.

PHILADELPHIA INDOOR CHAMPIONSHIPS, at Philadelphia: Rosemary Casals d. Françoise Durr, 6–2, 3–6, 6–2.

WLOD INVITATIONAL CHAMPIONSHIPS, at Ft. Lauderdale: Françoise Durr d. Billie Jean King, 6–3, 3–6, 6–3.

VIRGINIA SLIMS NATIONALS, at Winchester, Mass.: Billie Jean King d. Casals, 4–6, 6–2, 6–3; King and Casals d. Ann Jones and Françoise Durr, 6–4, 7–5.

K-MART INVITATIONAL, at Birmingham, Mich.: Billie Jean King d. Rosemary Casals, 3–6, 6–1, 6–2; Valerie Ziegenfuss and Mary

Ann Curtis d. Judy Dalton and Peaches Bartkowicz, 2–6, 6–2, 6–3.

VIRGINIA SLIMS INVITATIONAL OF NEW YORK, at New York City: Rosemary Casals d. Billie Jean King, 6–4, 6–4.

VIRGINIA SLIMS MASTERS, at St. Petersburg: Chris Evert d. Julie Heldman, 6–1, 6–2; Ann Jones and Françoise Durr d. Heldman and Judy Dalton, 7–6, 3–6, 6–3.

CAESAR'S PLACE WORLD PRO CHAMPIONSHIP, at Las Vegas: Ann Jones d. Billie Jean King, 7–5, 6–4; Jones and Françoise Durr d. King and Rosemary Casals, 0–6, 6–2, 6–4.

VIRGINIA SLIMS INVITATIONAL OF SAN DIEGO, at San Diego: Billie Jean King d. Rosemary Casals, 4–6, 7–5, 6–1; King and Casals d. Françoise Durr and Judy Dalton, 6–7, 6–2, 6–2.

VIRGINIA SLIMS INTERNATIONAL, at Houston: Billie Jean King d. Kerry Melville, 6–4, 4–6, 6–1; King and Rosemary Casals d. Judy Dalton and Françoise Durr, 2–6, 6–4, 6–3.

VIRGINIA SLIMS CLAY COURTS, at Chicago: Françoise Durr d. Billie Jean King, 6–4, 6–2; Durr and Judy Dalton d. King and Rosemary Casals, 6–4, 7–6.

VIRGINIA SLIMS GRASS COURTS, at Newport, R.I.: Billie Jean King d. Rosemary Casals,

Adrian Quist (*left*) won the Australian Championship in 1936, 1940, and 1948, while Viv McGrath (*right*) took it in 1937.

U.S. Pro Tournaments, 1967–1971 (cont.)

def.; Françoise Durr and Judy Dalton d. Kerry Melville and Kerry Harris, 6–2, 6–1.

VIRGINIA SLIMS THUNDERBIRD, at Phoenix: Kerry Melville d. Nancy Gunter, 6–2, 3–6, 7–6; Billie Jean King and Rosemary Casals d. Françoise Durr and Judy Dalton, 6–3, 6–2.

AUSTRALIAN CHAMPIONSHIPS—MEN'S SINGLES

1905	R. W. Heath
1906	Tony Wilding
1907	H. M. Rice
1908	Fred Alexander
1909	Tony Wilding
1910	R. W. Heath
1911	Norman Brookes
1912	J. C. Parke
1913	E. F. Parker
1914	Pat O'Hara Wood
1915	F. G. Lowe
1916–18	no competition
1919	R. F. Kingscote
1920	Pat O'Hara Wood
1921	R. G. Gemmell
1922	James Anderson

1923	Pat O'Hara Wood
1924	James Anderson
1925	James Anderson
1926	John Hawkes
1927	Gerald Patterson
1928	Jean Borotra
1929	J. C. Gregory
1930	E. F. Moon
1931	Jack Crawford
1932	Jack Crawford
1933	Jack Crawford
1934	Fred Perry
1935	Jack Crawford
1936	Adrian Quist
1937	Viv McGrath
1938	Don Budge
1939	John Bromwich
1940	Adrian Quist
1941–45	no competition
1946	John Bromwich
1947	Dinny Pails
1948	Adrian Quist
1949	Frank Sedgman
1950	Frank Sedgman
1951	Richard Savitt
1952	Ken McGregor
1953	Ken Rosewall
1954	Merv Rose
1955	Ken Rosewall
1956	Lew Hoad
1957	Ashley Cooper
1958	Ashley Cooper
1959	Alex Olmedo
1960	Rodney Laver
1961	Roy Emerson
1962	Rodney Laver
1963	Roy Emerson
1964	Roy Emerson
1965	Roy Emerson
1966	Roy Emerson
1967	Roy Emerson
1968	Bill Bowrey
1969*	Rodney Laver
1970*	Arthur Ashe
1971*	Ken Rosewall

Pat O'Hara Wood (*left*) and Gerald L. Patterson (*right*) were famed doubles players of the 1920's.

AUSTRALIAN CHAMPIONSHIPS—MEN'S DOUBLES

1905	T. Tachell and R. Lycett
1906	Tony Wilding and R. W. Heath
1907	H. A. Parker and W. A. Gregg
1908	Fred Alexander and Alfred Dunlop
1909	E. F. Parker and J. P. Keane
1910	H. Rice and A. Campbell
1911	R. W. Heath and R. Lycett
1912	J. C. Parke and C. P. Dixon
1913	E. F. Parker and A. H. Hedemann
1914	A. Campbell and Gerald Patterson
1915	H. M. Rice and C. V. Todd
1916–18	no competition
1919	Pat O'Hara Wood and R. V. Thomas
1920	Pat O'Hara Wood and R. V. Thomas

* Open championship.

Four Australian women stars of the 1930's and 1940's (*left to right*), Dot Stevenson, Nancye Wynne (later Mrs. Bolton), Mrs. Nell Hopman, and Thelma Coyne (Mrs. Long).

1921	R. H. Gennell and R. V. Thomas
1922	Gerald Patterson and John Hawkes
1923	Pat O'Hara Wood and C. B. St. John
1924	Norman Brookes and James Anderson
1925	Gerald Patterson and Pat O'Hara Wood
1926	Gerald Patterson and John Hawkes
1927	Gerald Patterson and John Hawkes
1928	Jean Borotra and Jacques Brugnon
1929	Jack Crawford and Harry Hopman
1930	Jack Crawford and Harry Hopman
1931	D. Donohoe and R. Dunlop
1932	Jack Crawford and E. F. Moon
1933	Ellsworth Vines and Keith Gledhill
1934	Fred Perry and George Hughes
1935	Jack Crawford and Viv McGrath
1936	Adrian Quist and D. P. Turnbull
1937	Adrian Quist and D. P. Turnbull
1938	Adrian Quist and John Bromwich
1939	Adrian Quist and John Bromwich
1940	Adrian Quist and John Bromwich
1941–45	no competition
1946	Adrian Quist and John Bromwich
1947	Adrian Quist and John Bromwich
1948	Adrian Quist and John Bromwich
1949	Adrian Quist and John Bromwich
1950	Adrian Quist and John Bromwich
1951	Frank Sedgman and Ken McGregor
1952	Frank Sedgman and Ken McGregor
1953	Lew Hoad and Ken Rosewall
1954	Rex Hartwig and Merv Rose
1955	Vic Seixas and Tony Trabert
1956	Lew Hoad and Ken Rosewall
1957	Lew Hoad and Neale Fraser
1958	Ashley Cooper and Neale Fraser
1959	Rodney Laver and Bob Mark
1960	Rodney Laver and Bob Mark
1961	Rodney Laver and Bob Mark
1962	Roy Emerson and Neale Fraser
1963	Bob Hewitt and Fred Stolle
1964	Bob Hewitt and Fred Stolle
1965	John Newcombe and Tony Roche
1966	Roy Emerson and Fred Stolle
1967	John Newcombe and Tony Roche
1968	Dick Crealy and Allen Stone
1969*	Roy Emerson and Rodney Laver
1970*	Robert Lutz and Stan Smith
1971*	John Newcombe and Tony Roche

AUSTRALIAN CHAMPIONSHIPS—WOMEN'S SINGLES

1922	Mrs. M. Molesworth
1923	Mrs. M. Molesworth
1924	S. Lance
1925	D. Akhurst
1926	D. Akhurst
1927	E. F. Boyd
1928	D. Akhurst
1929	D. Akhurst
1930	D. Akhurst
1931	Mrs. C. Buttsworth
1932	Mrs. C. Buttsworth
1933	J. Hartigan
1934	J. Hartigan
1935	D. Round
1936	J. Hartigan
1937	Nancye Wynne
1938	D. M. Bundy
1939	Mrs. V. Westacott
1940	Nancye Wynne
1941–45	no competition
1946	Mrs. N. W. Bolton
1947	Mrs. N. W. Bolton
1948	Mrs. N. W. Bolton
1949	Doris Hart
1950	A. Louise Brough
1951	Mrs. N. W. Bolton
1952	Mrs. C. Long
1953	Maureen Connolly
1954	Mrs. C. Long
1955	Beryl Penrose
1956	Mary Carter
1957	Shirley J. Fry
1958	Angela Mortimer
1959	Mrs. M. Reitano
1960	Margaret Smith
1961	Margaret Smith
1962	Margaret Smith
1963	Margaret Smith
1964	Margaret Smith
1965	Margaret Smith
1966	Margaret Smith
1967	Nancy Richey
1968	Mrs. Billie J. King
1969*	Mrs. Margaret S. Court
1970*	Mrs. Margaret S. Court
1971*	Mrs. Margaret S. Court

AUSTRALIAN CHAMPIONSHIPS—WOMEN'S DOUBLES

1922	E. F. Boyd and M. Mountain
1923	E. F. Boyd and S. Lance

* Open championship.

Australian Championships—Women's Doubles (cont.)

1924	D. Akhurst and S. Lance
1925	Mrs. R. R. Harper and D. Akhurst
1926	Mrs. P. O'Hara Wood and E. F. Boyd
1927	Mrs. P. O'Hara Wood and L. Bickerton
1928	D. Akhurst and E. F. Boyd
1929	D. Akhurst and L. Bickerton
1930	Mrs. M. Molesworth and E. Hood
1931	Mrs. D. A. Cozens and L. Bickerton
1932	Mrs. C. Buttsworth and Mrs. J. H. Crawford
1933	Mrs. M. Molesworth and Mrs. V. Westacott
1934	Mrs. M. Molesworth and Mrs. V. Westacott
1935	E. Dearman and N. Lyle
1936	T. Coyne and N. Wynne
1937	T. Coyne and N. Wynne
1938	T. Coyne and N. Wynne
1939	T. Coyne and N. Wynne
1940	T. Coyne and N. Wynne
1941–45	no competition
1946	J. Fetch and M. Bevis
1947	Mrs. T. C. Long and Mrs. N. W. Bolton
1948	Mrs. T. C. Long and Mrs. N. W. Bolton
1949	Mrs. T. C. Long and Mrs. N. W. Bolton
1950	A. Louise Brough and Doris Hart
1951	Mrs. T. C. Long and Mrs. N. W. Bolton
1952	Mrs. T. C. Long and Mrs. N. W. Bolton
1953	Maureen Connolly and Julia Sampson
1954	Mrs. M. Hawton and Beryl Penrose
1955	Mrs. M. Hawton and Beryl Penrose
1956	Mrs. M. Hawton and Mrs. T. C. Long
1957	Althea Gibson and Shirley Fry
1958	Mrs. M. Hawton and Mrs. T. C. Long
1959	Renée Schuurman and Sandra Reynolds
1960	Maria Bueno and Christine Truman
1961	Mrs. M. Reitano and Margaret Smith
1962	Margaret Smith and Robyn Ebbern
1963	Margaret Smith and Robyn Ebbern
1964	Judy Tegart and Lesley Turner
1965	Margaret Smith and Lesley Turner
1966	Mrs. C. C. Graebner and Nancy Richey
1967	Lesley Turner and Judy Tegert
1968	Karen Krantzcke and Kerry Melville
1969*	Mrs. M. S. Court and Judy Tegart
1970*	Mrs. M. S. Court and Mrs. J. T. Dalton
1971*	Mrs. M. S. Court and Evonne Goolagong

AUSTRALIAN CHAMPIONSHIPS—MIXED DOUBLES

1922	E. F. Boyd and John B. Hawkes
1923	S. Lance and Horace M. Rice
1924	D. Akhurst and John Willard
1925	D. Akhurst and John Willard
1926	E. F. Boyd and John B. Hawkes
1927	E. F. Boyd and John B. Hawkes
1928	D. Akhurst and Jean Borotra
1929	D. Akhurst and E. F. Moon
1930	N. Hall and Harry C. Hopman
1931	Mr. and Mrs. John H. Crawford
1932	Mr. and Mrs. John H. Crawford
1933	Mr. and Mrs. John H. Crawford
1934	J. Hartigan and E. F. Moon
1935	L. M. Bickerton and C. Boussus

* Open championship.

1936	Mr. and Mrs. Harry C. Hopman
1937	Mr. and Mrs. Harry C. Hopman
1938	M. Wilson and John Bromwich
1939	Mr. and Mrs. Harry C. Hopman
1940	N. Wynne and Colin Long
1941–45	no competition
1946	Mrs. N. Bolton and Colin Long
1947	Mrs. N. Bolton and Colin Long
1948	Mrs. N. Bolton and Colin Long
1949	Doris Hart and Frank Sedgman
1950	Doris Hart and Frank Sedgman
1951	Mrs. C. Long and George Worthington
1952	Mrs. C. Long and George Worthington
1953	Julia Sampson and Rex Hartwig
1954	Mrs. C. Long and Rex Hartwig
1955	Mrs. C. Long and George Worthington
1956	Beryl Penrose and Neale Fraser
1957	Fay Muller and Mal Anderson
1958	Mrs. Mary Hawton and Bob Howe
1959	Sandra Reynolds and Bob Mark
1960	Jan LeHane and Trevor Fancutt
1961	Jan LeHane and Bob Hewitt
1962	Lesley Turner and Fred Stolle
1963	Margaret Smith and Ken Fletcher
1964	Margaret Smith and Ken Fletcher
1965	unfinished
1966	Judy Tegart and Tony Roche
1967	Lesley Turner and Owen Davidson
1968	Mrs. Billie J. King and Dick Crealy
1969–71	not held

CANADIAN CHAMPIONSHIPS—MEN'S SINGLES

1890	E. E. Tanner
1891	F. S. Mansfield
1892	F. H. Hovey
1893	H. E. Avery
1894	R. W. P. Matthews
1895	W. A. Larned
1896	R. D. Wrenn
1897	L. E. Ware
1898	L. E. Ware
1899	M. D. Whitman
1900	M. D. Whitman
1901	W. A. Larned
1902	B. C. Wright
1903	B. C. Wright
1904	B. C. Wright
1905	no tournament
1906	I. C. Wright
1907	J. F. Foulkes
1908	T. Y. Sherwell
1909	J. F. Foulkes
1910	J. F. Foulkes
1911	B. P. Schwengers
1912	B. P. Schwengers
1913	R. Baird
1914	T. M. Sherwell
1915–18	no tournament
1919	Seijchiro Kashio
1920	Paul Bennett
1921	W. J. Bates
1922	Frank Anderson
1923	W. L. Rennie
1924	George M. Lott

1925   W. F. Crocker
1926   L. DeTurenne
1927   J. A. Wright
1928   Wilmer Allison
1929   J. A. Wright
1930   G. Lyttleton
1931   Jack Wright
1932   Frank Parker
1933   John Murio
1934   Marcel Rainville
1935   Eugene Smith
1936   Jack Tidball
1937   Walter Senior
1938   Frank Parker
1939   P. Morey Lewis
1940   Don McDiarmid
1941–45   no tournaments
1946   P. Morey Lewis
1947   James Evert
1948   William Tully
1949   Henri Rochon
1950   Brendan Macken
1951   Tony Vincent
1952   Richard Savitt
1953   Mervyn Rose
1954   Bernard Bartzen
1955   Robert Bedard
1956   Noel Brown
1957   Robert Bedard
1958   Robert Bedard
1959   Reynaldo Garrido
1960   Ladislav Legenstein
1961   Whitney Reed
1962   Juan Couder
1963   Whitney Reed
1964   Roy Emerson
1965   Ronald Holmberg
1966   Allen Fox
1967   Manuel Santana
1968   Ramanathan Krishnan
1969* Cliff Richey
1970   Mike Belkin
1970* Rod Laver
1971   Peter Burwash
1971* John Newcombe

CANADIAN CHAMPIONSHIPS—MEN'S DOUBLES

1919   G. D. Holmes and P. Bennett
1920   P. Bennett and F. W. Leistikow
1921   C. V. Todd and N. Peach
1922   F. T. and F. G. Anderson
1923   W. F. Crocker and Jack Wright
1924   G. M. Lott and Sam Hardy
1925   W. F. Crocker and Jack Wright
1926   L. DeTurenne and John Proctor
1927   B. Harrison and S. Lockwood
1928   J. Van Ryn and Wilmer Allison
1929   J. A. Wright and W. F. Crocker
1930   Fred Mercur and J. G. Hall
1931   Jack Wright and Marcel Rainville
1932   George Lott and Marcel Rainville
1933   John Murio and Martin Kenneally

  * Open championship.

American Julie Heldman won, among her many honors, the Canadian and Italian championships.

1934   Harold Surface and Philip Castlen
1935   Worth Oswold and Charles Weesner
1936   Jack Tidball and Charles Church
1937   Walter Martin and D. N. Jones, Jr.
1938   W. L. Allison, Jr. and Frank Parker
1939   P. M. Lewis and F. A. Froehling
1940   Ross Wilson and Phil Pearson
1941–45   no tournament
1946   Jim Macken and Brendan Macken
1947   James Evert and Jerry Evert
1948   Edgar Lanthier and Gordon MacNeil
1949   Edgar Lanthier and Gordon MacNeil
1950   Robert Abdesselam and Jean Ducos
1951   Brendan Macken and Lorne Main
1952   Kurt Nielsen and Richard Savitt
1953   Rex Hartwig and Mervyn Rose
1954   Luis Ayala and Lorne Main
1955   Robert Bedard and Donald Fontana
1956   Earl Baumgardner and Noel Brown
1957   Robert Bedard and Donald Fontana
1958   Robert Howe and Whitney Reed
1959   Robert Bedard and Donald Fontana
1960   Peter School and Ladislav Legenstein
1961   Whitney Reed and Michael Sangster
1962   Bill Hoogs and Jim McManus
1963   Joaquin Loyo-Mayo and Marcelo Lara
1964   Roy Emerson and Fred Stolle
1965   Ronald Holmberg and Lester Sack
1966   Keith Carpenter and Mike Carpenter

Canadian Championships—Men's Doubles (cont.)

1967   Roy Emerson and Manuel Santana
1968   Harry Fauquier and John Sharpe
1969* John Newcombe and Ron Holmberg
1970   Bob Bedard and Bob Puddicombe
1970* William Bowrey and Martin Riessen
1971   Peter Burwash and Ken Binnis
1971* Tom Okker and Martin Riessen

CANADIAN CHAMPIONSHIPS—WOMEN'S SINGLES

1919   Marion Zinderstein
1920   Mrs. H. Bickle
1921   Mrs. H. Bickle
1922   Mrs. H. Bickle
1923   F. Best
1924   Mrs. H. Bickle
1925   M. Leeming
1926   M. Leeming
1927   C. Swartz
1928   Marjorie Gladman
1929   Olive Wade
1930   Olive Wade
1931   Edith Cross
1932   Olive Wade
1933   Gracyn Wheeler
1934   Caroline Deacon
1935   Margaret Osborne
1936   Dr. Esther Bartosh
1937   Evelyn M. Dearman
1938   Mrs. R. Bolte
1939   Elizabeth Blackman
1940   Eleanor Young
1941–45   no tournament
1946   Mrs. B. Lewis
1947   Mrs. G. Kelleher
1948   Patricia Macken
1949   Mrs. B. Lewis
1950   Barbara Knapp
1951   Mrs. L. Davidson
1952   Melita Ramirez
1953   Melita Ramirez
1954   Karol Fageros
1955   Mrs. H. Sladek
1956   Jean Laird
1957   Mrs. L. Brown
1958   Eleanor Dodge
1959   Mary Martin
1960   Donna Floyd
1961   Ann Haydon
1962   Ann Barclay
1963   Ann Barclay
1964   Benita Senn
1965   Julie M. Heldman
1966   Rita Bentley
1967   Kathy Harter
1968   Jane Bartkowicz
1969* Faye Urban
1970   Andre Martin
1970* Mrs. M. S. Court
1971   Vicki Berner
1971* Françoise Durr

   * Open championship.

CANADIAN CHAMPIONSHIPS—WOMEN'S DOUBLES

1919   Mrs. H. Bickle and F. Best
1920   Mrs. H. Bickle and F. Best
1921   Mrs. H. Bickle and F. Best
1922   Mrs. H. Bickle and F. Best
1923   Mrs. H. Bickle and F. Best
1924   Mrs. H. Bickle and F. Best
1925   M. Leeming and K. Tatlow
1926   Mrs. D. Bourque and L. Fraser
1927   C. Swartz and Edith Cross
1928   Mrs. A. H. Chapin, Jr. and Marjorie Gladman
1929   Mrs. O. E. Gray and Olive Wade
1930   M. Leeming and H. Leeming
1931   Edith Cross and Mrs. D. Perow
1932   M. Leeming and Mrs. K. J. Salmond
1933   Mrs. H. V. Wilson and Mary Campbell
1934   Caroline Deacon and Eleanor Young
1935   Mrs. C. Rose and Mrs. M. Laird
1936   Mrs. G. M. Gross and Jean Milne
1937   Evelyn Dearman and J. Ingram
1938   Mrs. Frank Fisher and Mrs. W. Walson, Jr.
1939   E. and L. Blackman
1940   E. Young and E. Milne
1941–45   no tournaments
1946   Mrs. B. Lewis and Noreen Haney
1947   Mrs. G. Wheeler Kelleher and June Crow
1948   Mrs. Frank Fisher and Mary Green
1949   Mrs. B. Lewis and Edyth A. Sullivan
1950   Isabel Troccole and Carol Liguori
1951   Mrs. L. Davidson and Doris Popple
1952   Doris Ell and Melita Ramirez
1953   Mrs. Thelma Long and Melita Ramirez
1954   Karol Fageros and Ethel Norton
1955   C. Bowan and Ann Barclay
1956   Mrs. J. Lee and Pat Miller
1957   Mrs. L. Brown and Mrs. H. Doleschell
1958   Barbara Browning and Pam Davis
1959   Mrs. D. Head Knode and Mary Martin
1960   Donna Floyd and Belmar Gunderson
1961   M. Bundy and Eleanor Dodge
1962   Ann Barclay and Mrs. L. Brown
1963   Susan Butt and Vicki Berner
1964   Mrs. A. Tym and Hedy Rutzezeck
1965   Brenda Nunns and Faye Urban
1966   Vicki Berner and Faye Urban
1967   Vicki Berner and Faye Urban
1968   not held
1969* Vicki Berner and Faye Urban
1970   Andre Martin and Jane O'Hara
1970* Mrs. M. S. Court and Rosemary Casals
1971   Andre Martin and Jane O'Hara
1971* Rosemary Casals and Françoise Durr

CANADIAN CHAMPIONSHIPS—MIXED DOUBLES

1919   Marion Zinderstein and H. Taylor
1920   G. Maxwell and P. Bennett
1921   Mrs. H. Bickle and W. Bates
1922   G. Hutchings and L. K. Verley
1923   Mr. and Mrs. H. F. Wright
1924   P. Grierson and Sam Hardy
1925   M. Leeming and John Proctor
1926   D. Seaker and C. W. Aikman

1927   C. Swartz and S. Lockwood
1928   Mrs. A. H. Chaplin, Jr. and John Doeg
1929   tie, not decided
1930   M. Leeming and John Proctor
1931   Edith Cross and L. Driscod
1932   Olive Wade and Grant McLean
1933   Gracyn Wheeler and M. Kenneally
1934   Mrs. H. L. Beer and George Leclerc
1935   Mrs. M. Laird and Ray Casey
1936   Dr. Esther Bartosh and Verne Hughes
1937   Evelyn Dearman and M. Laird Watt
1938   Mr. and Mrs. Wilmer Allison
1939   E. Young and Wm. H. Pedlar
1940   Jean Milne and Phil Pearson
1941–45   no tournament
1946   Mr. and Mrs. Morey Lewis
1947   Mr. and Mrs. Robert Kelleher
1948   Mrs. P. Robinson and R. Buser
1949   Mrs. B. Lewis and Blair Hawley
1950   Barbara Knapp and Lorne Main
1951   Doris Popple and Paul Willey
1952   Melita Ramirez and Gustavo Palafox
1953   Melita Ramirez and Francisco Contreras
1954   Ethel Norton and Dan Sullivan
1955   canceled
1956   Jean Laird and Paul Willey
1957   Mrs. Anne Bagge Vieira and Robert Howe
1958   Farel Footman and Whitney Reed
1959   Marietta Laframboise and Robert Bedard
1960   Deirdre Catt and Michael Sangster
1961   Ann Haydon and Michael Sangster
1962   Eleanor Dodge and Keith Carpenter
1963   Vicki Berner and Keith Carpenter
1964   Mrs. Alice Tym and Owen Davidson
1965   Faye Urban and Tom Body
1967   Kathy Harter and Ray Keldie
1968   not held
1969   Andre Martin and Bill Higgins
1970–71   not held

France's Marcel Bernard won his country's title in 1946.

FRENCH CHAMPIONSHIPS—MEN'S SINGLES

1891   J. Briggs
1892   J. Schopfer
1893   L. Riboulet
1894   A. Vacherot
1895   A. Vacherot
1896   A. Vacherot
1897   P. Ayme
1898   P. Ayme
1899   P. Ayme
1900   P. Ayme
1901   A. Vacherot
1902   A. Vacherot
1903   M. Décugis
1904   M. Décugis
1905   M. Germot
1906   M. Germot
1907   M. Décugis
1908   M. Décugis
1909   M. Décugis
1910   M. Germot
1911   A. H. Gobert
1912   M. Décugis

Czechoslovakia's Jan Kodes took the French title in both 1970 and 1971.

French Championships—Men's Singles (cont.)

1913	M. Décugis
1914	M. Décugis
1915–19	no competition
1920	A. H. Gobert
1921	J. Samazeuith
1922	Henri Cochet
1923	P. Blanchy
1924	Jean Borotra
1925*	Jean René Lacoste
1926	Henri Cochet
1927	Jean René Lacoste
1928	Henri Cochet
1929	Jean René Lacoste
1930	Henri Cochet
1931	Jean Borotra
1932	Henri Cochet
1933	John H. Crawford
1934	G. von Cramm
1935	Fred J. Perry
1936	G. von Cramm
1937	H. Henkel
1938	J. Donald Budge
1939	W. Donald McNeill
1940	no competition
1941†	Bernard Destreman
1942†	Bernard Destreman
1943†	Yvon Petra
1944†	Yvon Petra
1945†	Yvon Petra
1946	Marcel Bernard
1947	Josef Asboth
1948	Frank A. Parker
1949	Frank A. Parker
1950	Budge Patty
1951	Jaroslav Drobny
1952	Jaroslav Drobny
1953	Kenneth Rosewall
1954	Tony Trabert
1955	Tony Trabert
1956	Lewis Hoad
1957	Sven Davidson
1958	Mervyn Rose
1959	Nicola Pietrangeli
1960	Nicola Pietrangeli
1961	Manuel Santana
1962	Rodney Laver
1963	Roy Emerson
1964	Manuel Santana
1965	Fred Stolle
1966	Tony Roche
1967	Roy Emerson
1968‡	Ken Rosewall
1969‡	Rodney Laver
1970‡	Jan Kodes
1971‡	Jan Kodes

FRENCH CHAMPIONSHIPS—MEN'S DOUBLES

1891	B. Desjoyau and T. Legrand
1892	J. Havet and D. Albertini

* Entries accepted from all countries.
† From 1941–45 the championship was called the "Tournoi de France."
‡ Open championship.

1893	J. Schopfer and F. Goldsmith
1894	L. Brosselin and J. Lesage
1895	A. Vacherot and C. Winzer
1896	F. N. Warden and J. Wynn
1897	P. Ayme and T. Lebreton
1898	A. Vacherot and X. E. Casdagli
1899	P. Ayme and T. Lebreton
1900	P. Ayme and T. Lebreton
1901	A. Vacherot and M. Vacherot
1902	M. Décugis and J. Worth
1903	M. Décugis and J. Worth
1904	M. Décugis and M. Germot
1905	M. Décugis and J. Worth
1906	M. Décugis and M. Germot
1907	M. Décugis and M. Germot
1908	M. Décugis and M. Germot
1909	M. Décugis and M. Germot
1910	M. Décugis and M. DuPont
1911	M. Décugis and M. Germot
1912	M. Décugis and M. Germot
1913	M. Décugis and M. Germot
1914	M. Décugis and M. Germot
1915–19	no competition
1920	M. Décugis and M. Germot
1921	A. H. Gobert and W. H. Laurentz
1922	J. Brugnon and M. DuPont
1923	P. Blanchy and J. Samarzeuilh
1924	Jean Borotra and Jean René Lacoste
1925	Jean Borotra and Jean René Lacoste
1926	Vincent Richards and H. Kinsey
1927	Henri Cochet and J. Brugnon
1928	Jean Borotra and J. Brugnon
1929	Jean Borotra and Jean René Lacoste
1930	Henri Cochet and J. Brugnon
1931	George M. Lott and John Van Ryn
1932	Henri Cochet and J. Brugnon
1933	G. P. Hughes and F. J. Perry
1934	Jean Borotra and J. Brugnon
1935	Jack Crawford and Adrian Quist
1936	Jean Borotra and Marcel Bernard
1937	Gottfried von Cramm and Henner Henkel
1938	Bernard Destremau and Yvon Petra
1939	Don McNeill and C. R. Harris
1940	no competition
1941†	Bernard Destremau and C. Boussus
1942†	Bernard Destremau and Yvon Petra
1943†	Marcel Bernard and Yvon Petra
1944†	Marcel Bernard and Yvon Petra
1945†	Henri Cochet and P. Pellizza
1946	Marcel Bernard and Yvon Petra
1947	Eustace Fannin and Eric Sturgess
1948	Lennart Bergelin and Jaroslav Drobny
1949	Frank Parker and Richard Gonzalez
1950	William Talbert and Tony Trabert
1951	Kenneth McGregor and Frank Sedgman
1952	Kenneth McGregor and Frank Sedgman
1953	Lewis Hoad and Kenneth Rosewall
1954	E. Victor Seixas, Jr. and Tony Trabert
1955	E. Victor Seixas, Jr. and Tony Trabert
1956	Don Candy and Robert Perry
1957	Malcolm J. Anderson and Ashley J. Cooper
1958	Ashley J. Cooper and Neale Fraser
1959	Nicola Pietrangeli and Orlando Sirola
1960	Neale Fraser and Roy Emerson

1961	Roy Emerson and Rodney Laver
1962	Roy Emerson and Neale Fraser
1963	Roy Emerson and Manuel Santana
1964	Roy Emerson and Ken Fletcher
1965	Roy Emerson and Fred Stolle
1966	Clark Graebner and Dennis Ralston
1967	John Newcombe and Tony Roche
1968*	Ken Rosewall and Fred Stolle
1969*	John Newcombe and Tony Roche
1970*	Ilie Nastase and Ion Tiriac
1971*	Arthur Ashe and Marty Riessen

FRENCH CHAMPIONSHIPS—WOMEN'S SINGLES

1897	F. Masson
1898	F. Masson
1899	F. Masson
1900	Mrs. J. Provost
1901	P. Girod
1902	F. Masson
1903	F. Masson
1904	K. Gillou
1905	K. Gillou
1906	Mrs. K. Fenwick
1907	Mrs. C. de Kermel
1908	Mrs. K. Fenwick
1909	J. Mattey
1910	J. Mattey
1911	J. Mattey
1912	J. Mattey
1913	M. Broquedis
1914	M. Broquedis
1915–19	no competition
1920	S. Lenglen

At nineteen years of age, Evonne Goolagong won both the French and Wimbledon Championships in 1971.

1921	S. Lenglen
1922	S. Lenglen
1923	S. Lenglen
1924	D. Vlasto
1925	S. Lenglen
1926	S. Lenglen
1927	K. Bouman
1928	Helen Wills
1929	Helen Wills
1930	Mrs. H. Wills Moody
1931	C. Aussem
1932	Mrs. H. Wills Moody
1933	M. C. Scriven
1934	M. C. Scriven
1935	Mrs. H. Sperling
1936	Mrs. H. Sperling
1937	Mrs. H. Sperling
1938	Mrs. R. Mathieu
1939	Mrs. R. Mathieu
1940	no competition
1941*	A. Weiwers
1942*	A. Weiwers
1943*	Mrs. N. Lafargue
1944*	L. Veber
1945*	Mrs. L. Dodille Payot
1946	Margaret Osborne
1947	Mrs. Patricia C. Todd
1948	Mrs. N. Landry
1949	Mrs. Margaret O. du Pont
1950	Doris Hart
1951	Shirley Fry
1952	Doris Hart
1953	Maureen Connolly
1954	Maureen Connolly
1955	Angela Mortimer
1956	Althea Gibson
1957	Shirley Bloomer
1958	Mrs. S. Koermoczi
1959	Christine Truman
1960	Darlene Hard
1961	Ann Haydon
1962	Margaret Smith
1963	Lesley Turner
1964	Margaret Smith
1965	Lesley Turner
1966	Mrs. A. H. Jones
1967	Françoise Durr
1968*	Nancy Richey
1969*	Mrs. M. S. Court
1970*	Mrs. M. S. Court
1971*	Evonne Goolagong

FRENCH CHAMPIONSHIPS—WOMEN'S DOUBLES

1925	S. Lenglen and D. Vlasto
1926	S. Lenglen and D. Vlasto
1927	Mrs. T. Peacock and E. L. Heine
1928	Mrs. J. Watson and E. Bennett
1929	L. de Alvarez and K. Bouman
1930	Mrs. H. Wills Moody and E. Ryan
1931	Mrs. Whittingstall and B. Nuthall
1932	Mrs. H. Wills Moody and E. Ryan
1933	Mrs. R. Mathieu and E. Ryan

* Open championships.

French Championships—Women's Doubles (cont.)

1934	Mrs. R. Mathieu and E. Ryan
1935	M. C. Scriven and K. Stammers
1936	Mrs. R. Mathieu and A. M. Yorke
1937	Mrs. R. Mathieu and J. Jedrzekowska
1938	Mrs. R. Mathieu and A. M. Yorke
1939	Mrs. R. Mathieu and J. Jedrzekowska
1940	no competition
1941*	A. Weiwers and D. St. Omer Roy
1942*	A. Weiwers and D. St. Omer Roy
1943*	A. Weiwers and D. St. Omer Roy
1944*	Mrs. B. Grosbois and Mrs. J. Manescau
1945*	Mrs. N. Lafargue and Mrs. P. Fritz
1946	A. Louise Brough and Margaret Osborne
1947	A. Louise Brough and Margaret Osborne
1948	Doris Hart and Mrs. Pat C. Todd
1949	Mrs. M. O. du Pont and A. Louise Brough
1950	Doris Hart and Shirley Fry
1951	Doris Hart and Shirley Fry
1952	Doris Hart and Shirley Fry
1953	Doris Hart and Shirley Fry
1954	Maureen Connolly and Mrs. N. Hopman
1955	Mrs. B. B. Fleitz and Darlene Hard
1956	Angela Buxton and Althea Gibson
1957	Shirley Bloomer and Darlene Hard
1958	Rosie Reyes and Yola Ramirez
1959	Sandra Reynolds and Renée Schuurman
1960	Maria Bueno and Darlene Hard
1961	Sandra Reynolds and Renée Schuurman
1962	Sandra Reynolds and Renée Schuurman
1963	Mrs. A. H. Jones and Renée Schuurman
1964	Margaret Smith and Lesley Turner
1965	Margaret Smith and Lesley Turner
1966	Judy Tegart and Margaret Smith
1967	Françoise Durr and Gail Sheriff
1968*	Françoise Durr and Mrs. A. H. Jones
1969*	Françoise Durr and Mrs. A. H. Jones
1970*	Mrs. C. S. Chanfreau and Françoise Durr
1971*	Mrs. C. S. Chanfreau and Françoise Durr

FRENCH CHAMPIONSHIPS—MIXED DOUBLES

1925	S. Lenglen and J. Brugnon
1926	S. Lenglen and J. Brugnon
1927	Mrs. M. Bordes and Jean Borotra
1928	E. Bennett and Henri Cochet
1929	E. Bennett and Henri Cochet
1930	C. Aussen and William T. Tilden II
1931	Betty Nuthall and P. D. Spence
1932	Betty Nuthall and Fred J. Perry
1933	M. C. Scriven and Jack H. Crawford
1934	C. Rosambert and Jean Borotra
1935	L. Pavot and M. Bernard
1936	A. M. Yorke and M. Bernard
1937	Mrs. R. Mathieu and Y. Petra
1938	Mrs. R. Mathieu and D. Mitic
1939	Mrs. S. P. Fabyan and Elwood T. Cooke
1940–45	no competition
1946	Pauline Betz and Budge Patty
1947	Mrs. S. Summers and Eric W. Sturgess
1948	Mrs. P. C. Todd and Jaroslav Drobny
1949	Mrs. S. Summers and Eric W. Sturgess
1950	Barbara Sudfield and Enrique Morea

* Open championships.

1951	Doris Hart and Frank Sedgman
1952	Doris Hart and Frank Sedgman
1953	Doris Hart and E. Victor Seixas, Jr.
1954	Maureen Connolly and Lew Hoad
1955	Darlene Hard and Gordon Forbes
1956	Mrs. T. C. Long and Luis Ayala
1957	V. Puzejova and J. Javorsky
1958	Shirley Bloomer and Nicoli Pietrangeli
1959	Yola Ramirez and William Knight
1960	Maria Bueno and Robert Howe
1961	Darlene Hard and Rod Laver
1962	Renée Schuurman and Robert Howe
1963	Margaret Smith and Ken Fletcher
1964	Margaret Smith and Ken Fletcher
1965	Margaret Smith and Ken Fletcher
1966	Annette van Zyl and Frew McMillan
1967	Mrs. B. J. King and Owen Davidson
1968*	Françoise Durr and Jean Claude Barclay
1969*	Mrs. M. S. Court and Martin Riessen
1970*	Mrs. B. J. King and Jean Claude Barclay
1971*	Françoise Durr and Jean Claude Barclay

GERMAN CHAMPIONSHIPS—MEN'S SINGLES

1892	W. Bonne
1893	G. Winzer

Germany's two best pre-World War II players, Heinrich Henkel (*left*) and Baron Gottfried von Cramm (*right*).

1894	G. Voss
1895	G. Voss
1896	G. Voss
1897	G. W. Hillyard
1898	S. M. Mahony
1899	C. Hobart
1900	G. W. Hillyard
1901	M. Décugis
1902	M. Décugis
1903	M. G. J. Ritchie
1904	M. G. J. Ritchie
1905	M. G. J. Ritchie
1906	M. G. J. Ritchie
1907	O. Froitzheim
1908	M. G. J. Ritchie
1909	O. Froitzheim
1910	O. Froitzheim
1911	O. Froitzheim
1912	O. von Muller
1913	H. Schomburgk
1914–19	no competition
1920	O. Kreuzer
1921	O. Froitzheim
1922	O. Froitzheim
1923	H. Landmann
1924	B. von Kehrling
1925	O. Froitzheim
1926	H. Molenhauer
1927	H. Molenhauer
1928	D. Prenn
1929	C. Boussus
1930	C. Boussus
1931	R. Menzel
1932	G. von Cramm
1933	G. von Cramm
1934	G. von Cramm
1935	G. von Cramm
1936	no competition
1937	H. Henkel
1938	O. Szigeti
1939	H. Henkel
1940–47	no competition
1948	G. von Cramm
1949	G. von Cramm
1950	J. Drobny
1951	L. Bergelin
1952	E. W. Sturgess
1953	B. Patty
1954	B. Patty
1955	A. Larsen
1956	L. A. Hoad
1957	M. G. Rose
1958	S. Davidson
1959	W. A. Knight
1960	N. Pietrangeli
1961	R. Laver
1962	R. Laver
1963	M. F. Mulligan
1964	W. P. Bungert
1965	E. C. Drysdale
1966	F. S. Stolle
1967	R. Emerson
1968	J. D. Newcombe

* Open championships.

1969*	A. D. Roche
1970*	T. Okker
1971*	A. Gimeno

GERMAN CHAMPIONSHIPS—MEN'S DOUBLES

1902	M. Décugis and M. Germot
1903	R. Kinzl and C. von Wessely
1904	M. G. J. Ritchie and W. E. Lane
1905	A. F. Wilding and E. Spitz
1906	M. G. J. Ritchie and G. F. Adler
1907	L. Trasenster and O. Froitzheim
1908	O. von Muller and H. Schomburgk
1909	F. W. Rahe and C. Bergmann
1910	O. von Muller and H. Schomburgk
1911	O. Froitzheim and F. Pipes
1912	L. Transenster and L. M. Heyden
1913	R. Kinzl and C. von Wessely
1914–19	not held
1920	G. Salm and O. Kruezer
1921	L. M. Heyden and H. Schomburgk
1922	O. Froitzheim and O. Kreuzer
1923	F. W. Rahe and B. von Kehrling
1924	F. W. Rahe and B. von Kehrling
1925	O. Froitzheim and O. Kreuzer
1926	F. W. Rahe and B. von Kehrling
1927	D. M. Greig and M. V. Summerson
1928	R. O. Cummings and E. F. Moon
1929	J. Brugnon and C. Boussus
1930	J. B. Crawford and E. F. Moon
1931	W. Dessart and E. Nourney
1932	J. B. Crawford and H. Hopman
1933	J. Satoh and R. Nuoni
1934	E. Maier and A. Quist
1935	H. Henkel and H. Denker
1936	not held
1937	J. B. Crawford and V. McGrath
1938	Y. Petra and J. Lesueur
1939	H. Henkel and R. Menzel
1940–47	no competition
1948	G. von Cramm and J. E. Harper
1949	G. von Cramm and J. E. Harper
1950	A. Quist and O. W. Sidwell
1951	K. Nielsen and T. Ulrich
1952	J. Drobny and W. Avre
1953	G. von Cramm and B. Patty
1954	G. von Cramm and B. Patty
1955	G. von Cramm and B. Patty
1956	L. Hoad and D. Candy
1957	M. G. Rose and D. Candy
1958	F. Contreras and M. Llamas
1959	L. Ayala and D. Candy
1960	R. Emerson and N. Fraser
1961	R. Hewitt and F. S. Stolle
1962	R. Hewitt and M. F. Mulligan
1963	R. Hewitt and F. S. Stolle
1964	J. L. Arilla and M. Santana
1965	I. Buding and C. Kuknke
1966	F. S. Stolle and T. Ulrich
1967	R. Hewitt and F. McMillan
1968	T. Okker and M. Riessen
1969*	T. Okker and M. Riessen
1970*	R. Hewitt and F. McMillan
1971*	A. Gimeno and J. Alexander

GERMAN CHAMPIONSHIPS—WOMEN'S SINGLES

1896　M. Thomsen
1897　Mrs. G. W. Hillyard
1898　E. Lane
1899　C. Cooper
1900　Mrs. G. W. Hillyard
1901　T. Lowther
1902　C. Ross
1903　V. Pinckney
1904　E. Lane
1905　E. Lane
1906　L. Berton
1907　F. de Madarasz
1908　F. de Madarasz
1909　D. Heimann
1910　M. Rieck
1911　M. Rieck
1912　D. Koring
1913　D. Koring
1914–19　no competition
1920　Mrs. I. Friedleben
1921　Mrs. I. Friedleben
1922　Mrs. I. Friedleben
1923　Mrs. I. Friedleben
1924　Mrs. I. Friedleben
1925　Mrs. N. Neppach
1926　Mrs. I. Friedleben
1927　C. Aussem
1928　D. Akhurst
1929　Mrs. H. von Reznicek
1930　C. Aussem
1931　C. Aussem
1932　L. Payot
1933　H. Krahwinkel
1934　Mrs. H. K. Sperling
1935　Mrs. H. K. Sperling
1936　no competition
1937　Mrs. H. K. Sperling
1938　Mrs. H. K. Sperling
1939　Mrs. H. K. Sperling
1940–47　no competition
1948　U. Rosenow
1949　Mrs. M. Weiss
1950　D. Head
1951　Mrs. N. Bolton
1952　D. Head
1953　Mrs. D. H. Knode
1954　Mrs. A. J. Mottram
1955　B. Penrose
1956　Mrs. N. C. Long
1957　Y. Ramirez
1958　L. Coghlan
1959　E. Buding
1960　S. Reynolds
1961　S. Reynolds
1962　Mrs. L. E. G. Price
1963　R. Schuurman
1964　M. Smith
1965　M. Smith
1966　M. Smith
1967　F. Durr
1968　Mrs. J. du Plooy

* Open championships.

1969*　J. A. M. Tegart
1970*　Mrs. H. Hoesl
1971*　Mrs. B. J. M. King

GERMAN CHAMPIONSHIPS—WOMEN'S DOUBLES

1925　Mrs. N. Neppach and Mrs. H. Kaeber
1926　Mrs. M. Galvao and E. Hoffmann
1927　Mrs. N. Neppach and Mrs. H. Petery Varady
1928　D. Akhurst and E. Boyd
1929　J. Fry and M. V. Chamberlain
1930　Mrs. L. A. Godfree and Mrs. H. Watson
1931　Mrs. L. A. Godfree and N. Trentham
1932　H. Krahwinkel and A. Peitz
1933　Mrs. J. B. Pittmann and K. Stammers
1934　E. M. Dearman and N. M. Lyle
1935　Mrs. A. Schneider and Mrs. M. Rollin
　　　　Couquerque
1936　no competition
1937　Mrs. H. K. Sperling and Mrs. M. Rollin
　　　　Conquerque
1938　N. Wynne and T. Coyne
1939　Mrs. H. K. Sperling and Mrs. A. Schneider
1940–47　no competition
1948　Mrs. M. Dietz and T. Heidtmann
1949　Mrs. A. von Tarnay and T. Zehden
1950　Mrs. J. Pohmann and D. Head
1951　Mrs. N. W. Bolton and Mrs. M. Procter
1952　D. Head and Mrs. A. J. Mottram
1953　Mrs. D. H. Knode and Mrs. A. J. Mottram
1954　Mrs. E. Vollmer and Mrs. A. J. Mottram
1955　B. Penrose and M. Carter
1956　E. F. Muller and B. Seeney
1957　A. Mortimer and P. Ward
1958　M. Hawton and Mrs. N. C. Long
1959　Y. Ramirez and R. M. Reyes
1960　E. Buding and C. Truman
1961　S. Reynolds and R. Schuurman
1962　L. R. Turner and J. Lehane
1963　L. Hunt and A. M. van Zyl
1964　M. Smith and L. R. Turner
1965　M. Smith and L. R. Turner
1966　M. Smith and Mrs. A. H. Jones
1967　J. Tegart and L. R. Turner
1968　Mrs. A. M. duPlooy and P. Walkden
1969*　H. Niessen and J. Tegart
1970*　K. Krantzcke and K. Melville
1971*　Mrs. B. J. King and R. Casals

GERMAN CHAMPIONSHIPS—MIXED DOUBLES

1906　N. Schmoller and O. Kreuzer
1907　Mrs. G. Neresheimer and L. Trasenster
1908　K. Osery and L. Trasenster
1909　M. Rieck and M. Galvao
1910　Mrs. G. Neresheimer and F. C. Uhl
1911　Mrs. G. Neresheimer and F. C. Uhl
1912　D. Koering and H. Schomburgk
1913　D. Koering and H. Schomburgk
1914–19　no competition
1920　Mrs. J. Friedleben and O. Kreuzer
1921　Mrs. H. Schomburgk and H. Schomburgk
1922　E. de Alvarez and L. M. Heyden
1923　E. de Alvarez and L. M. Heyden
1924　Mrs. N. Neppach and H. Kleinschroth

1925	Mrs. Neppach and A. Ludke
1926	C. Aussem and H. Moldenhauer
1927	J. Kallmeyer and D. M. Greig
1928	C. Aussem and R. R. Boyd
1929	E. L. Colyer and H. G. N. Lee
1930	Mrs. L. A. Godfree and J. C. Gregory
1931	L. Payot and H. C. Fisher
1932	H. Krahwinkel and G. von Cramm
1933	H. Krahwinkel and G. von Cramm
1934	Mrs. H. K. Sperling and G. von Cramm
1935	C. Aussem and H. Henkel
1936	no competition
1937	M. L. Horne and H. Denker
1938	N. Wynne and J. Lesueur
1939	G. Wheeler and M. Smith
1940–47	no competition
1948	V. Rosenow and E. Buchholz
1949	Mrs. J. Pohmann and T. Koch
1950	Mrs. M. Dietz and O. W. Sidwell
1951	Mrs. N. W. Bolton and J. Borotra
1952	D. Head and E. W. Sturgess
1953	P. Ward and A. J. Mottram
1954	Mrs. E. Vollmer and H. W. Stewart
1955	Mrs. E. Vollmer and H. W. Stewart
1956	Mrs. T. C. Long and L. Ayala
1957	E. Buding and M. G. Rose
1958	Y. Ramirez and J. Jansco
1959	Y. Ramirez and W. A. Knight
1960	S. Reynolds and I. Vermaak
1961	S. Reynolds and R. Hewitt
1962	L. R. Turner and K. Fletcher
1963	L. R. Turner and F. S. Stolle
1964	H. Schultze and N. Pilic
1965	M. Smith and N. Fraser
1966	M. Smith and J. Newcombe
1967	C. Sheriff and T. Okker
1968	Mrs. A. M. du Plooy and F. McMillan
1969*	J. Tegart and M. Riessen
1970*	J. T. Dalton and F. McMillan
1971	not held

All-England Championships (Wimbledon Championships)

The following record indicates the final match by which the championship was decided. From 1877 to 1921 the men's singles was decided on a challenge-round system, the previous year's winner standing out until a

Lew Hoad displays the "prize" of tennis, the Wimbledon Cup, which he won in both 1956 and 1957.

winner of the so-called All Comers' event qualified to challenge. The same system applied in the women's singles from 1886 to 1921 and in the men's doubles from 1886 to 1921. It never applied in the women's and mixed doubles. In those years the presence of the previous year's winner in the last match means that the title was decided in a challenge round.

The Championships were staged at the All-England Club, Worple Road, Wimbledon, London, from 1877 to 1921, when the club moved to Church Road, Wimbledon. Partial seeding by placing overseas competitors was introduced in 1924, full merit seeding in 1927. Wimbledon became "Open" in 1968.

ALL-ENGLAND CHAMPIONSHIPS—MEN'S SINGLES

	Winner	*Runner-Up*
1877	Spencer W. Gore	W. C. Marshall
1878	P. F. Hadow	Spencer W. Gore
1879	J. T. Hartley	V. "St. Leger" Gould
1880	J. T. Hartley	H. F. Lawford
1881	William Renshaw	J. T. Hartley
1882	William Renshaw	Ernest Renshaw
1883	William Renshaw	Ernest Renshaw
1884	William Renshaw	H. F. Lawford
1885	William Renshaw	H. F. Lawford

* Open championships.

All-England Championships—Men's Singles (*cont.*)

	Winner	Runner-Up
1886	William Renshaw	H. F. Lawford
1887	H. F. Lawford	Ernest Renshaw
1888	Ernest Renshaw	H. F. Lawford
1889	William Renshaw	Ernest Renshaw
1890	W. J. Hamilton	William Renshaw
1891	Wilfred Baddeley	Joshua Pim
1892	Wilfred Baddeley	Joshua Pim
1893	Joshua Pim	Wilfred Baddeley
1894	Joshua Pim	Wilfred Baddeley
1895	Wilfred Baddeley	Wilberforce V. Eaves
1896	H. S. Mahoney	Wilfred Baddeley
1897	Reggie F. Doherty	H. S. Mahoney
1898	Reggie F. Doherty	H. Laurie Doherty
1899	Reggie F. Doherty	Arthur W. Gore
1900	Reggie F. Doherty	Sidney H. Smith
1901	Arthur W. Gore	Reggie F. Doherty
1902	H. Laurie Doherty	Arthur W. Gore
1903	H. Laurie Doherty	Frank L. Riseley
1904	H. Laurie Doherty	Frank L. Riseley
1905	H. Laurie Doherty	Norman E. Brookes
1906	H. Laurie Doherty	Frank L. Riseley
1907	Norman E. Brookes	Arthur W. Gore
1908	Arthur W. Gore	H. Roper Barrett
1909	Arthur W. Gore	M. G. J. Ritchie
1910	Anthony F. Wilding	Arthur W. Gore
1911	Anthony F. Wilding	H. Roper Barrett
1912	Anthony F. Wilding	Arthur W. Gore
1913	Anthony F. Wilding	Maurice E. McLoughlin
1914	Norman E. Brookes	Anthony F. Wilding
1915–18	not held	
1919	Gerald L. Patterson	Norman E. Brookes
1920	William T. Tilden II	Gerald L. Patterson
1921	William T. Tilden II	Brian I. C. Norton
1922	Gerald L. Patterson	Randolph Lycett
1923	William M. Johnston	Francis T. Hunter
1924	Jean Borotra	Jean René Lacoste
1925	Jean René Lacoste	Jean Borotra
1926	Jean Borotra	Howard Kinsey
1927	Henri Cochet	Jean Borotra
1928	Jean René Lacoste	Henri Cochet
1929	Henri Cochet	Jean Borotra
1930	William T. Tilden II	Wilmer Allison
1931	Sidney Wood	Frank X. Shields
1932	Ellsworth Vines	Wilfred Austin
1933	Jack Crawford	Ellsworth Vines
1934	Fred C. Perry	Jack Crawford
1935	Fred J. Perry	Gottfried von Cramm
1936	Fred J. Perry	Gottfried von Cramm
1937	Donald Budge	Gottfried von Cramm
1938	Donald Budge	Wilfred Austin
1939	Bobby Riggs	Elwood Cooke
1940–45	not held	
1946	Yvon Petra	Geoff E. Brown
1947	Jack Kramer	Tom P. Brown
1948	Bob Falkenburg	John Bromwich
1949	Ted Schroeder	Jaroslav Drobny
1950	Budge Patty	Frank Sedgman
1951	Dick Savitt	Ken McGregor
1952	Frank Sedgman	Jaroslav Drobny
1953	Vic Seixas	Kurt Nielsen
1954	Jaroslav Drobny	Ken Rosewall
1955	Tony Trabert	Kurt Nielsen

	Winner	Runner-Up
1956	Lew Hoad	Ken Rosewall
1957	Lew Hoad	Ashley Cooper
1958	Ashley Cooper	Neale Fraser
1959	Alex Olmedo	Rod Laver
1960	Neale Fraser	Rod Laver
1961	Rod Laver	Chuck McKinley
1962	Rod Laver	Martin Mulligan
1963	Chuck McKinley	Fred Stolle
1964	Roy Emersom	Fred Stolle
1965	Roy Emerson	Fred Stolle
1966	Manuel Santana	Dennis Ralston
1967	John Newcombe	Wilhelm Bungert
1968*	Rod Laver	Tony Roche
1969*	Rod Laver	John Newcombe
1970*	John Newcombe	Ken Rosewall
1971*	John Newcombe	Stan Smith

ALL-ENGLAND CHAMPIONSHPS—MEN'S DOUBLES (*Played from 1879 to 1883 at Oxford*)

	Winner	Runner-Up
1879	L. R. Erskine and H. F. Lawford	F. Durant and G. E. Tabor
1880	William and Ernest Renshaw	O. E. Woodhouse and C. J. Cole
1881	William and Ernest Renshaw	W. J. Down and H. Vaughan
1882	J. T. Hartley and R. T. Richardson	J. G. Horn and C. B. Russell
1883	C. W. Grinstead and C. E. Welldon	C. B. Russell and R. T. Milford
1884	William and Ernest Renshaw	E. W. Lewis and E. L. Williams
1885	William and Ernest Renshaw	C. E. Farrar and A. J. Stanley
1886	William and Ernest Renshaw	C. E. Farrar and A. J. Stanley
1887	Herbert W. Wilberforce and P. B. Lyon	J. Hope Crispe and Barrat Smith
1888	William and Ernest Renshaw	Herbert Wilberforce and P. B. Lyon
1889	William and Ernest Renshaw	E. W. Lewis and G. W. Hillyard
1890	Joshua Pim and F. O. Stoker	E. W. Lewis and G. W. Hillyard
1891	Wilfred and Herbert Baddeley	Joshua Pim and F. O. Stoker
1892	E. W. Lewis and H. S. Barlow	Wilfred and Herbert Baddeley
1893	Joshua Pim and F. O. Stoker	E. W. Lewis and H. S. Barlow
1894	Wilfred and Herbert Baddeley	H. S. Barlow and C. H. Martin
1895	Wilfred and Herbert Baddeley	E. W. Lewis and W. V. Eaves
1896	Wilfred and Herbert Baddeley	R. F. Doherty and H. A. Nisbet
1897	Reggie F. and H. Laurie Doherty	Wilfred and Herbert Doherty
1898	Reggie F. and H. Laurie Doherty	H. A. Nisbet and C. Hobart
1899	Reggie F. and H. Laurie Doherty	H. A. Nisbet and C. Hobart
1900	Reggie F. and H. Laurie Doherty	H. Roper Barrett and H. A. Nisbet
1901	Reggie F. and H. Laurie Doherty	Dwight Davis and Holcombe Ward
1902	Sidney H. Smith and Frank Riseley	Reggie F. and H. Laurie Doherty
1903	Reggie F. and H. Laurie Doherty	H. S. Mahoney and M. G. J. Ritchie
1904	Reggie F. and H. Laurie Doherty	Sidney H. Smith and Frank Riseley
1905	Reggie F. and H. Laurie Doherty	Sidney H. Smith and Frank Riseley
1906	Sidney H. Smith and Frank Riseley	Reggie F. and H. Laurie Doherty
1907	Norman E. Brookes and Anthony Wilding	Beals C. Wright and Karl Behr
1908	Anthony Wilding and M. G. J. Ritchie	Arthur W. Gore and H. R. Barrett
1909	Arthur W. Gore and H. R. Barrett	Stanley Doust and H. A. Parker
1910	Anthony Wilding and M. G. J. Ritchie	Arthur W. Gore and H. R. Barrett
1911	André Gobert and Max Décugis	Anthony Wilding and M. G. J. Ritchie
1912	H. R. Barrett and Charles Dixon	André Gobert and Max Décugis
1913	H. R. Barrett and Charles Dixon	F. W. Rahe and H. Kleinschroth
1914	Norman E. Brookes and Anthony Wilding	H. R. Barrett and Charles Dixon
1915–18	not held	
1919	R. V. Thomas and Pat O'Hara Wood	Randolph Lycett and R. W. Heath
1920	R. N. Williams and C. S. Garland	A. R. F. Kingscote and J. C. Parke
1921	Randolph Lycett and Max Woosnam	Arthur H. and Frank G. Lowe
1922	J. O. Anderson and Randolph Lycett	Gerald Patterson and Pat O'Hara Wood

* Open championships.

All-England Championships—Men's Doubles (*cont.*)

	Winner	Runner-Up
1923	Leslie A. Godfree and Randolph Lycett	Count deGomar and E. Flaquer
1924	Frank Hunter and Vincent Richards	R. N. Williams and W. M. Washburn
1925	Jean Borotra and Jean René Lacoste	J. Hennessey and R. Casey
1926	Jacques Brugnon and Henri Cochet	H. Kingsey and Vincent Richards
1927	Frank Hunter and William Tilden II	Jacques Brugnon and Henri Cochet
1928	Jacques Brugnon and Henri Cochet	Gerald Patterson and J. B. Hawkes
1929	Wilmer Allison and John Van Ryn	J. Colin Gregory and Ian G. Collins
1930	Wilmer Allison and John Van Ryn	John H. Doeg and George M. Lott
1931	George M. Lott and John Van Ryn	Jacques Brugnon and Henri Cochet
1932	Jean Borotra and Jacques Brugnon	Fred J. Perry and G. Pat Hughes
1933	Jean Borotra and Jacques Brugnon	R. Nunoi and J. Satoh
1934	George M. Lott and Lester R. Stoefen	Jean Borotra and Jacques Brugnon
1935	Jack Crawford and Adrian Quist	Wilmer Allison and John Van Ryn
1936	G. Pat Hughes and Raymond Tuckey	Charles Hare and Frank Wilde
1937	Don Budge and Gene Mako	G. Pat Hughes and Raymond Tuckey
1938	Don Budge and Gene Mako	Henner Henkel and G. von Metaxa
1939	Ellwood Cooke and Bobby Riggs	Charles Hare and Frank Wilde
1940–45	not held	
1946	Tom Brown and Jack Kramer	Geoff Brown and Dinny Pails
1947	Bob Falkenburg and Jack Kramer	Tony Mottram and O. W. Sidwell
1948	John Bromwich and Frank Sedgman	Tom Brown and Gardnar Mulloy
1949	Richard Gonzalez and Frank Parker	Gardnar Mulloy and Ted Schroeder
1950	John Bromwich and Adrian Quist	Geoff Brown and O. W. Sidwell
1951	Ken McGregor and Frank Sedgman	Jaroslav Drobny and Eric Sturgess
1952	Ken McGregor and Frank Sedgman	Vic Seixas and Eric Sturgess
1953	Lew Hoad and Ken Rosewall	Rex Hartwig and Mervyn Rose
1954	Rex Hartwig and Mervyn Rose	Vic Seixas and Tony Trabert
1955	Rex Hartwig and Lew Hoad	Neale Fraser and Ken Rosewall
1956	Lew Hoad and Ken Rosewall	Nicola Pietrangeli and O. Sirola
1957	Budge Patty and Gardnar Mulloy	Neale Fraser and Lew Hoad
1958	Sven Davidson and Ulf Schmidt	Ashley Cooper and Neale Fraser
1959	Roy Emerson and Neale Fraser	Rod Laver and Bob Mark
1960	Rafael Osuna and Dennis Ralston	Mike Davies and Bobby Wilson
1961	Roy Emerson and Neale Fraser	Bob Hewitt and Fred Stolle
1962	Bob Hewitt and Fred Stolle	Boro Jovanovic and Nikki Pilic
1963	Rafael Osuna and Antonio Palafox	Jean C. Barclay and Pierre Darmon
1964	Bob Hewitt and Fred Stolle	Roy Emerson and Ken Fletcher
1965	John Newcombe and Tony Roche	Ken Fletcher and Bob Hewitt
1966	Ken Fletcher and John Newcombe	Bill Bowrey and Owen Davidson
1967	Bob Hewitt and Frew McMillan	Roy Emerson and Ken Fletcher
1968*	John Newcombe and Tony Roche	Ken Rosewall and Fred Stolle
1969*	John Newcombe and Tony Roche	Tom Okker and Marty Riessen
1970*	John Newcombe and Tony Roche	Ken Rosewall and Fred Stolle
1971*	Roy Emerson and Rod Laver	Dennis Ralston and Arthur Ashe

ALL-ENGLAND CHAMPIONSHIPS—WOMEN'S SINGLES

	Winner	Runner-Up
1884	Maud Watson	Lillian Watson
1885	Maud Watson	Blanche Bingley
1886	Blanche Bingley	Maud Watson
1887	Lottie Dod	Blanche Bingley
1888	Lottie Dod	Blanche Bingley Hillyard
1889	Blanche Bingley Hillyard	L. Rice
1890	L. Rice	L. Jacks
1891	Lottie Dod	Blanche Bingley Hillyard
1892	Lottie Dod	Blanche Bingley Hillyard
1893	Lottie Dod	Blanche Bingley Hillyard
1894	Blanche Bingley Hillyard	L. Austin
1895	Charlotte Cooper	H. Jackson
1896	Charlotte Cooper	Mrs. W. H. Pickering
1897	Blanche Bingley Hillyard	Charlotte Cooper

* Open championships.

	Winner	Runner-Up
1898	Charlotte Cooper	L. Martin
1899	Blanche Bingley Hillyard	Charlotte Cooper
1900	Blanche Bingley Hillyard	Charlotte Cooper
1901	Charlotte Cooper Sterry	Blanche Bingley Hillyard
1902	M. E. Robb	Charlotte Cooper Sterry
1903	Dorothea Douglas	E. W. Thompson
1904	Dorothea Douglas	Charlotte Cooper Sterry
1905	May Sutton	Dorothea Douglas
1906	Dorothea Douglas	May Sutton
1907	May Sutton	Dorothea Douglas Lambert Chambers
1908	Charlotte Cooper Sterry	A. M. Morton
1909	Dora Boothby	A. M. Morton
1910	Dorothea Douglas Lambert Chambers	Dora Boothby
1911	Dorothea Douglas Lambert Chambers	Dora Boothby
1912	E. W. Thomson Larcombe	Charlotte Cooper Sterry
1913	Dorothea Douglas Lambert Chambers	Mrs. R. J. McNair
1914	Dorothea Douglas Lambert Chambers	E. W. Thomson Larcombe
1915–18	not held	
1919	Suzanne Lenglen	Dorothea Douglas Lambert Chambers
1920	Suzanne Lenglen	Dorothea Douglas Lambert Chambers
1921	Suzanne Lenglen	Elizabeth Ryan
1922	Suzanne Lenglen	Molla Mallory
1923	Suzanne Lenglen	Kitty McKane
1924	Kitty McKane	Helen Wills
1925	Suzanne Lenglen	Joan Fry
1926	Kitty McKane Godfree	Lili Alvarez
1927	Helen Wills	Lili Alvarez
1928	Helen Wills	Lili Alvarez
1929	Helen Wills	Helen Jacobs
1930	Helen Wills Moody	Elizabeth Ryan
1931	Cilly Aussem	Hilda Krahwinkel
1932	Helen Wills Moody	Helen Jacobs
1933	Helen Wills Moody	Dorothy Round
1934	Dorothy Round	Helen Jacobs
1935	Helen Wills Moody	Helen Jacobs
1936	Helen Jacobs	Hilda Krahwinkel Sperling
1937	Dorothy Round	Jadwiga Jedrzejowska
1938	Helen Wills Moody	Helen Jacobs
1939	Alice Marble	Kay Stammers
1940–45	not held	
1946	Pauline Betz	A. Louise Brough
1947	Margaret Osborne	Doris Hart
1948	A. Louise Brough	Doris Hart
1949	A. Louise Brough	Margaret Osborne du Pont
1950	A. Louise Brough	Margaret Osborne du Pont
1951	Doris Hart	Shirley Fry
1952	Maureen Connolly	A. Louise Brough
1953	Maureen Connolly	Doris Hart
1954	Maureen Connolly	A. Louise Brough
1955	A. Louise Brough	Beverly Baker Fleitz
1956	Shirley Fry	Angela Buxton
1957	Althea Gibson	Darlene Hard
1958	Althea Gibson	Angela Mortimer
1959	Maria Bueno	Darlene Hard
1960	Maria Bueno	Sandra Reynolds
1961	Angela Mortimer	Christine Truman
1962	Karen Hantze Susman	Vera Puzejova Sukova
1963	Margaret Smith	Billie Jean Moffitt
1964	Maria Bueno	Margaret Smith
1965	Margaret Smith	Maria Bueno
1966	Billie Jean Moffitt King	Maria Bueno
1967	Billie Jean Moffitt King	Maria Bueno
1968*	Billie Jean Moffitt King	Judy Tegart

* Open championships.

The famed men's doubles team of Fred Stolle and Bob Hewitt.

When Angela Mortimer won the Ladies' Singles Championship in 1961 from Christine Truman, she was the first Briton to do so since 1937.

All-England Championships—Women's Singles (cont.)

Winner	Runner-Up
1969* Ann Haydon Jones	Billie Jean Moffitt King
1970* Margaret Smith Court	Billie Jean Moffitt King
1971* Evonne Goolagong	Margaret Smith Court

ALL-ENGLAND CHAMPIONSHIPS—WOMEN'S DOUBLES

Winner	Runner-Up
1913 Mrs. R. J. McNair and Doro Boothby	Charlotte Cooper Sterry and Dorothea Douglas L. Chambers
1914 A. M. Morton and Elizabeth Ryan	E. W. Thomson Larcombe and G. Hannam
1915–18 not held	
1919 Suzanne Lenglen and Elizabeth Ryan	E. W. Thomson Larcombe and Dorothea Douglas L. Chambers
1920 Suzanne Lenglen and Elizabeth Ryan	E. W. Thomson Larcombe and Dorothea Douglas L. Chambers
1921 Suzanne Lenglen and Elizabeth Ryan	Geraldine Beamish and Mrs. G. Peacock
1922 Suzanne Lenglen and Elizabeth Ryan	Kitty McKane and Mrs. A. D. Stocks
1923 Suzanne Lenglen and Elizabeth Ryan	Joan Austin and Edith Colyer
1924 Hazel Wightman and Helen Wills	Phyllis Covel and Kitty McKane
1925 Suzanne Lenglen and Elizabeth Ryan	Mrs. A. V. Bridge and Mrs. C. G. McIlquham
1926 Mary K. Browne and Elizabeth Ryan	Kitty McKane Godfree and Edith Colyer
1927 Helen Wills and Elizabeth Ryan	Mrs. G. Peacock and Bobie Heine
1928 Peggy Saunders and Phyllis Watson	Ermyntrude Harvey and Eileen Bennett
1929 Peggy Michell and Phyllis Watson	Phyllis Covel and Dorothy Shepherd Barron
1930 Helen Wills Moody and Elizabeth Ryan	Eleanor Cross and Sarah Palfrey
1931 Phyllis Mudford and Dorothy Shepherd Barron	Doris Metaxa and Josane Sigart
1932 Doris Metaxa and Josane Sigart	Helen Jacobs and Elizabeth Ryan
1933 Simone Mathieu and Elizabeth Ryan	Freda James and Billie Yorke
1934 Simone Mathieu and Elizabeth Ryan	Dorothy Andrus and Sylvia Henrotin
1935 Freda James and Kay Stammers	Simone Mathieu and Hilda Krahwinkel Sperling
1936 Freda James and Kay Stammers	Helen Jacobs and Sarah Palfrey Fabyan
1937 Simone Mathieu and Billie Yorke	Phyllis Mudford King and Elsie Pittman

* Open championships.

	Winner	*Runner-Up*
1938	Sarah Palfrey Fabyan and Alice Marble	Simone Mathieu and Billie Yorke
1939	Sarah Palfrey Fabyan and Alice Marble	Helen Jacobs and Billie Yorke
1940–45	not held	
1946	A. Louise Brough and Margaret Osborne	Pauline Betz and Doris Hart
1947	Pat Todd and Doris Hart	A. Louise Brough and Margaret Osborne
1948	A. Louise Brough and Margaret Osborne du Pont	Pat Todd and Doris Hart
1949	A. Louise Brough and Margaret Osborne du Pont	Pat Todd and Gussie Moran
1950	A. Louise Brough and Margaret Osborne du Pont	Doris Hart and Shirley Fry
1951	Doris Hart and Shirley Fry	A. Louise Brough and Margaret Osborne du Pont
1952	Doris Hart and Shirley Fry	A. Louise Brough and Maureen Connolly
1953	Doris Hart and Shirley Fry	Julie Sampson and Maureen Connolly
1954	A. Louise Brough and Margaret Osborne du Pont	Doris Hart and Shirley Fry
1955	Angela Mortimer and Anne Shilcock	Shirley Bloomer and Pat Ward
1956	Angela Buxton and Althea Gibson	Daphne Seeney and Fay Muller
1957	Althea Gibson and Darlene Hard	Thelma Long and Mary Hawton
1958	Maria Bueno and Althea Gibson	Margaret Osborne du Pont and Margaret Varner
1959	Jean Arth and Darlene Hard	Beverly Baker Fleitz and Christine Truman
1960	Maria Bueno and Darlene Hard	Sandra Reynolds and Renée Schuurman
1961	Karen Hantze and Billie Jean Moffitt	Ian Lehane and Margaret Smith
1962	Billie Jean Moffitt and Karen Hantze Susman	Sandra Reynolds Price and Renée Schuurman
1963	Maria Bueno and Darlene Hard	Robyn Ebbern and Margaret Smith
1964	Margaret Smith and Lesley Turner	Billie Jean Moffitt and Karen Hantze Susman
1965	Maria Bueno and Billie Jean Moffitt	Françoise Durr and Janine Lieffrig
1966	Maria Bueno and Nancy Richey	Margaret Smith and Judy Tegart
1967	Rosemary Casals and Billie Jean Moffitt King	Maria Bueno and Nancy Richey
1968*	Rosemary Casals and Billie Jean Moffitt King	Françoise Durr and Ann Haydon Jones
1969*	Margaret Smith Court and Judy Tegart	Patti Hogan and Peggy Michell
1970*	Rosemary Casals and Billie Jean Moffitt King	Françoise Durr and Virginia Wade
1971*	Rosemary Casals and Billie Jean Moffitt King	Margaret Smith Court and Evonne Goolagong

* Open championships.

Rosemary Casals and Mrs. Billie Jean King won the Ladies' Doubles Championship in 1967, 1968, 1970, 1971. Mrs. King also won the title with Karen Hantze (1961) and Maria Bueno (1965).

Lining up before their 1970 Wimbledon final in the Veterans' Doubles are: (*left to right*) George Mac-Call, Pancho Segura, Bobby Riggs, and Jaroslav Drobny. Match was won by Drobny and Riggs in straight sets.

ALL-ENGLAND CHAMPIONSHIPS—MIXED DOUBLES

	Winner	*Runner-Up*
1913	J. Hope Crispe and Mrs. C. O. Tuckey	J. C. Parke and E. W. Thomson Larcombe
1914	J. C. Parke and E. W. Thomson Larcombe	Anthony F. Wilding and Mlle. Broquedis
1915–18	not held	
1919	Randolph Lycett and Elizabeth Ryan	Albert Prebble and Dorothea Douglas Lambert Chambers
1920	Gerald Patterson and Suzanne Lenglen	Randolph Lycett and Elizabeth Ryan
1921	Randolph Lycett and Elizabeth Ryan	Max Woosnam and P. Howkins
1922	Pat O'Hara Wood and Suzanne Lenglen	Randolph Lycett and Elizabeth Ryan
1923	Randolph Lycett and Elizabeth Ryan	L. S. Deane and Dorothy Shepherd Barron
1924	J. Brian Gilbert and Kitty McKane	Leslie Godfree and Dorothy Shepherd Barron
1925	Jean Borotra and Suzanne Lenglen	Baron H. L. deMorpurgo and Elizabeth Ryan
1926	Leslie Godfree and Kitty McKane Godfree	Harold O. Kinsey and Mary K. Browne
1927	Francis T. Hunter and Helen Wills	Leslie Godfree and Kitty McKane
1928	Pat Spence and Elizabeth Ryan	Jack Crawford and Dorothy Akhurst
1929	Francis T. Hunter and Helen Wills	Ian Collins and Joan Fry
1930	Jack Crawford and Elizabeth Ryan	Daniel Prenn and Hilda Krahwinkel
1931	George M. Lott and Mrs. L. A. Harper	Ian Collins and Joan Ridley
1932	Enrique Majer and Elizabeth Ryan	Harry Hopman and Josane Sigart
1933	Gottfried von Cramm and Hilda Krahwinkel	Norman Farquharson and Mary Heeley
1934	Ryuki Mike and Dorothy Round	Bunny Austin and Dorothy Shepherd Barron
1935	Fred J. Perry and Dorothy Round	Harry and Nell Hopman
1936	Fred J. Perry and Dorothy Round	Don Budge and Sarah Palfrey Fabyan
1937	Don Budge and Alice Marble	Yvon Petra and Simone Mathieu
1938	Don Budge and Alice Marble	Henner Henkel and Sara Palfrey Fabyan
1939	Bobby Riggs and Alice Marble	Frank Wilde and Nina Brown
1940–45	not held	
1946	Tom Brown and A. Louise Brough	Geoff Brown and Dodo Bundy
1947	John Bromwich and A. Louise Brough	Colin Cong and Nancye Bolton
1948	John Bromwich and A. Louise Brough	Frank Sedgman and Doris Hart
1949	Eric Sturgess and Sheila Summers	John Bromwich and A. Louise Brough
1950	Eric Sturgess and A. Louise Brough	Geoff Brown and Pat Todd
1951	Frank Sedgman and Doris Hart	Mervyn Rose and Nancye Bolton
1952	Frank Sedgman and Doris Hart	Enrique Morea and Thelma Long
1953	Vic Seixas and Doris Hart	Enrique Morea and Shirley Fry
1954	Vic Seixas and Doris Hart	Ken Rosewall and Margaret Osborne du Pont
1955	Vic Seixas and Doris Hart	Enrique Morea and A. Louise Brough
1956	Vic Seixas and Shirley Fry	Gardnar Mulloy and Althea Gibson
1957	Mervyn Rose and Darlene Hard	Neale Fraser and Althea Gibson
1958	Bob Howe and Loraine Coghlan	Kurt Nielsen and Althea Gibson
1959	Rod Laver and Darlene Hard	Neale Fraser and Maria Bueno
1960	Rod Laver and Darlene Hard	Bob Howe and Maria Bueno
1961	Fred Stolle and Lesley Turner	Bob Howe and Edda Buding
1962	Neale Fraser and Margaret Osborne du Pont	Dennis Ralston and Ann Haydon
1963	Ken Fletcher and Margaret Smith	Bob Hewitt and Darlene Hard
1964	Fred Stolle and Lesley Turner	Ken Fletcher and Margaret Smith
1965	Ken Fletcher and Margaret Smith	Tony Roche and Judy Tegart
1966	Ken Fletcher and Margaret Smith	Dennis Ralston and Billie Jean Moffitt King
1967	Owen Davidson and Billie Jean Moffitt King	Ken Fletcher and Maria Bueno
1968*	Ken Fletcher and Margaret Smith Court	Alex Metreveli and Olga Morozova
1969*	Fred Stolle and Ann Jones	Tony Roche and Judy Tegart
1970*	Ilie Nastase and Rosemary Casals	Alex Metreveli and Olga Morozova
1971*	Owen Davidson and Billie Jean Moffitt King	Marty Riessen and Margaret Smith Court

BRITISH HARD COURTS—MEN'S SINGLES

1924	R. Lycett	1927	J. R. Lacoste
1925	P. D. B. Spence	1928	J. R. Lacoste
1926	J. Brugnon	1929	H. W. Austin

* Open championships.

The finalists in 1930 British Hard-Court Championship: Mrs. M. List (*left*) and Joan Fry (*right*). Miss Fry took the title.

1930	H. G. N. Lee
1931	C. Boussus
1932	F. J. Perry
1933	F. J. Perry
1934	F. J. Perry
1935	F. J. Perry
1936	F. J. Perry
1937	H. W. Austin
1938	Kho Sin Kie
1939	Kho Sin Kie
1940–45	no competition
1946	J. E. Harper
1947	E. W. Sturgess
1948	E. W. Sturgess
1949	P. Masip
1950	J. Drobny
1951	J. Drobny
1952	J. Drobny
1953	E. Morea
1954	A. J. Mottram
1955	S. Davidson
1956	B. Patty
1957	J. Drobny
1958	W. A. Knight
1959	L. A. Gerrard
1960	M. G. Davies
1961	R. Emerson
1962	R. Laver
1963	W. A. Knight
1964	W. A. Knight
1965	J. E. Lundquist
1966	K. N. Fletcher
1967	J. E. Lundquist
1968	K. R. Rosewall
1969	J. D. Newcombe
1970	M. Cox
1971	G. Battrick

BRITISH HARD COURTS—WOMEN'S SINGLES

1924	E. Ryan
1925	E. Ryan
1926	J. Fry
1927	B. Nuthall
1928	E. A. Goldsack
1929	E. L. Heine
1930	J. Fry
1931	Mrs. R. Mathieu
1932	Mrs. R. Mathieu
1933	D. E. Round
1934	D. E. Round
1935	K. E. Stammers
1936	K. E. Stammers
1937	A. Lizana
1938	M. C. Scriven
1939	K. E. Stammers
1940–45	no competition
1946	Mrs. E. W. A. Bostock
1947	Mrs. N. Bolton
1948	Mrs. B. E. Hilton
1949	P. J. Curry
1950	P. J. Curry
1951	D. Hart
1952	D. Hart
1953	D. Hart
1954	D. Hart
1955	A. Mortimer
1956	A. Mortimer
1957	S. J. Bloomer
1958	S. J. Bloomer
1959	A. Mortimer
1960	C. C. Truman
1961	A. Mortimer
1962	R. Schuurman
1963	Mrs. A. H. Jones
1964	Mrs. A. H. Jones
1965	Mrs. A. H. Jones
1966	Mrs. A. H. Jones
1967	V. Wade
1968	V. Wade
1969	Mrs. M. S. Court
1970	Mrs. M. S. Court
1971	Mrs. M. S. Court

BRITISH COVERED COURT (INDOOR) CHAMPIONSHIPS—MEN'S SINGLES

1935	J. Borotra
1936	K. Schroeder
1937	H. W. Austin
1938	J. Borotra

British Covered Court (Indoor) Championships—Men's Singles (cont.)

1939–47	no competition
1948	J. Borotra
1949	J. Borotra
1950	J. Drobny
1951	G. L. Paish
1952	J. Drobny
1953	J. Drobny
1954	J. Drobny
1955	V. Skonecki
1956	A. Huber
1957	M. G. Davies
1958	M. G. Davies
1959	R. K. Wilson
1960	W. A. Knight
1961	J. A. Pickard
1962	R. K. Wilson
1963	R. K. Wilson
1964	M. J. Sangster
1965	R. K. Wilson
1966–67	no competition
1968	R. A. J. Hewitt
1969	R. Laver
1970	R. Laver
1971	Ilie Nastase

BRITISH COVERED COURT (INDOOR) CHAMPIONSHIPS—WOMEN'S SINGLES

1935	M. C. Scriven
1936	A. Lizana
1937	M. C. Scriven
1938	M. C. Scriven
1939–47	no competition
1948	G. Hoahing
1949	P. J. Curry
1950	J. Quertier
1951	J. S. V. Partridge
1952	A. Mortimer
1953	A. Mortimer
1954	A. Mortimer
1955	J. A. Shilcock
1956	A. Buxton
1957	J. A. Shilcock
1958	J. A. Shilcock
1959	A. Mortimer
1960	A. Mortimer
1961	A. Mortimer
1962	A. Haydon
1963	D. M. Catt
1964	Mrs. A. H. Jones
1965	Mrs. A. H. Jones
1966–67	no competition
1968	Mrs. M. S. Court
1969	Mrs. A. H. Jones
1970	Mrs. B. J. M. King
1971	Mrs. B. J. M. King

IRISH CHAMPIONSHIPS—MEN'S SINGLES

1879	V. "St. Leger" Gould
1880	W. Renshaw
1881	W. Renshaw
1882	W. Renshaw
1883	E. Renshaw
1884	H. F. Lawford
1885	H. F. Lawford
1886	H. F. Lawford
1887	E. Renshaw
1888	E. Renshaw
1889	W. J. Hamilton
1890	E. W. Lewis
1891	E. W. Lewis
1892	E. Renshaw
1893	J. Pim
1894	J. Pim
1895	J. Pim
1896	W. Baddeley
1897	W. V. Eaves
1898	H. S. Mahony
1899	R. F. Doherty
1900	R. F. Doherty
1901	R. F. Doherty
1902	H. L. Doherty
1903	W. S. Drapes
1904	J. C. Parke
1905	J. C. Parke
1906	F. L. Riseley
1907	M. G. J. Ritchie
1908	J. C. Parke
1909	J. C. Parke
1910	J. C. Parke
1911	J. C. Parke
1912	J. C. Parke
1913	J. C. Parke
1914	C. J. Tindell Green
1915–18	no competition
1919	C. Campbell
1920	V. Miley
1921	C. Campbell
1922	no competition
1923	G. F. Mackay
1924	L. A. Meldon
1925	C. F. Scroope
1926	H. Landry
1927	G. R. O. Crole-Rees
1928	G. L. Rogers
1929	J. S. Oliff
1930	H. G. N. Lee
1931	E. A. McGuire
1932	S. B. Wood
1933	D. N. Jones
1934	C. E. Malfroy
1935	A. C. Stedman
1936	G. L. Rogers
1937	G. L. Rogers
1938	O. Anderson
1939	M. D. Deloford
1940–45	no competition
1946	D. Pails
1947	A. J. Mottram
1948	E. W. Sturgess
1949	N. Cockburn
1950	H. Weiss
1951	A. Segal
1952	N. Kumar
1953	N. Kumar
1954	H. Stewart
1955	H. Stewart

1956	B. Patty		1926	H. Wallis
1957	A. J. Cooper		1927	Mrs. M. Watson
1958	N. A. Fraser and M. G. Davies divided		1928	Mrs. Blair White
1959	J. W. Frost		1929	E. L. Heine
1960	R. D. Ralston		1930	H. Wallis
1961	W. Bond		1931	Mrs. Blair White
1962	R. Laver		1932	J. Jedrzejowska
1963	R. K. Wilson		1933	H. Wallis
1964	R. K. Wilson		1934	Mrs. H. K. Sperling
1965	A. D. Roche		1935	S. G. Chuter
1966	J. Cromwell		1936	A. Lizana
1967	K. Wooldridge		1937	T. R. Jarvis
1968*	T. Okker		1938	Mrs. H. W. Moody
1969*	R. Hewitt		1939	A. Marble
1970*	A. D. Roche		1940–45	no competition
1971*	C. Drysdale		1946	A. L. Brough
			1947	Mrs. E. W. A. Bostock
			1948	Mrs. S. Summers

IRISH CHAMPIONSHIPS—WOMEN'S SINGLES

			1949	Mrs. .T. C. Long
1879	M. Langrishe		1950	H. Weiss
1880	D. Meldon		1951	E. F. Lombard
1881	no competition		1952	M. Connolly
1882	H. Abercrombie		1953	A. Mortimer
1883	M. Langrishe		1954	M. Connolly
1884	M. Watson		1955	Mrs. J. Fleitz
1885	M. Watson		1956	S. J. Bloomer
1886	M. Langrishe		1957	S. Reynolds
1887	C. Dod		1958	Mrs. D. H. Knode
1888	Mrs. G. W. Hillyard		1959	Mrs. R. Schuurman
1889	L. Martin		1960	Mrs. D. H. Knode
1890	L. Martin		1961	A. S. Haydon
1891	L. Martin		1962	M. Schacht
1892	L. Martin		1963	B. J. Moffitt
1893	L. Stanuell		1964	M. E. Bueno
1894	Mrs. G. W. Hillyard		1965	M. E. Bueno
1895	C. Cooper		1966	M. Smith
1896	L. Martin		1967	A. Soady
1897	Mrs. G. W. Hillyard		1968*	Mrs. M. S. Court
1898	C. Cooper		1969*	Mrs. B. J. M. King
1899	L. Martin		1970*	V. Wade
1900	L. Martin		1971*	V. Wade
1901	M. E. Robb			
1902	L. Martin			
1903	L. Martin			
1904	W. A. Longhurst			**ITALIAN CHAMPIONSHIPS—MEN'S SINGLES**
1905	W. A. Longhurst			
1906	W. A. Longhurst		1930	William T. Tilden II
1907	M. Garfit		1931	Pat Hughes
1908	M. Garfit		1932	André Merlin
1909	M. Garfit		1933	Emanuele Sertorio
1910	A. Holder		1934	Giovanni Palmieri
1911	Mrs. D. R. Barry		1935	Wilmer Hines
1912	Mrs. A. Larcombe		1936–49	not held
1913	A. Barry		1950	Jaroslav Drobny
1914	I. Clarke		1951	Jaroslav Drobny
1915–18	no competition		1952	Frank Sedgman
1919	E. Ryan		1953	Jaroslav Drobny
1920	E. Ryan		1954	J. Edward Patty
1921	E. Ryan		1955	Fausto Gardini
1922	no competition		1956	Lewis Hoad
1923	H. Ryan		1957	Nicola Pietrangeli
1924	H. Wallis		1958	Mervyn Rose
1925	E. Boyd		1959	Luis Ayala
			1960	Barry MacKay
* Open championship.			1961	Nicola Pietrangeli

Italian Championships—Men's Singles (*cont.*)

1962	Rodney Laver
1963	Martin Mulligan
1964	Jan Erik Lundquist
1965	Martin Mulligan
1966	Tony Roche
1967	Martin Mulligan
1968	Tom Okker
1969*	John Newcombe
1970*	Ilie Nastase
1971*	Rodney Laver

ITALIAN CHAMPIONSHIPS—MEN'S DOUBLES

1930	William T. Tilden II and Wilbur Coen
1931	Alberto Del Bono and Pat Hughes
1932	Giorgio De Stefani and Pat Hughes
1933	J. Lesuer and Martin Legeay
1934	G. Palmieri and George Rogers
1935	Jack Crawford and Viv McGrath
1936–49	not held
1950	Bill Talbert and Tony Trabert
1951	Jaroslav Drobny and Dick Savitt
1952	Jaroslav Drobny and Frank Sedgman
1953	Lewis Hoad and Kenneth Rosewall
1954	Jaroslav Drobny and Enrique Morea
1955	Arthur Larsen and Enrique Morea
1956	Jaroslav Drobny and Lewis Hoad
1957	Lewis Hoad and Neale Fraser
1958	Kurt Nielsen and Anton Jansco
1959	Neale Fraser and Roy Emerson
1960	not completed
1961	Neale Fraser and Roy Emerson
1962	Rodney Laver and John Fraser
1963	Bob Hewitt and Fred Stolle
1964	Bob Hewitt and Fred Stolle
1965	John Newcombe and Tony Roche
1966	Roy Emerson and Fred Stolle
1967	Bob Hewitt and Frew McMillan
1968	Tom Okker and Martin Riessen
1969	not completed
1970*	Ilie Nastase and Ion Tiriac
1971*	John Newcombe and Tony Roche

ITALIAN CHAMPIONSHIPS—WOMEN'S SINGLES

1930	Lili Alvarez
1931	Lucia Valerio
1932	Ada Adamoff
1933	Elizabeth Ryan
1934	Helen Jacobs
1935	Hilda Sperling
1936–49	not held
1950	Angela Bossi
1951	Doris Hart
1952	Susan Partridge
1953	Doris Hart
1954	Maureen Connolly
1955	Patricia Ward
1956	Althea Gibson
1957	Shirley Bloomer
1958	Maria Bueno

* Open championship.

1959	Christine Truman
1960	Mrs. S. Kormoczi
1961	Maria E. Bueno
1962	Margaret Smith
1963	Margaret Smith
1964	Margaret Smith
1965	Maria Bueno
1966	Mrs. A. H. Jones
1967	Lesley Turner
1968	Mrs. L. T. Bowrey
1969*	Julie M. Heldman
1970*	Mrs. B. J. King
1971*	Virginia Wade

ITALIAN CHAMPIONSHIPS—WOMEN'S DOUBLES

1930	Lucia Valerio and Lili Alvarez
1931	Anna Luzzatti and R. Gagliardi
1932	C. Rosambert and Lolette Payot
1933	Mrs. D. Burke and I. Adamoff
1934	Helen Jacobs and Elizabeth Ryan
1935	Evelyn Dearman and Nancy Lyle
1936–49	not held
1950	Jean Quertier and Mrs. Jean Walker-Smith
1951	Doris Hart and Shirley Fry
1952	Mrs. T. Long and Mrs. Nell Hopman
1953	Maureen Connolly and Julia Sampson
1954	Patricia Ward and E. M. Watson
1955	Patricia Ward and Christine Marcelis
1956	Mrs. T. C. Long and Mrs. M. Hawton
1957	Mrs. T. C. Long and Mrs. M. Hawton
1958	Shirley Bloomer and Christine Truman
1959	Yola Ramirez and Rosie Reyes
1960	Yola Ramirez and Rosie Reyes
1961	Lesley Turner and Jan LeHane
1962	Maria Bueno and Darlene Hard
1963	Margaret Smith and Robyn Ebbern
1964	Margaret Smith and Lesley Turner
1965	Madonna Schacht and Annette van Zyl
1966	Norma Baylon and Annette van Zyl
1967	Rosemary Casals and Lesley Turner
1968	Mrs. M. S. Court and Virginia Wade
1969*	Françoise Durr and Mrs. Ann H. Jones
1970*	Rosemary Clark and Mrs. B. J. M. King
1971*	Mrs. H. N. Masthoff and Virginia Wade

ITALIAN CHAMPIONSHIPS—MIXED DOUBLES

1930	Lili Alvarez and J. L. DeMorpurgo
1931	Lucia Valerio and Pat Hughes
1932	Lolette Payot and J. Bonte
1933	Mrs. Dorothy Burke and Martin Legeay
1934	Elizabeth Ryan and Henry Culley
1935	Jadwiga Jedrzejowska and Harry Hopman
1936–49	not held
1950	not completed
1951	Shirley Fry and Felicissimo Ampon
1952	Arvilla McGuire and Kurt Nielsen
1953	Doris Hart and E. Victor Seixas, Jr.
1954	divided
1955	divided
1956	Mrs. T. C. Long and Luis Ayala
1957	Mrs. T. C. Long and Luis Ayala

1958   Shirley Bloomer and Giorgio Fachini
1959   Rosie Reyes and Francisco Contreras
1960   not played
1961   Margaret Smith and Roy Emerson
1962   Lesley Turner and Fred Stolle
1963   canceled
1964   Margaret Smith and John Newcombe
1965   Carmen Coronado and Edison Mandarino
1966   not played
1967   Lesley Turner and William Bowrey
1968   Mrs. M. S. Court and Martin Riessen
1969–71   not played

NEW ZEALAND CHAMPIONSHIPS—MEN'S SINGLES

1886   P. C. Fenwicke
1887   P. C. Fenwicke
1888   P. C. Fenwicke
1889   M. Fenwicke
1890   J. M. Marshall
1891   R. D. Harman
1892   M. Fenwicke
1893   M. Fenwicke
1894   J. R. Hooper
1895   H. A. Parker
1896   J. M. Marshall
1897   J. R. Hooper
1898   C. C. Cox
1899   J. R. Hooper
1900   A. W. Dunlop
1901   J. C. Peacocke
1902   H. A. Parker
1903   H. A. Parker
1904   H. A. Parker
1905   H. A. Parker
1906   A. F. Wilding
1907   H. A. Parker
1908   A. F. Wilding
1909   A. F. Wilding
1910   J. C. Peacocke
1911   G. Ollivier
1912   R. N. K. Swanston
1913   A. Wallace
1914   G. Ollivier
1915–18   no competition
1919   G. Ollivier
1920   W. T. Tilden II
1921   J. T. Laurentson
1922   G. Ollivier
1923   A. W. Sims
1924   G. Ollivier
1925   G. Ollivier
1926   E. D. Andrews
1927   G. Ollivier
1928   E. L. Bartleet
1929   C. Angas
1930   A. C. Stedman
1931   C. Angas
1932   E. D. Andrews
1933   C. E. Malfroy
1934   R. J. Perry
1935   V. B. McGrath
1936   D. C. Coombe

* Open championships.

1937   A. D. Brown
1938   N. V. Edwards
1939   J. E. Bromwich
1940–44   no competition
1945   R. S. McKenzie
1946   R. S. McKenzie
1947   R. S. McKenzie
1948   R. S. McKenzie
1949   J. E. Robson
1950   G. Worthington
1951   R. S. McKenzie
1952   J. E. Robson
1953   G. A. Worthington
1954   J. A. Barry
1955   J. A. Barry
1956   J. E. Robson
1957   M. G. Davies
1958   R. N. Howe
1959   R. N. Howe
1960   L. A. Gerrard
1961   L. A. Gerrard
1962   L. A. Gerrard
1963   L. A. Gerrard
1964   L. A. Gerrard
1965   B. Phillips-Moore
1966   K. Fletcher
1967   M. Cox
1968   B. Phillips-Moore
1969   C. W. Stodels
1969*   A. D. Roche
1970   B. Fairlie
1970*   R. Taylor
1971   O. Parun
1971*   C. Dibley

NEW ZEALAND CHAMPIONSHIPS—WOMEN'S SINGLES

1886   M. Lance
1887   E. Harman
1888   E. Gordon
1889   E. Gordon
1890   J. Rees
1891   N. Douslin
1892   J. Rees
1893   M. R. Speirs
1894   H. Hitchings
1895   K. M. Nunneley
1896   K. M. Nunneley
1897   K. M. Nunneley
1898   K. M. Nunneley
1899   K. M. Nunneley
1900   K. M. Nunneley
1901   K. M. Nunneley
1902   K. M. Nunneley
1903   K. M. Nunneley
1904   K. M. Nunneley
1905   K. M. Nunneley
1906   K. M. Nunneley
1907   K. M. Nunneley
1908   L. Powdrell
1909   L. Powdrell
1910   E. D. Travers

New Zealand Championships—Women's Singles (cont.)

1911	P. A. Stewart
1912	A. Gray
1913	A. Gray
1914	A. Gray
1915–18	no competition
1919	Mrs. S. C. Hodges
1920	N. Curtis
1921	N. Curtis
1922	S. Lance
1923	M. Speirs
1924	Mrs. W. J. Melody
1925	M. Speirs
1926	A. Howe
1927	M. Speirs
1928	M. Macfarlane
1929	D. Nicholls
1930	Mrs. H. M. Dykes
1931	J. Hartegan
1932	D. Nicholls
1933	L. Bickerton
1934	D. Nicholls
1935	D. Nicholls
1936	D. Nicholls
1937	M. Beverly
1938	M. Hardcastle
1939	N. Wynne
1940–44	no competition
1945	M. Beverly
1946	M. Beverly
1947	M. Beverly
1948	E. G. Attwood
1949	Mrs. J. J. McVay
1950	M. Beverly
1951	J. F. Burke
1952	J. MacGibbon
1953	J. F. Burke
1954	J. F. Burke
1955	J. F. Burke
1956	S. Cox
1957	R. Morrison
1958	S. Cox
1959	R. Morrison
1960	R. Morrison
1961	R. Morrison
1962	J. Davidson
1963	R. Morrison
1964	R. H. Bentley
1965	Mrs. R. Davy
1966	K. Melville
1967	B. Vercoe
1968	K. Melville
1969	M. Pryde
1969*	Mrs. A. H. Jones
1970	B. Vercoe
1970*	Mrs. A. H. Jones
1971	M. Pryde
1971*	E. Goolagong

SOUTH AFRICAN CHAMPIONSHIPS—MEN'S SINGLES

1891	L. A. Richardson
1892	L. A. Richardson

* Open championship.

1893	W. L. Edwards
1894	L. Giddy
1895	L. Giddy
1896	L. Giddy
1897	L. Giddy
1898	L. Giddy
1899	L. G. Heard
1900–02	no competition
1903	R. W. G. Clarke
1904	P. W. Sherwell
1905	H. A. Kitson
1906	J. Richardson
1907	Dr. A. Rowan
1908	H. A. Kitson
1909	R. F. Doherty
1910	A. F. Wilding
1911	H. A. Kitson
1912	G. H. Dodd
1913	H. A. Kitson
1914	C. L. Winslow
1915–19	no competition
1920	B. I. C. Norton
1921	L. Raymond
1922	L. Raymond
1923	L. Raymond
1924	L. Raymond
1925	I. J. Richardson
1926	J. Condon
1927	no competition
1928	G. Eaglestone
1929	C. J. J. Robbins
1930	L. Raymond
1931	L. Raymond
1932	Max Bertram
1933	C. J. J. Robbins
1934	N. G. Farquharson
1935	N. G. Farquharson
1936	N. G. Farquharson
1937	J. Palada
1938	N. G. Farquharson
1939	E. W. Sturgess
1940	E. W. Sturgess
1941–45	no competition
1946	E. W. Sturgess
1947	E. Fannin
1948	E. W. Sturgess
1949	E. W. Sturgess
1950	E. W. Sturgess
1951	E. W. Sturgess
1952	E. W. Sturgess
1953	E. W. Sturgess
1954	E. W. Sturgess
1955	W. R. Seymour
1956	J. C. Vermaak
1957	E. W. Sturgess
1958	U. Schmidt
1959	G. L. Forbes
1960	E. Buchholz
1961	G. L. Forbes
1962	R. Mark
1963	W. Bungert
1964	A. Segal
1965	C. Drysdale
1966	R. Emerson
1967	M. Santana

1968	T. Okker
1969*	R. Laver
1970*	R. Laver
1971*	K. Rosewall

SOUTH AFRICAN CHAMPIONSHIPS—WOMEN'S SINGLES

1891	H. Grant
1892	H. Grant
1893	H. Grant
1894	H. Grant
1895	R. Biddulph
1896	Mrs. H. Green
1897	N. Hickman
1898	N. Hickman
1899	N. Hickman
1900–02	no competition
1903	F. Kuys
1904	Mrs. H. A. Kirby
1905	Mrs. H. A. Kirby
1906	Mrs. H. A. Kirby
1907	Mrs. H. A. Kirby
1908	B. Kelly
1909	Mrs. G. Washington
1910	Mrs. H. A. Kirby
1911	Mrs. G. Washington
1912	Mrs. H. A. Kirby
1913	M. Coles
1914	G. Mathias
1915–19	no competition
1920	Mrs. C. L. Winslow
1921	N. Edwards
1922	Mrs. T. MacJannett
1923	Mrs. M. Pitt
1924	Mrs. I. E. Peacock
1925	Mrs. I. E. Peacock
1926	Mrs. I. E. Peacock
1927	no competition
1928	E. L. Heine
1929	Mrs. MacJannett
1930	R. D. Tapscott
1931	E. L. Heine
1932	Mrs. E. L. H. Miller
1933	Mrs. C. J. J. Robbins
1934	Mrs. C. J. J. Robbins
1935	Mrs. A. Allister
1936	Mrs. E. L. H. Miller
1937	Mrs. E. L. H. Miller
1938	Mrs. C. J. J. Robbins
1939	Mrs. O. Craze
1940	Mrs. O. Craze
1941–45	no competition
1946	Mrs. M. Muller
1947	Mrs. M. Muller
1948	Mrs. S. P. Summers
1949	Mrs. S. P. Summers
1950	S. J. Fry
1951	Mrs. S. P. Summers
1952	D. J. Hart
1953	Mrs. H. Redick-Smith
1954	Mrs. H. Redick-Smith
1955	Mrs. H. Redick-Smith
1956	D. Kilian

* Open championships.

1957	Mrs. H. Brewer
1958	B. Carr
1959	S. Reynolds
1960	Mrs. V. Vucovich
1961	S. Reynolds
1962	Mrs. A. Segal
1963	A. Van Zyl
1964	D. Hard
1965	C. C. Truman
1966	Mrs. B. J. M. King
1967	Mrs. B. J. M. King
1968	Mrs. M. S. Court
1969*	Mrs. B. J. M. King
1970*	Mrs. M. S. Court
1971*	Mrs. M. S. Court

WELSH CHAMPIONSHIPS—MEN'S SINGLES

1886	E. de S. H. Browne
1887	E. de S. H. Browne
1888	W. J. Hamilton
1889	W. J. Hamilton
1890	W. J. Hamilton
1891	H. S. Barlow
1892	H. S. Barlow
1893	G. C. Ball-Greene
1894	G. C. Ball-Greene
1895	W. V. Eaves
1896	no competition
1897	S. H. Smith
1898	S. H. Smith
1899	S. H. Smith
1900	S. H. Smith
1901	S. H. Smith
1902	S. H. Smith
1903	J. M. Boucher
1904	S. H. Smith
1905	S. H. Smith
1906	S. H. Smith
1907	J. M. Boucher
1908	J. M. Boucher
1909	J. M. Boucher
1910	C. P. Dixon
1911	C. P. Dixon
1912	H. A. Kitson
1913	C. P. Dixon
1914	C. P. Dixon
1915–19	no competition
1920	P. Freeman
1921	M. J. G. Ritchie
1922	M. Alonso
1923	J. M. Boucher
1924	G. R. O. Crobe-Rees
1925	J. M. Hillyard
1926	H. C. Fisher
1927	D. H. Williams
1928	E. C. Peters
1929	C. H. Kingsley
1930	D. H. Williams
1931	J. Satoh
1932	I. Tloczynski
1933	N. G. Farquharson
1934	D. Prenn
1935	H. W. Artens

Welsh Championships—Men's Singles (cont.)

1936	A. C. Stedman and C. Malfroy, divided
1937	A. C. Stedman
1938	G. L. Rogers
1939	C. Tananescu
1940–45	no competition
1946	C. Spychala
1947	C. Spychala
1948	C. Spychala and D. H. Slack, divided
1949	F. Ampon
1950	K. H. Ip and I. Tlockzynski, divided
1951	J. W. Cawthorn
1952	N. Kumar
1953	W. R. Seymour
1954	abandoned because of rain at semifinal stage
1955	O. G. Williams
1956	A. Huber
1957	J. Drobny
1958	R. Becker
1959	R. K. Wilson
1960	A. R. Mills
1961	A. F. Rawstone
1962	M. J. Sangster
1963	W. F. Jacques
1964	R. A. J. Hewitt
1965	R. Emerson
1966	R. A. J. Hewitt
1967	J. D. Newcombe
1968	W. W. Bowrey
1969*	M. Cox
1970*	K. Rosewall
1971*	K. Rosewall

WELSH CHAMPIONSHIPS—WOMEN'S SINGLES

1887	M. Watson
1888	Mrs. G. W. Hillyard
1889	C. Pope
1890	no competition
1891	C. Pope
1892	M. Sweet-Escott
1893	M. Cochrane
1894	P. Jackson
1895	N. Corder
1896	no competition
1897	H. Ridding
1898	A. E. Parr
1899	M. A. Robb
1900	C. Hill
1901	W. A. Longhurst
1902	W. A. Longhurst
1903	C. M. Wilson
1904	C. M. Wilson
1905	M. Sutton
1906	M. Sutton
1907	M. Sutton
1908	M. Garfit
1909	M. Garfit
1910	H. Aitchinson
1911	D. Boothby
1912	Mrs. H. Hannam
1913	Mrs. H. Hannam

* Open championships.

1914	Mrs. H. Hannam
1915–19	no competition
1920	Mrs. H. Hannam
1921	Mrs. M. Leisk
1922	Mrs. H. Hannam
1923	L. K. C. Raikes
1924	E. Ryan
1925	Mrs. P. C. Satterthwaite
1926	Mrs. J. Seel
1927	Mrs. P. C. Satterthwaite
1928	E. F. Rose
1929	E. F. Rose
1930	E. Hemmant
1931	E. Hemmant
1932	J. Jedrzejowska
1933	R. M. Hardwick
1934	Mrs. H. K. Sperling
1935	J. Jedrzejowska
1936	J. Jedrzejowska
1937	Mrs. R. Mattieu
1938	Mrs. R. Mathieu
1939	Mrs. R. Mathieu
1940–45	no competition
1946	G. Hoahing
1947	J. Curry
1948	J. Curry
1949	G. E. Woodgate
1950	B. Scofield
1951	A. Mortimer
1952	B. Penrose
1953	Mrs. W. Brewer
1954	S. Kamo and J. W. Middleton, divided
1955	Mrs. J. Weiss
1956	A. Haydon
1957	A. Mortimer
1958	A. Mortimer
1959	A. Mortimer
1960	A. Mortimer
1961	A. Haydon
1962	A. Haydon
1963	C. Rosser
1964	M. E. Bueno
1965	A. Van Zyl
1966	M. E. Bueno
1967	J. A. M. Tegart
1968	K. Pigeon
1969*	Mrs. M. S. Court
1970*	E. Goolagong
1971*	V. Wade

**OTHER MAJOR WORLD CHAMPIONSHIPS
(1968–1971)**

1968 Season

TASMANIAN CHAMPIONSHIP, at Hobart: Ray Ruffels d. Graham Stilwell (Great Britain), 3–6, 6–8, 7–5, 7–5, 6–2; Ruffels and Allan Stone d. Stilwell and Peter Curtis (Great Britain), 6–1, 11–9, 6–4; Billie Jean King d. Judy Tegart, 6–2, 6–4; Margaret Court and Gail Sherriff d. Tegart and Mary Ann Eisel

(U.S.), 8–6, 0–6, 6–4; Court and Stilwell d. Eisel and Curtis, 6–2, 6–2.

WESTERN AUSTRALIA CHAMPIONSHIP, at Perth: Bill Bowrey d. Ray Ruffels, 6–8, 11–9, 6–2, 17–19, 6–4; Graham Stilwell and Peter Curtis d. Bowrey and Ruffels, 6–4, 3–6, 6–4; Billie Jean King (U.S.) d. Margaret Court, 6–2, 6–4; King and Rosemary Casals (U.S.) d. Court and Gail Sherriff, 8–6, 4–6, 6–2; Court and Brian Bowman d. King and Ruffels, 5–7, 6–4, 6–4.

ASIAN CHAMPIONSHIP, at Madras, India: Alex Metreveli (U.S.S.R.) d. Ion Tiriac (Romania), 8–6, 6–3, 6–4.

NATAL CHAMPIONSHIP, at Durban: Bob Maud d. Wilheim Bungert (Germany), 3–6, 6–3, 6–4, 6–4; Clark Graebner (U.S.) and Marty Riessen (U.S.) d. Bob Hewitt and Frew McMillan, 8–10, 6–3, 6–2, 6–4; Annette van Zyl d. Carole Graebner (U.S.), 6–1, 6–1.

WESTERN PROVINCE CHAMPIONSHIP, at Capetown: Jan Leschly (Denmark) d. Bob Maud, 3–6, 6–3, 8–6; Pat Walkden (Rhodesia) d. Carole Graebner, 6–2, 1–6, 6–4; Annette van Zyl and Walkden d. Winnie Shaw (Great Britain) and Nell Truman (Great Britain), 3–6, 6–4, 6–4.

ORANGE FREE STATE CHAMPIONSHIP, at Bloemfontein, South Africa: Marty Riessen d. Tom Okker (Netherlands), 7–5, 6–3; Clark Graebner and Riessen d. Mark Cox and Paul Hutchins (Great Britain), 6–1, 6–2; Virginia Wade (Great Britain) d. Pat Walkden, 6–3, 6–3; Walkden and Annette van Zyl d. Winnie Shaw and Nell Truman, def.; Clark Graebner and Carole Graebner d. van Zyl and Frew McMillan, 2–6, 6–3, 6–2.

EASTERN PROVINCE CHAMPIONSHIP, at Port Elizabeth, South Africa: Marty Riessen d. Thomaz Koch (Brazil), 6–4, 6–4, 8–6; Torben Ulrich (Denmark) and Jan Leschly (Denmark) d. Koch and Edison Mandarino (Brazil), 6–2, 11–9; Pat Walkden d. Carole Graebner, 6–1, 6–1; Winnie Shaw and Nell Truman d. Walkden and Annette van Zyl, 1–6, 6–4, 6–3; van Zyl and Frew McMillan d. Graebner and Clark Graebner, 11–9, 6–3.

DANISH COVERED COURTS CHAMPIONSHIP, at Copenhagen: Jan Leschly d. Alex Metreveli, 4–6, 12–10, 6–3, 6–4; Ove Bengtsson (Sweden) and H. Andersson (Sweden) d. Leschly and Torben Ulrich, 10–8, 7–5, 6–4; Virginia Wade d. Joyce Williams (Great

Britain), 6–1, 6–2; Wade and Williams d. Anna Dmitrieva (U.S.S.R.) and Galina Baksheyeva (U.S.S.R.), 6–4, 6–3.

GERMAN COVERED COURTS CHAMPIONSHIP, at Bremen: Ismail El Shafei (UAR) d. Daniel Contet (France), 6–2, 6–2, 9–7; Uwe Gottschalk (Germany) and Bob Carmichael (Australia) d. El Shafei and Istvan Gulyas (Hungary), 5–7, 4–6, 6–3, 13–11, 7–5; Joyce Williams d. Helga Niessen, 6–2, 6–1; Niessen and Heide Orth d. Williams and Frances MacLennan (Great Britain), 1–6, 6–3, 8–6; Olga Morozova (U.S.S.R.) and Vyacheslav Egorov (U.S.S.R.) d. Galina Baksheyeva (U.S.S.R.) and Ann Dmitriyeva, 6–3, 9–7.

FRENCH COVERED COURTS CHAMPIONSHIP, at Paris: Milan Holecek (Czechoslovakia) d. Bob Carmichael, 6–4, 10–8, 3–6, 6–3; Patrice Beust and Daniel Contet d. Carmichael and Ismail El Shafei, 4–6, 10–8, 6–2, 19–17; Nell Truman d. Evelyn Terras, 6–4, 6–1; Monique Salfati and Rosie Darmon d. Janine Lieffrig and Jacqueline Venturino, 3–6, 6–0, 6–3; Truman and Gerald Battrick (Great Britain) d. Terras and Jean Pierre Courcol, 6–2, 1–6, 6–3.

AUSTRALIAN NATIONAL CHAMPIONSHIP, at Melbourne: Bill Bowrey d. Juan Gisbert (Spain), 7–5, 2–6, 9–7, 6–4; Dick Crealy and Allan Stone d. Ray Heldie and Terry Addison, 10–8, 6–4, 6–3; Billie Jean King d. Margaret Court, 6–1, 6–2; Karen Krantzcke and Kerry Melville d. Lesley Turner and Judy Tegart, 6–4, 3–6, 6–2; King and Crealy d. Court and Stone, def.

WILLS NEW ZEALAND CHAMPIONSHIP, at Auckland: Barry Phillips-Moore (Australia) d. Onny Parun, 6–3, 6–8, 1–6, 6–3, 6–2; Dick Crealy (Australia) and Phillips-Moore d. Mike Belkin (Canada) and Juan Gisbert, 6–3, 6–4; Kerry Melville (Australia) d. Gail Sherriff (Australia), 8–6, 6–1; Melville and Sherriff d. Astrid Suurbeek (Netherlands) and Ada Bakker (Netherlands) 6–0, 6–2; Sherriff and Gisbert d. Melville and Crealy, 7–5, 13–11.

ALTAMIRA INTERNATIONAL INVITATION, at Caracas: Marty Riessen d. Cliff Richey, 6–1, 8–6, 6–1; Riessen and Tom Okker (Netherlands) d. Manuel Orantes (Spain) and Lis Arilla (Spain), 7–5, 9–7; Ann Jones (Great Britain) d. Julie Heldman (U.S.), 6–4, 11–9; Jones and Françoise Durr (France) d. Lesley

Altamira International, 1968 (*cont.*)

Turner Bowrey (Australia) and Judy Tegart, 6–0, 6–2.

CIUDAD DE BARRANQUILLA, at Barranquilla, Colombia: Tom Okker d. Marty Riessen, 8–6, 6–3, 6–3; Riessen and Okker d. Mike Sangster (Great Britain) and Mark Cox (Great Britain), 5–7, 6–2, 11–9; Nancy Richey d. Lesley Turner Bowrey, 6–2, 6–0; Ann Jones and Françoise Durr d. Bowrey and Judy Tegart, 6–4, 9–7, 6–4; Richey and Okker d. Jones and Riessen, 6–3, 3–6, 6–3.

MEXICO INTERNATIONAL CHAMPIONSHIP, at Mexico City: Rafe Osuna d. Joaquin Loyo-Mayo, 6–4, 6–4, 6–4; Manuel Orantes and Lis Arilla d. Osuna and Loyo-Mayo, 5–7, 4–6, 8–6, 16–14, 10–8; Julie Heldman d. Ann Jones, def.; Elena Subirats and Yola Ramirez Ochoa d. Jones and Françoise Durr, def.

CURACAO INTERNATIONAL CHAMPIONSHIP, at Caracas, Netherlands-Antilles: Marty Riessen d. Tom Okker, 7–5, 3–6, 9–11, 6–2, 6–2; Riessen and Okker d. Jan Kukal and Jan Kodes, 6–3, 10–8; Nancy Richey d. Judy Tegart, 2–6, 6–1, 6–2; Richey and Valerie Ziegenfuss d. Helga Niessen (Germany) and Faye Urban, 6–2, 7–9, 6–3.

CAIRO INTERNATIONAL CHAMPIONSHIP, at Cairo: Milan Holecek d. Ismail El Shafei, 4–6, 6–3, 6–1, 6–2; Ken Fletcher (Hong Kong) and El Shafei d. Jean Pierre Courcol and Patrice Beust, 4–6, 7–5, 6–4, 0–6, 9–7; Gail Sherriff d. Monique Salfati, 6–4, 6–2.

MOSCOW INDOORS CHAMPIONSHIP, at Moscow: Alex Metreveli d. Toomas Lejus, 6–4, 4–6, 9–7, 6–4; Patrice Beust and Daniel Contet d. Metreveli and Sergei Likhachev, 6–1, 6–4, 10–8; Virginia Wade d. Galina Baksheyeva, 6–1, 6–8, 6–4; Ann Dmitriyeva and Baksheyeva d. Olga Morozova and Rauza Islanova, 2–6, 9–7, 7–5.

CANNES INTERNATIONAL CHAMPIONSHIP, at Cannes: Ion Tiriac (Romania) d. Alex Metreveli, 6–1, 6–3; Metreveli and Sergei Likhachev d. Tiriac and Ilie Nastase (Romania), 6–4, 4–6, 7–5; Roberta Beltrame (Italy) d. Helen Gourlay (Australia), 6–2, 6–4; Tine Zwann (Netherlands) and Lidy Venneboer (Netherlands) d. Maria Nasuelli and Beltrame, 1–6, 6–3, 6–3; Robin Lloyd (Great Britain) and Metreveli d. Beltrame and Wieslaw Gasiorek (Poland), 6–1, 6–3.

SOUTH AFRICAN NATIONAL CHAMPIONSHIP,

at Johannesburg: Tom Okker d. Marty Riessen, 12–10, 6–1, 6–4; Okker and Riessen d. Frew McMillan and Bob Hewitt, 6–2, 6–3, 3–6, 4–6, 6–3; Margaret Court d. Virginia Wade, 6–4, 6–4; Annette Van Zyl and Pat Walkden d. Court and Wade, 0–6, 6–4, 7–5; Walkden and Riessen d. Court and Bob Hewitt, 6–8, 6–4, 6–4.

NAIROBI NATIONAL CHAMPIONSHIP, at Nairobi: Allan Stone d. Juan Manuel Couder (Spain), 6–3, 7–5; Virginia Wade d. Kerstin Seelbach (Germany), 4–6, 6–1, 6–2; Wade and Frances MacLennan d. Seelbach and Kora Schediwy (Germany), 6–1, 6–3.

KAMPALA CHAMPIONSHIP, at Kampala, Uganda: Brian Fairlie (New Zealand) d. Allan Stone, 6–4, 6–3; Ian Fletcher (Australia) and Stone d. Terry Addison and Ray Keldie, 10–8, 6–1; Virginia Wade d. Margaret Court, 7–5, 6–4; Court and Fletcher d. Wade and Stone, 8–6, 6–4.

AIX-EN-PROVENCE CHAMPIONSHIP, at Aix-en-Provence: Pierre Darmon d. Daniel Contet, 7–5, 6–1, 8–6; Ken Fletcher and Barry Phillips-Moore d. Patrice Beust and Contet, 8–6, 6–4, 6–4; Gail Sherriff d. Rosie Darmon, 6–2, 6–4; Sherriff and Marilyn Aschner (U.S.) d. Ilse Buding (Germany) and Darmon, 8–6, 6–3.

NICE CHAMPIONSHIP, at Nice: Alex Metreveli d. Barry Phillips-Moore, 9–7, 5–7, 6–2, 6–4; Metreveli and Sergei Likhachev d. Gerald Battrick and Paul Hutchins, 6–2, 6–2; Gail Sherriff d. Robin Lloyd, 9–7, 6–4; Sherriff and Carol Sherriff d. Roberta Beltrame and Helen Gourlay, 3–6, 7–5, 7–5.

MONTE CARLO CHAMPIONSHIP, at Monte Carlo: Nicola Pietrangeli d. Alex Metreveli, 6–2, 6–2; Sergei Likhachev and Metreveli d. Patrice Beust and Daniel Contet, 4–6, 9–7, 6–4, 5–7, 7–5; Vlasta Vapickova (Czechoslovakia) d. Marilyn Aschner, 6–4, 3–6, 6–3; Gail Sherriff and Carol Sherriff d. Roberta Beltrame and Francesca Gordigiani (Italy), 8–6, 7–5.

BRITISH OPEN HARD COURT CHAMPIONSHIP, at Bournemouth: Ken Rosewall d. Andres Gimeno, 3–6, 6–2, 6–0, 6–3; Roy Emerson and Rod Laver d. Gimeno and Pancho Gonzalez, 8–6, 4–6, 6–3, 6–2; Virginia Wade d. Winnie Shaw, 6–4, 6–1; Christine Truman Janes and Nell Truman d. Faye Toyne Moore (Australia) and Annette van Zyl, 6–4, 6–3;

Wade and Bob Wade d. Moore and Jimmy Moore (Australia) 6–3, 6–2.

CATANIA CHAMPIONSHIP, at Catania, Italy: Marty Mulligan (Australia) d. Ion Tiriac, 8–6, 6–4, 6–3; Tiriac and Ilie Nastase d. Pat Cornejo (Chile) and Jamie Pinto-Bravo (Chile), 6–3, 6–1, 6–0; Helen Gourlay d. Judith Dibar (Romania), 6–3, 6–3.

PALERMO CHAMPIONSHIP, at Palermo, Italy: Ion Tiriac d. Marty Riessen, 8–6, 6–0, 1–6, 6–4; Nicki Pietrangeli and Marty Mulligan d. Tiriac and Ilie Nastase, 3–6, 6–3, 4–6, 6–3, 6–1; Helen Gourlay d. Virginia Caceres (Peru), 6–3, 6–0.

ISRAELI SPRING CHAMPIONSHIPS, at Tel Aviv: Ian Fletcher d. Eleazar Davidman, 6–4, 8–6, 6–4; Laura Rossouiv (South Africa) d. Nadine Netter (U.S.), 6–2, 6–0.

PARIS INTERNATIONAL CHAMPIONSHIP, at Paris: Bob Carmichael d. Pierre Darmon, 6–3, 8–6, 12–10; Thomaz Koch and Edison Mandarino d. Georges Goven and Jean Claude Barclay, 6–1, 1–6, 11–9, 10–12, 8–6; Gail Sherriff d. Helen Amos (Australia), 6–1, 6–0; Amos and Sherriff d. Rosie Darmon and Monique Salfati, 6–2, 6–3.

LONDON HARD COURTS CHAMPIONSHIPS, at London: Ken Fletcher d. Keith Wooldridge, 6–1, 9–7; Margaret Court d. Virginia Wade, 6–3, 6–2.

NAPLES CHAMPIONSHIP, at Naples: Pat Mulligan d. Nicki Pietrangeli, 6–1, 6–2, 6–2; Helen Gourlay d. Lesley Hunt, 6–4, 6–3.

REGGIO CALABRIA CHAMPIONSHIP, at Reggio Calabria: Marty Riessen d. Ilie Nastase, 3–6, 3–6, 6–4, 6–2; Riessen and Allan Stone d. Nastase and Ion Tiriac, 4–6, 8–6, 6–2, 7–5; Helen Gourlay d. Alice Tym (U.S.), 6–4, 8–6.

ITALIAN NATIONAL CHAMPIONSHIP, at Rome: Tom Okker d. Hewitt, 10–8, 6–8, 6–1, 3–6, 6–0; Marty Riessen and Okker d. Allan Stone and Nick Kalo (Germany), 6–3, 6–3, 6–2; Lesley Turner Bowrey d. Margaret Court, 2–6, 6–2, 6–3; Court and Virginia Wade d. Annette du Plooy and Pat Walkden, 6–2, 7–5; Court and Riessen d. Wade and Okker, 8–6, 6–3.

SURREY GRASS COURT CHAMPIONSHIP, at Surbiton, England: Keith Wooldridge d. Ken Fletcher, 3–6, 6–3, 7–5; Judy Tegart d. Christine Janes, 10–8, 6–4.

WEST OF ENGLAND CHAMPIONSHIP, at

Bristol: Arthur Ashe d. Clark Graebner, 6–4, 6–3; Bob Hewitt and Frew McMillan d. Graebner and Jim Osborne, 6–4, 6–3; Kerry Melville d. Karen Krantzcke, 6–0, 6–1; Krantzcke and Melville d. Robin Moore and Pat Walkden, 6–8, 6–4, 6–0.

NORTH OF ENGLAND CHAMPIONSHIP, at Manchester: Ken Fletcher d. Luis Ayala (Chile), 6–3, 6–2; Ayala and Premjit Lall (India) d. Lars Olander (Sweden) and John de Mendoza, 6–3, 6–2; Margaret Court d. Virginia Wade, 6–4, 4–6, 6–4; Court and Wade d. Judy Tegart and Betty Pratt (U.S.), 6–3, 6–4.

KENT OPEN CHAMPIONSHIP, at Beckenham: Fred Stolle (Australia) d. Roy Emerson, 6–3, 6–1; Emerson and Stolle d. Bob Howe and John Barrett, 6–2, 6–4; Margaret Court d. Ann Jones, 11–9, 6–2; Maria Bueno (Brazil) and Court d. Jones and Françoise Durr, 6–3, 6–2.

FRENCH NATIONAL OPEN CHAMPIONSHIP, at Paris: Ken Rosewall d. Rod Laver, 6–3, 6–1, 2–6, 6–2; Rosewall and Fred Stolle d. Laver and Roy Emerson, 6–3, 6–4, 6–3; Nancy Richey d. Ann Jones, 5–7, 6–4, 6–1; Françoise Durr and Jones d. Rosemary Casals and Billie Jean King, 7–5, 4–6, 6–4; Durr and Jean Claude Barclay d. King and Owen Davidson, 6–1, 6–4.

BERLIN CHAMPIONSHIP, at Berlin: Manolo Santana d. Tom Okker, 6–8, 6–4, 6–1, 6–2; Helga Schultze d. Margaret Court, 6–1, 7–5.

HELSINKI INTERNATIONAL CHAMPIONSHIP, at Helsinki: Manolo Santana d. Thomas Lejus, 6–1, 6–1, 6–4; Marty Riessen and Tom Okker d. Harald Eischenbroich (Germany) and Uwe Gottschalk, 6–2, 4–6, 6–1; Lesley Bowrey d. Birgitta Lindstrom, 6–1, 6–1.

BRUSSELS INTERNATIONAL CHAMPIONSHIP, at Brussels: Brian Fairlie d. Bob Carmichael, 6–4, 6–3, 4–6, 6–4; Nich Kalo and Carmichael d. Ingo Buding (Germany) and Ray Keldie, 4–6, 6–4, 8–6; Gail Sherriff d. Marilyn Aschner, 6–3, 6–2.

SWISS INTERNATIONAL CHAMPIONSHIP, at Lugano: Ian Tiriac d. Tom Okker, 6–8, 7–5, 6–0; Okker and Marty Riessen d. Bill Bowrey and Ray Ruffels, 6–4, 6–4; Annette du Plooy d. Helga Niessen, 6–4, 6–1; Lesley Bowrey and du Plooy d. Edda Buding and Helga Niessen, 6–4, 6–3.

GSTAAD OPEN CHAMPIONSHIP, at Gstaad, Switzerland: Cliff Drysdale d. Tom Okker,

Gstaad Open, 1968 (cont.)

6–3, 6–3, 6–0; John Newcombe and Dennis Ralston d. Okker and Mal Anderson (Australia), 8–10, 12–10, 12–14, 6–8, 6–3; Annette du Plooy d. Julie Heldman, 6–0, 6–1; Rosie Darmon and du Plooy d. Helen Amos and Elena Subirats, 6–1, 6–3; Heldman and Torben Ulrich d. Subirats and Massimo Di Domenico (Italy), 6–2, 6–2.

ALL-ENGLAND CHAMPIONSHIP, at Wimbledon: Rod Laver d. Tony Roche, 6–3, 6–4, 6–2; John Newcombe and Roche d. Ken Rosewall and Fred Stolle, 6–3, 6–8, 5–7, 14–12, 6–3; Billie Jean King d. Judy Tegart, 9–7, 7–5; Rosemary Casals and King d. Françoise Durr and Ann Jones, 3–6, 6–4, 7–5; Margaret Court and Ken Fletcher d. Olga Morozova and Alex Metreveli, 6–1, 14–12.

IRISH OPEN CHAMPIONSHIP, at Dublin: Tom Okker d. Lew Hoad, 6–1, 6–2; Ken Fletcher and Mark Cox d. Hoad and Okker, 6–4, 2–6, 11–9; Margaret Court d. Ann Jones, 6–3, 6–1; Jones and Rosemary Casals d. Court and Patti Hogan, 6–3, 7–5; Court and Fletcher d. Jones and Okker, 6–4, 6–3.

WELSH OPEN CHAMPIONSHIP, at Newport: Bill Bowrey d. Owen Davidson, 9–7, 6–4; Kristy Pigeon d. Faye Moori (Australia), 6–2, 6–0; Judy Tegart and Lesley Bowrey d. Christine Janes and Nell Truman, 5–7, 8–6, 6–1.

BAVARIAN CHAMPIONSHIPS, at Munich: Marty Mulligan d. Ion Tiriac, 6–3, 3–6, 7–5, 6–3; Rob Maud and Frew McMillan d. Jan Kodes and Milan Holecek, 6–4, 6–4, 6–4; Julie Heldman d. Helga Niessen, 4–6, 6–3, 6–3; Virginia Wade and Pat Walkden d. Ada Bakker and Astrid Suurbeek, 12–10, 6–4.

GERMAN OPEN CHAMPIONSHIPS, at Hamburg: John Newcombe d. Cliff Drysdale, 6–3, 6–2, 6–4; Tom Okker and Marty Riessen d. Newcombe and Tony Roche, 6–4, 6–4, 7–5; Annette du Plooy d. Judy Tegart, 6–1, 7–5; Pat Walkden and du Plooy d. Winnie Shaw and Tegart, 6–3, 7–5; du Plooy and Frew McMillan d. Walkden and Mal Anderson, 6–1, 12–10.

HILVERSUM CHAMPIONSHIPS, at Hilversum, Netherlands: Bob Maud d. Istvan Gulyas, 7–9, 7–5, 6–0, 1–6, 13–11; Jan Kodes and Jan Kukal (Czechoslovakia) d. Harold Elschenbroich and Ingo Buding, 6–3, 6–1; Margaret Court d. Judy Tegart, 8–6, 6–0;

Annette du Plooy and Pat Walkden d. Tegart and Astrid Suurbeek, 6–2, 3–6, 6–3; du Plooy and Maud d. Court and Tom Okker, 6–3, 7–5.

ISTANBUL INTERNATIONAL CHAMPIONSHIP, at Istanbul: Mark Cox d. Patricio Rodriguez (Chile), 6–3, 6–3, 2–6, 6–4; Frew McMillan and Bob Maud d. Bill Bowrey and Ray Ruffels, 6–2, 6–4, 6–2; Gail Sherriff d. Lesley Bowrey, 6–2, 7–5.

ROMANIAN INTERNATIONAL CHAMPIONSHIP, at Mamaia: Ion Nastase d. John Alexander, 6–4, 11–9, 6–2; Ion Tiriao and Ilie Nastase d. Alexander and Phil Dent (Australia), 3–6, 7–5, 10–8, 6–0; Lesley Hunt d. Kerry Harris, 4–6, 6–1, 6–2; Hunt and Harris d. Eleonora Dumitrescu and Mariana Ciogolea, 6–1, 6–3.

BRITISH COVERED COURTS CHAMPIONSHIPS, at London: Bob Hewitt d. Bob Lutz, 4–6, 6–2, 6–4, 10–8; Stan Smith and Lutz d. Bob Howe and Mike Sangster, 6–1, 7–5, 6–2; Margaret Court d. Virginia Wade, 10–8, 6–1; Mary Ann Eisel and Winnie Shaw d. Christine Janes and Nell Truman, 6–2, 6–3; Court and Smith d. Eisel and Peter Curtis, 5–7, 7–5, 8–6.

SOUTH AMERICAN OPEN CHAMPIONSHIP, at Buenos Aires: Roy Emerson d. Rod Laver, 9–7, 6–4, 6–4; Andres Gimeno and Fred Stolle d. Laver and Emerson, 6–3, 4–6, 7–5, 6–1; Ann Jones d. Nancy Richey, def.; Ann Jones and Rosemary Casals d. Julie Heldman and Mabel Vrancovich, 6–1, 6–2; Heldman and Herb FitzGibbon d. Norma Baylon Puiggros and Edison Mandarino, 6–3, 6–4.

CRYSTAL PALACE INDOOR CHAMPIONSHIP, at London: Stan Smith d. Mark Cox, 6–4, 6–4; Bob Hewitt and Owen Davidson d. Bob Lutz and Smith, 9–11, 6–3, 13–11; Virginia Wade d. Margaret Court, 6–3, 6–4; Court and Pat Walkden d. Mary Ann Eisel and Winnie Shaw, 4–6, 6–3, 6–4.

SOUTH AUSTRALIAN CHAMPIONSHIP, at Adelaide: Bill Bowrey d. Allen Stone, 6–4, 6–3, 4–6, 6–4; Bowrey and Ray Ruffels d. Phil Bent and John Alexander, 9–7, 6–3, 7–5; Karen Krantzcke d. Lesley Hunt, 4–6, 9–7, 6–1; Krantzcke and Terry Melville d. Judy Tegart and Hunt, 6–1, 6–2; Tegart and Allan Stone d. Hunt and D. Turner (New Zealand), 6–2, 6–4.

QUEENSLAND CHAMPIONSHIPS, at Brisbane: Arthur Ashe d. Stan Smith, 6–4, 1–6, 9–7, 4–6, 7–5; Smith and Bob Lutz d. Terry

Addison and Ray Keldie, 7–5, 6–4, 13–11; Karen Krantzcke d. Kerry Melville, 6–3, 6–4.

1969 Season

TASMANIAN CHAMPIONSHIPS, at Hobart: Fred Stolle (Australia) d. Tony Roche (Australia), 6–3, 0–6, 6–4, 6–1; Mal Anderson (Australia) and Roger Taylor (England) d. Roche and Stolle, 7–5, 6–3, 4–6, 1–6, 6–4. Kerry Melville (Australia) d. Rosie Casals (U.S.), 6–3, 6–3; Billie Jean Moffitt King (U.S.) and Casals d. Karen Krantzcke (Australia) and Melville, 2–6, 6–2, 6–3.

WESTERN AUSTRALIA CHAMPIONSHIPS, at Perth: Marty Riessen (U.S.) d. Ken Rosewall (Australia), 6–3, 6–4, 2–6, 6–1; Riessen and Rosewall d. John Alexander and Phil Dent (both Australia), 6–3, 7–5, 3–6, 7–5. Margaret Smith Court (Australia) d. Lesley Hunt (Australia), 7–5, 6–1; Judy Tegart (Australia) and Court d. Françoise Durr (France) and Ann Haydon Jones (England), 6–4, 6–4.

VICTORIAN OPEN, at Melbourne: Stan Smith (U.S.) d. Arthur Ashe (U.S.), 14–12, 6–8, 6–3, 8–6; Allan Stone and Dick Crealy (both Australia) d. Bill Bowrey and Ray Ruffels (both Australia), 9–7, 6–4, 6–4. Margaret Court d. Kerry Harris (Australia), 6–1, 6–4; Judy Tegart and Court d. Karen Krantzcke and Kerry Melville, 3–6, 6–3, 6–2.

NEW SOUTH WALES OPEN, at Sydney: Tony Roche d. Rod Laver, 6–4, 4–6, 9–7, 12–10; Roy Emerson (Australia) and Laver d. John Newcombe (Australia) and Roche, 14–12, 6–4, 6–3. Margaret Court d. Rosie Casals, 6–1, 6–2; Judy Tegart and Court d. Billie Jean King and Casals, 15–13, 4–6, 6–3.

AUSTRALIAN OPEN, at Brisbane: Rod Laver d. Andres Gimeno, 6–3, 6–4, 7–5; Roy Emerson and Laver d. Ken Rosewall and Fred Stolle, 6–4, 6–4. Margaret Court d. Billie Jean King, 6–4, 6–1; Judy Tegart and Court d. Rosie Casals and King, 6–4, 6–4.

NEW ZEALAND OPEN, at Auckland: Tony Roche d. Rod Laver, 6–1, 6–4, 4–6, 6–3; Ray Moore (South Africa) and Roger Taylor d. Tom Lejus (U.S.S.R.) and Mal Anderson, 13–15, 6–3, 8–6. Ann Jones d. Karen Krantzcke, 6–1, 6–1; Billie Jean King and Jones d. Helen Gourlay (Australia) and Krantzcke, 6–2, 10–8.

SOUTH AFRICAN OPEN, at Johannesburg: Rod Laver d. Tom Okker (Netherlands),

6–3, 10–8, 6–3; Pancho Gonzalez (U.S.) and Ray Moore d. Frew McMillan and Bob Hewitt (both South Africa), 6–3, 6–4, 1–6, 6–3. Billie Jean King d. Nancy Richey (U.S.), 6–3, 6–4; Ann Jones and Françoise Durr d. Virginia Wade (England) and Richey, 6–2, 3–6, 6–4.

NATAL OPEN, at Durban, South Africa: Bob Maud d. Julian Krinsky, 8–6, 4–6, 6–1, 6–4; Cliff Drysdale and Keith Diepraam (both South Africa) d. Bob Hewitt and Frew McMillan, 3–6, 9–7, 3–6, 9–7, 6–3. Billie Jean King d. Annette Van Zyl du Plooy (South Africa), 6–4, 6–1; Rosie Casals and King d. Pat Walkden (Rhodesia) and du Plooy, 6–3, 1–6, 6–2.

MONACO OPEN, at Monte Carlo: Tom Okker d. John Newcombe, 8–10, 6–1, 7–5, 6–3; Owen Davidson (Australia) and Newcombe d. Dennis Ralston (U.S.) and Pancho Gonzalez, 7–5, 11–13, 6–2, 6–1. Ann Jones d. Virginia Wade, 6–1, 6–3; Jones and Wade d. Gail Sherriff Chanfreau (France) and Françoise Durr, 1–6, 6–4, 6–3.

ITALIAN OPEN, at Rome: John Newcombe d. Tony Roche, 6–3, 4–6, 6–4, 5–7, 6–3; doubles unfinished, Okker and Riesen vs. Newcombe and Roche. Julie Heldman (U.S.) d. Kerry Melville, 7–5, 6–3; Ann Jones and Françoise Durr d. Rosie Casals and Billie Jean King, 6–3, 3–6, 6–2.

BRITISH HARD-COURT OPEN, at Bournemouth: John Newcombe d. Bob Hewitt, 6–8, 6–3, 5–7, 6–4; Frew McMillan and Hewitt d. Jean-Claude Barclay (France) and Bobby Wilson (England), 6–4, 6–2, 2–6, 9–7. Margaret Court d. Winnie Shaw (Scotland), 5–7, 6–4, 6–4; Judy Tegart and Court d. Ada Bakker and Marjike Schaar (both Netherlands), 6–1, 6–4.

BELGIAN OPEN, at Brussels: Tom Okker d. Zeljko Franulovic (Yugoslavia), 6–4, 1–6, 6–2, 6–2; John Newcombe and Okker d. Bob Hewitt and Frew McMillan, 7–5, 6–4, 4–6, 8–6. Ann Jones d. Rosie Casals, 6–4, 6–0; Françoise Durr and Jones d. Rosa Reyes Darmon (France) and Gail Chanfreau, 7–9, 6–3, 6–1.

WEST BERLIN OPEN, at West Berlin: Ray Moore d. Cliff Drysdale, 1–6, 6–1, 7–5, 6–8, 7–5; Bob Hewitt and Frew McMillan d. Marty Riessen and Moore, 6–4, 6–4, 6–1. Karen Krantzcke d. Lesley Bowrey, 3–6, 6–2, 6–2;

West Berlin Open, 1969 (cont.)

Kerry Melville and Krantzcke d. Kristy Pigeon and Mary Ann Curtis (both U.S.), 7–5, 6–3.

FRENCH OPEN, at Paris: Rod Laver d. Ken Rosewall, 6–4, 6–3, 6–4; John Newcombe and Tony Roche d. Roy Emerson and Laver, 4–6, 6–1, 3–6, 6–4, 6–4. Margaret Court d. Ann Jones, 6–1, 4–6, 6–3; Françoise Durr and Jones d. Nancy Richey (U.S.) and Court, 6–0, 4–6, 7–5.

WEST OF ENGLAND OPEN, at Bristol: Ken Rosewall d. Pierre Barthes (France), 7–9, 6–3, 6–1; John Newcombe and Marty Riessen d. Roger Taylor and Cliff Drysdale, 4–6, 15–13, 6–3. Margaret Court d. Billie Jean King, 6–3, 6–3; Judy Tegart and Court d. Rosie Casals and King, 6–4, 6–2.

LONDON OPEN, at Queens Club, London: Fred Stolle d. John Newcombe, 6–3, 22–20; Owen Davidson (Australia) and Dennis Ralston (U.S.) d. Ove Bengsston (Sweden) and Tom Koch (Brazil), 8–6, 6–3. Ann Jones d. Winnie Shaw (Scotland), 6–0, 6–1; Rosie Casals and Billie Jean King d. Françoise Durr and Jones, 8–6, 6–4.

ALL-ENGLAND OPEN CHAMPIONSHIPS (Wimbledon), at London: Rod Laver d. John Newcombe, 6–4, 5–7, 6–4, 6–4; Tony Roche and Newcombe d. Marty Riessen and Tom Okker, 7–5, 11–9, 6–3. Ann Jones d. Billie Jean King, 3–6, 6–3, 6–2; Judy Tegart and Margaret Court d. Patti Hogan and Peggy Michel (both U.S.), 9–7, 6–2.

IRISH OPEN, at Dublin: Bob Hewitt d. Niki Pilic (Yugoslavia), 6–3, 6–2; Frew McMillan and Hewitt d. Roger Taylor and Pilic, 6–4, 2–6, 7–5. Billie Jean King d. Virginia Wade (England), 6–2, 6–2; Karen Krantzcke and Kerry Melville d. Rosie Casals and King, 5–7, 6–2, 6–4.

GOLDEN RACQUET OPEN, at Aix-en-Provence, France: Roy Emerson d. Harald Eischenbroich (West Germany), 6–3, 6–4, 8–6; Mal Anderson and Emerson d. Cliff Drysdale and Roger Taylor, 6–3, 6–4. Ann Jones d. Françoise Durr, 6–1, 6–1; Durr and Jones d. Kazuko Sawamatsu and Junko Sawamatsu (both Japan), 6–1, 5–7, 6–0.

SWISS OPEN, at Gstaad: Roy Emerson d. Tom Okker, 6–1, 12–14, 6–4, 6–4; Marty Riessen and Okker d. Owen Davidson and Fred Stolle, 6–1, 6–4. Françoise Durr d. Rosie Casals, 6–4, 4–6, 6–2; Billie Jean King and Casals d. Ann Jones and Durr, 8–6, 6–3.

WEST GERMAN OPEN, at Hamburg: Tony Roche d. Tom Okker, 6–1, 5–7, 7–5, 8–6; Marty Riessen and Okker d. Jurgen Fassbender (W. Germany) and Jean-Claude Barclay, 6–1, 6–2, 6–4. Judy Tegart d. Helga Niessen (W. Germany), 6–3, 6–4. Niessen and Tegart d. Edda Buding Duchting and Helga Schultze Hoesl (both W. Germany), 6–1, 6–4.

DUTCH OPEN, at Hilversum: Tom Okker d. Roger Taylor, 10–8, 7–9, 6–4, 6–4; Okker and Taylor d. Jan Kodes and Jan Kukal (both Czechoslovakia), 6–3, 6–2, 6–4. Kerry Melville d. Karen Krantzcke, 6–2, 3–6, 6–3; Melville and Krantzcke d. Helen Goultray (Australia) and Pat Walkden (Rhodesia), 1–6, 6–4, 6–3.

CANADIAN OPEN, at Toronto: Cliff Richey (U.S.) d. Butch Buchholz (U.S.), 6–3, 5–7, 6–4, 6–0; Ron Holmberg (U.S.) and John Newcombe d. Ray Moore and Buchholz, 6–3, 6–4; Faye Urban (Canada) d. Vicki Berner (Canada), 6–2, 6–0; Urban and Berner d. Jane O'Hara and Vivienne Strong (both Canada), 6–1, 6–1.

ARGENTINE OPEN, at Buenos Aires: François Jauffret (France) d. Zeljko Franulovic, 3–6, 6–2, 6–4, 6–3; Pat Cornejo and Jaime Fillol d. Roy Emerson and Frew McMillan, by default. Helga Niessen (Germany) d. Rosie Casals, 1–6, 6–4, 6–2. Billie Jean King and Casals d. Kora Schediwy (Germany) and Niessen, 6–1, 7–5.

BRITISH INDOOR OPEN, at London: Rod Laver d. Tony Roche, 6–4, 6–1, 6–3; Roy Emerson and Laver d. Pancho Gonzalez and Bob Hewitt, 6–3, 8–6; Ann Jones d. Billie Jean King, 9–11, 6–2, 9–7; Virginia Wade and Jones d. Rosie Casals and King, 6–2, 6–4.

STOCKHOLM INDOOR OPEN, at Stockholm: Niki Pilic d. Ilie Nastase (Romania), 6–4, 4–6, 6–2; Rod Laver and Roy Emerson d. Andres Gimeno and Fred Stolle, 6–4, 6–2. Billie Jean King d. Julie Heldman, 9–7, 6–2; Rosie Casals and King d. Françoise Durr and Heldman, 6–4, 6–4.

1970 Season

AUSTRALIAN OPEN, at Sydney: Arthur Ashe d. Dick Crealy, 6–4, 9–7, 6–2; Bob Lutz and

Two young overseas stars: (*left*) Zeljko Franulovic of Yugoslavia and (*right*) Ray Moore of South Africa.

Stan Smith d. Phil Dent and John Alexander, 8–6, 6–3, 6–4. Margaret Court d. Kerry Melville, 6–3, 6–1; Judy Dalton and Court d. Karen Krantzcke and Melville, 6–1, 6–3.

NEW ZEALAND OPEN, at Auckland: Roger Taylor d. Tom Okker, 6–4, 6–4, 6–1; Dick Crealy and Ray Ruffels d. Phil Dent and John Alexander, 6–4, 3–6, 6–3, 8–6. Ann Jones d. Kerry Melville, 6–3, 4–6, 6–2; Virginia Wade and Jones d. Karen Krantzcke and Melville, 6–0, 6–4.

DUNLOP OPEN, at Sydney: Rod Laver d. Ken Rosewall, 3–6, 6–2, 6–2, 6–3; Fred Stolle and Rosewall d. Bill Bowrey and Roger Taylor, 6–3, 7–5. Billie Jean King d. Margaret Court, 6–2, 4–6, 6–3.

SOUTH AFRICAN OPEN, at Johannesburg: Rod Laver d. Frew McMillan, 4–6, 6–2, 6–1, 6–2; Bob Hewitt and McMillan d. Cliff Drysdale and Roger Taylor, 6–3, 6–3, 6–2. Margaret Court d. Billie Jean King, 6–4, 1–6, 6–3; Rosie Casals and King d. Karen Krantzcke and Kerry Melville, 6–2, 6–2.

NATAL OPEN, at Durban: Bob Hewitt d. Cliff Drysdale, 6–4, 3–6, 6–4, 6–3; Frew McMillan and Hewitt d. Mark Cox and Graham Stilwell, 6–2, 6–2, 6–3. Billie Jean King d. Margaret Court, 6–4, 4–6, 6–2; Rosie Casals and King d. Judy Dalton and Court, 7–5, 6–3.

MONAGASQUE OPEN, at Monte Carlo: Zeljko Franulovic d. Manolo Orantes, 7–5, 6–3, 4–6, 6–1; Roger Taylor and Marty Riessen d. Pierre Barthes and Nikki Pilic, 6–3, 6–4, 6–2. Helga Niessen d. Kerry Melville, 6–4, 6–1; Gail Chanfreau and Françoise Durr d. Virginia Wade and Winnie Shaw, 6–2, 6–3.

ITALIAN OPEN, at Rome: Ilie Nastase d. Jan Kodes, 6–3, 1–6, 6–3, 8–6; Ion Tiriac and Nastase d. Bill Bowrey and Owen Davidson, 0–6, 10–8, 6–3, 6–8, 6–1. Billie Jean King d. Julie Heldman, 6–1, 6–3; Rosie Casals and King d. Françoise Durr and Virginia Wade, 6–2, 3–6, 9–7.

ROTHMAN'S BRITISH HARD-COURT OPEN*, at Bournemouth: Mark Cox d. Bob Hewitt, 6–1, 6–2, 6–3; Tom Okker and Tony Roche d. Bill Bowrey and Owen Davidson, 2–6, 6–4, 6–4, 6–4, 6–4. Margaret Court d. Virginia Wade, 6–2, 6–3; Judy Dalton and Court d. Rosie Casals and Billie Jean King, 6–2, 6–8, 7–5.

BELGIAN OPEN, at Brussels: Tom Okker d. Ilie Nastase, 6–3, 6–4, 0–6, 4–6, 6–4; Ion Tiriac and Nastase d. Bill Bowrey and Marty Riessen, 6–2, 3–6, 11–9, 6–4. Julie Heldman d. Peaches Bartkowicz, 6–1, 6–2, Mary Ann Curtis and Heldman d. Winnie Shaw and Bartkowicz, 6–3, 6–4.

EGYPTIAN OPEN, at Cairo: Manolo Santana d. Alex Metreveli, 7–5, 6–2, 6–4; Jan Kukal and Ismail El Shafei d. Vladimir Korotkov and Metreveli, 9–7, 3–6, 4–6, 6–3, 9–7. Olga Morozova d. Lea Pericoli, 6–3, 3–6, 9–7.

FRENCH OPEN*, at Paris: Jan Kodes d. Zeljko Franulovic, 6–2, 6–4, 6–0; Ilie Nastase and Ion Tiriac d. Arthur and Charlie Pasarell, 6–2, 6–4, 6–3. Margaret Court d. Helga Niessen, 6–2, 6–4; Françoise Durr and Gail Chanfreau d. Billie Jean King and Rosie Casals, 6–1, 3–6, 6–3.

SOUTH OF ENGLAND OPEN, at Eastbourne: Ken Rosewall d. Bob Hewitt, 6–2, 6–1; Fred Stolle and Rosewall d. Allan Stone and Bob Maud, 6–3, 7–5. Ann Jones d. Virginia Wade,

Asterisks throughout major tournaments indicate Pepsi Grand Prix Tournaments. See page 454.

South of England Open, 1970 (*cont.*)

8–6, 6–1; Judy Dalton and Jones d. Françoise Durr and Wade, 4–6, 6–3, 6–4.

WEST OF ENGLAND OPEN, at Bristol: Nikki Pilic d. Rod Laver, 6–3, 1–6, 6–3; Dennis Ralston and Laver d. Tom Okker and Marty Riessen, 6–3, 7–5. Margaret Court d. Françoise Durr, 6–1, 6–1; Judy Dalton and Court d. Karen Krantzcke and Kerry Melville, 6–2, 6–3.

LONDON OPEN, at Queens, London: Rod Laver d. John Newcombe, 6–4, 6–3; Tom Okker and Marty Riessen d. Arthur Ashe and Dennis Ralston, 6–4, 6–4. Margaret Court d. Winnie Shaw, 2–6, 8–6, 6–2; Billie Jean King and Rosie Casals d. Kerry Melville and Karen Krantzcke, 6–4, 6–3.

ALL-ENGLAND OPEN CHAMPIONSHIPS (Wimbledon), at London: John Newcombe d. Ken Rosewall, 5–7, 6–3, 6–2, 3–6, 6–1; Tony Roche and Newcombe d. Fred Stolle and Rosewall, 10–8, 6–3, 6–1. Margaret Court d. Billie Jean King, 14–12, 11–9; Rosie Casals and King d. Françoise Durr and Virginia Wade, 6–3, 6–2.

MIDLANDS OPEN, at Leicester, England: Tom Okker d. Roger Taylor, 6–1, 10–8; Cliff Drysdale and Taylor d. Owen Davidson and Bill Bowrey, 7–5, 6–3. Evonne Goolagong d. Patti Hogan, 6–2, 6–2; Pat Edwards and Goolagong d. Judy Dalton and Kerry Melville, 7–5, 5–7, 6–3.

SWEDISH OPEN*, at Båstad: Dick Crealy d. Georges Goven, 6–3, 6–1, 6–1; Allan Stone and Crealy d. Jan Kodes and Zeljko Franulovic, 2–6, 6–2, 12–10. Peaches Bartkowicz d. Ingrid Bentzner, 6–1, 6–1; Ann Maria Arias (Argentina) and Bartkowicz d. Eva Lundquist (Sweden) and Kathy Harter (U.S.), 6–4, 6–4.

IRISH OPEN, at Dublin: Tony Roche d. Rod Laver, 6–3, 6–1; Bob Hewitt and Laver d. Marty Riessen and Tom Okker, 6–1, 6–1. Virginia Wade d. Valerie Ziegenfuss, 6–3, 6–3; Kerry Melville and Karen Krantzcke d. Julie Heldman and Wade, 6–2, 7–5.

WELSH OPEN, at Newport: Ken Rosewall d. John Newcombe, 6–3, 6–4; Owen Davidson and Newcombe d. Nikki Pilic and Rosewall, 5–7, 6–4, 6–2. Evonne Goolagong d. Patti Hogan, 6–0, 8–6; Rosie Casals and Judy Dalton d. Ann Jones and Hogan, 6–3, 6–2.

SWISS OPEN, at Gstaad: Tony Roche d. Tom Okker, 6–3, 7–5, 6–3; Cliff Drysdale and

Roger Taylor d. Marty Riessen and Okker, 6–2, 6–3, 6–2. Rosie Casals d. Françoise Durr, 6–2, 5–7, 6–2; Casals and Durr d. Betty Stove (Netherlands) and Helga Niessen, 6–2, 6–2.

ROTHMAN'S CANADIAN OPEN, at Toronto: Rod Laver d. Roger Taylor, 6–0, 4–6, 6–3; Bill Bowrey and Marty Riessen d. Fred Stolle and Cliff Drysdale, 6–3, 6–2. Margaret Court d. Rosie Casals, 6–8, 6–4, 6–4. Court and Casals d. Pat Walkden and Helen Gourlay, 6–0, 6–1.

NORTH OF ENGLAND OPEN, at Holylake, England: John Newcombe d. Owen Davidson, 4–6, 9–7, 6–4; Bill Bowrey and Davidson d. Ismail El Shafei and Newcombe, 4–6, 6–2, 6–4. Evonne Goolagong d. Kerry Melville, 2–6, 6–2, 6–1; Karen Krantzcke and Melville d. Judy Dalton and Julie Heldman, 6–2, 12–10.

BAVARIAN OPEN*, at Munich: Ion Tiriac d. Nikki Pilic, 2–6, 9–7, 6–3, 6–4; Owen Davidson and Pilic d. Bob Hewitt and Frew McMillan, 6–4, 7–5, 6–4. Evonne Goolagong d. Karen Krantzcke, 3–6, 6–2, 6–4; Brenda Kirk and Laura Roussow (both South Africa) d. Nell Truman and Faye Moore, 6–4, 6–4.

WEST GERMAN OPEN, at Hamburg: Tom Okker d. Ilie Nastase, 4–6, 6–3, 6–3, 6–4; Bob Hewitt and Frew McMillan d. Nikki Pilic and Okker, 6–3, 7–5, 6–2. Helga Hoesl (W. Germany), d. Helga Niessen, 6–3, 6–3; Kerry Melville and Karen Krantzcke d. Virginia Wade and Winnie Shaw, 6–0, 6–1.

DUTCH OPEN*, At Hilversum: Tom Okker d. Roger Taylor, 4–6, 6–0, 6–1, 6–3; Bill Bowrey and Owen Davidson d. John Alexander and Phil Dent, 6–3, 6–4, 6–2. Margaret Court d. Kerry Melville, 6–1, 6–1; Karen Krantzcke and Melville d. Helga Niessen and Court, 3–6, 9–7, 7–5.

SPANISH OPEN, at Barcelona: Manolo Santana d. Rod Laver, 6–3, 6–4, 6–3; Lew Hoad (Australia) and Santana d. Andres Gimeno and Laver, 6–4, 9–7, 7–5. Helga Hoesl d. Sue Alexander (Australia), 6–1, 6–1.

PARIS INDOOR*, at Paris: Arthur Ashe d. Marty Riessen, 7–6, 6–4, 6–3; Pancho Gonzalez (U.S.) and Ken Rosewall d. Tom Okker and Riessen, 6–4, 7–6, 7–6.

EMBASSY INDOOR OPEN*, at London: Rod Laver d. Cliff Richey, 6–3, 6–4, 6–4; Stan Smith and Ken Rosewall d. Ion Tiriac and

Ilie Nastase, 6–4, 6–3, 6–2. Billie Jean King d. Ann Jones, 8–6, 3–6, 6–1; Virginia Wade and Jones d. Valerie Ziegenfuss and Mary Ann Curtis, 6–1, 8–6.

STOCKHOLM INDOOR OPEN*, at Stockholm: Stan Smith d. Arthur Ashe, 5–7, 6–4, 6–4; Ashe and Smith d. Bob Carmichael and Owen Davidson, 6–0, 5–7, 7–5.

ARGENTINE OPEN*, at Buenos Aires: Zeljko Franulovic d. Manolo Orantes, 6–4, 6–2, 6–0; Bob Carmichael and Ray Ruffels d. Jan Kodes and Franulovic, 7–5, 6–2, 5–7, 6–7, 6–3. Beatriz Araujo d. Raquel Giscafre, 6–4, 6–4; Ines Roget and Araujo d. Graciela Moran and Alice Tym, 6–4, 6–4.

ASIAN INTERNATIONAL, at Delhi, India: Alex Metreveli (U.S.S.R.) d. Premjit Lall, 6–3, 6–4, 2–6, 3–6, 6–3; Shyam Minotra and Shir Prakash Misra d. Lall and Jaidys Mukerjea, 6–2, 9–7, 6–4; I. Aybandaye (U.S.S.R.) d. Aleksandra Ivanova (U.S.S.R.), 9–7, 6–3.

VICTORIA STATE CHAMPIONSHIPS, at Melbourne, Australia: Newcombe d. Roche, 6–4, 6–4, 4–6, ret.; Smith and Lutz d. McManus and Gorman, 6–3, 6–4, 6–4; Court d. Melville, 6–1, 6–1; Court and Dalton d. Melville and Krantzcke, 6–3, 6–4.

SCANDINAVIAN CHAMPIONSHIPS, at Oslo, Norway: Lundquist d. Aaberg, 6–4, 6–3, 6–2; Clifton and Hutchins d. Yahr and Nerell, 4–6, 7–5, 10–12, 8–6, 8–6. Joyce Williams (Great Britain) d. Nell Truman, 6–1, 6–1; Williams and Truman d. Ingrid Lofdahl Bentyer (Sweden) and Gundrun Rcsin (Sweden), 6–2, 6–3.

COVERED COURT CHAMPIONSHIPS OF FRANCE, at Lyon: Goven d. Yednik, 6–3, 6–2, 6–1; Barclay and Beust d. Yednik and Pala, 16–14, 6–3, 6–2; DeRoulin d. Chanfreau, 6–2, 6–2.

INTERNATIONAL CHAMPIONSHIPS OF LEBANON, at Beirut: Pietrangeli d. H. Phillips-Moore, 6–1, 6–0, 6–2; Hombergen and Drossart d. Phillips-Moore and Bartlett, 16–14, 4–6, 7–5, 8–6; Martin d. O'Hara, 4–6, 6–2, 6–3.

INTERNATIONAL CHAMPIONSHIPS OF WEST BERLIN, at West Berlin: Goven d. Kuhnke, 6–2, 2–6, 6–1, 6–3; Carmichael and Addison d. Elschenbroich and Davidson, 9–7, 6–4, 6–4; Wade d. Niessen, 10–8, 6–1; Wade and Dalton d. Hoesl and Krantzcke, 4–6, 7–5, 6–0.

INTERNATIONAL CHAMPIONSHIPS OF MOROCCO, at Casablanca: Newcombe d. Gimeno, 6–4, 6–4, 6–4; Cox and Stilwell d. Taylor and Riessen, 6–4, 6–4.

INTERNATIONAL TOURNAMENT AT LE TOUQUET, at Le Touquet, France: Jauffret d. Panatta, 6–3, 7–5, 6–8, 6–4; Courcol and Jauffret d. Bartlett (Australia) and Masters, 6–3, 4–6, 6–4; Hunt d. deRoubin, 6–4, 6–4.

INTERNATIONAL CHAMPIONSHIPS OF CZECHOSLOVAKIA, at Bratislava: Kodes d. Holecek, 3–6, 6–3, 6–2, 7–5; Machan and Syoke d. Kodes and Kukal, 7–5, 8–6; Vopickova d. Yiegenfuos, 6–4, 6–4; Holubova and Kodesova d. Vopickova and Neumannova, 6–3, 9–7.

INTERNATIONAL TOURNAMENT, at La Baule, France: F. Jauffret d. Contet, 6–4, 6–1, 6–1; F. Jauffret and Pierre Jauffret d. Barclay and Contet, 6–4, 4–6, 6–2; Guedy d. Michele Boulle Rodriguey, 6–4, 7–5.

INTERNATIONAL CHALLENGE CUP, at Le Touquet, France: Proisy d. Leclercq, 5–7, 8–6, 6–3, 6–1; Elena Subirats (Mexico) d. M. Proisy, 6–2, 7–5.

INTERNATIONAL TOURNAMENT, at Broumana, Lebanon: Gulyas d. Alexander, 6–3, 14–12, 6–8, 7–5; Alexander and Dent d. Gulyas and Baranyi, 6–3, 6–4, 6–4; Shaw d. Jones, 1–6, 6–2, 6–1.

SECOND EUROPEAN CHAMPIONSHIPS FOR AMATEURS, at Sofia, Bulgaria: Metreveli d. Baranyi, 6–0, 6–3, 6–2; Metreveli and Likhachev d. Lejus and Korotkov, 6–1, 5–7, 6–2, 6–3; Moroyova d. Borka, 6–4, 6–2; Moroyova and Tiiu Kivi d. Iyopaitis and Krasina, 6–2, 6–1.

COUPE PORÉE, at Paris, France: Jauffret d. Proisy, 6–4, 6–1, 6–1; DeRoribin d. Boriteleux, 3–6, 6–2, 6–1; Hombergen and Montrenaud d. Meyer and Wanare N'Godrella, 6–4, 6–4; Chanfreau and Darmon d. de Roubin and Rovire, 6–2, 6–1.

1971 Season

WESTERN AUSTRALIAN CHAMPIONSHIP, at Perth: Alex Metreveli (U.S.S.R.) d. John Alexander, 7–5, 6–2, 6–2; Margaret Court d. Virginia Wade (Great Britain), 6–1, 6–2; Syd Ball and Bob Giltinan d. Metreveli and John Bartlett, 10–8, 6–3, 6–3; Court and Evonne Goolagong d. Wade and Winnie

Western Australian, 1971 (cont.)

Shaw, 6–4, 7–5; Metreveli and Olga Morozova (U.S.S.R.), d. Ian Fletcher and Patti Hogan (U.S.), 10–8, 6–3.

TASMANIAN OPEN, at Hobart: Alex Metreveli d. John Alexander, 7–6, 6–3, 4–6, 6–3; Gail Chanfreau (France) d. Kerry Harris, 6–1, 2–6, 6–2; Alexander and Phil Dent d. Milan Holecek (Czechoslovakia) and Vladimir Zednik (Czechoslovakia), 6–3, 6–2, 7–6; Patti Hogan and Olga Morozova d. Laura Rossouw (South Africa) and Brenda Kirk (South Africa), 6–2, 6–0.

NEW SOUTH WALES CHAMPIONSHIP, at Sydney: Phil Dent d. John Alexander, 6–3, 6–4, 6–4; Margaret Court d. Olga Morozova, 6–2, 6–2; John Alexander and Phil Dent d. Mal Anderson and Alex Metreveli, 6–7, 2–6, 6–3, 7–6, 7–6; Court and Morozova d. Helen Gourlay and Kerry Harris, 6–2, 6–0.

WELLINGTON CHAMPIONSHIP, at Wellington, New Zealand: Brian Fairlie d. Onny Parun, 6–3, 6–3, 7–6; Kathy Harter (U.S.) d. Beverley Vercoe, 6–2, 6–2; Onny Parun and Kevin Woolcott d. Hans Kary (Austria) and Ian Beverley, 6–4, 5–7, 6–3, 7–5; Harter and Sue Blakely d. Vercoe and Bev Ward, 6–7, 6–4, 6–4; Harter and Paul Thomson d. Barbara Wright and Billy Wright, 7–5, 6–7, 7–5.

AUCKLAND GRASS COURT CHAMPIONSHIP, at Auckland, New Zealand: Brian Fairlie d. Onny Parun, 3–6, 6–2, 6–1, 7–5; Kathy Harter d. Shelley Monds, 6–1, 6–0; Fairlie and Jeff Simpson d. Parun and Hans Kary, 11–9, 7–5, 3–6, 7–5; Harter and Patsy Stevens d. E. Stephan and H. Stevans, 6–1, 6–2; Harter and Mark Elliott (U.S.) d. Stephan and Peter Becroft, 6–1, 6–4.

MOSCOW INDOOR OPEN, at Moscow, U.S.S.R.: Vladimir Korotkov d. Vyacheslav Yegorov, 6–2, 6–6, 6–4, 6–3; Rauza Islanova d. Yevgeniya Biryukova, 6–3, 6–4; Yegorov and Korotkov d. Alex Ivanov and Vladimir Palman, 7–6, 7–6, 6–1; Biryukova and L. Novashinskaya d. Anna Yeremeyeva and Tatiana Lagoiskaya, 2–6, 6–3, 6–4.

MEXICAN NATIONALS, at Mexico City: Joaquin Loyo-Mayo d. Marcelo Lara, 6–8, 6–1, 6–3, 9–7; Yola Ramirez Ochoa d. Elena Subirats, 6–0, 6–0; Luis Garcia and Lara d. Loyo-Mayo and Raul Ramirez, 8–6, 16–14, 6–4; Subirats and Patricia Reyes d. Ochoa and Susana Zenea, 6–4, 6–3.

ROTHMAN'S TENNIS SPECTACULAR, at Kingston, Jamaica: Gerald Battrick (Great Britain) d. Joaquin Loyo-Mayo (Mexico), 6–2, 1–6, 6–1; David Pratt and Haroon Rahim (Pakistan) d. Richard Russell and Compton Russell, 6–0, 7–5.

GERMAN INDOOR CHAMPIONSHIPS, at Bremen: Jorgen Ulrich (Denmark) d. David Lloyd (Great Britain), 6–4, 10–8, 4–6, 4–6, 6–3; Nell Truman (Great Britain) d. Heide Orth, 6–3, 6–3; Jean-Claude Barclay (France) and Pat Hombergen (Belgium) d. Eric Drossart (Belgium) and Bernard Mignot (Belgium), 6–4, 9–7, 1–6, 6–0; Orth and Mrs. H. Niessen Masthoff d. Ingrid Bentzer (Sweden) and Eva Lundquist (Sweden), 6–3, 5–7, 6–1; Orth and Jurgen Fassbender d. Truman and Barclay, 2–6, 6–0, 6–4.

VICTORIAN CHAMPIONSHIPS, at Kooyong: Alex Metreveli d. Phil Dent, 6–4, 6–2; Evonne Goolagong d. Margaret Court, 7–6, 7–6.

B. P. NEW ZEALAND CHAMPIONSHIP, at Auckland: Colin Dibley (Australia) d. Bob Giltinan (Australia), 6–1, 6–4, 6–4; Evonne Goolagong (Australia) d. Betty Stove (Netherlands), 6–1, 6–4; Milan Holecek and Vladimir Zednick d. Dibley and Giltinan, 3–6, 4–6, 6–2, 6–4, 6–4; Winnie Shaw (Great Britain) and Kathy Harter d. Gail Chanfreau (France) and Goolagong, 6–4, 4–6, 7–6; Chanfreau and Jean Loup Rouyer (France) d. Goolagong and Giltinan, 6–4, 6–4.

BENSON AND HEDGES OPEN, at Auckland: Bob Carmichael (Australia) d. Allan Stone (Australia), 7–6, 7–6, 6–3; Margaret Court d. Evonne Goolagong, 3–6, 7–6, 6–2; Carmichael and Ray Ruffels (Australia) d. Brian Fairlie and Ray Moore (South Africa), 6–3, 6–7, 6–4, 4–6, 6–3; Court and Goolagong d. Winnie Shaw and Lesley H. Bowrey (Australia), 7–6, 6–0; Court and Colin Dibley d. Bowrey and Bill Bowrey, 6–2, 6–1.

AUSTRALIAN DUNLOP OPEN, at Sydney: Ken Rosewall d. Arthur Ashe (U.S.), 6–1, 7–5, 6–3; John Newcombe and Tony Roche d. Tom Okker (Netherlands) and Marty Riessen (U.S.), 6–2, 7–6; Margaret Court d. Evonne Goolagong, 2–6, 7–6, 7–5; Court and Goolagong d. Lesley Hunt and Jill Emmerson, 6–0, 6–0.

ROTHMAN'S INTERNATIONAL CHAMPIONSHIP, at London: Tony Roche (Australia) d. Marty Riessen, 7–5, 6–2; Roy Emerson (Australia) and Rod Laver (Australia) d. Roger Taylor and Andres Gimeno (Spain), 6–0, 6–4, 6–3.

MOSCOW INTERNATIONAL INDOORS CHAMPIONSHIPS, at Moscow: Alex Metreveli d. Anatoly Volkov, 6–3, 2–6, 6–4; Metreveli and Sergei Likhachev d. Frantisek Pala (Czechoslovakia) and Pavel Hutka (Czechoslovakia), 5–7, 6–4, 4–6, 7–6; Olga Morozova d. Maria Kull, 6–1, 7–5; Marina Kroshina and Yevyeniya Biryukova d. Morozova and Yelena Granaturova, 7–6, 5–7, 7–5; Morozova and Metreveli d. Biryukova and Likhachev, 6–3, 6–4.

KENYA NATIONALS, at Nairobi: Aly El Daoudi (UAR) d. Yashvin Shretta, 6–4, 6–4, 3–6, 6–4; Bernard Montreaud (France) and Bernard Paul (France) d. Peter Burwash (Canada) and Bernard Mignot (Belgium), 5–7, 6–2, 2–6, 6–4, 7–5; Nirupa Mankad (India) d. Jenny Paterson, 6–0, 6–0; Mankad and Paterson d. Mrs. W. Vincenzini and Mrs. V. M. Nash, 6–2, 6–2; Mankad and Mootaz Sonbol (UAR) d. Corrine O'Tolle and Mignot, 6–2, 6–1.

UGANDA NATIONALS, at Kampala: Mootaz Sonbol d. Bernard Mignot, 6–1, 6–4; Aly El Daoudi and Sonbol d. Yashvin Shretta (Kenya) and Lars Olander (Sweden), 2–6, 7–5, 6–1; Nirupa Mankad d. Phil McEwen, 6–0, 6–1; Mankad and Doreen Hinchliffe d. McEwen and Margaret Walker, 6–1, 6–0.

UAR OPEN CHAMPIONSHIPS, at Cairo: Alex Metreveli d. Ismail El Shafei, 8–6, 9–7, 6–4; Pierre Barthes (France) and Jean Baptiste Chanfreau d. El Shafei and Brian Fairlie, 9–7, 7–5, 6–3.

JAPANESE NATIONAL INDOOR CHAMPIONSHIPS, at Tokyo: Ian Fletcher (Australia) d. Takeshi Koura, 7–5, 6–4; Jun Kamuvazumi and Toshiro Sakai d. Junizo Kawamori and Koura, 7–6, 5–7, 6–3; Yaeko Matsuda d. Kimiyo Hatanaka, 5–7, 6–4, 6–4; Junko Sawamatsu and Kazuko Sawamatsu d. Chikado Murakami and Hatanaka, 7–6, 6–1.

CARACAS INTERNATIONAL CHAMPIONSHIP, at Caracas: Thomaz Koch (Brazil) d. Manuel Orantes (Spain), 7–6, 6–1, 6–3; Koch and Edison Mandarino (Brazil) d. Gerald Battrick (Great Britain) and Peter Curtis (Great Britain), 6–4, 3–6, 6–7, 6–4, 7–6.

PALERMO INTERNATIONAL*, at Palermo, Italy: Roger Taylor (Great Britain) d. Pierre Barthes, 6–3, 4–6, 7–6, 6–2; Georges Goven and Barthes (both of France) d. Ilie Nastase and Ion Tiriac, def.; Helga Schultze Hoesl (Germany) d. Gail Chanfreau (France), 6–3, 4–6, 7–6; Chanfreau and Hoesl d. Miroslava Holubova and Maria Neumannova (both of Czech.), 6–4, 6–3.

CATANIA INTERNATIONAL*, at Catania, Italy: Jan Kodes (Czechoslovakia) d. Georges Goven, 6–3, 6–0, 6–2; Pierre Barthes and François Jauffret (France) d. Jan Kukal (Czechoslovakia) and Kodes, 6–4, 3–6, 6–3; Virginia Wade d. Gail Chanfreau, 1–6, 7–6, 6–2; Helga Hoesl and Chanfreau d. Pam Teeguarden (U.S.), 6–4, 6–4.

MONTE CARLO OPEN CHAMPIONSHIP*, at Monte Carlo: Ilie Nastase (Romania) d. Tom Okker, 3–6, 8–6, 6–1, 6–1; Nastase and Ion Tiriac (Romania) d. Okker and Roger Taylor (Great Britain), 1–6, 6–3, 6–3, 8–6; Gail Chanfreau d. Betty Stove, 6–4, 4–6, 6–4; Katja Ebbinghaus (Germany) and Stove d. Lea Pericoli (Italy) and Lucia Bassi (Italy), 6–4, 6–3.

NICE OPEN CHAMPIONSHIP*, at Nice: Ilie Nastase d. Jan Kodes (Czechoslovakia), 10–8, 11–9, 6–1; Nastase and Ion Tiriac d. Pierre Barthes and François Jauffret, 6–3, 6–3; Jill Cooper (Great Britain) d. Marijke Schaar, 6–1, 6–1; Lea Pericoli and Lucia Bassi d. Betty Stove and Trudy Walhof (Netherlands), def.; Gail Chanfreau and Barthes d. Miroslava Holubova (Czechoslovakia) and Frantisek Pala (Czechoslovakia), 6–4, 6–2.

DURBAN OPEN CHAMPIONSHIP, at Durban: Bob Hewitt d. Manuel Santana (Spain), 7–6, 6–1, 6–1; Santana and Hewitt d. Dave Phillips and C. Diederichs, 6–3, 6–1; Margaret Court d. Patti Hogan (U.S.), 6–2, 6–1; Court and Evonne Goolagong d. Winnie Shaw and Kerry Harris, 6–3, 3–6, 6–3.

SOUTH AFRICAN OPEN, at Johannesburg: Ken Rosewall (Australia) d. Fred Stolle (Australia), 6–4, 6–0, 6–4; Rosewall and Stolle d. Bob Hewitt and Frew McMillan, 5–7, 6–2, 6–1, 6–2; Margaret Court d. Evonne Goolagong, 6–3, 6–1; Court and Goolagong d. Brenda Kirk and Laura Rossouw, 6–4, 7–5; Court and Stolle d. Ray Ruffels and Pat Walkden (Rhodesia), 6–3, 7–6.

ROTHMAN'S OPEN HARD-COURT CHAMPIONSHIP*, at Bournemouth: Gerald Battrick d.

Rothman's Open Hard Court, 1971 *(cont.)*

Zeljko Franulovic (Yugoslavia), 6–3, 6–2, 5–7, 6–0; Bill Bowrey and Owen Davidson d. Jaime Fillol (Chile) and Pat Cornejo (Chile), 8–6, 6–2, 3–6, 4–6, 6–3; Margaret Court d. Evonne Goolagong, 7–5, 6–1; Françoise Durr (France) and Mary Ann Curtis d. Court and Goolagong, 6–3, 5–7, 6–4.

BIO-STRATH LONDON HARD-COURT CHAMPIONSHIP*, at London: Jaime Fillol d. Gerald Battrick, 7–5, 6–3; Margaret Court d. Françoise Durr, 6–0, 6–3; Rosemary Casals (U.S.) and Billie Jean King (U.S.) d. Court and Evonne Goolagong, 6–1, 6–4.

ARYAMEHR CUP, at Teheran: Marty Riessen d. John Alexander, 6–7, 6–1, 6–3, 7–6; Tony Roche and John Newcombe d. Bob Carmichael and Ray Ruffels, 6–4, 6–7, 6–1.

KENT CHAMPIONSHIP, at Beckenham: Stan Smith d. Premjit Lall (India), 7–9, 6–4, 6–2; Syd Ball (Australia) and Geoff Masters (Australia) d. Terry Addison (Australia) and Ray Keldie (Australia), 6–3, 3–6, 6–3; Kerry Melville (Australia) d. Kristy Pigeon (U.S.), 6–0, 3–6, 9–7; Christine Janes and Nell Truman d. Zaiga Yansone (U.S.S.R.) and Olga Morozova, 6–3, 9–7.

ROTHMAN'S LONDON OPEN CHAMPIONSHIP*, at London: Stan Smith d. John Newcombe, 8–6, 6–3; Tom Okker and Marty Riessen d. Smith and Erik Van Dillen, 8–6, 4–6, 10–8; Margaret Court d. Billie Jean King, 6–3, 3–6, 6–3; Rosemary Casals and King d. Mary Ann Curtis and Val Ziegenfuss, 6–3, 6–2.

ALL-ENGLAND OPEN CHAMPIONSHIP*, at Wimbledon: John Newcombe d. Stan Smith, 6–3, 5–7, 2–6, 6–4, 6–4; Roy Emerson and Rod Laver d. Arthur Ashe and Dennis Ralston (U.S.), 4–6, 9–7, 6–8, 6–4, 6–4; Evonne Goolagong d. Margaret Court, 6–4, 6–1; Rosemary Casals and Billie Jean King d. Court and Goolagong, 6–3, 6–2; King and Owen Davidson d. Court and Marty Riessen, 3–6, 6–2, 15–13.

WELSH OPEN CHAMPIONSHIP*, at Newport: Ken Rosewall d. Roger Taylor, 6–1, 9–8; Rosewall and Taylor d. John Paish and John Clifton, 7–5, 3–6, 6–2; Virginia Wade d. Judy Dalton, 6–3, 6–4; Helen Gourlay and Kerry Harris d. Gail Chanfreau and Winnie Shaw, 6–3, 8–6; Dalton and Frew McMillan d. Gourlay and Hank Irvine (Rhodesia), 4–6, 6–0, 6–4.

ROTHMAN'S NORTH OF ENGLAND OPEN*, at Holylake: Andrew Pattison (South Africa) d. Jaidip Muskerjea (India), 6–2, 5–7, 6–2; John Paish and Bobby Wilson d. Bob Hewitt (South Africa) and Ray Keldie, 17–15, 6–3; Billie Jean King d. Rosemary Casals, 6–3, 6–3; Casals and King d. Margaret Court and Evonne Goolagong, def.

GREEN SHIELD MIDLAND OPEN, at Leicester: Syd Ball d. Bob Hewitt, 8–6, 6–3; Hank Irvine and Ball d. Hewitt and Ray Keldie, 6–4, 1–6, 6–4; Evonne Goolagong d. Patti Hogan, 6–2, 6–1; Goolagong and Judy Dalton d. Hogan and Barbara Hawcroft, 6–3, 6–2; Goolagong and Hewitt d. Helen Gourlay and Irvine, 6–2, 6–2.

IRISH OPEN CHAMPIONSHIP, at Dublin: Cliff Drysdale d. Clark Graebner (U.S.), 10–8, 6–3; Bill Bowrey and Owen Davidson d. Jaime Fillol and Pat Cornejo, 8–6, 6–3; Margaret Court d. Evonne Goolagong, 6–3, 2–6, 6–3; Lesley Bowrey and Betty Stove d. Court and Goolagong, 7–5, 6–3; Goolagong and Fred Stolle d. Court and Davidson, 6–3, 6–2.

SWEDISH OPEN CHAMPIONSHIP*, at Båstad: Ilie Nastase d. Jan Leschly, 6–7, 6–2, 6–1, 6–4; Nastase and Ion Tiriac d. Jaime Pinto-Bravo (Chile) and Butch Seewagen (U.S.), 7–6, 7–1; Helga Masthoff d. Ingrid Bentzer, 4–6, 6–1, 6–3; Masthoff and Heidi Orth d. Arias Pinto-Bravo (Argentina) and Linda Tuero (U.S.), 6–2, 6–1.

SWISS INTERNATIONAL OPEN CHAMPIONSHIP*, at Gstaad: John Newcombe d. Okker, 6–2, 5–7, 1–6, 7–5, 6–3; John Alexander and Phil Dent d. Newcombe and Okker, 5–7, 6–3, 6–4; Françoise Durr d. Lesley Hunt, 6–3, 6–3; Laura Rossouw and Brenda Kirk d. Durr and Lea Pericoli, 8–6, 6–3; Rossouw and Rober Maud (South Africa) d. Hunt and Colin Dibley (Australia) 6–3, 6–4.

AUSTRIAN CHAMPIONSHIP, at Kitzbuehel: Clark Graebner drew with Manuel Orantes, 6–1, 7–5, 6–7, 5–7, 4–4 (unfinished); Billie Jean King d. Laura Rossouw, 6–2, 4–6, 7–5; Graebner and Ion Tiriac d. Hans Turgen Pohmann (Germany) and Jurgen Fassbender, 6–4, 6–4, 7–5; King and Rosemary Casals d. Helga Masthoff and Heide Orth, 6–2, 6–4.

YUGOSLAV INTERNATIONAL CHAMPIONSHIP, at Belgrade: Zeljko Franulovic d. Manuel Orantes (Spain), 6–1, 6–2, 6–2; Orantes and Juan Gisbert (Spain) d. Franulovic and Boro

Jovanovic, 2–0, ret.; Yulia Berberjan (Bulgaria) d. Judith Dibar (Romania), 5–7, 6–4, 6–0; Dibar and Berberjan d. Jelene Gencio and C. Toklin, 6–2, 6–3.

ITALIAN OPEN CHAMPIONSHIP, at Rome: Rod Laver d. Jan Kodes, 7–5, 6–3, 6–3; John Newcombe and Tony Roche d. Andres Gimeno and Roger Taylor, 5–7, 6–2, 6–2; Virginia Wade (Great Britain) d. Helga Niessen Masthoff, 6–4, 6–4; Wade and Masthoff d. Helen Gourlay (Australia) and Lesley Bowrey (Australia), 5–7, 6–2, 6–2.

GERMAN CHAMPIONSHIP*, at Hamburg: Andres Gimeno d. Peter Szoke (Hungary), 6–3, 6–2, 6–2; Gimeno and John Alexander (Australia) d. Allan Stone (Australia) and Dick Crealy (Australia), 6–4, 7–5, 7–9, 6–4; Billie Jean King d. Helga Niessen Masthoff, 6–3, 6–4; King and Rosemary Casals d. Masthoff and Heide Orth Schildknecht, 6–2, 6–1.

MADRID INTERNATIONAL CHAMPIONSHIP, at Madrid: Ion Tiriac d. Ilie Nastase, 7–5, 6–1, 6–0; Winnie Shaw d. Lesley Hunt (Australia), 5–7, 6–1, 6–1.

CITY OF PARIS CHAMPIONSHIP*, at Paris: Stan Smith (U.S.) d. François Jauffret, 6–2, 6–4, 7–5; Smith and Tom Gorman (U.S.) d. Pierre Barthes and Jauffret, 3–6, 7–5, 6–2; Helga Schultz Hoesl (Germany) d. Brenda Kirk (South Africa), 4–6, 6–2, 6–1; Gail Chanfreau and Rosie Darmon d. Kirk and Laura Rossouw, 6–2, 10–8; Darmon and Jan Leschly (Denmark) d. Chanfreau and Jean Loup Rouyer, 6–4, 12–10.

FRENCH NATIONAL OPEN CHAMPIONSHIP*, at Paris: Jan Kodes d. Ilie Nastase, 8–6, 6–2, 2–6, 7–5; Arthur Ashe and Marty Riessen d. Tom Gorman and Stan Smith, 6–8, 4–6, 6–3, 6–4, 11–9; Evonne Goolagong d. Helen Gourlay, 6–3, 7–5; Gail Chanfreau and Françoise Durr d. Gourlay and Kerry Harris, 6–4, 6–1; Durr and Jean-Claude Barclay d. Winnie Shaw and Thomas Lejus (U.S.S.R.), 6–2, 6–4.

BELGIAN INTERNATIONAL OPEN CHAMPIONSHIP*, at Brussels: Cliff Drysdale (South Africa) d. Ilie Nastase, 6–0, 6–1, 7–5.

FORD CAPRI CHAMPIONSHIP, at Venice: Helga Masthoff d. Rosemary Casals, 3–6, 6–4, 6–3; Billie Jean King and Judy Dalton d. Gail Chanfreau and Françoise Durr, 3–6, 6–4, 6–4.

QUEBEC INTERNATIONAL CHAMPIONSHIP, at Quebec: Tom Okker d. Rod Laver, 6–3, 7–6, 6–7, 6–1; Laver and Roy Emerson d. Okker and Marty Riessen, 7–6, 6–2.

ROTHMAN'S CANADIAN OPEN, at Toronto: John Newcombe d. Tom Okker, 7–6, 3–6, 6–2, 7–6; Okker and Marty Riessen d. Arthur Ashe and Dennis Ralston, 6–3, 6–3; Françoise Durr d. Evonne Goolagong, 6–4, 6–2; Rosemary Casals and Durr d. Goolagong and Lesley Bowrey, 6–3, 6–3.

RIVER PLATE, at Buenos Aires: Jaime Fillol d. Julian Ganzabal, 6–4, 6–3, 6–3; Pat Cornejo and Fillol d. Thomaz Koch and Edison Mandarino, 7–5, 8–6; Olga Morozova d. Maria Nasuelli (Italy), 6–3, 6–4; Morozova and Betty Stove d. Beatriz Araujo and Ines Roget, 7–5, 6–1; Morozova and Vyacheslav Yegorov (U.S.S.R.) d. Stove and Tomas Lejus (U.S.S.R.), 6–3, 6–1.

SENEGALLIA OPEN*, at Senegallia, Italy: Andiano Panatta (Italy) d. Marty Mulligan (Italy), 6–3, 7–5, 6–1; Atet Wijono (Indonesia) and Gondo Widjojo (Indonesia) d. Massimo Di Domenico (Italy) and Antonio Zugarelli (Italy), 6–7, 7–5, 6–3; Lanny Kaligis (Indonesia) d. Lita Liem (Indonesia), 7–5, 3–6, 6–2.

ATHENS INTERNATIONAL, at Athens: Nick Kalogeropoulos (Greece) d. Patrice Dominguez (France), 6–3, 7–5, 6–2; John Bartlett (Australia) and Kalogeropoulos d. Pietro Marzano (Italy) and Dominguez, 6–3, 7–9, 6–4, 6–4; Brenda Kirk d. Fiorella Bonicelli (Uruguay), 9–7, 6–0; Kirk and Marzano d. Bonicelli and Dominguez, 6–4, 7–9, 7–5.

ROTHMAN'S VANCOUVER INTERNATIONAL, at Vancouver, Canada: Ken Rosewall d. Tom Okker, 6–2, 6–2, 6–4; Rod Laver and Roy Emerson d. John Alexander and Phil Dent, 5–7, 6–7, 6–0, 7–5, 7–6.

REAL MADRID, at Madrid, Spain: Harald Eischenbroich (Germany) d. Juan Gisbert, 6–4, 6–4, 6–3; Lew Hoad (Australia) and Manuel Santana d. Marty Mulligan and Eischenbroich, 7–5, 6–2.

PHILIP MORRIS INVITATIONAL, at Zaragoza, Spain: Manuel Santana d. Harald Eischenbroich, 6–4, 6–4, 8–6; Jamie Pinto-Bravo and Bernard Mignot (Belgium) d. Bill Alvarez (Colombia) and Santana, 4–6, 9–7, 7–5, 8–6; M. Guardaz (Spain) d. Monique Van Haver (Belgium), 6–3, 6–3; Van Haver and Guardaz d. Sue Alexander (Australia) and R. Murphy (Spain), 6–4, 6–1.

SPANISH INTERNATIONAL, at Barcelona:

Spanish International, 1971 (cont.)

Manuel Orantes (Spain) d. Bob Lutz (U.S.),
6–4, 6–3, 6–4; Zeljko Franulovic and Juan
Gisbert d. Andres Gimeno and Cliff Drysdale,
7–6, 6–2, 6–2; Helga Hoesl d. Ana Maria
Pinto-Bravo (Argentina), 6–2, 6–1; C. Gisbert and Hoesl d. Guthia Sieler (Spain) and
Pinto-Bravo, 6–4, 6–2.

PROFI-TENNIS-WELLMEISTERSCHAFT, at Cologne, Germany: Bob Lutz d. Jeff Borowiak
(U.S.), 6–3, 6–7, 6–3, 6–2; Tom Okker and
Marty Riessen d. Roy Emerson and Rod
Laver, 6–7, 3–6, 7–6, 6–3, 6–4.

EDINBURGH-DEWAR CUP, at Edinburgh: Bob
Hewitt d. Gerald Battrick, 7–6, 6–3; Rayno
Seegers (South Africa) and Hewitt d. Jaime
Fillot and Ray Moore (South Africa), 6–2,
7–6; Evonne Goolagong d. Françoise Durr,
6–0, 6–4; Julie Heldman (U.S.) and Goolagong d. Patti Hogan (U.S.) and Nell Truman
(Great Britain), 6–3, 6–0.

BILLINGHAM-DEWAR CUP, at Billingham,
England: Jaime Fillol d. Gerald Battrick,
2–6, 6–4, 6–3; Ion Tiriac and Battrick d.
Ray Moore and Fillol, 6–1, 6–4; Virginia
Wade d. Julie Heldman, 4–6, 7–5, 6–3;
Evonne Goolagong and Heldman d. Françoise
Durr and Wade, 6–3, 4–6, 6–2.

QUEENSLAND CHAMPIONSHIP, at Brisbane,
Australia: Mal Anderson (Australia) d. John
Cooper (Australia), 6–4, 6–4, 6–7, 7–6;
Evonne Goolagong d. Helen Gourlay, 6–2,
7–6.

NEW ZEALAND OPEN, at Auckland: Ray
Ruffels d. John Alexander, 6–4, 6–4, 7–6;
Kerry Melville d. Rosemary Casals, 6–4, 6–0;
Billie Jean King and Casals d. Françoise Durr
and Judy Dalton, 7–6, 4–6, 7–5.

BOLOGNA OPEN, at Bologna, Italy: Rod
Laver d. Arthur Ashe, 6–3, 6–4, 6–4; Ken
Rosewall and Fred Stolle d. Robert Maud and
Frew McMillan, 6–7, 6–2, 6–3, 6–3.

STOCKHOLM OPEN, at Stockholm, Sweden:
Arthur Ashe d. Jan Kodes, 6–1, 3–6, 6–2,

1–6, 6–4; Stan Smith and Tom Gorman d.
Bob Lutz and Ashe, 6–3, 6–4.

ABERAVON-DEWAR CUP, at Aberavon, Wales:
Bob Hewitt d. Gerald Battrick, 7–5, 6–4;
Rayno Seegers and Hewitt d. John Clifton
(Great Britain) and John Paish (Great
Britain), 6–2, 6–4; Virginia Wade d. Evonne
Goolagong, 7–6, 6–3; Françoise Durr and
Wade d. Julie Heldman and Goolagong, 7–5,
6–4.

EMBASSY INDOOR CHAMPIONSHIP*, at Wembley, England: Ilie Nastase d. Rod Laver,
3–6, 6–3, 3–6, 6–4, 6–4; Bob Hewitt and
Frew McMillan d. Bill Bowrey and Owen
Davidson, 7–5, 9–7, 6–2; Billie Jean King d.
Françoise Durr, 6–1, 5–7, 7–5; Virginia Wade
and Durr d. Evonne Goolagong and Julie
Heldman, 3–6, 7–5, 6–3.

TORQUAY-DEWAR CUP, at Torquay, England: Bob Hewitt d. Gerald Battrick, 3–6,
6–1, 6–2; Jamie Fillol and Ion Teriac d.
Rayno Seegers and Hewitt, 6–3, 6–4; Evonne
Goolagong d. Françoise Durr, 6–1, 6–0;
Julie Heldman and Goolagong d. Virginia
Wade and Durr, 7–6, 6–4.

DEWAR CUP FINALS, at London, England:
Gerald Battrick d. Bob Hewitt, 0–6, 6–1, 6–3;
Rayno Seegers and Hewitt d. John Paish and
Battrick, 7–6, 6–3; Virginia Wade d. Julie
Heldman, 6–1, 6–3; Evonne Goolagong and
Heldman d. Françoise Durr and Wade, 7–5,
6–4.

Professional World Tournament

While professional tournaments in the
United States started in 1926 (see Section II),
they were played in Europe soon after World
War I. (The French Professional Championship started in 1920.) But the oldest contested
international world tournament is the one held
at Wembley Stadium in England. Here are the
results since it was first played in 1934:

PROFESSIONAL WORLD SINGLES TOURNAMENT

	Winner	Runner-up
1934	H. Ellsworth Vines	Hans Nusslein
1935	H. Ellsworth Vines	William T. Tilden II
1936	H. Ellsworth Vines	William T. Tilden II
1937	Hans Nusslein	William T. Tilden II
1938	Hans Nusslein	William T. Tilden II
1939–45	not held	

1946	not held	
1947	Donald Budge	Robert L. Riggs
1948	Robert L. Riggs	Donald Budge
1949	John A. Kramer	Robert L. Riggs
1950	Richard A. Gonzalez	Welby Van Horn
1951	Richard A. Gonzalez	Francisco Segura
1952	Richard A. Gonzalez	John A. Kramer
1953	Frank A. Sedgman	Richard A. Gonzalez
1954–55	not held	
1956	Richard A. Gonzalez	Frank A. Sedgman
1957	Kenneth Rosewall	Francisco Segura
1958	Frank A. Sedgman	M. Anthony Trabert
1959	Malcolm J. Anderson	Francisco Segura
1960	Kenneth Rosewall	Francisco Segura
1961	Kenneth Rosewall	Lewis Hoad
1962	Kenneth Rosewall	Lewis Hoad
1963	Kenneth Rosewall	Lewis Hoad
1964	Rodney Laver	Kenneth Rosewall
1965	Rodney Laver	Andres Gimeno
1966	Rodney Laver	Kenneth Rosewall
1967	Rodney Laver	Kenneth Rosewall
1968	Kenneth Rosewall	John Newcombe
1969	Kenneth Rosewall	John Newcombe
1970	Rodney Laver	Kenneth Rosewall
1971	Ilie Nastase	Rodney Laver

PROFESSIONAL WORLD DOUBLES TOURNAMENT

1934	William T. Tilden II and H. Ellsworth Vines
1935	William T. Tilden II and H. Ellsworth Vines
1936	William T. Tilden II and H. Ellsworth Vines
1937	William T. Tilden II and Henri Cochet

1938	William T. Tilden II and H. Ellsworth Vines
1939–46	not held
1947	not available
1948	Fred Perry and Donald Budge
1949	Fred Perry and Donald Budge
1950	Richard A. Gonzalez and Donald Budge
1951	Richard A. Gonzalez and Francisco Segura
1952	Richard A. Gonzalez and Francisco Segura
1953	Frank A. Sedgman and Donald Budge
1954–55	not held
1956	Richard A. Gonzalez and M. Anthony Trabert
1957	Lewis Hoad and Kenneth Rosewall
1958	Richard A. Gonzalez and Kenneth Rosewall
1959	Lewis Hoad and M. Anthony Trabert
1960	Frank A. Sedgman and Kenneth Rosewall
1961	Lewis Hoad and Kenneth Rosewall
1962	Lewis Hoad and Kenneth Rosewall
1963	Frank A. Sedgman and Alex Olmedo
1964	Lewis Hoad and Kenneth Rosewall
1965	Rodney Laver and Earl Buchholz
1966	Lewis Hoad and Kenneth Rosewall
1967	Rodney Laver and Andres Gimeno
1968	John Newcombe and Tony Roche
1969	John Newcombe and Tony Roche
1970	John Newcombe and Tony Roche
1971	not held

Andres Gimeno after he won the 1968 Madison Square Garden Challenge Trophy.

International Lawn Tennis Challenge Trophy (Davis Cup)

In 1900 Dwight Filley Davis of St. Louis, Missouri, then a 21-year-old just graduated

The Davis Cup as it appeared in the early 1900's (*left*) and as it appears today (*right*).

International Lawn Tennis Challenge Trophy (Davis Cup) (*cont.*)

from Harvard College, and a leading American player, put into competition the International Lawn Tennis Challenge Trophy. He envisioned a yearly tournament that would advance friendship and goodwill internationally among sportsmen who visited one another's country for matches.

The success of his idea was almost immediate, and quickly the sterling silver bowl became known simply as the Davis Cup. A total of 63 nations have appeared in the competition, but only four have won: The United States (23 times), Australia (22), Great Britain (9), and France (6). Through 1971, the champion nation stood out, meaning that the victor of one year defends the Cup the following year in the grand final called the Challenge Round against the nation which wins its way through an elimination tournament involving four zones: European Zones A and B, American Zone, and Eastern Zone. A challenging nation must usually win five or six matches to reach the Challenge Round. In 1971 the Challenge Round was dropped in favor of all-comers format.

Eight nations, besides the four winners, have appeared in the Challenge Round: Belgium, Japan, Italy, Mexico, Spain, India, Romania, West Germany.

Davis Cup matches were inaugurated in 1900, and with the exception of 1901 and 1910, contests were held annually until 1914, the challenge round of that year being played just prior to the outbreak of World War I. Competition was suspended during the war and was not resumed until 1919. In 1904, 1912, and 1919 the United States did not compete. There was no Cup play during 1940–1945, due to World War II.

British Isles (now Great Britain) was the only nation to challenge for the Cup in 1900, and the first match was played at Dwight Davis's club, Longwood Cricket Club in Boston, August 8, 9, and 10. Davis captained the United States team and won a singles match as well as the decisive doubles (with Holcombe Ward) in a 3–0 triumph. Until 1904 the British were the only challengers. Then France and Belgium entered the tournament. In 1905 the nation that would compile the best record, Australia, came in, known until 1924 as Australasia (a combination of Australia and New Zealand).

The International Lawn Tennis Challenge Trophy is under the jurisdiction of the Davis Cup nations. The representatives of these Davis Cup nations (nations entered in the current competition and/or having played in one or more of the five last preceding competitions and which are still eligible to compete) meet annually in London during the period between June 14 and July 31. Each nation may be represented at the Annual General Meeting (and at any general meeting that may be held from time to time at the discretion of the champion nation or upon request to the champion nation by not less than one-third of the nations and within six months after receipt of such request by the champion nation) by not more than two accredited representatives, and each nation is entitled to one vote.

Davis Cup competition is conducted by the Committee of Management appointed annually by the lawn tennis association (for an example), or corresponding organization of the champion nation. This committee has power to co-opt other persons for the purpose of carrying out all or any of its duties and to set up a Zonal Committee of Management to manage the zones or sections of the competition in the geographical area in which the champion nation is not situated, with a special committee being appointed for the European Zone.

The rules of lawn tennis, as adopted by the International Lawn Tennis Federation, govern Davis Cup play. While having full authority over the Davis Cup competition, the Davis Cup nations recognize the ILTF's interest in all international competition by providing in the Davis Cup regulations that the Committee of Management of the ILTF may nominate an additional representative to membership of the Davis Cup Committee of Management. This representative may attend all meetings of the Davis Cup Committee of Management and the annual general meeting of the Davis Cup nations.

The format is a three-day match of two singles the first day, a doubles the second, and two singles the third.

The challenge round format was dropped after 1971 competition and the all-comers' type has replaced it. Competition is divided into three geographic zones: European Zone (all European nations, Middle East and Africa); American Zone (both North and South America plus the nations of the Caribbean); and Eastern Zone (the nation of Asia, plus Australia and New Zealand). The choice of site for the finals is determined by the ILTF, but no nation may be the host for two consecutive years. The venue date and surface of the court will be decided by the home nation.

Davis Cup Challenge Rounds

1900—UNITED STATES d. BRITISH ISLES, 3–0

Longwood Cricket Club, Boston, Massachusetts

(Captains: British Isles, Arthur W. Gore; U.S., Dwight F. Davis)

British Isles was the only challenger.

Malcolm D. Whitman (U.S.) d. Arthur W. Gore, 6–1, 6–3, 6–2; Dwight F. Davis (U.S.) d. E. D. Black, 4–6, 6–2, 6–4, 6–4; Malcolm D. Whitman (U.S.) d. E. D. Black, unplayed; Dwight F. Davis (U.S.) d. Arthur W. Gore, 9–7, 9–9, unfinished; Holcombe Ward and Dwight F. Davis (U.S.) d. E. D. Black and H. Roper Barrett, 6–4, 6–4, 6–4.

1901—no match

1902—UNITED STATES d. BRITISH ISLES, 3–2

Crescent Athletic Club, Brooklyn, N.Y.

(Captains: British Isles, William H. Collins; U.S., Malcolm D. Whitman).

British Isles was the only challenger.

Reginald F. Doherty (B.I.) d. William A. Larned, 2–6, 3–6, 6–3, 6–4; Malcolm D. Whitman (U.S.) d. Dr. Joshua Pim, 6–1, 6–1, 1–6, 6–0; William A. Larned (U.S.) d. Dr. Joshua Pim, 6–3, 6–2, 6–3; Malcolm D. Whitman (U.S.) d. Reginald F. Doherty, 6–1, 7–5, 6–4; Reginald F. Doherty and Hugh L. Doherty (B.I.) d. Holcombe Ward and Dwight F. Davis, 3–6, 10–8, 6–3, 6–4.

1903—BRITISH ISLES d. UNITED STATES, 4–1

Longwood Cricket Club, Boston, Massachusetts

(Captains: British Isles, William H. Collins; U.S., William A. Larned).

British Isles was the only challenger.

Hugh L. Doherty (B.I.) d. Robert D. Wrenn, 6–0, 6–3, 6–4; William A. Larned (U.S.) d. Reginald F. Doherty, default; Hugh L. Doherty (B.I.) d. William A. Larned, 6–3, 6–8, 6–0, 2–6, 7–5; Reginald F. Doherty (B.I.) d. Robert D. Wrenn, 6–4, 3–6, 6–3, 6–4; Reginald F. Doherty and Hugh L. Doherty (B.I.) d. Robert D. Wrenn and George L. Wrenn, 7–5, 9–7, 2–6, 6–3.

1904—BRITISH ISLES d. BELGIUM, 5–0

Wimbledon, London

(Captains: Belgium, Paul de Borman; British Isles, William H. Collins).

Two challenging nations entered competition.

Davis Cup Challenge Round, 1904 (cont.)

Hugh L. Doherty (B.I.) d. Paul de Borman, 6–4, 6–1, 6–1; Frank L. Riseley (B.I.) d. W. Lemaire, 6–1, 6–4, 6–2; Hugh L. Doherty (B.I.) d. William Lemaire, default; Frank L. Riseley (B.I.) d. Paul de Borman, 4–6, 6–2, 8–6, 7–5; Reginald F. Doherty and Hugh L. Doherty (B.I.) d. Paul de Borman and W. Lemaire, 6–0, 6–1, 6–3.

1905—BRITISH ISLES d. UNITED STATES, 5–0

Wimbledon, London

(Captains: U.S., Paul Dashiell; British Isles, William H. Collins)

Four challenging nations entered competition.

Hugh L. Doherty (B.I.) d. Holcombe Ward, 7–9, 4–6, 6–1, 6–2, 6–0; Sidney H. Smith (B.I.) d. William A. Larned, 6–4, 6–4, 5–7, 6–4; Sidney H. Smith (B.I.) d. William J. Clothier, 4–6, 6–1, 6–4, 6–3; Hugh L. Doherty (B.I.) d. William A. Larned, 6–4, 2–6, 6–8, 6–4, 6–2; Reginald F. Doherty and Hugh L. Doherty, (B.I.) d. Holcombe Ward and Beals C. Wright, 8–10, 6–2, 6–2, 4–6, 8–6.

1906—BRITISH ISLES d. UNITED STATES, 5–0

Wimbledon, London

(Captains: U.S., Beals Wright; British Isles, William H. Collins)

Two challenging nations entered competition.

Sidney H. Smith (B.I.) d. Raymond D. Little, 6–4, 6–4, 6–1; Hugh L. Doherty (B.I.) d. Holcombe Ward, 6–2, 8–6, 6–3; Sidney H. Smith (B.I.) d. Holcombe Ward, 6–1, 6–0, 6–4; Hugh L. Doherty (B.I.) d. Raymond D. Little, 3–6, 6–3, 6–8, 6–1, 6–3; Reginald F. Doherty and Hugh L. Doherty (B.I.) d. Holcombe Ward and Raymond D. Little, 3–6, 11–9, 9–7, 6–1.

1907—AUSTRALASIA d. BRITISH ISLES, 3–2

Wimbledon, London

(Captains: Australasia, Norman E. Brookes; British Isles, S. A. E. Hickson)

Two challenging nations entered competition.

Norman E. Brookes (A) d. Arthur W. Gore, 7–5, 6–1, 7–5; Anthony F. Wilding (A) d. H. Roper Barrett, 1–6, 6–4, 6–3, 7–5; Norman E. Brookes (A) d. H. Roper Barrett, 6–2, 6–0, 6–3; Arthur W. Gore (B.I.) d.

Anthony F. Wilding, 3–6, 6–3, 7–5, 6–2; Arthur W. Gore and H. Roper Barrett (B.I.) d. Norman E. Brookes and Anthony F. Wilding, 3–6, 4–6, 7–5, 6–2, 13–11.

1908—AUSTRALASIA d. UNITED STATES, 3–2

Warehousemen's Grounds, Melbourne, Australia

(Captains: U.S., Beals Wright; Australasia, Norman E. Brookes)

Two challenging nations entered competition.

Norman E. Brookes (A) d. Fred B. Alexander, 5–7, 9–7, 6–2, 4–6, 6–3; Beals C. Wright (U.S.) d. Anthony F. Wilding, 3–6, 7–5, 6–3, 6–1; Anthony F. Wilding (A) d. Fred B. Alexander, 6–3, 6–4, 6–1; Beals C. Wright (U.S.) d. Norman E. Brookes, 0–6, 3–6, 7–5, 6–2, 12–10; Norman E. Brookes and Anthony F. Wilding (A) d. Beals C. Wright and Fred B. Alexander, 6–4, 6–2, 5–7, 1–6, 6–4.

1909—AUSTRALASIA d. UNITED STATES, 5–0

Double Bay Grounds, Sydney, Australia

(Captains: U.S., Maurice E. McLoughlin; Australasia, Norman E. Brookes)

Two challenging nations entered competition.

Norman E. Brookes (A) d. Maurice E. McLoughlin, 6–2, 6–2, 6–4; Anthony F. Wilding (A) d. Melville H. Long, 6–2, 7–5, 6–1; Norman E. Brookes (A) d. Melville H. Long, 6–4, 7–5, 8–6; Anthony F. Wilding (A) d. Maurice E. McLoughlin, 3–6, 8–6, 6–2, 6–3; Norman E. Brookes and A. F. Wilding (A) d. Maurice E. McLoughlin and Melville H. Long, 12–10, 9–7, 6–3.

1910—no match

1911—AUSTRALASIA d. UNITED STATES, 5–0

Hagley Park, Christchurch, New Zealand

(Captains: U.S., William A. Larned; Australasia, Norman E. Brookes)

Two challenging nations entered competition.

Norman E. Brookes (A) d. Beals C. Wright, 6–4, 2–6, 6–3, 6–3; Rodney W. Heath (A) d. William A. Larned, 2–6, 6–1, 7–5, 6–2; Norman E. Brookes (A) d. Maurice E. McLoughlin, 6–4, 3–6, 4–6, 6–3, 6–4; Rodney W. Heath (A) d. Beals C. Wright. Default. Norman E. Brookes and Alfred W. Dunlop (A) d. Beals C. Wright and Maurice E. McLoughlin, 6–4, 5–7, 7–5, 6–4.

1912—BRITISH ISLES d. AUSTRALIA, 3–2

Warehousemen's Grounds, Melbourne, Australia

(Captains: British Isles, Charles P. Dixon; Australasia, Norman E. Brookes)

Two challenging nations entered competition.

J. Cecil Parke (B.I.) d. Norman E. Brookes, 8–6, 6–3, 5–7, 6–2; Charles P. Dixon (B.I.) d. Rodney W. Heath, 5–7, 6–4, 6–4, 6–4; J. Cecil Parke (B.I.) d. Rodney W. Heath, 6–2, 6–4, 6–4; Norman E. Brookes (A) d. Charles P. Dixon, 6–2, 6–4, 6–4; Norman E. Brookes and Alfred W. Dunlop (A) d. J. Cecil Parke and Alfred E. Beamish, 6–4, 6–1, 7–5.

1913—UNITED STATES d. BRITISH ISLES, 3–2

Wimbledon, London

(Captains: U.S., Harold H. Hackett; British Isles, Roger J. McNair)

Seven challenging nations entered competition.

J. Cecil Parke (B.I.) d. Maurice E. McLoughlin, 8–10, 7–5, 6–4, 1–6, 7–5; R. Norris Williams II (U.S.) d. Charles P. Dixon, 8–6, 3–6, 6–2, 1–6, 7–5; Maurice E. McLoughlin (U.S.) d. Charles P. Dixon, 8–6, 6–3, 6–2; J. Cecil Parke (B.I.) d. R. Norris Williams II, 6–2, 5–7, 5–7, 6–4, 6–2; Harold H. Hackett and Maurice E. McLoughlin (U.S.) d. H. Roper Barrett and Charles P. Dixon, 5–7, 6–1, 2–6, 7–5, 6–4.

1914—AUSTRALASIA d. UNITED STATES, 3–2

West Side Tennis Club, Forest Hills, N.Y.

(Captains: Australasia, Norman E. Brookes; U.S., Maurice E. McLoughlin)

Six challenging nations entered competition.

The 1920 United States Davis Cup team: (*left to right*) William M. Johnston, R. N. Williams II, Samuel Hardy (captain), William T. Tilden II, Charles S. Garland, and Watson Washburn.

Davis Cup Challenge Round, 1914 (cont.)

Norman E. Brookes (A) d. R. Norris Williams II, 6–1, 6–2, 8–10, 6–3; Maurice E. McLoughlin (U.S.) d. Anthony F. Wilding, 6–2, 6–3, 2–6, 6–2; Anthony F. Wilding (A) d. R. Norris Williams II, 7–5, 6–2, 6–3; Maurice E. McLoughlin (U.S.) d. Norman E. Brookes, 17–15, 6–3, 6–3; Norman E. Brookes and A. F. Wilding (A) d. Maurice E. McLoughlin and Thomas C. Bundy, 6–3, 8–6, 9–7.

1915–18—no match

1919—AUSTRALASIA d. BRITISH ISLES, 4–1
> Double Bay Grounds, Sydney, Australia
> (Captains: British Isles, Algernon R. F. Kingscote; Australasia, Norman E. Brookes).
> Four challenging nations entered competition.

Gerald L. Patterson (A) d. Arthur H. Lowe, 6–4, 6–3, 2–6, 6–3; Algernon R. F. Kingscote (B.I.) d. James O. Anderson, 7–5, 6–2, 6–4; Gerald Patterson (A) d. Algernon R. F. Kingscote, 6–4, 6–4, 8–6; James O. Anderson (A) d. Arthur H. Lowe, 6–4, 5–7, 6–3, 4–6, 12–10; Norman E. Brookes and Gerald L. Patterson (A) d. Algernon R. F. Kingscote and Alfred E. Beamish, 6–0, 6–0, 6–2.

1920—UNITED STATES d. AUSTRALASIA, 5–0
> Domain Cricket Ground, Auckland, New Zealand
> (Captains: U.S., Sam Hardy; Australasia, Norman E. Brookes).
> Five challenging nations entered competition.

William T. Tilden II (U.S.) d. Norman E. Brookes, 10–8, 6–4, 1–6, 6–4, William M. Johnston (U.S.) d. Gerald L. Patterson, 6–3, 6–1, 6–1; William T. Tilden II (U.S.) d. Gerald L. Patterson, 5–7, 6–2, 6–3, 6–3; William M. Johnston (U.S.) d. Norman E. Brookes, 5–7, 7–5, 6–3; William T. Tilden II and William M. Johnston (U.S.) d. Norman E. Brookes and Gerald L. Patterson, 4–6, 6–4, 6–0, 6–4.

1921—UNITED STATES d. JAPAN, 5–0
> West Side Tennis Club, Forest Hills, N.Y.
> (Captains: Japan, Ichiya Kumagae; U.S., R. Norris Williams II)
> Eleven challenging nations entered competition

William T. Tilden II (U.S.) d. Zenzo Shimizu, 5–7, 4–6, 7–5, 6–2, 6–1; William M. Johnston (U.S.) d. Ichiya Kumagae, 6–2, 6–4, 6–2; William T. Tilden II (U.S.) d. Ichiya Kumagae, 9–7, 6–4, 6–1; William M. Johnston (U.S.) d. Zenzo Shimizu, 6–3, 5–7, 6–2, 6–4; R. Norris Williams II and Watson M. Washburn (U.S.) d. Zenzo Shimizu and Ichiya Kumagae, 6–2, 7–5, 4–6, 7–5.

1922—UNITED STATES d. AUSTRALASIA, 4–1
> West Side Tennis Club, Forest Hills, N.Y.
> (Captains: Australasia, James O. Anderson; U.S., R. Norris Williams II)
> Ten challenging nations entered competition.

William T. Tilden II (U.S.) d. Gerald L. Patterson, 7–5, 10–8, 6–0; William M. Johnston (U.S.) d. James O. Anderson, 6–1, 6–2, 6–3; William M. Johnston (U.S.) d. Gerald L. Patterson, 6–2, 6–2, 6–1; William T. Tilden II (U.S.) d. James O. Anderson, 6–4, 5–7, 3–6, 6–4, 6–2; Gerald L. Patterson and Pat O'Hara Wood (A) d. William T. Tilden II and Vincent Richards, 6–3, 6–0, 6–4.

1923—UNITED STATES d. AUSTRALASIA, 4–1
> West Side Tennis Club, Forest Hills, N.Y.
> (Captains: Australasia, Gerald L. Patterson; U.S., R. Norris Williams II)
> Sixteen challenging nations entered competition.

James O. Anderson (A) d. William M. Johnston, 4–6, 6–2, 2–6, 7–5, 6–2; William T. Tilden II (U.S.) d. John B. Hawkes, 6–4, 6–2, 6–1; William M. Johnston (U.S.) d. John B. Hawkes, 6–0, 6–2, 6–1; William T. Tilden II (U.S.) d. James O. Anderson, 6–2, 6–3, 1–6, 7–5; William T. Tilden II and R. Norris Williams II (U.S.) d. James O. Anderson and John B. Hawkes, 17–15, 11–13, 2–6, 6–3, 6–2.

1924—UNITED STATES d. AUSTRALASIA, 5–0
> Germantown Cricket Club, Philadelphia, Pa.
> (Captains: Australasia, Gerald L. Patterson; U.S., R. Norris Williams II)
> Twenty-two nations entered competition.

William T. Tilden II (U.S.) d. Gerald L. Patterson, 6–4, 6–2, 6–2; Vincent Richards (U.S.) d. Pat O'Hara Wood, 6–3, 6–2, 6–4; William T. Tilden II (U.S.) d. Pat O'Hara

President Calvin Coolidge making the initial draw in the 1924 Davis Cup drawings in the presence of diplomatic representatives and Dwight F. Davis on the White House lawn.

Wood, 6–2, 6–1, 6–1; Vincent Richards (U.S.) d. Gerald L. Patterson, 6–3, 7–5, 6–4; William T. Tilden II and William M. Johnston (U.S.) d. Gerald L. Patterson and Pat O'Hara Wood, 5–7, 6–3, 6–4, 6–1.

1925—UNITED STATES d. FRANCE, 5–0

    Germantown Cricket Club, Philadelphia, Pa.

    (Captains: France, Max Décugis; U.S., R. Norris Williams II)

    Twenty-two challenging nations entered competition.

William T. Tilden II (U.S.) d. Jean Borotra, 4–6, 6–0, 2–6, 9–7, 6–4; William M. Johnston (U.S.) d. Jean René Lacoste, 6–1, 6–8, 6–3; William T. Tilden II (U.S.) d. Jean René Lacoste, 3–6, 10–12, 8–6, 7–5, 6–2; William M. Johnston (U.S.) d. Jean Borotra, 6–1, 6–4, 6–0; Vincent Richards and R. Norris Williams II (U.S.) d. Jean René Lacoste and Jean Borotra, 6–4, 6–4, 6–3.

1926—UNITED STATES d. FRANCE, 4–1

    Germantown Cricket Club, Philadelphia, Pa.

    (Captains: France, Pierre Gillou; U.S., R. Norris Williams II)

    Twenty-three challenging nations entered competition.

William M. Johnston (U.S.) d. Jean René Lacoste, 6–0, 6–4, 0–6, 6–0; William T. Tilden II (U.S.) d. Jean Borotra, 6–2, 6–3, 6–3; William M. Johnston (U.S.) d. Jean Borotra, 8–6, 6–4, 9–7; Jean René Lacoste (F) d. William T. Tilden II, 4–6, 6–4, 8–6, 8–6; R. Norris Williams II and Vincent Richards (U.S.) d. Henri Cochet and Jacques Brugnon, 6–4, 6–4, 6–2.

1927—FRANCE d. UNITED STATES, 3–2

    Germantown Cricket Club, Philadelphia, Pa.

    (Captains: France, Pierre Gillou; U.S., Charles Garland)

    Twenty-three challenging nations entered competition.

Jean René Lacoste (F) d. William M. Johnston, 6–3, 6–2, 6–2; William T. Tilden II (U.S.) d. Henri Cochet, 6–4, 2–6, 6–2, 8–6; Jean René Lacoste (F) d. William T. Tilden II, 6–3, 4–6, 6–3, 6–2; Henri Cochet (F) d. William M. Johnston, 6–4, 4–6, 6–2, 6–4; William T. Tilden II and Francis T. Hunter (U.S.) d. Jean Borotra and Jacques Brugnon, 3–6, 6–3, 6–3, 4–6, 6–0.

The 1928 United States Davis Cup team sails for the Inter-Zone matches aboard the *Ile de France: (left to right)* Wilbur Coen, George Lott, Samuel Peacock (manager), Bill Tilden, and John Hennessey. In the Challenge Round, Francis T. Hunter replaced Coen on the team. Incidentally, Coen was the youngest American player to play in a Davis Cup match.

1928—FRANCE d. UNITED STATES, 4–1
Stade Roland Garros, Auteuil, Paris
(Captains: U.S., Joseph Wear; France, Pierre Gillou)
Thirty-three challenging nations entered competition.
William T. Tilden II (U.S.) d. Jean René Lacoste, 1–6, 6–4, 6–4, 2–6, 6–3; Henri Cochet (F) d. John F. Hennessey, 5–7, 9–7, 6–3, 6–0; Henri Cochet (F) d. William T. Tilden II, 9–7, 8–6, 6–4; Jean René Lacoste (F) d. John F. Hennessey, 4–6, 6–1, 7–5, 6–3; Henri Cochet and Jean Borotra (F) d. William T. Tilden II and Francis T. Hunter, 6–4, 6–8, 7–5, 4–6, 6–2.

1929—FRANCE d. UNITED STATES, 3–2
Stade Roland Garros, Auteuil, Paris
(Captains: U.S., Fitz-Eugene Dixon;

France, Pierre Gillou)
Twenty-eight challenging nations entered competition.
Henri Cochet (F) d. William T. Tilden II, 6–3, 6–1, 6–2; Jean Borotra (F) d. George M. Lott, Jr., 6–1, 3–6, 6–4, 7–5; William T. Tilden II (U.S.) d. Jean Borotra, 4–6, 6–1, 6–4, 7–5; Henri Cochet (F) d. George M. Lott, Jr., 6–1, 3–6, 6–0, 6–3; John Van Ryn and Wilmer L. Allison (U.S.) d. Henri Cochet and Jean Borotra, 6–1, 8–6, 6–4.

1930—FRANCE d. UNITED STATES, 4–1
Stade Roland Garros, Auteuil, Paris
(Captains: U.S., Fitz-Eugene Dixon; France, Pierre Gillou)
Twenty-seven challenging nations entered competition.
William T. Tilden II (U.S.) d. Jean Borotra,

2–6, 7–5, 6–4, 7–5; Henri Cochet (F) d. George M. Lott, Jr., 6–4, 6–2, 6–2; Jean Borotra (F) d. George M. Lott, Jr., 5–7, 6–3, 2–6, 6–2, 8–6; Henri Cochet (F) d. William T. Tilden II, 4–6, 6–3, 6–1, 7–5; Henri Cochet and Jacques Brugnon (F) d. Wilmer L. Allison and John Van Ryn, 6–3, 7–5, 1–6, 6–2.

1931—FRANCE d. GREAT BRITAIN, 3–2

Stade Roland Garros, Auteuil, Paris
(Captains: Britain, Herbert Roper Barrett; France, Jean René Lacoste)
Twenty-nine challenging nations entered competition.

Henri Cochet (F) d. Henry W. Austin, 3–6, 11–9, 6–2, 6–4; Frederick J. Perry (G.B.) d. Jean Borotra, 4–6, 10–8, 6–0, 4–6, 6–4; Henry W. Austin (G.B.) d. Jean Borotra, 7–5, 6–3, 3–6, 7–5; Henri Cochet (F) d. Frederick J. Perry, 6–4, 1–6, 9–7, 6–3; Henri Cochet and Jacques Brugnon (F) d. George P. Hughes and Charles H. Kingsley, 6–1, 5–7, 6–3, 8–6.

1932—FRANCE d. UNITED STATES, 3–2

Stade Roland Garros, Auteuil, Paris
(Captains: U.S., Bernon Prentice; France, Jean René Lacoste)
Twenty-eight challenging nations entered competition.

Jean Borotra (F) d. H Ellsworth Vines, Jr., 6–4, 6–2, 3–6, 6–4; Henri Cochet (F) d. Wilmer L. Allison, 5–7, 7–5, 7–5, 6–2; Jean Borotra (F) d. Wilmer L. Allison, 1–6, 3–6, 6–4, 6–2, 7–5; H. Ellsworth Vines, Jr. (U.S.) d. Henri Cochet, 4–6, 0–6, 7–5, 8–6, 6–2; Wilmer L. Allison and John Van Ryn (U.S.) d. Henri Cochet and Jacques Brugnon, 6–3, 11–13, 7–5, 4–6, 6–4.

1933—GREAT BRITAIN d. FRANCE, 3–2

Stade Roland Garros, Auteuil, Paris
(Captains: Britain, Herbert Roper Barrett; France, Jean René Lacoste)
Twenty-nine challenging nations entered competition.

Henry W. Austin (G.B.) d. André Merlin, 6–3, 6–4, 6–0; Frederick J. Perry (G.B.) d. Henri Cochet, 8–10, 6–4, 8–6, 3–6, 6–1; Henri Cochet (F) d. Henry W. Austin, 5–7,

The 1932 United States Davis Cup team: (*left to right*) Frank Shields, Wilmer Allison, Bernon Prentice (captain), John Van Ryn, Ellsworth Vines, Jr.

The 1937 United States Davis Cup team: (*left to right*) Wayne Sabin, Bryan (Bitsy) Grant, Donald Budge, Gene Mako, Walter Pate (captain), Frank Parker.

Davis Cup Challenge Round, 1933 (*cont.*)
6–4, 4–6, 6–4, 6–4; Frederick J. Perry (G.B.) d. André Merlin, 4–6, 8–6, 6–2, 7–5; Jean Borotra and Jacques Brugnon (F) d. George P. Hughes and Harold G. N. Lee, 6–3, 8–6, 6–2.

1934—GREAT BRITAIN d. UNITED STATES, 4–1
    Wimbledon, London
    (Captains: U.S., R. Norris Williams II; Britain, Herbert Roper Barrett)
    Twenty-six challenging nations entered competition.

Henry W. Austin (G.B.) d. Francis X. Shields, 6–4, 6–4, 6–1; Frederick J. Perry (G.B.) d. Sidney B. Wood, Jr., 6–1, 4–6, 5–7, 6–0, 6–3; Frederick J. Perry (G.B.) d. Francis X. Shields, 6–4, 4–6, 6–2, 15–13; Henry W. Austin (G.B.) d. Sidney B. Wood, Jr., 6–4, 6–0, 6–8, 6–3; George M. Lott, Jr., and Lester R. Stoefen (U.S.) d. George P. Hughes and Harold G. N. Lee, 7–5, 6–0, 4–6, 9–7.

1935—GREAT BRITAIN d. UNITED STATES, 5–0
    Wimbledon, London
    (Captains: U.S., Joseph Wear; Britain, Herbert Roper Barrett)
    Twenty-seven challenging nations entered competition.

Henry W. Austin (G.B.) d. Wilmer L. Allison, 6–2, 2–6, 4–6, 6–3, 7–5; Frederick J. Perry

(G.B.) d. J. Donald Budge, 6–0, 6–8, 6–3, 6–4; Henry W. Austin (G.B.) d. J. Donald Budge, 6–2, 6–4, 6–8, 7–5; Frederick J. Perry (G.B.) d. Wilmer L. Allison, 4–6, 6–4, 7–5, 6–3; George P. Hughes and Charles R. D. Tuckey (G.B.) d. Wilmer L. Allison and John Van Ryn, 6–2, 1–6, 6–8, 6–3, 6–3.

1936—GREAT BRITAIN d. AUSTRALIA, 3–2
Wimbledon, London
(Captains: Australia, Cliff Sproule; Britain, Herbert Roper Barrett)
Twenty-three challenging nations entered competition.

Henry W. Austin (G.B.) d. John H. Crawford, 4–6, 6–3, 6–1, 6–1; Frederick J. Perry (G.B.) d. Adrian K. Quist, 6–1, 4–6, 7–5, 6–2; Adrian K. Quist (A) d. Henry W. Austin, 6–4, 3–6, 7–5, 6–3; Frederick J. Perry (G.B.) d. John H. Crawford, 6–2, 6–3, 6–3; John H. Crawford and Adrian K. Quist (A) d. George P. Hughes and Charles R. D. Tuckey, 6–4, 2–6, 7–5, 10–8.

1937—UNITED STATES d. GREAT BRITAIN, 4–1
Wimbledon, London
(Captains: U.S., Walter Pate; Britain, Herbert Roper Barrett)
Twenty-four challenging nations entered competition.

Henry W. Austin (G.B.) d. Frank A. Parker, 6–3, 6–2, 7–5; J. Donald Budge (U.S.) d. Charles E. Hare, 15–13, 6–1, 6–2; Frank A. Parker (U.S.) d. Charles E. Hare, 6–2, 6–4, 6–2; J. Donald Budge (U.S.) d. Henry W. Austin, 8–6, 3–6, 6–4, 6–3; J. Donald Budge and C. Gene Mako (U.S.) d. Charles R. D. Tuckey and Frank H. D. Wilde, 6–3, 7–5, 7–9, 12–10.

1938—UNITED STATES d. AUSTRALIA, 3–2
Germantown Cricket Club, Philadelphia, Pa.
(Captains: Australia, Harry Hopman; U.S., Walter Pate)
Twenty-three challenging nations entered competition.

Robert L. Riggs (U.S.) d. Adrian K. Quist, 4–6, 6–0, 8–6, 6–1; J. Donald Budge (U.S.) d. John E. Bromwich, 6–2, 6–3, 4–6, 7–5; J. Donald Budge (U.S.) d. Adrian K. Quist, 8–6, 6–1, 6–2; John E. Bromwich (A) d. Robert L. Riggs, 6–4, 4–6, 6–0, 6–2; Adrian K. Quist and John E. Bromwich (A) d. J. Donald Budge and C. Gene Mako, 0–6, 6–3, 6–4, 6–2.

1939—AUSTRALIA d. UNITED STATES, 3–2
Merion Cricket Club, Haverford, Pa.
(Captains: Australia, Harry Hopman; U.S., Walter Pate)
Twenty-five challenging nations entered competition.

Robert L. Riggs (U.S.) d. John E. Bromwich, 6–4, 6–0, 7–5; Frank A. Parker (U.S.) d. Adrian K. Quist, 6–3, 6–4, 1–6, 7–5; Adrian K. Quist (A) d. Robert L. Riggs, 6–1, 6–4, 3–6, 3–6, 6–4; John E. Bromwich (A) d. Frank A. Parker, 6–0, 6–3, 6–1; Adrian K. Quist and John E. Bromwich (A) d. John A. Kramer and Joseph R. Hunt, 5–7, 6–2, 7–5, 6–2.

1940–1945—no matches, World War II

1946—UNITED STATES d. AUSTRALIA, 5–0
Kooyong Tennis Club, Melbourne, Australia
(Captains: U.S., Walter Pate; Australia, Gerald L. Patterson)
Eighteen challenging nations entered competition.

Frederick R. Schroeder, Jr. (U.S.) d. John E. Bromwich, 3–6, 6–1, 6–2, 0–6, 6–3; John A. Kramer (U.S.) d. Dinny Pails, 8–6, 6–2, 9–7; John A. Kramer (U.S.) d. John E. Bromwich, 8–6, 6–4, 6–4; Gardnar Mulloy (U.S.) d. Dinny Pails, 6–3, 6–3, 6–4; John A. Kramer, and Frederick R. Schroeder, Jr. (U.S.) d. John E. Bromwich and Adrian K. Quist, 6–2, 7–5, 6–4.

1947—UNITED STATES d. AUSTRALIA, 4–1
West Side Tennis Club, Forest Hills, N.Y.
(Captains: Australia, Roy Cowling; U.S., Alrick Man)
Twenty-one challenging nations entered competition.

John A. Kramer (U.S.) d. Dinny Pails, 6–2, 6–1, 6–2; Frederick R. Schroeder, Jr. (U.S.) d. John E. Bromwich, 6–4, 5–7, 6–3, 6–4; Frederick R. Schroeder, Jr. (U.S.) d. Dinny Pails, 6–3, 8–6, 4–6, 9–11, 10–8; John A. Kramer (U.S.) d. John E. Bromwich, 6–3, 6–2, 6–2; John E. Bromwich and Colin Long (A) d. John A. Kramer and Frederick A. Schroeder, Jr., 6–4, 2–6, 6–2, 6–4.

1948—UNITED STATES d. AUSTRALIA, 5–0
West Side Tennis Club, Forest Hills, N.Y.
(Captains: Australia, Adrian K. Quist; U.S., Alrick Man).

The 1946 United States Davis Cup team: (*left to right*) Gardnar Mulloy, William Talbert, Walter Pate (captain), Frank Parker, and Jack Kramer.

Davis Cup Challenge Round, 1948 (*cont.*)

Twenty-eight challenging nations entered competition.

Frank A. Parker (U.S.) d. O. William Sidwell, 6–4, 6–4, 6–4; Frederick R. Schroeder, Jr. (U.S.) d. O. William Sidwell, 6–2, 6–1, 6–1; Frank A. Parker (U.S.) d. Adrian K. Quist, 6–2, 6–2, 6–3; Frederick R. Schroeder, Jr. (U.S.) d. Adrian K. Quist, 6–3, 4–6, 6–0, 6–0; William F. Talbert and Gardnar Mulloy (U.S.) d. O. William Sidwell and Colin Long, 8–6, 9–7, 2–6, 7–5.

1949—UNITED STATES d. AUSTRALIA, 4–1

West Side Tennis Club, Forest Hills, N.Y.

(Captains: Australia, John Bromwich; U.S., Alrick Man)

Twenty-six challenging nations entered competition.

Frederick R. Schroeder, Jr. (U.S.) d. O. William Sidwell, 6–1, 5–7, 4–6, 6–2, 6–3; Richard Gonzalez (U.S.) d. Frank Sedgman, 8–6, 6–4, 9–7; Frederick R. Schroeder, Jr. (U.S.) d. Frank Sedgman, 6–4, 6–3, 6–3; Richard Gonzalez (U.S.) d. O. William Sidwell, 6–1, 6–3, 6–3; O. William Sidwell and John Bromwich (A) d. William F. Talbert and

Gardnar Mulloy, 3–6, 4–6, 10–8, 9–7, 9–7.

1950—AUSTRALIA d. UNITED STATES, 4–1

West Side Tennis Club, Forest Hills, N.Y.

(Captains: Australia, Harry Hopman; U.S., Alrick Man)

Twenty-five challenging nations entered competition.

Frank Sedgman (A) d. Thomas P. Brown, Jr. 6–0, 8–6, 9–7; Kenneth McGregor (A) d. Frederick R. Schroeder, Jr., 13–11, 6–3, 6–4; Frank Sedgman (A) d. Frederick R. Schroeder, Jr., 6–2, 6–2, 6–2; Thomas P. Brown, Jr. (U.S.) d. Kenneth McGregor, 9–11, 8–10, 11–9, 6–1, 6–4; Frank Sedgman and John Bromwich (A) d. Frederick R. Schroeder, Jr., and Gardnar Mulloy, 4–6, 6–4, 6–2, 4–6, 6–4.

1951—AUSTRALIA d. UNITED STATES, 3–2

White City Courts, Sydney, Australia

(Captains: U.S. Frank Shields; Australia, Harry Hopman)

Twenty-six challenging nations entered competition.

E. Victor Seixas, Jr., (U.S.) d. Mervyn Rose, 6–3, 6–4, 9–7; Frank Sedgman (A) d. Frederick R. Schroeder, Jr., 6–4, 6–3, 4–6, 6–4;

Frederick R. Schroeder, Jr. (U.S.) d. Mervyn Rose, 6–4, 13–11, 7–5; Frank Sedgman (A) d. E. Victor Seixas, Jr., 6–4, 6–2, 6–2; Kenneth McGregor and Frank Sedgman (A) d. Frederick R. Schroeder, Jr. and Tony Trabert, 6–2, 9–7, 6–3.

1952—AUSTRALIA d. UNITED STATES, 4–1
> Memorial Drive Courts, Adelaide, Australia
> (Captains: U.S., E. Victor Seixas, Jr.; Australia, Harry Hopman)
> Twenty-seven challenging nations entered competition.

Frank Sedgman (A) d. E. Victor Seixas, Jr., 6–3, 6–4, 6–2; Kenneth McGregor (A) d. Tony Trabert, 11–9, 6–4, 6–1; Frank Sedgman (A) d. Tony Trabert, 7–5, 6–4, 10–8; E. Victor Seixas, Jr. (U.S.) d. Kenneth McGregor, 6–3, 8–6, 6–8, 6–3; Kenneth McGregor and Frank Sedgman (A) d. E. Victor Seixas, Jr., and Tony Trabert, 6–3, 6–4, 1–6, 6–2.

1953—AUSTRALIA d. UNITED STATES, 3–2
> Kooyong Stadium, Melbourne, Australia
> (Captains: U.S., William Talbert; Australia, Harry Hopman)
> Twenty-eight challenging nations entered competition.

Lewis Hoad (A) d. E. Victor Seixas, Jr., 6–4, 6–2, 6–3; Tony Trabert (U.S.) d. Kenneth Rosewall, 6–3, 6–4, 6–4; Lewis Hoad (A) d. Tony Trabert, 13–11, 6–3, 2–6, 3–6, 7–5; Kenneth Rosewall (A) d. E. Victor Seixas, Jr., 6–2, 2–6, 6–3, 6–4; E. Victor Seixas, Jr. and Tony Trabert (U.S.) d. Rex Hartwig and Lewis Hoad, 6–2, 6–4, 6–4.

1954—UNITED STATES d. AUSTRALIA, 3–2
> White City Stadium, Sydney, Australia
> (Captains: U.S., William Talbert; Australia, Harry Hopman)
> Thirty challenging nations entered competition.

Tony Trabert (U.S.) d. Lewis Hoad, 6–4, 2–6, 12–10, 6–3; E. Victor Seixas, Jr. (U.S.) d. Kenneth Rosewall, 8–6, 6–8, 6–4, 6–3; Kenneth Rosewall (A) d. Tony Trabert, 9–7, 7–5, 6–3; Rex Hartwig (A) d. E. Victor Seixas, Jr., 4–6, 6–3, 6–2, 6–3; E. Victor Seixas, Jr. and Tony Trabert (U.S.) d. Lewis

Frank Parker (*left*) of the United States defeats Billy Sidwell (Australia) in the first match of the 1948 challenge round. The United States swept all matches.

Davis Cup Challenge Round, 1954 (*cont.*)
Hoad and Kenneth Rosewall, 6–2, 4–6, 6–2, 10–8.
1955—AUSTRALIA d. UNITED STATES, 5–0
> West Side Tennis Club, Forest Hills, N.Y.
> (Captains: Australia, Harry Hopman; U.S., William Talbert)
> Thirty-four challenging nations entered competition.

Kenneth Rosewall (A) d. E. Victor Seixas, Jr., 6–3, 10–8, 4–6, 6–2; Lewis Hoad (A) d. Tony Trabert, 4–6, 6–3, 6–3, 8–6; Lewis Hoad (A) d. E. Victor Seixas, Jr., 7–9, 6–1, 6–4; Kenneth Rosewall (A) d. Hamilton Richardson, 6–4, 3–6, 6–1, 6–4; Lewis Hoad and Rex Hartwig (A) d. Tony Trabert and E. Victor Seixas, Jr., 12–14, 6–4, 6–3, 3–6, 7–5.
1956—AUSTRALIA d. UNITED STATES, 5–0
> Memorial Drive Stadium, Adelaide, Australia
> (Captains: U.S., William Talbert; Australia, Harry Hopman)
> Thirty-two challenging nations entered competition.

Lewis Hoad (A) d. Herbert Flam, 6–2, 6–3, 6–3; Kenneth Rosewall (A) d. E. Victor Seixas, Jr., 6–1, 6–4, 4–6, 6–1; Kenneth Rosewall (A) d. Samuel Giammalva, 4–6, 6–1, 8–6, 7–5; Lewis Hoad (A) d. E. Victor Seixas, Jr., 6–2, 7–5, 6–3; Lewis Hoad and Kenneth Rosewall (A) d. Samuel Giammalva and E. Victor Seixas, Jr., 1–6, 6–1, 7–5, 6–4.
1957—AUSTRALIA d. UNITED STATES, 3–2
> Kooyong Stadium, Melbourne, Australia
> (Captains: U.S., William Talbert; Australia, Harry Hopman)
> Thirty-five challenging nations entered competition.

Malcolm J. Anderson (A) d. Barry MacKay, 6–3, 7–5, 3–6, 7–9, 6–3; Ashley J. Cooper (A) d. E. Victor Seixas, Jr., 3–6, 7–5, 6–1, 1–6, 6–3; E. Victor Seixas, Jr. (U.S.) d. Malcolm I. Anderson, 6–3, 4–6, 6–3, 0–6, 13–11; Barry MacKay (U.S.) d. Ashley J. Cooper, 6–4, 1–6, 4–6, 6–4, 6–3; Malcolm J. Anderson and Mervyn Rose (A) d. Barry MacKay and E. Victor Seixas, Jr., 6–4, 6–4, 8–6.
1958—UNITED STATES d. AUSTRALIA, 3–2
> Milton Courts, Brisbane, Australia
> (Captains: U.S., Perry Jones; Australia, Harry Hopman)

Thirty-six challenging nations entered competition.

Alejandro Olmedo (U.S.) d. Malcolm J. Anderson, 8–6, 2–6, 9–7, 8–6; Ashley J. Cooper (A) d. Barry MacKay, 4–6, 6–3, 6–2, 6–4; Alejandro Olmedo (U.S.) d. Ashley J. Cooper, 6–3, 4–6, 6–4, 8–6; Malcolm J. Anderson (A) d. Barry MacKay, 7–5, 13–11, 11–9; Alejandro Olmedo and Hamilton Richardson (U.S.) d. Malcolm J. Anderson and Neale Fraser, 10–12, 3–6, 16–14, 6–3, 7–5.
1959—AUSTRALIA d. UNITED STATES, 3–2
> West Side Tennis Club, Forest Hills, N.Y.
> (Captains: Australia, Harry Hopman; U.S., Perry Jones)
> Thirty-nine challenging nations entered competition.

Neale A. Fraser (A) d. Alejandro Olmedo, 8–6, 6–8, 6–4, 8–6; Barry MacKay (U.S.) d. Rodney Laver, 7–5, 6–4, 6–1; Alejandro Olmedo (U.S.) d. Rodney Laver, 9–7, 4–6, 10–8, 12–10; Neale A. Fraser (A) d. Barry MacKay, 8–6, 3–6, 6–2, 6–4; Neale A. Fraser and Roy Emerson (A) d. Alejandro Olmedo and Earl Buchholz, Jr., 7–5, 7–5, 6–4.
1960—AUSTRALIA d. ITALY, 4–1
> White City Stadium, Sydney, Australia
> (Captains: Italy, Vanni Canapele; Australia, Harry Hopman)
> Forty challenging nations entered competition.

Neale A. Fraser (A) d. Orlando Sirola, 4–6, 6–3, 6–3, 6–3; Rodney G. Laver (A) d. Nicola Pietrangeli, 8–6, 6–4, 6–3; Rodney G. Laver (A) d. Orlando Sirola, 9–7, 6–2, 6–3; Nicola Pietrangeli (I) d. Neale A. Fraser, 11–9, 6–3, 1–6, 6–2; Neale A. Fraser and Roy Emerson (A) d. Nicola Pietrangeli and Orlando Sirola, 10–8, 5–7, 6–2, 6–4.
1961—AUSTRALIA d. ITALY, 5–0
> Kooyong Stadium, Melbourne, Australia
> (Captains: Italy, Vanni Canapele; Australia, Harry Hopman)
> Forty-two challenging nations entered competition.

Roy Emerson (A) d. Nicola Pietrangeli, 8–6, 6–4, 6–0; Rodney G. Laver (A) d. Orlando Sirola, 6–1, 6–4, 6–3; Rodney G. Laver (A) d. Nicola Pietrangeli, 6–3, 3–6, 4–6, 6–3, 8–6; Roy Emerson (A) d. Orlando Sirola, 6–3, 6–3, 4–6, 6–2; Neale A. Fraser and Roy

The 1963 United States Davis Cup team presents the Cup to President Johnson. (*left to right*) Bob, Kelleher (captain), Dennis Ralston, Chuck McKinley, the President, Mrs. McKinley, Marty Riessen, and Edward Turville, President of USLTA. Two other members of the team, Frank Froehling and Gene Scott, were unable to be present at the ceremony.

Emerson (A) d. Nicola Pietrangeli and Orlando Sirola, 6–2, 6–3, 6–4.

1962—AUSTRALIA d. MEXICO, 5–0
  Milton Courts, Brisbane, Australia
  (Captains: Mexico, Francisco Contreras; Australia, Harry Hopman)
  Forty-one challenging nations entered competition.
Rodney G. Laver (A) d. Rafael Osuna, 6–2, 6–1, 7–5; Neale A. Fraser (A) d. Antonio Palafox, 7–9, 6–3, 6–4, 11–9; Neale A. Fraser (A) d. Rafael Osuna, 3–6, 11–9, 6–1, 3–6, 6–4; Rodney G. Laver (A) d. Antonio Palafox, 6–1, 4–6, 6–4, 8–6; Roy Emerson and Rodney G. Laver (A) d. Rafael Osuna and Antonio Palafox, 7–5, 6–2, 6–4.

1963—UNITED STATES d. AUSTRALIA, 3–2
  Memorial Drive Stadium, Adelaide, Australia
  (Captains: U.S., Robert Kellcher; Australia, Harry Hopman)

Forty-eight challenging nations entered competition.
R. Dennis Ralston (U.S.) d. John Newcombe, 6–4, 6–1, 3–6, 4–6, 7–5; Roy Emerson (A) d. Charles R. McKinley, 6–3, 3–6, 7–5, 7–5; Roy Emerson (A) d. R. Dennis Ralston, 6–2, 6–3, 3–6, 6–2; Charles R. McKinley (U.S.) d. John Newcombe, 10–12, 6–2, 9–7, 6–2; Charles R. McKinley and R. Dennis Ralston (U.S.) d. Roy Emerson and Neale A. Fraser, 6–3, 4–6, 11–9, 11–9.

1964—AUSTRALIA d. UNITED STATES, 3–2
  Harold T. Clark Courts, Cleveland Heights, Ohio
  (Captains: Australia, Harry Hopman; U.S., E. Victor Seixas, Jr.)
  Forty-eight challenging nations entered competition.
Charles R. McKinley (U.S.) d. Fred Stolle, 6–1, 9–7, 4–6, 6–2; Roy Emerson (A) d. R. Dennis Ralston, 6–3, 6–4, 6–2; Fred Stolle

The 1968 United States Davis Cup team: (*left to right*) Stan Smith, Jim Osborne, Clark Graebner, Donald Dell (captain), Arthur Ashe, Jr., Robert Lutz, Charles Pasarell.

Two reasons Romania challenged the United States in 1969 and 1971: Ilie Nastase (*left*) and Ion Tiriac (*right*).

Davis Cup Challenge Round, 1964 (cont.)

(A) d. R. Dennis Ralston, 7–5, 6–3, 3–6, 9–11; 6–4; Roy Emerson (A) d. Charles R. McKinley, 3–6, 6–2, 6–4, 6–4; Charles R. McKinley and R. Dennis Ralston (U.S.) d. Roy Emerson and Fred Stolle, 6–4, 4–6, 4–6, 6–3, 6–4.

1965—AUSTRALIA d. SPAIN, 4–1

> White City Stadium, Sydney, Australia
> (Captains: Spain, Jaime Bartoli; Australia, Harry Hopman)
> Forty-three challenging nations entered competition.

Fred Stolle (A) d. Manuel Santana, 10–12, 3–6, 6–1, 6–4, 7–5; Roy Emerson (A) d. Juan Gisbert, 6–3, 6–2, 6–2; Manuel Santana (S) d. Roy Emerson, 2–6, 6–3, 6–4, 15–13; Fred Stolle (A) d. Juan Gisbert, 6–2, 6–4, 8–6; John Newcombe and Tony Roche (A) d. Jose Luis Arilla and Manuel Santana, 6–3, 4–6, 7–5, 6–2.

1966—AUSTRALIA d. INDIA, 4–1

> Kooyong Stadium, Melbourne, Australia
> (Captains: India, Raj Kanna; Australia, Harry Hopman)
> Forty-five challenging nations entered competition.

Fred Stolle (A) d. Ramanathan Krishnan, 6–3, 6–2, 6–4; Roy Emerson (A) d. Jaidip Mukerjea, 7–5, 6–4, 6–2; Roy Emerson (A) d. Ramanathan Krishnan, 6–0, 6–2, 10–8; Fred Stolle (A) d. Jaidip Mukerjea, 7–5, 6–8, 6–3, 5–7, 6–3; Ramanathan Krishnan and Jaidip Mukerjea (I) d. John Newcombe and Tony Roche, 4–6, 7–5, 6–4, 6–4.

1967—AUSTRALIA d. SPAIN, 4–1

> Milton Courts, Brisbane, Australia
> (Captains: Spain, Jaime Bartroli; Australia, Harry Hopman)
> Forty-seven challenging nations entered competition.

Roy Emerson (A) d. Manuel Santana, 6–4, 6–1, 6–1; John Newcombe (A) d. Manuel Orantes, 6–3, 6–3, 6–2; Manuel Santana (S) d. John Newcombe, 7–5, 6–4, 6–2; Roy Emerson (A) d. Manuel Orantes, 6–1, 6–1, 2–6, 6–4; Roy Emerson and John Newcombe (A) d. Manuel Orantes and Manuel Santana, 6–4, 6–4, 6–4.

1968—UNITED STATES d. AUSTRALIA, 4–1

> Memorial Drive Stadium, Adelaide, Australia
> (Captains: U.S., Donald Dell; Australia, Harry Hopman)
> Forty-nine challenging nations entered competition.

Clark Graebner (U.S.) d. William Bowrey, 8–10, 6–4, 8–6, 3–6, 6–1; Arthur Ashe, Jr. (U.S.) d. Ray Ruffels, 6–8, 7–5, 6–3, 6–3; Clark Graebner (U.S.) d. Ray Ruffels, 3–6, 8–6, 2–6, 6–3, 6–1; William Bowrey (A) d. Arthur Ashe, Jr., 2–6, 6–3, 11–9, 8–6; Robert Lutz and Stan Smith (U.S.) d. John Alexander and Ray Ruffels, 6–4, 6–4, 6–2.

1969—UNITED STATES d. ROMANIA, 5–0

> Harold T. Clark Courts, Cleveland Heights, Ohio
> (Captains: Romania, Georgy Cobzucs; U.S., Donald Dell)
> Fifty challenging nations entered competition.

Arthur Ashe, Jr. (U.S.) d. Ilie Nastase, 6–2, 15–13, 7–5; Stan Smith (U.S.) d. Ion Tiriac, 6–8, 6–3, 5–7, 6–4, 6–4; Stan Smith (U.S.) d. Ilie Nastase, 4–6, 4–6, 6–4, 6–1, 11–9; Arthur Ashe, Jr. (U.S.) d. Ion Tiriac, 6–3, 8–6, 3–6, 4–0, def.; Robert Lutz and Stan Smith (U.S.) d. Ilie Nastase and Ion Tiriac, 8–6, 6–1, 11–9.

1970—UNITED STATES d. WEST GERMANY, 5–0

> Harold T. Clark Courts, Cleveland Heights, Ohio
> (Captains: West Germany, Ferdinance Henkel; U.S., Edward Turville)
> Fifty challenging nations entered competition.

Arthur Ashe, Jr. (U.S.) d. Wilhelm Bungert, 6–2, 10–8, 6–2; Cliff Richey (U.S.) d. Christian Kuhnke, 6–3, 6–4, 6–2; Cliff Richey (U.S.) d. Wilhelm Bungert, 6–4, 6–4, 7–5; Arthur Ashe, Jr. (U.S.) d. Christian Kuhnke, 6–8, 10–12, 9–7, 13–11, 6–4; Bob Lutz and Stan Smith (U.S.) d. Christian Kuhnke and Wilhelm Bungert, 6–3, 7–5, 6–4.

1971—UNITED STATES d. ROMANIA, 3–2

> Julian Clark Stadium, Charlotte, N.C.
> (Captains: Romania, Stefan Georgescu; U.S., Edward Turville)
> Fifty challenging nations entered competition.

Stan Smith (U.S.) d. Ilie Nastase, 7–5, 6–3, 6–1; Frank Froehling (U.S.) d. Ion Tiriac, 3–6, 1–6, 6–1, 6–3, 8–6; Stan Smith (U.S.) d. Ion Tiriac, 8–6, 6–3, 6–0; Ilie Nastase (R) d. Frank Froehling, 6–3, 6–1, 4–6, 6–4; Ilie Nastase and Ion Tiriac (R) d. Stan Smith and Erik van Dillen, 6–3, 6–1, 4–6, 6–4.

The 1959 Junior Davis Cup team: (*left to right*) Paul Palmer, Martin Riessen, William Bond, Dennis Ralston, Ramsey Earnhart, and Charles McKinley. Three members of this team—Marty Riessen, Denny Ralston, and Chuck McKinley—later played for the famed Cup.

Challenge Round Standings

	Won	Lost	Percent
France	6	3	.667
Australia	22	15	.563
Great Britain	9	7	.563
United States	23	24	.489
Belgium	0	1	.000
Japan	0	1	.000
Mexico	0	1	.000
India	0	1	.000
West Germany	0	2	.000
Romania	0	1	.000
Italy	0	2	.000
Spain	0	2	.000

Final Rounds of Davis Cup (*right to be challenger*)

	Winner	Loser	Score
1904	Belgium	France	3–2
1905	United States	Australasia	5–0
1906	United States	Australasia	3–2

1907	Australasia	United States	3–2
1908	United States	British Isles	4–1
1909	United States	British Isles	5–0
1910	not held		
1911	United States	British Isles	4–1
1912	British Isles	United States	withdraw
1913	United States	Canada	3–0
1914	Australasia	British Isles	3–0
1915–18	not held		
1919	British Isles	France	3–2
1920	United States	Holland	withdraw
1921	Japan	Australasia	4–1
1922	Australasia	Spain	4–1

Inter-Zone Finals of Davis Cup (*right to be challenger*)

	Winner	*Loser*	*Score*
1923	Australasia	France	4–1
1924	Australasia	France	3–2
1925	France	Australia	3–1
1926	France	Japan	3–2
1927	France	Japan	3–0
1928	United States	Italy	4–0
1929	United States	Germany	5–0
1930	United States	Italy	4–1
1931	Great Britain	United States	3–2
1932	United States	Germany	3–2
1933	Great Britain	United States	4–1
1934	United States	Australia	3–2
1935	United States	Germany	4–1
1936	Australia	Germany	4–1
1937	United States	Germany	3–2
1938	Australia	Germany	5–0
1939	Australia	Yugoslavia	4–1
1940–45	not held		
1946	United States	Sweden	5–0
1947	Australia	Czechoslovakia	4–1
1948	Australia	Czechoslovakia	3–2
1949	Australia	Italy	5–0
1950	Australia	Sweden	3–2
1951	United States	Sweden	5–0
1952	United States	Italy	5–0
1953	United States	Belgium	4–1
1954	United States	Sweden	5–0
1955	Australia	Italy	5–0
1956	United States	Italy	4–1
1957	United States	Belgium	3–2
1958	United States	Italy	5–0
1959	Australia	Italy	4–1
1960	Italy	United States	3–2
1961	United States	Italy	4–1
1962	Mexico	India	5–0
1963	United States	India	5–0
1964	Australia	Sweden	5–0
1965	Spain	India	3–2
1966	India	Brazil	3–2
1967	Spain	South Africa	3–2
1968	United States	India	4–1
1969	Romania	Great Britain	3–2
1970	West Germany	India	5–0
1971	Romania	Brazil	3–2

United States Rivalries

	Challenge Rounds		Zone Matches		Overall	
	U.S. Won	U.S. Lost	U.S. Won	U.S. Lost	U.S. Won	U.S. Lost
Australia (was Australasia—Australia and New Zealand—until 1924)	13	14	6	2	19	16
Britain	4	5	5	2	9	7
France	2	5	2	0	4	5
Romania	2	0	–	–	2	0
Japan	1	0	6	0	7	0
Mexico	–	–	19	1	19	1
Canada	–	–	15	0	15	0
Italy	–	–	5	2	5	2
Caribbean Commonwealth (formerly British West Indies	–	–	7	0	7	0
Germany	1	0	5	0	6	0
Venezuela	–	–	4	0	4	0
India	–	–	4	0	4	0
Sweden	–	–	3	0	3	0
Ecuador	–	–	2	1	2	1
Philippines	–	–	3	0	3	0
Belgium	–	–	2	0	2	0
Spain	–	–	1	1	1	1
Brazil	–	–	2	1	2	1
China	–	–	2	0	2	0
Cuba	–	–	3	0	3	0
Argentina	–	–	3	0	3	0
Iran	–	–	1	0	1	0
Total	23	24	100	10	123	34

King's Cup

The King's Cup—the men's international team championship on indoor courts of Europe—is formally "H. M. King Gustav V of Sweden Cup." Here are the winning countries since its inception in 1936:

1936	France
1937	France
1938	Germany
1939–51	not held
1952	Denmark
1953	Denmark
1954	Denmark
1955	Sweden
1956	Sweden
1957	Sweden
1958	Sweden
1959	Denmark
1960	Denmark
1961	Sweden
1962	Denmark
1963	Yugoslavia
1964	Great Britain
1965	Great Britain
1966	Great Britain
1967	Great Britain
1968	Sweden
1969	Czechoslovakia
1970	France
1971	France

Dubler Cup

The Dubler Cup, commonly known throughout the world as "The Davis Cup for

King Gustav of Sweden presented the King's Cup to indoor tennis.

The 1969 United States Dubler Cup team: (*left to right*) Gardnar Mulloy, Nicholas E. Powell (captain), Leon Dubler (donor of the Cup), Emery Neale, and Robert Sherman.

Veterans," was offered by Leon Dubler of Switzerland for competition by members of the Veteran International Tennis Association (VITA). This association consists of some twenty-five nations including such far-away places as Pakistan, Israel, China, Japan, Brazil, and the Philippines, Australia, and New Zealand. The United States joined VITA in 1968. Matches were inaugurated in 1958, with the following challenge round results:

1958	Italy d. Germany, 3–1
1959	Switzerland d. Italy, 4–1
1960	Italy d. Switzerland, 5–0
1961	Italy d. Austria, 4–1
1962	Italy d. France, 3–2
1963	Italy d. Belgium, 4–1
1964	Italy d. Germany, 5–0
1965	Italy d. Sweden, 3–0
1966	Sweden d. Italy, 4–1
1967	France d. Sweden, 3–2
1968	United States d. France, 5–0
1969	United States d. Sweden, 4–1

1970	United States d. Sweden, 4–1
1971	United States d. Sweden, 4–1

Stevens Cup

For the six years of its existence (1964 to 1969), the Stevens Cup, donated by Richard Stevens in honor of his father—who in the years 1892–1905 was eight times nationally ranked in the top ten players—was as an international senior team competition, involving teams from the United States, Canada, Mexico, Great Britain, and India. In 1971, the Stevens was rededicated as the "World Senior Tennis Championships," and pits a team from the North American continent, composed of the top seniors in all age brackets against its counterpart from the European continent. This competition is under the auspices of USLTA and VITA and follows international cup-match rules. The results of the Stevens Cup are as follows:

	Winner	Runner-up
1964	United States	India
1965	United States	Canada
1966	United States	Canada
1967	United States	Canada
1968	United States	Canada
1969	United States	Canada
1970	United States	Great Britain
1971	United States	Australia

Mitre Cup

The Mitre Cup is the Davis Cup of South American lawn tennis and the winning nations since it was first played in 1921 are as follows:

1921	Argentina
1922	Argentina
1923	Chile
1924	Argentina
1925	Argentina
1926	Argentina
1927	Argentina
1928	Argentina
1929	Argentina
1930	Argentina
1931	Argentina
1932	Brazil
1933	Argentina
1934	Brazil
1935	Brazil
1936	Argentina
1937	no competition
1938	Argentina
1939	no competition
1940	Argentina
1941–43	no competition
1944	Argentina
1945–46	no competition
1947	Argentina
1948	Peru
1949	Argentina
1950	Argentina
1951	Chile
1952	Chile
1953	Chile
1954	Chile
1955	Chile
1956	no competition
1957	Argentina
1958	Chile
1959	Brazil
1960	Chile
1961	Argentina
1962	Ecuador
1963	Chile
1964	Brazil
1965	Brazil
1966	Brazil
1967	Chile
1968	Chile
1969	Chile
1970	Chile
1971	Chile

Galea Cup

The Galea Cup is an under-21 European male team event which follows the basic Davis Cup format of play. The semifinals and finals are now held at Vichy, France. The results of the Galea Cup are as follows:

	Winner	Runner-up	Score
1950	Italy	France	4–1
1951	France	Germany	5–0
1952	Italy	France	4–1
1953	France	Italy	4–1
1954	Italy	Yugoslavia	8–2
1955	Italy	Spain	5–0
1956	Spain	Italy	4–1
1957	Spain	Italy	4–1
1958	Spain	Germany	3–2
1959	Germany	U.S.S.R.	4–1
1960	France	U.S.S.R.	3–2
1961	France	Spain	3–2
1962	France	U.S.S.R.	3–2
1963	Czechoslovakia	Italy	3–2
1964	U.S.S.R.	Czechoslovakia	3–2
1965	Czechoslovakia	U.S.S.R.	3–2
1966	Czechoslovakia	U.S.S.R.	4–1
1967	France	Great Britain	3–1
1968	Spain	France	3–2
1969	Spain	Czechoslovakia	3–2
1970	Czechoslovakia	Spain	3–2
1971	Sweden	France	5–0

Annie Soisbault Cup

The Annie Soisbault Cup is an under-21 European girls' team event which follows the basic Davis and Galea cups format of play. The winning countries are as follows:

1965 Netherlands
1966 France
1967 Netherlands
1968 U.S.S.R.
1969 U.S.S.R.
1970 U.S.S.R.
1971 France

Sunshine Cup

The Sunshine Cup is an under-18 boys' international team event that follows the basic Davis Cup format of play. It is played each January at Miami Beach, Florida. The winning nations are as follows:

1959 Brazil
1960 Spain
1961 United States
1962 United States
1963 United States
1964 Mexico
1965 Australia
1966 United States
1967 United States
1968 United States
1969 Australia
1970 United States
1971 United States

Wightman Cup

In 1923 Mrs. George W. Wightman of Boston, the former Hazel Hotchkiss, who stands as one of the game's all-time champions, presented a sterling vase to the USLTA for international women's team competition. Great Britain challenged the United States for the cup that year, and the match was the first to be played in the newly constructed stadium of the West Side Tennis Club at Forest Hills, N.Y. This began a rivalry that found favor in both countries, and it was decided that the trophy, known as the Wightman Cup, would be confined to an annual match between British and American women. Mrs. Wightman captained the United States team and joined Eleanor Goss to make a doubles point in the opener, won by the U.S., 7–0.

The United States leads in the series, 36 matches to 7:

1923—UNITED STATES d. GREAT BRITAIN, 7–0
West Side Tennis Club, Forest Hills, N.Y.
(Captains: Britain, Anthony Sabelli; U.S., Mrs. George W. Wightman)
Helen Wills (U.S.) d. Kathleen McKane, 6–2, 7–5; Mrs. Molla B. Mallory (U.S.) d. Mrs. R. C. Clayton, 6–1, 8–6; Eleanor Goss (U.S.) d. Mrs. W. Geraldine Beamish, 6–2, 0–6, 7–5; Helen Wills (U.S.) d. Mrs. R. C. Clayton, 6–2, 6–3; Mrs. Molla B. Mallory (U.S.) d. Kathleen McKane, 6–2, 6–3; Mrs. George W. Wightman and Eleanor Goss

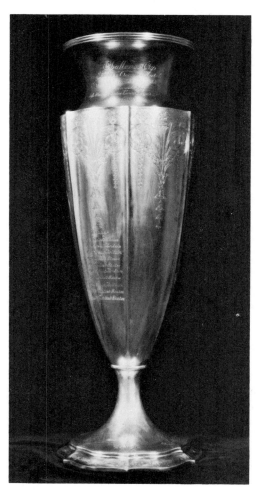

The Wightman Cup.

Wightman Cup Winners, 1923 (cont.)

(U.S.) d. Kathleen McKane and Mrs. B. C. Covell, 10–8, 5–7, 6–4; Mrs. Molla B. Mallory and Helen Willis (U.S.) d. Mrs. W. Geraldine Beamish and Mrs. R. C. Clayton, 6–3, 6–2.

1924—GREAT BRITAIN d. UNITED STATES, 6–1
    Wimbledon, London
        (Captains: Britain, Mrs. Lambert Chambers; U.S., Mrs. George W. Wightman)

Mrs. B. C. Covell (G.B.) d. Helen Wills, 6–2, 6–4; Kathleen McKane (G.B.) d. Mrs. Molla B. Mallory, 6–3, 6–3; Kathleen McKane (G.B.) d. Helen Wills, 6–2, 6–2; Mrs. B. C. Covell (G.B.) d. Mrs. Molla B. Mallory, 6–2, 5–7, 6–3; Mrs. W. Geraldine Beamish (G.B.) d. Eleanor Goss, 6–1, 8–10, 6–3; Mrs. B. C. Covell and Mrs. D. C. Shepherd-Barron (G.B.) d. Mrs. Marion Z. Jessup and Eleanor Goss, 6–2, 6–2; Mrs. George W. Wightman and Helen Wills (U.S.) d. Kathleen McKane and Evelyn L. Colyer, 2–6, 6–2, 6–4.

1925—GREAT BRITAIN d. UNITED STATES, 4–3
    West Side Tennis Club, Forest Hills, N.Y.
        (Captains: Britain, Mrs. Lambert Chambers; U.S., Mary K. Browne)

Kathleen McKane (G.B.) d. Mrs. Molla B. Mallory, 6–4, 5–7, 6–0; Helen Wills (U.S.) d. Joan C. Fry, 6–0, 7–5; Mrs. Lambert Chambers (G.B.) d. Eleanor Goss, 7–5, 3–6, 6–1; Helen Wills (U.S.) d. Kathleen McKane, 6–1, 1–6, 9–7; Mrs. Molla B. Mallory (U.S.) d. Joan C. Fry, 6–3, 6–0; Mrs. Lambert Chambers and Ermyntrude H. Harvey (G.B.) d. Mrs. Molla B. Mallory and Mrs. May Sutton Bundy, 10–8, 6–1; Kathleen McKane and Evelyn L. Colyer (G.B.) d. Helen Wills and Mary K. Browne, 6–0, 6–3.

1926—UNITED STATES d. GREAT BRITAIN, 4–3
    Wimbledon, London
        (Captains: Britain, Mrs. Lambert Chambers, U. S., Mary K. Browne)

Elizabeth Ryan (U.S.) d. Joan C. Fry, 6–1, 6–3; Mrs. Kathleen McKane Godfree (G.B.) d. Mary K. Browne, 6–1, 7–5; Joan C. Fry (G.B.) d. Mary K. Browne, 3–6, 6–0, 6–4; Mrs. Kathleen McKane Godfree (G.B.) d. Elizabeth Ryan, 6–1, 5–7, 6–4; Mrs. Marion Z. Jessup and Eleanor Goss (U.S.) d. Mrs. Lambert Chambers and Mrs. D. C.

Shepherd-Barron, 6–4, 6–2; Mary K. Browne and Elizabeth Ryan (U.S.) d. Mrs. Kathleen McKane Godfree and Evelyn L. Colyer, 3–6, 6–2, 6–4.

1927—UNITED STATES d. GREAT BRITAIN, 5–2
    West Side Tennis Club, Forest Hills, N.Y.
        (Captains: Britain, Maj. Dudley Larcombe; U.S., Mrs. George W. Wightman)

Helen N. Wills (U.S.) d. Joan Fry, 6–2, 6–0; Mrs. Molla B. Mallory (U.S.) d. Mrs. Kathleen McKane Godfree, 6–4, 6–2; Betty Nuthall (G.B.) d. Helen Jacobs, 6–3, 2–6, 6–1; Helen N. Wills (U.S.) d. Mrs. Kathleen McKane Godfree, 6–1, 6–1; Mrs. Molla B. Mallory (U.S.) d. Joan Fry, 6–2, 11–9; Gwendolyn Sterry and Mrs. John Hill (G.B.) d. Eleanor Goss and Mrs. Alfred H. Chapin, Jr., 5–7, 7–5, 7–5; Helen N. Wills and Mrs. George W. Wightman (U.S.) d. Mrs. Kathleen McKane Godfree and Ermyntrude Harvey, 6–4, 4–6, 6–3.

1928—GREAT BRITAIN d. UNITED STATES, 4–3
    Wimbledon, London
        (Captains: Britain, Ermyntrude H. Harvey; U.S., Eleanor Goss)

Helen N. Wills (U.S.) d. Mrs. P. Watson, 6–1, 6–2; Eileen Bennett (G.B.) d. Mrs. Molla B. Mallory, 6–1, 6–3; Helen N. Wills (U.S.) d. Eileen Bennett, 6–3, 6–2; Mrs. P. Watson (G.B.) d. Mrs. Molla B. Mallory, 2–6, 6–1, 6–2; Helen Jacobs (U.S.) d. Betty Nuthall, 6–3, 6–1; Ermyntrude H. Harvey and Peggy Saunders (G.B.) d. Eleanor Goss and Helen Jacobs, 6–4, 6–1; Eileen Bennett and Mrs. P. Watson (G.B.) d. Helen N. Wills and Penelope Anderson, 6–2, 6–1.

1929—UNITED STATES d. GREAT BRITAIN, 4–3
    West Side Tennis Club, Forest Hills, N.Y.
        (Captains: Britain, Mrs. B. C. Covell; U.S., Mrs. George W. Wightman)

Helen N. Wills (U.S.) d. Mrs. P. Watson, 6–1, 6–4; Helen Jacobs (U.S.) d. Betty Nuthall, 7–5, 8–6; Mrs. A. G. Watson (G.B.) d. Helen Jacobs, 6–3, 6–2; Edith Cross (U.S.) d. Mrs. Peggy Saunders Michell, 6–3, 3–6, 6–3; Helen N. Wills (U.S.) d. Betty Nuthall, 8–6, 8–6; Mrs. P. Watson and Mrs. Peggy Saunders Michell (G.B.) d. Helen N. Wills and Edith Cross, 6–4, 6–1; Mrs. B. C. Covell

The United States Wightman Cup Squad of 1927—one of the strongest teams in history. (*left to right*) Helen Wills, Eleanor Goss, Mrs. J. Dallas Corbiere, Helen Jacobs, Mrs. Molla Mallory, Margaret Blake, Mrs. Charlotte Chapin, and Penelope Anderson.

and Mrs. D. C. Shepherd-Barron (G.B.) d. Mrs. George W. Wightman and Helen Jacobs, 6–2, 6–1.

1930—GREAT BRITAIN d. UNITED STATES, 4–3
    Wimbledon, London
    (Captains: Britain, Mrs. Phoebe Watson; U.S., Mrs. Helen Wills Moody)
Mrs. Helen Wills Moody (U.S.) d. Joan Fry, 6–1, 6–1; Mrs. P. Watson (G.B.) d. Helen Jacobs, 2–6, 6–2, 6–4; Mrs. Helen Wills Moody (U.S.) d. Mrs. P. Watson, 7–5, 6–1; Helen Jacobs (U.S.) d. Joan Fry, 6–0, 6–3; Phyllis Mudford (G.B.) d. Sarah Palfrey, 6–0, 6–2; Joan Fry and Ermyntrude Harvey (G.B.) d. Sarah Palfrey and Edith Cross, 2–6, 6–2, 6–4; Mrs. P. Watson and Mrs. K. McK. Godfree (G.B.) d. Mrs. Helen Wills Moody and Helen Jacobs, 7–5, 1–6, 6–4.

1931—UNITED STATES d. GREAT BRITAIN, 5–2
    West Side Tennis Club, Forest Hills, N.Y.
    (Captains: Britain, Mrs. D. C. Shepherd-Barron; U.S., Mrs. George W. Wightman)
Mrs. Helen Wills Moody (U.S.) d. Phyllis Mudford, 6–1, 6–4; Helen Jacobs (U.S.) d. Betty Nuthall, 8–6, 6–4; Mrs. Lawrence A. Harper (U.S.) d. Dorothy E. Round, 6–3, 4–6, 9–7; Helen Jacobs (U.S.) d. Phyllis Mudford, 6–4, 6–2; Mrs. Helen Wills Moody (U.S.) d. Betty Nuthall, 6–4, 6–2; Phyllis Mudford and Mrs. D. C. Shepherd-Barron (G.B.) d. Sarah Palfrey and Mrs. George W. Wightman, 6–4, 10–8; Betty Nuthall and Mrs. Eileen Bennett Whittingstall (G.B.) d. Mrs. Helen Wills Moody and Mrs. Lawrence A. Harper, 8–6, 5–7, 6–3.

1932—UNITED STATES d. GREAT BRITAIN, 4–3
    Wimbledon, London
    (Captains: Britain, Mrs. D. C. Shepherd-Barron; U.S., Mrs. Helen Wills Moody)
Helen Jacobs (U.S.) d. Dorothy E. Round, 6–4, 6–3; Mrs. Helen Wills Moody (U.S.) d. Mrs. Eileen Bennett Whittingstall, 6–2, 6–4; Mrs. Helen Wills Moody (U.S.) d. Dorothy E. Round, 6–2, 6–3; Mrs. Eileen Bennett Whittingstall (G.B.) d. Helen Jacobs, 6–4, 2–6, 6–1; Mrs. Phyllis Mudford King (G.B.) d. Mrs. Lawrence A. Harper, 3–6, 6–3, 6–1; Mrs. Lawrence A. Harper and Helen Jacobs (U.S.) d. Mrs. Peggy Saunders Michell and Dorothy E. Round, 6–4, 6–1; Mrs. Eileen Bennett Whittingstall and Betty Nuthall

The 1935 British Wightman Cup team: (*left to right*) Freda James, Mrs. Phyllis Mudford King, Evelyn Dearman, Kay Stammers, Nancy Lyle, Dorothy Round.

Wightman Cup Winners, 1932 (*cont.*)
(G.B.) d. Mrs. Helen Wills Moody and Sarah Palfrey, 6–3, 1–6, 10–8.

1933—UNITED STATES d. GREAT BRITAIN, 4–3
West Side Tennis Club, Forest Hills, N.Y.
(Captains: Britain, Malcolm Horn; U.S., Mrs. George W. Wightman)
Helen Jacobs (U.S.) d. Dorothy E. Round, 6–4, 6–2; Sarah Palfrey (U.S.) d. Margaret Scriven, 6–3, 6–1; Betty Nuthall (G.B.) d. Carolin Babcock, 1–6, 6–1, 6–3; Dorothy E. Round (G.B.) d. Sarah Palfrey, 6–4, 10–8; Helen Jacobs (U.S.) d. Margaret Scriven, 5–7, 7–2, 7–5; Helen Jacobs and Sarah Palfrey (U.S.) d. Dorothy E. Round and Mary Heeley, 6–4, 6–2; Betty Nuthall and Freda James (G.B.) d. Alice Marble and Mrs. Marjorie Gladman Van Ryn, 7–5, 6–2.

1934—UNITED STATES d. GREAT BRITAIN, 5–2
Wimbledon, London
(Captains: Britain, Malcolm Horn; U.S., James Cushman)
Sarah Palfrey (U.S.) d. Dorothy E. Round, 6–3, 3–6, 8–6; Helen Jacobs (U.S.) d. Margaret Scriven, 6–1, 6–1; Helen Jacobs (U.S.) d. Dorothy E. Round, 6–4, 6–4; Sarah Palfrey (U.S.) d. Margaret Scriven, 4–6, 6–2, 8–6; Betty Nuthall (G.B.) d. Carolin Babcock, 5–7, 6–3, 6–4; Nancy Lyle and Evelyn Dearman (G.B.) d. Carolin Babcock and Josephine Cruickshank, 7–5, 7–5; Helen Jacobs and Sarah Palfrey (U.S.) d. Mrs. Kathleen Godfree and Betty Nuthall, 5–7, 6–3, 6–2.

1935—UNITED STATES d. GREAT BRITAIN, 4–3
West Side Tennis Club, Forest Hills, N.Y.
(Captains: Britain, Malcolm Horn; U.S., Mrs. George W. Wightman)
Katharine Stammers (G.B.) d. Helen Jacobs, 5–7, 6–1, 9–7; Dorothy E. Round (G.B.) d. Mrs. Ethel Burkhardt Arnold, 6–0, 6–3; Mrs. Sarah Palfrey Fabyan (U.S.) d. Mrs. Phyllis Mudford King, 6–0, 6–3; Helen Jacobs (U.S.) d. Dorothy E. Round, 6–3, 6–2; Mrs. Ethel Burkhardt Arnold (U.S.) d. Katharine Stammers, 6–2, 1–6, 6–3; Helen Jacobs and Mrs. Sarah Palfrey Fabyan (U.S.) d. Katharine Stammers and Freda James, 6–3, 6–2; Nancy Lyle and Evelyn Dearman (G.B.) d. Mrs.

Dorothy Andrus and Carolin Babcock, 3–6, 6–4, 6–1.

1936—UNITED STATES d. GREAT BRITAIN, 4–3
    Wimbledon, London
        (Captains: Britain, Malcolm Horn; U.S., James Cushman)

Katharine Stammers (G.B.) d. Helen Jacobs, 12–10, 6–1; Dorothy E. Round (G.B.) d. Mrs. Sarah Palfrey Fabyan, 6–3, 6–4; Mrs. Sarah Palfrey Fabyan (U.S.) d. Katharine Stammers, 6–3, 6–4; Dorothy E. Round (G.B.) d. Helen Jacobs, 6–3, 6–3; Carolin Babcock (U.S.) d. Mary Hardwick, 6–4, 4–6, 6–2; Carolin Babcock and Mrs. Marjorie Gladman Van Ryn (U.S.) d. Evelyn Dearman and Nancy Lyle, 6–2, 1–6, 6–3; Helen Jacobs and Mrs. Sarah Palfrey Fabyan (U.S.) d. Katharine Stammers and Freda James, 1–6, 6–3, 7–5.

1937—UNITED STATES d. GREAT BRITAIN, 6–1
    West Side Tennis Club, Forest Hills, N.Y.
        (Captains: Britain, Malcolm Horn; U.S., Mrs. George W. Wightman)

Alice Marble (U.S.) d. Mary Hardwick, 4–6, 6–2, 6–4; Helen Jacobs (U.S.) d. Katharine Stammers, 6–1, 4–6, 6–4; Helen Jacobs (U.S.) d. Mary Hardwick, 2–6, 6–4, 6–2; Alice Marble (U.S.) d. Katharine Stammers, 6–3, 6–1; Mrs. Sarah Palfrey Fabyan (U.S.) d. Margot Lumb, 6–3, 6–1; Alice Marble and Mrs. Sarah Palfrey Fabyan (U.S.) d. Evelyn Dearman and Joan Ingram, 6–3, 6–2; Katharine Stammers and Freda James (G.B.) d. Mrs. Marjorie Van Ryan and Dorothy M. Bundy, 6–3, 10–8.

1938—UNITED STATES d. GREAT BRITAIN, 5–2
    Wimbledon, London
        (Captains: Britain, Mrs. M. C. King; U.S., Mrs. George W. Wightman)

Katharine Stammers (G.B.) d. Alice Marble, 3–6, 7–5, 6–3; Mrs. Helen Wills Moody (U.S.) d. Margaret Scriven, 6–0, 7–5; Mrs. Sarah Palfrey Fabyan (U.S.) d. Margot Lumb, 5–7, 6–2, 6–3; Alice Marble (U.S.) d. Margaret Scriven, 6–3, 3–6, 6–0; Mrs. Helen Wills Moody (U.S.) d. Katharine Stammers, 6–2, 3–6, 6–3; Alice Marble and Mrs. Sarah Palfrey Fabyan (U.S.) d. Margot Lumb and Freda James, 6–4, 6–2; Evelyn M. Dearman and Joan Ingram (G.B.) d. Mrs. Helen Wills Moody and Dorothy M. Bundy, 6–2, 7–5.

The Duchess of Kent presents the Wightman Cup to its donor, Mrs. George Wightman, captain of the 1938 United States team. The team members are (*left to right*) Mrs. Sarah Palfrey Fabyan, Dorothy Bundy, Mrs. Helen Wills Moody, and Alice Marble.

The 1946 United States Wightman Cup team: (*left to right*) Mrs. Pat Todd, A. Louise Brough, Pauline Betz, Mrs. George Wightman (captain), Margaret Osborne, and Doris Hart.

Wightman Cup Winners (*cont.*)

1939—UNITED STATES d. GREAT BRITAIN, 5–2
West Side Tennis Club, Forest Hills, N.Y.
(Captains: Britain, Betty Nuthall; U.S., Mrs. George W. Wightman)
Alice Marble (U.S.) d. Mary Hardwick, 6–3, 6–4; Katharine Stammers (G.B.) d. Helen Jacobs, 6–2, 1–6, 6–3; Valerie Scott (G.B.) d. Mrs. Sarah Palfrey Fabyan, 6–3, 6–4; Alice Marble (U.S.) d. Katharine Stammers, 3–6, 6–3, 6–4; Helen Jacobs (U.S.) d. Mary Hardwick, 6–2, 6–2; Dorothy M. Bundy and Mary Arnold (U.S.) d. Betty Nuthall and Nina Brown, 6–3, 6–1; Alice Marble and Mrs. Sarah Palfrey Fabyan (U.S.) d. Katharine Stammers and Mrs. Freda James Hammersley, 7–5, 6–2.

1940–45—no matches, World War II

1946—UNITED STATES d. GREAT BRITAIN, 7–0
Wimbledon, London
(Captains: Britain, Mrs. Nancy Lyle Glover; U.S., Mrs. George W. Wightman)
Pauline Betz (U.S.) d. Mrs. Jean Bostock, 6–2, 6–4; Margaret Osborne (U.S.) d. Mrs. Jean Bostock, 6–1, 6–4; Margaret Osborne (U.S.) d. Mrs. Kay Stammers Menzies, 6–3, 6–2; A. Louise Brough (U.S.) d. Joan Curry, 8–6, 6–3; Pauline Betz (U.S.) d. Mrs. Kay Stammers Menzies, 6–4, 6–4; Margaret Osborne and A. Louise Brough (U.S.) d. Mrs. Jean Bostock and Mrs. Mary Halford, 6–2, 6–1; Pauline Betz and Doris Hart (U.S.) d.

Mrs. Betty Passingham and Molly Lincoln, 6–1, 6–3.

1947—UNITED STATES d. GREAT BRITAIN, 7–0
West Side Tennis Club, Forest Hills, N.Y.
(Captains: Britain, Ted Avory; U.S., Mrs. George W. Wightman)
Margaret Osborne (U.S.) d. Mrs. Jean Bostock, 6–4, 2–6, 6–2; A. Louise Brough (U.S.) d. Mrs. Kay Stammers Menzies, 6–4, 6–2; Doris Hart (U.S.) d. Mrs. Betty Hilton, 4–6, 6–3, 7–5; A. Louise Brough (U.S.) d. Mrs. Jean Bostock, 6–4, 6–4; Margaret Osborne (U.S.) d. Mrs. Kay Stammers Menzies, 7–5, 6–2; Doris Hart and Mrs. Patricia Todd (U.S.) d. Joy Gannon and Jean Quertier, 6–1, 6–2; Margaret Osborne and A. Louise Brough (U.S.) d. Mrs. Jean Bostock and Mrs. Betty Hilton, 6–1, 6–4.

1948—UNITED STATES d. GREAT BRITAIN, 6–1
Wimbledon, London
(Captains: Britain, Mrs. Kay Stammers Menzies; U.S., Mrs. George W. Wightman)
Mrs. Margaret Osborne du Pont (U.S.) d. Mrs. Jean Bostock, 6–4, 8–6; Louise Brough (U.S.) d. Mrs. Betty Hilton, 6–1, 6–1; Mrs. Margaret Osborne du Pont (U.S.) d. Mrs. Betty Hilton, 6–3, 6–4; A. Louise Brough (U.S.) d. Mrs. Jean Bostock, 6–3, 4–6, 7–5; Doris Hart (U.S.) d. Kay Stammers Menzies and Mrs. Betty Hilton, 6–2, 6–2; Mrs. Jean Bostock and Mrs. Molly Lincoln Blair (G.B.) d. Doris Hart and Mrs. Patricia Canning Todd, 6–3, 6–4.

1949—UNITED STATES d. GREAT BRITAIN, 7–0
Merion Cricket Club, Haverford, Pa.
(Captains: Britain, Mrs. Kay Stammers Menzies; U.S., Mrs. Marjorie Gladman Van Ryn Buck)
Doris Hart (U.S.) d. Mrs. Jean Walker-Smith, 6–3, 6–1; Mrs. Margaret Osborne du Pont (U.S.) d. Mrs. Betty Hilton, 6–1, 6–3; Doris Hart (U.S.) d. Mrs. Betty Hilton, 6–1, 6–3; Mrs. Margaret Osborne du Pont (U.S.) d. Mrs. Jean Walker-Smith, 6–4, 6–2; Beverly Baker (U.S.) d. Jean Quertier, 6–4, 7–5; Doris Hart and Shirley Fry (U.S.) d. Jean Quertier and Mrs. Molly Lincoln Blair, 6–1, 6–2; Gertrude Moran and Mrs. Patricia Canning Todd (U.S.) d. Mrs. Betty Hilton and Kay Tuckey, 6–4, 8–6.

1950—UNITED STATES d. GREAT BRITAIN, 7–0

Wimbledon, London

(Captains: Britain, Mrs. D. C. Shepherd-Barron; U.S., Mrs. Marjorie Gladman Van Ryn Buck)

Mrs. Margaret Osborne du Pont (U.S.) d. Mrs. Betty Hilton, 6–3, 6–4; Doris Hart (U.S.) d. Joan Curry, 6–2, 6–4; A. Louise Brough (U.S.) d. Mrs. Betty Hilton, 2–6, 6–2, 7–5; Mrs. Margaret Osborne du Pont (U.S.) d. Mrs. Jean Walker-Smith, 6–3, 6–2; A. Louise Brough (U.S.) d. Mrs. Jean Walker-Smith, 6–0, 6–0; Mrs. Patricia Canning Todd and Doris Hart (U.S.) d. Mrs. Jean Walker-Smith and Jean Quertier, 6–2, 6–3; A. Louise Brough and Mrs. Margaret Osborne du Pont (U.S.) d. Mrs. Betty Hilton and Kay Tuckey, 6–2, 6–0.

1951—UNITED STATES d. GREAT BRITAIN, 6–1

Longwood Cricket Club, Chestnut Hills, Mass.

(Captains: Britain, Mrs. D. C. Shepherd-Barron; U.S., Mrs. Marjorie Gladman Van Ryn Buck)

Doris Hart (U.S.) d. Jean Quertier, 6–4, 6–4; Shirley Fry (U.S.) d. Mrs. Jean Walker-Smith, 6–1, 6–4; Maureen Connolly (U.S.) d. Kay Tuckey, 6–1, 6–3; Doris Hart (U.S.) d. Mrs. Jean Walker-Smith, 6–4, 2–6, 7–5; Jean Quertier (G.B.) d. Shirley Fry, 6–3, 8–6; Mrs. Patricia Canning Todd and Nancy Chaffee (U.S.) d. Pat Ward and Mrs. Joy Gannon Mottram, 7–5, 6–3; Shirley Fry and Doris Hart (U.S.) d. Jean Quertier and Kay Tuckey, 6–3, 6–3.

1952—UNITED STATES d. GREAT BRITAIN, 7–0

Wimbledon, London

(Captains: Britain, Col. Duncan Macaulay; U.S., Mrs. Marjorie Gladman Van Ryn Buck)

Doris Hart (U.S.) d. Mrs. Jean Quertier Rinkel, 6–3, 6–3; Maureen Connolly (U.S.) d. Mrs. Jean Walker-Smith, 3–6, 6–1, 7–5; Doris Hart (U.S.) d. Mrs. Jean Walker-Smith, 7–5, 6–2; Maureen Connolly (U.S.) d. Mrs. Jean Quertier Rinkel, 9–7, 6–2; Shirley Fry (U.S.) d. Susan Partridge, 6–0, 8–6; Shirley Fry and Doris Hart (U.S.) d. Helen Fletcher and Mrs. Jean Quertier Rinkel, 8–6, 6–4; A. Louise Brough and Maureen Connolly (U.S.) d. Mrs. Joy Gannon Mottram and Pat Ward, 6–0, 6–3.

1953—UNITED STATES d. GREAT BRITAIN, 7–0

Westchester Country Club, Rye, N.Y.

The 1955 British Wightman Cup team: (*left to right, kneeling*) Angela Buxton and Patricia Ward; (*standing*) Angela Mortimer, Shirley Bloomer, and Mrs. Mary Halford (captain).

(Captains: Britain, Col. Duncan Macaulay; U.S., Mrs. Margaret Osborne du Pont)

Maureen Connolly (U.S.) d. Angela Mortimer, 6–1, 6–1; Doris Hart (U.S.) d. Helen Fletcher, 6–4, 7–5; Shirley Fry (U.S.) d. Mrs. Jean Quertier Rinkel, 6–2, 6–4; Maureen Connolly (U.S.) d. Helen Fletcher, 6–1, 6–1; Doris Hart (U.S.) d. Angela Mortimer, 6–1, 6–1; Maureen Connolly and A. Louise Brough (U.S.) d. Angela Mortimer and Anne Shilcock, 6–2, 6–3; Doris Hart and Shirley Fry (U.S.) d. Mrs. Jean Quertier Rinkel and Helen Fletcher, 6–2, 6–1.

1954—UNITED STATES d. GREAT BRITAIN, 6–0

Wimbledon, London

(Captains: Britain, Mrs. Mary Halford; U.S., Mrs. Margaret Osborne du Pont)

Maureen Connolly (U.S.) d. Helen Fletcher, 6–1, 6–3; Doris Hart (U.S.) d. Anne Shilcock, 6–4, 6–1; Doris Hart (U.S.) d. Helen Fletcher, 6–1, 6–8, 6–2; A. Louise Brough (U.S.) d. Angela Buxton, 8–6, 6–2; Maureen Connolly (U.S.) d. Anne Shilcock, 6–2, 6–2; A. Louise Brough and Mrs. Margaret Osborne du Pont (U.S.) d. Angela Buxton and Pat Hird, 2–6, 6–4, 7–5; Helen Fletcher and

Anne Shilcock (G.B.) vs. Shirley Fry and Doris Hart (U.S.), unplayed.

1955—UNITED STATES d. GREAT BRITAIN, 6–1
Westchester Country Club, Rye, N.Y.
(Captains: Britain, Mrs. Mary Halford; U.S., Mrs. Margaret Osborne du Pont)

Angela Mortimer (G.B.) d. Doris Hart, 6–4, 1–6, 7–5; A. Louise Brough (U.S.) d. Shirley Bloomer, 6–2, 6–4; A. Louise Brough (U.S.) d. Angela Mortimer, 6–0, 6–2; Mrs. Dorothy Head Knode (U.S.) d. Angela Buxton, 6–3, 6–3; Doris Hart (U.S.) d. Shirley Bloomer, 7–5, 6–3; A. Louise Brough and Mrs. Margaret Osborne du Pont (U.S.) d. Shirley Bloomer and Patricia Ward, 6–3, 6–3; Doris Hart and Shirley Fry (U.S.) d. Angela Mortimer and Angela Buxton, 3–6, 6–2, 7–5.

1956—UNITED STATES d. GREAT BRITAIN, 5–2
Wimbledon, London
(Captains: Britain, Mrs. Mary Halford; U.S., A. Louise Brough)

A. Louise Brough (U.S.) d. Angela Mortimer, 3–6, 6–4, 7–5; Shirley Fry (U.S.) d. Angela Buxton, 6–2, 6–8, 7–5; A. Louise Brough (U.S.) d. Angela Buxton, 3–6, 6–3, 6–4; Shirley Bloomer (G.B.) d. Mrs. Dorothy Head Knode, 6–4, 6–4; Angela Mortimer (G.B.) d. Shirley Fry, 6–4, 6–3; Mrs. Dorothy Head Knode and Mrs. Beverly Baker Fleitz (U.S.) d. Shirley Bloomer and Patricia Ward, 6–1, 6–4; A. Louise Brough and Shirley Fry (U.S.) d. Angela Buxton and Angela Mortimer, 6–2, 6–2.

1957—UNITED STATES d. GREAT BRITAIN, 6–1
Edgeworth Club, Sewickley, Pa.
(Captains: Britain, Mrs. Mary Halford; U.S., Mrs. Margaret Osborne du Pont)

Althea Gibson (U.S.) d. Shirley Bloomer, 6–4, 4–6, 6–2; Mrs. Dorothy Head Knode (U.S.) d. Christine Truman, 6–2, 11–9; Ann Haydon (G.B.) d. Darlene Hard, 6–3, 3–6, 6–4; Mrs. Dorothy Head Knode (U.S.) d. Shirley Bloomer, 5–7, 6–1, 6–2; Althea Gibson (U.S.) d. Christine Truman, 6–4, 6–2; Althea Gibson and Darlene Hard (U.S.) d. Shirley Bloomer and Sheila Armstrong, 6–3, 6–4; A. Louise Brough and Mrs. Margaret Osborne du Pont (U.S.) d. Anne Shilcock and Ann Haydon, 6–4, 6–1.

1958—GREAT BRITAIN d. UNITED STATES, 4–3

Wimbledon, London
(Captains: Britain, Mrs. Mary Halford; U.S., Mrs. Margaret Osborne du Pont)

Althea Gibson (U.S.) d. Shirley Bloomer, 6–3, 6–4; Christine Truman (G.B.) d. Mrs. Dorothy Head Knode, 6–4, 6–4; Mrs. Dorothy Head Knode (U.S.) d. Shirley Bloomer, 6–4, 6–2; Christine Truman (G.B.) d. Althea Gibson, 2–6, 6–3, 6–4; Ann Haydon (G.B.) d. Miriam Arnold, 6–3, 5–7, 6–3; Christine Truman and Shirley Bloomer (G.B.) d. Karol Fageros and Mrs. Dorothy Head Knode, 6–2, 6–3; Althea Gibson and Janet Hopps (U.S.) d. Anne Shilcock and Pat Ward, 6–4, 3–6, 6–3.

1959—UNITED STATES d. GREAT BRITAIN, 4–3
Edgeworth Club, Sewickley, Pa.
(Captains: Britain, Mrs. Bea Walter; U.S., Janet Hopps)

Mrs. Beverly Baker Fleitz (U.S.) d. Angela Mortimer, 6–2, 6–1; Christine Truman (G.B.) d. Darlene Hard, 6–4, 2–6, 6–3; Darlene Hard (U.S.) d. Angela Mortimer, 6–3, 6–8, 6–4; Mrs. Beverly Baker Fleitz (U.S.) d. Christine Truman, 6–4, 6–4; Ann Haydon (G.B.) d. Sally Moore, 6–1, 6–1; Darlene Hard and Jeanne Arth (U.S.) d. Christine Truman and Mrs. Shirley Bloomer Brasher, 9–7, 9–7; Ann Haydon and Angela Mortimer (G.B.) d. Janet Hopps and Sally Moore, 6–2, 6–4.

1960—GREAT BRITAIN d. UNITED STATES, 4–3
Wimbledon, London
(Captains: Britain, Mrs. Bea Walter; U.S., Janet Hopps)

Ann Haydon (G.B.) d. Karen Hantze, 2–6, 11–9, 6–1; Darlene Hard (U.S.) d. Christine Truman, 4–6, 6–3, 6–4; Darlene Hard (U.S.) d. Ann Haydon, 5–7, 6–2, 6–1; Christine Truman (G.B.) d. Karen Hantze, 7–5, 6–3; Angela Mortimer (G.B.) d. Janet Hopps, 6–8, 6–4, 6–1; Karen Hantze and Darlene Hard (U.S.) d. Ann Haydon and Angela Mortimer, 6–0, 6–0; Christine Truman and Mrs. Shirley Bloomer Brasher (G.B.) d. Janet Hopps and Mrs. Dorothy Head Knode, 6–4, 9–7.

1961—UNITED STATES d. GREAT BRITAIN, 6–1
Saddle and Cycle Club, Chicago, Ill.
(Captains: Britain, Mrs. Bea Walter; U.S., Mrs. Margaret Osborne du Pont)

Karen Hantze (U.S.) d. Christine Truman, 7–9, 6–1, 6–1; Billie Jean Moffitt (U.S.) d.

Ann Haydon, 6–4, 6–4; Karen Hantze (U.S.) d. Ann Haydon, 6–1, 6–4; Christine Truman (G.B.) d. Billie Jean Moffitt, 6–3, 6–2; Justina Bricka (U.S.) d. Angela Mortimer, 10–8, 4–6, 6–3; Karen Hantze and Billie Jean Moffitt (U.S.) d. Christine Truman and Deirdre Catt, 7–5, 6–2; Mrs. Margaret Osborne du Pont and Margaret Varner (U.S.) d. Angela Mortimer and Ann Haydon, default.

1962—UNITED STATES d. GREAT BRITAIN, 4–3

Wimbledon, London

(Captains: Britain, Mrs. Bea Walter; U.S., Mrs. Margaret Osborne du Pont)

Darlene Hard (U.S.) d. Christine Truman, 6–2, 6–2; Ann Haydon (G.B.) d. Mrs. Karen Hantze Susman, 10–8, 7–5; Deirdre Catt (G.B.) d. Nancy Richey, 6–1, 7–5; Darlene Hard (U.S.) d. Ann Haydon, 6–3, 6–8, 6–4; Mrs. Karen Hantze Susman (U.S.) d. Christine Truman, 6–4, 7–5; Mrs. Margaret Osborne du Pont and Margaret Varner (U.S.) d. Deirdre Catt and Elizabeth Starkie, 6–2, 3–6, 6–2; Christine Truman and Ann Haydon (G.B.) d. Darlene Hard and Billie Jean Moffitt, 6–4, 6–3.

1963—UNITED STATES d. GREAT BRITAIN, 6–1

Cleveland Skating Club, Cleveland, Ohio

(Captains: Britain, Mrs. Bea Walter; U.S., Mrs. Margaret Osborne du Pont)

Mrs. Ann Haydon Jones (G.B.) d. Darlene Hard, 6–1, 0–6, 8–6; Billie Jean Moffitt (U.S.) d. Christine Truman, 6–4, 19–17; Nancy Richey (U.S.) d. Deirdre Catt, 14–12, 6–3; Darlene Hard (U.S.) d. Christine Truman, 6–3, 6–0; Billie Jean Moffitt (U.S.) d. Mrs. Ann Haydon Jones, 6–4, 4–6, 6–3; Darlene Hard and Billie Jean Moffitt (U.S.) d. Christine Truman and Mrs. Ann Haydon Jones, 4–6, 7–5, 6–2; Nancy Richey and Mrs. Donna Floyd Fales (U.S.) d. Deirdre Catt and Elizabeth Starkie, 6–4, 6–8, 6–2.

1964—UNITED STATES d. GREAT BRITAIN, 5–2

Wimbledon, London

(Captains: Britain, Angela Mortimer; U.S., Mrs. Donna Floyd Fales)

Nancy Richey (U.S.) d. Deirdre Catt, 4–6, 6–4, 7–5; Billie Jean Moffitt (U.S.) d. Mrs. Ann Haydon Jones, 4–6, 6–2, 6–3; Carole Caldwell (U.S.) d. Elizabeth Starkie, 6–4, 1–6, 6–3; Nancy Richey (U.S.) d. Mrs. Ann

Haydon Jones, 7–5, 11–9; Billie Jean Moffitt (U.S.) d. Deirdre Catt, 6–3, 4–6, 6–3; Deirdre Catt and Mrs. Ann Haydon Jones (G.B.) d. Carole Caldwell and Billie Jean Moffitt, 6–2, 4–6, 6–0; Angela Mortimer and Elizabeth Starkie (G.B.) d. Nancy Richey and Mrs. Donna Floyd Fales, 2–6, 6–3, 6–4.

1965—UNITED STATES d. GREAT BRITAIN, 5–2

Harold T. Clark Stadium, Cleveland, Ohio

(Captains: Britain, Angela Mortimer; U.S., Mrs. Margaret Osborne du Pont)

Mrs. Ann Haydon Jones (G.B.) d. Billie Jean Moffitt, 6–2, 6–4; Nancy Richey (U.S.) d. Elizabeth Starkie, 6–1, 6–0; Mrs. Carole Caldwell Graebner (U.S.) d. Virginia Wade, 3–6, 10–8, 6–4; Billie Jean Moffitt (U.S.) d. Elizabeth Starkie, 6–3, 6–2; Mrs. Ann Haydon Jones (G.B.) d. Nancy Richey, 6–4, 8–6; Mrs. Carole Caldwell Graebner and Nancy Richey (U.S.) d. Nell Truman and Elizabeth Starkie, 6–1, 6–0; Billie Jean Moffitt and Mrs. Karen Hantze Susman (U.S.) d. Mrs. Ann Haydon Jones and Virginia Wade, 6–3, 8–6.

1966—UNITED STATES d. GREAT BRITAIN, 4–3

Wimbledon, London

(Captains: Britain, Angela Mortimer; U.S., Margaret Varner)

Mrs. Ann Haydon Jones (G.B.) d. Nancy Richey, 2–6, 6–4, 6–3; Mrs. Billie Jean King (U.S.) d. Virginia Wade, 6–2, 6–3; Winnie Shaw (G.B.) d. Mary Ann Eisel, 6–3, 6–3; Nancy Richey (U.S.) d. Virginia Wade, 2–6, 6–2, 7–5; Mrs. Billie Jean King (U.S.) d. Mrs. Ann Haydon Jones, 5–7, 7–2, 6–3; Mrs. Ann Haydon Jones and Virginia Wade (G.B.) d. Mrs. Billie Jean King and Jane Albert, 7–5, 6–2; Nancy Richey and Mary Ann Eisel (U.S.) d. Rita Bentley and Elizabeth Starkie, 6–1, 6–2.

1967—UNITED STATES d. GREAT BRITAIN, 6–1

Harold T. Clark Stadium, Cleveland, Ohio

(Captains: Britain, Mrs. Angela Mortimer Barrett; U.S., Mrs. Betty Rosenquest Pratt)

Mrs. Billie Jean King (U.S.) d. Virginia Wade, 6–3, 6–2; Nancy Richey (U.S.) d. Mrs. Ann H. Jones, 6–2, 6–2; Christine Truman (G.B.) d. Rosemary Casals, 3–6, 7–5, 6–1; Nancy Richey (U.S.) d. Virginia Wade, 3–6, 8–6, 6–2; Mrs. Billie Jean King (U.S.)

The 1970 United States Wightman Cup team: (*left to right*) Nancy Richey, Mrs. Billie Jean King, Doris Hart (captain), Peaches Bartkowicz, Julie Heldman, and Mary Ann Curtis.

Wightman Cup Winners, 1967 (*cont.*)
d. Mrs. Ann H. Jones, 6–1, 6–2; Rosemary Casals and Mrs. Billie Jean King (U.S.) d. Mrs. Ann H. Jones and Virginia Wade, 10–8, 6–4; Mary Ann Eisel and Mrs. Carole C. Graebner (U.S.) d. Winnie Shaw and Joyce Williams, 8–6, 12–10.

1968—GREAT BRITAIN d. UNITED STATES, 4–3
    Wimbledon, London
    (Captains: Britain, Mrs. Angela Mortimer Barrett; U.S., Mrs. Betty Rosenquest Pratt)
Nancy Richey (U.S.) d. Mrs. Christine T. Janes, 6–1, 8–6; Virginia Wade (G.B.) d.

The 1962 Junior Wightman Cup Squad: (*left to right*) Joyce Davenport, Susan Behlmar, Carole Caldwell, Judy Alvarez, Carol Hanks, Chris Safford, Connie Jaster, Tory Fretz, Marilyn Montgomery, and Carol Southmayd.

Mary Ann Eisel, 6–0, 6–1; Jane Bartkowicz (U.S.) d. Winnie Shaw, 7–5, 3–6, 6–4; Mary Ann Eisel (U.S.) d. Mrs. Christine T. Janes, 6–4, 6–3; Virginia Wade (G.B.) d. Nancy Richey, 6–4, 2–6, 6–3; Virginia Wade and Winnie Shaw (G.B.) d. Nancy Richey and Mary Ann Eisel, 5–7, 6–4, 6–3; Nell Truman and Mrs. Christine Janes (G.B.) d. Stephanie DeFina and Kathy Harter, 6–3, 2–6, 6–3.

1969—UNITED STATES d. GREAT BRITAIN, 5–2
  Harold T. Clark Courts, Cleveland Heights, Ohio
  (Captains: Britain, Mrs. Angela Mortimer Barrett; U.S., Mrs. Betty Rosenquest Pratt)
Julie M. Heldman (U.S.) d. Virginia Wade, 3–6, 6–1, 8–6; Nancy Richey (U.S.) d. Winnie Shaw, 8–6, 6–2; Peaches Bartkowicz (U.S.) d. Mrs. Christine Truman Janes, 8–6, 6–0; Mrs. Christine T. Janes and Nell Truman (G.B.) d. Mrs. Mary Ann E. Curtis and Valerie Ziegenfuss, 6–1, 3–6, 6–4; Virginia Wade (G.B.) d. Nancy Richey, 6–3, 2–6, 6–4; Julie M. Heldman (U.S.) d. Winnie Shaw, 6–3, 6–4; Julie Heldman and Peaches Bartkowicz (U.S.) d. Winnie Shaw and Virginia Wade, 6–4, 6–2.

1970—UNITED STATES d. GREAT BRITAIN, 4–3
  Wimbledon, London
  (Captains: Britain, Mrs. Angela Mortimer Barrett; U.S., Doris Hart)
Mrs. Billie Jean King (U.S.) d. Virginia Wade, 8–6, 6–4; Mrs. Ann H. Jones (G.B.) d. Nancy Richey, 6–3, 6–3; Julie M. Heldman (U.S.) d. Joyce Williams, 6–3, 6–2; Virginia Wade (G.B.) d. Nancy Richey, 6–3, 6–2; Mrs. Billie Jean King (U.S.) d. Mrs. Ann H. Jones, 6–4, 6–2; Mrs. Ann H. Jones and Joyce Williams (G.B.) d. Mrs. Mary Ann E. Curtis and Julie M. Heldman, 6–3, 6–2; Mrs. Billie Jean King and Peaches Bartkowicz (U.S.) d. Virginia Wade and Winnie Shaw, 7–5, 6–8, 6–2.

1971—UNITED STATES d. GREAT BRITAIN, 4–3
  Harold T. Clark Courts, Cleveland Heights, Ohio
  (Captains: Britain, Mrs. Ann Haydon Jones; U.S., Mrs. Carole Caldwell Graebner)
Chris Evert (U.S.) d. Winnie Shaw, 6–0, 6–4; Virginia Wade (G.B.) d. Julie M. Heldman, 7–5, 7–5; Joyce Williams (G.B.) d. Kristy Pigeon, 7–5, 3–6, 6–4; Mary Ann Eisel and Valerie Ziegenfuss (U.S.) d. Mrs. Christine T. Janes and Nell Truman, 6–1, 6–4; Valerie Ziegenfuss (U.S.) d. Winnie Shaw, 6–4, 4–6, 6–3; Chris Evert (U.S.) d. Virginia Wade, 6–1, 6–1; Virginia Wade and Winnie Shaw (G.B.) d. Chris Evert and Mrs. Carole C. Graebner, 10–8, 4–6, 6–1.

The Federation Cup

The Federation Cup was launched in 1963 by the International Lawn Tennis Federation as a worldwide team competition for women in the spirit of the Davis Cup but with a slightly different format. All entrants gather at one site to play an elimination tournament. Unlike Davis Cup, the champion nation does not stand out until the final. Two singles and one doubles constitute a match. The championship is completed in a week or less. The team of Billie Jean Moffitt (now Mrs. King), Darlene Hard, and Carole Caldwell (now Mrs. Graebner) won the first Federation Cup in London over Australia in the final, 2–1. United States captain was William Kellogg. Although the first matches were played in June of 1963 at Queens Club, they took place indoors because of rain.

Australia, with five victories, and the United States, with four, are the only countries to win the Cup. The Federation Cup Championship finals are as follows:

1963—UNITED STATES d. AUSTRALIA, 2–1
  Queens Club, London
Margaret Smith (A) d. Darlene Hard, 6–3, 6–0; Billie Jean Moffitt (U.S.) d. Lesley Turner, 5–7, 6–0, 6–3; Darlene Hard and Billie Jean Moffitt (U.S.) d. Margaret Smith and Lesley Turner, 3–6, 13–11, 6–3.

1964—AUSTRALIA d. UNITED STATES, 2–1
  Germantown Cricket Club, Philadelphia, Pa.
Margaret Smith (A) d. Billie Jean Moffitt, 6–2, 6–3; Lesley Turner (A) d. Nancy Richey, 7–5, 6–1; Billie Jean Moffitt and Mrs. Karen Hantze Susman (U.S.) d. Margaret Smith and Lesley Turner, 4–6, 7–5, 6–1.

1965—AUSTRALIA d. UNITED STATES, 2–1
  Melbourne, Australia
Lesley Turner (A) d. Mrs. Carole C. Graebner, 6–3, 2–6, 6–3; Margaret Smith (A) d. Billie Jean Moffitt, 6–4, 8–6; Billie Jean Moffitt and Mrs. Carole C. Graebner (U.S.) d.

The 1969 Federation Cup team: (*left to right*) Mrs. Donna Floyd Fales (captain), Nancy Richey, Peaches Bartkowicz, and Julie Heldman.

The 1971 Federation Cup winners: the Australian team (*left to right*) Lesley Hunt, captain, Mrs. Margaret Court, and Evonne Goolagong.

The Federation Cup, 1965 (*cont.*)

Margaret Smith and Judy Tegart, 7–5, 4–6, 6–4.

1966—UNITED STATES d. WEST GERMANY, 3–0
    Turin, Italy

Julie M. Heldman (U.S.) d. Helga Niessen, 4–6, 7–5, 6–1; Mrs. Billie Jean King (U.S.) d. Edda Buding, 6–3, 3–6, 6–1; Mrs. Carole C. Graebner and Mrs. Billie Jean King (U.S.) d. Helga Schultz and Edda Buding, 6–4, 6–2.

1967—UNITED STATES d. ENGLAND, 2–0
    Berlin, Germany

Rosemary Casals d. Virginia Wade, 9–7, 8–6; Mrs. Billie Jean King d. Mrs. Ann H. Jones, 6–3, 6–4; doubles match called at set-all.

1968—AUSTRALIA d. NETHERLANDS, 3–0
    Paris, France

Kerry Melville (A) d. Marijke Jansen, 4–6, 7–5, 6–3; Mrs. Margaret S. Court (A) d. Astrid Suurbeek, 6–1, 6–3; Mrs. Margaret S. Court and Kerry Melville d. Astrid Suurbeek and L. J. Venneboar, 6–3, 6–8, 7–5.

1969—UNITED STATES d. AUSTRALIA, 2–1
    Athens, Greece

Nancy Richey (U.S.) d. Kerry Melville, 6–4, 6–3; Mrs. Margaret S. Court (A) d. Julie M. Heldman, 6–1, 8–6; Peaches Bartkowicz and Nancy Richey (U.S.) d. Mrs. Margaret S. Court and Judy Tegart, 6–4, 6–4.

1970—AUSTRALIA d. WEST GERMANY, 3–0
    Freiburg, West Germany

Karen Krantzcke (A) d. Helga Schultz Hoesl, 6–2, 6–3; Judy Tegart Dalton (A) d. Helga Niessen, 4–6, 6–3, 6–3; Karen Krantzke and Judy Tegart Dalton (A) d. Helga Schultz Hoesl and Helga Niessen, 6–2, 7–5.

1971—AUSTRALIA d. GREAT BRITAIN, 3–0
    Perth, Australia

Margaret Smith Court (A) d. Ann H. Jones, 6–8, 6–3, 6–2; Evonne Goolagong (A) d. Virginia Wade, 6–4, 6–1; Margaret Smith Court and Lesley Hunt (A) d. Virginia Wade and Winnie Shaw, 6–4, 6–4.

United States Federation Cup Rivalries (with 13 other nations)

	Final Matches		Other Rounds		Overall	
	U.S. Won	U.S. Lost	U.S. Won	U.S. Lost	U.S. Won	U.S. Lost
Argentina	–	–	1	0	1	0
Australia	2	2	–	–	2	2
France	–	–	2	0	2	0
Great Britain	1	0	4	1	5	1
Ireland	–	–	1	0	1	0
Italy	–	–	4	0	4	0

Results of Major Tournaments and Lawn Tennis Championships

	Final Matches		Other Rounds		Overall	
	U.S. Won	U.S. Lost	U.S. Won	U.S. Lost	U.S. Won	U.S. Lost
Netherlands	–	–	2	1	2	1
Rhodesia	–	–	1	0	1	0
South Africa	–	–	3	0	3	0
Sweden	–	–	1	0	1	0
Switzerland	–	–	1	0	1	0
West Germany	1	0	1	1	2	1
Yugoslavia	–	–	2	0	2	0
	4	2	23	3	27	5

SECTION VI

Lawn Tennis Greats

NATIONAL LAWN TENNIS HALL OF FAME

The National Lawn Tennis Hall of Fame and Tennis Museum (NLTHFTM) was founded in 1954 and it was decided that its headquarters should be in the historic buildings of the Newport Casino, Newport, R.I. It must be remembered that it was with the building of the Newport Casino that the history of Championship Lawn Tennis in the United States really began. The Casino was built in 1880 under the sponsorship of James Gordon Bennett, owner of the New York *Herald*. As the result of a controversy with the Newport Reading Room, an old and conservative men's club, he engaged Stanford White, the noted architect of the firm of McKim, Mead and White, to design the buildings for a new club to be located opposite his residence on Bellevue Avenue. Upon completion, the club was turned over to the "Newport Casino" corporation formed by a group of summer residents.

The opening of the Casino coincided with the organization of the United States Lawn Tennis Association in 1881, and it was decided to hold their first official championship tournament at the Casino in August of that year. The National Men's Singles Championships were held there through 1914, and an important Invitation Tournament including many of the world's leading amateur tennis players was continued annually through 1967. An annual Professional Tournament has been held there since 1965.

The idea of the National Lawn Tennis Hall

of Fame originated with James H. Van Alen in 1952. A dedicated tennis player and enthusiast, and President of the Newport Casino, Van Alen considered the Casino, as the cradle of American Lawn Tennis, to be the logical place for a national museum. The United States Lawn Tennis Association gave official permission for its establishment in 1954. At an organizational meeting in New York in September of that year, the name of National Lawn Tennis Hall of Fame and Tennis Museum, Inc. was selected, and William J. Clothier, National Champion in 1906, was chosen the first President.

Later in 1954 an appeal was made through tennis organizations and interested individuals, which resulted in the donation of a significant collection of tennis trophies and other memorabilia, as well as financial support. A part of the south wing of the Casino was renovated to house the museum collection and set up an office. The museum has since received many gifts of championship trophies, antique rackets, and other historic tennis equipment, photographs, books, statuary, a model court tennis court, and other interesting items associated with the games of lawn tennis and court tennis. Today, thousands of persons from all over the world visit this shrine of American lawn tennis each year to browse among the ever-expanding display of tennis memorabilia, and to view the notable Stanford White architecture and the beauti-

A lawn tennis tournament at Newport in the 1880's as viewed from the upper balcony of the Casino.

ful grass tennis courts of the Newport Casino.

One of the most important features of Tennis Week at the Casino in August of each year is the enshrinement ceremonies. Selection for enshrinement in the National Lawn Tennis Hall of Fame is based on sportsmanship, skill, character, and contribution to the game of tennis. The following American lawn tennis players have been elected to enshrinement in the Hall of Fame:

1955

OLIVER SAMUEL CAMPBELL (born February 25, 1871; died July 11, 1953). He was National Singles Champion 1890, 1891, and 1892. At age 19 years, 6 months, 9 days, Campbell has been the youngest man ever to win the United States Singles Championship. He was National Doubles Champion with Valentine G. Hall in 1888, and with Robert P. Huntington, Jr., in 1891 and 1892. He was ranked first in 1890, 1891, 1892; third in 1889, and eighth in 1888. Campbell is

generally considered to be America's first net-rusher.

JOSEPH SILL CLARK (born November 30, 1861; died April 14, 1956). He was the first winner of the intercollegiate in 1883. In that year, with his brother C. M. Clark, he defeated R. D. Sears and Dr. James Dwight in doubles trials, first in Boston and then in New York. The Clark brothers played the first international tennis match against the Renshaw brothers at Wimbledon, losing in four sets. Joseph Clark was National Doubles Champion with R. D. Sears in 1885 and was ranked in the top ten from 1885 to 1889. He was Secretary of the USNLTA in 1885 and 1886; Vice-president in 1887 and 1888 and from 1894 to 1901; and President from 1889 to 1891.

DR. JAMES DWIGHT (born July 14, 1852; died July 13, 1917). He is generally considered to be the "father" of American lawn tennis. Ranked second to R. D. Sears in 1885 and 1886, Dr. Dwight was doubles champion with

Robert Duffield Wrenn.

Joseph Sill Clark.

him in 1882, 1883, 1884, 1886, and 1887. He was a member of the first Executive Committee of USNLTA and was President of the Association from 1882 to 1884, and from 1894 to 1911.

RICHARD DUDLEY SEARS (born October 26, 1861; died April 8, 1943). He was the first United States Singles Champion, and the only man to win that title seven consecutive years, 1881 to 1887 inclusive, retiring undefeated. He also won the United States Doubles title with Dr. James Dwight in 1882, 1883, and 1884; with Joseph S. Clark in 1885; and again with Dr. Dwight in 1886 and 1887. He was President of the USNLTA in 1887 and 1888.

HENRY WARNER SLOCUM, JR. (born May 28, 1862; died January 22, 1948). He was National Singles Champion in 1888 and 1889. After winning the All-Comers Round in 1887, he was ranked second to R. D. Sears in that year. The next two years, of course, he was ranked number one in the United States. He was Secretary of the USNLTA in 1887; Treasurer in 1888; Vice-president from 1889 to 1891, and again in 1912 and 1913; President in 1892 and 1893. For many years, he represented the Association in international negotiations.

MALCOLM D. WHITMAN (born March 15, 1877; died December 28, 1932). He was National Singles Champion in 1898, 1899, and 1900. He represented the United States in Davis Cup matches in 1900 and 1902 in singles, without a defeat.

ROBERT DUFFIELD WRENN (born September 20, 1873; died November 12, 1952). He was National Singles Champion in 1893, 1894, 1896 and 1897 and was National Doubles Champion with Malcolm G. Chace in 1895. Wrenn was six times in the best-ten rankings. He played on the United States Davis Cup Team in 1903 singles, and with George L. Wrenn in doubles. He was Vice-president of the USNLTA from 1902–1911 and was President from 1912 to 1915.

1956

MRS. MAY SUTTON BUNDY (born September 25, 1887). Mrs. Bundy was the first woman to be enshrined in the National Lawn Tennis Hall of Fame and was the first American to win at Wimbledon. She won the Women's Singles championship there in 1905 and 1907, having won the championship of

William J. Clothier.

Champion with Holcombe Ward in 1899, 1900, and 1901, retiring undefeated; won the All-Comers doubles at Wimbledon in 1901. In singles he ranked fourth in 1898; second in 1899 and 1900; and fourth in 1902, when he retired. He played on the winning first two Davis Cup Teams in 1900 and 1902. He was President of the USLTA in 1923. He served as Governor General of the Philippine Islands and as Secretary of War, and was a Major-General in World War II.

WILLIAM A. LARNED (born December 30, 1872; died December 16, 1926). He was seven times United States Singles Champion, retiring undefeated in 1911; ranked first in the United States eight times; second five times; third four times; fifth and sixth once, continuously from 1892 to 1911, except when absent in the Spanish War in 1898. He played four times in the Davis Cup Challenge Round.

HOLCOMBE WARD (born November 23, 1878; died 1967). He was six times Doubles Champion of the United States; first with Dwight F. Davis in 1899, 1900, and 1901 (with whom he also won the All-Comers title at Wimbledon); and with Beals C. Wright in 1904, 1905, 1906 (retiring undefeated); he was United States Singles Champion in 1904, and played four years in the Davis Cup Challenge Round. He was President of the USLTA

Dwight Filley Davis.

the United States in 1904. For several years thereafter, though not competing in the national championship or abroad, she was considered the strongest woman player. When she later resumed national tournament play, she ranked fourth in 1921 and fifth in 1922 and 1928.

WILLIAM J. CLOTHIER (born September 27, 1881; died 1962). He was Singles Champion of the United States in 1900, and won the All-Comers in 1909. He was a member of the first Davis Cup Team to go across in 1905 and played on the team for two years. He ranked first in 1905, second in 1904 and 1909; third in 1903 and 1913; fourth in 1905, 1908, and 1912; and fifth in 1902 and 1914. He was elected President of the National Lawn Tennis Hall of Fame in 1954.

DWIGHT FILLEY DAVIS (born July 5, 1879; died November 28, 1945). He was the donor of International Lawn Tennis Challenge Bowl (the Davis Cup); United States Doubles

Holcombe Ward.

from 1937 to 1947.

BEALS COLEMAN WRIGHT (born December 19, 1879; died 1961). He was singles champion of the United States in 1905, and doubles champion with H. Ward in 1904, 1905, and 1906. He won the All-Comers in 1908. He represented the United States four years in Davis Cup play, and beat A. F. Wilding and N. E. Brookes in singles in the Challenge Round in Australia in 1908, and (with K. Behr) beat them in doubles of the Final Tie in England in 1907. He ranked first in 1905; fourth in 1900, 1903, 1904; second in 1901, 1907, and 1908; and third in 1902, 1906, and 1910.

1957

MARY K. BROWNE (born 1897). Played one of the best games of any American woman tennis champion. Miss Browne ranks among the finest volleyers developed in the women's ranks. She was one of the most popular champions, particularly with her fellow players. Her racket was always at service in a worthy cause. She went on tour with Suzanne Lenglen for the benefit of the Fund for Devastated France following World War I. During World War II she worked overseas with the American Red Cross.

Miss Browne won the National Women's Championship in 1912, 1913, and 1914, and was runner-up to Mrs. Molla Mallory in 1921. She won the National Doubles title in 1912, 1913, 1914, 1921, and 1925, the last year with Helen Wills. She won many other titles, including National Mixed Doubles. She was ranked first in 1913 and 1914, second in 1921, and 1924, and sixth in 1925. She played on the Wightman Cup Team in 1925 and 1926.

MAURICE EVANS MC LOUGHLIN (born January 7, 1890; died December 10, 1957). Known as the California Comet, he was one of the most spectacular of America's tennis champions. His tremendous service behind which he was fairly irresistible with the volley, was one of the most effective, and he was decisive overhead. His service was a big factor in his most celebrated victory over Norman Brookes of Australia at Forest Hills in 1914. The first set went to the record score of 17–15 and Brookes never was able to break through service.

McLoughlin was National Champion in 1912 and 1913 and runner-up in 1911, 1914, and 1915. He won the National Doubles with Thomas Bundy in 1912, 1913, and 1914. He played in the Davis Cup Challenge Round in 1909, 1911, 1913, and 1914. He was ranked in the first ten from 1909 through 1915. He was No. 1 in 1912, 1913, and 1914. McLoughlin's career as a tournament player was relatively short. He did not compete after World War I. The general belief was that he had "burned himself out" with his fiery style of play.

RICHARD NORRIS WILLIAMS II (born January 29, 1892; died 1968). He was one of the most daring players to ever win the National Championship. In his heyday his blinding brilliance was almost unbelievable as he stood in close and took the ball on the rise and volleyed and half-volleyed from positions that are untenable for most players. Because of the riskiness of his attack, with its narrow margin of safety as he played for the lines and a winning shot, errors marred his game when he did not have the "touch." But when he was at his best he was unbeatable.

National Tennis Hall 1957 Enshrinement Ceremony: (*left to right*) R. Norris Williams II, Mary K. Browne, Hazel H. Wightman, Maurice McLoughlin, with James H. Van Alen.

Williams won the National Championship in 1914 and 1916. He was runner-up to McLoughlin in 1913. He won the National Doubles with Vincent Richards in 1925 and 1926. These same two years he and Richards played the Davis Cup doubles against France. He also paired with William Tilden in the 1923 Davis Cup Challenge Round against Australia, and with Watson Washburn in 1921 against Japan. Williams played singles in the Challenge Rounds of 1913 against the British Isles and 1914 against Australia. Ten times Williams was ranked in the first ten, from 1912 through 1916 and, after the war, from 1919 through 1923. He was ranked first in 1916. In 1914 he was ranked second to McLoughlin despite the fact that he won the national title, and there was a considerable furore over this. This is the only time this occurred.

MRS. HAZEL HOTCHKISS WIGHTMAN (born December 20, 1886). Hazel Wightman, donor of the Wightman Cup, has one of the most remarkable records ever compiled in tennis. She started winning National Championships in 1909 and she is still active and winning tournaments in Senior competition. At the same time she has worked with young players and helped to bring them to the top, and her hospitality in taking players into her home during tournaments at the Longwood Cricket Club near Boston is known across the country.

Mrs. Wightman won the National Championship in 1909, 1910, 1911, and 1919. She was runner-up to Molla Bjurstedt (later Mrs. Mallory) in 1915. She won the National Doubles in 1909, 1910, 1911, 1915, 1924, and 1928, Helen Wills being her partner the last two years. She won the Mixed Doubles five times, the indoor singles twice, and the indoor doubles nine times, and the Senior Doubles eleven times. The last time was in 1954. In all, she has won approximately fifty national titles. She was ranked in the first ten, first instituted for women in 1913, in 1915,

William M. Johnston.

1918, and 1919. The international team match between women's teams representing Great Britain and the United States for the Wightman Cup was started in 1923, when Mrs. Wightman put up the trophy. She played on the first team and again in 1924, 1927, 1929, and 1931, each time in the doubles.

1958

WILLIAM M. JOHNSTON (born November 2, 1894; died May 1, 1946). Known as "Little Bill," he won the National Championship in 1915, defeating the defending champion, Maurice McLoughlin. He won again in 1919 over a rising player answering to the name of William T. Tilden II. In 1920, 1922, 1923, 1924, and 1925, Johnston was runner-up to Tilden. In 1923 Johnston won the Wimbledon title, defeating Francis T. Hunter in the final.

A Californian, Johnston ranked in the first ten of the country twelve times in fourteen years. His first appearance was at number four in 1913. He ranked first in 1915 and 1919, and second in 1916 and from 1920 to 1923, and also in 1925. He won three National Doubles Championships in 1915, 1916 and 1920, with Clarence J. Griffin. He won the National Mixed Doubles in 1921 with Mary K. Browne,

and the National Clay Court title in 1919. He was Pacific Coast Champion seven times between 1913 and 1922. Johnston was a member of the celebrated team which brought back the Davis Cup from Australia in 1920. His overall Davis Cup Challenge Round record included thirteen wins and three loses. He died in 1946 at the age of 51. One of the greatest volleyers the game has known, and armed with a mighty Western topspin forehand drive, Johnston ranks among the world's all-time giants of the court, although he was one of the smallest men to win the championship. He was also one of the game's most beloved players, a sportsman of the first rank.

MRS. MOLLA BJURSTEDT MALLORY (born 1892; died 1959). She won the National title

Mrs. Molla Bjurstedt Mallory.

seven times and also won the Patriotic Tournament that took the place of the Championship in 1917. She was champion in 1915, 1916, and 1918 as Molla Bjurstedt, and in 1920, 1921, 1922, and 1926 after her marriage to Franklin Mallory. In 1922 she defeated Helen Wills for the title, and in 1923 and 1924 she was runner-up to Miss Wills. With Eleanora Sears she won the National Doubles crown in 1916 and 1917. She and Irving C. Wright were National Mixed Doubles Champions in 1917, and she won with William Tilden in 1922 and 1923. Mrs. Mallory played on five Wightman Cup teams in the years 1923 through 1928. In 1922 she was a finalist at Wimbledon, losing to Suzanne Lenglen. She defeated the great French player at Forest Hills in the 1921 championship, Mlle. Lenglen defaulting after losing the first set of one of the most famous matches in tennis history. Mrs. Mallory was ranked in the first ten thirteen times between 1915 and 1928. She was first seven times. Her winning of the National title seven times has been equaled only by Mrs. Helen Wills Moody.

Mrs. Mallory's forehand and her fighting heart won her a place among the greatest players. She had a tremendous competitive spirit.

ROBERT LINDLEY MURRAY (born November 3, 1893; died 1970). He won the Patriotic Tournament of 1917 and the National Championship in 1918, defeating Tilden in the final. He was left-handed and his service was one of the strongest points of his game. He ranked fourth in 1914 and 1916, first in 1918, and fourth in 1919.

MRS. MAUD BARGER WALLACH (born 1871; died April 2, 1954). She won the Women's Singles Championship in 1908. She was runner-up in 1906. There were no women's rankings until 1913, and she was fifth in 1915 and tenth the following year. Mrs. Barger Wallach maintained a keen interest in tennis for many years, up to the time of her death in 1954. She was a patron of the game and gave her support particularly to the Newport Invitation Tournament.

1959

MRS. HELEN WILLS MOODY ROARK (born October 6, 1905). By capturing the English Ladies' 1938 Singles Championship at Wimbledon, Mrs. Roark (then Mrs. Moody) brought to a climax a tennis career which had covered a period of eighteen years; which had kept her in the front rank of women tennis players of the world during a majority of that time and enabled her to win more than thirty National and International championships. She won her first national championship, Girls' Singles and doubles, at fifteen. She reached the finals of the women's singles in 1922 and won the doubles with Mrs. Jessup. The next year she won her first Women's Singles at Forest Hills, defeating players many years her senior, including Kitty McKane, the English star, and Mrs. Mallory, then for several years the holder, in the final. She visited Europe for the first time in 1924 as a member of the United States Olympic team, won the Olympic singles and doubles in Paris, and reached the final of the Wimbledon singles; successfuly defended her American singles title, won the doubles with Mrs. Wightman and the mixed doubles with Vincent Richards. In 1925 she retired her first singles trophy, and won the doubles and mixed doubles again. Her first setback came the following year in the famous match against Suzanne Lenglen at Cannes, following which she underwent an appendicitis operation in Paris and was unable to play either in England or the United States the remainder of the season. Her great triumph in 1927 was her first Wimbledon win, being the second American woman ever to win the English title (Mrs. May Sutton Bundy was the first in 1905). But Mrs. Moody made a record by winning the United States title again the same year. She bettered this in 1928 by adding the French title to the other two, a feat never equaled by any other woman player. Moreover she never lost a set in the doing. By this time a lost set for Miss Wills would have been front-page news. She repeated herself in 1929, three major titles without the loss of a set. In 1930 she defended her French and English titles successfully but did not defend at Forest Hills. Back again in 1931 she regained her American title and made a trip to Japan, a renowned celebrity. Her playing in 1932 was confined to England and the Continent, dominating major and minor tournaments as usual.

Illness called a halt to her 1933 activities. After winning the Wimbledon championship for the sixth time she was forced to withdraw from Wightman Cup play (she had played in No. 1 position in these matches 1923–1932 with the exception of 1927) and defaulted to Miss Jacobs midway in the American championship final. Two years later she entered the Wimbledon championships, defeating Miss Helen Jacobs in a sensational recovery when within one point of defeat.

Most tennis "experts" agree that Helen Wills Roark is the greatest woman player in the annals of lawn tennis. Always a shrewd and methodical performer, she seemed, as one writer said, to look at each match as a separate rung to the ladder, carefully apportioning the requisite amount of effort needed to outplay each opponent and not allowing herself to be drawn into wasting an ounce of energy, knowing accurately just when to raise her game to an attacking force and when to let a rival defeat herself.

WILLIAM TATEM TILDEN II (born February 10, 1893; died June 5, 1953). He ruled the game in the 1920's, "Sport's Golden Age." He won the United States Singles Championship seven times—1920–1925 inclusive and 1929—equaling the records of Richard D. Sears and William A. Larned. In addition he was five times the National Doubles Champion (three times with Vincent Richards and once with Brian I. C. Norton and Francis T. Hunter), four times the National Mixed Doubles Champion (twice each with Mary K. Browne and Mrs. Molla Bjurstedt Mallory). Tilden also won the United States Clay Championship seven times, Indoor Singles Championship once, and Indoor Doubles four times. He was the first American player to win the men's singles at Wimbledon, in 1920, by defeating Zenzo Shimizer of Japan in the All-Comers and Gerald L. Patterson of Australia in the Challenge Round. He won the Wimbledon Singles Championship two more times and the Doubles once. He was also Singles, Doubles, and Mixed Doubles Champion of Australia in 1930; Singles and Doubles Champion of Holland in 1920 and 1930; Singles Champion of New Zealand in 1921 and of Italy in 1930. He was ranked in the first ten 12 times (ten times at No. 1, two times at No. 2) in the years 1918 to 1929.

He turned professional in 1930 and was a great pro until the late 1940's.

"Big Bill" Tilden and "Little Bill" Johnston were the twin aces who won the Davis Cup from Australasia in 1920 and kept it in this country through 1926, with asistance from Vincent Richards, R. Norris Williams II, and Watson Washburn. In those seven years Tilden lost only one match in singles in the challenge round. Overall, he won 17 out of 22 Davis Cup singles matches he played from 1920 to 1930, and in addition won four Davis Cup Doubles matches.

There are many who rank Tilden as the greatest player of all time. He had tremendous hitting power from both forehand and backhand. He had one of the finest services the game has known. He was a master of spin and of tactics. He had a marvelous physique for the game and raced across the court on the nimblest of feet. He was the absolute master of the tennis world from 1920 through 1925.

1960
No enshrinements

1961
FRED BEASLEY ALEXANDER (born August 14, 1880; died 1969). After winning the Intercollegiate Doubles Championship in 1900 and Intercollegiate Singles Championship in 1901, he went on to win the United States Doubles with Harold H. Hackett from 1907 to 1910. He also won the Doubles Championship of the Patriotic Tournament with Harold A. Throckmorton. In addition, in that 1917 tournament, he was Captain and Manager of the players who played in tournaments and exhibition matches and who raised funds to purchase ambulances and personnel to man them under the direction of the United States Lawn Tennis Association for the benefit of the Red Cross. All of the tournaments and championships of that year were called Patriotic Tournaments and Championships and all of the profits were devoted to supplying the ambulances and personnel to the Red Cross. Each club that contributed a prescribed amount had a plate placed upon the ambulance with the club name. When the war was over these plates were returned to the Club that gave the ambulance. Fred Alexander

Fred Beasley Alexander.

did a magnificent job as leader to the various players that participated.

HAROLD HUMPHREY HACKETT (born July 17, 1878; died November 20, 1937). He was a member of the famous doubles team of Alexander and Hackett which won four National Doubles Championships four successive years (1907 to 1910). He also captured the 1912 Davis Cup team which defeated the British Isles 3 matches to 2. He won the deciding doubles match with Maurice Mc-Loughlin in a close five-set match.

FRANCIS TOWNSEND HUNTER (born June 28, 1894). He was National Indoors Singles Champion in 1922 and 1930, and Indoors Doubles Champion with Vincent Richards in 1922, 1924 and 1929. He was National Champion with Bill Tilden in 1927. In 1924 Paris Olympic Games, he and Richards won the doubles gold medal, while in 1928 he won the International Championship which was held in connection with the Olympic Games in Holland, defeating Jean Borotra in the final round in straight sets. He was on two Davis Cup teams (1927 and 1928), which were defeated by France in the Challenge Round. He joined Tilden in the professional ranks in 1931.

VINCENT RICHARDS (born March 20, 1903; died September 28, 1959). He won most of the United States titles—both amateur and professional—except National Singles. He won his first USNLTA doubles title with Bill Tilden at the age of 15 years, 4 months and 26 days—the youngest player to win a National Championship. He won the Doubles crown four more times—twice with Tilden

Francis Townsend Hunter.

John Hope Doeg.

Helen Hull Jacobs.

and twice with R. Norris Williams. He won the National Mixed Doubles with Marion Ainderstein in 1919 and with Helen Wills in 1928. He won the Indoors Singles in 1919, 1923, and 1924 and Doubles in 1919, 1920, 1921, 1923, and 1924. He was ranked five times in the top ten.

Richards played in the first international match in 1922 against Australasia, defeating Gerald Patterson. He had a record in Davis Cup competition of two victories in singles and three in doubles. He was never beaten in Davis Cup play. He also won two gold medals —singles and doubles—in the 1924 Olympic Games in Paris.

Richards was the United States' first "named" player to turn professional (1926) and won most of the world's professional titles. His last one, in 1945, was the United States Professional Doubles Title with Bill Tilden.

1962

JOHN HOPE DOEG (born December 7, 1908). He won the national title in 1930, defeating William T. Tilden in the semifinals and Francis X. Shields in the final. He was the Junior Champion of the country in 1926, and ranked Number 8 nationally the following year and in 1928. In 1929 he moved

up to third place, and headed the ranking the following year. He won the National Doubles Title for two years in succession (1929 and 1930) with George M. Lott, Jr., and was runner-up for the Wimbledon doubles in 1930 with I. G. Collins, the British player. A slashing, fighting left-hander, Doeg is best remembered for his powerful serve and topspin forehand, and for his great courage and endurance as a match player.

HELEN HULL JACOBS (born August 8, 1908). She was a famous number two who eventually won most of the big ones herself. From 1927 to 1941, with the exception of two years of noncompetition, she was at or near the top of the national rankings. For four straight years (1932–1935) she ranked first, and she was in the Number 2 slot no less than ten times. Her celebrated rivalry with Helen Wills (now Mrs. Helen Wills Roark) went back as far as 1928, when Miss Wills beat her in the Forest Hills final. In 1933, Miss Jacobs lost the Wimbledon final to the same opponent, but in 1933 she beat her for the United States Championship. All told, Miss Jacobs won the National Singles four times and was runner-up an equal number. She was four-time Wimbledon finalist, finally carrying off the Championship there in 1936 by defeating Fraulein Sperling. Other national titles in her long record include: U.S. Girls' Singles, 1924–25; National Doubles with Sarah Palfrey (1932, '33, and '35); and National Mixed Doubles in 1934 with George Lott.

In Wightman Cup play, during twelve years, Miss Jacobs has an overall record in singles and doubles of 18 victories and 11 defeats. She developed the chop forehand to a high level of accuracy and steadiness. She hit a classic, sweeping backhand and excelled in both serve and volley. Her match play and sportsmanship were both exemplary.

HENRY ELLSWORTH VINES, JR. (born September 28, 1911). He hit the ball as hard and fast as any man ever did. He was the United States Singles Champion in 1931 and 1932, beating Lott and Henri Cochet in the respective finals. He won the National Clay Court title in 1931 and the Wimbledon Championship over H. W. (Bunny) Austin a year later. Wimbledon finalist again in 1933, he lost to

Wilmer Lawson Allison.

Jack Crawford, the great Australian. Paired with Keith Gladhill, he held the Junior Doubles Championship in 1929 and the National title, as well as the Clay Court title, two years later. In the Davis Cup Challenge Round of 1932, Vines beat Cochet in five sets but lost to Jean Borotra in four.

In his short, meteoric career, he ranked Number 8 in the country in 1930, and first for the two succeeding years. He turned professional in 1933 and later gained new fame as a professional golfer. Vines had every shot in the game and hit them with every ounce of strength in his lean frame. His smash, serve, and forehand are perhaps best remembered.

1963

WILMER LAWSON ALLISON (born December 8, 1904). He was United States national champion in 1935. In the final he beat Fred Perry of England. In 1930 he was runner-up to Tilden at Wimbledon after he had beaten the great Henri Cochet of France. He won the doubles championship of the United States with John Van Ryn in 1931 and 1935, and they were finalists in 1930, 1932, 1934, and 1936. They were Wimbledon titlists in 1929

and 1930 and runners-up in 1935. Allison was ranked third in 1930, second in 1932 and 1933, and first in 1934 and 1935.

MRS. SARAH PALFREY DANZIG (born Sept. 18, 1912). Mrs. Danzig was one of the world's leading women players for many years. She ranked in the first ten thirteen times between 1929 and 1945. She was National Champion in 1941 and 1945—and runner-up in 1934 and 1935 to Helen Jacobs. She had a remarkable record in doubles, winning the title nine times. With Alice Marble she won the Wimbledon crown twice, 1938 and 1939. She was a winner of seven Wightman Cup matches with Miss Jacobs from 1933 to 1936, and with Miss Marble from 1937 to 1939. Mrs. Danzig was best known for her sweeping backhand and keen competitive spirit.

JULIAN S. MYRICK (born March 1, 1880; died January 4, 1969). The elder statesman of tennis is a former President of the United States Lawn Tennis Association, Chairman of the Davis Cup and Wightman Cup Commit-

John William Van Ryn with his wife, the former Marjorie Gladman—a fine player in her own right.

tees. He was a leader of international prominence in the vast development and growth of the game. During his administration programs for the development of junior boys' and girls' tennis were started and the number of clubs in the USLTA was increased all across the nation. He was largely responsible for the inauguration of the international women's matches with Britain for the Wightman Cup. Through the years he was a steadfast advocate of strict amateurism and the highest standards of sportsmanship.

JOHN WILLIAM VAN RYN (born June 30, 1906). He was one of the great doubles players of his time, and with Wilmer Allison formed one of the most famous combinations the game has known. With Allison he won the United States Doubles title in 1931 and 1935 and was a finalist in 1930, 1932, 1934, and 1936. They were Wimbledon champions in 1929 and 1930 and runners-up in 1935. In the Davis Cup Challenge Round they defeated Henri Cochet and Jean Borotra in 1929 and Cochet and Jacques Brugnon in 1932. In addition to the honors he gained with Allison, Van Ryn won the Wimbledon and French doubles championships with George Lott in 1931. He was ranked sixth in singles in 1927 and 1928, fifth in 1929, ninth in 1930, and fourth in 1931.

George Martin Lott, Jr.

1964

GEORGE T. ADEE (born 1874; died 1948). He was famous as a Yale football player before he gained renown in tennis. He was named all-American quarterback by Walter Camp in 1894. He gave many years of devoted service to tennis. He was chairman of the Davis Cup Committee and Amateur Rule Committee and served on numerous other committees.

JOHN DONALD BUDGE (born June 13, 1915). He ranks among the greatest men champions of all time. Budge is particularly famous for scoring the first grand slam in tennis. In 1938 he swept the world's four major championships—Wimbledon, Forest Hills, the French and the Australian. He was champion of the United States in 1937 and won Wimbledon that year also. With Gene Mako he won the Wimbledon doubles in 1937 and 1938 and the United States doubles in 1936 and 1938. He was a member of the team that won the Davis Cup in 1937 and that successfully defended it in 1938. He ranked in the first ten five times before turning professional late in 1938 and was ranked first in 1936, 1937, and 1938. In 1937, he was the first tennis player to receive the James E. Sullivan Memorial Trophy for being America's top amateur athlete.

ALICE MARBLE (born September 28,

George T. Adee.

Francis Xavier Shields.

1913). Miss Marble was national champion four times, in 1936, 1938, 1939, and 1940, and was noted for her volleying ability and aggressive style of play. She was Wimbledon champion in 1939. With Sarah Palfrey Danzig she won the national doubles title from 1937 through 1940 and the Wimbledon doubles with Helen Jacobs in 1938 and 1939. She was a member of four winning Wightman Cup teams in 1933, 1937, 1938, and 1939. She ranked in the top ten seven times and was Number 1 from 1936 through 1940. Miss Marble ranks among the greatest women champions of all time.

GEORGE MARTIN LOTT, JR. (born October 16, 1906). Lott is rated as one of the greatest doubles players and he was finalist in the singles against Ellsworth Vines in 1931. He won the national doubles five times with three different partners. They were John Doeg (twice), Lester Stoefen (twice), and John Hennessey. He won the Wimbledon doubles with John Van Ryn in 1931 and with Stoefen in 1934 and in 1931 also won the French doubles with Van Ryn. He played in the Davis Cup challenge round in 1929, 1930, and 1934 and ranked in the first ten nine times.

FRANCIS X. SHIELDS (born November 18, 1910). Shields won international fame early. He was runner-up to John Doeg for the national championship in 1930. In 1931 he got to the final at Wimbledon but had to default to Wood owing to an ankle injury suffered in the semifinals. He was on the Davis Cup challenge round team in 1934 and he ranked in the first ten eight times.

Sidney B. Wood, Jr.

Mrs. Pauline Betz Addie.

The first Men's Singles champion (Richard D. Sears, 1881) and the first Women's Singles champion (Mrs. Ellen Hansell Allerdice, 1887) receiving championship medallions from Secretary of Navy Charles Francis Adams during the Golden Jubilee celebration of the USLTA.

SIDNEY B. WOOD, JR. (born November 1, 1911). He was Wimbledon champion in 1931 and runner-up to Wilmer Allison for the national title in 1935. He played in the Davis Cup challenge round in 1934 and ranked in the first ten no less than ten times.

1965

MRS. PAULINE BETZ ADDIE (born August 6, 1919). She was perhaps the most agile of the American players who dominated the women's game during World War II. She was champion of the United States four times—in 1942, 1943, 1944, and 1946. She was runner-up to Sarah Palfrey in 1941 and 1945. In 1946 Mrs. Addie won the Wimbledon crown without losing a set, and won her two singles matches and the doubles with Doris Hart in the Wightman Cup matches. She also won the French Mixed Doubles championship with Budge Patty in 1946. Mrs. Addie ranked in the first ten eight times and was first four times.

MRS. ELLEN FORDE HANSELL ALLERDICE

(born [date not available]; died 1937). She was the first winner of the women's United States championship in 1887. She was honored, with Richard D. Sears, the first men's champion, at the Golden Jubilee celebration of the USLTA in 1931 at Forest Hills, New York.

W. DONALD MCNEILL (born April 30, 1918). He won the French championship in 1939 in singles and in doubles with Charles Harris. In 1944 he was doubles champion of the United States with Robert Falkenburg, and in 1946 he was runner-up with Frank Guernsey. He was the United States Singles Indoor Champion in 1938 and 1940, and was Indoor Doubles Champion in 1941, 1949, 1950, and 1951. McNeill ranked in the first

W. Donald McNeill.

ten six times and was number one in 1940. His career was interrupted by World War II, and the Davis Cup matches were suspended when he was in his prime.

JAMES H. VAN ALEN (born Sept. 19, 1902). He won distinction in both lawn tennis and court tennis, the ancient forerunner of the modern game. Both sports are encompassed in the National Lawn Tennis Hall of Fame and Tennis Museum. In court tennis Van Alen was national champion repeatedly. His skill was not comparable in lawn tennis, but he has won his greatest fame for his distinguished service to lawn tennis.

As President of the Newport Casino, Van Alen was responsible for the establishment of the Hall of Fame there. Following his election as President of the NLTHF, succeeding William J. Clothier, Sr., he assured the permanence of the Casino home by gaining controlling shares for the Hall of Fame as donations from stockholders. Also as Casino President he became the director of the Newport Invitation Tournament and infused new life into it when it seemed it might be dropped permanently and the Casino might be sold. He has been a benefactor too of court tennis, and he has won wide attention recently for his VASSS (Van Alen Simplified Scoring System).

WATSON WASHBURN (born June 13, 1894). He was a high-ranking player who represented the United States on Davis Cup and Olympic Teams and for years he has rendered valuable service to the USLTA. With Richard Norris Williams II, he won the Davis Cup Challenge Round doubles in 1921, and they were runners-up in the United States doubles in 1921 and 1923 and at Wimbledon in 1924. He ranked in the first ten seven times. He has served on many USLTA committees, and was chairman of the Constitution and Rules Committee, the Ball Committee, and Intercollegiate Committee.

1966

JOSEPH R. HUNT (born February 17, 1919; died February 2, 1944). Hunt, a graduate of the United States Naval Academy, won the National championship in 1943. He was a lieutenant in the Navy at the time and played in the championship on a brief leave after serving as a deck officer in the Atlantic theater of the war and before starting training

as a pilot. He was killed in training in Florida.

Hunt played in the 1939 Davis Cup challenge round against Australia, pairing in the doubles with Jack Kramer. He ranked in the first ten five times.

FRANK A. PARKER (born January 31, 1916). He ranked in the first ten seventeen consecutive years from 1933 through 1949 and won the championship in 1944 and 1945 as an Army sergeant. He was French champion in 1948 and 1949 and won the Wimbledon and French doubles with Richard (Pancho) Gonzalez in 1949 and the United States doubles with Kramer in 1943. Parker won United States Clay Court Singles Championship 1933, 1939, 1941, 1946, and 1947 and the Doubles in 1939. He was the United States Indoor Champion with G. S. Mangin. He played singles with Donald Budge on the team that won the Davis Cup for the United States in 1937 for the first time since 1927. He was also a member of the team that lost the cup to Australia in 1939 and again on the winning team in 1949.

THEODORE R. PELL (born 1879; died 1966). Pell, who ranked in the first ten five times from 1910 to 1918 and was national indoor champion three times, is particularly famous for his backhand. It was rated as the greatest the game had seen. He is honored not only for his playing ability but also for the esteem in which he has been held for half a century.

FREDERICK R. SCHROEDER (born July 20, 1921). He was national champion in 1942 and Wimbledon champion in 1949. He won the United States doubles with Jack Kramer in 1940, 1941, and 1947 and the mixed doubles with Louise Brough in 1942. Schroeder was United States Clay Court Doubles champion in 1941 and 1947. He was a member of the winning Davis Cup team in 1946, 1947, 1948, and 1949 and was also on the 1950 and 1951 teams that lost to Australia. He ranked in the first ten eight times.

1967

MRS. A. LOUISE BROUGH CLAPP (born March 11, 1923). She was one of the greatest athletes women's tennis has ever known. She captured four Wimbledon Singles titles (1948, 1949, 1950, 1955) and was runner-up three times. She won the United States Singles crown in 1947 and was runner-up five times. She won the Australian Singles once in 1950. In Women's Doubles she won Wimbledon five times (1946, 1948, 1949, 1950, 1954), United States 12 times (1942–1950, 1955–1957), Australia once (1950), and France three times (1946, 1947, 1949), a total of 21. In Mixed Doubles she won Wimbledon four times and United States four times. In Wightman Cup play from 1946 to 1957, she played in 22 matches and won all 22. She was ranked in the first ten each year commencing with 1941, excepting 1951, a total of 16 times. [This exceeds all male records also excepting Bill Larned (19) and Frankie Parker (17).] In 1948 she was named as the winner of the Service Bowl, which is awarded annually to the woman making the most outstanding contribution to tennis.

MRS. MARGARET OSBORNE DU PONT (born March 4, 1918). An excellent volleyer, she was National Champion in 1948, 1949, and 1950, and runner-up in 1944 and 1947. In Doubles she and Mrs. Louise Brough Clapp won the National Doubles title 12 times from 1942 to 1950, and 1955 through 1957. Mrs. du Pont also won with Mrs. Sarah Palfrey Danzig in 1941. She was Wimbledon Champion in 1947 and finalist in 1949 and 1950, and Champion of France in 1946 and 1949. She and Mrs. Clapp won the Wimbledon Doubles in 1946, 1948, 1949, 1950, and 1954, and the French Doubles in 1946, 1947, and 1949. In Wightman Cup competition Mrs. du Pont won both of her singles matches in 1946 and 1950, and doubles with Mrs. Clapp in 1946, 1947, 1948, 1950, 1954, 1955, and 1957, and with Margaret Varner in 1961 and 1962. She was ranked in the first ten fourteen times. She was seventh in 1938, fourth in 1941, third in 1942, fourth in 1943, second in 1944, third in 1945, second in 1946 and 1947, first in 1948, 1949, and 1950, fifth in 1953, fourth in 1956, and fifth in 1958.

ROBERT LORIMER RIGGS (born February 25, 1918). He was one of the cleverest and strongest defensive players the game has known. Riggs won the Singles Championship of the United States in 1939 and 1941, and was mixed doubles champion with Alice Marble in 1940. He was Champion of Wimbledon in 1939, the last year the tournament was held before the war forced its cancellation until 1946, and Doubles Champion with Elwood Cooke. He was United States Clay Court Singles Champion in 1936, 1937, and 1938 and was doubles champion with Wayne Sabin in 1936. He also won the United States indoor singles, doubles, and mixed doubles championships in 1940. He was a member of the victorious Davis Cup Team in 1935 with Don Budge, defeating Adrian Quist and losing to John Bromwich. In 1939 Riggs defeated Bromwich and bowed to Quist as the United States lost the Cup. He ranked fourth in 1936, second in 1937, 1938, and 1940, and first in 1939 and 1941.

WILLIAM F. TALBERT (born September 4, 1918). He was one of the world's outstanding doubles players and an authority on the tactics of that form of the game. With Gardnar Mulloy he won the United States doubles crown in 1942, 1945, 1946, and 1948. He won the United States Clay Court doubles in 1942 (with William Reedy), 1944 and 1945 (with Francisco Segura), and 1946 (with Gardnar Mulloy). Talbert with three different partners won the Indoor doubles championships in 1949–1952 and in 1954. With Tony Trabert he won French and Italian doubles in 1950. With Margaret Osborne he captured the United States Mixed Doubles title four times (1943–1946). He was United States Indoor Singles Champion in 1948. Talbert won the Davis Cup Challenge Round Doubles match with Mulloy in 1948 against Australia and lost the Doubles in 1949. He ranked in the first ten thirteen times. He was tenth in 1941, fifth in 1942, 1947, 1950, 1951, fourth in 1943 and 1948, second in 1944 and 1945, third in 1949, sixth in 1946, 1952, and ninth in 1954.

1968

MRS. MAUREEN CONNOLLY BRINKER (born September 17, 1934; died 1969). The brief but amazing record of "Little Mo" Connolly ranks her easily among the top 10 women who have played the game. Winner of three consecutive United States singles titles (1951–1953), beginning at the age of 17, as well as three successive Wimbledon titles (1952–1954). In 1953, she won the grand slam of tennis—Australian, French, Wimbledon, and United States singles titles. She also won the

Italian championship in 1954 as well as the French doubles and mixed doubles. She also was United States clay court singles champion in 1953, and 1954 and the doubles with Doris Hart in 1954. Besides being the Australian doubles champion in 1954, she won nine out of nine Wightman Cup matches from 1951 to 1954. In national rankings, she was No. 10 in 1950, No. 1 in 1951 to 1953. If an unfortunate accident to her leg hadn't cruelly cut short her career, there is no telling how many titles she might eventually have racked up.

ALLISON DANZIG (born Feb. 27, 1898). He was the highly respected dean of United States tennis writers while with the *New York Times* for over 45 years. Danzig wrote with a keen awareness and appreciation of the game, all embellished by a lovely fluent prose that made his accounts a rare pleasure to read. He also performed many a distinguished service for tennis, in recognition of which he has now been inducted into the Hall of Fame, the first writer to be so honored.

RICHARD A. GONZALEZ (born May 9, 1928). He won the United States singles crown in 1948 at age nineteen and repeated in 1949. Also he won the French doubles championship in 1949 (with Frank Parker), United States Clay Court Singles in 1948 and 1949, and United States Indoor Singles in 1949. He played in 1949 Davis Cup Challenge Round, winning two singles matches without losing a set. He turned pro in 1949. After a few years there, he became the undisputed world champion for the incredible span of more than a decade.

JACK ALBERT KRAMER (born August 5, 1921). His big serve-and-volley game did more than anyone else's to perfect the modern, postwar attacking game, bringing it down to fine science. He won the United States singles championship in 1946 and 1947, and the Wimbledon crown in 1947. He won the United States doubles in 1940, 1941, and 1947 with Frederick Schroeder and in 1943 with Frank Parker. At Wimbledon, Kramer won the doubles in 1946 (with Tom Brown) and in 1947 (with Bob Falkenburg). In 1941, he won the United States Mixed Doubles with Mrs. Sarah Palfrey Cooke. He also was United States Clay Court doubles champion in 1941 and Indoor champion in both singles and doubles in 1947. After being in the top ten of the National rankings five times (twice as No. 1), he became a professional in 1947 and later became the leading impressario of the professional game.

ELEANORA SEARS (born 1881; died July 9, 1967). The daughter of a Boston "Brahmin" family, she was an unusually gifted sportswoman who won more than 240 trophies on the tennis and squash courts and in horse show rings. In tennis, she was four times national doubles champion (1911, 1915–1917).

1969

KARL HOWELL BEHR (born May 30, 1885; died October 15, 1949). He was ranked in the first ten seven times from 1906 through 1915. With Beals Wright he went to England in 1907 as the United States Davis Cup team to play Australasia. After Brookes defeated Wright, he lost to Wilding after leading two

Jack Albert Kramer (*left*) and Frank Parker (*right*).

Doris J. Hart.

sets to one. He and Wright beat Brookes and Wilding in the doubles and on the final day Wright defeated Wilding and Behr lost to Brookes after volleying sensationally to win the first set.

When on his game, Behr was phenomenally brilliant and in 1907 he scored several victories over William Larned, seven times winner of the national championship.

DORIS J. HART (born June 20, 1925). She won each of the four major singles championships, Australia (1949), France (1950, 1952), Great Britain (1951), and United States (1954, 1955), plus those of Italy (1951, 1953) and South Africa (1952). She also has won United States Clay Courts singles (1950), and British hard court championships (1951–1954). She won the women's doubles championship at Wimbledon three times with Shirley Fry and once with Mrs. Patricia C. Todd; the French doubles title once with Mrs. Todd and four times with Miss Fry; and the United States doubles four years also with Miss Fry. In 1954, she did "the hat trick" by winning the United States singles, doubles, and mixed doubles (with Vic Seixas). It was her fourth offensive win of the mixed doubles (three with Seixas and

two with Frank Sedgman). Miss Hart also has won the Wimbledon mixed doubles title four times (twice with Sedgman and twice with Seixas) and the French mixed doubles three times (twice with Sedgman, once with Seixas). She also won the Australian doubles (1950), Australian mixed doubles (1949, 1950), Italian doubles (1951), Italian mixed doubles (1953), South African doubles (1950, 1952), and South African mixed doubles (1950). She also won the United States Clay Courts doubles (1950, 1954), United States Indoors doubles (1947, 1948) and mixed doubles (1947, 1948) and British hard court doubles (1951–1954) and mixed doubles (1951, 1954). Miss Hart was a member of the Wightman Cup Team from 1946 through 1955 and lost one match in the ten years. Fourteen consecutive years (1942–1955) she ranked in the first ten.

CHARLES S. GARLAND (born October 29, 1898; died January 28, 1971). He was a member of the Davis Cup team in 1920 when the United States won back the trophy from Australia and began its seven-year reign as champion nation. He ranked in the first ten in 1918, 1919 and 1920, and in 1920 he won the Wimbledon doubles with Richard Norris Williams II, Bill Tilden and Bill Johnston, falling before them in the semifinals. Garland won prominence not only as a player but also as an officer of the United States Lawn Tennis Association and a committeeman. He served as secretary in 1921 and 1922 and vice president in 1942 and 1943. The Davis Cup Committee was among those on which he served.

ARTHUR LARSEN (born April 6, 1925). He was champion of the United States in 1950 and with Enrique Morea won the Italian doubles the same year. He was United States Clay court champion in 1952 and the next year he added the indoor title. With Herb Flam in 1950 and Grant Golden in 1953 he took the United States Clay Court title while with K. Nielsen in 1953, he won United States doubles championship. He played in Davis Cup competition in 1951, 1952, winning four out of four matches. Ranked in the top ten, eight times from 1949 through 1956, his career on the courts was ended prematurely when he was badly injured while riding his motor-scooter. Small in size, Larsen lacked

Marie Wagner.

power and the big serve but he was a clever touch player and excelled in tactical play and volleying skill.

MARIE WAGNER (born February 3, 1883). She was very popular and one of the best-known figures in tennis in the Metropolitan New York area for nearly half a century as a player and as a member of tournament and ranking committees. She was runner-up to Mary K. Browne for the United States championship in 1914 and she won the United States indoor title six times, a record, between 1908 and 1917. She ranked in the top ten eight times beween 1913 and 1922 and might have been ranked many times more had the ranking started before 1913. She won the United States Indoor doubles title four times (1910, 1913, 1916, 1917).

1970

CLARENCE J. GRIFFIN (born Sept. 4, 1888). Better known as "Peck," he and "Little Bill" Johnston won the doubles championship in 1915, 1916, and 1920. "Peck," whose brothers, Elmer and Mervyn, were also tennis players of note, won the United States clay court championship in 1914 and the doubles title with John Strachan. He ranked seventh in 1915, sixth in 1916 and 1920, and tenth in 1924.

SHIRLEY FRY IRVIN (born June 30, 1927). She was champion of the United States and Wimbledon in 1956 and runner-up in both in 1951, when she won the French title. She also won the United States clay court (1956), the South African (1950) and Australian (1957) championships. With Doris Hart, she won the United States doubles in 1951–1954 and the Wimbledon doubles in 1951–1953. With various doubles partners, Mrs. Irvin won the French (1950–53), British hard court (1951–1953), United States Clay court (1946, 1950, 1956), Italian (1951), Australian (1957), and South African (1950 and 1952) championships. She also won the Wimbledon mixed doubles with Vic Seixas in 1956 and Italian mixed doubles with Felicissmo Ampon in 1951. Mrs. Irvin was a member of the Wightman Cup Team from 1949 through 1956, except in 1950. She ranked in the top ten from 1944 through 1956, being No. 1 in 1956, second in 1955, and third in 1951, 1952, and 1953.

PERRY JONES (born May 6, 1888; died February 16, 1970). Known as "Mr. Tennis" on the Pacific Coast, he devoted his adult life to the service of tennis. He did more for the development of junior tennis than probably anyone else in the history of tennis in southern California. He raised funds and marshalled the help of ranking players and club and civic officials in providing equipment and instruction for boys and girls in clinics, and he set standards of sportsmanship and personal neatness for the youth. Most of the young players who come East from southern California to win national and world renown were started on their way by Jones.

MARION ANTHONY TRABERT (born August 16, 1930). He won the championship of the United States in 1953 and 1955, and was the last player of this country to do so until Arthur Ashe triumphed in 1968. Trabert also won at Wimbledon in 1955, and was champion of France in 1954 and 1955. He was a member of the Davis Cup Team from 1951 through 1955. He won the United States doubles with Victor Seixas in 1954, the French doubles in 1954 and 1955, and the Australian doubles in 1955. He won the French and Italian doubles with William Talbert in 1950. Trabert won the United States clay court singles title in 1951 and 1955, and the doubles in 1954 and 1955. He also captured the United States indoor singles championship in 1955 and doubles in 1954 and 1955. He was ranked first in the United States in 1953 and 1955, second in 1954, and third in 1951. He served in the Navy in 1952 and left the amateur ranks after the 1955 season.

1971

ALTHEA GIBSON DARBEN (born August 25, 1927). Won both the United States and Wimbledon Championships in 1957 and 1958, the first black player to be crowned. She was runner-up for the United States title in 1956, when she won the French and Italian Championships. She won the Wimbledon Doubles with Angela Buxton in 1956, with Darlene Hard in 1957 and Maria Bueno in 1958; the French Doubles with Miss Buxton in 1956; and the Australian Doubles with Shirley Fry in 1957. Mrs. Darben was a member of the Wightman Cup team in 1957 and 1958. She ranked in the first ten 6 times between 1952 and 1958 and was No. 1 in 1957 and 1958.

ELIZABETH MOORE (born June 6, 1876; died July 29, 1944). Won the Women's Championship of the United States in 1896, 1901, 1903, and 1905. She was runner-up for the title four times, in 1892, 1902, 1904 and 1906. She was Doubles Champion with Juliette Atkinson in 1896 and with Carrie Neely in 1903.

ARTHUR NIELSEN (born January 2, 1894). Chairman of the A. C. Nielsen Company, world-wide marketing research organization, he has been one of the most generous philanthropists to contribute to tennis. He and his wife gave a four-court indoor tennis building to the Park District in the village of Winnetka, Illinois, and following this, in 1966, he offered more than a million dollars to the University of Wisconsin for the construction of a building for tennis and squash courts. His gifts are estimated to total more than $3,000,000. He was captain of the Wisconsin tennis team from 1916 to 1918.

ELIAS VICTOR SEIXAS, JR. (born August 30, 1923) won the championships of the United States in 1954 and was runner-up in 1951 and 1953. He won the National Doubles with Mervyn Rose of Australia in 1952 and with Tony Trabert in 1954. He was Wimbledon Champion in 1953 and he won the French and Australian Doubles titles with Trabert. Seixas played on the United States Davis Cup team from 1951 through 1957. He ranked in the first ten 12 times between 1948 and 1966 and was No. 1 in 1951, 1954 and 1957.

WORLD TENNIS ROLL OF HONOR

The following are the all-time greats of tennis —foreign players and those Americans not already elected to the Hall of Fame—and a listing of their major victories:

ANDERSON, JAMES O. (Australia); born September 17, 1895, at Enfield, New South Wales; died July 19, 1960.

Wimbledon champion, doubles 1924. Australian champion, singles 1922, 1924, 1925; doubles 1924. Member of Davis Cup team.

ANDERSON, MALCOLM JAMES (Australia); born March 5, 1935, at Rockhampton, Queensland.

United States champion, singles 1957. Australian champion, mixed doubles (with F. Muller) 1957; French champion, doubles (with A. J. Cooper) 1957. Member of Davis Cup team 1957, 1958.

ASHE, ARTHUR ROBERT (United States); born July 10, 1943, in Richmond, Va.

United States champion singles 1968. United States Open champion, singles 1968. United States clay court champion, singles 1968. United States Hard Court champion, singles 1963. United States indoor champion, doubles 1967, 1970. United States Clay Court Open champion, doubles, 1970. Australian champion, singles, 1970. Member of Davis Cup team 1963 to 1968.

AUSSEM, CILLY (Germany); born January 4, 1909, in Cologne, Germany.

Wimbeldon champion, singles 1931; French champion, singles 1931; mixed doubles (with W. T. Tilden) 1930; German champion, singles 1927, 1930, 1931; mixed doubles 1926, 1928, 1935.

BADDELEY, WILFRED (Great Britain); born January 11, 1872; died January 30, 1929.

Wimbledon champion, singles 1891, 1892, 1895; doubles (with his twin brother Herbert)

James O. Anderson.

1891, 1894–96. The youngest men's singles winner of Wimbledon. He was 19 years 5 months 23 days old when he won the title in 1891.

BERNARD, MARCEL (France); born May 18, 1914, in Lille, France.

French champion, singles 1946; doubles 1936, 1946; mixed doubles 1935, 1936. Member of Davis Cup team 1935 to 1956.

BOLTON, MRS. NANCY WYNNE (Australia); born June 10, 1917, in Melbourne.

Australian champion, singles 1937, 1940, 1946–1948, 1951; doubles 1936–1940, 1947–1949, 1952; mixed doubles 1940, 1947, 1948.

BOROTRA, JEAN (France); born August 13, 1898, in Arbonne, Basses-Pyrénées.

United States champion, mixed doubles 1926. Wimbledon champion, singles 1924, 1926; doubles 1925, 1932, and 1933; mixed doubles 1925. French champion singles 1924, 1931; doubles 1925, 1928, 1929, 1934, 1936; mixed doubles 1927, 1934. Australian champion, singles 1928; doubles 1928; mixed doubles 1928. British covered court champion, singles 11 times (1926 to 1949), mixed doubles 5 times (1932 to 1948). French covered court champion, singles 12 times (1922 to 1947), doubles 11 times (1923 to 1937), mixed doubles 12 times (1922 to 1952). United States indoor champion, singles 4 times (1925 to 1931), doubles 3 times (1925 to 1931). Member of Davis Cup team 1922 to 1947.

BOWREY, WILLIAM W. (Australia); born December 25, 1943, in Sydney.

Australian champion, singles 1968.

BOWREY, MRS. LESLEY TURNER (Austra-lia); born August 16, 1942, in New South Wales.

United States champion, doubles, 1961. Wimbledon champion, doubles 1964; mixed doubles 1961, 1964. French champion, singles 1963, 1965; doubles 1964, 1965. Australian champion, doubles 1964, 1965, 1967; mixed doubles 1962, 1967. Italian champion singles 1967, 1968; doubles 1961, 1964, 1967; mixed doubles 1962, 1967. German champion, doubles 1962, 1964, 1965, 1967; mixed doubles 1962, 1963.

BRASHER, MRS. SHIRLEY BLOOMER (Great Britain); born June 13, 1934, at Grimsby.

French champion, singles 1957; doubles 1957; mixed doubles 1958. Italian champion, singles 1957; doubles 1958; mixed doubles 1958. Scandinavian covered court champion, doubles 1958; mixed doubles 1958. British hard court champion, singles 1957, 1958; doubles 1955, 1957; mixed doubles 1958–60. British covered court champion, doubles 1960; mixed 1960.

BROMWICH, JOHN EDWARD (Australia); born November 14, 1918, at New South Wales.

United States champion, doubles 1939, 1949, 1950; mixed doubles 1947. Wimbledon champion, doubles 1948, 1950; mixed doubles 1947, 1948; Australian champion, singles 1939, 1946; doubles 1938–40; 1946–50; mixed doubles 1938. Member of Davis Cup team 1937 to 1950.

BROOKES, SIR NORMAN EVERARD (Austra-lia); born November 14, 1877, in Melbourne; died January 10, 1968.

United States champion, doubles 1919. Wimbledon champion, singles 1907, 1914; doubles 1907, 1914. Australian champion, singles 1911; doubles 1924. Member of Davis Cup team 1905 to 1920.

BROWN, TOM (United States); born November 26, 1922, in San Francisco, Calif.

United States champion, mixed doubles 1948; Wimbledon champion, doubles 1946; mixed doubles 1946. Member of Davis Cup team 1950, 1953.

BRUGNON, JACQUES (France); born May 11, 1895, in Paris.

Wimbledon champion, doubles 1926, 1928, 1932, 1933. French champion, doubles 1927, 1928, 1930, 1932, 1934; mixed doubles 1925, 1926. Australian champion, doubles 1928.

BUCHHOLZ, EARL H. (United States); born

Earl H. Buchholz.

September 16, 1940, in St. Louis, Mo.

South African champion, singles 1960; member of Davis Cup team 1959, 1960. Achieved a unique record as a junior when he won the junior titles of Australia, France,

Dorothea Lambert Douglas Chambers.

Wimbledon, and United States in sequence 1958–1959.

BUENO, MARIA ESTHER (Brazil); born October 11, 1939, in São Paulo.

United States champion, singles 1959, 1960, 1964; doubles 1960, 1962, 1966, 1968. United States Open champion, doubles 1968. Wimbledon champion, singles 1959, 1960, 1964; doubles 1958, 1960, 1963, 1965, 1966. French champion, doubles 1960; mixed doubles 1960.

CASALS, ROSEMARY (United States); born September 16, 1948, in San Francisco, Calif.

United States champion, doubles 1967, 1971. United States Hard Court, singles 1965; doubles 1966, 1967; mixed doubles 1966. United States Indoor, doubles 1966, 1967, 1968. Wimbledon champion, doubles 1967, 1968, 1970, 1971; mixed doubles 1970. Italian champion, doubles 1967, 1970. South African champion, doubles 1967–1970. Irish champion, doubles, 1968; Welsh champion, doubles 1970; mixed doubles 1970. Canadian champion, doubles 1970. Swiss champion, singles 1970; doubles 1970. Swedish champion, doubles 1970. Argentine champion, doubles 1968. Member of Wightman Cup (1967) and Federation Cup team (1967).

CHAMBERS, DOROTHEA LAMBERT DOUGLASS (Great Britain); born 1872, in Ealing; died October 4, 1960.

Wimbledon champion, singles 1903, 1904, 1906, 1910, 1911, 1913, 1914; doubles 1903, 1904; mixed doubles 1903, 1906.

COCHET, HENRI (France); born December 14, 1901, in Lyons.

United States champion, singles 1928; mixed doubles 1927. Wimbledon champion, singles 1927, 1929; doubles 1926, 1928. French champion, singles 1922, 1926, 1928, 1930, 1932; doubles 1927, 1930, 1932; mixed doubles 1922, 1923, 1928, 1929. Member of Davis Cup team 1922 to 1933.

COOPER, ASHLEY JOHN (Australia); born September 15, 1936, in Melbourne.

United States champion, singles 1958; doubles 1957. Wimbledon champion, singles 1958. French champion, doubles 1957, 1958. Australian champion, singles 1957, 1958; doubles 1958. Member of Davis Cup team in 1957, 1958.

COURT, MARGARET SMITH (Australia); born July 16, 1942, in Albury, New South Wales.

Ashley John Cooper.

United States, singles 1962, 1965, 1968, 1969; doubles 1963, 1968, 1969; mixed doubles 1963–1965. United States Open, singles 1969, 1970; doubles 1968, 1970; mixed doubles, 1969, 1970. Wimbledon champion, singles 1963, 1965, 1970; doubles 1964, 1965, 1969; mixed doubles 1963, 1965, 1966, 1968. French champion, singles 1962, 1964, 1969, 1970; doubles 1964, 1965; mixed doubles 1963–1965, 1969. Australian champion, singles 1960–1966, 1969–1971; doubles 1961–1963, 1965, 1969–1971; mixed doubles 1963, 1964. Italian champion, singles 1962–1964; doubles 1963, 1964, 1968; mixed 1961, 1968. Canadian champion, singles 1970; doubles 1970. German champion, singles 1964–1966; doubles 1964–1969; mixed 1965, 1966. Irish champion, singles 1968. South African champion, singles 1968–1971; doubles 1966; mixed doubles 1966. Welsh champion, singles 1969. Member of Federation Cup team from 1963 to 1971.

CRAWFORD, JOHN HERBERT (Australia); born March 22, 1908, in Alburg, New South Wales.

Wimbledon champion, singles 1933; doubles 1935; mixed doubles 1930. French champion, singles 1933; doubles 1935; mixed 1933. Australian champion, singles 1931–3,

doubles 1929, 1930, 1932, 1935; mixed 1931–33. Member of Davis Cup team from 1928 to 1937.

DAVIDSON, SVEN (Sweden); born July 13, 1928, in Boras.

Wimbledon champion, doubles 1958. French champion, singles 1957. German champion, singles 1958. Member of Davis Cup team from 1950 to 1960.

DECUGIS, MAX (France); born February 21, 1882, at Paris; died 1949.

Wimbledon champion, doubles 1911; French champion, singles 1903, 1904, 1907–1909, 1912–1914; doubles 1902–1909, 1911–1914, 1920; mixed doubles 1904–1910, 1912–1914, 1920, 1921. German champion, singles 1901, 1902. Member of Davis Cup team.

DOD, CHARLOTTE (Great Britain); born September 24, 1871, at Bebington; died October 10, 1962.

Wimbledon champion, singles 1887, 1888, 1891–1893; ("Lottie" Dod was Wimbledon's youngest champion when, in 1887, she won the title at 15 years 10 months); doubles, 1886–1888; mixed doubles 1889, 1892. Irish champion, singles 1887; mixed doubles 1887.

DOHERTY, HUGH LAWRENCE (Great Britain); born October 8, 1876, at London; died August 11, 1919.

United States champion, singles 1903;

Sven Davidson.

doubles 1902, 1903; ("Laurie" Doherty was first overseas player to win the United States title). Wimbledon champion, singles 1902–1906; doubles 1897–1901, 1903–1905. British covered court champion, singles 1901–1906; doubles 1898 to 1906; mixed doubles 1902, 1903. Member of Davis Cup team from 1902 to 1906.

DOHERTY, REGINALD FRANK (Great Britain); born October 16, 1874; died December 29, 1910.

United States champion, doubles 1902, 1903; Wimbledon champion, singles 1897–1900; doubles 1897 to 1901, 1903 to 1905. South African champion, singles 1909; doubles 1909. Member of Davis Cup team.

DROBNY, JAROSLAV (Czechoslovakia); born October 12, 1921, at Prague.

Wimbledon champion, singles 1954. French champion, singles 1951, 1952; doubles 1948; mixed doubles 1948. Italian champion, singles 1950, 1951, 1953; doubles 1951, 1952, 1954, 1956. German champion, singles 1950; doubles 1952. South African champion 1954. Member of Davis Cup team 1946 to 1949.

DRYSDALE, CLIFFORD (South Africa); born May 26, 1941, at Nelsprint, Transvaal.

German champion, singles 1965; South African champion, singles 1965; doubles 1964.

DU PLOOY, MRS. ANNETTE VAN ZYL (South Africa); born September 25, 1943, at Pretoria.

French champion, mixed doubles 1966; Italian champion, doubles 1965, 1966. German champion, singles 1968; doubles 1963, 1968; mixed doubles 1968. South African champion, singles 1963; doubles 1962, 1963, 1965, 1966, 1968.

DURR, FRANÇOISE (France); born December 25, 1942, at Beziers.

French champion, singles 1967; doubles 1967–1971; mixed doubles 1968, 1971. German champion, singles 1967.

EMERSON, ROY (Australia); born November 3, 1936, at Kingsway, Queensland.

United States champion, 1961, 1964; doubles 1959, 1960, 1965, 1966. Wimbledon champion, singles 1964, 1965; doubles 1959, 1961. French champion, singles 1963, 1967; doubles 1960–1965. Australian champion, singles 1961, 1963–1967; doubles 1962, 1966, 1969. Italian champion, doubles 1959, 1961, 1966; mixed doubles 1961. German cham-

Roy Emerson.

pion, singles 1967; doubles 1960. South African champion, singles 1966; doubles 1966. Member of Davis Cup team from 1957 to 1967.

FALKENBURG, ROBERT (United States and Brazil); born January 29, 1926, at Los Angeles.

United States champion, doubles 1944. Wimbledon champion, singles 1948; doubles 1947. Member of Brazilian Davis Cup team.

FLETCHER, KENNETH (Australia); born June 15, 1940, in Queensland.

United States champion, mixed doubles 1963. Wimbledon champion, doubles 1966; mixed doubles 1963, 1965, 1966, 1968. French champion, doubles 1964; mixed doubles 1963–1965. Australian champion, mixed doubles 1963, 1964; German champion, mixed doubles 1962.

FRASER, NEALE ANDREW (Australia); born October 3, 1933 at St. Kilda, Melbourne.

United States champion, singles 1959, 1960; doubles 1957, 1959, 1960; mixed doubles 1958–1960. Wimbledon champion, singles 1960; doubles 1959, 1961; mixed doubles 1962. French champion, doubles 1958, 1960, 1962. Australian champion,

Clark Graebner.

Wimbledon champion, singles 1901, 1908, 1909; doubles 1909. Member of Davis Cup team in 1900, 1907 and 1912.

GRAEBNER, MRS. CAROLE CALDWELL (United States); born June 24, 1943, at Pittsburgh, Pa.

United States champion, doubles 1965. Australian champion, doubles 1966. United States clay court champion, doubles 1964, 1965. Member of Wightman Cup (1964, 1965, 1967) and Federation Cup (1963, 1965, 1966) teams.

GRAEBNER, CLARK EDWARD (United States); born November 4, 1943, at Cleveland, Ohio.

French champion, doubles 1966; United States Clay court champion, singles 1968; doubles 1963, 1965–1967, 1969, 1970. United States Indoor champion, singles 1971. United States Hard Court, singles 1969. Member of Davis Cup team 1963 to 1970.

HAYGARTH, MRS. RENÉE SCHNUURMAN (South Africa); born October 26, 1939, at Durban, Natal.

French champion, doubles 1959, 1961–1963; mixed 1962. Australian champion,

doubles 1957, 1958, 1962; mixed 1956. Italian champion, doubles 1959, 1961. German champion, doubles 1960. Member of Davis Cup team from 1958 to 1963.

GODFREE, MRS. KATHLEEN MCKANE (Great Britain)

United States champion, doubles 1923, 1927; mixed doubles 1925. Wimbledon champion, singles 1924, 1926; mixed doubles 1924, 1926. German champion, doubles 1930, 1931; mixed doubles 1930. United States Indoor champion, doubles 1922, 1923.

GOOLAGONG, EVONNE (Australia); born July 31, 1951. Wimbledon Champion, Singles 1971. French Champion, Singles 1971.

GORE, ARTHUR WENTWORTH (Great Britain); born January 2, 1896, at Lyndhurst, Hampshire; died December 1, 1928.

Mrs. Nancy Richey Gunther.

Darlene R. Hard.

doubles 1959. South African champion, doubles 1958, 1960, 1961. German champion, singles 1963; doubles 1961. United States clay court champion, doubles 1959.

HENKEL, HENNER ERNST OTTO (Germany); born October 9, 1915, at Posen; killed at Stalingrad, 1942.

United States champion, doubles 1937. French champion, singles 1937; doubles 1937. German champion singles 1937, 1939; doubles 1935, 1939; mixed doubles 1935. Member of Davis Cup team 1934 to 1939.

HEWITT, ROBERT A. J. (South Africa); born January 12, 1940, in New South Wales, Australia.

Wimbledon champion, doubles 1962, 1964, 1967. Australian champion, doubles 1963, 1964; mixed 1961. Italian champion, doubles 1963, 1964, 1967. German champion, doubles 1961–3, 1967. South African champion, doubles 1967. United States clay court champion, doubles 1960.

HILLYARD, MRS. BLANCHE BINGLEY (Great Britain); born November 3, 1863, at Greenford, Middlesex; died November 16, 1938.

Wimbledon champion, singles 1886, 1889, 1894, 1897, 1899, 1900; doubles 1893–1897, 1906, 1907; mixed doubles 1888, 1893, 1907. German champion, singles 1897, 1900. Irish champion, singles 1888, 1894, 1897. Welsh champion, singles 1888.

HOAD, LEWIS A. (Australia); born November 23, 1934, at Glebe, New South Wales.

United States champion, doubles 1956. Wimbledon champion, singles 1956, 1957; doubles 1953, 1955, 1956. French champion, singles 1956; doubles 1953; mixed 1954. Australian champion, singles 1956; doubles 1953, 1956, 1957. Italian champion, doubles 1953, 1956, 1957. German champion, singles 1956; doubles 1956. Member of Davis Cup team 1953 to 1956.

HOPMAN, HARRY C. (Australia); born December 8, 1906.

United States champion, mixed doubles 1939. Australian champion, doubles 1929, 1930; mixed 1930, 1936, 1937, 1939. Italian champion, mixed 1935. German champion, doubles 1932. Member of Davis Cup team 1928 to 1932.

HUGHES, GEORGE PATRICK (Great Britain); born December 21, 1902, at Sutton, Coldfield.

Wimbledon champion, doubles 1936; French champion, doubles 1933; Australian champion, doubles 1934. Member of Davis Cup team.

Mrs. Dorothy Head Knode.

JANES, MRS. CHRISTINE TRUMAN (Great Britain); born January 16, 1941, at Loughton, Essex.

French champion, singles 1959. Australian champion, doubles 1960. Italian champion, singles 1959; doubles 1958; German champion, doubles 1960. Member of Wightman Cup team.

JONES, MRS. ADRIANNE SHIRLEY HARDON (Great Britain); born October 17, 1938, at Birmingham.

Wimbledon champion, singles 1969; mixed doubles 1969. French champion, singles 1961, 1966; doubles 1963, 1968, 1969. Italian champion, singles 1966; doubles 1969. Member of Wightman Cup team 1957 to 1971.

KING, MRS. BILLIE JEAN MOFFITT (United States); born November 22, 1943, at Long Beach, Calif.

United States champion, singles 1967, 1971; doubles 1964, 1967; mixed 1967. Wimbledon champion, singles 1966–1968; doubles 1961, 1962, 1965, 1967, 1968, 1970, 1971; mixed doubles 1967. Australian champion, singles 1968; mixed doubles 1968. French champion, mixed doubles 1967, 1970. German champion, singles 1971; doubles 1971. Italian champion, singles 1970; doubles 1970. South African champion, singles 1966, 1967, 1969; doubles 1967–1970, mixed doubles 1967. Irish champion, singles 1963–1969; doubles, 1963; mixed doubles 1969. New Zealand champion, doubles 1969. Argentine champion, singles 1967. Swiss champion, doubles 1969. United States indoor champion, singles 1966–1967; doubles 1966, 1967, 1971; mixed doubles 1966, 1967. United States hard court champion, singles 1966; doubles, 1966. United States clay court champion, doubles 1960. Member of Wightman Cup (1961–1967, 1970) and Federation Cup (1963–1967) teams.

KNODE, MRS. DOROTHY HEAD (United States); born July 4, 1925, at Richmond, Calif.

German champion, singles 1950; doubles 1950, 1952; mixed doubles 1952. United States clay court champion, singles 1955, 1958, 1960; doubles 1955, 1956, 1958. Member of Wightman Cup team.

LACOSTE, RENÉ (France); born July 2, 1905, at Paris.

United States champion, singles 1926, 1927. Wimbledon champion, singles 1925, 1928; doubles 1925. French champion, singles 1925, 1927, 1929; doubles 1924, 1925, 1929. United States indoor champion singles 1926. Member of Davis Cup team 1923 to 1928.

LARCOMBE, MRS. ETHEL THOMSON (Great Britain); born June 22, 1879, at Hampton Hill, Middlesex; died August 11, 1965.

Wimbledon champion, singles 1912; doubles 1911–1913; mixed doubles 1912, 1914.

LAVER, RODNEY GEORGE (Australia); born August 9, 1938, at Rockhampton, Queensland.

United States champion, singles 1962. United States Open champion, singles 1969. Wimbledon champion, singles 1961, 1962, 1968, 1969; doubles 1971; mixed doubles 1959, 1960. Canadian champion, singles 1970. French champion, singles 1962, 1969; doubles 1961; mixed doubles 1962. German champion, singles 1961, 1962. Australian champion, singles 1960, 1962, 1969; doubles 1959–1961, 1969. Italian champion, singles 1962, 1971; doubles 1962. South African champion, singles 1969, 1970. Member of Davis Cup team 1959 to 1962.

LENGLEN, SUZANNE (France); born May 24, 1899, at Compiegne; died May 27, 1938.

Wimbledon champion, singles 1919–1923, 1925; doubles 1919–1923, 1925; mixed doubles 1920, 1922, 1925. French champion, singles 1914, 1920–1923, 1925, 1926; doubles 1914, 1920–1923, 1925, 1926; mixed doubles 1914, 1920–1923, 1925, 1926. World hard court champion, singles 1914, 1921–1923; doubles 1914, 1921, 1922; mixed doubles 1921–1923. Olympic champion, singles 1920; mixed doubles 1920.

LITTLE, MRS. DOROTHY ROUND (Great Britain); born July 13, 1909, at Dudley, Worcestershire.

Wimbledon champion, singles 1934, 1937; mixed doubles 1934, 1935, 1937. Australian champion, singles 1935. Member of Wightman Cup team.

LONG, MRS. THELMA COYNE (Australia); born May 30, 1918, at Sydney.

Australian champion, singles 1952, 1954; doubles 1936–1940, 1947–1949, 1951, 1952, 1956, 1958; mixed doubles 1951, 1952, 1954, 1955. German champion, singles 1956. Irish champion, singles 1949, Italian champion, doubles 1952, 1956, 1957; mixed doubles 1956, 1957.

LUTZ, ROBERT CHARLES (United States); born August 29, 1947, at Lancaster, Pa.

United States champion, doubles 1968. United States Open champion, doubles 1968. Australian champion, doubles 1970. United States indoor champion, doubles 1966–1969. United States clay court champion, doubles 1968. United States hard court champion, doubles 1966, 1969. Member of Davis Cup team 1968 to 1970.

MACKAY, BARRY BRUCE (United States); born August 31, 1935 at Cincinnati, Ohio.

Italian champion, singles 1960. United States clay court champion, singles 1960; doubles 1958. United States indoor champion, singles 1960, doubles 1957–1959. Member of Davis Cup team 1956 to 1960.

MAKO, C. GENE (United States); born January 24, 1916, in Budapest, Hungary.

United States champion, doubles 1936, 1938; mixed doubles 1936; Wimbledon champion, doubles 1937, 1938. United States clay court champion, doubles 1934, 1939. Member of Davis Cup team 1935 to 1938.

MATHIEU, MRS. RENÉ SIMONE (France); born January 31, 1908, at Neuilly-sur-Seine.

Wimbledon champion, doubles 1933, 1934, 1937. French champion, singles 1938, 1939; doubles 1933, 1934, 1936–1939; mixed doubles 1937, 1938.

McGRATH, VIVIAN (Australia); born February 17, 1916, in New South Wales.

Australian champion, singles 1937; doubles 1935. Italian champion, doubles 1935; German champion, doubles 1937. Member of Davis Cup team.

McGREGOR, KEN (Australia); born June 2, 1929, at Adelaide.

United States champion, doubles 1951; mixed doubles 1950; Wimbledon champion, doubles 1951, 1952. Australian champion, singles 1952; doubles 1951, 1952. French champion, doubles 1951, 1952. Member of Davis Cup team 1950 to 1952.

McKINLEY, CHARLES (United States); born January 5, 1941, at St. Louis, Mo.

United States champion, doubles 1961, 1963, 1964. Wimbledon champion, singles 1963. United States clay court champion, singles 1962, 1963; doubles 1961, 1964.

René Simone Mathieu.

United States indoor champion, singles 1962, 1964; doubles 1962, 1963, 1965. Member of Davis Cup team 1960 to 1965.

McMILLAN, FREW DONALD (South Africa); May 20, 1942, at Springs.

Wimbledon champion, doubles 1967. French champion, mixed doubles 1966; South

Gardnar Mulloy.

African champion, doubles 1965, 1967; mixed doubles 1965. German champion, doubles 1967. Italian champion, doubles 1967. Member of Davis Cup team 1965 to 1968.

MENZIES, MRS. STAMMERS (Great Britain); born April 3, 1914, St. Albans, Hertfordshire.

Wimbledon champion, doubles 1935, 1936; French champion, doubles South African champion, doubles 1948. Member of Wightman Cup team.

MORTIMER, ANGELA (Great Britain); born April 21, 1932, at Plymouth.

Wimbledon champion, singles 1961; doubles 1955; French champion, singles 1955; Australian champion, singles 1958; German champion, doubles 1957. Welsh champion, singles 1951, 1957–1960. Member of Wightman Cup team.

MULLOY, GARDNAR (United States); born November 22, 1914, at Miami, Fla.

United States champion, doubles 1942, 1945, 1946, 1948. Wimbledon champion, doubles 1957. United States clay court champion, doubles 1946. Member of Davis Cup team 1946 to 1957.

NEWCOMBE, JOHN (Australia); born May 23, 1944, at Sydney, New South Wales.

United States champion, singles 1967; doubles 1967. French champion, doubles 1967, 1969. Australian champion, doubles 1965, 1967, 1970, 1971; doubles 1965, 1966, 1968–1970. Italian champion, singles 1969; doubles 1971; mixed doubles 1964. German champion, singles 1968; mixed doubles 1966. Welsh champion, singles 1967. Canadian champion, doubles 1969. Wimbledon champion, singles 1970, 1971. Member of Davis Cup team 1963 to 1967.

NIELSEN, KURT (Denmark); born November 19, 1930, at Copenhagen.

United States champion, mixed doubles 1957. United States indoor champion, singles 1957; doubles 1953. Member of Davis Cup team from 1948 to 1960.

NUTHALL, BETTY MAY (Great Britain); born May 23, 1911, at Surbiton.

United States champion, singles 1930; doubles 1930, 1931, 1933; mixed doubles 1929, 1931. French champion, doubles 1931; mixed doubles 1931, 1932. Member of Wightman Cup team.

OKKER, TOM (Netherlands); born February 22, 1944, at Haarlem.

Italian champion, singles 1968; doubles 1968. German champion, singles 1970; doubles 1968; mixed doubles 1967. South

Tom Okker.

African champion, singles 1968; doubles 1968. Irish champion, singles 1968. Member of Davis Cup team 1964 to 1968.

OLMEDO, ALEJANDRO (Peru); born March 24, 1936, at Arequipa.

United States champion, doubles 1958. Wimbledon champion, singles 1959. Australian champion, singles 1959. United States clay court champion, doubles 1956. United States indoor champion, singles 1959; doubles 1959. Member of United States Davis Cup team 1958, 1959.

OSUNA, RAFAEL (Mexico); born September 15, 1938, at Mexico City.

United States champion, singles 1963; doubles 1962. Wimbledon champion, doubles 1960, 1963. Member of Davis Cup team 1958 to 1968.

PARKE, JAMES CECIL (Great Britain); born July 26, 1881, at Clones, Ireland; died 1942.

Wimbledon champion, mixed doubles, 1910, 1912, 1914. Australian champion, singles 1912; doubles 1912. Member of Davis Cup team.

PATTERSON, GERALD L. (Australia); born December 17, 1895, at Melbourne; died June 13, 1967.

Frederick John Perry.

United States champion, doubles 1919. Wimbledon champion, singles 1919, 1922; mixed doubles 1920. Australian champion, singles 1927; doubles 1914, 1922, 1925–1927. Member of Davis Cup team 1919 to 1928.

PATTY, J. EDWARD (United States); born February 11, 1924, at Little Rock, Ark.

Wimbledon champion, singles 1950; doubles 1957. French champion, singles 1950; mixed doubles 1946. Italian champion, singles 1954. German champion, singles 1953, 1954; doubles 1953–1955. South African champion, doubles 1954. United States indoor champion, mixed doubles, 1950. Member of Davis Cup team 1951.

PERRY, FREDERICK JOHN (Great Britain); born May 18, 1909, at Stockport.

United States champion, singles 1933, 1934, 1936; mixed doubles 1932. Wimbledon champion, singles 1934–1936; mixed doubles 1935, 1936. French champion, singles 1935; doubles 1933; mixed doubles 1932. Australian champion, singles 1934; doubles 1934. Member of Davis Cup team 1931 to 1936.

PETRA, YVAN (France); born March 18, 1916, in Indo-China.

Wimbledon champion, singles 1946. French champion, singles 1945; doubles 1938, 1946; mixed doubles 1937. Member of Davis Cup team 1937 to 1947.

PIETRANGELI, NICOLA (Italy); born September 11, 1933, in Tunis.

French champion, singles 1959, 1960; doubles 1959; mixed doubles 1958. Italian champion, singles 1957, 1961. German champion, singles 1960. South African champion, mixed doubles 1962. Member of Davis Cup team 1954 to 1968.

PIM, JOSHUA (Great Britain); born May 20, 1869, in Ireland; died April 15, 1942.

Wimbledon champion, singles 1893, 1894; doubles 1890; 1893. Irish champion, singles 1893–1895; doubles 1890, 1891, 1893–1895. Member of Davis Cup team 1902.

PRICE, MRS. SANDRA REYNOLDS (South Africa); born March 4, 1939, at Bloemfontein.

French champion, doubles 1959, 1961, 1962. Australian champion, doubles 1959; mixed 1959. German champion, singles 1960–62; doubles 1961. South African cham-

William Renshaw and Ernest Renshaw.

RENSHAW, ERNEST (Great Britain); born January 3, 1861; died September 2, 1899.

Wimbledon champion, singles 1888; doubles 1880, 1881, 1884–1886, 1888, 1889; mixed doubles 1888. Irish champion, singles 1883, 1887, 1888, 1892; doubles 1881, 1883–1885.

RENSHAW, WILLIAM (Great Britain); born January 3, 1861; died August 12, 1904.

Wimbledon champion, singles 1881–1886, 1889; doubles 1880, 1881, 1884–1886, 1888, 1889. Irish champion, singles 1880–1882; doubles 1881, 1883–1885.

RICHEY, GEORGE CLIFFORD, JR. (United States); born December 31, 1946, at San Angelo, Tex.

Canadian champion, singles 1969. Argentine champion, singles 1966, 1967. United States clay court champion, singles 1966; United States open clay court champion, singles. United States indoor champion, singles 1968. Member of Davis Cup team 1966 to 1970.

pion, singles 1959, 1961; doubles 1959–61; mixed 1962. United States clay court champion 1959.

QUIST, ADRIAN KARL (Australia); born August 4, 1913, at Medindia, South Australia.

United States champion, doubles 1939. Wimbledon champion, doubles 1935, 1950. French champion, doubles 1935. Australian champion, singles 1936, 1940, 1948; doubles 1936–40, 1946–1950. German champion, doubles 1934. Member of Davis Cup team 1933 to 1948.

RALSTON, RICHARD DENNIS (United States); born July 27, 1942, at Bakersfield, Calif.

United States champion, doubles 1961, 1963, 1964. Wimbledon champion, doubles 1960. French champion, doubles 1966. Argentine champion, doubles 1966. United States clay court champion, singles 1964, 1965; doubles 1961, 1964, 1966. United States hard court champion, singles 1964, 1965; doubles 1964, 1965. United States indoor champion, 1963; doubles 1963–1965.

Martin Riessen.

Anthony Dalton Roche.

RIESSEN, MARTIN CLARE (United States); born December 4, 1941, at Hinsdale, Ill.

United States champion, mixed doubles 1969, 1970. Italian champion, doubles 1968; mixed doubles 1968. German champion, doubles 1969; mixed doubles 1969; Canadian champion, doubles 1970. Swiss champion, doubles 1969. French champion, mixed doubles 1969. South African champion, mixed doubles 1968. Member of Davis Cup team 1961 to 1967.

ROCHE, ANTHONY DALTON (Australia); born May 17, 1945, at Tarcutta, New South Wales.

United States champion, doubles 1967. Wimbledon, 1965, 1968–1970. French champion, singles 1966; doubles 1967, 1969. Australian champion, doubles 1965, 1967. Italian champion, singles 1966. Swiss champion, singles 1970. Irish champion, singles 1970. United States Pro Championship, singles 1970. Member of Davis Cup team 1965 to 1967.

ROSE, MERVYN (Australia); born January 23, 1930, at Coffs Harbor, New South Wales.

United States champion, doubles 1952, 1953. Wimbledon champion, doubles 1954; mixed 1957. Australian champion, singles 1954; doubles 1954. French champion, singles 1958. Italian champion, singles 1958; German champion, singles 1957; doubles 1957; mixed 1957. Member of Davis Cup team 1951 to 1957.

ROSEWALL, KENNETH R. (Australia); born November 2, 1934, at Sydney.

United States champion, singles 1956; doubles 1956; mixed doubles 1956. United States Open champion, singles 1970; doubles 1969. Wimbledon champion, doubles 1953, 1956. Australian champion, singles 1953, 1955; doubles 1953, 1956. French champion, singles 1953; doubles 1953. Italian champion, doubles 1953. Member of Davis Cup team 1953 to 1956.

RYAN, ELIZABETH (United States) born 1894, at Los Angeles.

United States champion, doubles 1926; mixed doubles 1926, 1933. Wimbledon champion, doubles 1914, 1919–1923, 1925–1927, 1930, 1933, 1934; mixed doubles 1919, 1921, 1923, 1927, 1928, 1930, 1932. French champion, doubles 1914, 1922, 1930, 1932–1934. Italian champion, singles 1933; doubles 1934; mixed doubles 1934. United States indoor champion, singles 1926; doubles 1926. Member of Wightman Cup team.

SANTANA, MANUEL (Spain); born May 10, 1938, at Madrid.

United States champion, singles 1965. Wimbledon champion, singles 1966. French champion, singles 1961, 1964; doubles 1963. South African champion, singles 1967. United States indoor champion, doubles 1964. Mem-

Kenneth R. Rosewall.

Elizabeth Ryan.

1951, 1952; mixed doubles 1951, 1952. Australian champion, singles 1949, 1950; doubles 1951, 1952; mixed doubles 1949, 1950. Italian champion, singles 1952, doubles 1952. Member of Davis Cup team 1949 to 1952.

SEGURA, FRANCISCO (Ecuador); born June 20, 1921, at Guayaquil.

United States clay court champion, singles 1944; doubles 1945. United States indoor champion, singles 1946.

SMITH, STANLEY ROGER (United States); born December 14, 1946, at Pasadena, Calif.

United States champion, singles 1971, doubles 1968, 1971. Australian champion, doubles 1970. United States indoor champion, singles 1969, 1970, 1966–1970. United States Open indoor champion, doubles 1970; United States clay court, doubles 1968. United States hard court, singles 1966–1968; doubles 1966. Member of Davis Cup team 1968 to 1971.

ber of Davis Cup team 1958 to 1968.

SAVITT, RICHARD (United States); born March 4, 1927, at Bayonne, N.J.

Wimbledon champion, singles 1951. Australian champion, singles 1951. Italian champion, doubles 1951. United States indoor champion, singles 1952, 1958, 1961. Member of Davis Cup team in 1951.

SEDGMAN, FRANK (Australia); born October 29, 1927, at Mont Albert, Victoria.

United States champion, singles 1951, 1952; doubles 1950, 1951; mixed doubles 1951, 1952. Wimbledon champion, singles 1952; doubles 1948, 1951, 1952; mixed doubles 1951, 1952. French champion, doubles

Manuel Santana.

SPERLING, MRS. HILDA KRAHWINKEL (Germany and Denmark).

Wimbledon champion, mixed doubles 1933. French champion, singles 1935. German champion, singles 1934, 1935, 1937–1939; doubles 1932, 1937; mixed doubles 1932–1934.

STERRY, MRS. CHARLOTTE COOPER (Great Britain); born at Ealing; died May 10, 1966.

Wimbledon champion, singles 1895, 1896, 1898, 1901, 1908; doubles 1908; mixed doubles 1894–1898, 1900, 1908. German champion, singles 1899. Irish champion, singles 1895, 1898.

STOEFEN, LESTER ROLLO (United States); born March 30, 1911, at Des Moines, Iowa; died February 10, 1970.

United States champion, doubles 1933, 1934. Wimbledon champion, doubles 1934. United States indoor champion, singles 1934; doubles 1934.

STOLLE, FRED (Australia); born October 8, 1938 at Hornsby, New South Wales.

United States champion, singles 1966; doubles 1965, 1966; mixed doubles 1962, 1965. Wimbledon champion, doubles 1962, 1964; mixed doubles 1961, 1964. French champion, singles 1965; doubles 1965, 1968. Australian champion, doubles 1963, 1964, 1966; mixed doubles 1962. Italian champion, doubles 1963, 1964; mixed doubles 1962. German champion, singles 1966; doubles 1961, 1963, 1966; mixed doubles 1963. South African champion, doubles 1966; mixed doubles 1966.

STURGESS, ERIC (South Africa); born May 10, 1920, at Johannesburg.

United States champion, mixed doubles 1949. Wimbledon champion, mixed doubles 1949, 1950. French champion, doubles 1947; mixed doubles 1947, 1949. German champion, singles 1952; mixed doubles 1952. South African champion, singles 1939, 1940, 1946, 1948–1954, 1957; doubles 1946–1948, 1951–1953, 1955, 1957; mixed doubles 1940, 1946–1948, 1951, 1953. Member of Davis Cup team 1947 to 1951.

SUSMAN, MRS. KAREN HANTZE (United States); born December, 1942, at San Diego, Calif.

United States champion, doubles 1964; Wimbledon champion, singles 1962; doubles 1961, 1962. Member of Wightman Cup team.

TODD, MRS. PATRICIA CANNING (United States); born July 22, 1922, at San Francisco, Calif.

Wimbledon champion, doubles 1947. French champion, singles 1947; doubles 1948; mixed doubles 1948. United States clay court champion, doubles 1951. United States indoor champion 1942, 1948; doubles 1952. Member of Wightman Cup team.

VIVIEN, MRS. MARGARET CRAFT SCRIVEN (Great Britain); born August 18, 1912, at Leeds.

French champion, singles 1933, 1934; doubles 1935; mixed doubles 1933. Member of Wightman Cup team.

VON CRAMM, BARON GOTTFRIED (Germany); born July 7, 1909, at Berlin.

United States champion, doubles 1937. Wimbledon champion, mixed doubles 1933. German champion, singles 1932–1935, 1948, 1949; doubles 1948, 1949, 1953–1954; mixed doubles 1932–1934. Member of Davis Cup team 1932 to 1953.

WADE, SARAH VIRGINIA (Great Britain); born October 7, 1945, at Bournemouth.

United States Open champion, singles Italian champion, singles 1971; doubles 1968,

Margaret Scriven Vivien.

1971. Member of Wightman Cup team 1965 to 1971.

WATSON, MAUD (Great Britain); born 1863; died November 16, 1934.

Wimbledon champion, singles 1884, 1885. Irish champion, singles 1884, 1885.

WILDING, ANTHONY FREDERICK (New Zealand); born October 31, 1883, at Christchurch; killed in action, France, May 9, 1915.

Wimbledon champion, singles 1910–1913; doubles 1907, 1908, 1910, 1914. Australian champion, singles 1906, 1909; doubles 1906. German champion, doubles 1905. Member of Davis Cup team 1905 to 1914.

Leading Tennis Players of Today

Name	Country	Date of Birth
John Alexander	Australia	July 4, 1951
Bill Alvarez	Colombia	December 15, 1936
Malcolm (Mal) Anderson	Australia	March 3, 1935
Beatriz Araujo	Argentina	July 14, 1955
Ana Maria Arias	Argentina	July 24, 1946
Arthur Ashe	United States	July 10, 1943
Ada Bakker	Netherlands	April 8, 1948
Galina Baksheeva	U.S.S.R.	July 12, 1945
Szabolis Baranyi	Hungary	January 31, 1944
Jean Claude Barclay	France	December 30, 1942
Roy Barth	U.S.A.	March 30, 1947
Pierre Barthes	France	September 13, 1941
Jane (Peaches) Bartkowicz	U.S.A.	April 4, 1949
Gerald Battrick	Great Britain	May 27, 1947
Lindsey Beaven	Great Britain	January 1, 1950
Mike Belkin	Canada	June 29, 1945
Ove Bengtson	Sweden	April 5, 1945
Ingrid Bentzer	Sweden	December 6, 1943
Byron Bertram	South Africa	October 29, 1952
Jeff Borowiak	U.S.A.	September 25, 1949
Bill (Tex) Bowrey	Australia	December 25, 1943
Lesley Bowrey	Australia	August 16, 1942
Shirley Brasher	Great Britain	June 13, 1934
Marianne Brummer	South Africa	November 24, 1949
Ingo Buding	West Germany	January 9, 1942
Maria Bueno	Brazil	October 11, 1939
Wilhelm Bungert	West Germany	April 1, 1939
Veronica Burton	Great Britain	January 27, 1952
Bob Carmichael	Australia	July 4, 1940
Rosemary Casals	U.S.A.	September 16, 1948
Gail Chanfreau	France	April 3, 1945
Jean Baptiste Chanfreau	France	December 5, 1943
John Clifton	Great Britain	February 19, 1946
Jim Connors	U.S.A.	September 2, 1952
Daniel Contet	France	November 3, 1943
Jill Cooper	Great Britain	April 14, 1949
John Cooper	Australia	May 10, 1947
Margaret Court	Australia	July 16, 1942
Mark Cox	Great Britain	July 5, 1943
Dick Crealy	Australia	September 18, 1944
Mary Ann Eisel	U.S.A.	November 25, 1946
Peter Curtis	Great Britain	August 29, 1945
Judy Dalton	Australia	December 12, 1937
Pierre Darmon	France	January 14, 1934
Rosie Darmon	France	October 9, 1939
Owen Davidson	Australia	October 4, 1943
Philip Dent	Australia	February 14, 1950
Roger Dowdeswell	Rhodesia	February 16, 1944
Cliff Drysdale	South Africa	May 26, 1941

Edda Duchting	West Germany	November 13, 1936
Annette du Plooy	South Africa	September 25, 1943
Françoise Durr	France	December 25, 1942
Harold Eischenbroich	West Germany	June 19, 1941
Esme Emanuel	South Africa	June 14, 1947
Roy Emerson	Australia	November 3, 1936
Chris Evert	U.S.A.	December 21, 1954
Brian Fairlie	New Zealand	June 13, 1948
Ian Fletcher	Australia	December 1, 1948
Zeljko Franulovic	Yugoslavia	June 13, 1947
Tory Ann Fretz	U.S.A.	August 8, 1942
Frank Froehling	U.S.A.	May 19, 1942
Wieslaw Gasiorek	Poland	January 13, 1936
Wendy Gilchrist	Australia	May 17, 1950
Bob Giltinan	Australia	July 4, 1949
Andres Gimeno	Spain	August 3, 1937
Juan Gisbert	Spain	July 10, 1944
Evonne Goolagong	Australia	July 31, 1951
Pancho Gonzalez	U.S.A.	May 9, 1928
Tom Gorman	U.S.A.	January 19, 1946
Helen Gourlay	Australia	December 23, 1946
Georges Goven	France	April 27, 1948
Clark Graebner	U.S.A.	November 4, 1943
Istvan Gulyas	Hungary	October 14, 1931
Nancy Richey Gunther	U.S.A.	August 23, 1942
Francisco (Pancho) Guzman	Ecuador	May 24, 1946
Betty Ann Hansen	U.S.A.	February 26, 1950
Gail Hansen	U.S.A.	April 21, 1951
Kerry Harris	Australia	September 19, 1949
Kathy Harter	U.S.A.	October 27, 1946
Julie Heldman	U.S.A.	December 8, 1945
Bob Hewitt	South Africa	January 12, 1940
Lew Hoad	Australia	November 23, 1934
Helga Hoesi	West Germany	February 2, 1940
Patti Hogan	U.S.A.	December 21, 1949
Milan Holecek	Czechoslovakia	October 23, 1943
Ron Holmberg	U.S.A.	January 27, 1938
Patrick Hombergen	Belgium	September 8, 1946
Bob Howe	Australia	August 3, 1925
Lesley Hunt	Australia	May 29, 1950
Paul Hutchins	Great Britain	April 5, 1945
Douglas "Hank" Irvine	Rhodesia	September 1, 1943
Christine Janes	Great Britain	January 16, 1941
François Jauffret	France	February 9, 1942
Ann Jones	Great Britain	October 17, 1938
Nicky Kalogeropoulos	Greece	February 18, 1945
Ray Keldie	Australia	January 17, 1946
Keith Kiepraam	South Africa	September 11, 1942
Billie Jean King	U.S.A.	November 22, 1943
Brenda Kirk	South Africa	January 11, 1951
Tiiu Kivi	U.S.S.R.	November 3, 1943
Thomas Koch	Brazil	May 11, 1945
Jan Kodes	Czechoslovakia	March 1, 1946
Vladimir Korotkov	U.S.S.R.	April 23, 1948
Karen Krantzcke	Australia	February 1, 1947
Ramanathan Krishnan	India	April 11, 1937
Jan Kukal	Czechoslovakia	September 13, 1942
Christian Kuknke	West Germany	April 13, 1939
Premjit Lall	India	October 20, 1940
Rod Laver	Australia	August 9, 1938
Tomas Lejus	U.S.S.R.	August 28, 1941

Name	Country	Date of Birth
Jan Leschly	Denmark	September 11, 1940
Sergei Likhachev	U.S.S.R.	March 20, 1940
David Lloyd	Great Britain	January 3, 1948
Ingrid Loeys	Belgium	January 12, 1948
Joaquin Loyo-Mayo	Mexico	August 16, 1945
Lance Lumsden	British Caribbean	February 16, 1946
Jan-Eric Lundquist	Sweden	April 14, 1937
Bob Lutz	U.S.A.	August 29, 1947
Edison Mandarino	Brazil	March 26, 1941
Cecilia Martinez	U.S.A.	May 24, 1947
Stanley Matthews	Great Britain	November 20, 1945
Robert Maud	South Africa	August 12, 1946
Allan McDonald	Australia	March 1, 1951
John McDonald	New Zealand	February 4, 1931
Jim McManus	U.S.A.	September 16, 1940
Frew McMillan	South Africa	May 20, 1942
Kerry Melville	Australia	August 7, 1947
John de Mendoza	Great Britain	August 22, 1949
Alexander Metreveli	U.S.S.R.	November 2, 1944
Margaret (Peggy) Michell	U.S.A.	February 2, 1949
Corinne Molesworth	Great Britain	June 18, 1949
Fay Moore	Australia	December 18, 1943
Ray Moore	South Africa	August 24, 1946
Olga Morozova	U.S.S.R.	May 3, 1949
Jaidip Mukerjea	India	April 21, 1942
Martin Mulligan	Italy	October 18, 1940
Antonio Munoz	Spain	March 1, 1951
Ilie Nastase	Rumania	July 19, 1946
John Newcombe	Australia	May 23, 1944
Helga Niessen	West Germany	November 11, 1941
Tom Okker	Netherlands	February 22, 1944
Manuel Orantes	Spain	February 6, 1949
James H. Osborne	U.S.A.	February 1945
John Paish	Great Britain	March 25, 1948
Adriano Panatta	Italy	July 3, 1952
Onny Parun	New Zealand	April 15, 1947
Charles Pasarell	U.S.A.	February 12, 1944
Andrew Pattison	South Africa	January 30, 1949
Lea Pericoli	Italy	April 11, 1943
Barry Phillips-Moore	Australia	June 9, 1938
Nicola Pietrangeli	Italy	September 11, 1933
Kristy Pigeon	U.S.A.	August 15, 1950
Nikki Pilic	Yugoslavia	August 27, 1939
Hans-Joachim Plotz	West Germany	February 26, 1944
Robin Primrose	Great Britain	February 21, 1944
Maryna Procter	South Africa	September 9, 1944
Marillyn Pryde	New Zealand	June 11, 1953
Dennis Ralston	U.S.A.	July 27, 1942
Cliff Richey	U.S.A.	December 31, 1946
Martin Riessen	U.S.A.	December 4, 1941
Tony Roche	Australia	May 17, 1945
Patricio Rodriguez	Chile	December 20, 1938
Ken Rosewall	South Africa	November 2, 1934
Laura Rossouw	South Africa	July 15, 1946
Ray Ruffels	Australia	March 23, 1946
Richard Russell	British Caribbean	September 8, 1945
Terry Ryan	South Africa	April 27, 1942
Christina Sandberg	Sweden	January 11, 1948
Mike Sangster	Great Britain	September 11, 1940
Manuel Santana	Spain	May 10, 1938
Kazuko Sawamatsu	Japan	January 5, 1951
Marijke Schaar	Netherlands	November 12, 1944

Abe Segal	South Africa	October 23, 1930
Ismail el Shafei	United Arab Republic	November 15, 1947
Winnie Shaw	Great Britain	January 18, 1947
Stan Smith	U.S.A.	December 19, 1946
Harold Solomon	U.S.A.	September 17, 1952
Nicola Spear	Yugoslavia	February 22, 1944
Graham Stilwell	Great Britain	November 15, 1945
Fred Stolle	Australia	October 8, 1938
Allan Stone	Australia	October 14, 1935
Betty Stove	Netherlands	June 24, 1945
Dimitri Sturdza	Switzerland	October 11, 1938
Astrid Suurbeek	Netherlands	February 15, 1947
Roscoe Tanner	U.S.A.	October 15, 1951
Frances Taylor	Great Britain	December 20, 1943
Roger Taylor	Great Britain	October 14, 1941
Ion Tiriac	Rumania	May 9, 1939
Janice Townsend	Great Britain	June 11, 1947
Denise Carter Triolo	U.S.A.	July 31, 1950
Neil Truman	Great Britain	December 12, 1945
Linda Tuero	U.S.A.	October 21, 1950
Jorgen Ulrich	Denmark	August 21, 1936
Torben Ulrich	Denmark	October 4, 1928
Erik Van Dillen	U.S.A.	February 21, 1951
Vlasta Vopickova	Czechoslovakia	March 26, 1944
Virginia Wade	Great Britain	July 10, 1945
Patricia Walkden	South Africa	February 12, 1946
Sharon Walsh	U.S.A.	February 24, 1952
Stephen Warboys	Great Britain	October 25, 1953
Alena West	Czechoslovakia	January 7, 1945
Joyce Williams	Great Britain	July 22, 1944
Bobby Wilson	Great Britain	November 22, 1935
Haakan Zahr	Sweden	June 4, 1948
Vladimir Zednik	Czechoslovakia	February 1, 1947
Valerie Ziegenfuss	U.S.A.	June 29, 1949

AGE OF MEN NATIONAL CHAMPIONS

There is no predicting when a man will be ready to win the United States singles championship. Several have arrived as teen-agers—Oliver Campbell, Dick Sears (our first champion, 1881), Bob Wrenn, and Ellsworth Vines winning at 19. Another, Vic Seixas, persisted until seven days after his thirty-first birthday before he became champion. The traditional entry to manhood—age 21—most frequently has been the breakthrough year for first championships. Six men—Ted Schroeder, Malcolm Whitman, Johnny Doeg, Bobby Riggs, Ken Rosewall, Ashley Cooper—made it at 21. In winning the USLTA's first seven tourneys, Dick Sears reigned through his twenty-fifth year. Bill Larned, also winner of seven titles although his success did not begin until 1901 when he was 28. This made Bill our oldest National champion, in 1911, at 38.

Year When First Won, Date of Final Match and Exact Age When First Won

Champion	Date of Birth	Final Match	Age Yrs.	Mos.	Days
Oliver S. Campbell	Feb. 25, 1871	Sept. 3, 1890	19	6	9
Richard D. Sears	Oct. 26, 1861	Sept. 3, 1881	19	10	8
Robert D. Wrenn*	Sept. 20, 1873	Aug. 30, 1893	19	11	10
H. Ellsworth Vines, Jr.	Sept. 28, 1911	Sept. 12, 1931	19	11	15
Richard A. Gonzalez	May 9, 1928	Sept. 19, 1948	20	4	10
William Johnston	Nov. 2, 1894	Sept. 7, 1915	20	10	5
Frederick R. Schroeder, Jr.	July 20, 1921	Sept. 7, 1942	21	1	18
Malcolm D. Whitman	March 5, 1877	Aug. 23, 1898	21	5	18
Robert L. Riggs	Feb. 25, 1918	Sept. 17, 1939	21	6	23
John H. Doeg*	Dec. 7, 1908	Sept. 13, 1930	21	9	6
Kenneth Rosewall	Nov. 2, 1934	Sept. 9, 1956	21	10	7
Ashley J. Cooper	Sept. 15, 1936	Sept. 7, 1958	21	11	22
Jean René Lacoste	July 2, 1904	Sept. 18, 1926	22	2	16
J. Donald Budge	June 13, 1915	Sept. 11, 1937	22	2	29
W. Donald McNeill	April 30, 1918	Sept. 9, 1940	22	4	10
Malcolm J. Anderson	March 5, 1935	Sept. 8, 1957	22	6	3
Maurice E. McLoughlin	Jan. 7, 1890	Aug. 26, 1912	22	7	19
M. Anthony Trabert	Aug. 16, 1930	Sept. 7, 1953	23	0	22
John Newcombe	May 23, 1944	Sept. 10, 1967	23	3	13
R. N. Williams II	Jan. 29, 1891	Sept. 1, 1914	23	7	3
Stanley R. Smith	Dec. 14, 1946	Sept. 15, 1971†	24	2	29
Frank A. Sedgman	Oct. 29, 1927	Sept. 4, 1951	23	10	6
Fred J. Perry	May 18, 1909	Sept. 10, 1933	24	3	23
Joseph R. Hunt	Feb. 17, 1919	Sept. 6, 1943	24	6	20
R. Lindley Murray*	Nov. 3, 1893	Sept. 3, 1918	24	10	0
Roy Emerson	Nov. 3, 1936	Sept. 10, 1961	24	10	7
William J. Clothier	Sept. 27, 1881	Aug. 29, 1906	24	11	2
Rodney Laver*	Aug. 9, 1938	Sept. 8, 1963	25	1	0
John A. Kramer	Aug. 1, 1921	Sept. 8, 1946	25	1	7
Arthur R. Ashe, Jr.	July 10, 1943	Sept. 8, 1968†	25	1	29
Arthur D. Larsen*	April 17, 1925	Sept. 5, 1950	25	4	18
Beals C. Wright*	Dec. 19, 1879	Aug. 31, 1905	25	8	12
Holcombe Ward	Nov. 23, 1878	Aug. 24, 1904	25	9	1
Neale A. Fraser*	Oct. 3, 1933	Sept. 13, 1959	25	11	10
Rafael Osuna	Sept. 15, 1938	Sept. 13, 1964	25	11	29
Henry W. Slocum, Jr.	May 28, 1862	Aug. 25, 1888	26	2	28
Henri Cochet	Dec. 14, 1901	Sept. 17, 1928	26	9	3
Hugh L. Doherty	Oct. 8, 1876	Aug. 27, 1903	26	10	19
Fred H. Hovey	Oct. 7, 1868	Aug. 27, 1895	26	10	20
Manuel Santana	May 10, 1938	Sept. 12, 1965	27	4	2
William T. Tilden II	Feb. 10, 1893	Sept. 6, 1920	27	6	27
Fred Stolle	Oct. 8, 1938	Sept. 11, 1966	27	11	3
Frank A. Parker	Jan. 31, 1916	Sept. 4, 1944	28	7	4
William A. Larned	Dec. 30, 1872	Aug. 21, 1901	28	7	22
Wilmer L. Allison, Jr.	Dec. 8, 1904	Sept. 12, 1935	30	9	4
E. Victor Seixas, Jr.	Aug. 30, 1923	Sept. 6, 1954	31	0	7

* Left-handed player.
† Open.

USLTA RANKINGS

When the first Top Ten was determined in 1885 by the USLTA men's ranking committee, with national champion Dick Sears of Boston in the foremost position, the competition was not so extensive as today. The first national championship, at the Newport (R.I.) Casino had been held only four years before, Sears felling Briton W. E. Glyn in the final. Now, room at the top is greatly sought. Hundreds of players, competing in scores of tournaments, are scheming to crash the Top Ten. In 1970, for example, the USLTA ranked 57 men and 31 women, and the low-liest of those is an exceptional player. It is something to have been ranked at all, but to be in the Top Ten—that is arrival, an accomplishment to be cherished.

Men's Ranking

1885

1. R. D. Sears
2. James Dwight
3. W. V. R. Berry
4. G. M. Brinley
5. J. S. Clark
6. A. Moffat
7. R. L. Beeckman
8. H. A. Taylor
9. F. S. Mansfield
10. W. P. Knapp

1886

1. R. D. Sears
2. James Dwight
3. R. L. Beeckman
4. H. A. Taylor
5. J. S. Clark
6. H. W. Slocum
7. G. M. Brinley
8. F. S. Mansfield
9. A. Moffat
10. J. S. Conover

1887

1. R. D. Sears
2. H. W. Slocum
3. R. L. Beeckman
4. H. A. Taylor
5. J. S. Clark
6. F. S. Mansfield
7. P. S. Sears
8. G. M. Brinley
9. E. P. MacMullen
10. Q. A. Shaw, Jr.

1888

1. H. W. Slocum
2. H. A. Taylor
3. James Dwight
4. J. S. Clark
5. C. A. Chase
6. P. S. Sears
7. E. P. MacMullen
8. O. S. Campbell
9. R. L. Beeckman
10. F. S. Mansfield

1889

1. H. W. Slocum
2. W. A. Shaw, Jr.
3. O. S. Campbell
4. H. A. Taylor
5. C. A. Chase
6. J. S. Clark
7. W. P. Knapp
8. R. P. Huntington, Jr.
9. R. S. Sears
10. F. S. Mansfield

1890

1. O. S. Campbell
2. R. P. Huntington, Jr.
3. W. P. Knapp
4. H. W. Slocum
5. F. H. Hovey
6. Clarence Hobart
7. P. S. Sears
8. H. A. Taylor
9. C. A. Chase
10. V. G. Hall

1891

1. O. S. Campbell
2. Clarence Hobart
3. R. P. Huntington, Jr.
4. F. H. Hovey
5. E. L. Hall
6. V. G. Hall
7. P. S. Sears
8. S. T. Chase
9. C. T. Lee
10. M. D. Smith

1892

1. O. S. Campbell
2. E. L. Hall
3. E. P. Knapp
4. Clarence Hobart
5. F. H. Hovey
6. W. A. Larned
7. M. G. Chace
8. R. D. Wrenn
9. Richard Stevens
10. C. P. Hubbard

1893

1. R. D. Wrenn
2. Clarence Hobart
3. F. H. Hovey
4. M. G. Chace
5. W. A. Larned
6. E. L. Hall
7. Richard Stevens
8. A. E. Foote
9. John Howland
10. C. R. Budlong

USLTA Rankings (*cont.*)

1894

1. R. D. Wrenn
2. W. A. Larned
3. M. F. Goodbody*
4. F. H. Hovey
5. M. G. Chace
6. Clarence Hobart
7. Richard Stevens
8. C. R. Budlong
9. A. E. Foote
10. W. G. Parker

1895

1. F. H. Hovey
2. W. A. Larned
3. M. G. Chace
4. John Howland
5. R. D. Wrenn
6. C. B. Neel
7. Clarence Hobart
8. Richard Stevens
9. A. E. Foote
10. C. R. Budlong

1896

1. R. D. Wrenn
2. W. A. Larned
3. C. B. Neel
4. F. H. Hovey
5. E. P. Fisher
6. G. L. Wrenn, Jr.
7. Richard Stevens
8. M. D. Whitman
9. L. E. Ware
10. G. P. Sheldon, Jr.

1897

1. R. D. Wrenn
2. W. A. Larned
3. W. V. Eaves*
4. H. A. Nisbet*
5. H. S. Mahoney*
6. G. L. Wrenn, Jr.
7. M. D. Whitman
8. Kreigh Collins
9. E. P. Fisher
10. W. S. Bond

1898

1. M. D. Whitman
2. L. E. Ware
3. W. S. Bond
4. D. F. Davis
5. C. R. Budlong
6. E. P. Fisher
7. G. L. Wrenn, Jr.
8. Richard Stevens
9. S. C. Millett
10. G. K. Belden

1899

1. M. D. Whitman
2. D. F. Davis
3. W. A. Larned
4. J. P. Paret
5. Kreigh Collins
6. G. L. Wrenn, Jr.
7. L. E. Ware
8. B. C. Wright
9. Holcombe Ward
10. R. P. Huntington, Jr.

1900

1. M. D. Whitman
2. D. F. Davis
3. W. A. Larned
4. B. C. Wright
5. Kreigh Collins
6. G. L. Wrenn, Jr.
7. Holcombe Ward
8. L. E. Ware
9. J. A. Allen
10. R. D. Little

1901

1. W. A. Larned
2. B. C. Wright
3. D. F. Davis
4. L. E. Ware
5. Clarence Hobart
6. R. D. Little
7. Holcombe Ward
8. Kreigh Collins
9. E. P. Fisher
10. W. J. Clothier

1902

1. W. A. Larned
2. M. D. Whitman
3. B. C. Wright
4. Holcombe Ward
5. W. J. Clothier
6. L. E. Ware
7. R. D. Little
8. Kreigh Collins
9. H. H. Hackett
10. Clarence Hobart

1903

1. W. A. Larned
2. Holcombe Ward
3. W. J. Clothier
4. B. C. Wright
5. Kreigh Collins
6. E. P. Larned
7. H. F. Allen
8. E. W. Leonard
9. R. H. Carleton
10. Kenneth Horton

* Foreign players included in USLTA ranking.

1904

1. Holcombe Ward
2. W. J. Clothier
3. W. A. Larned
4. B. C. Wright
5. Kreigh Collins
6. R. D. Little
7. F. B. Alexander
8. Richard Stevens
9. A. E. Bell
10. E. W. Leonard

1905

1. B. C. Wright
2. Holcombe Ward
3. W. A. Larned
4. W. J. Clothier
5. F. B. Alexander
6. Clarence Hobart
7. Richard Stevens
8. Kreigh Collins
9. R. D. Little
10. F. G. Anderson

1906

1. W. J. Clothier
2. W. A. Larned
3. B. C. Wright
4. F. B. Alexander
5. K. H. Behr
6. R. D. Little
7. H. H. Hackett
8. F. G. Anderson
9. E. B. Dewhurst
10. I. C. Wright

1907

1. W. A. Larned
2. B. C. Wright
3. K. H. Behr
4. R. D. Little
5. Robert LeRoy
6. Clarence Hobart
7. E. P. Larned
8. R. C. Seaver
9. I. C. Wright
10. F. C. Colston

1908

1. W. A. Larned
2. B. C. Wright
3. F. B. Alexander
4. W. J. Clothier
5. R. D. Little
6. Robert LeRoy
7. Nat Emerson
8. N. W. Niles
9. W. F. Johnson
10. R. H. Palmer

1909

1. W. A. Larned
2. W. J. Clothier
3. W. F. Johnson
4. N. W. Niles
5. R. D. Little
6. M. E. McLoughlin
7. M. H. Long
8. K. H. Behr
9. E. P. Larned
10. Robert LeRoy

1910

1. W. A. Larned
2. T. C. Bundy
3. B. C. Wright
4. M. E. McLoughlin
5. M. H. Long
6. N. W. Niles
7. G. F. Touchard
8. T. R. Pell
9. F. C. Colston
10. C. R. Gardner

1911

1. W. A. Larned
2. M. E. McLoughlin
3. T. C. Bundy
4. G. F. Touchard
5. M. H. Long
6. N. W. Niles
7. T. R. Pell
8. R. D. Little
9. K. H. Behr
10. W. M. Hall

1912

1. M. E. McLoughlin
2. R. N. Williams II
3. W. F. Johnson
4. W. J. Clothier
5. N. W. Niles
6. T. C. Bundy
7. K. H. Behr
8. R. D. Little
9. G. P. Gardner, Jr.
10. G. F. Touchard

1913

1. M. E. McLoughlin
2. R. N. Williams II
3. W. J. Clothier
4. W. M. Johnson
5. T. R. Pell
6. N. W. Niles
7. W. F. Johnson
8. G. F. Touchard
9. G. P. Gardner, Jr.
10. J. R. Strachan

USLTA Rankings (*cont.*)

1914

1. M. E. McLoughlin
2. R. N. Williams II
3. K. G. Behr
4. R. L. Murray
5. W. J. Clothier
6. W. M. Johnson
7. G. M. Church
8. F. B. Alexander
9. W. M. Washburn
10. E. F. Fottrell

1915

1. W. M. Johnson
2. R. N. Williams II
3. M. E. McLoughlin
4. K. H. Behr
5. T. R. Pell
6. N. W. Niles
7. C. J. Griffin
8. W. M. Washburn
9. G. M. Church
10. W. M. Hall

1916

1. R. N. Williams II
2. W. M. Johnson
3. G. M. Church
4. R. L. Murray
5. Ichiya Kumagae*
6. C. J. Griffin
7. W. M. Washburn
8. W. E. Davis
9. J. J. Armstrong
10. Dean Mathey

As only Patriotic Tournaments were held in 1917, no ranking was made for that year.

1918

1. R. L. Murray
2. W. T. Tilden II
3. F. B. Alexander
4. W. M. Hall
5. W. T. Hayes
6. N. H. Niles
7. Ichiya Kumagae*
8. C. S. Garland
9. S. H. Voshell
10. T. R. Pell

1919

1. W. M. Johnson
2. W. T. Tilden II
3. Ichiya Kumagae*
4. R. L. Murray
5. W. F. Johnson

* Foreign players included in USLTA ranking.

6. R. N. Williams II
7. Roland Roberts
8. C. S. Garland
9. W. T. Hayes
10. W. M. Washburn

1920

1. W. T. Tilden II
2. W. M. Johnson
3. R. N. Williams II
4. Ichiya Kumagae*
5. W. E. Davis
6. C. J. Griffin
7. W. M. Washburn
8. C. S. Garland
9. N. W. Niles
10. W. F. Johnson

1921

1. W. T. Tilden II
2. W. M. Johnson
3. Vincent Richards
4. W. F. Johnson
5. W. M. Washburn
6. R. N. Williams II
7. Ichiya Kumagae*
8. S. H. Voshell
9. L. B. Rice
10. N. W. Niles

1922

1. W. T. Tilden II
2. W. M. Johnston
3. Vincent Richards
4. R. N. Williams II
5. W. F. Johnson
6. Robert Kinsey
7. Zenzo Shimizu*
8. Howard Kinsey
9. Francis T. Hunter
10. W. M. Washburn

1923

1. W. T. Tilden II
2. W. M. Johnston
3. R. N. Wililams II
4. Vincent Richards
5. Francis T. Hunter
6. Howard Kinsey
7. Carl Fischer
8. Brian I. C. Norton*
9. Harvey Snodgrass
10. Robert Kinsey

1924

1. W. T. Tilden II
2. Vincent Richards
3. W. M. Johnston
4. Howard Kinsey

5. W. F. Johnson
6. Harvey Snodgrass
7. John F. Hennessey
8. Brian I. C. Norton*
9. Geo. M. Lott, Jr.
10. C. J. Griffin

1925

1. W. T. Tilden II
2. W. M. Johnston
3. Vincent Richards
4. R. N. Williams II
5. Manuel Alonso*
6. Howard Kinsey
7. Takeichi Harada*
8. Cranston W. Holman
9. Brian I. C. Norton*
10. Wray D. Brown

1926

1. W. T. Tilden II
2. Manuel Alonso*
3. Takeichi Harada*
4. W. M. Johnston
5. Edw. G. Chandler
6. Lewis N. White
7. A. J. Chapin, Jr.
8. Brian I. C. Norton*
9. Geo. M. Lott, Jr.
10. George King

1927

1. W. T. Tilden II
2. Francis T. Hunter
3. Geo. M. Lott, Jr.
4. Manuel Alonso*
5. John F. Hennessey
6. John Van Ryn
7. Arnold W. Jones
8. John H. Doeg
9. Lewis N. White
10. Cranston W. Holman

1928

1. W. T. Tilden II
2. Francis T. Hunter
3. Geo. M. Lott, Jr.
4. John F. Hennessey
5. Wilmer L. Allison
6. John Van Ryn
7. Frederick Mercur
8. John H. Doeg
9. Julius Seligson
10. Frank X. Shields

1929

1. W. T. Tilden II
2. Francis T. Hunter
3. John H. Doeg

4. George M. Lott, Jr.
5. John Van Ryn
6. Frederick Mercur
7. Wilmer L. Allison
8. Wilber F. Coen, Jr.
9. R. Berkeley Bell
10. Gregory S. Mangin

1930

1. John H. Doeg
2. Frank X. Shields
3. Wilmer L. Allison
4. Sidney B. Wood, Jr.
5. Clifford S. Sutter
6. Gregory S. Mangin
7. George M. Lott, Jr.
8. H. Ellsworth Vines, Jr.
9. John Van Ryn
10. Bryan M. Grant, Jr.

1931

1. H. Ellsworth Vines, Jr.
2. Geo. M. Lott, Jr.
3. Frank X. Shields
4. John Van Ryn
5. John H. Doeg
6. Clifford S. Sutter
7. Sidney B. Wood, Jr.
8. Keith Gledhill
9. Wilmer L. Allison
10. R. Berkeley Bell

1932

1. H. Ellsworth Vines, Jr.
2. Wilmer L. Allison
3. Clifford S. Sutter
4. Sidney B. Wood, Jr.
5. Frank X. Shields
6. Lester R. Stoefen
7. Gregory S. Mangin
8. Keith Gledhill
9. John Van Ryn
10. David N. Jones

1933

1. Frank X. Shields
2. Wilmer L. Allison
3. Lester R. Stoefen
4. Clifford S. Sutter
5. Gregory S. Mangin
6. Sidney B. Wood, Jr.
7. Bryan M. Grant, Jr.
8. Frank A. Parker
9. Keith Gledhill
10. George M. Lott, Jr.

1934

1. Wilmer L. Allison
2. Sidney B. Wood, Jr.

* Foreign players included in USLTA ranking.

USLTA Rankings (*cont.*)

3. Frank X. Shields
4. Frank A. Parker
5. Lester R. Stoefen
6. Geo. M. Lott, Jr.
7. R. Berkeley Bell
8. Clifford S. Sutter
9. J. Donald Budge
10. Bryan M. Grant, Jr.

1935

1. Wilmer L. Allison
2. J. Donald Budge
3. Bryan M. Grant, Jr.
4. Frank X. Shields
5. Sidney B. Wood, Jr.
6. Gregory S. Mangin
7. Frank A. Parker
8. J. Gilbert Hall
9. Wilmer M. Hines
10. R. Berkeley Bell

1936

1. J. Donald Budge
2. Frank A. Parker
3. Bryan M. Grant, Jr.
4. Robert L. Riggs
5. Gregory S. Mangin
6. John Van Ryn
7. John McDiarmid
8. Charles R. Harris
9. Joseph R. Hunt
10. Arthur H. Hendrix

1937

1. J. Donald Budge
2. Robert L. Riggs
3. Frank A. Parker
4. Bryan M. Grant, Jr.
5. Joseph R. Hunt
6. Wayne R. Sabin
7. Harold Surface, Jr.
8. C. Gene Mako
9. W. Donald McNeill
10. John Van Ryn

1938

1. J. Donald Budge
2. Robert L. Riggs
3. C. Gene Mako
4. Sidney B. Wood, Jr.
5. Joseph R. Hunt
6. Bryan M. Grant, Jr.
7. Elwood T. Cooke
8. Frank A. Parker
9. Gilbert A. Hunt, Jr.
10. Francis L. Kovacs II

1939

1. Robert L. Riggs
2. Frank A. Parker

3. W. Donald McNeill
4. S. Welby Van Horn
5. Wayne R. Sabin
6. Elwood T. Cooke
7. Bryan M. Grant, Jr.
8. Gardnar Mulloy
9. Gilbert A. Hunt, Jr.
10. Henry J. Prusoff

1940

1. W. Donald McNeill
2. Robert L. Riggs
3. Francis L. Kovacs II
4. Joseph R. Hunt
5. Frank A. Parker
6. John A. Kramer
7. Gardnar Mulloy
8. Henry J. Prusoff
9. Elwood T. Cooke
10. F. R. Schroeder, Jr.

1941

1. Robert L. Riggs
2. Francis L. Kovacs II
3. Frank A. Parker
4. W. Donald McNeill
5. F. R. Schroeder, Jr.
6. Wayne R. Sabin
7. Gardnar Mulloy
8. Bryan M. Grant, Jr.
9. John A. Kramer
10. William F. Talbert

1942

1. F. R. Schroeder, Jr.
2. Frank A. Parker
3. Gardnar Mulloy
4. Francisco Segura*
5. William F. Talbert
6. Sidney B. Wood, Jr.
7. Seymour Greenberg
8. George Richards
9. E. Victor Seixas, Jr.
10. Ladislav Hecht*

1943

1. Joseph R. Hunt
2. John A. Kramer
3. Francisco Segura*
4. William F. Talbert
5. Seymour Greenberg
6. Sidney B. Wood, Jr.
7. Robert Falkenberg
8. Frank A. Parker
9. James Brink
10. Jack Tuero

1944

1. Frank A. Parker
2. William F. Talbert

* Foreign players included in USLTA ranking.

3. Francisco Segura*
4. W. Donald McNeill
5. Seymour Greenberg
6. Robert Falkenberg
7. Jack Jossi
8. Charles W. Oliver
9. Jack McManis
10. J. Gilbert Hall

1945

1. Sgt. Frank A. Parker
2. William F. Talbert
3. Francisco Segura*
4. Elwood T. Cooke
5. Sidney B. Wood, Jr.
6. Lt. Gardnar Mulloy
7. Frank X. Shields
8. Lt. Harold Surface, Jr.
9. Lt. Seymour Greenberg
10. Jack McManis

1946

1. John A. Kramer
2. F. R. Schroeder, Jr.
3. Frank A. Parker
4. Thos. P. Brown, Jr.
5. Gardnar Mulloy
6. William F. Talbert
7. W. Donald McNeill
8. Robert Falkenberg
9. Edward Moulan
10. Francisco Segura*

1947

1. John A. Kramer
2. Frank A. Parker
3. F. R. Schroeder, Jr.
4. Gardnar Mulloy
5. William F. Talbert
6. Francisco Segura*
7. Robert Falkenberg
8. Edward Moylan
9. Earl H. Cochell
10. Seymour Greenberg

1948

1. Richard A. Gonzalez
2. F. R. Schroeder, Jr.
3. Frank A. Parker
4. William F. Talbert
5. Robert Falkenberg
6. Earl H. Cochell
7. E. Victor Seixas, Jr.
8. Gardnar Mulloy
9. Herbert Flam
10. Harry E. Likas, Jr.

1949

1. Richard A. Gonzalez
2. F. R. Schroeder, Jr.

* Foreign players included in USLTA ranking.

3. William F. Talbert
4. Frank A. Parker
5. Gardnar Mulloy
6. Arthur D. Larsen
7. Earl H. Cochell
8. Samuel Match
9. Edward Moylan
10. Herbert Flam

1950

1. Arthur D. Larsen
2. Herbert Flam
3. F. R. Schroeder, Jr.
4. Gardnar Mulloy
5. William F. Talbert
6. Richard Savitt
7. Earl H. Cochell
8. E. Victor Seixas, Jr.
9. Thos. P. Brown, Jr.
10. Samuel Match

1951

1. E. Victor Seixas, Jr.
2. Richard Savitt
3. Tony Trabert
4. Herbert Flam
5. William F. Talbert
6. Arthur D. Larsen
7. F. R. Schroeder, Jr.
8. Gardnar Mulloy
9. Hamilton Richardson
10. J. Ed. (Budge) Patty

1952

1. Gardnar Mulloy
2. E. Victor Seixas, Jr.
3. Arthur D. Larsen
4. Richard D. Savitt
5. Herbert Flam
6. William F. Talbert
7. Hamilton Richardson
8. Thos. P. Brown, Jr.
9. Noel Brown
10. Harry E. Likas, Jr.

1953

1. Tony Trabert
2. E. Victor Seixas, Jr.
3. Arthur D. Larsen
4. Gardnar Mulloy
5. L. Straight Clark
6. Hamilton Richardson
7. Bernard Bartzen
8. Thos. P. Brown, Jr.
9. Noel Brown
10. Grant Golden

1954

1. E. Victor Seixas, Jr.
2. Tony Trabert

USLTA Rankings (*cont.*)
3. Hamilton Richardson
4. Arthur D. Larsen
5. Gardnar Mulloy
6. Thos. P. Brown, Jr.
7. Edward Moylan
8. Bernard Bartzen
9. William F. Talbert
10. Gilbert J. Shea

1955

1. Tony Trabert
2. E. Victor Seixas, Jr.
3. Arthur D. Larsen
4. Bernard Bartzen
5. Edward Moylan
6. Gilbert J. Shea
7. Hamilton Richardson
8. Herbert Flam
9. Samuel Giammalva
10. Thos. P. Brown, Jr.

1956

1. Hamilton Richardson
2. Herbert Flam
3. E. Victor Seixas, Jr.
4. Edward Moylan
5. Bernard Bartzen
6. Robert M. Perry
7. Samuel Giammalva
8. Arthur D. Larsen
9. Gilbert J. Shea
10. Grant Golden

1957

1. E. Victor Seixas, Jr.
2. Herbert Flam
3. Richard Savitt
4. Gilbert J. Shea
5. Barry MacKay
6. Ronald Holmberg
7. Thos. P. Brown, Jr.
8. Whitney Reed
9. Bernard Bartzen
10. William Quillian

1958

1. Hamilton Richardson
2. Alejandro Olmedo*
3. Barry MacKay
4. Bernard Bartzen
5. Herbert Flam
6. Richard Savitt
7. Samuel Giammalva
8. E. Victor Seixas, Jr.
9. Earl Buchholz, Jr.
10. Thos. P. Brown, Jr.

1959

1. Alejandro Olmedo*
2. Bernard Bartzen

* Foreign players included in USLTA ranking.

3. Barry MacKay
4. Ronald Holmberg
5. Richard Savitt
6. Earl Buchholz, Jr.
7. Myron J. Franks
8. Noel Brown
9. Whitney Reed
10. E. Victor Seixas, Jr.

1960

1. Barry MacKay
2. Bernard Bartzen
3. Earl Buchholz, Jr.
4. Charles McKinley
5. R. Dennis Ralston
6. Jon Douglas
7. Ronald Holmberg
8. Whitney Reed
9. Donald Dell
10. Chris Crawford

1961

1. Whitney Reed
2. Charles McKinley
3. Bernard Bartzen
4. Jon Douglas
5. Donald Dell
6. F. Froehling III
7. Ronald Holmberg
8. Allen Fox
9. Jack Frost
10. William Bond

1962

1. Charles R. McKinley
2. F. A. Froehling, III
3. Hamilton Richardson
4. Allen E. Fox
5. Jon A. Douglas
6. Whitney R. Reed
7. Donald L. Dell
8. Eugene L. Scott
9. Martin Riessen
10. Charles Pasarell

1963

1. Charles R. McKinley
2. R. Dennis Ralston
3. F. A. Froehling, III
4. Eugene L. Scott
5. Martin Riessen
6. Arthur Ashe, Jr.
7. Hamilton Richardson
8. Allen Fox
9. Tom Edlefsen
10. Charles Pasarell

1964

1. R. Dennis Ralston
2. Charles R. McKinley

3. Arthur Ashe, Jr.
4. F. A. Froehling III
5. Eugene L. Scott
6. Ronald Holmberg
7. Hamilton Richardson
8. Allen E. Fox
9. Clark Graebner
10. Martin Riessen

1965

1. R. Dennis Ralston
2. Arthur Ashe
3. Cliff Richey
4. Charles R. McKinley
5. Charles Pasarell
6. Hamilton Richardson
7. Mike Belkin
8. Martin Riessen
9. Ronald E. Holmberg
10. Tom Edlefsen

1966

1. R. Dennis Ralston
2. Arthur Ashe, Jr.
3. Clark Graebner
4. Charles Pasarell
5. Cliff Richey
6. Ronald E. Holmberg
7. Martin Riessen
8. F. A. Froehling III
9. E. Victor Seixas, Jr.
10. Charles R. McKinley

1967

1. Charles Pasarell
2. Arthur Ashe, Jr.
3. Cliff Richey
4. Clark Graebner
5. Martin Riessen
6. Ronald E. Holmberg
7. Stanley R. Smith
8. Allen E. Fox
9. Eugene L. Scott
10. Robert Lutz

1968

1. Arthur Ashe, Jr.
2. Clark Graebner
3. Stan Smith
4. Cliff Richey
5. Robert Lutz
6. Ronald Holmberg
7. Charles Pasarell
8. James Osborne
9. James McManus
10. Eugene Scott

1969

1. Stanley Smith
2. Arthur Ashe, Jr.

3. Cliff Richey
4. Clark Graebner
5. Charles Pasarell
6. Robert Lutz
7. Tom Edlefsen
8. Roy Barth
9. Jim Osborne
10. Jim McManus

1970

1. Cliff Richey
2. Stan Smith
3. Arthur Ashe
4. Clark Graebner
5. Bob Lutz
6. Tom Gorman
7. Jim Osborne
8. Jim McManus
9. Barry MacKay
10. Charles Pasarell

1971

1. Stan Smith
2. Cliff Richey
3. Clark Graebner
4. Tom Gorman
5. Jimmy Connors
6. Erik Van Dillen
7. F. A. Froehling III
8. Roscoe Tanner
9. Alex Olmedo
10. Harold Solomon

Women's Ranking

Not until 1913 did the ladies begin social climbing with racket in hand. Although their first national championship was held in 1887, there was no feminine Top Ten for 26 years. Mary K. Browne became the first leading lady by defeating Dorothy Green in the 1913 final.

1913

1. Mary K. Browne
2. Mrs. Ethel Sutton Bruce
3. Florence Sutton
4. Mrs. Helen Homans McLean
5. Mrs. Louise Williams
6. Marie Wagner
7. Mrs. Dorothy Green Briggs
8. Edith E. Rotch
9. Anita Myers
10. Gwendolyn Rees

1914

1. Mary K. Browne
2. Florence Sutton

USLTA Rankings (*cont.*)
3. Marie Wagner
4. Mrs. Louise H. Raymond
5. Edith E. Rotch
6. Eleanora Sears
7. Mrs. Louise Williams
8. Mrs. Sarita Van Vliet Wood
9. Mrs. H. A. Niemeyer
10. Sara Livingstone

1915

1. Molla Bjurstedt
2. Mrs. Hazel H. Wightman
3. Mrs. Helen Homans McLean
4. Florence Sutton
5. Mrs. Maud Barger-Wallach
6. Marie Wagner
7. Anita Myers
8. Sara Livingstone
9. Clare Cassel
10. Eleanora Sears

1916

1. Molla Bjurstedt
2. Mrs. Louise H. Raymond
3. Evelyn Sears
4. Anita Myers
5. Sara Livingstone
6. Marie Wagner
7. Mrs. Homer S. Green
8. Martha Gunthrie
9. Eleanora Sears
10. Mrs. Maud Barger-Wallach

1917

As only Patriotic Tournaments were held in 1917, no ranking was made for that year.

1918

1. Molla Bjurstedt
2. Mrs. Hazel H. Wightman
3. Mrs. Homer S. Green
4. Eleanor Goss
5. Marie Wagner
6. Carrie B. Neely
7. Corinne Gould
8. Helene Pollak
9. Edith B. Handy
10. Clare Cassel

1919

1. Mrs. Hazel H. Wightman
2. Eleanor Goss
3. Mrs. Molla B. Mallory
4. Marion Zinderstein
5. Helen Baker
6. Mrs. Louise H. Raymond
7. Helen Gilleaudeau
8. Marie Wagner
9. Corinne Gould
10. Helene Pollak

1920

1. Mrs. Molla B. Mallory
2. Marion Zinderstein
3. Eleanor Tennant
4. Helen Baker
5. Eleanor Goss
6. Mrs. Louise H. Raymond
7. Marie Wagner
8. Mrs. Helene Pollak Falk
9. Edith Siguorney
10. Margaret Grove

1921

1. Mrs. Molla B. Mallory
2. Mary K. Browne
3. Mrs. Marion Z. Jessup
4. Mrs. May Sutton Bundy
5. Eleanor Goss
6. Helen Gilleaudeau
7. Mrs. B. E. Cole
8. Leslie Bancroft
9. Mrs. Louise H. Raymond
10. Margaret Grove

1922

1. Mrs. Molla B. Mallory
2. Leslie Bancroft
3. Helen N. Wills
4. Mrs. Marion Z. Jessup
5. Mrs. May Sutton Bundy
6. Martha Bayard
7. Helen Gilleaudeau
8. Mollie D. Thayer
9. Marie Wagner
10. Florence A. Ballin

1923

1. Helen N. Wills
2. Mrs. Molla B. Mallory
3. Eleanor Goss
4. Lillian Scharman
5. Mrs. Helen G. Lockhorn
6. Mayme MacDonald
7. Edith Sigourney
8. Leslie Bancroft
9. Martha Bayard
10. Helen Hooker

1924

1. Helen N. Wills
2. Mary K. Browne
3. Mrs. Molla B. Mallory
4. Eleanor Goss
5. Mrs. Marion Z. Jessup
6. Martha Bayard
7. Mayme MacDonald
8. Mrs. B. E. Cole
9. Mollie B. Thayer
10. Leslie Bancroft

1925

1. Helen N. Wills
2. Elizabeth Ryan
3. Mrs. Molla B. Mallory
4. Mrs. Marion Z. Jessup
5. Eleanor Goss
6. Mary K. Browne
7. Martha Bayard
8. Mrs. May Sutton Bundy
9. Charlotte Hosmer
10. Edith Sigourney

1926

1. Mrs. Molla B. Mallory
2. Elizabeth Ryan
3. Eleanor Goss
4. Martha Bayard
5. Mrs. Charlotte H. Chapin
6. Mrs. J. Dallas Corbiere
7. Margaret Blake
8. Penelope Anderson
9. Mrs. Edna Houselt Roeser
10. Mrs. William Endicott

1927

1. Helen N. Wills
2. Mrs. Molla B. Mallory
3. Mrs. Charlotte H. Chapin
4. Helen Jacobs
5. Eleanor Goss
6. Mrs. J. Dallas Corbiere
7. Penelope Anderson
8. Margaret Blake
9. Mrs. Edna H. Roeser
10. Alice Francis

1928

1. Helen N. Wills
2. Helen Jacobs
3. Edith Cross
4. Mrs. Molla B. Mallory
5. Mrs. May Sutton Bundy
6. Marjorie Morrill
7. Marjorie K. Gladman
8. Mrs. Anna McCune Harper
9. Mrs. Charlotte H. Chapin
10. Mrs. J. Dallas Corbiere

1929

1. Mrs. Helen Wills Moody
2. Helen Jacobs
3. Edith Cross
4. Sarah Palfrey
5. Mrs. Anna McC. Harper
6. Mary Greef
7. Eleanor Goss
8. Ethel Burkhardt
9. Marjorie K. Gladman
10. Josephine Cruickshank

1930

1. Mrs. Anna McC. Harper
2. Marjorie Morrill
3. Dorothy Weisel
4. Virginia Hilleary
5. Josephine Cruikshank
6. Ethel Burkhardt
7. Mrs. Marjorie G. Van Ryn
8. Sarah Palfrey
9. Mary Greef
10. Edith Cross

1931

1. Mrs. Helen W. Moody
2. Helen Jacobs
3. Mrs. Anna McC. Harper
4. Mrs. Marion Z. Jessup
5. Mary Greef
6. Marjorie Morrill
7. Sarah Palfrey
8. Mrs. Marjorie G. Van Ryn
9. Virginia Hilleary
10. Mrs. Dorothy Andrus Burke

1932

1. Helen Jacobs
2. Mrs. Anna McC. Harper
3. Carolin Babcock
4. Mrs. Marjorie M. Painter
5. Josephine Cruickshank
6. Virginia Hilleary
7. Alice Marble
8. Mrs. Marjorie G. Van Ryn
9. Virginia Rice
10. Marjorie Sachs

1933

1. Helen Jacobs
2. Mrs. Helen W. Moody
3. Alice Marble
4. Sarah Palfrey
5. Carolin Babcock
6. Josephine Cruickshank
7. Baroness Maud Levi
8. Mrs. Majorie G. Van Ryn
9. Virginia Rice
10. Mrs. Agnes S. Lamme

1934

1. Helen Jacobs
2. Mrs. Sarah P. Fabyan
3. Carolin Babcock
4. Mrs. Dorothy Andrus
5. Baroness Maud Levi
6. Jane Sharp
7. Mrs. Marjorie M. Painter
8. Mrs. Mary Greef Harris
9. Marjorie Sachs
10. Catherine Wolf

USLTA Rankings (cont.)

1935

1. Helen Jacobs
2. Mrs. E. Burkhardt Arnold
3. Mrs. Sarah P. Fabyan
4. Carolin Babcock
5. Mrs. Marjorie G. Van Ryn
6. Gracyn W. Wheeler
7. Mrs. Mary G. Harris
8. Mrs. Agnes S. Lamme
9. Mrs. Dorothy Andrus
10. Catherine Wolf

1936

1. Alice Marble
2. Helen Jacobs
3. Mrs. Sarah P. Fabyan
4. Gracyn W. Wheeler
5. Carolin Babcock
6. Helen A. Pedersen
7. Mrs. Marjorie G. Van Ryn
8. Dorothy M. Bundy
9. Katharine Winthrop
10. Mrs. Mary G. Harris

1937

1. Alice Marble
2. Helen Jacobs
3. Dorothy M. Bundy
4. Mrs. Marjorie G. Van Ryn
5. Gracyn W. Wheeler
6. Mrs. Sarah P. Fabyan
7. Mrs. Dorothy Andrus
8. Helen A. Pedersen
9. Katharine Winthrop
10. Mrs. Carolin Babcock Stark

1938

1. Alice Marble
2. Mrs. Sarah P. Fabyan
3. Dorothy M. Bundy
4. Barbara A. Winslow
5. Gracyn W. Wheeler
6. Dorothy E. Workman
7. Margaret E. Osborne
8. Helen A. Pedersen
9. Virginia Wolfenden
10. Katharine Winthrop

1939

1. Alice Marble
2. Helen Jacobs
3. Mrs. Sarah P. Fabyan
4. Helen I. Bernhard
5. Virginia Wolfenden
6. Dorothy M. Bundy
7. Dorothy E. Workman
8. Pauline Betz
9. Katharine Winthrop
10. Mary Arnold

1940

1. Alice Marble
2. Helen Jacobs
3. Pauline Betz
4. Dorothy M. Bundy
5. Mrs. Gracyn W. Kelleher
6. Mrs. Sarah P. Cooke
7. Virginia Wolfenden
8. Helen I. Bernhard
9. Mary Arnold
10. Hope Knowles

1941

1. Mrs. Sarah P. Cooke
2. Pauline Betz
3. Dorothy M. Bundy
4. Margaret Osborne
5. Helen Jacobs
6. Helen I. Bernhard
7. Hope Knowles
8. Mary Arnold
9. Mrs. Virginia W. Kovacs
10. A. Louise Brough

1942

1. Pauline Betz
2. A. Louise Brough
3. Margaret Osborne
4. Helen I. Bernhard
5. Mary Arnold
6. Doris Hart
7. Mrs. Patricia C. Todd
8. Mrs. Helen P. Rihbany
9. Mrs. Madge H. Vosters
10. Katharine Winthrop

1943

1. Pauline Betz
2. A. Louise Brough
3. Doris Hart
4. Margaret Osborne
5. Dorothy M. Bundy
6. Mary Arnold
7. Dorothy Head
8. Helen I. Bernhard
9. Mrs. Helen P. Rihbany
10. Katharine Winthrop

1944

1. Pauline Betz
2. Margaret Osborne
3. A. Louise Brough
4. Dorothy M. Bundy
5. Mary Arnold
6. Doris Hart
7. Mrs. Virginia W. Kovacs
8. Shirley J. Fry
9. Mrs. Patricia C. Todd
10. Dorothy Head

1945

1. Mrs. Sarah P. Cooke
2. Pauline Betz
3. Margaret Osborne
4. A. Louise Brough
5. Mrs. Patricia C. Todd
6. Doris Hart
7. Shirley J. Fry
8. Mrs. Mary A. Prentiss
9. Dorothy M. Bundy
10. Mrs. Helen P. Rihbany

1946

1. Pauline Betz
2. Margaret Osborne
3. A. Louise Brough
4. Doris Hart
5. Mrs. Patricia C. Todd
6. Mrs. Dorothy B. Cheney
7. Shirley J. Fry
8. Mrs. Mary A. Prentiss
9. Mrs. Virginia W. Kovacs
10. Dorothy Head

1947

1. A. Louise Brough
2. Mrs. Margaret O. du Pont
3. Doris Hart
4. Mrs. Patricia C. Todd
5. Shirley J. Fry
6. Barbara Krase
7. Dorothy Head
8. Mrs. Mary A. Prentiss
9. Gertrude Moran
10. Mrs. Helen P. Rihbany

1948

1. Mrs. Margaret O. du Pont
2. A. Louise Brough
3. Doris Hart
4. Gertrude Moran
5. Beverly Baker
6. Mrs. Patricia C. Todd
7. Shirley J. Fry
8. Mrs. Helen Pastall Perez
9. Mrs. Virginia W. Kovacs
10. Mrs. Helen P. Rihbany

1949

1. Mrs. Margaret O. du Pont
2. A. Louise Brough
3. Doris Hart
4. Mrs. Patricia C. Todd
5. Mrs. Helen Pastall Perez
6. Shirley J. Fry
7. Gertrude Moran
8. Mrs. Beverly B. Beckett
9. Dorothy Head
10. Barbara Scofield

1950

1. Mrs. Margaret O. du Pont
2. Doris Hart
3. A. Louise Brough
4. Beverly Baker
5. Mrs. Patricia C. Todd
6. Nancy Chaffee
7. Barbara Scofield
8. Shirley J. Fry
9. Mrs. Helen Pastall Perez
10. Maureen Connolly

1951

1. Maureen Connolly
2. Doris Hart
3. Shirley J. Fry
4. Mrs. Nancy Chaffee Kiner
5. Mrs. Patricia C. Todd
6. Mrs. Beverly Baker Fleitz
7. Dorothy Head
8. Mrs. Betty R. Pratt
9. Mrs. Magda Rurac
10. Mrs. Baba M. Lewis

1952

1. Maureen Connolly
2. Doris Hart
3. Shirley J. Fry
4. A. Louise Brough
5. Mrs. Nancy C. Kiner
6. Anita Kaner
7. Mrs. Patricia C. Todd
8. Mrs. Baba M. Lewis
9. Althea Gibson
10. Julia Ann Sampson

1953

1. Maureen Connolly
2. Doris Hart
3. Shirley J. Fry
4. A. Louise Brough
5. Mrs. Margaret O. du Pont
6. Mrs. Helen Pastall Perez
7. Althea Gibson
8. Mrs. Baba M. Lewis
9. Anita Kanter
10. Julia Ann Sampson

1954

1. Doris Hart
2. A. Louise Brough
3. Mrs. Beverly B. Fleitz
4. Shirley J. Fry
5. Mrs. Betty R. Pratt
6. Barbara Breit
7. Darlene Hard
8. Lois Felix
9. Mrs. Helen Pastall Perez
10. Mrs. Barbara S. Davidson

USLTA Rankings (*cont.*)
1955

1. Doris Hart
2. Shirley J. Fry
3. A. Louise Brough
4. Mrs. Dorothy Head Knode
5. Mrs. Beverly B. Fleitz
6. Mrs. Barbara S. Davidson
7. Barbara Breit
8. Althea Gibson
9. Darlene Hard
10. Mrs. Dorothy B. Cheney

1956

1. Shirley J. Fry
2. Althea Gibson
3. A. Louise Brough
4. Mrs. Margaret O. du Pont
5. Mrs. Betty R. Pratt
6. Mrs. Dorothy H. Knode
7. Darlene Hard
8. Karol Fageros
9. Janet S. Hopps
10. Miriam Arnold

1957

1. Althea Gibson
2. A. Louise Brough
3. Mrs. Dorothy H. Knode
4. Darlene Hard
5. Karol Fageros
6. Miriam Arnold
7. Jeanne Arth
8. Sally M. Moore
9. Janet S. Hopps
10. Mary Ann Mitchell

1958

1. Althea Gibson
2. Mrs. Beverly B. Fleitz
3. Darlene Hard
4. Mrs. Dorothy H. Knode
5. Mrs. Margaret O. du Pont
6. Jeanne Arth
7. Janet S. Hopps
8. Sally M. Moore
9. Gwyneth Thomas
10. Mary Ann Mitchell

1959

1. Mrs. Beverly B. Fleitz
2. Darlene Hard
3. Mrs. Dorothy H. Knode
4. Sally M. Moore
5. Janet S. Hopps
6. Karen J. Hantze
7. Mrs. Barbara G. Weigandt
8. Karol Fageros
9. Miriam Arnold
10. Lois Felix

1960

1. Darlene Hard
2. Karen Hantze
3. Nancy Richey
4. Billie Jean Moffitt
5. Donna Floyd
6. Janet Hopps
7. Gwyneth Thomas
8. Victoria Palmer
9. Kathy Chabot
10. Carol Hanks

1961

1. Darlene Hard
2. Karen Hantze
3. Billie Jean Moffitt
4. Katherine Chabot
5. Justina Bricka
6. Gwyneth Thomas
7. Marilyn Montgomery
8. Judy Alvarez
9. Carole Caldwell
10. Donna Floyd

1962

1. Darlene Hard
2. Mrs. Karen H. Susman
3. Billie Jean Moffitt
4. Carole Caldwell
5. Donna Floyd
6. Nancy Richey
7. Victoria Palmer
8. Gwyneth Thomas
9. Justina Bricka
10. Judy Alvarez

1963

1. Darlene Hard
2. Billie Jean Moffitt
3. Nancy Richey
4. Carole Caldwell
5. Gwyneth Thomas
6. Judy Alvarez
7. Carol Hanks
8. Tory A. Fretz
9. Mrs. Donna F. Fales
10. Carole Hanks

1964

1. Nancy Richey
2. Billie Jean Moffitt
3. Mrs. Carole C. Graebner
4. Mrs. Karen H. Susman
5. Mrs. Carol H. Aucamp
6. Jane Albert
7. Julie Heldman
8. Justina Bricka
9. Tory Fretz
10. Mary Ann Eisel

1965

1. Mrs. Billie Jean M. King
2. Nancy Richey
3. Mrs. Carole C. Graebner
4. Jane Albert
5. Mary Ann Eisel
6. Mrs. Carol H. Aucamp
7. Kathleen Harter
8. Julie M. Heldman
9. Tory Ann Fretz
10. Mrs. Donna F. Fales

1966

1. Mrs. Billie J. King
2. Nancy Richey
3. Rosemary Casals
4. Tory Fretz
5. Jane Bartkowicz
6. Mary Ann Eisel
7. Mrs. Donna F. Fales
8. Mrs. Carol H. Aucamp
9. Stephanie DeFina
10. Peachy Kellmeyer

1967

1. Mrs. Billie J. King
2. Nancy Richey
3. Mary Ann Eisel
4. Jane Bartkowicz
5. Rosemary Casals
6. Mrs. Carole C. Graebner
7. Stephanie DeFina
8. Kathleen M. Harter
9. Lynne Abbes
10. Vicky Rogers

1968

1. Nancy Richey
2. Julie Heldman
3. Vicky Rogers
4. Mary Ann Eisel

5. Kathleen Harter
6. Kristie Pigeon
7. Jane Bartkowicz
8. Linda Tuero
9. Stephanie DeFina
10. Patti Hogan

1969

1. Nancy Richey
2. Julie Heldman
3. Mrs. Mary Ann E. Curtis
4. Jane Bartkowicz
5. Patti Hogan
6. Kristie Pigeon
7. Betty Ann Grubb
8. Denise Carter
9. Valerie Ziegenfuss
10. Linda Tuero

1970

1. Mrs. Billie Jean M. King
2. Rosemary Casals
3. Mrs. Nancy Richey Gunter
4. Mrs. Mary Ann E. Curtis
5. Patti St. Ann Hogan
6. Jane Bartkowicz
7. Valerie Jean Ziegenfuss
8. Kristie Sue Pigeon
9. Mrs. Stephanie Johnson
10. Mrs. Denise Carter Triolo

1971

1. Mrs. Billie Jean M. King
2. Rosemary Casals
3. Chris Evert
4. Mrs. Nancy Richey Gunter
5. Mary Ann Eisel
6. Julie Heldman
7. Jane Bartkowicz
8. Linda Tuero
9. Patti St. Ann Hogan
10. Mrs. Denise Carter Triolo

Leading Members of the First Ten

Men	Total Years	Between	Years No. 1
Bill Larned	19	1892 and 1911	8
Frank Parker	17	1933 and 1949	2
Gardnar Mulloy	14	1939 and 1954	1
Bill Talbert	13	1941 and 1954	0
Vic Seixas	13	1942 and 1966	3
Bill Tilden	12	1918 and 1929	10
Bill Johnston	12	1913 and 1926	2
Ham Richardson	11	1951 and 1965	2
Beals Wright	11	1899 and 1910	1
William Clothier	11	1901 and 1914	1
R. D. Little	11	1900 and 1912	0
Nat Niles	10	1908 and 1921	0

Leading Members of the First Ten

Women	Total Years	Between	Years No. 1
Louise Brough	16	1941 and 1957	1
Margaret Osborne du Pont	14	1938 and 1958	3
Doris Hart	14	1942 and 1955	2
Molla Bjurstedt Mallory	13	1915 and 1928	7
Helen Jacobs	13	1927 and 1941	4
Sarah Palfrey	13	1929 and 1945	2
Shirley Fry	13	1944 and 1956	1
Dorothy Head Knode	11	1943 and 1959	0
Dorothy Bundy Cheney	11	1936 and 1955	0
Nancy Richey Gunter	11	1960 and 1971	3
Darlene Hard	10	1954 and 1963	4
Eleanor Goss	10	1918 and 1929	0
Pat Canning Todd	10	1942 and 1952	0
Billie Jean Moffit King	10	1960 and 1971	5
Helen Wills Moody	9	1922 and 1933	7

ALL-AMERICAN TOP TEN

In 1970, the USLTA made an All-American ranking for men, selecting the top ten players regardless of their status as amateurs or professionals, or whether they are independent or contract professionals. The All-American ranking is an adjunct to the usual USLTA rankings which include only players (amateur and independent pros) under the jurisdiction of the USLTA during the ranking period.

1. G. Clifford Richey, Jr.
2. Stanley R. Smith
3. Martin C. Riessen
4. Arthur R. Ashe, Jr.
5. R. Dennis Ralston
6. Richard A. Gonzalez
7. Clark E. Graebner
8. Robert C. Lutz
9. Thomas W. Gorman
10. Earl Buchholz, Jr.

1971

1. Stanley R. Smith
2. Arthur R. Ashe, Jr.
3. Martin C. Riessen
4. G. Clifford Richey, Jr.
5. Clark E. Graebner
6. Thomas W. Gorman
7. James Connors
8. Erik Van Dillen
9. F. A. Froehling III
10. Robert C. Lutz

WORLD RANKINGS

There has never been an "official" world ranking of tennis players. The rankings that appear here from 1914 through 1938 were made by A. Wallis Myers of the London *Daily Telegraph*. There were no rankings from 1915 to 1918, and the ladies were first rated by Myers in 1925. Sir F. Gordon Lowe did the ranking in 1939. No rankings were given from 1940 through 1945. Pierre Gillow made the rankings in 1946 and 1951, while John Dlliff did them from 1947 to 1950. Since 1952, Lance Tingay of the London *Daily Telegraph* has made the rankings. The world rankings by this group are as follows:

Men's Ranking

1914

1. M. E. McLoughlin (U.S.A.)
2. N. E. Brookes (Australia)
3. A. F. Wilding (New Zealand)
4. O. Froitzheim (Germany)
5. R. N. Williams (U.S.A.)
6. J. C. Parke (Ireland)
7. A. H. Lowe (England)
8. F. G. Lowe (England)
9. H. Kleinschroth (Germany)
10. M. Decugis (France)

Bill Larned (*left*) and Mrs. Louise Brough Clapp (*right*) have appeared on the Men's and Women's USLTA top-ten ranks the most of any players.

1919

1. G. L. Patterson (Australia)
2. W. M. Johnston (U.S.A.)
3. A. H. Gobert (France)
4. W. T. Tilden (U.S.A.)
5. N. E. Brookes (Australia)
6. A. R. F. Kingscote (England)
7. R. N. Williams (U.S.A.)
8. P. M. Davson (England)
9. Willis Davis (U.S.A.)
10. W. H. Laurentz (France)

1920

1. W. T. Tilden (U.S.A.)
2. W. M. Johnston (U.S.A.)

3. A. R. F Kingscote (England)
4. J. C. Parke (Ireland)
5. A. H. Gobert (France)
6. N. E. Brookes (Australia)
7. R. N. Williams (U.S.A.)
8. W. H. Laurentz (France)
9. Z. Shimizu (Japan)
10. G. L. Patterson (Australia)

1921

1. W. T. Tilden (U.S.A.)
2. W. M. Johnston (U.S.A.)
3. Vincent Richards (U.S.A.)
4. Z. Shimizu (Japan)
5. G. L. Patterson (Australia)
6. J. O. Anderson (Australia)

World Rankings—Men's (cont.)

7. B. I. C. Norton (S. Africa)
8. M. Alonso (Spain)
9. R. N. Williams (U.S.A.)
10. A. H. Gobert (France)

1922

1. W. T. Tilden (U.S.A.)
2. W. M. Johnston (U.S.A.)
3. G. L. Patterson (Australia)
4. Vincent Richards (U.S.A.)
5. J. O. Anderson (Australia)
6. H. Cochet (France)
7. P. O'Hara Wood (Australia)
8. R. N. Williams (U.S.A.)
9. A. R. F. Kingscote (England)
10. A. H. Gobert (France)

1923

1. W. T. Tilden (U.S.A.)
2. W. M. Johnston (U.S.A.)
3. J. O. Anderson (Australia)
4. R. N. Williams (U.S.A.)
5. F. T. Hunter (U.S.A.)
6. Vincent Richards (U.S.A.)
7. B. I. C. Norton (S. Africa)
8. M. Alonso (Spain)
9. J. Washer (Belgium)
10. H. Cochet (France)

1924

1. W. T. Tilden (U.S.A.)
2. Vincent Richards (U.S.A.)
3. J. O. Anderson (Australia)
4. W. M. Johnston (U.S.A.)
5. R. Lacoste (France)
6. J. Borotra (France)
7. H. Kinsey (U.S.A.)
8. G. L. Patterson (Australia)
9. H. Cochet (France)
10. M. Alonso (Spain)

1925

1. W. T. Tilden (U.S.A.)
2. W. M. Johnston (U.S.A.)
3. Vincent Richards (U.S.A.)
4. R. Lacoste (France)
5. R. N. Williams (U.S.A.)
6. J. Borotra (France)
7. G. L. Patterson (Australia)
8. M. Alonso (Spain)
9. B. I. C. Norton (S. Africa)
10. T. Harada (Japan)

1926

1. R. Lacoste (France)
2. J. Borotra (France)
3. H. Cochet (France)
4. W. M. Johnston (U.S.A.)
5. W. T. Tilden (U.S.A.)

6. Vincent Richards (U.S.A.)
7. T. Harada (Japan)
8. M. Alonso (Spain)
9. H. Kingsey (U.S.A.)
10. J. Brugnon (France)

1927

1. R. Lacoste (France)
2. W. T. Tilden (U.S.A.)
3. H. Cochet (France)
4. J. Borotra (France)
5. M. Alonso (Spain)
6. F. T. Hunter (U.S.A.)
7. G. M. Lott (U.S.A.)
8. J. F. Hennessey (U.S.A.)
9. J. Brugnon (France)
10. J. Koseluh (Czechoslovakia)

1928

1. H. Cochet (France)
2. R. Lacoste (France)
3. W. T. Tilden (U.S.A.)
4. F. T. Hunter (U.S.A.)
5. J. Borotra (France)
6. G. M. Lott (U.S.A.)
7. H. W. Austin (England)
8. J. F. Hennessey (U.S.A.)
9. H. L. de Morpurgo (Italy)
10. J. B. Hawkes (Australia)

1929

1. H. Cochet (France)
2. R. Lacoste (France)
3. J. Borotra (France)
4. W. T. Tilden (U.S.A.)
5. F. T. Hunter (U.S.A.)
6. G. M. Lott (U.S.A.)
7. J. Doeg (U.S.A.)
8. J. Van Ryn (U.S.A.)
9. H. W. Austin (England)
10. H. L. de Morpurgo (Italy)

1930

1. H. Cochet (France)
2. W. T. Tilden (U.S.A.)
3. J. Borotra (France)
4. J. H. Doeg (U.S.A.)
5. F. X. Shields (U.S.A.)
6. W. L. Allison (U.S.A.)
7. G. M. Lott (U.S.A.)
8. H. L. de Morpurgo (Italy)
9. S. Boussus (France)
10. H. W. Austin (England)

1931

1. H. Cochet (France)
2. H. W. Austin (England)
3. H. E. Vines (U.S.A.)
4. F. J. Perry (England)

5. F. X. Shields (U.S.A.)
6. S. B. Wood (U.S.A.)
7. J. Borotra (France)
8. G. M. Lott (U.S.A.)
9. J. Satoh (Japan)
10. J. Van Ryn (U.S.A.)

1932

1. H. E. Vines (U.S.A.)
2. H. Cochet (France)
3. J. Borotra (France)
4. W. L. Allison (U.S.A.)
5. C. Sutter (U.S.A.)
6. D. Prenn (Germany)
7. F. J. Perry (England)
8. G. von Cramm (Germany)
9. H. W. Austin (England)
10. J. H. Crawford (Australia)

1933

1. J. H. Crawford (Australia)
2. F. J. Perry (England)
3. J. Satoh (Japan)
4. W. H. Austin (England)
5. H. E. Vines (U.S.A.)
6. H. Cochet (France)
7. F. X. Shields (U.S.A.)
8. S. B. Wood (U.S.A.)
9. G. von Cramm (Germany)
10. L. R. Stoefen (U.S.A.)

1934

1. F. J. Perry (England)
2. J. H. Crawford (Australia)
3. G. von Cramm (Germany)
4. H. W. Austin (England)
5. W. L. Allison (U.S.A.)
6. S. B. Wood (U.S.A.)
7. R. Menzel (Czechoslovakia)
8. F. X. Shields (U.S.A.)
9. G. de Stefani (Italy)
10. C. Boussus (France)

1935

1. F. J. Perry (England)
2. J. H. Crawford (Australia)
3. G. von Cramm (Germany)
4. W. L. Allison (U.S.A.)
5. H. W. Austin (England)
6. J. D. Budge (U.S.A.)
7. F. X. Shields (U.S.A.)
8. V. B. McGrath (Australia)
9. C. Boussus (France)
10. S. B. Wood (U.S.A.)

1936

1. F. J. Perry (England)
2. G. von Cramm (Germany)
3. J. D. Budge (U.S.A.)

4. A. K. Quist (Australia)
5. H. W. Austin (England)
6. J. H. Crawford (Australia)
7. W. L. Allison (U.S.A.)
8. B. M. Grant (U.S.A.)
9. H. Henkel (Germany)
10. V. B. McGrath (Australia)

1937

1. J. D. Budge (U.S.A.)
2. G. von Cramm (Germany)
3. H. Henkel (Germany)
4. H. W. Austin (England)
5. R. L. Riggs (U.S.A.)
6. B. M. Grant (U.S.A.)
7. J. H. Crawford (Australia)
8. R. Menzel (Czechoslovakia)
9. F. A. Parker (U.S.A.)
10. C. E. Hare (England)

1938

1. J. D. Budge (U.S.A.)
2. H. W. Austin (England)
3. J. Bromwich (Australia)
4. R. L. Riggs (U.S.A.)
5. S. B. Wood (U.S.A.)
6. A. K. Quist (Australia)
7. R. Menzel (Czechoslovakia)
8. J. Yamagishi (Japan)
9. G. G. Mako (U.S.A.)
10. F. Puncec (Yugoslavia)

1939

1. R. L. Riggs (U.S.A.)
2. J. E. Bromwich (Australia)
3. A. K. Quist (Australia)
4. F. Puncec (Yugoslavia)
5. Frank A. Parker (U.S.A.)
6. H. Henkel (Germany)
7. W. D. McNeill (U.S.A.)
8. Elwood T. Cooke (U.S.A.)
9. Welby Van Horn (U.S.A.)
10. Joseph R. Hunt (U.S.A.)

1946

1. J. Kramer (U.S.A.)
2. F. R. Schroeder (U.S.A.)
3. J. Drobny (Czechoslovakia)
4. Y. Petra (France)
5. M. Bernard (France)
6. J. Bromwich (Australia)
7. T. Brown (U.S.A.)
9. F. Parker (U.S.A.)
10. G. Brown (Australia)

1947

1. J. Kramer (U.S.A.)
2. F. R. Schroeder (U.S.A.)

World Rankings—Men's (cont.)

3. F. Parker (U.S.A.)
4. J. E. Bromwich (Australia)
5. J. Drobny (Czechoslovakia)
6. D. Pails (Australia)
7. T. Brown (U.S.A.)
8. B. Patty (U.S.A.)
9. J. Asboth (Hungary)
10. G. Mulloy (U.S.A.)

1948

1. F. Parker (U.S.A.)
2. R. F. Schroeder (U.S.A.)
3. R. Gonzalez (U.S.A.)
4. J. E. Bromwich (Australia)
5. J. Drobny (Czechoslovakia)
6. E. W. Sturgess (S. Africa)
7. R. Falkenburg (U.S.A.)
8. J. Asboth (Hungary)
9. L. Bergelin (Sweden)
10. A. K. Quist (Australia)

1949

1. R. Gonzalez (U.S.A.)
2. F. R. Schroeder (U.S.A.)
3. W. F. Talbert (U.S.A.)
4. F. Sedgman (Australia)
5. R. Parker (U.S.A.)
6. E. W. Sturgess (S. Africa)
7. J. Drobny (Czechoslovakia)
8. B. Patty (U.S.A.)
9. G. Mulloy (U.S.A.)
10. O. W. Sidwell (Australia)

1950

1. B. Patty (U.S.A.)
2. F. Sedgman (Australia)
3. A. Larsen (U.S.A.)
4. J. Drobny (Egypt)
5. H. Flam (U.S.A.)
6. F. R. Schroeder (U.S.A.)
7. E. V. Seixas (U.S.A.)
8. K. McGregor (Australia)
9. W. F. Talbert (U.S.A.)
10. E. W. Sturgess (S. Africa)

1951

1. F. Sedgman (Australia)
2. R. Savitt (U.S.A.)
3. J. Drobny (Egypt)
4. E. V. Seixas (U.S.A.)
5. T. Trabert (U.S.A.)
6. F. R. Schroeder (U.S.A.)
7. K. McGregor (Australia)
8. H. Flam (U.S.A.)
9. A. Larsen (U.S.A.)
10. M. G. Rose (Australia)

1952

1. F. Sedgman (Australia)
2. J. Drobny (Egypt)

3. K. McGregor (Australia)
4. M. G. Rose (Australia)
5. E. V. Seixas (U.S.A.)
6. H. Flam (U.S.A.)
7. G. Mulloy (U.S.A.)
8. E. W. Sturgess (S. Africa)
9. R. Savitt (U.S.A.)
10. K. Rosewall (Australia)
    L. Hoad (Australia)

1953

1. T. Trabert (U.S.A.)
2. K. Rosewall (Australia)
3. E. V. Seixas (U.S.A.)
4. J. Drobny (Egypt)
5. L. Hoad (Australia)
6. M. G. Rose (Australia)
7. K. Nielsen (Denmark)
8. B. Patty (U.S.A.)
9. S. Davidson (Sweden)
10. E. Morea (Argentina)

1954

1. J. Drobny (Egypt)
2. T. Trabert (U.S.A.)
3. K. Rosewall (Australia)
4. E. V. Seixas (U.S.A.)
5. R. Hartwig (Australia)
6. M. G. Rose (Australia)
7. L. Hoad (Australia)
8. B. Patty (U.S.A.)
9. A. Larsen (U.S.A.)
10. E. Morea (Argentina)
    H. Richardson (U.S.A.)
    S. Davidson (Sweden)

1955

1. T. Trabert (U.S.A.)
2. K. Rosewall (Australia)
3. L. Hoad (Australia)
4. E. V. Seixas (U.S.A.)
5. R. Hartwig (Australia)
6. B. Patty (U.S.A.)
7. H. Richardson (U.S.A.)
8. K. Nielsen (Denmark)
9. J. Drobny (Egypt)
10. S. Davidson (Sweden)
    M. G. Rose (Australia)

1956

1. L. Hoad (Australia)
2. K. Rosewall (Australia)
3. H. Richardson (U.S.A.)
4. E. V. Seixas (U.S.A.)
5. S. Davidson (Sweden)
6. N. A. Fraser (Australia)
7. A. J. Cooper (Australia)
8. R. Savitt (U.S.A.)
9. H. Flam (U.S.A.)
10. B. Patty (U.S.A.)
    N. Pietrangeli (Italy)

1957

1. A. J. Cooper (Australia)
2. M. J. Anderson (Australia)
3. S. Davidson (Sweden)
4. H. Flam (U.S.A.)
5. N. A. Fraser (Australia)
6. M. G. Rose (Australia)
7. E. V. Seixas (U.S.A.)
8. B. Patty (U.S.A.)
9. N. Pietrangeli (Italy)
10. R. Savitt (U.S.A.)

1958

1. A. J. Cooper (Australia)
2. M. J. Anderson (Australia)
3. M. G. Rose (Australia)
4. N. A. Fraser (Australia)
5. L. Ayala (Chile)
6. H. Richardson (U.S.A.)
7. N. Pietrangeli (Italy)
8. U. Schmidt (Sweden)
9. B. MacKay (U.S.A.)
10. S. Davidson (Sweden)

1959

1. N. A. Fraser (Australia)
2. A. Olmedo (U.S.A.)
3. N. Pietrangeli (Italy)
4. B. MacKay (U.S.A.)
5. R. Laver (Australia)
6. L. Ayala (Chile)
7. R. Emerson (Australia)
8. R. Bartzen (U.S.A.)
9. R. Krishnan (India)
10. I. Vermaak (S. Africa)

1960

1. N. A. Fraser (Australia)
2. R. Laver (Australia)
3. N. Pietrangeli (Italy)
4. B. MacKay (U.S.A.)
5. E. Buchholz (U.S.A.)
6. R. Emerson (Australia)
7. L. Ayala (Chile)
8. R. Krishnan (India)
9. J. E. Lundquist (Sweden)
10. R. D. Ralston (U.S.A.)

1961

1. R. Laver (Australia)
2. R. Emerson (Australia)
3. M. Santana (Spain)
4. N. Pietrangeli (Italy)
5. C. McKinley (U.S.A.)
6. R. Krishnan (India)
7. L. Ayala (Chile)
8. N. A. Fraser (Australia)
9. J. E. Lundquist (Sweden)
10. U. Schmidt (Sweden)

1962

1. R. Laver (Australia)
2. R. Emerson (Australia)
3. M. Santana (Spain)
4. N. A. Fraser (Australia)
5. C. McKinley (U.S.A.)
6. R. H. Osuna (Mexico)
7. M. F. Mulligan (Australia)
8. R. Hewitt (Australia)
9. R. Krishnan (India)
10. W. Bungert (Germany)

1963

1. R. H. Osuna (Mexico)
2. C. McKinley (U.S.A.)
3. R. Emerson (Australia)
4. M. Santana (Spain)
5. F. S. Stolle (Australia)
6. F. Froehling (U.S.A.)
7. R. D. Ralston (U.S.A.)
8. B. Jovanovic (Yugoslavia)
9. M. J. Sangster (England)
10. M. F. Mulligan (Australia)

1964

1. R. Emerson (Australia)
2. F. S. Stolle (Australia)
3. J. E. Lundquist (Sweden)
4. W. Bungert (Germany)
5. C. McKinley (U.S.A.)
6. M. Santana (Spain)
7. N. Pietrangeli (Italy)
8. C. Kuhnke (Germany)
9. R. D. Ralston (U.S.A.)
10. R. H. Osuna (Mexico)

1965

1. R. Emerson (Australia)
2. M. Santana (Spain)
3. F. S. Stolle (Australia)
4. C. Drysdale (S. Africa)
5. R. D. Ralston (U.S.A.)
6. M. F. Mulligan (Australia)
7. J. E. Lundquist (Sweden)
8. A. D. Roche (Australia)
9. J. Newcombe (Australia)
10. A. R. Ashe (U.S.A.)

1966

1. M. Santana (Spain)
2. F. S. Stolle (Australia)
3. R. Emerson (Australia)
4. A. D. Roche (Australia)
5. R. D. Ralston (U.S.A.)
6. J. Newcombe (Australia)
7. A. R. Ashe (U.S.A.)
8. I. Gulyas (Hungary)
9. C. Drysdale (S. Africa)
10. K. Fletcher (Australia)

World Rankings—Men's (cont.)

1967

1. J. Newcombe (Australia)
2. R. Emerson (Australia)
3. M. Santana (Spain)
4. M. F. Mulligan (Australia)
5. A. D. Roche (Australia)
6. R. Hewitt (S. Africa)
7. N. Pilic (Yugoslavia)
8. C. Graebner (U.S.A.)
9. A. R. Ashe (U.S.A.)
10. J. Leschly (Denmark)
    W. Bungert (Germany)
    C. Drysdale (S. Africa)

1968

1. R. Laver (Australia)
2. A. R. Ashe (U.S.A.)
3. K. R. Rosewall (Australia)
4. T. Okker (Netherlands)
5. A. D. Roche (Australia)
6. J. Newcombe (Australia)
7. C. Graebner (U.S.A.)
8. R. D. Ralston (U.S.A.)
9. C. Drysdale (S. Africa)
10. R. Gonzalez (U.S.A.)

1969

1. R. Laver (Australia)
2. A. D. Roche (Australia)
3. J. Newcombe (Australia)
4. T. Okker (Netherlands)
5. K. R. Rosewall (Australia)
6. A. R. Ashe (U.S.A.)
7. C. Drysdale (S. Africa)
8. R. Gonzalez (U.S.A.)
9. A. Gimeno (Spain)
10. F. S. Stolle (Australia)

1970

1. J. Newcombe (Australia)
2. K. R. Rosewall (Australia)
3. A. D. Roche (Australia)
4. R. Laver (Australia)
5. A. R. Ashe (U.S.A.)
6. I. Nastase (Rumania)
7. T. Okker (Netherlands)
8. R. Taylor (Great Britain)
9. J. Kodes (Czechoslovakia)
10. C. Richey (U.S.A.)

1971

1. J. Newcombe (Australia)
2. S. R. Smith (U.S.A.)
3. R. Laver (Australia)
4. K. R. Rosewall (Australia)
5. J. Kodes (Czechoslovakia)
6. A. R. Ashe (U.S.A.)
7. T. Okker (Netherlands)
8. M. C. Riessen (U.S.A.)

9. C. Drysdale (South Africa)
10. I. Nastase (Rumania)

Women's Ranking

1925

1. S. Lenglen (France)
2. H. Wills (U.S.A.)
3. K. McKane (England)
4. E. Ryan (U.S.A.)
5. Mrs. M. B. Mallory (U.S.A.)
6. E. Goss (U.S.A.)
7. Mrs. Lambert Chambers (England)
8. J. Fry (England)
9. Mrs. B. Billout (France)
10. Mrs. M. Z. Jessup (U.S.A.)

1926

1. S. Lenglen (France)
2. Mrs. K. M. Godfree (England)
3. L. d'Alvarez (Spain)
4. Mrs. M. B. Mallory (U.S.A.)
5. E. Ryan (U.S.A.)
6. M. Browne (U.S.A.)
7. J. Fry (England)
8. Mrs. P. H. Watson (England)
9. Mrs. M. Z. Jessup (U.S.A.)
10. D. Vlasto (France)

1927

1. H. Wills (U.S.A.)
2. L. d'Alvarez (Spain)
3. E. Ryan (U.S.A.)
4. Mrs. M. B. Mallory (U.S.A.)
5. Mrs. K. M. Godfree (England)
6. B. Nuthall (England)
7. E. L. Heine (S. Africa)
8. J. Fry (England)
9. K. Bouman (Holland)
10. Mrs. C. H. Chapin (U.S.A.)

1928

1. H. Wills (U.S.A.)
2. L. d'Alvarez (Spain)
3. D. Akhurst (Australia)
4. E. Bennett (England)
5. Mrs. P. H. Watson (England)
6. E. Ryan (U.S.A.)
7. C. Aussem (Germany)
8. K. Bouman (Holland)
9. H. Jacobs (U.S.A.)
10. E. Boyd (Australia)

1929

1. H. Wills (U.S.A.)
2. Mrs. P. H. Watson (England)
3. H. Jacobs (U.S.A.)
4. B. Nuthall (England)

5. E. L. Heine (S. Africa)
6. Mrs. R. Mathieu (France)
7. E. Bennett (England)
8. P. von Reznicek (Germany)
9. Mrs. L. R. Michell (England)
10. E. A. Goldsack (England)

1930

1. Mrs. H. W. Moody (U.S.A.)
2. C. Aussem (Germany)
3. Mrs. P. H. Watson (England)
4. E. Ryan (U.S.A.)
5. Mrs. R. Mathieu (France)
6. H. Jacobs (U.S.A.)
7. J. Mudford (England)
8. L. d'Alvarez (Spain)
9. B. Nuthall (England)
10. H. Krahwinkel (Germany)

1931

1. Mrs. H. W. Moody (U.S.A.)
2. C. Aussem (Germany)
3. Mrs. F. Whittingstall (England)
4. H. Jacobs (U.S.A.)
5. B. Nuthall (England)
6. H. Krahwinkel (Germany)
7. Mrs. R. Mathieu (France)
8. L. d'Alvarez (Spain)
9. P. Mudford (England)
10. Mrs. E. A. G. Pittman (England)

1932

1. Mrs. H. W. Moody (U.S.A.)
2. H. Jacobs (U.S.A.)
3. Mrs. R. Mathieu (France)
4. L. Payot (Switzerland)
5. H. Krahwinkel (Germany)
6. M. Heeley (England)
7. Mrs. J. Whittingstall (England)
8. M. Horn (Germany)
9. K. Stammers (England)
10. J. Sigart (Belgium)

1933

1. Mrs. H. W. Moody (U.S.A.)
2. H. Jacobs (U.S.A.)
3. D. E. Round (England)
4. H. Krahwinkel (Germany)
5. M. C. Scriven (England)
6. Mrs. R. Mathieu (France)
7. S. Palfrey (U.S.A.)
8. B. Nuthall (England)
9. L. Payot (Switzerland)
10. A. Marble (U.S.A.)

1934

1. D. E. Round (England)
2. H. Jacobs (U.S.A.)
3. Mrs. H. K. Sperling (Denmark)
4. S. Palfrey (U.S.A.)

5. M. C. Scriven (England)
6. Mrs. R. Mathieu (France)
7. L. Payot (Switzerland)
8. J. Hartigan (Australia)
9. C. Aussem (Germany)
10. C. Babcock (U.S.A.)

1935

1. Mrs. H. W. Moody (U.S.A.)
2. H. Jacobs (U.S.A.)
3. K. Stammers (England)
4. Mrs. H. K. Sperling (Denmark)
5. Mrs. S. P. Fabyan (U.S.A.)
6. D. E. Round (England)
7. Mrs. H. Ardnold (U.S.A.)
8. Mrs. R. Mathieu (France)
9. J. Hartigan (Australia)
10. M. C. Scriven (England)

1936

1. H. Jacobs (U.S.A.)
2. Mrs. H. K. Sperling (Denmark)
3. D. E. Round (England)
4. A. Marble (U.S.A.)
5. Mrs. R. Mathieu (France)
6. J. Jedrzejowska (Poland)
7. K. Stammers (England)
8. A. Lizana (Chile)
9. Mrs. S. P. Fabyan (U.S.A.)
10. C. Babcock (U.S.A.)

1937

1. A. Lizana (Chile)
2. Mrs. K. Little (England)
3. J. Jedrzejowska (Poland)
4. Mrs. H. K. Sperling (Denmark)
5. Mrs. R. Mathieu (France)
6. H. Jacobs (U.S.A.)
7. A. Marble (U.S.A.)
8. M. Horn (Germany)
9. R. M. Hardwick (England)
10. D. M. Bundy (U.S.A.)

1938

1. Mrs. H. W. Moody (U.S.A.)
2. H. Jacobs (U.S.A.)
3. A. Marble (U.S.A.)
4. Mrs. H. K. Sperling (Denmark)
5. Mrs. R. Mathieu (France)
6. J. Jedrzejowska (Poland)
7. Mrs. S. P. Fabyan (U.S.A.)
8. Mrs. H. Miller (S. Africa)
9. K. Stammers (England)
10. N. Wynne (Australia)

1939

1. A. Marble (U.S.A.)
2. K. Stammers (England)
3. H. Jacobs (U.S.A.)

World Rankings—Women's (cont.)

4. Mrs. H. K. Sperling (Denmark)
5. Mrs. R. Mathieu (France)
6. Mrs. S. P. Fabyan (U.S.A.)
7. J. Jedrzejowska (Poland)
8. R. M. Hardwick (England)
9. V. E. Scott (England)
10. V. Wolfenden (U.S.A.)

1946

1. P. Betz (U.S.A.)
2. M. Osborne (U.S.A.)
3. A. L. Brough (U.S.A.)
4. D. Hart (U.S.A.)
5. Mrs. P. C. Todd (U.S.A.)
6. D. Bundy (U.S.A.)
7. Mrs. N. Landry (France)
8. Mrs. M. Menzies (England)
9. S. J. Fry (U.S.A.)
10. Mrs. F. Kovacs (U.S.A.)

1947

1. M. Osborne (U.S.A.)
2. A. L. Brough (U.S.A.)
3. D. Hart (U.S.A.)
4. Mrs. N. Bolton (Australia)
5. Mrs. P. C. Todd (U.S.A.)
6. Mrs. S. Summers (S. Africa)
7. Mrs. W. A. Bostock (England)
8. B. Krase (U.S.A.)
9. Mrs. B. Hilton (England)
10. Mrs. M. Rurac (Rumania)

1948

1. Mrs. W. du Pont (U.S.A.)
2. A. L. Brough (U.S.A.)
3. Mrs. D. Hart (U.S.A.)
4. Mrs. N. Bolton (Australia)
5. Mrs. P. C. Todd (U.S.A.)
6. Mrs. E. W. A. Bostock (England)
7. Mrs. S. Summers (S. Africa)
8. S. J. Fry (U.S.A.)
9. Mrs. M. Rurac (Rumania)
10. Mrs. N. Landry (France)

1949

1. Mrs. W. du Pont (U.S.A.)
2. A. L. Brough (U.S.A.)
3. D. Hart (U.S.A.)
4. Mrs. N. Bolton (Australia)
5. Mrs. P. C. Todd (U.S.A.)
6. Mrs. B. Hilton (England)
7. Mrs. S. Summers (S. Africa)
8. Mrs. A. Bossi (Italy)
9. Mrs. P. J. Curry (England)
10. Mrs. J. J. Walker-Smith (England)

1950

1. Mrs. W. du Pont (U.S.A.)
2. A. L. Brough (U.S.A.)

3. D. Hart (U.S.A.)
4. Mrs. P. C. Todd (U.S.A.)
5. Mrs. B. Scofield (U.S.A.)
6. N. Chaffee (U.S.A.)
7. B. Baker (U.S.A.)
8. S. J. Fry (U.S.A.)
9. Mrs. A. Bossi (Italy)
10. Mrs. H. Weiss (Argentina)

1951

1. D. Hart (U.S.A.)
2. M. Connolly (U.S.A.)
3. S. J. Fry (U.S.A.)
4. Mrs. N. C. Kiner (U.S.A.)
5. Mrs. Walker-Smith (England)
6. J. Quertier (England)
7. A. L. Brough (U.S.A.)
8. Mrs. J. Fleitz (U.S.A.)
9. Mrs. P. C. Todd (U.S.A.)
10. Mrs. J. Maule (England)

1952

1. M. Connolly (U.S.A.)
2. D. Hart (U.S.A.)
3 A. L. Brough (U.S.A.)
4. S. J. Fry (U.S.A.)
5. Mrs. P. C. Todd (U.S.A.)
6. Mrs. N. C. Kiner (U.S.A.)
7. Mrs. T. C. Long (Australia)
8. Mrs. J. Walker-Smith (England)
9. Mrs. I. Rinkel-Quertier (England)
10. Mrs. D. Knode (U.S.A.)

1953

1. M. Connolly (U.S.A.)
2. D. Hart (U.S.A.)
3. A. L. Brough (U.S.A.)
4. S. J. Fry (U.S.A.)
5. Mrs. W. du Pont (U.S.A.)
6. Mrs. D. Knode (U.S.A.)
7. Mrs. S. Kormoczy (Hungary)
8. A. Mortimer (England)
9. H. Fletcher (England)
10. Mrs. I. Rinkel-Quertier (England)

1954

1. M. Connolly (U.S.A.)
2. D. Hart (U.S.A.)
3. Mrs. B. Fleitz (U.S.A.)
4. A. L. Brough (U.S.A.)
5. Mrs. W. du Pont (U.S.A.)
6. S. J. Fry (U.S.A.)
7. Mrs. S. Pratt (Jamaica)
8. H. Fletcher (England)
9. A. Mortimer (England)
10. Mrs. T. C. Long (Australia)

1955

1. A. L. Brough (U.S.A.)
2. D. Hart (U.S.A.)

3. Mrs. B. Fleitz (U.S.A.)
4. A. Mortimer (England)
5. Mrs. D. Knode (U.S.A.)
6. B. Breit (U.S.A.)
7. D. Hard (U.S.A.)
8. B. Penrose (Australia)
9. P. E. Ward (England)
10. Mrs. S. Kormoczy (Hungary)
    S. J. Fry (U.S.A.)

1956

1. S. J. Fry (U.S.A.)
2. A. Gibson (U.S.A.)
3. A. L. Brough (U.S.A.)
4. A. Mortimer (England)
5. Mrs. S. Kormoczy (Hungary)
6. A. Buxton (England)
7. S. J. Bloomer (England)
8. P. E. Ward (England)
9. Mrs. S. Pratt (Jamaica)
10. Mrs. W. du Pont (U.S.A.)
    D. Hard (U.S.A.)

1957

1. A. Gibson (U.S.A.)
2. D. Hard (U.S.A.)
3. S. J. Bloomer (England)
4. A. L. Brough (U.S.A.)
5. Mrs. D. Knode (U.S.A.)
6. V. Puzejova (Czechoslovakia)
7. A. Haydon (England)
8. Y. Ramirez (Mexico)
9. C. C. Truman (England)
10. Mrs. W. du Pont (U.S.A.)

1958

1. A. Gibson (U.S.A.)
2. Mrs. S. Kormoczy (Hungary)
3. Mrs. B. Fleitz (U.S.A.)
4. D. Hart (U.S.A.)
5. S. Bloomer (England)
6. C. C. Truman (England)
7. A. Mortimer (England)
8. A. S. Haydon (England)
9. M. E. Bueno (Brazil)
10. Mrs. D. Knode (U.S.A.)

1959

1. M. E. Bueno (Brazil)
2. C. C. Truman (England)
3. D. Hard (U.S.A.)
4. Mrs. B. Fleitz (U.S.A.)
5. S. Reynolds (S. Africa)
6. A. Mortimer (England)
7. A. S. Haydon (England)
8. Mrs. S. Kormoczy (Hungary)
9. S. Moore (U.S.A.)
10. Y. Ramirez (Mexico)

1960

1. M. E. Bueno (Brazil)
2. D. Hard (U.S.A.)

3. S. Reynolds (S. Africa)
4. C. C. Truman (England)
5. Mrs. S. Kormoczy (Hungary)
6. A. S. Haydon (England)
7. A. Mortimer (England)
8. J. Lehane (Australia)
9. Y. Ramirez (Mexico)
10. R. Schuurman (S. Africa)

1961

1. A. Mortimer (England)
2. D. Hard (U.S.A.)
3. A. S. Haydon (England)
4. M. Smith (Australia)
5. S. Reynolds (S. Africa)
6. Y. Ramirez (Mexico)
7. C. C. Truman (England)
8. Mrs. S. Kormoczy (Hungary)
9. R. Schuurman (S. Africa)
10. K. Hantze (U.S.A.)

1962

1. M. Smith (Australia)
2. M. E. Bueno (Brazil)
3. D. Hard (U.S.A.)
4. Mrs. J. R. Susman (U.S.A.)
5. Mrs. V. Sukova (Czechoslovakia)
6. Mrs. L. Price (S. Africa)
7. L. Turner (S. Africa)
8. A. S. Haydon (England)
9. R. Schuurman (S. Africa)
10. A. Mortimer (England)

1963

1. M. Smith (Australia)
2. L. Turner (Australia)
3. M. E. Bueno (Brazil)
4. B. J. Moffitt (U.S.A.)
5. A. H. Jones (England)
6. D. Hard (U.S.A.)
7. J. Lehane (Australia)
8. R. Schuurman (S. Africa)
9. N. Richey (U.S.A.)
10. Mrs. V. Sukova (Czechoslovakia)

1964

1. M. Smith (Australia)
2. M. E. Bueno (Brazil)
3. L. Turner (Australia)
4. Mrs. C. Graebner (U.S.A.)
5. H. Schultze (Germany)
6. N. Richey (U.S.A.)
7. B. J. Moffitt (U.S.A.)
8. Mrs. R. J. Susman (U.S.A.)
9. R. Ebbern (Australia)
10. J. Lehane (Australia)

1965

1. M. Smith (Australia)
2. M. E. Bueno (Brazil)
3. L. Turner (Australia)

World Rankings—Women's (cont.)

4. B. J. Moffitt (U.S.A.)
5. Mrs. A. H. Jones (England)
6. A. Van Zyl (S. Africa)
7. C. C. Truman (England)
8. N. Richey (U.S.A.)
9. Mrs. C. Graebner (U.S.A.)
10. F. Durr (France)

1966

1. Mrs. B. J. King (U.S.A.)
2. M. Smith (Australia)
3. M. E. Bueno (Brazil)
4. Mrs. A. H. Jones (England)
5. N. Richey (U.S.A.)
6. A. Van Zyl (S. Africa)
7. N. Baylon (Argentina)
8. F. Durr (France)
9. R. Casals (U.S.A.)
10. K. Melville (Australia)

1967

1. Mrs. B. J. King (U.S.A.)
2. Mrs. A. H. Jones (England)
3. F. Durr (France)
4. N. Richey (U.S.A.)
5. L. Turner (Australia)
6. R. Casals (U.S.A.)
7. M. E. Bueno (Brazil)
8. S. V. Wade (England)
9. K. Melville (Australia)
10. J. A. M. Tegart (Australia)

1968

1. Mrs. B. J. King (U.S.A.)
2. Miss S. V. Wade (England)
3. N. Richey (U.S.A.)
4. M. E. Bueno (Brazil)
5. M. S. Court (Australia)
6. Mrs. A. H. Jones (England)

7. J. A. M. Tegart (Australia)
8. Mrs. J. du Plooy (S. Africa)
9. Mrs. W. W. Bowrey (Australia)
10. R. Casals (U.S.A.)

1969

1. Mrs. M. S. Court (Australia)
2. Mrs. A. H. Jones (England)
3. Mrs. B. J. King (U.S.A.)
4. N. Richey (U.S.A.)
5. J. Heldman (U.S.A.)
6. R. Casals (U.S.A.)
7. K. Melville (Australia)
8. J. Bartkowicz (U.S.A.)
9. S. V. Wade (England)
10. Mrs. W. W. Bowrey (Australia)

1970

1. Mrs. M. S. Court (Australia)
2. Mrs. B. J. King (U.S.A.)
3. R. Casals (U.S.A.)
4. S. V. Wade (England)
5. H. Niessen (Germany)
6. K. Melville (Australia)
7. J. Heldman (U.S.A.)
8. K. Krantzcke (Australia)
9. F. Durr (France)
10. Mrs. N. R. Gunter (U.S.A.)

1971

1. E. Goolagong (Australia)
2. Mrs. B. J. King (U.S.A.)
3. Mrs. M. S. Court (Australia)
4. R. Casals (U.S.A.)
5. S. V. Wade (England)
6. F. Durr (France)
7. Mrs. H. N. Masthoff (Germany)
8. K. Melville (Australia)
9. Mrs. N. R. Gunter (U.S.A.)
10. Mrs. J. T. Dalton (Australia)

Leading Members of the World's First Ten

Men	Total Years	Between	Years No. 1
W. T. Tilden (U.S.A.)	12	1919 and 1930	6
H. Cochet (France)	11	1922 and 1933	4
H. W. Austin (England)	11	1928 and 1938	0
J. Drobny (Czechoslovakia and Egypt)	10	1946 and 1955	1
R. Emerson (Australia)	9	1959 and 1967	2
J. Borotra (France)	9	1924 and 1932	0
W. M. Johnson (U.S.A.)	8	1919 and 1926	0
Women			
H. Jacobs (U.S.A.)	12	1928 and 1939	1
A. L. Brough (U.S.A.)	12	1946 and 1957	1
Mrs. A. H. Jones (England)	12	1957 and 1969	0
Mrs. R. Mathieu (France)	11	1929 and 1939	0
Mrs. H. W. Moody (U.S.A.)	10	1925 and 1938	9
M. E. Bueno (Brazil)	10	1958 and 1968	2
D. Hart (U.S.A.)	10	1946 and 1955	1

Mrs. Ann Haydon Jones (*left*) has been in the world's first ten for 12 years, while H. W. "Bunny" Austin (*right*) has appeared for 11 years, but neither has been ranked number one. Austin never won a major international event; however, he was an outstanding player in the 1930's.

ALL-TIME RECORDS

With "sudden death" play (see page 187) in use, most of the following records will remain intact:

Men's Singles

126 games. Roger Taylor, England, d. Wieslaw Gasiorek, Poland, 27–29, 31–29, 6–4. King's Cup match, Warsaw, 1966.

112 games. Pancho Gonzalez, Los Angeles, d. Charlie Pasarell, Santurce, P.R., 22–24, 1–6, 16–14, 6–3, 11–9. First round, Wimbledon, 1969.

107 games. Dick Knight, Seattle, d. Mike Sprengelmeyer, Dubuque, Iowa, 32–30, 3–6, 19–17. Qualifying round, Meadow Club Invitation, Southampton, N.Y., 1967.

100 games. F. D. Robbins, Salt Lake City, d. Dick Dell, Bethesda, Md., 22–20, 9–7, 6–8,

8–10, 6–4. First round, U.S. Open, Forest Hills, 1969.

100 games (not completed). Jaroslav Drobny, Czechoslovakia, tied with Budge Patty, France, 21–19, 8–10, 21–21. Lyons Covered Courts Invitation, Lyons, France, 1955.

95 games. Vic Seixas, Philadelphia, d. Bill Bowrey, Australia, 32–34, 6–4, 10–8. Third round. Pennsylvania Grass Championships, Merion Cricket Club, Philadelphia, 1966.

94 games. Dennis Ralston, Bakersfield, Calif., d. John Newcombe, Australia, 19–17, 20–18, 4–6, 6–4. Quarter-final, Australian Open, Sydney, 1970.

93 games. Jaroslav Drobny d. Budge Patty, 8–6, 16–18, 3–6, 8–6, 2–10. Third round, Wimbledon, 1953.

92 games. Allan Stone, Australia, d. Phil Dent, Australia, 6–3, 20–22, 6–1, 8–10, 9–7. First round, Victorian Championships, Melbourne, 1968.

90 games. Rod Laver, Australia, d. Tony Roche, Australia, 7–5, 22–20, 9–11, 1–6, 6–3. Semifinal, Australian Open, Brisbane, 1969.

Men's Doubles

147 games. Dick Leach, Arcadia, Calif., and Dick Dell, Bethesda, Md., d. Len Schloss, Baltimore, and Tom Mozur, Sweetwater, Tenn., 3–6, 49–47, 22–20. Second round, Newport Casino, Newport, R.I., 1967.

144 games. Bobby Wilson and Mark Cox, both England, d. Ron Holmberg, Highland Falls, N.Y., and Charlie Pasarell, Santurce, P.R., 26–24, 17–19, 30–28. Quarter-final, National Indoors, Salisbury, Md., 1968.

134 games. Ted Schroeder, La Crescenta, Calif., and Bob Falkenburg, Los Angeles, d. Pancho Gonzalez, Los Angeles, and Hugh Stewart, San Marino, Calif., 36–34, 2–6, 4–6, 6–4, 19–17. Final, Southern California Champions, Los Angeles, 1949.

106 games. Len Schloss and Tom Mozur d. Chris Bovett, England, and Butch Seewagen, Bayside, N.Y., 7–5, 48–46. Second round, Meadow Club, 1967.

105 games. Cliff Drysdale and Ray Moore, both South Africa, d. Roy Emerson, Australia, and Ron Barnes, Brazil, 29–31, 8–6, 3–6, 8–6, 6–2. Quarter-final, National Doubles, Longwood Cricket Club, Boston. 1967.

105 games. Jim Osborne, Honolulu, and Bill Bowrey, Australia, d. Terry Addison and Ray Keldie, both Australia, 3–6, 43–41, 7–5. Semifinal Pennsylvania Grass, Merion Cricket Club, Philadelphia, 1969.

105 games. Joaquin Loyo-Mayo and Marcelo Lara, both of Mexico, d. Manolo Santana, Spain, and Luis Garcia, Mexico, 10–12, 24–22, 11–9, 3–6, 6–2. Third round, National Doubles, Longwood, 1966.

102 games. Don White, Coronado, Calif., and Bob Galloway, La Jolla, Calif., d. Hugh Sweeney and Lamar Roemer, both Houston, 6–4, 17–15, 4–6, 18–20, 7–5. First round, National Doubles, Longwood, 1964.

102 games. Russell Bobbitt and Bitsy Grant, both Atlanta, d. Ed Amark, San Francisco, and Robin Hippenstiel, San Bernardino, Calif., 14–12, 15–17, 6–4, 4–6, 13–11. Second round, National Doubles, Longwood 1941.

100 games. Bob Lutz, Los Angeles, Joaquin Loyo-Mayo, Mexico, d. Bill Bond, La Jolla, Calif., and Dick Leach, 19–17, 33–31. Quarter-final, Thunderbird, Phoenix, 1969.

Women's Singles

62 games. Kathy Blake, Pacific Palisades, Calif., d. Elena Subirats, Mexico, 12–10, 6–8, 14–12. First round, Piping Rock, Locust Valley, N.Y., 1966.

60 games. Kristie Pigeon, Danville, Calif., d. Karen Krantzcke, Australia, 17–15, 2–6, 11–9. First round, Kingston Invitation, Kingston, Jamaica, 1969.

56 games. Helen Jacobs, Berkeley, Calif., d. Ellen Whittingstall, England, 9–11, 6–2, 15–13. Quarter-final, British Hard Courts, Bournemouth, 1933.

54 games A. Weiwers, France, d. Mrs. O. Anderson, U.S., 8–10, 14–12, 6–4. Second round, Wimbledon, 1948.

53 games. Mary Ann Eisel, St. Louis, d. Karen Krantzcke, Australia, 3–6 16–14, 8–6. Final, Piping Rock, 1968.

53 games. Corinne Molesworth, England, d. Pam Teeguarden, Los Angeles, 3–6, 7–5, 17–15. Third round, Palace Indoor, Torquay, England, 1968.

51 games. Juliette Atkinson d. Marion Jones, 6–3, 5–7, 6–4, 2–6, 7–5 (best of 5 sets). Final, National Singles, Philadelphia Cricket Club, Philadelphia, 1898.

54 games. Molly Hannas, Kansas City, Mo., d. Lourdes Diaz, Mexico, 9–7, 13–15, 6–4. First round, National Girls 18 Championships, Philadelphia Cricket Club, Philadelphia, 1969.

49 games. Mabel Cahill d. Elizabeth Moore, 5–7, 6–3, 6–4, 4–6, 6–2 (best of 5 sets). Final, National Singles, Philadelphia, 1891.

48 games. Mrs. Margaret Osborne du Pont, Wilmington, Del., d. Louise Brough, Beverly Hills, Calif., 4–6, 6–4, 15–13. Final, National Singles, West Side Tennis Club, Forest Hills, 1948.

48 games. Janet Hopps, Seattle, d. Mary Ann
Mitchell, San Leandro, Calif., 4–6, 6–4,
15–13. Seattle Championships, 1956. Seattle, Wash.

Women's Doubles

81 games. Nancy Richey, San Angelo, Tex.,
and Mrs. Carole Caldwell Graebner, New
York, d. Justina Bricka and Carol Hanks,
both St. Louis, 31–33, 6–1, 6–4. Semifinal
Eastern Grass, Orange Lawn Tennis Club,
South Orange, N.J., 1964.

48 games. Pat Brazier and Christabel Wheat-
croft, both England, d. Mildred Nonweiller
and Betty Soames, both England, 11–9, 5–
7, 9–7. First round, Wimbledon, 1933.

48 games. Mrs. Billie Jean Moffitt King, Long
Beach, Calif., and Rosie Casals, San Francisco, d. Mrs. Ann Haydon Jones, England,
and Françoise Durr, France, 6–8, 8–6, 11–
9. Final Pacific Southwest Open, Los
Angeles, 1969.

Mixed Doubles

71 games. Mrs. Margaret Osborne du Pont,
Wilmington, Del., and Bill Talbert, New
York, d. Gussie Moran, Santa Monica,
Calif., and Bob Falkenburg, Los Angeles,
27–25, 5–7, 6–1. Semifinal, National
Mixed, West Side Tennis Club, Forest Hills,
1948.

61 games. Jane Albert, Pebble Beach, Calif.,
and Dave Reed, Glendale, Calif., d. Kathy
Blake, Pacific Palisades, Calif., and Gene
Scott, New York, 6–3, 7–9, 19–17. Semifinal, Thunderbird, Phoenix, Ariz., 1965.

58 games. Virginia Wade, England, and Dick
Crealy, Australia, d. Mrs. Joyce Barclay
Williams and Bob Howe, both England,
7–5, 17–19, 6–4. Third round, U.S. Open,
Forest Hills, 1969.

52 games. C. Lyon and W. Dixon, both
England, d. Ann Barclay, Canada, and
O. K. French, Australia, 2–6, 9–7, 15–13.
Second Round, Wimbledon, 1963.

Longest Sets (Men's Singles)

70 games. John Brown, Australia, d. Bill
Brown, Omaha, 36–34, 6–1. Third round,

One of the greatest professional matches of all
times was Poncho Gonzalez's five-set victory over
favored Ron Laver in the final match of the 1969
Madison Square Garden Classic. (*above*) Gonzalez serves in the fourth set.

Heart of America, Kansas City, Mo., 1968.

66 games. Vic Seixas d. Bill Bowrey, *32–34,*
6–4, 10–8. Merion.

64 games. Roger Taylor d. Taddeus Nowicki,
Poland, *33–31,* 6–1. King's Club, 1966.

62 games. Dick Knight d. Mike Sprengelmeyer, *32–30,* 3–6, 19–17. Southampton,
1967.

56–60 games. Roger Taylor d. Wieslaw Gasiorek, *27–29, 31–29,* 6–4. King's Cup, 1966.

54 games. Frank Froehling III, Coral Gables,
Fla., d. Marty Riessen, Evanston, Ill., 7–5,
28–26. Quarter-final, Pennsylvania Grass,
Merion, Philadelphia, 1964.

Longest Sets (Men's Doubles)

96 games. Dick Leach and Dick Dell d. Len Schloss and Tom Mozur, 3–6, *49–47*, 22–20. Newport, 1966.

94 games. Schloss and Mozur d. Chris Bovett and Butch Seewagen, 7–5, *48–46*. Southampton, 1967.

84 games. Jim Osborne and Bill Bowrey d. Terry Addison and Ray Keldie, 3–6, *43–41*, 7–5. Merion, 1969.

70 games. Ted Schroeder and Bob Falkenburg d. Pancho Gonzalez and Hugh Stewart, *36–34*, 3–6, 4–6, 6–4, 19–17. Southern California, 1949.

64 games. Bob Lutz and Joaquin Loyo-Mayo d. Bill Bond and Dick Leach, 19–17, *33–31*. Thunderbird, 1969.

62 games. Pancho Segura and Alex Olmedo, both Los Angeles, d. Abe Segal and Gordon Forbes, both South Africa, *32–30*, 5–7, 6–4, 6–4. Second round, Wimbledon, 1968.

60 games. Budge Patty, Paris, and Tony Trabert, Cincinnati, d. Frank Sedgman and Ken McGregor, both Australia, 6–4, *31–29*, 7–9, 6–2. Quarter-final, Wimbledon, 1950.

60 games. Cliff Drysdale and Ray Moore d. Roy Emerson and Ron Barnes, *29–31*, 8–6, 3–6, 8–6, 6–2. National Doubles, 1967.

Longest Sets (Women's Singles)

36 games. Billie Jean Moffitt d. Christine Truman, England, 6–4, *19–17*. Wightman Cup, Cleveland Skating Club, Cleveland, 1963.

34 games. Lesley Hunt, Australia, d. Cerzsebat Polgar, Hungary, *18–16*, 6–3. Semifinal, Montana Invitation, Montana, Switzerland, 1969.

32 games. Kristie Pigeon d. Karen Krantzcke, *17–15*, 2–6, 11–9. Kingston, Jamaica, 1969.

Longest Sets (Women's Doubles)

64 games. Nancy Richey and Mrs. Carole Caldwell Graebner d. Justina Bricka and Carol Hanks, *31–33*, 6–1, 6–4. Easterns, 1964.

Most Games Won in Succession

In two successive 1925 tournaments—Nassau Country Club and Agawam Hunt—William T. Tilden II won 57 games in a row and 63 games out of 64 played in this streak. This remarkable run began in the final match at Nassau when, playing Alfred Chapin, Jr., he was 3–4 in the first set and did not lose another game. He had previously won two love sets from Takeichi Harada. Going on to Providence for the Agawam tournament, Tilden won his first three matches without the loss of a game. He then won the first set from Carl Fischer at love, making his fifty-seventh.

Shortest time on record for one set in a tournament match.

In 1925, *American Lawn Tennis* magazine recorded a 6–0 set that required only nine minutes. Ray Casey, United States, beat Pat Wheatley, Great Britain, in an international match at Eastbourne. The score, 6–0, 6–1, 6–3. "It is doubtful," commented ALT at the time, "whether there is any authenticated case of a set being won in less than nine minutes."

It is interesting to examine the problem involved in winning a set in less than nine minutes. The following analysis appeared in *ALT:*

A 6–0 set requires a minimum of 24 points. There must be three changes of sides. If the winner of the 6–0 set serves first, he can win three service games with four service aces in each, or 12 in all. He can also win the three in which his opponent serves by aceing the 12 serves. That is 24 strokes plus the 12 in the other three games, or 36 strokes in all. This is assuming that the first serve in each game is good. Players have served four consecutive aces in a game. Tilden, Anderson, and Williams have all done so; and McLoughlin aced four first services of Wilding in one game in 1914.

If the minimum of 24 points and 36 strokes is achieved it is still somewhat of a feat to crowd them into nine minutes. Even if the three changes of sides are not taken into consideration, that is 15 seconds to a stroke. Fast work!

Of course, there has never been such an

achievement as 24 consecutive points scored in a set, each of the first services being good and each of the returns of service being an ace. Mrs. Hazel Hotchkiss

Wightman did win a 6–0, 6–0 tournament match in which her opponent failed to win a point, but no record was kept of the point details of the two sets.

THE GRAND SLAMS OF TENNIS

First to win a Grand Slam—the championships of Australia, France, England, and the United States in the same season—was Don Budge of Oakland, Calif., in 1938. Then came Maureen Connolly of San Diego in 1953 and Rod Laver, the Australian, in 1962, as an amateur, and again in 1969 when the Slam first became open to all competitors. Margaret Smith Court won the Grand Slam of women's tennis in 1970. Slams also have been made in doubles by Frank Sedgman and Ken McGregor, Australians, in 1951, and in mixed doubles by Margaret Smith Court and Ken Fletcher, Australians, in 1963.

The complete record of all Grand Slams follows:

Don Budge, 1938, Singles

AUSTRALIA, at Adelaide: d. Les Hancock, 6–2, 6–3, 6–4; H. Whillans, 6–1, 6–0, 6–1; L. A. Schwarts, 6–4, 6–3, 10–8; Adrian Quist, 5–7, 6–4, 6–1, 6–2; John Bromwich, 6–4, 6–2, 6–1.

FRANCE, at Roland Garros, Paris: d. Antoine Gentien, 6–1, 6–2, 6–4; Ghaus Mohammed, 6–1, 6–1, 5–7, 6–0; Franz Kukuljevic, 6–2, 8–6, 2–6, 1–6, 6–1; Bernard Destremeau, 6–4, 6–3, 6–4; Josip Pallada, 6–2, 6–3, 6–3; Roderic Menzel, 6–3, 6–2, 6–4.

ENGLAND, at Wimbledon, London: d. Kenneth Gandar-Dower, 6–2, 6–3, 6–3; Henry Billington, 7–5, 6–1, 6–1; George Lyttleton Rogers, 6–0, 7–5, 6–1; Ronald Shayes, 6–3, 6–4, 6–1; Franz Cejnar, 6–3, 6–0, 7–5; Henner Henkel, 6–2, 6–4, 6–0; Henry Austin, 6–1, 6–0, 6–3.

UNITED STATES, at Forest Hills: d. Welby Van Horn, 6–0, 6–0, 6–1; Bob Kamrath, 6–3, 7–5, 9–7; Charles Hare, 6–3, 6–4, 6–0; Harry Hopman, 6–3, 6–1, 6–3; Sidney Wood, 6–3, 6–3, 6–3; Gene Mako, 6–3, 6–8, 6–2, 6–1.

Maureen Connolly, 1953, Singles

AUSTRALIA, at Kooyong, Melbourne: d. C. Boreilli, 6–0, 6–1; Mrs. R. W. Baker, 6–1, 6–0; P. Southcombe, 6–0, 6–1; Mary Haw-

ton, 6–2, 6–1; Julie Sampson, 6–3, 6–2.

FRANCE, at Roland Garros, Paris: d. Christiane Mercelis, 6–1, 6–3; Raymonde Verber Jones, 6–3, 6–1; Susan Patridge Chatrier, 3–6, 6–2, 6–2; Dorothy Head Knode, 6–3, 6–3; Doris Hart, 6–2, 6–4.

ENGLAND, at Wimbledon, London: d. D. Killian, 6–0, 6–0; J. M. Petchell, 6–1, 6–1; Anne Shilcock, 6–0, 6–1; Erika Vollmer, 6–3, 6–0; Shirley Fry, 6–1, 6–1; Doris Hart, 8–6, 7–5.

UNITED STATES, at Forest Hills: d. Jean Fallot, 6–1, 6–0; Pat Stewart, 6–3, 6–1; Jeanne Arth, 6–1, 6–3; Althea Gibson, 6–2, 6–3; Shirley Fry, 6–1, 6–1; Doris Hart, 6–2, 6–4.

Rod Laver, 1962, Singles

AUSTRALIA, at White City, Sydney: d. Fred Sherriff, 8–6, 6–2, 6–4; Geoff Pares, 10–8, 18–16, 7–9, 7–5; Owen Davidson, 6–4, 9–7, 6–4; Bob Hewitt, 6–1, 4–6, 6–4, 7–5; Roy Emerson, 8–6, 0–6, 6–4, 6–4.

Don Budge was the first player to complete the Grand Slam of Tennis.

Grand Slams (*cont.*)

FRANCE, at Roland Garros, Paris: d. Michele Pirro, 6–4, 6–0, 6–2; Tony Pickard, 6–2, 9–7, 4–6, 6–1; Sergio Jacobini, 4–6, 6–3, 7–5, 6–1; Marty Mulligan, 6–4, 3–6, 2–6, 10–8, 6–2; Neale Fraser, 3–6, 6–3, 6–2, 3–6, 7–5; Roy Emerson, 3–6, 2–6, 6–3, 9–7, 6–2.

ENGLAND, at Wimbledon, London: d. Naresh Kumar, 7–5, 6–1, 6–2; Tony Pickard, 6–1, 6–2, 6–2; Whitney Reed, 6–4, 6–1, 6–4; Pierre Darmon, 6–3, 6–2, 13–11; Manolo Santana, 14–16, 9–7, 6–2; Neale Fraser, 10–8, 6–1, 7–5; Marty Mulligan, 6–2, 6–2, 6–1.

UNITED STATES, at Forest Hills: d. Eleazar Davidman, 6–3, 6–2, 6–3; Eduardo Zuleta, 6–3, 6–3, 6–1; Bodo Nitsche, 9–7, 6–1, 6–1; Tonio Palafox, 6–1, 6–2, 6–2; Frank Froehling, 6–3, 13–11, 4–6, 6–3; Rafe Osuna, 6–1, 6–3, 6–4; Roy Emerson, 6–2, 6–4, 5–7, 6–4.

Rod Laver, 1969 Singles

AUSTRALIA, at Milton Courts, Brisbane: d. Massimo di Domenico, 6–2, 6–3, 6–3; Roy Emerson, 6–2, 6–3, 3–6, 9–7; Fred Stolle, 6–4, 18–16, 6–2; Tony Roche, 7–5, 22–20, 9–11, 1–6, 6–3; Andres Gimeno, 6–3, 6–4, 7–5.

FRENCH, at Roland Garros, Paris: d. Koji Watanabe, 6–1, 6–1, 6–1; Dick Crealy, 3–6, 7–9, 6–2, 6–2, 6–4; Pietro Marzano, 6–1, 6–0, 8–6; Stan Smith, 6–4, 6–2, 6–4; Andres Gimeno, 3–6, 6–3, 6–4, 6–3; Tom Okker, 4–6, 6–0, 6–2, 6–4; Ken Rosewall, 6–4, 6–3, 6–4.

BRITISH, at Wimbledon, London: d. Nicola Pietrangeli, 6–1, 6–2, 6–2; Premjit Lall, 3–6, 4–6, 6–3, 6–0, 6–0; Jan Leschly, 6–3, 6–3, 6–3; Stan Smith, 6–4, 6–2, 7–9, 3–6, 6–3; Cliff Drysdale, 6–4, 6–2, 6–3; Arthur Ashe, 2–6, 6–2, 9–7, 6–0; John Newcombe, 6–4, 5–7, 6–4, 6–4.

UNITED STATES, at Forest Hills: d. Luis Garcia, 6–2, 6–4, 6–2; Jaime Pinto-Bravo, 6–4, 7–5, 6–2; Jaime Fillol, 8–6, 6–1, 6–2; Dennis Ralston, 6–4, 4–6, 4–6, 6–2, 6–3; Roy Emerson, 4–6, 8–6, 13–11, 6–4; Arthur Ashe, 8–6, 6–3, 14–12; Tony Roche, 7–9, 6–1, 6–2, 6–2.

Margaret Smith Court, 1970 Singles

AUSTRALIA, at White City, Sydney: d. Evonne Goolagong, 6–3, 6–1; Karen Krantzcke, 6–1, 6–3; Kerry Melville, 6–3, 6–1.

FRENCH, at Roland Garros, Paris: d. Marijke Jansen Schaar, 6–1, 6–1; Olga Morozova, 3–6, 8–6, 6–1; Lesley Hunt, 6–2, 6–1; Rosie Casals, 7–5, 6–2; Julie Heldman, 6–0, 6–2; Helga Niessen, 6–2, 6–4.

BRITISH, at Wimbledon, London: d. Sue Alexander, 6–0, 6–1; Maria Guzman, 6–0, 6–1; Vlasta Vopickvoa, 6–3, 6–3; Helga Niessen, 6–8, 6–0, 6–0; Rosie Casals, 6–4, 6–1; Billie Jean Moffitt King, 14–2, 11–9.

UNITED STATES, at Forest Hills, New York: d. Pam Austin, 6–1, 6–0; Patti Hogan, 6–1, 6–1; Pat Faulkner, 6–0, 6–2; Helen Gourlay, 6–2, 6–2; Nancy Richey, 6–1, 6–3; Rosie Casals, 6–2, 2–6, 6–1.

Frank Sedgman and Ken McGregor, 1951 Doubles

AUSTRALIAN, at White City, Sydney: d. Rocavert and J. Gilchrist, 6–1, 6–3, 13–11; J. A. Mehaffey and Clive Wilderspin, 6–4, 6–4, 6–3; Merv Rose and Don Candy, 8–6, 6–4, 6–3; Adrian Quist and John Bromwich, 11–9, 2–6, 6–3, 4–6, 6–3.

FRENCH, at Roland Garros, Paris: d. A. Gentien and P. Grandguillot, 6–0, 6–0, 6–0; M. Bergamo and Beppe Meriod, 6–3, 7–5, 6–1; Bob Abdesselam and Paul Remy, 6–2, 6–2, 4–6, 6–3. Merv Rose and Ham Richardson, 6–3, 7–5, 6–2; Gardnar Mulloy and Dick Savitt, 6–2, 2–6, 9–7, 7–5.

ENGLISH, at Wimbledon, London: d. Vladimir Petrovic and P. Milojkovic, 6–1, 6–1, 6–3; Raymundo Deyro and Gene Garrett, 6–4, 6–4, 6–3; Bernard Destremeau and Torsten Johansson, 3–6, 6–3, 6–2, 9–7; Gianni Cucelli and Marcello del Bello, 6–4, 7–5, 16–14; Budge Patty and Ham Richardson, 6–4, 6–2, 6–3; Eric Sturgess and Jaroslav Drobny, 3–6, 6–2, 6–3, 3–6, 6–3.

UNITED STATES, at Longwood Cricket Club, Boston: d. Harrison Rowbotham and Sumner Rodman, 6–2, 6–3, 6–3; Dave Mesker and Ed Wesely, 6–1, 6–1, 6–1; Earl Cochell and Merv Rose, 10–8, 4–6, 6–4, 7–5 (final round match played at Forest Hills, moved from Boston because of heavy rains).

Margaret Smith and Ken Fletcher, 1963 Mixed Doubles

AUSTRALIAN, at Memorial Drive, Adelaide: d. Faye Toyne and Bill Bowry, 6–2, 6–2; Jill Blackman and Roger Taylor, 6–3, 6–3; Liz Starkie and Mark Cox, 7–5, 6–4; Lesley Turner and Fred Stolle, 7–5, 5–7, 6–4.

FRENCH, at Roland Garros, Paris: d. C. Rouire and M. Lagard, 6–2, 6–1; d. Marie Dusapt and Ion Tiriac, 6–0, 6–2; Mary Habicht and Peter Strobl, 6–3, 6–0; Margaret Hunt and Cliff Drysdale, 7–5, 4–6, 6–1; Judy Tegart and Ed Rubinoff, 6–3, 6–1; Lesley Turner and Fred Stolle, 6–1, 6–2.

ENGLISH, at Wimbledon, London: d. Judy Tegart and Ed Rubinoff, 6–2, 6–2; Judy Alvarez and John Fraser, 6–2, 9–7; Senor and Senora Alfonso Ochoa, 6–4, 6–4; Renée Schuurman and Wilhelm Bungert, 6–2, 6–1; Ann Jones and Dennis Ralston, 6–1, 7–5; Darlene Hard and Bob Hewitt, 11–9, 6–4.

UNITED STATES, at Forest Hills: d. Heidi Schilnecht and Peter Scholl, 6–2, 6–3; Mr. and Mrs. Alan Mills, 6–4, 3–6, 6–1; Robyn Ebbern and Owen Davidson, 6–2, 6–2; Billie Jean Moffitt and Donald Dell, 5–7, 8–6, 6–4; Judy Tegart and Ed Rubinoff, 3–6, 8–6, 6–2.

USLTA TENNIS AWARDS

The William M. Johnston Award

The William M. Johnston Trophy is awarded to that man player who by his character, sportsmanship, manners, spirit of cooperation, and contribution to the growth of the game ranks first in the opinion of the Selection Committee for the year ending at the time of the USLTA Men's Singles Championship. This includes help which the player renders not only to players in his own class, but to the Junior players as well.

The award is the result of a suggestion by the late "Little Bill" Johnston, who gave one of his championship cups to the International Lawn Tennis Club of the United States to be used for this purpose. The name of the winner of the award is engraved on the trophy and a small silver tray suitably inscribed is given to the recipient as a memento of the award.

The William M. Johnston Trophy has been awarded to the following:

1947   John A. Kramer
1948   E. Victor Seixas, Jr.
1949   Frederick R. Schroeder
1950   J. Gilbert Hall
1951   W. Donald McNeill
1952   Francis X. Shields
1953   William F. Talbert
1954   L. Straight Clark
1955   Chauncey Depew Steele, Jr.
1956   Hamilton Richardson
1957   not awarded
1958   Thomas P. Brown, Jr.
1959   Bernard V. Bartzen
1960   not awarded
1961   Eugene Scott
1962   Jon A. Douglas
1963   Martin Riessen
1964   Arthur Ashe, Jr.
1965   Charles R. McKinley
1966   R. Dennis Ralston

1967   not awarded
1968   Stanley R. Smith
1969   Charles Pasarell
1970   Tom Gorman
1971   Jim McManus

USLTA Junior and Boys' Sportsmanship Award

In 1957, shortly after the death of Dr. Allen B. Stowe, a long-time director of the National Junior and Boys' Tennis Championships, a group of Kalamazoo tennis enthus-

The 1969 winner of the William M. Johnston award was Charles Pasarell.

Junior and Boys' Sportsmanship Award (cont.)

iasts sought to establish a fitting and lasting memorial to the former Kalamazoo College professor and tennis coach. The group contributed a sum of money for a trophy to be presented annually to the Junior player who, in the opinion of the National Junior and Boys' Championships Committee, best combined the qualities of outstanding sportsmanship and oustanding ability. Past winners are:

1958	Paul Palmer
1959	Bill Lenoir
1960	Charles Pasarell
1961	Davis Reed
1962	Jim Bests
1963	George Seewagen
1964	Armistead Neely
1965	Roy Barth
1966	Mac Claflin
1967	Bill Colson
1968	Charles Owens
1969	Danny Birchmore
1970	Brian Gottfried
1971	Compton Russell

USLTA Girls' Sportsmanship Trophy Award

The United States Lawn Tennis Association Girls' Sportsmanship Trophy is awarded annually at the close of the United States Lawn Tennis Association Girls' Championship to the player in the Championship who, in the opinion of the Committee of Judges, most nearly approaches the ideal in Sportsmanship, Appearance, Court Manners, and Tactics. The Trophy was presented in 1936 by Mrs. Harrison Smith and the Award has been made annually ever since.

The Trophy is a sterling-silver plate. The name of the recipient of the Award is engraved on the Trophy each year and she receives a small silver plate similar to the Trophy in design and engraving. The following players have received the award:

1936	Eleanor Dawson
1937	Mary Olivia Morrill
1938	Helen Irene Bernhard
1939	Dorothy Wightman
1940	Mary Jane Metcalf
1941	Barbara Krase
1942	Judy Atterbury
1943	Doris Jane Hart*
	Betty Rosenquest*
1944	Barbara Van Alen Scofield

* Joint award.
† Honorable Mention.

1945	Shirley June Fry
1946	Nancy Anne Chaffee
	Mary Cunningham†
1947	Doris Marie Newcomer
	Martha Miller†
1948	Barbara Jane Scarlett
1949	Rosalie Meluney
1950	Natalie Cobough
1951	Elaine Marie Lewicki*
	Bonnie Jean MacKay*
1952	Judy Iselin
1953	Jeanne Arth
	Mary Ann Eilenberger†
	Gwenyth Howell Johnson†
1954	Mary Elizabeth Wellford
1955	Patricia Jean Shaffer
1956	Rosa Maria Reyes
1957	Susan Hodgman
1958	Gwyneth Thomas
	Albertina C. Rodi†
1959	Karen Hantze
1960	Pamela Davis
1961	Katherine D. Chabot
1962	Peachy Kellmeyer
1963	Nancy L. Falkenberg
1964	Kathleen M. Harter*
	Kathleen A. Blake*
1965	Wendy Overton
	Gretchen A. Vosters†
1966	Patsy Rippy
	Julia K. Anthony
1967	Valerie Ziengenfuss*
	Lynn Abbes*
	Vicki Rogers†
1968	Betty Ann Grubb
1969	Gail Hansen
1970	Sharon Walsh
1971	Ann Kiyomura

The Samuel Hardy Award

The Samuel Hardy Award is made each year by the USLTA at its Annual Meeting to the person selected by the Directors of the National Tennis Educational Foundation, Inc., for outstanding service rendered to the tennis educational program.

The Hardy Award is a large sterling tray commemorating numerous events won by Samuel Hardy in competition on the French Riviera and given by him to the USLTA. The name of each winner of the award is engraved on the tray and the recipient receives a small silver tray, suitably inscribed as a memento of the award.

Following are the winners of the Samuel Hardy Award:

1953	Dr. Allen B. Stowe
1954	Mrs. Harrison Smith

Sam Hardy was an outstanding player in the early 1920's.

1955	Perry T. Jones
1956	William Matson Tobin
1957	Percy C. Rogers
1958	Dr. Howard Z. Dredge
1959	Lawrence A. Baker
1960	Victor Denny
1961	Martin L. Tressel
1962	George E. Barnes
1963	James B. Moffet
1964	David L. Freed
1965	Robert H. Pease
1966	Harrison F. Rowbotham
1967	Mr. and Mrs. Monroe C. Lewis
1968	William J. Clothier II
1969	Edward A. Turville
1970	Robert J. Kelleher
1971	Daniel S. Johnson

The Harold A. Lebair Memorial Trophy

The Harold A. Lebair Memorial Trophy is to be awarded annually at the National Open Tennis Championships to that player, man or woman, who by virtue of his or her sportsmanship, conduct on and off the court, and playing of the game, best examplifies the finest traditions of tennis. The trophy is a perpetual one and will be inscribed with the winner's name and year of award. A small replica, suitably inscribed, will be given annually to the recipient of the award. The winner is to be named by a vote of the Lebair Memorial Trophy Committee, appointed each year by the President of the USLTA from officials of the USLTA, press representatives, and other knowledgeable and interested persons. The following have received the trophy:

1968	Arthur Ashe, Jr.
1969	Stanley R. Smith
1970	Ken Rosewall
1971	Chris Evert

The John T. McGovern Umpires' Award

The late John T. (Terry) McGovern was a well-known leader in amateur sports. He was for many years legal advisor to the United States Olympic Committee, a former president of the Cornell University Alumni Association, and president of the Sandlot Baseball Association. Almost from the inception of the USLTA Umpires Association, he was a devoted tennis linesman.

In 1949 he presented a beautiful gold-plated trophy for annual award to that umpire or linesman who contributed most to the cause of tennis officiating during the previous year. In addition to the perpetual trophy, Mr. McGovern contributed gold-plated medalettes to be given annually for the permanent possession of the recipient, as well as silver-plated medalettes to be given on a similar basis to junior officials. The Committee of Award consists of the chairman of the USLTA Umpires Committee and all previous recipients of the award.

This trophy has been awarded to:

1949	Donald M. Dickson
1950	Craufurd Kent
1951	Harold A. Lebair
1952	David S. Niles
1953	Louis W. Shaw
1954	Frank J. Tybeskey
1955	Hubert J. Quinn
1956	H. LeVan Richards
1957	Winslow Blanchard
1958	Edward Mellor
1959	Harold E. Ammerman
1960	J. Clarence Davies, Jr.
1961	Herbert J. Lewis
1962	Frank Dowling
1963	John G. Kroel
1964	William Macassin
1965	Ernest J. Oberlaender, Jr.
1966	John B. Stahr
1967	S. R. Bumann
1968	John Coman
1969	Frank Hammond
1970	E. Brooks Keffer
1971	Titus Sparrow

The Service Bowl Award

"To the Player Who Yearly Makes the Most Notable Contribution to the Sportsmanship, Fellowship, and Service of Tennis." This inscription is engraved on The Service Bowl trophy which, after being limited for four years to women players in New England, has been awarded on a nationwide basis since 1944 during the week of the National Doubles Championships at the Longwood Cricket Club, with the President of the New England Lawn Tennis Association acting as Master of Ceremonies. The award is the outgrowth of an association of thirty New England women players who earlier had been organized informally for a number of years in an annual "tennis party" given by the donor of the award, Mrs. Lyman H. B. Olmstead. The award has been made to the following:

New England Winners:

1940 Mrs. Hazel H. Wightman
1941 Mrs. William S. Shedden
1942 Mrs. J. Lewis Bremer
1943 Mrs. Marjorie Morrill Painter

National Winners:

1944 Mrs. Dorothy Bundy Cheney
1945 Mrs. Margaret Osborne du Pont
1946 Mrs. Hazel H. Wightman
1947 Mrs. John B. Prizer
1948 A. Louise Brough
1949 Mrs. Madge Harshaw Vosters
1950 Nancy P. Norton
1951 Mrs. Gladys Medalie Heldman
1952 Mrs. Maureen Connolly Brinker
1953 Mrs. John B. Moore
1954 Mrs. Marjorie Gladman Buck
1955 Doris Hart
1956 Mrs. Patricia Henry Yeomans
1957 Mrs. Dorothy Head Knode
1958 Katharine Hubbell
1959 Mrs. Barbara Krase Chandler
1960 Mrs. Sylvia K. Simonin
1961 Mrs. Gail Stewart
1962 Mimi Arnolds
1963 Marilyn Montgomery
1964 Mrs. Helen Fulton Shockley and
      Mrs. Theodore Hackett (co-winners)
1965 Mrs. Rosalind Greenwood
1966 Mrs. Billie Jean Moffitt King
1967 Mrs. Donna Floyd Fales
1968 Mrs. Betty R. Pratt
1969 Mrs. Doris Harrison

1970 Mrs. Nancy Jeffett
1971 Mrs. Ruth Lay

Seniors' Service Award

A perpetual trophy for service to Senior tennis is awarded each year at the National Championships to the person who, in the judgment of the USLTA Senior's Committee, has been, through his efforts, willingness, co-operation and participation, most deserving of the respect and honor of all Seniors, either in play or organizational work for the betterment and furtherance of Senior Competition. Each year the winner's name and the year are engraved on the trophy and a replica of the trophy is given to the winners, who are as follows:

1958 W. Dickson Cunningham
1959 William L. Nassau, Jr.
1960 Henry L. Benisch
1961 Dr. Irving Bricker
1962 Monte L. Ganger
1963 Caspar H. Nannes
1964 Joseph Lipshutz
1965 Gardnar Mulloy
1966 J. Clarence Davies, Jr.
1967 C. Alphonso Smith
1968 Col. Nicholas E. Powel
1969 Robert L. Galloway
1970 E. Jefferson Mendal
1971 Emery Neale

The Colonel James H. Bishop Award

The Colonel James H. Bishop Award is made during the USLTA Men's Singles Championships to that U.S. Junior Davis Cup squad member who, in the opinion of his captain and team mates, has best exemplified during the year the objectives of the Junior Davis Cup Program in regard to highest standards of character, conduct, sportsmanship, appearance, amateurism on and off the tennis court, and tennis accomplishment.

The award, a sterling-silver tray, was donated by Dorothy W. and Thomas E. Price to the USLTA in the memory of the late Colonel James H. Bishop—the founder of the Junior Davis Cup Program in 1937 (the forerunner of the Junior Wightman Cup Program in 1938) and a well-known and highly regarded friend of youth, educator, and tennis leader until his untimely death in 1961.

The name of the recipient of the Award

is engraved on the tray and a suitably inscribed small silver replica is given to the recipient as a memento of the award. The following U.S. Junior Davis Cup squad members have earned this award:

1962   David Reed
1963   James Parker
1964   David Power
1965   Jim Pickens
1966   Stan Smith
1967   James Osborne
1968   Robert McKinley
1969   Richard Stockton
1970   not awarded
1971   Roscoe Tanner

Tennis Educational Merit Award

The Tennis Educational Merit Award is made annually by the USLTA to the person selected by the Directors of the National Tennis Educational Foundation, Inc., for outstanding service rendered to the tennis educational program by a teaching professional and/or instructor.

It is the desire of the USLTA to honor and recognize such services to the development of the game through leadership, inspiration, and junior programs in the schools, colleges, clubs, parks, and playgrounds benefiting the nation's youth. Winners of the award are as follows:

1967   Harry A. Leighton
1968   William C. Lufler
1969   Dennis Van der Meer
1970   Harry James
1971   John Conroy

The Ralph W. Westcott Award

This award was initiated by Martin L. Tressel, President of the USLTA, in 1965 to emphasize that tennis is a family game. Ralph W. Westcott donated a large silver tray as a Perpetual Award. This trophy was given by him upon retiring as President of the Chicago District Tennis Association. He has also been President of the Western Sectional Association and Secretary of the USLTA.

The award is made annually to the family who has done the most to promote amateur tennis during the past twelve months. The names of the recipients are engraved on this

tray and a small silver replica suitably inscribed is given to the National Tennis Family of the Year as a memento of the award. Each District, each Section, and each Region selects a Tennis Family of the Year. From the four Regional finalists a National Winner is selected by a committee appointed by the President of the USLTA. The trophy is presented at the USLTA Singles Championships at Forest Hills in September.

The Ralph Westcott Trophy has been awarded to the following:

1965   The John F. Sullivan Family
1966   The Will Rompf Family
1967   The Charles Pasarell Family
1968   The Bundy-Cheney Family
1969–71   not awarded

The Leadership Award for Women

The Leadership Award for Women is made annually to the woman physical educator who has made outstanding contributions to the development and growth of tennis for girls and women. The recipient is named at the USLTA Women's Collegiate Championships.

A large permanent silver trophy has been donated by Judy Barta upon which the name of the recipient is engraved. A smaller replica is given to the awardee. Winners are as follows:

1969   Mrs. Luell Weed Guthrie
1970   Mrs. Jean Johnson
1971   not awarded

The Maureen Connolly Brinker Award

The Maureen Connolly Brinker Outstanding Junior Girl Award was approved in February, 1969, at the annual meeting of the USLTA. The award created by the Maureen Connolly Brinker Foundation, Inc., will be presented each year following the finals of the National Girls' 18 Championships in Philadelphia at the Philadelphia Cricket Club.

The award and the foundation were the dream of the late Maureen Connolly Brinker. This award will be presented each year to the girl player considered by the committee to have had the most outstanding full season performance. She must be exceptional in

Maureen Connolly Brinker Award (cont.)

ability, sportsmanship, and in competitive spirit.

The magnificent silver bowl which will be kept at the Philadelphia Cricket Club will have inscribed the name of each year's winner. The recipient of the award will receive a small engraved silver tray and a lifetime enrollment in the USLTA. Winners are as follows:

1969 Eliza Pande
1970 Sharon Walsh
1971 Chris Evert

LEADING ACHIEVERS IN DAVIS CUP PLAY

Most of the world's great tennis players have played in the Davis Cup competition. Here are some of their records:

Davis Cup Stalwarts of All-Times

Although Nikki Pietrangeli was unable to win the Davis Cup for Italy, he did retire with the distinction of having played more Cup matches for his homeland than any other man in the competition stretching back 70 years. In 62 international battles he ap-

peared on the court 159 times in singles and doubles, winning 116 times. Twice, in 1960 and 1961, Pietrangeli led Italy to the Challenge Round final. Nobody in the list of Davis Cup stalwarts is close to him, and among them only Willy Bungert of West Germany remains active. It is unlikely that non-Europeans will crack the list since more matches are involved for those playing in the larger European Zones. Ram Krishnan of India, who started Cup play at 16 in 1953, is the lone outsider on the roll.

	TOTAL GAMES		SINGLES		DOUBLES		
	Played	Won	Played	Won	Played	Won	Matches
Nikki Pietrangeli (Italy, 1954–69)	159	116	108	76	51	40	62
Jackie Brichant (Belgium, 1949–65)	121	71	80	52	41	19	42
Manolo Santana (Spain, 1958–69)	117	90	83	67	34	23	45
Gottfried von Cramm (Germany, 1932–53)	102	82	69	58	33	24	37
Willy Bungert (W. Germany, 1958–71)	102	66	79	52	23	14	43
Ulf Schmidt (Sweden, 1954–64)	102	66	69	44	33	22	38
Philippe Washer (Belgium, 1946–51)	102	66	64	46	38	20	39
Torben Ulrich (Denmark, 1948–68)	98	46	63	31	35	15	39
Ram Krishnan (India, 1953–69)	97	69	69	50	28	19	39
Kurt Nielsen (Denmark, 1948–60)	96	53	65	42	31	11	33
Jan Lundquist (Sweden, 1957–69)	89	64	61	47	28	17	34
Orlando Sirola (Italy, 1953–69)	89	57	46	22	43	35	45
Lennart Bergelin (Sweden, 1946–65)	88	62	60	43	28	19	36
Roderic Menzel (Czechoslovakia, 1928–38) (Germany, 1939)	84	61	60	47	24	14	35
Sven Davidson (Sweden, 1950–60)	84	61	53	39	31	22	35

Davis Cup Stalwarts Among the Leaders

Of the four nations who have won the cup —the United States, Australia, Great Britain, and France—the United States has played with 83 men, while only 52 played for Australia, 71 have played for Great Britain, and 38 for France. (Incidentally, the 1971 Challenge Round was the 157th Davis Cup match for the United States—no other nation has had so many.)

Of the four winning nations, Bobby Wilson of Great Britain and Pierre Darmon of France have played in the most matches.

		TOTAL GAMES		SINGLES		DOUBLES		
		Played	Won	Played	Won	Played	Won	Matches
Australia								
Jack Crawford	1928–37	58	36	40	23	18	13	23
Adrian Quist	1933–48	55	42	33	23	22	19	28
John Bromwich	1937–50	52	39	31	19	21	20	23
Gerald Patterson	1919–28	46	32	31	21	15	11	16
Roy Emerson	1959–67	40	36	24	22	16	14	18

Four Davis Cup doubles players: (*left to right*) Quist, Schroeder, Kramer, and Bromwich, of 1946 challenge round, anxiously watch the fall of Australian Adrian Quist's racket to decide first service. The Australians won the toss, but Jack Kramer and Ted Schroeder won the match and Davis Cup for the United States.

Davis Cup Stalwarts

		TOTAL GAMES		SINGLES		DOUBLES		
		Played	Won	Played	Won	Played	Won	
Great Britain								
Mike Sangster	1960–68	65	43	48	29	17	14	26
Bobby Wilson	1955–68	62	41	29	16	33	25	34
Tony Mottram	1947–55	56	36	38	25	18	11	19
Fred Perry	1930–36	52	45	38	34	14	11	20
Bunny Austin	1929–37	48	36	48	36	0	0	24
France								
Pierre Darmon	1956–67	69	47	62	44	7	3	34
Henri Cochet	1922–33	58	44	42	34	16	10	26
Jean Borotra	1922–47	54	36	31	19	23	17	32
Paul Remy	1949–58	53	33	29	16	24	16	25
René Lacoste	1923–28	51	40	40	32	11	8	26
United States								
Vic Seixas	1951–57	55	38	36	24	19	14	19
Wilmer Allison	1929–36	45	32	29	18	16	14	20
Bill Tilden	1920–30	41	34	30	25	11	9	17
Chuck McKinley	1960–65	38	30	22	17	16	13	16
Tony Trabert	1951–55	35	27	21	16	14	11	14
Dennis Ralston	1960–66	35	25	20	14	15	11	15

Challenge-Round Stalwarts

In Challenge Rounds, that English notable at the turn of the century, Laurie Doherty leads with a perfect record of 12 singles and doubles victories in five Challenge appearances. Bill Tilden, the legendary American who appeared in more Challenge Rounds than anyone else (11), won 21 of 28 matches. With the change in Davis Cup format (see page 333) all of the following challenge-round records will stand:

	Matches Played	Won	Average	Challenge Rounds
Laurie Doherty (Great Britain, 1902–06)	12	12	1.000	5
Fred Perry (Great Britain, 1931–36)	10	9	.900	5
Roy Emerson (Australia, 1959–67)	18	15	.833	9
Bill Johnston (United States, 1920–27)	16	13	.813	8
Frank Sedgman (Australia, 1949–52)	11	9	.818	4
Bill Tilden (United States, 1920–30)	28	21	.750	11
Neale Fraser (Australia, 1958–63)	11	8	.727	6
Lew Hoad (Australia, 1953–56)	11	8	.727	4
Henri Cochet (France, 1926–33)	20	14	.700	8
Ken Rosewall (Australia, 1953–56)	10	7	.700	4
Norman Brookes (Australia, 1907–20)	22	15	.682	8

Tony Wilding (Australia, 1907–14)	12	8	.667	4
Bunny Austin (Great Britain, 1931–37)	12	8	.667	6
Ted Schroeder (United States, 1946–51)	15	9	.600	6
John Bromwich (Australia, 1938–50)	14	7	.500	6
Adrian Quist (Australia, 1936–48)	12	5	.417	5
Maurice McLoughlin (United States, 1909–14)	11	4	.364	4
Jean Borotra (France, 1925–33)	17	6	.353	9
Gerald Patterson (Australia, 1919–24)	12	4	.333	4
Tony Trabert (United States, 1951–55)	12	4	.333	5
Vic Seixas (United States, 1951–57)	20	6	.300	7

Vital Challenge-Round Matches

Laurie Doherty also leads in "vital" Challenge Round matches, that is, those matches played while the issue was still in doubt. He was flawless, winning nine for nine.

	Matches Played	Won	Average
Laurie Doherty	9	9	1.000
Fred Perry	9	8	.889
Ray Emerson	15	13	.867
Bill Tilden	18	14	.778
Frank Sedgman	9	7	.778
Neale Fraser	9	7	.778
Bill Johnston	12	9	.750
Henri Cochet	17	12	.706
Tony Wilding	10	7	.700
Norman Brookes	19	13	.684
Lew Hoad	9	6	.667
Bunny Austin	8	5	.625
Ted Schroeder	13	8	.615
Ken Rosewall	7	4	.571
John Bromwich	11	6	.545
Jean Borotra	13	6	.462
Adrian Quist	11	5	.455
Gerald Patterson	10	4	.400
Tony Trabert	10	4	.400
Maurice McLoughlin	8	3	.375
Vic Seixas	15	4	.267

Longest Davis Cup Matches

Singles

86 Games. Arthur Ashe, U.S. d. Christian Kuhnke, Germany, 6–8, 10–12, 9–7, 13–11, 6–4. Challenge Round, Cleveland, 1970.

83 Games. Arthur Ashe, U.S. d. Manolo Santana, Spain, 11–13, 7–5, 6–3, 13–15, 6–4. Zone Match, Cleveland, 1968.

79 Games. Barry MacKay, U.S. d. Nicola Pietrangeli, Italy, 8–6, 3–6, 8–10, 8–6, 13–11. Zone Match, Perth, Australia, 1960.

78 Games. Jaroslav Drobny, Czechoslovakia d. Adrian Quist, Australia, 6–8, 3–6, 18–16, 6–3, 7–5. Zone Match, Boston, 1948.

75 Games. Tom Brown, U.S. d. Ken McGregor, Australia, 9–11, 8–10, 11–9, 6–1, 6–4. Challenge Round, New York, 1950.

Doubles

95 games. Wilhelm Bungert and Christian Kuhnke, Germany d. Mark Cox and Peter Curtis, England, 10–8, 17–19, 13–11, 3–6, 6–2. Zone Match, Birmingham, England, 1969.

94 Games. Roy Emerson and Fred Stolle, Australia d. Rafe Osuna and Antonio Palafox, Mexico, 18–16, 7–9, 7–9, 6–4, 10–8. Zone Match, Mexico City, 1964.

82 Games. Alex Olmedo and Ham Richardson, U.S. d. Neal Fraser and Mal Anderson, Australia, 10–12, 3–6, 16–14, 6–3, 7–5. Challenge Round, Brisbane, Australia, 1958.

81 Games. Bill Tilden and Dick William, U.S. d. Jim Anderson and John Hawkes, Australia, 17–15, 11–13, 2–6, 6–3, 6–2. Challenge Round, New York, 1923.

79 Games. Carlos Fernandes and Armardo

Longest Davis Cup Matches (*cont.*)

Vieira, Brazil d. Eleazar Davidman and A. Avidan, Israel, 1–6, 4–6, 6–4, 6–2, 23–21. Zone Match, Montreal, 1957.

75 Games. Nicola Pietrangeli and Orlando Sirola, Italy d. Chuck McKinley and Earl Buchholz, United States, 3–6, 10–8, 6–4, 6–8, 13–11. Zone Match, Perth, 1960.

United States Davis Cup Who's Who

Eighty-two men are on America's tennis honor roll, having played for their country in the Davis Cup since the first balls were struck August 8, 1900, in Boston by Malcolm Whitman of the home side and the loser, A. W. Gore of Britain. Of this number, 54 have played in the grand final, the Challenge Round. Most illustrious of course was "Big Bill" Tilden, whose 11 years of Challenge Rounds are high for American players. No one of any other country has surpassed his 11 Challenge Round appearances (during which the United States won the Cup seven times), nor his number of individual victories (21) and matches (28). Only Roy Emerson of Australia played on more Cup-winning teams than Tilden—eight.

MALCOLM WHITMAN, 1900, '02. Challenge Rounds (2): 3–0 in singles, 1–0 in doubles.

DWIGHT DAVIS, 1900, '02. Challenge Rounds (2): 1–0 in singles, 1–1 in doubles.

HOLCOMBE WARD, 1900, '02, '05, '06. Challenge Rounds (4): 0–3 in singles, 1–3 in doubles. Zone Matches (3): 3–1 in singles, 3–0 in doubles. Overall: 7–7 for 7 matches.

BOB WRENN, 1903. Challenge Round (1): 0–2 in singles, 0–1 in doubles.

BILL LARNED, 1902, '03, '05, '08, '09, '11. Challenge Rounds (4): 2–5 in singles. Zone Matches (4): 8–0 in singles. Overall: 10–5 for 8 matches.

GEORGE WRENN, 1903. Challenge Round (1): 0–1 in doubles.

BEALS WRIGHT, 1905, '07, '08, '11. Challenge Rounds (3): 2–2 in singles, 0–3 in doubles. Zone Matches (4): 6–2 in singles, 3–0 in doubles. Overall 11–7 for 7 matches.

BILL CLOTHIER, 1905, '09. Challenge Round (1): 0–1 in singles. Zone Matches (2): 4–0 in singles. Overall: 4–1 for 3 matches.

RAYMOND LITTLE, 1906, '09, '11. Challenge Round (1): 0–2 in singles, 0–1 in doubles.

Zone Matches (3): 1–1 in singles, 2–1 in doubles. Overall: 3–5 for 4 matches.

KARL BEHR, 1907. Zone Match (1): 0–2 in singles, 1–0 in doubles.

FRED ALEXANDER, 1908. Challenge Round (1): 0–2 in singles, 0–1 in doubles. Zone Match (1): 1–0 in doubles. Overall: 1–3 for 2 matches.

HAROLD HACKETT, 1908, '09, '13. Challenge Round (1): 0–1 in doubles. Zone Matches (5): 4–1 in doubles. Overall: 5–1 for 6 matches.

MELVILLE LONG, 1909. Challenge Round (1): 0–2 in singles, 0–1 in doubles.

MAURICE McLOUGHLIN, 1909, '11, '13, '14. Challenge Rounds (4): 3–4 in singles, 1–3 in doubles. Zone Matches (4): 6–0 in singles, 2–1 in doubles. Overall: 12–8 for 8 matches.

TOM BUNDY, 1911, '14. Challenge Round (1): 0–1 in doubles. Zone Match (1): 0–1 in doubles. Overall: 0–2 for 2 matches.

RICHARD WILLIAMS, 1913, '14, '21, '23, '25, '26. Challenge Rounds (6): 1–3 in singles, 4–0 in doubles. Zone Matches (3): 5–0 in singles. Overall: 10–3 for 9 matches.

BILL JOHNSTON, 1920 through 1927. Challenge Rounds (8): 11–3 in singles, 2–0 in doubles. Zone Matches (2): 3–0 in singles, 2–0 in doubles. Overall: 18–3 for 10 matches.

WALLACE JOHNSON, 1913. Zone Match (1): 1–0 in singles.

BILL TILDEN, 1920 through 1930. Challenge Rounds (11): 17–5 in singles, 5–1 in doubles. Zone Matches (6): 8–0 in singles, 5–0 in doubles. Overall: 35–6 for 17 matches.

WATSON WASHBURN, 1921. Challenge Round (1): 1–0 in doubles.

VINCENT RICHARDS, 1922, '24, '25, '26. Challenge Rounds (4): 2–0 in singles, 3–0 in doubles.

FRANK HUNTER, 1927, '28, '29. Challenge Rounds (2): 1–1 in doubles. Zone Matches (2): 3–1 in singles. Overall: 4–2 for 4 matches.

ARNOLD JONES, 1928. Zone Match (1): 1–0 in doubles.

JOHN HENNESSEY, 1928, '29. Challenge Round (1): 0–2 in singles. Zone Matches (7): 10–0 in singles, 3–0 in doubles. Overall: 13–2 for 8 matches.

GEORGE LOTT, 1928 through 1931, '33, '34. Challenge Rounds (3): 0–4 in singles, 1–0 in doubles. Zone Matches (14): 7–0 in singles, 10–0 in doubles. Overall: 18–4 for 17 matches.

WILBUR COEN, 1928. Zone Matches (2): 1–0 in singles, 1–0 in doubles.

JOHN VAN RYN, 1929 through 1936. Challenge Rounds (4): 2–2 in doubles. Zone Matches (20): 7–1 in singles, 9–0 in doubles. Overall 18–3 for 24 matches.

WILMER ALLISON, 1929 through 1933, '35, '36. Challenge Rounds (4): 0–4 in singles, 2–2 in doubles. Zone Matches (19): 17–6 in singles, 12–0 in doubles. Overall: 31–12 for 23 matches.

JOHN DOEG, 1930. Zone Matches (2): 2–0 in singles.

FRANK SHIELDS, 1931, '32, '34. Challenge Round (1): 0–2 in singles. Zone Matches (12): 16–4 in singles, 3–0 in doubles. Overall: 19–6 for 13 matches.

SIDNEY WOOD, 1931, '34. Challenge Round (1): 0–2 in singles. Zone Matches (6): 5–4 in singles, 3–0 in doubles. Overall: 8–6 for 7 matches.

CLIFF SUTTER, 1931, '33. Zone Matches (2): 3–0 in singles.

ELLSWORTH VINES, 1932, '33. Challenge Round (1): 1–1 in singles. Zone Matches (7): 12–2 in singles. Overall: 13–3 for 8 matches.

LES STOEFEN, 1934. Challenge Round (1): 1–0 in doubles. Zone Matches (2): 3–0 in singles, 2–0 in doubles. Overall: 6–0 for 4 matches.

BRYAN (BITSY) GRANT, 1935 through 1938. Zone Matches (5): 8–2 in singles.

DON BUDGE, 1935 through 1938. Challenge Rounds (3): 4–2 in singles, 1–1 in doubles. Zone Matches (8): 15–0 in singles, 5–1 in doubles. Overall: 25–4 for 11 matches.

GENE MAKO, 1935 through 1938. Challenge Rounds (2): 1–1 in doubles. Zone Matches (6): 0–1 in singles, 5–1 in doubles. Overall: 6–3 for 8 matches.

FRANK PARKER, 1937, '39, '46, '48. Challenge Rounds (3): 4–2 in singles. Zone Matches (4): 8–0 in singles. Overall: 12–2 for 7 matches.

BOBBY RIGGS, 1938, '39. Challenge Rounds (2): 2–2 in singles.

JOE HUNT, 1939. Challenge Round (1): 0–1 in doubles.

JACK KRAMER, 1939, '46, '47. Challenge Rounds (3): 3–0 in singles, 1–2 in doubles.

ZONE Match (1): 2–0 in singles. Overall: 6–2 for 4 matches.

BILL TALBERT, 1946, '48, '49, '51, '52, '53. Challenge Rounds (2): 1–1 in doubles. Zone Matches (6): 2–0 in singles, 6–0 in doubles. Overall: 9–1 for 8 matches.

TED SCHROEDER, 1946 through 1951. Challenge Rounds (6): 9–3 in singles, 1–3 in doubles. Zone Matches (2): 2–0 in singles, 1–0 in doubles. Overall: 13–6 for 8 matches.

GARDNAR MULLOY, 1946, '48, '49, '50, '52, '53, '57. Challenge Rounds (4): 1–0 in singles, 1–2 in doubles. Zone Matches (8): 2–0 in singles, 7–1 in doubles. Overall: 11–3 for 12 matches.

RICHARD (PANCHO) GONZALEZ, 1949. Challenge Round (1): 2–0 in singles.

TOM BROWN, 1950, '53. Challenge Round (1): 1–1 in singles. Zone Match (1):1–1 in singles, 1–0 in doubles. Overall: 3–2 for 2 matches.

DICK SAVITT, 1951. Zone Matches (2): 3–0 in singles.

HERB FLAM, 1951, '52, '56, '57. Challenge Round (1): 0–1 in singles. Zone Matches (7): 10–1 in singles, 2–0 in doubles. Overall: 12–2 for 8 matches.

TONY TRABERT, 1951 through 1955. Challenge Rounds (5): 2–5 in singles, 2–3 in doubles. Zone Matches (9): 14–0 in singles, 9–0 in doubles. Overall: 27–8 for 14 matches.

ART LARSEN, 1951, '52. Zone Matches (3): 4–0 in singles.

VIC SEIXAS, 1951 through 1957. Challenge Rounds (7): 4–10 in singles, 2–4 in doubles. Zone Matches (16): 20–2 in singles, 12–1 in doubles. Overall: 38–17 for 23 matches.

BUDGE PATTY, 1951. Zone Match (1): 1–0 in singles, 1–0 in doubles.

HUGH STEWART, 1952, '61. Zone Matches (2): 2–0 in singles, 2–0 in doubles.

BERNARD BARTZEN, 1952, '53, '57, '60, '61. Zone Matches (9): 15–0 in singles, 1–0 in doubles.

BOB PERRY, 1952, '53. Zone Matches (2): 1–1 in singles, 1–0 in doubles.

HAMILTON RICHARDSON, 1952 through 1956, '58, '65. Challenge Rounds (2): 0–1 in singles, 1–0 in doubles. Zone Matches (12): 17–0 in singles, 2–1 in doubles. Overall: 20–2 for 14 matches.

RON HOLMBERG, 1956. Zone Match (1): 1–0 in doubles.

Davis Cup Who's Who (cont.)

STRAIGHT CLARK, 1953, '54. Zone Matches (3): 3–0 in singles, 2–0 in doubles.

HAL BURROWS, 1954. Zone Matches (2): 2–0 in singles, 2–0 in doubles.

BARRY MACKAY, 1956 through 1960. Challenge Rounds (3): 2–4 in singles, 0–1 in doubles. Zone Matches (12): 15–3 in singles, 5–1 in doubles. Overall: 22–9 for 15 matches.

SAM GIAMMALVA, 1956, '57, '58. Challenge Round (1): 0–1 in singles, 0–1 in doubles. Zone Matches (6): 4–0 in singles, 3–1 in doubles. Overall: 7–3 for 7 matches.

MIKE GREEN, 1956, '57. Zone Matches (3): 1–2 in singles.

GRANT GOLDEN, 1957. Zone Matches (2): 1–1 in singles, 1–0 in doubles.

BILL QUILLIAN, 1958. Zone Match (1): 1–0 in singles, 1–0 in doubles.

WHITNEY REED, 1958, '61. Zone Matches (3): 2–3 in singles, 0–1 in doubles.

JACK DOUGLAS, 1959, '61, '62. Zone Matches (5): 5–3 in singles, 1–0 in doubles.

ALEX OLMEDO, 1958, '59. Challenge Rounds (2): 3–1 in singles, 1–1 in doubles. Zone Match (1): 2–0 in singles, 1–0 in doubles. Overall: 7–2 for 3 matches.

EARL (BUTCH) BUCHHOLZ, JR., 1959, '60. Challenge Round (1): 0–1 in doubles. Zone Matches (5): 3–1 in singles, 3–1 in doubles. Overall: 6–3 for 6 matches.

CHUCK MCKINLEY, 1960 through 1965. Challenge Rounds (2): 2–2 in singles, 2–0 in doubles. Zone Matches (14): 14–4 in singles, 11–3 in doubles. Overall: 29–9 for 16 matches.

DENNIS RALSTON, 1960 through 1966. Challenge Rounds (2): 1–3 in singles, 2–0 in doubles. Zone Matches (13): 13–2 in singles, 9–4 in doubles. Overall: 25–9 for 15 matches.

DONALD DELL, 1961, '63. Zone Matches (3): 1–0 in singles, 2–1 in doubles.

CHRIS CRAWFORD, 1961. Zone Match (1): 2–0 in singles.

GENE SCOTT, 1963, '65. Zone Matches (2): 3–0 in singles, 1–0 in doubles.

ALLEN FOX, 1963. Zone Match (1): 2–0 in singles.

MARTY RIESSEN, 1963, '65, '67. Zone Matches (6): 2–0 in singles, 4–1 in doubles.

ARTHUR ASHE, 1963 and 1965 through 1970. Challenge Rounds (3): 5–1 in singles. Zone Matches (12): 19–2 in singles, 1–1 in

doubles. Overall: 25–4 for 15 matches.

FRANK FROEHLING, 1963, '65, '71. Challenge Round (1): 1–1 in singles. Zone Matches (2): 2–2 in singles. Overall: 3–3 for 3 matches.

CLIFF RICHEY, 1966, '67, '70. Challenge Round (1): 2–0 in singles. Zone Matches (6): 8–3 in singles. Overall: 10–3 for 7 matches.

CHARLES PASARELL, 1966, '67, '68. Zone Matches (3): 2–0 in singles, 1–1 in doubles.

CLARK GRAEBNER, 1965 through 1968. Challenge Round (1): 2–0 in singles. Zone Matches (10): 9–2 in singles, 5–2 in doubles. Overall: 16–4 for 11 matches.

BOB LUTZ, 1968, '69, '70. Challenge Rounds (3): 3–0 in doubles. Zone Matches (4): 1–0 in singles, 4–0 in doubles. Overall: 8–0 for 7 matches.

STAN SMITH, 1968, '69, '70, '71. Challenge Rounds (4): 4–0 in singles, 3–1 in doubles. Zone Matches (3): 3–0 in doubles. Overall: 10–1 for 7 matches.

ERIK VAN DILLEN, 1971. Challenge Round (1): 0–1 in doubles.

American Davis Cup Highs

Most Years Played

11	Bill Tilden, 1920 through 1930
8	Bill Johnston, 1920 through 1927

Most Challenge Rounds

11	Bill Tilden
8	Bill Johnston

Most Challenge Round Wins

22	Bill Tilden—17 in singles, 5 in doubles
13	Bill Johnston—11 in singles, 2 in doubles

Most Challenge Round Individual Matches

28	Bill Tilden
20	Vic Seixas, 1951 through 1957

Most Zone Matches

20	John Van Ryn, 1929 through 1936
19	Wilmer Allison, 1929 through 1933, 1935, 1936

Most Zone Match Individual Wins

32 Vic Seixas—20 in singles, 12 in doubles
29 Wilmer Allison—17 in singles, 12 in doubles

Most Team Matches Overall

24 John Van Ryn
23 Wilmer Allison
23 Vic Seixas

Most Individual Wins Overall

38 Vic Seixas—24 in singles, 14 in doubles
35 Bill Tilden—25 in singles, 10 in doubles

Wightman Cup Leaders

Playing for their country in the Wightman Cup Series have been 55 American and 56 British women. Most successful of these was American Louise Brough, who played nine years and was unbeaten in 22 matches—12 singles and 10 doubles. Helen Jacobs of the United States and Ann Haydon Jones of Great Britain were selected the most times—12. Miss Jacobs and Helen Wills Moody appeared on court the most times for the United States in 30 singles and doubles matches. But Mrs. Jones holds the record for both sides with 32 matches. Of those Mrs. Jones won 10 singles and five doubles, high for Great Britain.

The longest Wightman match, 46 games, was a singles won by Billie Jean Moffitt of the United States (now Mrs. King) over Christine Truman (now Mrs. Janes), 19–17, 6–4, in 1963. Hazel Hotchkiss Wightman, donor of the Cup, played in and won the longest doubles, 40 games, alongside Eleanor Goss of the United States when they defeated Mrs. B. C. Covell and Kathleen McKane, 10–8, 5–7, 6–4, in the series opener of 1923.

United States Wightman Cup Who's Who

HELEN WILLS MOODY, 1923, '24, '25, '27 through '32, '38. 18–2 in singles, 3–7 in doubles. Overall: 21–9 for 10 matches.

MOLLA BJURSTEDT MALLORY, 1923, '24, '25, '27, '28. 5–5 in singles, 1–1 in doubles. Overall: 6–6 for 5 matches.

ELEANOR GOSS, 1923 through 1928. 1–2 in singles, 2–3 in doubles. Overall: 3–5 for 6 matches.

HAZEL HOTCHKISS WIGHTMAN, 1923, '24, '27, '29, '31. 3–2 in doubles.

MARION ZINDERSTEIN JESSUP, 1924, '26. 1–0 in singles, 1–1 in doubles. Overall: 2–1 for 2 matches.

MAY SUTTON BUNDY, 1925. 0–1 in doubles.

MARY K. BROWNE, 1925, '26. 0–2 in singles, 1–1 in doubles. Overall: 1–3 for 2 matches.

ELIZABETH RYAN, 1926. 1–1 in singles, 1–0 in doubles.

HELEN JACOBS, 1927 through 1937, '39. 14–7 in singles, 5–4 in doubles. Overall: 19–11 for 12 matches.

CHARLOTTE HOSMER CHAPIN, 1927. 0–1 in doubles.

PENELOPE ANDERSON, 1928. 0–1 in doubles.

EDITH CROSS, 1929, '30. 1–0 in singles, 0–2 in doubles. Overall: 1–2 for 2 matches.

SARAH PALFREY FABYAN, 1930 through 1939. 7–4 in singles, 7–3 in doubles. Overall: 14–7 for 10 matches.

ANNA McCUNE HARPER, 1931, '32. 1–1 in singles, 1–1 in doubles. Overall: 2–2 for 2 matches.

CAROLIN BABCOCK, 1933 through 1936. 1–2 in singles, 1–2 in doubles. Overall: 2–4 for 4 matches.

ALICE MARBLE, 1933, '37, '38, '39. 5–1 in singles, 3–1 in doubles. Overall 8–2 for 4 matches.

MARJORIE GLADMAN VAN RYN, 1933, '36, '37. 1–2 in doubles.

JOSEPHINE CRUICKSHANK, 1934. 0–1 in doubles.

ETHEL BURKHARDT ARNOLD, 1935. 1–1 in singles.

DOROTHY ANDRUS, 1935. 0–1 in doubles.

DOROTHY BUNDY, 1937, '38, '39. 1–2 in doubles.

MARY ARNOLD, 1939. 0–1 in doubles.

PAULINE BETZ, 1946. 2–0 in singles, 1–0 in doubles.

MARGARET OSBORNE DU PONT, 1946 through 1950, '54, '55, '57, '62. 10–0 in singles, 8–0 in doubles. Overall: 18–0 for 9 matches.

LOUISE BROUGH, 1946, '47, '48, '50, '52

Wightman Cup Who's Who (cont.)

through '57. 12–0 in singles, 10–0 in doubles. Overall: 22–0 for 10 matches.

DORIS HART, 1946 through 1955. 14–0 in singles, 8–1 in doubles. Overall: 22–1 for 10 matches.

PATRICIA CANNING TODD, 1947 through 1951. 4–1 in doubles.

BEVERLY BAKER FLEITZ, 1949, '56, '59. 3–0 in singles, 1–0 in doubles.

SHIRLEY FRY, 1949, '51, '52, '53, '55, '56. 4–2 in singles, 6–0 in doubles. Overall: 10–2 for 6 matches.

GERTRUDE MORAN, 1949. 1–0 in doubles.

MAUREEN CONNOLLY, 1951 through 1954. 7–0 in singles, 2–0 in doubles. Overall: 9–0 for 4 matches.

NANCY CHAFFEE, 1951. 1–0 in doubles.

DOROTHY HEAD KNODE, 1955, '56, '57, '58, '60. 4–2 in singles, 1–2 in doubles. Overall: 5–4 for 5 matches.

ALTHEA GIBSON, 1957, '58. 3–1 in singles, 2–0 in doubles. Overall: 5–1 for 2 matches.

DARLENE HARD, 1957, '59, '60, '62, 63. 6–3 in singles, 4–1 in doubles. Overall 10–4 for 5 matches.

MIRIAM ARNOLD, 1958. 0–1 in singles.

KAROL FAGEROS, 1958. 0–1 in doubles.

JANET HOPPS, 1958, '59, '60. 0–1 in singles, 1–2 in doubles. Overall: 1–3 for 3 matches.

SALLY MOORE, 1959. 0–1 in singles, 0–1 in doubles.

JEANNE ARTH, 1959. 0–1 in doubles.

KAREN HANTZ SUSMAN, 1960, '61, '62, '65. 3–3 in singles, 3–0 in doubles. Overall: 6–3 for 4 matches.

BILLIE JEAN MOFFITT KING, 1961 through 1967, 1970. 12–2 in singles, 5–3 in doubles. Overall: 17–5 for 8 matches.

JUSTINA BRICKA, 1961. 1–0 in singles.

NANCY RICHEY GUNTER, 1962 through 1968. 9–7 in singles, 3–2 in doubles. Overall: 12–9 for 7 matches.

MARGARET VARNER, 1961, '62. 1–0 in doubles.

DONNA FLOYD FALES, 1963, '64. 1–1 in doubles.

CAROLE CALDWELL GRAEBNER, 1964, '65, '67. 2–0 in singles, 2–1 in doubles. Overall: 4–1 for 4 matches.

MARY ANN EISEL CURTIS, 1966 through 1971. 1–2 in singles, 3–3 in doubles. Overall: 4–5 for 6 matches.

JANE ALBERT, 1966. 0–1 in doubles.

ROSEMARY CASALS, 1967. 0–1 in singles, 1–0 in doubles.

JANE BARTKOWICZ, 1968, '69, '70. 2–0 in singles, 2–0 in doubles. Overall: 4–0 for 3 matches.

STEPHANIE DEFINA JOHNSON, 1968. 0–1 in doubles.

KATHLEEN HARTER, 1968. 0–1 in doubles.

JULIE HELDMAN, 1969, '70, '71. 3–1 in singles, 1–1 in doubles. Overall: 4–2 for 3 matches.

VALERIE ZIEGENFUSS, 1969, '71. 1–0 in singles, 1–1 in doubles. Overall: 2–1 for 2 matches.

KRISTIE PIGEON, 1971. 0–1 in singles.

CHRIS EVERT, 1971. 2–0 in singles, 0–1 in doubles. Overall: 2–1 for 1 match.

Leading British Wightman Cup Players

KATHLEEN MCKANE GODFREE, 1923 through 1927, '30, '34. 5–5 in singles, 2–5 in doubles, Overall: 7–10 for 7 matches.

Two of the outstanding Wightman Cup players of the last 1930 period: Alice Marble of the United States (*left*) and Mrs. Kay Stammers Menzies of Great Britain (*right*).

BETTY NUTHALL, 1927, '28, '29, '31, '32, '33, '34, '39. 3–5 in singles, 3–2 in doubles. Overall: 6–7 for 8 matches.

PHOEBE WATSON, 1928, '29, '30. 3–3 in singles, 3–0 in doubles. Overall: 6–3 for 3 matches.

KAY STAMMERS MENZIES, 1935 through 1939, '46, '47, '48. 4–9 in singles, 1–4 in doubles. Overall: 5–13 for 8 matches.

ANGELA MORTIMER, 1953, '55, '56, '59, '60, '61. 3–7 in singles, 2–4 in doubles. Overall: 5–11 for 6 matches.

ANN HAYDON JONES, 1957 through 1967, 1970. 10–12 in singles, 5–5 in doubles. Overall: 15–17 for 12 matches.

CHRISTINE TRUMAN JANES, 1957 through 1963, '67, '68, '69. 5–11 in singles, 5–3 in doubles. Overall: 10–14 for 10 matches.

VIRGINIA WADE, 1965 through 1970. 4–7 in singles, 2–4 in doubles. Overall: 6–11 for 6 matches.

Federation Cup Leaders

Twelve women have competed for the United States in Federation Cup. Mrs. Billie Jean Moffitt King in five years played 19 engagements against other countries and won 31 of 35 matches. The following have been members of the United States team:

DARLENE HARD, 1963. 3–1 in singles, 3–0 in doubles.

MRS. BILLIE JEAN MOFFITT KING, 1963 through 1967. 15–4 in singles, 16–0 in doubles. Overall: 31–4 for 19 matches.

MRS. CAROLE CALDWELL GRAEBNER, 1963, '65, '66. 2–1 in singles, 10–0 in doubles. Overall: 12–1 for 10 matches.

MRS. NANCY RICHEY GUNTER, 1964, '68, '69. 10–1 in singles, 5–1 in doubles. Overall: 15–2 for 11 matches.

MRS. KAREN HANTZE SUSMAN, 1964. 4–0 in doubles. Overall: 4–4 for 4 matches.

JULIE HELDMAN, 1966, '69, '70. 9–2 in singles, 2–1 in doubles. Overall: 11–3 for 11 matches.

ROSIE CASALS, 1967. 4–0 in singles, 3–0 in doubles. Overall: 7–0 for 4 matches.

MRS. MARY ANN EISEL CURTIS, 1968, '70. 1–2 in singles, 4–2 in doubles. Overall: 5–4 for 6 matches.

KATHY HARTER, 1968. 1–0 in doubles.

JANE (PEACHES) BARTKOWICZ, 1969, '70. 3–0 in singles, 4–0 in doubles. Overall: 7–0 for 7 matches.

SHARON WALSH, 1971. 1–2 in singles, 2–1 in doubles. Overall: 3–3 for 3 matches.

PATTI HOGAN, 1971. 2–1 in singles, 2–1 in doubles. Overall: 4–2 for 3 matches.

All-Time Federation Leading Players (Based on number of victories)

MRS. MARGARET SMITH COURT, Australia, 1963, '64, '65, '68, '69, '71. 20–0 in singles, 14–5 in doubles. Overall: 34–5 for 20 matches.

MRS. BILLIE JEAN MOFFITT KING, United States, 1963 through 1967. 15–4 in singles, 16–0 in doubles. Overall: 31–4 for 19 matches.

MRS. ANN HAYDON JONES, Britain, 1963 through 1967, 1971. 10–7 in singles, 12–4 in doubles. Overall: 22–11 for 18 matches.

VIRGINIA WADE, Britain, 1967 through 1971. 10–7 in singles, 11–3 in doubles. Overall 21–10 for 14 matches.

MRS. JUDY TEGART DALTON, Australia, 1965, '66, '67, '69, '70. 6–1 in singles, 11–3 in doubles. Overall: 17–4 for 14 matches.

FRANÇOISE DURR, France, 1963 through 1967, 1971. 7–5 in singles, 7–5 in doubles. Overall: 14–10 for 13 matches.

MRS. NANCY RICHEY GUNTER, United States, 1964, '69. 10–1 in singles, 5–1 in doubles. Overall: 15–2 for 11 matches.

FR. HELGA NIESSEN MASTHOFF, West Germany, 1965, '66, '67, '68, '70. 10–4 in singles, 3–3 in doubles. Overall: 13–7 for 14 matches.

Longest Federation Cup Matches

Mrs. King played in the longest Club match, 42 games, a doubles in which she and Darlene Hard clinched the 1963 Cup over Australians Lesley Turner (now Mrs. Bowrey) and Margaret Smith (now Mrs. Court), 3–6, 13–11, 6–3.

Mrs. King also played in the second longest singles, 38 games, a 12–10, 9–7 win over Argentinian Norma Baylon.

The longest Cup singles was 41 games, Andrée Martin of Canada over Katalin Borka of Hungary, 3–6, 7–5, 11–9, in 1969.

Cliff Richey (*left*) won the Pepsi Grand Prix of Tennis in 1970, but Stan Smith (*right*) captured the Masters' Round Robin.

Prize Money List (Men's)

1969 was the first time all the leading men players were competing for prize money, in opens, pro tournaments, or "player" events. The ten leading money winners from 1969 on are as follows:

1969

1.	Rod Laver	$124,000
2.	Tony Roche	75,045
3.	Tom Okker	65,451
4.	Roy Emerson	62,629
5.	John Newcombe	52,610
6.	Ken Rosewall	46,796
7.	Pancho Gonzalez	46,288
8.	Marty Riessen	43,441
9.	Fred Stolle	43,160
10.	Arthur Ashe	42,030

1970

1.	Rod Laver	$201,453
2.	Arthur Ashe	141,018
3.	Ken Rosewall	140,455
4.	Cliff Richey	97,000
5.	Roy Emerson	96,485
6.	Stan Smith	95,251
7.	John Newcombe	78,251
8.	Pancho Gonzalez	77,365
9.	Clark Graebner	68,000
10.	Tony Roche	67,232

1971

1.	Rod Laver	$292,717
2.	Ken Rosewall	138,317
3.	Tom Okker	120,465
4.	Ilie Nastase	114,000
5.	Arthur Ashe	104,642
6.	Stan Smith	103,806
7.	John Newcombe	101,514
8.	Marty Riessen	87,310
9.	Clark Graebner	75,400
10.	Cliff Richey	75,000

Prize Money List (Women's)

The women professional tennis players came into their own in 1971 with their tour. It proved to be a great success, and Mrs. Billie Jean King became the first woman professional athlete to win over $100,000 in one season. The ten leading money winners in 1971 were as follows:

1.	Mrs. Billie Jean M. King	$117,000
2.	François Durr	65,000
3.	Rosemary Casals	62,000
4.	Mrs. Judy Dalton	33,867
5.	Kerry Melville	29,767
6.	Mrs. Dan H. Jones	26,148
7.	Virginia Wade	24,000
8.	Mrs. Nancy R. Gunter	15,300
9.	Mary Ann Eisel	15,000
10.	Valerie Viegenfuss	14,000

Pepsi/ILTF Grand Prix of Tennis

In conjunction with the International Lawn Tennis Federation, the Pepsi-Cola Company established the International Lawn Tennis Grand Prix involving a set number of international tournaments (see Section V). Points are awarded according to these results, and the high point player receives a cash award. Then the first six point scorers play a Masters Round Robin for additional money. In 1970, only men were included, while in 1971 both men and women had a grand prix. The final standings and results of the Grand Prix are as follows:

1970 Final Standings	Points	Money
Cliff Richey	60	$25,000
Arthur Ashe	55	17,000
Ken Rosewall	53	15,000
Rod Laver	51	12,000
Stan Smith	47	10,500
Zeljko Franulovic	35	9,500
John Newcombe	35	8,500
Jan Kodes	35	7,500
Tony Roche	32	6,500
Bob Carmichael	31	6,000

Results of the Masters Round Robin STANDINGS—Smith, 4–1 ($15,000); Laver, 4–1 ($9,000); Rosewall, 3–2 ($7,500); Ashe, 3–2 ($6,000); Franulovic, 1–4 ($4,500); Kodes, 0–5 ($3,000). Smith and Laver tied with 4–1 records, but Smith won first prize because he beat Laver.

1971

Men's Final Standings	Points	Money
Stan Smith	187	$25,000
Ilie Nastase	172	17,000
Zeljko Franulovic	129	15,000
Jan Kodes	124	12,000
Cliff Richey	98	10,500
Pierre Barthes	82	9,500
Clark Graebner	79	8,500
Tom Gorman	69	7,500
Frank Froehling	68	6,500
Roger Taylor	60	6,000

Results of the Masters Round Robin Standings: Nastase, 6–0 ($15,000); Smith, 4–2 ($9,000); Richey, 3–3 ($7,500); Barthes, 3–3 ($6,000); Kodes, 3–3 ($4,500); Franulovic, 1–5 ($1,500); Graebner, 1–5 ($1,500).

1971

Women's Final Standings	Points	Money
Mrs. Billie Jean M. King	181	$10,000
Françoise Durr	119	7,500
Helen Gourlay	83	6,500
Mrs. Judy Dalton	70	5,250
Virginia Wade	69	4,000
Winnie Shaw	51	3,500
Mrs. Gail S. Chanfreau	49	3,000
Lesley Hunt	43	2,500
Betty Stove	32	2,000
L. Liem	23	1,500

SECTION VII

Glossary of Lawn Tennis Terms

Tennis is a wonderful game . . . and it is fascinating to speculate just who originated the various terms that are so common to everyone who has ever swung a racket. For instance, as was stated in Section I, the name first applied to court tennis and later to lawn tennis is elusive and mysterious. Its origin, long said to be "unknown," is obscure. The word that began as *tenes* and ended as *tennis* has passed through twenty-four transformations, four variations of five letters, twelve of six letters, seven of seven letters, and one of eight letters. It would almost seem as though the word changed its form to escape the etymologists.

As noted in the first English treatise on tennis, published anonymously in 1822 and later attributed to one R. Lukin: "The unsettled state . . . of our orthography at that period [fifteenth century] forbids these varieties from becoming the ground-work of any speculations; nor does it seem at all expedient to lengthen out this note . . . by offering conjectures, which the reader may multiply at pleasure without much hope perhaps of arriving at the truth."

There are certain derivations that have never been substantiated, and may be disposed of at the outset to avoid confusion. Lukin himself offers two theories not found elsewhere: one that tennis came from the French word *tente*, referring to a covered building in which the game was played, and another that it came from an old Norman word meaning "bound," this referring to the "cords or ten-dons" which were formerly wound around the hand to protect it in playing *jeu de paume* (tennis).

Other authors have claimed that tennis comes from the Latin word *teniludium*, meaning "play of tennis," and from a so-called Greek word *phennis*. The word *teniludium* is not endorsed by the leading Latin scholars, although *teniludus* and *teniludius* appear in a compilation of medieval expressions by a Dominican friar of Norfolk, England, in 1440. There is not a shadow of Greek authority, however, for the word *phennis* as indicating tennis.

Other theories to be consigned to the realm of the imagination are: one, that tennis comes from the German *tanz,* the bounding or ricochet motion of the tennis ball, being a "tanz" or dance of the ball around the court; another, that *tenne* is German for threshing floor, which was used at an early time for a primitive tennis court; another, that tennis is old English for *tens,* and that the game is really double fives; another, that *tence* (tennis) meant combat or batting to and fro, and hence knocking a ball back and forth with a racket, it being said that *tence* is used with this meaning in early English works; another that, as Tennyson and Denison have been found to be the same originally, Saint Denis was probably Saint Tennis, who became a patron saint, and lent his name to the game.

The most accepted etymology, however, is that *tennis* in English comes from the French word *tenez*. But, the derivation from the

French *tenez* really rests upon the assumption that this expression was used by the French when they were about to strike the ball. Let us examine the evidence. From 1324, and all through the fourteenth century thereafter, the word *tennis* in its various forms appears, but during this period no French literature records any mention of the players calling *tenez* at the beginning of play. The first literature that makes such a suggestion does not appear in France but in England, and it does not appear until the seventeenth century. In 1617 a London lexicographer made a vast compilation in eleven languages, and this compilation contains the following: "Tennis, play . . . *tenez* . . . which word the Frenchmen, the only tennis players, use to speak when they strike the ball, at tennis."

Like so many words in our language, while the weight of authority favors the *tenez* theory, the more the subject is studied the less satisfactory the theory becomes. It fails to convince a great many students of tennis history. The French had a universally adopted name for their game before *tenez* appeared in their literature. *Jeu de paume,* meaning tennis, was mentioned as early as 1200, and probably began to take form from 1150 to 1200. It is difficult to believe that an established name should have been changed from a mere exclamation at play. Furthermore, the transition from *tenez* to *tennis* is not an easy one.

Are you bewildered or confused? Then how about the origin of scoring? Most players of today who call the scores so glibly may be surprised to know that they speak a language which has been a puzzle for centuries. While the use of "fifteen" in tennis scoring still remains obscure, as pointed out in Section IV, the use of the word *love* is the great mystery. It is so mysterious that it is not discussed in an authoritative way by any of the historians. Although of comparatively recent origin, for the word has no foreign equivalent and was first used by the English, no one really knows why it was used, nor exactly when it was first used. Only a few casual references or bold assertions appear in tennis literature. For example, one author states didactically that the word comes from an old Scotch word *luff,* meaning "nothing," and this has been repeatedly quoted. According to the authorities,

however, no such word has been used at any time in the Scotch language. Most writers who mention "love" at all dismiss it with a hopeless gesture. There are, however, certain theories, legendary and otherwise, that are interesting to consider.

One of these, which has come down by word of mouth for many years, is to the effect that the French, the earliest exponents of court tennis, in marking up a zero to indicate no score, wrote the figure in an elliptical form. This figure often had the appearance of an egg, and so the French called it *l'oeuf* (the egg). It has been said that when the English learned the game from the French they heard the French calling *l'oeuf* for no score, and this sounded to them like the word *love,* so they called it "love," and have continued to do so ever since.

To support this theory an analogy is drawn from the game of cricket. In that game the zero or "0" placed against the batsman's name in the scoring sheet when he fails to score is used to designate "nothing," and this score for a long time has been called "the duck's egg" or "duck egg." An analogy is also drawn from the slang expression "goose egg" as applied in other games. It is said that this expression originated in the United States, *The New York Times* being referred to as giving the following description of a baseball game in 1886: "The New York players presented the Boston men with nine unpalatable goose eggs in their (baseball) contest on the Polo Grounds yesterday."

While most lexicographers believe the use by the French of *l'oeuf* to indicate "no score" is the basis of *love* in today's tennis, there are other theories, too. For example, the use of the word *love* to suggest "nothing" is as old as the English language. In the year 971 we find the equivalent of the expression "neither for love nor money," "ne for feu, ne for nanes mannes lufou." Similar expressions have been in common use for centuries. Later, by an easy antithesis, there developed the expression in competitive games "to play for love," meaning "to play for nothing," as contrasted with playing for money. Similarly, a labor of love, though originally meaning a labor one delights in, came to mean a labor done for favor, for love, or for nothing.

In fact, it is quite usual to say, "Let's play

for love," when we mean to play for nothing, and in view of the antiquity of this expression it would seem most natural for the English to have used the word to indicate no score when they first began to play the game.

As you go further in the language of tennis, you will find every phase of the sport has words of interesting derivations. A study of the service, for instance, naturally leads to a consideration of the let, because the word *let* is most often applied to a service, otherwise good, that touches the net. The word *let* means literally "obstruction." It is now almost obsolete, but appears in the current expression "without let or hindrance." It is easy to see how the word was used to apply to a ball that was hindered or obstructed by a person or object in such a way that the point had to be played over again.

The rules in the first two editions of Major Wingfield's *Sphairistike* in December, 1873, and November, 1874, make no mention of the let. Further, the first official rules of lawn tennis adopted by the Marylebone Cricket Club in 1875 provide that "it is a good service or return, although the ball touches the net or either of the posts." By 1878 the words "or either of the posts" were omitted, according to Jefferies' modern rules published in that year. In fact, the first mention of a *let* in lawn tennis appears in 1878, where it is stated that a *let* should be allowed for outside obstruction or interference, such as "an obtrusive dog running across the court, or anything of that kind," but should not be allowed "for anything which constitutes a part of court." In other words, no *let* was allowed for a service that touched the net.

In 1880, however, the Marylebone Cricket Club and the All-English Croquet and Lawn Tennis Club definitely established the *let* in their decision that "if the ball served touch the net, the service, provided it be otherwise good, counts for nothing." This rule was adopted in substance in the United States in 1881.

We could go on almost indefinitely on the derivations of tennis words. For the uninitiated, however, this could become bewildering and rather confusing. Instead, for those who are not familiar with the vocabulary of this sport, the following is a glossary of common tennis terms.

Ace. An earned point as distinguished from one scored by opponent's error.

Ace on service. A point earned on serving a ball that cannot be returned.

Ad in. The server's advantage.

Ad out. The receiver's advantage.

Advantage. A point won by player after deuce. If he wins the next point, he wins the game; if he loses it, the score returns to deuce.

All. An equal score. For example, "thirty-all" refers to points in a game; or "one-all" refers to games (sometimes called *games all*) in a set.

All-court game. A term usually applied to ability of a player to play all the strokes, from any part of the court. *All-around* play means a good ground game supplemented by a good net game.

Alley. The area on each side of the singles court employed to enlarge the court for doubles play.

Amateur. One who does not receive, or has not received, directly or indirectly, pecuniary advantage by the playing, teaching, demonstrating, or pursuit of the game of tennis.

American twist. A type of serve in which the racket strikes the ball with an upward motion, causing the ball to spin in its flight and to take a high bounce when it hits the ground.

Angle volley. A volleying stroke angled past an opponent.

Angle game. A style of play in which the angles of the court are used. Specifically, it refers to the short angles. E.g, the player hits a forehand cross court which lands inside his opponent's service line and close to the opponent's forehand sideline.

Anticipatory position. A position assumed while waiting for the ball to be served or returned. Same as a *waiting* or *readiness position*.

Approach shot. A hard, deep-to-the-corner shot that puts an opponent on the defensive. A type of forcing shot.

Australian formation. A positioning of players in a doubles game in which the server's partner stands on the same side of court from which he is serving.

Backcourt. The area between the base line and service line.

Backhand. A stroke made with the playing arm and racket across the body. Any stroke played on the left side of a right-handed player, or on the right side of a left-handed player.

Back room. The space between the base line and the court's backstop or fence. Also called *runback*.

Backspin. The reverse or backward rotation of the ball while in its flight. The spinning of the ball caused by a straight cut or a chop stroke, the ball spinning back toward the striker. Opposite of *forward spin.*

Backswing. The initial swing of the racket in a backward direction in preparation for the forward stroking movement. Also called *racket-back position.*

Backstop. The netting or other obstruction behind the court to prevent the balls from rolling away.

Bad ball. A ball that does not land in the playing court area.

Ball. The cloth-covered sphere used in playing lawn tennis. Also the term used for the result of a stroke. Thus, a "good-length ball" is a stroke which makes the ball hit the ground near the base line.

Ball boy. A person who retrieves the balls for the players.

Band. The strip of canvas attached to the top of the net.

Base line. The back line at either end of the court.

Base-line game. A style of play in which the player stays on or near the base line and seldom moves into the forecourt. Same as *base-line player.*

Being beaten by the ball. Arriving too late; being passed or almost passed; or too late for optimal position.

Big game. A style of play in which the emphasis is on a big service and a net attack.

Big server. A man with a powerful service.

Blocked ball. A ball returned without the swing of a racket, by simply meeting it with a stiff wrist and stationary racket; generally, a "stop-volley."

Bound. The rising of the ball from the court surface. Also the trajectory from first and second impact on the court surface.

Break. The action of a bounding ball as it leaves the ground; used chiefly in speaking of cut or twist strokes, when the ball bounds unnaturally.

Broken service. A game won by the opponent of the server.

Bullet. A hard-hit ball.

Bye. The right to enter the next round without playing, given by chance in the drawing to players for whom there is no antagonist. Same as a *walk-in.*

Cannonball. An extremely fast, flat service.

Center mark. The mark bisecting the base line, defining one of the limits of the service position.

Center service line. The line dividing the service court into halves and separating the right and left service courts.

Center strop. Two-inch-wide piece of canvas that secures the net at the center of the court on some surfaces.

Chalk. The white material often used to mark lines on some tennis surfaces. When a ball strikes exactly on a line, white dust often flies into the air, and players then speak of *seeing chalk,* meaning that a disputed ball was good because it raised white dust.

Challenge cups. Trophies offered in lawn tennis, the holders of which are open to challenge for their possession. The customary requirements are that the holder must meet the winner of an event held once each year, and if the trophy be won three times by the same player, it passes into his permanent possession. In England, some of these cups must be won three times in succession, but this is not the case in America.

Challenger. The player who wins an event for which there is a challenge cup, or title, and thus earns the right to challenge the holder for the trophy.

Challenge round. The extra round in which a match is played between the challenger and holder for any trophy or title.

Champion barred. The conditions of most events for championships, the holder of the title being debarred from entering for the prizes, and meeting the winner in the challenge round.

Championship. The title held by virtue of winning any tournament held for supremacy of any given section. Also, the event held for the right to challenge for the title or trophy.

Change of length. Shots that are made with varying lengths; one deep, followed by a short shot, or vice versa.

Change of pace. The game strategy or tactic of changing the speed of your shots or reversing the spin on the ball.

Changing courts. The process whereby players, at the end of every odd game during a set, change to opposite sides of the net.

Chip. A short, angled shot, often sliced, to return a serve.

Choke. To grip the racket handle up toward the head rather than at its end.

Chop. A slicing stroke made by drawing the racket down sharply with a chopping motion when striking the ball, giving it a sharp backspin or underspin.

Circuit. Term used when referring to the various tournaments on a player's schedule. Same as *tour.*

Closed-face racket. A racket whose face is tilted forward in the direction of the oncoming ball.

Consolation. A prize event, or match, open (in

America) to any player beaten in the first match actually played, or (in England) generally to all players beaten in the first and second rounds. Similar to *plate,* as used abroad.

Continental grip. Used to maintain the same grip for forehand and backhand; sometimes called the *service grip.*

Conventional stroking. In the orthodox manner.

Court. The playing area on which the game of tennis is played.

Court material. The surface of the court—grass, clay, hard, synthetic, etc.

Cover. Turning the face of the racket from the perpendicular forward, usually giving topspin to the ball.

Covered court. An indoor court for winter play, generally with wood or synthetic surface, always with roof—used chiefly in England. In the United States, called an *indoor court.*

Crack. A slang expression abbreviated from "crack-a-Jack," meaning a very expert player.

Cross-court. A stroke that drives the ball across the court diagonally from one side to the other.

Curl. The twist, cut, or spin on a ball resulting from a sharp cut stroke.

Cut. The twist, spin, or curl of a ball when it has been sliced in hitting.

Cut stroke. A stroke in which the racket strikes a glancing blow and is drawn sharply to one side or another in striking.

Dead. A ball is dead after it has ceased to be "in play"; that is, when it has hit the ground twice anywhere or once out of court, when it has fallen into the net, or when either player has lost the point by any infraction of the rules. Also said of a ball that has been placed or smashed out of the reach of an antagonist; a "killed" ball.

Deep-court game. A style of play in which the player stays deep or in the backcourt.

Deep shot. A shot that bounces near the base line or deep into the playing area.

Default. The victory given to a player whose opponent is absent or declines to play; also, the absence or act of declining to play. Same as *walk-over.*

Defensive volley. A volleying stroke made from below the level of the net. Also called *low volley.*

Delivery. A service.

Deuce. An even score after six points of a game or ten games of a set.

Die. Descriptive of a ball that scarcely bounces at all.

Dink. A ball hit easily (usually close to the net) so that the opponent cannot reach it before it bounces twice. Also called *softie.*

Dipping balls. Balls that barely clear the net, then drop fast and short.

Double fault. Two successive faults in serving.

Double hit. A ball stroked twice on the same play —an illegal play.

Doubles. A game of four players (two on each side).

Down-the-line shot. A ball hit parallel and close to a side line.

Draft. The draw; the list of players entered for any event written out and bracketed in the order in which they are drawn to play.

Draw. The act of deciding by chance the order in which the players in any tournament will play, and against whom they will play. Also, the draft; the list of players entered.

Drive. A hard-hit ground stroke, either by forehand or backhand.

Drive volley. A hard-hit volleying stroke, either by forehand or backhand.

Drop. The unnatural down curve of a ball when hit with a "lifting" stroke that gives a top curl or forward spin.

Drop stroke. A stroke made with a sharp lift of the racket as it meets the ball, which makes the ball twist forward rapidly and "drop" unnaturally after it crosses the net. Also, a short stroke made so that the ball drops just over the net.

Drop volley. A volleying stroke hit softly and easily just over the net.

Duffer. A poor player.

Earned point. A point won by skillful play rather than by an opponent's error or fault.

Eastern grip. The most common grip for a racket, (see page 94).

Echelon formation. A positioning of players in a doubles game in which one player stands close to the net and his partner plays deep.

Error. Failure to make a legal return after the ball touches the racket.

Event. Any complete competition on the program of a tournament.

Face. Either side of the stringing of a racket; the flat surface in the head or blade of a racket which is strung.

Falls. Dies; the second bound of a ball in play, or its first bound if out of court.

Fast court. A court on which a moderately hard-hit ball tends to have a long skid and low bounce and on which a ball with spin is not greatly diverted.

Fault. A served ball that does not strike in the proper court or is not properly served.

Feeder stroke. A drop-and-hit swing used in practicing or to return a ball to the server after a point.

Fifteen. One point scored for either player.

Fifteen-all. The score when each side has won one stroke.

Fifteen-(thirty-, or forty-) love. The score when the server has won one (fifteen), two (thirty), or three (forty) points and the opponent none.

Final round. The last round, in which the two surviving players or teams are opposed to each other; commonly referred to as the "finals."

Finishing shot. A shot that cannot be returned by an opponent.

First return. The first stroke made by the "striker-out," in returning the service.

Flat serve. A service hit very hard with little or no spin. Same as *cannonball serve.*

Flat shot. A very hard-hit shot that travels almost in a straight, flat line with little or no spin. Same as *plain shot.*

Flub. To miss an easy shot.

Fluke. A slang expression meaning an accidental return, or one that was intended in some other way. Also, the victory of a poorer player over a stronger player, through chance or luck; an "upset."

Follow-through. The completion of the swing after impact. Same as *follow-after.*

Foot fault. An improper or illegal position or movement of the feet before or during the service.

Forced error. An error made by a player because of a good shot on the part of his opponent.

Forcing shot. A shot or series of shots that keep the opponent on the defensive or out of position.

Forecourt. The area between the service line and the net.

Forehand. A stroke used to hit a ball by a player on his right if right-handed; on his left if left-handed.

Fork. An iron upright stuck in the ground at the center of the court to keep the net at exactly the required height.

Form. The style in which a player carries him- and makes his strokes. Also, his playing skill.

Forty. Three points scored for either player.

Forward impulse. The straight forward portion of the swing of any shot.

Forward spin. A forward rotation of the ball in the direction of its flight. Opposite of "back-spin."

Forward swing. The motion of the racket toward and through the ball.

Frame. The wooden or metal portion of the racket which holds the strings.

Full stroke. Any stroke in which the player swings arm, racket, and body to the fullest extent possible.

Gallery. The spectators watching any game or match.

Gallery play. A slang expression meaning fancy strokes made for the purpose of attracting the attention of the spectators, or a spectacular stroke made in the regular course of a game.

Game. The unit of scoring next higher than the point; scored when either player has won four points, unless the other player has meantime won three; in that case (deuce score) the player first gaining a lead of two points.

Game point. The point which, if won by the player who is ahead, wins the game.

Games-all. The score of a set when the games are even at five-all, six-all, or higher. Same as "deuce" in the score of a set.

Game score. Points are reckoned as "15," "30," "40," and "game" rather than "1," "2," "3," and "4." A player must win a game by at least two points. Therefore, if each player has three points, the score is called "deuce" or "40-40" or "40-all." The player who wins the next point has "advantage" (not "50-40"). If he loses the next point, the score goes back to deuce.

Good. A ball that strikes in the proper court. Same as *good ball.*

Grip. The manner of holding a racket in the hand. Also, the racket handle covering, generally made of leather.

Grooved stroke. A stroke with which the player is so familiar that he performs it automatically.

Ground game. A style of play that depends mainly on ground strokes and is played in the backcourt.

Ground stroke. A stroke used to hit a ball after it has bounced on the playing surface. Opposite of volley.

Gut. An animal product (generally from lambs or hogs) sometimes used to string tennis rackets.

Guy-rope. The rope stays used to support the poles between which the net is suspended.

Hack. To make a clumsy swing at a ball.

Half-court line. The line dividing the service court into halves and separating the right and left service courts. Same as *center service line.*

Half volley. A stroke hit just as a ball is leaving the ground. Sometimes called *pickup shot.*

Handicap. Odds given or owed to a poorer player to equalize skill. Also, an event or match in which odds are assigned to unequal players, in order to equalize the chances of winning.

Handle. The end of the racket by which it is held.

Head. The upper part of a racket in which the stringing is fastened. Same as *blade.*

Hit out on the line of flight. A return on the same line as the shot received.

Hitting deep. Hitting to an area on or within 2 or 3 feet of the baseline.

Hitting short. Hitting into an area in the vicinity of the service line.

Hold service. The winning of a game by the person who is serving. Opposite of *break service*.

Hop. The bound of the ball.

How? The call of a player for the decision of the linesman or umpire on any doubtful ball.

ILTF. Abbreviation for International Lawn Tennis Federation.

In. A ball that strikes in the proper court. Same as *good* or *right*.

Invitation tournament. A meeting which is open only to players who are invited to enter.

Kill. To place a ball into some part of the opponent's court where it cannot be returned, or to smash it so fast that he cannot return it.

Knock-up. Practice play generally to warm up before a match, and often played without serving or scoring; sometimes only knocking the balls back and forth over the net regardless of the court lines.

Latitudinally. From side to side.

Length. The distance a ball travels after crossing the net; specifically, how close it strikes to the base line.

Let. A served ball that touches the net and yet goes into the proper court. It is then played over again without penalty. Also any stroke that does not count and is played over. Same as *net-cord stroke*.

Let it touch! The warning called out by a player to his partner in doubles, when he thinks a ball is going out.

Lift stroke. A stroke made with the racket nearly or quite vertical, and drawn up sharply as it meets the ball, apparently lifting the ball over the net.

Line ball. A ball that strikes any portion of the line (outside edge, middle, or inside edge). Such a ball is considered to be good.

Line of flight. The direction of the shot.

Line pass. A stroke made from the side of the court so as to drive the ball past the player at the net, the ball passing parallel with and inside the side line.

Lines. The various lines or markings that indicate the boundaries and playing areas on a tennis court.

Linesman. An official of the match, whose duty it is to decide whether balls are inside or outside side lines and base lines.

Live hand. A firm but not viselike grip; not frozen or tightened up. Same as *life-in-the-hand*.

Lob. A stroke in which the ball is lifted high in the air. An *offensive lob* is a ball stroked high into the air, deep into the opponent's court. A *defensive lob* is a ball hit high into the air enabling a player to regain his proper court position.

Lob volley. A volleying stroke hit over the head of an opponent.

Long. Refers to a service or ground stroke which lands outside the baseline or the service line.

Longitudinally. From back to front.

Loop drive. A ground stroke that is hit softer than the conventional drive. The ball travels in an arc rather than on a direct line.

Love. A scoring term indicating zero.

Love-fifteen (-thirty, or -forty). A term used in scoring to indicate that the server has not made a point and the opponent has made one (fifteen), two (thirty), or three (forty) points.

Love game. A game in which one side has not scored a point.

Love-one. (-two, -three, -four, or -five). A term used in scoring sets to indicate that the server has not won a game.

Love-set. A set in which one side did not win a single game. In England, winning six successive games is called a love set, even though the antagonist had already scored when the run began.

Marker. An implement for marking out the lines of the court. Also, a person who keeps the score.

Match. A predetermined number of sets, usually two out of three or three out of five sets, which decide the winner. Also a competition arranged between two clubs, teams, counties, states, nations, or other bodies, each being represented by an equal number of players who play a series of matches (as per first definition) against each other.

Match point. The final point of a match. Same as *match ball*.

Mid-court. The central area of a player's court in front of and behind the service line.

Miss. Failure to hit the ball with the racket.

Mixed doubles. A match between two teams each consisting of a male and a female.

Mix-up. Changing the pace of play; varying your shots.

Modifying the stroke. Adapting the stroke to incorrect body position in relation to the ball.

Net. The netting placed across the middle of the court. It is suspended by a cord or metal cable, the ends of which are attached to two posts.

Net ball. After the service, a ball that touches the net; the ball remains in play.

Net game. A game strategy in which a player plays in the forecourt, close to the net, and volleys.

Net man. The partner in doubles play who stays close to the net while his teammate serves. Same as *net player*.

Net play. The action which takes place near the net.

Net stick. Used to support the net during singles play at 42 inches when placed on singles side line. Same as *singles stick* or *side stick*.

No-man's land. The area on the court between the base line and the service line in which a player should not stand while waiting for the ball.

Nonporous court. A court on which water does not penetrate, but runs off the surface. Same as an *impervious court*.

Not up. The call made by the official when a player narrowly misses reaching a ball before it touches down a second time; often, informally called "two bounces" or "double bounce." Also applies to balls hit near the ground that go from the racket to the ground and *then* over the net.

Objective hit. A planned shot carefully directed to a point in the opposite court to do the striker most good and the opponent least good.

Offensive volley. A volleying stroke made from above net level. Also called *high volley*.

One- (two-, three-, etc.) love. A term used in scoring to indicate that the server has one (two, three, etc.) games and the opponent none.

Open-face racket. A racket whose face is tilted backward from the direction of the oncoming ball. The opposite of "covering" the ball.

Opening. A defensive lapse or mistake which permits a player an opportunity to score a point.

Open tennis. Refers to tournaments in which both amateurs and professionals may compete.

Out. A term applied to a ball which lands outside of the playing area.

Out-of-position shot. A stroke made when not in the optimal position.

Overdrive. To stroke or drive the ball over the opponent's base line so that it lands outside of the playing court for an error.

Overhand. With the racket above the shoulder.

Overhead. With the racket above the head.

Overhead shot. A ball hit in the air above one's head, generally off a lob.

Overhead smash. Shot made with a hard overhead stroke so that the ball comes down sharply into the opponent's court. This shot is usually referred to as the "smash" or "kill."

Overspin. The motion of a ball hit with the racket starting below the ball and coming up over it, imparting accentuated forward motion. Same as *topspin*.

Pace. The speed or amount of speed of play.

Parallel formation. A positioning of players in a doubles game in which the partners keep abreast of each other on the court.

Pass. To hit the ball past an opponent so that he cannot return it. Also a stroke that drives the ball past an opponent at the net, inside the court, but beyond his reach, as a *passing shot*.

Pat-ball delivery. A soft service.

Permanent fixtures. The umpire, linesmen, and spectators and their chairs or stands, net, posts, back and side stops, and any other objects situated around the court.

Place. To hit the ball accurately to a desired location on the court.

Placement. A shot placed where an opponent cannot reach or return the ball.

Play. A warning called by the server just before serving. Also, the response of a linesman or umpire when appealed to for a decision on a ball that is good; an order to continue play.

Played. An abbreviation of "well played." Used as applause for a clever stroke. Also, the manner in which a ball is returned.

Player. A participant in the game of tennis. Also, according to ILTF rules, a "player" is one who has reached the age of 18 years, accepts the authority of his national lawn tennis association at all times, and is authorized to derive pecuniary advantage from tennis.

Plugging the side line. A game strategy or tactic in which the player keeps playing his opponent's backhand until he is moved sufficiently out of position to be vulnerable for a forehand drop shot.

Poach. To hit a ball in doubles that should have been played by one's partner, usually applied to play at the net.

Point. The smallest unit of the score. Four points scored win a game, unless both sides have won three points, when the score is deuce and one player must gain a lead of two points to win the game.

Point of impact. The point at which the racket meets the ball.

Porous court. A court which permits water to filter through the surface. Same as a *pervious court*.

Position. Where a player stands in relation to the lines of the court, the net, the opponent, and the ball.

Position play. Playing each shot in such a manner

so as to get an opponent out of position. Playing to create an opening.

Post. One of the wooden or metal uprights supporting the net. Same as *pole*.

Precision hitting. Clear clean-cut hitting off the center of the racket.

Preliminary round. In tournament play, the first series of matches when the number of entries does not exactly equal a power of two. Same as *first round*.

Press. To force, to attack. Also a device used to hold the racket firmly so that it will not warp.

Professional. One who receives pecuniary advantage by playing, teaching, demonstrating or pursuit of the game of tennis. There are two major classes: (1) *Independent* or *registered professional*—one who has reached the age of 18 years, accepts the authority of his national lawn tennis association at all times, and is authorized to derive pecuniary advantage from tennis; and (2) *touring* or *contract professional*—one who is under contract with an organization other than a national lawn tennis association or its affiliated bodies and who gains pecuniary advantage from taking part in events which are not organized by the national association of the country where they are held.

Put away. To hit so well that no return is made.

Racket. The implement used to strike or hit the ball. The *rough side* of a racket is that on which the thin binding strings at the throat and at the top form loops around the regular stringing. The other side is known as the *smooth side*.

Rallying. A prolonged series of strokes (ground strokes and/or volleys). Also playing the ball to each other for practice or for warming up.

Ranking. A process by which players are listed according to their performances of the preceding year.

Reaching up and out. Making the service swing at the length of the arm and over the right (or left) shoulder.

Ready position. Ready for any stroke—weight on toes, knees bent, shoulders hunched.

Receiver. The player who receives the service.

Referee. The official in charge of a tournament.

Retire. For one player to give his opponent a "walk-over," or allow him to win by default by refusing to continue a match.

Retrieve. To make a good return of a ball which is difficult to handle or reach.

Retriever. A player whose style is primarily defensive and relies on running down and returning shots rather than putting away.

Return. To knock a ball back over the net while in play.

Reverse twist. A stroke made by drawing the racket across the body in striking the ball.

Round. A series of matches in a tournament, the winners of which must equal an even power of two.

Round robin. A method of playing a tournament by which each player meets all of the others in turn.

Runner-up. The loser in the final round of any tournament or event.

Running-in shot. A stroke made and followed to the net.

Rush. To advance to the net.

Rushing the net. A game strategy in which the player runs up close to the net after hitting the ball in hopes that the opponent's return can be killed from this vantage spot.

Seeding. Placing the most highly skilled performers in tournament competition in such a way as to prevent their meeting in early-round play; in effect, allowing the tournament committee a chance to pick or predict the winner by seeding him number one.

Semfinal round. The round preceding the final round.

Semifinals. The two matches in the round before the finals; the matches of the semifinal round.

Serve. To deliver the ball from the base line by throwing it into the air with the hand and knocking it into the opponent's service court; the opening stroke of each point; the act of putting the ball into play.

Server. The player whose privilege it is to serve, or put the ball in play.

Service. The ball that has been served.

Service ace. An ace scored by service; a point earned by a served ball that is placed out of the reach of the striker-out but in the right court.

Service break. See *broken service*.

Service court. The space on each side of the net between the service line and the net, and between the singles side lines. The *center line* divides this area into two equal parts—the *right service court* and the *left service court*.

Service line. The line 21 feet from the net that bounds the service courts.

Set. The unit of scoring next higher than the game, scored when either player has won six games, unless the other player has meantime won five; in that case (a deuce set) the player first gaining a lead of two games wins.

Setless. Without a set; when a player loses a match in *"straight sets."*

Set point. That game point which, if won, will also win the set.

Setup. An easy shot, usually a short, high ball,

which a competent player can hit away for an outright winner.

Shadow tennis. A practice procedure in footwork and strokes done without the use of a ball. Similar to shadow boxing performed by prize fighters.

Shag. To collect or retrieve idle balls knocked out of the court; the work of the ball boys.

Short ball. A ball that drops just over the net when the opponent is back in his court, intended to win because it is out of his reach. Generally a "stop volley."

Side line. The line at either side of the court that marks the outside edge of the playing surface.

Side pass. A stroke that drives the ball along the side of the court, out of the reach of an opponent at the net. Same as *line* pass.

Side service line. The line forming the boundary of the service courts at the right and left sides. In singles the side service lines are also part of the side lines.

Side spin. A spin, usually accomplished by a slice stroke, that causes the ball to bounce to one side or the other.

Singles. A game in which only two players take part, one on each side of the court.

Skittles. A contemptuous slang expression to describe the poor play in a game where the ball is knocked back and forth with little attempt to win.

Slap-dash shots. Not objective hitting.

Slice. A stroke hit with the racket that imparts a side spin. Also a type of service.

Slow court. A court on which a moderately hard hit ball tends not to skid very much and the bounce is generally higher than on a fast court. The ball hit with spin is considerably diverted.

Smash. A hard, overhead swing on a descending ball.

Spikes. Shoes in which nails protrude from the soles or heels to keep the player from slipping. Same as steel points.

Spin. The rotation or twist of a ball in its flight.

Spinning. A method of determining which player serves first, and from which side of the net. It is accomplished by one player spinning his racket rapidly and letting it fall to the ground. While the racket is spinning, the other player calls "rough" or "smooth," referring to the manner in which the trimming cord at the top and throat of the racket face is wound around the stringing. See also *toss*.

Stop volley. A volleying stroke intended to drop the ball barely over the net.

Straight sets. A match won without losing a set; setless.

Strap. A canvas strap in the center of the net which is anchored to the ground to hold the net

secure and at its proper height (3 feet at the center).

Strategy. The general plan of play in a specific match usually based on the opponent's weaknesses. Also called *game strategy*.

Striker or striker-out. The player whose turn it is to return the service.

Stringing. The filament (animal gut, nylon, or silk) in the head of the racket.

Stroke. The act of striking or hitting the ball with the racket.

Sudden death. An expression meaning a set decided by one game, after the score has been even at five-all, in contradistinction to playing deuce-and-vantage sets.

Tactics. The carrying out of the strategical plans; the ways and means used in the presence of the opponent.

Take the net. To move in close to the net.

Tape. The "band" of canvas bound on the top of the net. Aso, the court line (derived from the occasional use of tapes for lines on clay courts).

Tennis elbow. An inflammation and swelling of the elbow joint, resulting from too much playing.

Tennis leg. A rupture of some of the muscle fibers in the calf of the leg, resulting from a sudden twist or strain.

Tennis stroke. A stroke made by cutting or slicing the ball under so that it twists backward. Same as *cut stroke*.

Thirty. A term used in scoring to denote two points. Also, in handicap matches, two points given on every game.

Thirty-all. A term used in scoring to denote that each side has scored two points.

Three (or two) straight. A match won in successive sets; a setless victory. Same as *straight sets*.

Throat. The portion of the racket where the head meets the handle.

Top. To hit the ball on top, causing it to spin downward; the ball tends to bounce backward when it hits the ground.

Topspin. Forward revolving motion of the ball. Same as *forward spin, overspin,* or *top curl*.

Toss. A method to determine which player serves first, and from which side of the net. This is usually accomplished by spinning a racket and the player who wins the toss has his choice of serving or receiving, or the choice of side. He cannot choose both. Also throwing a ball into the air to start a serve.

Touch. A term used to describe a player who hits a ball with style and grace, as if *he* were actually touching it rather than the racket. Also the act of the ball when it strikes the ground.

Also the feeling of the ball with a player's racket.

Tournament. An official competition.

Twist. The spin that is applied to curve the service ball.

Umpire. The official in charge of a tournament.

Undercut. To hit the ball on the bottom, thus causing reverse spin. Same as an *underspin* or *backspin*.

Underhand. A stroke made with the racket below the level of the shoulders.

Up. An equal score; same as *all*.

USLTA. Abbreviation for United States Lawn Tennis Association.

Vantage. The score of a game after either side has won a point from "deuce." Same as *advantage*.

Vantage-all. A term used in scoring, when the usual method of deuce-and-vantage games or sets is not used. When the best two out of three points (for games) or games (for sets) decide the game or set, the score is vantage-all when each side has won one point or game after deuce.

Vantage game. The next game won by either side in a deuce-and-vantage set, after the score of games has been at deuce.

Vantage-in. A term used to indicate that the server has won the "vantage" point (opposite of "vantage-out"). Same as *vantage-server*.

Vantage-out. A term used in scoring to indicate that the striker-out has won the "vantage" point (opposite of "vantage-in"). Same as *vantage-striker*.

Vantage sets. Sets in which deuce-and-vantage has been or is to be played.

VASSS. Abbreviation for Van Alen Simplified Scoring System.

Veteran. A player over (men) 45 years of age; (women) 40 years of age. Same as *senior player*.

Volley. A stroke made by hitting the ball before it has touched the ground.

Volleyer. A player who uses the "net game"; one who volleys by preference (opposite to a baseline player).

Western grip. A method of gripping the racket. (see page 95).

Wide. A term generally given to a ball that lands out of the playing court beyond the side lines.

Wide-breaking slice. A slice service with so much spin that it pulls the receiver into or beyond the alley.

Wood shot. A shot in which the ball strikes the wooden portion of the racket rather than on the stringing. While this shot is legal, it is not a desirable one.

Wrist action. The "action" imparted by the wrist to any stroke.

Illustration Credits are listed by page numbers. The illustrations on pages 93 through 132 except those on pages 110 and 127 are through the courtesy of Russ Adams Productions; all other illustrations courtesy of United States Lawn Tennis Association except those listed below.

2 Tennis Hall of Fame
3 Australian News and Information Bureau
6 Tennis Hall of Fame
9 Tennis Hall of Fame
12 Tennis Hall of Fame
14 Tennis Hall of Fame
17 Edwin Levick
19 (left) Wide World Photos
   Tennis Hall of Fame
25 (bottom) International Film Service, Inc.
25 (top) Tennis Hall of Fame
26 (top) Edwin Levick
26 (bottom) Edwin Levick
27 Tennis Hall of Fame
28 (top) U.S. Army Signal Corps
31 (top) Paul Thompson
31 (bottom, left) Edwin Levick
32 Wide World Photos
33 (top) Edwin Levick
34 (bottom, left) William Fox
36 (top) Edwin Levick
36 (bottom) Wide World Photos
37 (top) Acme News; (bottom, left) International Film Service, Inc.
38 (top) Acme News; (bottom) Edwin Levick
39 Edwin Levick
40 Edwin Levick
41 Wide World Photos
44 (bottom) French Lines
46 (bottom) Edwin Levick
47 (top) Wide World Photos
48 Charles Baulard
51 Max Peter Haas
53 Max Peter Haas
54 Thelner Hoover
56 Russel Kingman
57 Derek Bayes
58 (left) Derek Bayes
59 Acme News
60 Edwin Levick
61 Madison Square Garden, Inc.
68 Russ Adams Productions
72 Chemold Corporation
74 (left) Bancroft Sporting Goods Company (center) Garcia Ski and Tennis Corporation (right) Charger Corporation
76 Ball-Boy Company
79 (top, left) Prince Manufacturing Company
80 (top, left) Bancroft Ski and Tennis Corporation
87 (top) Kalamazoo *Gazette;* (bottom) Sheltair, Inc.
90 Philadelphia *Sunday Bulletin*
110 (left) Central Press Photos, Ltd.
127 Mary Puschak
135 Madison Square Garden, Inc.
155 Australian News and Information Bureau
156 Australian News and Information Bureau
159 Australian News and Information Bureau

160 Australian News and Information Bureau
169 Robert F. Warner, Inc.
170 (top) Robert F. Warner, Inc.
172 (top) Madison Square Garden, Inc.; (bottom) British Travel Association
175 Australian News and Information Bureau
230 Madison Square Garden, Inc.
236 Barbara Dodge
240 Rotofotos, Inc.
260 Telegraph Newspare Company, Ltd.
261 Russ Adams Productions
284 (left) Les Walsh; (right) Whitestone Photos
290 Edwin Levick
295 (top) Keystone View Company
297 Australian News and Information Bureau
306 (left) Derek Bayes; (right) Fox Photos, Ltd.
307 (right) Le-Roye Productions, Ltd.
309 Robert Stuart
331 Madison Square Garden, Inc.
337 Henry Miller
342 Max Peter Haas
343 Acme News
345 Wide World Photos
348 Max Peter Haas
355 Edwin Levick
356 Edwin Levick
358 Ben Schnall
359 Cunard Line
362 (bottom) Max Peter Haas
368 Tennis Hall of Fame
371 Tennis Hall of Fame
372 Tennis Hall of Fame
373 (top) Edwin Levick; (bottom) Edwin Levick
376 (top, left) Edwin Levick
377 Edwin Levick
378 (left) Edwin Levick; (right) Edwin Levick
379 (bottom) London *Daily Mirror;* (top) Edwin Levick
380 (top) Edwin Levick; (bottom, left) Edwin Levick; (bottom, right) Morris Engel
381 (top) European Picture Service
384 (right) International News Photos
385 Ben Schnall
386 Edwin Levick
388 Edwin Levick
390 (bottom) The Telegraph Newspaper Company, Ltd.
393 (top) International News Photos; (bottom) Max Peter Haas
396 (bottom) Russ Adams Productions
398 (top) Tennis Hall of Fame
399 (top) Chemold Corporation
400 (top) Wide World Photos; (bottom) Russ Adams Productions
401 Sport & General Press Agency, Ltd.
423 (right) Max Peter Haas
433 (right) Sport & General Press Agency, Ltd.
435 Madison Square Garden, Inc.
445 Press Association, Inc.

Index

Names of players have been omitted from the index to avoid repetition but most of the players' names can be found in the appropriate category in Section VI.

All-American Top Ten, 422
All-England championships, *see* Wimbledon
all-time records, 433–7, 447–8, 453
Amateur Code rule, 29–30, 32, 51, 62, 63, 194–5
American Tennis Association champions, 281–4
  men's doubles, 282
  men's singles, 282
  mixed doubles, 283
  women's doubles, 283
  women's singles, 282–3
Annie Soisbault Cup, 353
Australian championships, 33, 54, 290–2
  men's doubles, 290–1
  men's singles, 290
  mixed doubles, 292
  women's doubles, 291–2
  women's singles, 291
Australian formation, 157

backboards, 77–8, 79
backhand, 95–6, 109–12, 114, 117, 122, 123, 125
  drive, 109, 125
  lob, 114
  slice, 111–12
  stop volley, 123
  volley, 117, 122, 123
Bagnall-Wilde handicap, 166, 204–5
ball, tennis, 1, 8, 10, 11, 69–71, 74, 85
  buying, 71
  care of, 71
  manufacture of, 70–1
ball boys, 213
ball-throwing machine, 78, 79
British championship, 5, 7–8, 20, 21, 25, 33, 38, 39–42, 54, 55–8, 301–8
British covered court champions, 309–10

British covered court champions (*cont'd*)
  men's singles, 309–310
  women's singles, 310
British hard court champions, 306–9
  men's singles, 309–10
  women's singles, 310
Butler Cup, 45–7

camps, tennis, 88–90
Canadian championship, 292–5
  men's doubles, 293–4
  men's singles, 292–5
  mixed doubles, 294–5
  women's doubles, 294
  women's singles, 294
cannonball service, 130, 131
Champion of America, 11–12, 20
center theory, 133–4, 143–4
chop stroke, 105–7, 108, 113
Church Cup, 264–5
clay court champions, 84, 166, 251–6
clothing, 9, 23, 24, 28, 69, 76–7
competition types, 194, 207–9
consolation tournament, 207–8
courts, tennis, 1, 2–4, 6, 8–9, 10, 69, 79–85, 145–6
  clay, 82, 83, 84–5, 145
  concrete, 82, 83, 84–5, 145
  dimensions, 81–3
  hard, 85, 145
  grass, 80, 83–4, 145
  indoor, 83
  layout, 81–3
  surface, 82–6, 145–6
  synthetic, 85–6, 145
  wood, 85, 145
court tactics, 139–47
  tennis, 2–4
  strategy, 139–53

Davis Cup, 16, 19–22, 29, 30, 31–3, 34, 42–5, 49, 51–

Davis Cup (*cont'd*)
  3, 56, 60, 61, 90, 167, 172, 215, 331–50, 444–51
  all-time records, 447–8
  all-time stalwarts, 444
  American highs, 450–1
  challenge rounds, 333–47
  challenge round standing, 348
  challenge round stalwarts, 445–7
  final rounds, 348–9
  Inter-zone finals, 349
  United States rivalries, 350
  United States who's who, 448–50
  vital matches, 447
doubles court, 80, 82
doubles play, 93, 155–63, 190–1
  tips, 161–2
double elimination tournament, 207–8
draw, 204–7
  making, 204–5
  seeding, 205–7
drive, 104–5, 109, 112, 125
  volley, 119, 125
drop shot, 38, 102, 107, 123–5
  volley, 123
Dubler Cup, 350–1
elimination tournaments, 207–8
equipment, 69–86
etiquette, 151–2, 216–19
  galley, 219
  player, 151–2, 216–18

Federation Cup, 172, 363–5, 453
  leaders, 453
  records, 453
  United States rivalries, 364–5
first-aid on court, 209–10
flat service, 130, 131
foot-fault judge, 215
footwork, 93, 101–2, 107, 126–7

forehand drive, 104–5, 112, 125
ground strokes, 95–6, 103–8, 135
half volley, 124
lob, 113–14
low volley, 123
stop volley, 123
volley, 117
Forest Hills, 16–17, 35, 38, 45, 53, 82, 83, 168, 170, 215, 221, 227
form, tennis, 96–102
French championships, 33, 36, 54, 55, 295–8
men's doubles, 296–7
men's singles, 295–6
mixed doubles, 298
women's doubles, 297–8
women's singles, 297
fundamentals of tennis, 93–163

Galea Cup, 352
German championships, 298–301
men's doubles, 299
men's singles, 298–9
mixed doubles, 300–1
women's doubles, 300
women's singles, 300
Germantown Cricket Club, 29, 43, 44, 62, 168
Grand Prix of Tennis, 455
Grand Slam of Tennis, 33, 54, 55, 57, 437–9
grip, 94–6, 105, 108, 109, 110, 118, 126, 137
Continental, 95, 105, 109, 118, 126, 137
Eastern, 94–5, 105, 109, 137
two-handed, 95, 110
Western, 95, 105, 137
ground strokes, 95, 102, 103–15

half volley, 102, 125
handicapping, 192–3, 207, 208, 209
handicap tournament, 208
hard court champions, 166, 245–51
history of tennis, 1–67
hitting the ball, 93, 97–101
horizontal volleying, 116–22

indoor championship, 28, 45, 197, 238–45, 309–10, 350
intercollegiate championship, 16, 166, 257–60
interscholastic championship, 166, 197–8, 256
International Lawn Tennis Federation (ILTF), 18, 20, 25, 32, 49–50, 62, 63–6, 69–70, 71, 166–7, 171–5, 187, 191, 195, 454
members, 172–5
Irish championships, 310–11
men's singles, 310–11
women's singles, 311
Italian championships, 311–13
men's doubles, 312

Italian championships (cont'd)
men's singles, 311–12
mixed doubles, 312–13
women's doubles, 312
women's singles, 312

junior championships, 166, 167, 194, 197–8, 199–203, 231–5, 238, 242–4, 247–9, 254, 262–4
Junior Davis Cup, 167, 198
Junior Wightman Cup, 167

King's Cup, 45, 350

ladder tournament, 207, 209
leading players of today, 402–5
lessons, kinds of, 153
taking, 153–5
linesman, duties of, 211, 212, 213, 214, 218, 219
lob, 102, 112–15, 137, 143–4, 148, 158, 159–61
volley, 102
Longwood Cricket Club, 15, 21, 59, 168, 215

Madison Square Garden, 60, 62, 172, 187
match play, 151–2
Merion Cricket Club, 45, 168, 171
Mitre Cup, 45, 352
mixed doubles, 23, 24, 25, 28, 35, 36, 40, 41, 162–3, 227
move-up move-down tournament, 207, 208–9

national champions, 14–18, 28, 32–5, 50–1, 62, 82, 221–56
age, 405–6
national collegiate champions, 16, 166, 257–60
college winners, 260
doubles, 258–9
singles, 257–8
National Lawn Tennis Hall of Fame, 367–87
National Public Park champions, 260–4
boys' 14 doubles, 263
boys' 14 singles, 263
boys' 16 doubles, 263
boys' 16 singles, 263
boys' 12 doubles, 263
boys' 12 singles, 263
girls' 18 doubles, 263
girls' 18 singles, 263
girls' 14 singles, 263–4
girls' 16 doubles, 263
girls' 16 singles, 263
girls' 12 singles, 264
junior doubles, 262
junior singles, 262
men's doubles, 261
men's senior doubles, 264
men's senior singles, 264
men's singles, 260–1
men's 35 doubles, 264

National Public Park Champions (cont'd)
men's 35 singles, 264
mixed doubles, 262
women's doubles, 262
women senior's doubles, 264
women senior's singles, 264
women's singles, 261–2
Newport, 11, 15, 16–17, 20, 166, 168, 170, 187, 205, 215, 221, 367–8
New Zealand championships, 313–14,
men's singles, 313
women's singles, 313–14
net, height of, 6, 10, 15, 81
net umpire, duties of, 214–15

officials, duties of, 210–16
Olympic Games, 47–9
open tennis, 62–7
Orange Bowl championships, 167
overhead smash, 102
volley, 102, 119–21

par tennis, 193
Patino Cup, 45
Patriotic Tournament, 17, 18, 35, 221, 222, 225, 228, 229, 253
Philadelphia Cricket Club, 23, 35, 227
pickup shot, 125
playing wind, 146–7
practice, 77–9, 152–4
board, 77–8, 79
devices, 77–9
kinds, 154
Prentice Cup, 45
prize money list, 454–5
men's, 454
women's, 454–5
professional tennis, 29–31, 57, 58–62, 284–90, 330–1, 454–5
World Tournament, 330–1
doubles, 331
singles, 330–1
psychology of tennis, 147–52
pyramid tournament, 207, 209

rackets, 1, 10, 69, 71–6, 77, 96
bag, 76, 77
balance, 73, 74
care of, 75, 76
flexibility, 75
frame materials, 73, 74–5, 76
size, 73–4, 96
strings, 75
weight, 72–3, 74
ranking, 207, 406–21, 422–32
USLTA, 406–21
world, 422–32
rebound ball, 79, 80
net, 78–9
referee, duties of, 195, 211–12
registered player, 63, 67
return-of-service strategy, 158–9
singles, 233

round-robin tournament, 207, 208, 209
rules, 4–5, 11, 69–70, 71–2, 93, 157, 166, 175–86, 216, 219

scoring, 1–2, 4, 93, 165, 186–91
  doubles, 190–1
  games, 188, 189–91
  match, 188–9
  set, 188
  singles, 189–90
  tie-breaker, 189–91
Sears Cup, 265–6
seeding, 205–7
service, 97, 102, 125–37, 141, 143–4, 157, 158–9
  return of, 134–7, 141, 143–4, 158–9
  strategy, 132–4, 157
  strokes, 96, 102, 125–32
shoes, tennis, 76–7, 85
single elimination tournament, 207–8
slice stroke, 105–6, 107, 111–12, 130–1
smash, 102, 119–22
South African championships, 314–15
  men's singles, 314–15
  women's singles, 315
Staten Island Cricket Club, 8–9, 11–12, 13, 20, 23, 29, 80
Stevens Cup, 351–2
stop volley, 102, 123
strategy, tennis, 132–7, 147–52, 157–61
  doubles, 157–61
  during rallies, 159–61
  service, 132–7, 157
Sunshine Cup, 167, 353
swing, tennis, 93, 97–101, 127–31

team matches, 198, 209
tennis centers, 200–1, 203–4
  clubs, 77, 86–7
  elbow, 210
  teacher's methods, 153–4
  Umpires' Association, 215–16
timing in tennis, 93, 102
tips for parents, 90–1
tournaments, 193–203, 205–9, 211
  championship, 195–203
  regulations, 195–203, 205–7, 211
  types, 194, 207–9
twist service, 38, 131–2

umpire, duties of, 211, 212–16, 219
United States Lawn Tennis Association (USLTA), 12–14, 15, 18, 22, 29–32, 48, 49–50, 58–67, 70, 71, 86, 87, 90, 93, 165–71, 175–86, 194–203, 205, 215, 221, 406–21, 439–44

United States Lawn Tennis Association (USLTA) (cont'd)
  awards, 439–44
  enrollment, 195
  ranking, 406–21
    men's 406–15
    women's, 439–44
  sectional associations, 168–71, 194, 199–200, 201, 202–3
USLTA champions, 221–57
  amateur, 224, 226, 229, 231
    men's doubles, 226
    men's singles, 224
    mixed doubles, 231
    women's doubles, 231
    women's singles, 229
  amateur grass court, 166, 196, 237
    men's doubles, 237
    men seniors' 55 doubles, 237
    men seniors' 55 singles, 237
    men seniors' 70 doubles, 237
    men seniors' 70 singles, 237
    men seniors' 60 doubles, 237
    men seniors' 60 singles, 237
    men seniors' 65 doubles, 237
    men seniors' 65 singles, 237
    men's singles, 237
    women's doubles, 237
    women's singles, 237
  clay court championships, 84, 166, 251–6
    amateur men's doubles, 254
    amateur men's singles, 254
    amateur women's doubles, 254
    amateur women's singles, 254
    boys' 16 doubles, 254
    boys' 16 singles, 254
    father and son, 254
    girls' 18 doubles, 254
    girls' 18 singles, 254
    junior doubles, 254
    junior singles, 254
    men's doubles, 252–3
    men seniors' 50 doubles, 255
    men seniors' 50 singles, 255
    men seniors' 55 doubles, 255
    men seniors' 55 singles, 255
    men seniors' singles, 254
    men seniors' 60 doubles, 255
    men seniors' 60 singles, 255
    men seniors' 65 doubles, 255

USLTA champions, clay court championships (cont'd)
    men seniors' 65 singles, 255
    men's singles, 253
    men's 35 doubles, 254–5
    men's 35 singles, 254
    women's doubles, 253–4
    women's singles, 253
  hard court champions, 166, 245–51
    boys' 14 doubles, 247
    boys' 14 singles, 247
    boys' 16 doubles, 247
    boys' 16 singles, 247
    boys' 12 doubles, 248
    boys' 12 singles, 247–8
    father and son, 249
    girls' 18 doubles, 248
    girls' 18 singles, 248
    girls' 14 doubles, 249
    girls' 14 singles, 249
    girls' 16 doubles, 249
    girls' 16 singles, 248–9
    girls' 12 doubles, 249
    girls' 12 singles, 249
    junior doubles, 247
    junior singles, 247
    men's doubles, 245–6
    men seniors' 50 doubles, 251
    men seniors' 50 singles, 251
    men seniors' 55 doubles, 251
    men seniors' 55 singles, 251
    men seniors' 70 doubles, 251
    men seniors' 70 singles, 251
    men seniors' 60 doubles, 251
    men seniors' 60 singles, 251
    men seniors' 65 doubles, 251
    men seniors' 65 singles, 251
    men's singles, 245
    men's 35 doubles, 250–1
    men's 35 singles, 250
    mixed doubles, 246–7
    seniors' doubles, 249–50
    seniors' mixed doubles, 250
    seniors' singles, 249
    women's doubles, 246
    women's seniors' 50 doubles, 251
    women seniors' 50 singles, 251
    women seniors' doubles, 250
    women seniors' singles, 250
    women's 35 doubles, 251
    women's 35 singles, 251
  husband-wife championship, 166
  junior grass court, 233
    doubles, 233

USLTA champions, hard court champions (*cont'd*)
indoor champions, 28, 45, 197, 238–45, 309–10, 350
boys' 16 doubles, 243
boys' 16 singles, 243
girls' 18 doubles, 243–4
girls' 18 singles, 243
girls' 16 doubles, 244
girls' 16 singles, 244
junior doubles, 242–3
junior singles, 242
men's doubles, 239–40
men seniors' doubles, 244
men seniors' 55 doubles, 245
men seniors' 55 singles, 245
men seniors' 70 doubles, 245
men seniors' 70 singles, 245
men seniors' singles, 244
men seniors' 60 doubles, 245
men seniors' 60 singles, 245
men seniors' 65 doubles, 245
men seniors' 65 singles, 245
men's singles, 238–9
men's 35 doubles, 244–5
men's 35 singles, 244
mixed doubles, 241–2
seniors' mixed doubles, 245
women's doubles, 240–1
women seniors' doubles, 245
women seniors' singles, 245
women's singles, 241
interscholastic champions, 166, 197–8, 256
singles, 256
doubles, 256
national champions, 14–18, 23–9, 32–9, 50–8, 62, 82, 196–203, 221–56
boys' 14 doubles, 199–203, 233
boys' 14 singles, 199–203, 233
boys' 16 doubles, 199–203, 233
boys' 16 singles, 199–203, 233

USLTA champions, national champions (*cont'd*)
boys' 12 doubles, 199–203, 233
boys' 12 singles, 199–203, 233
girls' 18 doubles, 199–203, 234
girls' 18 singles, 199–203, 234
girls' 14 doubles, 199–203, 235
girls' 14 singles, 199–203, 235
girls' 16 doubles, 199–203, 235
girls' 16 singles, 199–203, 234–5
girls' 12 doubles, 199–203, 235
girls' 12 singles, 199–203, 235
father and son champions, 197, 235
junior champions, 199–203, 231–2
doubles, 199–203, 232
singles, 199–203, 231–2
Men's doubles, 17–18, 33–5, 51, 196, 224–6
men seniors' doubles, 196, 236–7
men seniors' singles, 196, 235–6
men's singles, 14–17, 28, 32–3, 50–1, 62, 82, 196, 220–3, 405–6
mixed doubles, 196, 227, 231
women's doubles, 24–5, 28, 35, 36, 38, 196, 227, 229–30
women seniors' doubles, 196, 238
women seniors' singles, 196, 237–8
women's singles, 23–7, 28–9, 35–9, 41, 53–5, 196, 227–9
open champions, 67, 166, 189, 223
men's doubles, 226
men's seniors' doubles, 237
men's singles, 223
mixed doubles, 231
women's doubles, 230
women's singles, 229

USLTA champions, open champions (*cont'd*)
women's collegiate champions, 198–9, 256–7
doubles, 257
singles, 256–7
United States Professional Tennis Association, 58–60, 284–6
champions, 284–6
doubles, 285
over 55 doubles, 285–6
over 55 singles, 285
over 45 doubles, 286
over 45 singles, 286
over 35 doubles, 285
over 35 singles, 285
singles, 284–5
United States professional tour, 286–90
United States title matches, 266–81
VASSS, 187, 191, 192–3, 209
handicap, 192–3, 209
round-robin play, 209
scoring, 187, 191
volley, 7, 38, 95, 102, 107, 115–25, 133, 141, 143, 158, 159–60, 163

Welsh champions, 315–16
men's singles, 315–16
women's singles, 316
where to play tennis, 86–7
Wightman Cup, 26, 36, 45, 48, 61, 353–63, 451–3
leaders, 451–3
Wimbledon, 5–8, 11, 18, 23, 25, 29, 38, 39–42, 45, 53, 54–8, 61, 65, 82, 83, 172, 210, 301, 308
champions, 301–8
men's doubles, 303–4
men's singles, 301–3
mixed doubles, 308
women's doubles, 306–7
women's singles, 304–6
winter tennis, 87–8
World Cup, 68
world championships (1968–1971), 316–30
World Championship Tennis, 187, 190
world rankings, 422–32
men's, 422–8
women's, 428–32
World Tennis Roll of Honor, 387–402